REF 820.9
Encyclopedia of British
writers, 1800 to the

OVER NIGHT

Y0-EIJ-704

Encyclopedia of British Writers, 1800 to the Present

Second Edition

19TH CENTURY

Encyclopedia of British Writers, 1800 to the Present

Second Edition

19th Century

Dr. George Stade
General Editor
Professor Emeritus Department of
English and Comparative Literature
Columbia University

Dr. Karen Karbiener
General Editor
Liberal Studies Program
New York University

Dr. Karen H. Meyers
Adviser
Department of Continuing Education
Bowling Green State University

Dr. Christine Krueger
General Editor, 1st Edition
Department of English
Marquette University

Dr. Thomas Recchio
Adviser, 1st Edition
Department of English
University of Connecticut, Storrs

Facts On File
An imprint of Infobase Publishing

Encyclopedia of British Writers, 1800 to the Present, Second Edition

19th Century

Copyright © 2009 by DWJ BOOKS, LLC

All rights reserved. No part of this book may be reproduced or utilized in any form or by any means, electronic or mechanical, including photocopying, recording, or by any information storage or retrieval systems, without permission in writing from the publisher. For information contact:

Facts On File, Inc.
An imprint of Infobase Publishing
132 West 31st Street
New York NY 10001

Library of Congress Cataloging-in-Publication Data

Encyclopedia of British writers, 1800 to the present / general editors, Karen Karbiener, George Stade.—2nd ed.
　　p. cm.
　　Rev. ed. of: Encyclopedia of British writers, 19th and 20th centuries. 2003.
　　Includes bibliographical references and index.
　　ISBN 978-0-8160-7385-6 (v. 1 : alk. paper) 1. English literature—19th century—Bio-bibliography—Dictionaries. 2. English literature—20th century—Bio-bibliography—Dictionaries. 3. Authors, English—19th century—Biography—Dictionaries. 4. Authors, English—20th century—Biography—Dictionaries. I. Karbiener, Karen, 1965– II. Stade, George. III. Encyclopedia of British writers, 19th and 20th centuries.
　　PR451.E55 2009
　　820.9'008'03—dc22　　　　　　2008022264

Facts On File books are available at special discounts when purchased in bulk quantities for businesses, associations, institutions, or sales promotions. Please call our Special Sales Department in New York at (212) 967-8800 or (800) 322-8755.

You can find Facts On File on the World Wide Web at http://www.factsonfile.com

Text design by James Scotto-Lavino

Written and developed by DWJ BOOKS

Printed in the United States of America

VB Hermitage 10 9 8 7 6 5 4 3 2 1

This book is printed on acid-free paper and contains 30 percent postconsumer recycled content.

CONTENTS

Preface	vii
Note to the New Edition	ix
Introduction	xi
Authors' Time Line	xv
Entries A to Z	1
Selected Bibliography	421
Index	428

PREFACE

The 19th-century British writers represented in this volume produced a dauntingly large body of literature on diverse subjects in a wide array of genres. This encyclopedia offers a literary map to this vast landscape in the hope that it will appear, not forbidding or remote, but enticing. We have chosen to mark outstanding pinnacles, such as the works of Jane Austen and Alfred, Lord Tennyson, as well as significant but little-visited spots, such as the historical writing of Mary Anne Everett Green, the art criticism of Anna Jameson, the plays of Harriet Lee, and the literary criticism of George Saintsbury. Although our map is not exhaustive, we hope that it points you in directions that enable you to blaze new trails in the field.

If you are encountering 19th-century writers for the first time, this volume will help you to identify major figures, who are treated in long entries, as well as key schools and genres, and to appreciate the full scope of literary production in the period. If you are investigating the careers of major figures, it will provide you with biographical information, overviews of their publications, and, in some cases, critical analyses of their most important works. You also will find information on lesser-known writers in all genres, including critics and other nonfiction authors, poets, playwrights, and novelists. Cross-references, indicated in SMALL CAPITAL LETTERS, will lead you to the key influences on writers' careers.

Just as the film adaptations of *Pride and Prejudice* or *Dracula* are no substitute for reading Jane Austen and Bram Stoker, neither can this reference work replace firsthand encounters with the works it discusses. Entries have been written, then, not only to be of sufficient intrinsic interest and clarity to inspire curiosity in users of this volume, but also to offer guides to *reading*. Believing that informed reading is also more pleasurable reading, we intend the historical and critical perspectives offered here to enhance appreciation for the formal innovations made by 19th-century writers, for the ways that writing of the 19th century still entertains us and, moreover, for its continuing relevance to our understanding of individual development and social relations. Lists of works by and about writers, following their entries, also will lead you beyond this reference guide to further reading.

Much of the writing discussed in this volume is in print in editions that are readily accessible, and much of it is studied in secondary school and college literature courses. But users of this volume should also be encouraged to explore those works that are no longer in print. Many are available on the Internet, in used bookstores, and in libraries.

These works deserve to endure, and will do so if informed and curious readers seek them out. Like the places into which 19th-century writers ventured in their texts—from Afghanistan and the Congo to imaginary utopias and the innermost thoughts of characters—19th-century literature is itself a landscape inviting new adventurers who will be rewarded with exciting discoveries and enchanting experiences.

Christine L. Krueger
General Editor, First Edition

Note to the New Edition

The thrill of discovering alternative voices, of encountering fresh points of view, or simply relishing a new read, is not reserved for the initiates to 19th-century British literature. Even seasoned readers and critics—including the editors of this volume—continue to find forgotten treasures to reconsider, as well as innovative ways to understand old favorites. Progressive scholarship and technologies steadily expand the cultural landscape, so much so that this edition of the *Encyclopedia of British Writers, 1800 to the Present,* is greatly revised from our first edition (titled *Encyclopedia of British Writers, 19th and 20th centuries*) of some years ago. In this expanded and updated volume, new entries on 21 more authors have been added, along with 36 additional sections of Critical Analysis on writers ranging from Dorothy Wordsworth to George Sand. These essays enable readers to gain a deeper understanding and appreciation of the artistry and impact of the authors' most notable works.

This volume of the second edition of this encyclopedia is a testament to how many 19th-century writers and their works continue to live on and inspire, even from a historical distance of well over a century. Perusing the entries, you may linger over a revealing detail about a familiar name. For example, did you know that John Muir, the naturalist instrumental in the establishment of Yosemite and Grand Canyon national parks, was Scottish by birth? Or perhaps you will be intrigued by a more recently discovered talent, such as John Stuart Mill's outspoken and radical stepdaughter Helen Taylor or the Egyptologist Lucie Duff Gordon. From the quirky characters of Thomas Love Peacock's novels to the dreamy poetic visions of Arthur O'Shaughnessy to the eccentric life of Irish poet James Clarence Mangan to the delicious limericks of Edward Lear, the entries provide countless departure points for your armchair adventures. The editors of this volume invite you to discover—and rediscover—the British writers of the 19th century along with us.

Karen Karbiener and George Stade
General Editors, Revised Edition

Introduction

Nineteenth-century British writers practiced their art within unprecedented social conditions, and, in turn, helped readers to imagine new ways of being. Percy Bysshe Shelley declared in 1821 that "poets are the unacknowledged legislators of the world." In the face of the growing authority of science, economics, and mathematics, Shelley insisted on the crucial role the literary imagination played in forming a compassionate society and just social structures. His assertion resonates down to our own time, and we may look to 19th-century writers for models of how literature contributes to a more comprehensive and humane understanding of life and resists forces that would diminish us all to mere statistics or soulless consumers.

Although not all 19th-century authors would have shared Shelley's social goals for writing—much less his radical politics—they have left us an extraordinary artistic legacy that can still inspire, challenge, and amuse us. From William Wordsworth's poetic celebrations of the common man, to Emily Brontë's novelistic depictions of wild passions in wilder landscapes, to Elizabeth Gaskell's critiques of capitalism or Lewis Carroll's delightful wonderland, 19th-century writers produced enduring responses to their brave new world.

Fundamental changes in British life during the 19th century called for tremendous literary innovation. Britain's population had been primarily rural; in the course of the 19th century, industrialization concentrated workers around factories in urban areas. London's population, for example, soared from just over 1 million in 1801 to more than 6.5 million in 1901. Although workers labored long hours, evangelical religious movements and radical political movements, which thrived among these concentrated populations, encouraged members of the laboring classes to learn to read.

As the factories burgeoned, so did the ranks of the middle classes, who enjoyed leisure time for reading. Thanks to technological advances in printing processes, which made possible cheap, mass-produced publications, literature came within the buying power even of a significant proportion of the working class. Middle-class readers who could not afford books could, for a fee, borrow them by mail from Mudie's Circulating Library, founded in 1842, and all readers might borrow books without charge from new free lending libraries. With dramatically increasing literacy rates, and the advent of mass-publication technologies, 19th-century writers certainly had the opportunity to address a much wider audience than had earlier writers. These new conditions changed the nature of authorship and of literature itself.

It is important to remember that before the 19th century, the majority of people experienced poetry and stories not in written, but in oral form. The very forces that contributed to the expansion of literacy accelerated a centuries-long trend away from oral culture—sung or recited poems and stories—toward print culture. The production of literature was increasingly removed from individuals who could sing or who could tell a good story, and placed in the hands of those with access to printing presses. Printed literature was more susceptible to government censorship and to market forces. Government censorship was especially severe in the wake of the French and American revolutions; for example, the poet William Blake was tried for seditious libel. Censorship was relaxed in the course of the 19th century, but constraints of a market economy posed new challenges, requiring that literary publications make a profit. Romantic theories of literary creation that downplayed the hard work of composition and the monetary motives of many writers developed in these circumstances. These theories emphasized the quasidivine genius of the writer and the spiritual sources of his creativity to disguise the fact that what was printed might have had less to do with what was inspired than with what would sell. Wordsworth, who in 1800 declared that "poetry is the spontaneous overflow of powerful feelings," was by 1838 writing sonnets demanding new copyright laws that would protect not only his financial interests but also those of his heirs.

The spread of literacy, however, expanded the ranks and diversity of authors. Throughout the 18th century, middle-class writers who earned their living by their pens had come to replace aristocratic writers for whom authorship was a leisure activity and authors who served the interests of their wealthy patrons. After 1800, the number of female writers continued to grow, as it had in the 18th century, and a new group of authors from the laboring classes also emerged, such as the "factory-girl poet" Ellen Johnston, and Israel Zangwill, the "Dickens of the Ghetto."

Thus, in general, authorship became less an amateur or polite pastime and more of a profession. Writers from all backgrounds were forced to negotiate with publishers and printers, gauge readers' tastes, and demand greater control over their intellectual property. In 1884 the Royal Society of Authors was founded to enhance both the prestige and the bargaining power of writers and to regulate who could be considered a "proper" writer. In short, although many more people—and more kinds of people—were publishing literature at the end of the 19th century than at its beginning, the newly professionalized authors became class stratified. Some, such as Charles Dickens, were able to earn a comfortable living, while many could barely survive on their writing income. The novelist George Gissing, himself a struggling writer, called this latter group "Grub Street," because they had to grub for a living.

The cultural transformations that brought about the commercialization of literature also changed the kind of literature that was published. Poetry was the most popular kind of literature at the beginning of the century. By the century's close, the novel had become the most widely circulated genre. Poetry remained popular throughout the century, but even as early as the mid-18th century its nature had begun to change. Whereas poems modeled on classical Greek and Latin poetic forms, especially the epic, had long been held in the highest regard, lyric and narrative poetry were favored by many of the romantic poets. The lyric and the narrative seemed better able to convey personal, individual experience; to capture spontaneous feelings; and to approximate everyday language. William Wordsworth, among others, appropriated elements of the oral ballad: its verse forms, simple language, and subject matter. It might be said that romanticism sought a more democratic voice for poetry, which represented common people's tastes. Romantic verse was often nostalgic about rural life, which the factory system was destroying, and was filled with the supernatural—fairies, ghosts, and the like.

Victorian heirs of romanticism, such as Alfred, Lord Tennyson and Elizabeth Barrett Browning, were enormously popular poets, and tried to retain a sense of the spiritual and mystical even in the ordinary events of life. Their work embodied what Thomas Carlyle termed "Natural Supernaturalism," or the awesome qualities the imagination revealed in natural, mundane things.

Many of the same forces shaped the development of the 19th-century novel, which was characterized by the interrelated modes of realism and sensationalism. From at least the late 17th century, the novel had negotiated between the rigorous adherence to the facts of scientific observation and the supernatural features of religious writing and fantastical romances, such as the Arthurian legends. The most popular novels of the early 19th century, those by Sir Walter Scott, aptly illustrate these combined impulses. Most of Scott's novels deal with the Scottish past and mix historical research with stories of ghosts, witches, and feats of heroic derring-do. The influential novels of Scott's contemporary, Jane Austen, on the other hand, resolutely avoid the supernatural (indeed, in the 1818 *Northanger Abbey* she parodied the supernatural elements of the 18th-century Gothic novel), yet we find in her realistic heirs a significant element of "Natural Supernaturalism."

For such writers as Charles Dickens and even George Eliot, some aspects of the supernatural were part of reality and therefore had to be represented in realistic fiction. Sensation novels were filled with extraordinary events, improbable coincidences, and Gothic terrors. Nevertheless, they also dealt with such staple themes of the realist novel as marriage and family relationships, inheritance, scientific investigation, and political rights.

What may have led to the novel's emergence as the dominant literary form by the end of the century was its adaptability to the constraints of literary marketing and its ability to represent the complexity of Britain as it evolved into a democratic state and a global empire. By contrast, lyric poetry seemed to some to lead to the dead end of self-absorbed despair. Matthew Arnold complained in his "Preface to Poems" (1853) that 19th-century lyric poetry was marked by the "dialogue of the mind with itself" and caused readers to feel that there "was everything to be endured, and nothing to be done." The intricate plots of long novels could help readers find their place in a newly complex world. What George Eliot's character Will Ladislaw says in *Middlemarch* regarding historical imagination might be said of the Victorian novel in general: It reveals the "suppressed connections" between apparently distinct people, places, and events.

Cheap mass-publication newspapers and periodicals emerging at midcentury supplied a mass audience with a steady stream of short, entertaining fiction. But long novels could be serialized in magazines or published in brief, inexpensive installments—that is, in pamphlets containing a chapter or two. Publishers found a mass readership who could afford the first chapter and then were hooked into buying subsequent numbers.

It is partially true that such marketing caused 19th-century novels to grow in length (into what Henry James termed "loose, baggy monsters"). Yet it is also the case that, unlike poetry that focused on the emotions of an individual, the expansiveness of the novel allowed authors to explore the vast web of interconnections—between men and women, among various classes and races, between nation and empire—that characterized British experience.

The novel also benefited from its close affiliation with drama. Some novelists engaged in performance as well as print. In addition to giving public readings of his works, Dickens acted in and directed plays, and his fellow novelists Wilkie Collins and Charles Reade reached a wider audience through dramatic adaptations of their fiction.

Nineteenth-century critics such as Samuel Taylor Coleridge and Matthew Arnold celebrated Shakespeare as the preeminent English author, although they considered his plays more as poetry to be read than as drama to be performed. Indeed, Coleridge deserves much of the credit for the prominent place Shakespeare occupies in modern taste and curricula. Shakespeare performances, nevertheless, were wildly popular throughout the century. Two hundred years and more after Shakespeare's death, his language and that of the contemporaneous King James Version of the Bible were enormously influential not only on literature but also on ordinary speech.

Nineteenth-century forms of drama thrived as well, at least among a popular audience. Melodramas were performed in makeshift theaters and in the major houses of London, Dublin, Edinburgh, and Liverpool. These plays might be seen as the forerunners of soap operas, thrillers, and special-effects films in the way they combined emotionalism, politics, and catastrophic events, as well as in their increasingly elaborate scenery.

The rise of club theaters and private theaters, which could survive with smaller audiences than the vast Haymarket or Drury Lane theaters of London, helped to encourage a new generation of British playwrights, including Arthur Wing Pinero, Oscar Wilde, and George Bernard Shaw.

Although Britain did not commit itself to providing universal education until the Education Act of 1870, the vast expansion of literacy and printed materials helped to popularize a wide range of general education subjects in fiction and nonfiction genres. The Society for the Diffusion of Useful Knowledge was founded in 1826 to serve just this end. Many other examples can be cited. For instance, Eliza Cook promoted scientific theories of housekeeping and cookery to working- and middle-class women through *Eliza Cook's Journal*. John Ruskin, author of learned works of art history and theory, lectured to Working Men's Institutes, and then published those lectures. Harriet Martineau published stories illustrating the principles of Political Economy. Hosts of amateur scientists spread the geological discoveries of Sir Charles Lyell and the evolutionary theories of Charles Darwin. A vast network of antiquarians and historians published works of history aimed at a general readership.

Writers like James Hogg and George Saintsbury built reputations as literary critics; careers were sometimes made, but often broken, by reviewers in powerful journals such as *Blackwood's*. Indeed, supporters of John Keats claimed that it was hostile critics as much as tuberculosis that killed the young poet. But such criticism also helped to foster the academic study of English (as opposed to Greek and Latin) literature and influenced the development of literature curricula.

As Virginia Woolf remarked in her novel *Orlando* (1928), a history of 19th-century British literature would require eight volumes, or one paragraph. The astonishing body of literary material produced in the 19th century eludes mastery—either in a brief introduction or in a lifetime of study. Indeed, despite the vast number of books, periodicals, pamphlets, broadsheets, newspapers, and manuscripts that have been preserved, many have disappeared, and many unique copies disintegrate or are otherwise lost to us every day. Even the most learned scholar must recognize, therefore, what cannot be known about 19th-century writers. Still, we can generalize about 19th-century literature enough to say that it helped to create the modern world by shaping how we in the 21st century feel about society, belief, nature, history, and, above all, ourselves. What the critic Raymond Williams said about the 19th-century novel might be applied to all the literature of the period: that it provided readers with "structures of feeling" with which to organize their often disturbing experiences and to approach their complex world. The reward for reading 19th-century writers is not only intellectual accomplishment, or the satisfaction of historical curiosity, therefore, but a deeper appreciation for the lasting contribution they made to humanity.

Christine L. Krueger
General Editor, First Edition

Authors' Time Line

Dates	Author
1729–1797	Burke, Edmund
1731–1800	Cowper, William
1741–1810	Trimmer, Sarah
1743–1805	Paley, William
1743–1825	Barbauld, Anna Laetitia
1745–1797	Equiano, Olaudah
1745–1809	Holcroft, Thomas
1745–1833	More, Hannah
1746–1810?	Radcliffe, Mary Ann
1747–1809	Seward, Anna
1748–1832	Bentham, Jeremy
1749–1806	Smith, Charlotte
1752–1840	Burney, Fanny
1753–1821	Inchbald, Elizabeth
1754–1820	Drennan, William
1754–1832	Crabbe, George
1755–1838	Grant, Anne
1756–1836	Godwin, William
1757–1827	Blake, William
1757–1851	Lee, Harriet
1758–1800	Robinson, Mary
1758–1816	Hamilton, Elizabeth
1758–1852	West, Jane
1759–1796	Burns, Robert
1759–1797	Wollstonecraft, Mary
1759–1813	Little, Janet

Dates	Author
1760–1838	Polwhele, Richard
1760–1846	Clarkson, Thomas
1761–1827	Williams, Helen Maria
1762–1851	Baillie, Joanna
1762–1859	Bowles, William Lisle
1763–1835	Cobbett, William
1764?–1845	Roche, Maria Regina
1764–1823	Radcliffe, Ann
1764–1847	Lamb, Mary Ann
1766–1817	Staël, Madame de
1766–1834	Malthus, Thomas
1768–1849	Edgeworth, Maria
1769–1846	Frere, John Hookham
1769–1853	Opie, Amelia
1770–1827	Canning, George
1770–1831	Hope, Thomas
1770–1835	Hogg, James
1770–1850	Wordsworth, William
1771–1832	Scott, Sir Walter
1771–1834	Bloomfield, Robert
1771–1845	Smith, Sydney
1771–1854	Montgomery, James
1771–1855	Wordsworth, Dorothy
1772–1810	Tighe, Mary
1772–1823	Ricardo, David
1772–1834	Coleridge, Samuel Taylor

Dates	Author
1772–1849	Egan, Pierce
1773–1836	Mill, James
1773–1850	Jeffrey, Francis
1774–1843	Southey, Robert
1775–1817	Austen, Jane
1775–1818	Lewis, Matthew Gregory
1775–1834	Lamb, Charles
1775–1841	White, Joseph Blanco
1775–1851	Sherwood, Mary
1775–1864	Landor, Walter Savage
1776–1850	Porter, Jane
1776–1859	Owenson, Sydney
1777–1832	Lathom, Francis
1777–1844	Campbell, Thomas
1778?–1844	Holcroft, Frances
1778–1818	Brunton, Mary
1778–1830	Hazlitt, William
1779–1839	Galt, John
1779–1852	Moore, Thomas
1779–1863	Trollope, Frances
1780–1824	Maturin, C. R.
1780–1832	Porter, Anne Maria
1780–1849	Morier, James
1781–1864	Aiken, Lucy
1782?–1825	Dacre, Charlotte
1782–1835	Pocock, Isaac
1782–1854	Ferrier, Susan
1782–1856	Bowdler, Thomas
1784–1859	Hunt, Leigh
1785–1828	Lamb, Lady Caroline
1785–1848	Wheeler, Anna
1785–1854	North, Christopher
1785–1859	De Quincey, Thomas
1785–1866	Peacock, Thomas Love
1786–1846	Haydon, Benjamin Robert
1787–1855	Mitford, Mary Russell
1788–1824	Byron, George Gordon, Lord
1788–1833	Prince, Mary
1790–1846	Tonna, Charlotte Elizabeth
1790–1849	Blessington, Marguerite Gardiner, Countess of
1791–1871	Babbage, Charles
1792–1822	Shelley, Percy Bysshe

Dates	Author
1792–1848	Marryat, Frederick
1792–1866	Keble, John
1792–1879	Howitt, William
1792–1881	Trelawny, Edward John
1793–1835	Hemans, Felicia Dorothea
1793–1842	Maginn, William
1793–1864	Clare, John
1794–1854	Lockhart, J. G.
1794–1857	Moncrieff, William Thomas
1794–1860	Jameson, Anna
1794–1895	Greville, Charles Cavendish Fulke
1795–1821	Keats, John
1795–1842	Arnold, Thomas
1795–1881	Carlyle, Thomas
1796–1849	Coleridge, Hartley
1796–1874	Strickland, Agnes
1797–1851	Shelley, Mary
1797–1869	Eden, Emily
1797–1875	Lyell, Sir Charles
1799–1845	Hood, Thomas
1799–1859	Acton, Eliza
1799–1860	James, George Payne
1799–1888	Howitt, Mary
1800–1833	Jewsbury, Maria Jane
1800–1861	Gore, Catherine
1800–1861	Macaulay, Thomas
1800?–1876	Crowe, Catherine
1800–1879	Wells, Charles Jeremiah
1800–1882	Pusey, Edward Bouverie
1800–1886	Taylor, Henry
1801?–1854?	Jones, Hannah Maria
1801–1866	Carlyle, Jane Welsh
1801–1873	Clive, Caroline ("V.")
1801–1886	Barnes, William
1801–1890	Newman, John Henry Cardinal
1802–1838	Landon, Letitia Elizabeth
1802–1871	Chambers, Robert
1802–1876	Martineau, Harriet
1802–1879	Buckstone, J. B.
1802–1882	Bulwer-Lytton, Rosina
1803–1881?	Stone, Elizabeth
1803–1849	Beddoes, Thomas Lovell

Dates	Author	Dates	Author
1803–1849	Mangan, James Clarence	1812–1880	Jewsbury, Geraldine
1803–1857	Jerrold, Douglas	1812–1885	Fullerton, Lady Georgiana
1803–1868	Coyne, Joseph Stirling	1812–1887	Mayhew, Henry
1803–1873	Bulwer-Lytton, Edward	1812–1888	Lear, Edward
1803–1881	Borrow, George	1812–1889	Browning, Robert
1804–1873	Hawker, R. S.	1812–1904	Smiles, Samuel
1804–1876	Sand, George	1813–1865	Aytoun, William Edmondstoune
1804–1881	Disraeli, Benjamin		
1805–1864	Surtees, Robert	1814–1863	Faber, Frederick
1805–1882	Ainsworth, W. H.	1814–1873	Le Fanu, Joseph Sheridan
1805–1892	Cooper, Thomas	1814–1879	Reynolds, G. M. W.
1806–1861	Browning, Elizabeth Barrett	1814–1880	Kingston, W. H. G.
1806–1872	Lever, Charles	1814–1883	Colenso, John William
1806–1873	Mill, John Stuart	1814–1884	Reade, Charles
1807–1855	Montgomery, Robert	1814–1887	Wood, Ellen
1807–1858	Mill, Harriet Taylor	1814–1902	De Vere, Aubrey Thomas
1808–1871	Burns, James Dawson	1815?–1880?	Smedley, Menella Bute
1808–1874	Strauss, David Friedrich	1815–1882	Trollope, Anthony
1808–1876	Taylor, Philip Meadows	1815–1906	Sewell, Elizabeth Missing
1808–1877	Norton, Caroline	1816–1847	Aguilar, Grace
1808–1879	Turner, Charles Tennyson	1816–1855	Brontë, Charlotte
1809–1870	Lemon, Mark	1816–1874	Brooks, Shirley
1809–1882	Darwin, Charles	1816–1909	Martin, Theodore
1809–1883	Fitzgerald, Edward	1817–1878	Lewes, G. H.
1809–1884	Tucker, Charlotte	1817–1894	Layard, Sir Austen Henry
1809–1885	Milnes, Richard Monkton	1817–1901	Victoria, Queen of England
1809–1891	Kinglake, Alexander William	1818–1848	Brontë, Emily
1809–1892	Tennyson, Alfred Lord	1818–1883	Marx, Karl
1809–1893	Kemble, Fanny	1818–1889	Cook, Eliza
1809–1898	Clarke, Mary Cowden	1818–1894	Froude, James Anthony
1809–1898	Gladstone, William	1818–1895	Green, Mary Anne Everett
1810–1852	Warburton, Eliot	1819–1861	Clough, Arthur Hugh
1810–1865	Gaskell, Elizabeth	1819–1868	Jones, Ernest Charles
1810–1871	Alford, Henry	1819–1875	Kingsley, Charles
1810–1878	Doyle, Sir Francis Hastings	1819–1880	Eliot, George
1810–1888	Gosse, Philip Henry	1819–1900	Ruskin, John
1810–1892	Trollope, Thomas Adolphus	1820/22–1890	Boucicault, Dion
1811–1833	Hallam, Arthur	1820–1849	Brontë, Anne
1811–1863	Thackeray, William Makepeace	1820–1878	Sewell, Anna
1811–1891	Morton, John Maddison	1820–1895	Engels, Friedrich
1812–1870	Dickens, Charles	1820–1897	Ingelow, Jean
1812–1872	Ellis, Sarah Stickney	1820–1903	Spencer, Herbert
1812–1876	Forster, John	1820–1910	Nightingale, Florence

Dates	Author	Dates	Author
1821–1869	Gordon, Lucie Duff	1829–1925	Belloc, Bessie Rayner Parkes
1821–1878	Whyte-Melville, George	1829–1871	Robertson, Thomas
1821–1882	Greenwell, Dora	1829–1888	Oliphant, Laurence
1821–1889	Charles, Elizabeth	1829–1890	Booth, Catherine
1821–1890	Burton, Richard Francis	1829–1912	Booth, William
1821–1896	Wilde, Jane Francesca (Speranza)	1830–1867	Smith, Alexander
		1830–1894	Rossetti, Christina
1821–1899	Skene, Felicia	1830–1897	Brown, Thomas Edward
1822–1888	Arnold, Matthew	1831–1892	Edwards, Amelia
1822–1896	Hughes, Thomas	1831–1894	Yates, Edmund
1822–1898	Linton, Eliza Lynn	1831–1907	Taylor, Helen
1821–1902	Temple, Frederick	1831–1909	Fenn, George Manville
1822–1904	Cobbe, Frances Power	1831–1913	White, William Hale
1822–1912	Ogilvy, Eliza	1831–1923	Harrison, Frederic
1823–1896	Patmore, Coventry	1832–1898	Carroll, Lewis
1823–1901	Yonge, Charlotte	1832–1904	Stephen, Leslie
1824–1874	Dobell, Sydney	1832–1906	Riddell, Charlotte Elizabeth
1824–1877	Kavanagh, Julia	1832–1911	Stretton, Hesba
1824–1889	Allingham, William	1832–1914	Watts-Dunton, Theodore
1824–1889	Collins, Wilkie	1833–1885	Gordon, Charles George
1824–1897	Palgrave, Francis Turner	1833–1900	Dixon, Richard Watson
1824–1905	Macdonald, George	1834–1882	Thomson, James
1825–1864	Procter, Adelaide Anne	1834–1896	Du Maurier, George
1825–1894	Ballantyne, R. M.	1834–1896	Morris, William
1825–1895	Huxley, T. H.	1834–1903	Shorthouse, Joseph Henry
1825–1900	Blackmore, Richard	1834–1924	Baring-Gould, Sabine
1826–1877	Bagehot, Walter	1834–1925	Fitzgerald, Percy
1826–1887	Craik, Mrs. (Dinah Maria Mulock)	1835?–1873	Johnston, Ellen
		1835–1902	Butler, Samuel
1826–1894	Alexander, William	1835–1913	Austin, Alfred
1826–1915	Boldrewood, Rolf	1836–1865	Beeton, Isabella
1827–1864	Speke, John Henry	1836–1901	Besant, Walter
1827–1876	Collins, Mortimer	1836–1904	Hopkins, Ellice
1827–1876	Lawrence, George Alfred	1836–1911	Gilbert, W. S.
1827–1886	Evans, Matilda	1837–1891	à Beckett, Gilbert
1827–1890	Pfeiffer, Emily	1837–1894	Webster, Augusta
1827–1891	Bodichon, Barbara Leigh Smith	1837–1899	Marryat, Florence
1828–1879	Dallas, E. S.	1837–1909	Swinburne, Algernon Charles
1828–1882	Rossetti, Dante Gabriel	1837–1915	Braddon, Mary Elizabeth
1828–1897	Oliphant, Margaret	1837–1919	Ritchie, Anne
1828–1906	Butler, Josephine	1838–1903	Farjeon, Benjamin
1828–1909	Meredith, George	1838–1914	Muir, John
1829–1862	Siddal, Elizabeth	1839–1894	Pater, Walter

Authors' Time Line

Dates	Author
1839–1908	Ouida
1839–1916	Todhunter, John
1839–1921	Molesworth, Mary Louisa
1840–1893	Symonds, John Addington
1840–1904	Dilke, Lady Emilia
1840–1916	Booth, Charles
1840–1920	Broughton, Rhoda
1840–1921	Dobson, Henry Austin
1840–1928	Hardy, Thomas
1841–1885	Ewing, Juliana
1841–1896	Blind, Mathilde
1841–1898	Black, William
1841–1901	Buchanan, Robert
1841–1904	Stanley, Henry Morton
1841–1922	Hudson, William Henry
1843–1916	James, Henry
1844–1881	O'Shaughnessy, Arthur
1844–1899	Hopkins, Gerard Manley
1844–1912	Lang, Andrew
1844–1914	Meade, Lillie T.
1844–1926	Cambridge, Ada
1844–1929	Carpenter, Edward
1844–1930	Bridges, Robert
1845–1895	Bevington, Louisa S.
1845–1915	Walford, Lucy
1845–1933	Saintsbury, George
1846–1898	Dowling, Richard
1846–1928	O'Grady, Standish
1847–1912	Stoker, Bram
1847–1922	Meynell, Alice
1847–1929	Fawcett, Millicent
1847–1929	Steel, Flora Annie
1847–1933	Besant, Annie
1848–1887	Jefferies, Richard
1848–1899	Allen, Charles Grant
1848–1915	Bradley, Katherine Harris (Michael Field)
1849–1903	Henley, W. E.
1849–1923	Mallock, William Hurrell
1849–1924	Burnett, Frances Hodgson
1849–1928	Gosse, Edmund
1850?–1912	Adams, Bertha Jane Leith
1850–1887	Marston, Philip Bourke

Dates	Author
1850–1894	Stevenson, Robert Louis
1850–1904	Hearn, Lafcadio
1851–1920	Ward, Mary
1851–1929	Jones, Henry Arthur
1851–1935	Praed, Rosa
1852–1931	Malet, Lucas
1852–1933	Moore, George
1853–1931	Caine, T. H. Hall
1854–1900	Wilde, Oscar
1854–1943	Grand, Sarah
1855–1898	Marx, Eleanor
1855–1905	Sharp, William
1855–1920	Schreiner, Olive
1855–1924	Corelli, Maria
1855–1934	Pinero, Arthur Wing
1856–1909	Probyn, May
1856–1911	Stannard, Henrietta
1856–1925	Haggard, H. Rider
1856–1931	Harris, Frank
1856–1935	Lee, Vernon
1856–1950	Shaw, George Bernard
1857–1903	Gissing, George
1857–1907	Davidson, John
1857–1924	Conrad, Joseph
1857–1932	Dixon, Ella Hepworth
1858–1889	Naden, Constance
1858–1920	Radford, Dollie
1858–1924	Nesbit, E.
1858–1932	Caird, Mona
1858–1935	Watson, Sir William
1859–1907	Thompson, Francis
1859–1925	Cholmondeley, Mary
1859–1926	Brooke, Emma Frances
1859–1927	Jerome, Jerome K.
1859–1930	Doyle, Sir Arthur Conan
1859–1936	Housman, A. E.
1859–1939	Ellis, Havelock
1860–1913	Rolfe, Frederick William
1860–1945	Egerton, George (Mary Dunne)
1861–1889	Levy, Amy
1861–1907	Coleridge, Mary
1862–1893	Adams, Francis
1862–1900	Kingsley, Mary

Dates	Author	Dates	Author
1862–1903	Scott, Hugh Stowell	1865–1936	Kipling, Rudyard
1862–1913	Cooper, Edith Emma (Michael Field)	1865–1945	Symons, Arthur
		1866–1947	Le Gallienne, Richard
1862–1933	Leverson, Ada	1867–1900	Dowson, Ernest
1862–1938	Newbolt, Henry	1867–1902	Johnson, Lionel
1862–1960	Phillpotts, Eden	1867–1906	Craigie, Pearl
1863–1943	Jacobs, William Wymark	1867–1945	Dowie, Menie Muriel
1863–1944	Quiller-Couch, Arthur (Q)	1869–1928	Mew, Charlotte
1863–1945	Morrison, Arthur	1870–1945	Douglas, Lord Alfred
1864–1916	Danby, Frank	1872–1898	Beardsley, Aubrey
1864–1926	Zangwill, Israel	1872–1956	Beerbohm, Max
1864–1950	Hichens, Robert		

à Beckett, Gilbert (1837–1891) *playwright, editor, nonfiction writer*

Gilbert Abbott à Beckett was born in Hammersmith, England, and attended Westminster School. He later became a successful lawyer and was appointed a judge at age 38.

Though à Beckett wrote as many as 60 plays, he is best known as a satiric magazine writer. He was on the original staff of the weekly magazine *Punch,* which was devoted to political and social satire, and edited another humor magazine, *Figaro in London.* He wrote for various newspapers, including the *Times* and the *Morning Herald,* and contributed amusing articles to the *Illustrated London News* under the pseudonym Perambulating Philosopher.

Among à Beckett's best known works are *The Comic History of England* (1847–48) and *The Comic History of Rome* (1852), which he said he was prompted to write "by a very serious desire to instruct those who, though willing to acquire information, seek to do so with as much amusement as possible." One of his hit plays was *The Chimes at Midnight,* an adaptation of a short story of the same title by CHARLES DICKENS.

Other Work by Gilbert à Beckett
The Comic Blackstone. London: Ashford, 1985.

Acton, Eliza (1799–1859) *poet, cookbook writer*

Born in Suffolk, England, Eliza Acton was the oldest daughter of John Acton, an Ipswich brewer. As a young woman she experienced poor health and spent time recuperating in Paris, where she began writing poetry. She was briefly engaged to a French officer, and her earliest poems question his honor and fidelity. After returning to England, she continued to write poetry while operating a boarding house. Acton collected her early works in *Poems* (1826), and she occasionally published poems in the *Sudbury Pocket Book.*

Acton's poems unite romantic images of natural beauty, death, and betrayal with a classic, Sapphic narrative in which a female speaker urges her friends to remember former times of happiness. For example, in "Where, oh! where, on his restless wing," (1826), the narrator confides that she has once "been where passionate hearts beat high." But she now rejects her unfaithful lover, telling him to "ne'er again in thy roamings come" because, "though rapture dwell in thy sunny smile / Despair comes fast on thy steps the while."

In the early 1840s Acton's publisher, Thomas Longman, rejected the idea of another volume of poetry, suggesting instead that Acton produce a cookbook. The result, *Modern Cookery* (1845), was instantly successful and was reprinted several times during its first year. The book was so popular, in fact, that Acton used the preface of the 1855 edition to complain about the widespread plagiarism of its contents. The book's popularity sprang first from its specificity and detail. For instance, in her jam recipes, Acton associates the quality of the jam with the time of the season in which the fruit was picked. She also provides a history for each recipe and explains why her version is superior to other regional varieties. Finally, Acton was the first cookbook writer to include precise measurements for the ingredients in her recipes.

Her book's popularity eventually declined because its culinary tastes were more reflective of the late 18th century than of the emerging Victorian culture. *Modern Cookery* was replaced by such books as ISABELLA BEETON's *Household Management*. But because of Acton's innovative presentation of her recipes, *Modern Cookery* is still considered the most influential cookbook of the 19th century. The critic Elizabeth David describes it as "the final expression, the crystallisation, of pre-Industrial England's taste in food and attitude to cookery."

Other Work by Eliza Acton
Ray, Elizabeth, ed. *The Best of Eliza Acton*. New York: Penguin, 1974.

Adams, Bertha Jane Leith (1837?–1912)
novelist, short story writer, journalist

The daughter of a solicitor, Frederick Grundy, Bertha Jane Grundy was born in Cheshire, England. In 1859 she married Andrew Leith Adams, an army surgeon whose military service took the couple on extensive travels. One of England's earliest women journalists, Adams worked on the staff of *All the Year Round* beginning in 1878. In 1883, a year after her husband's death, Adams remarried. While her new husband, the Reverend Robert Stuart De Courcy Laffan, performed his duties as rector of St. Stephen Walbrook and pursued his active interest in higher education for the working classes, Adams wrote fiction.

Her most popular novel, *Geoffrey Stirling* (1883), told the melodramatic story of a wife's revenge on her husband's murderer. Influenced by the serial installments of fiction published in *All the Year Round,* Adams sought young, especially female, readers with such novels as *Aunt Hepsy's Foundling* (1881), praised by the *Saturday Review* as "an almost perfect novel of its kind," and *Bonnie Kate* (1891), a novel about marital conflict, subtitled *A Story from a Woman's Point of View.*

For *A Garrison Romance* (1892) and the patriotic *Colour Sergeant No. 1 Company* (1894), Adams drew upon her earlier travels with her first husband to create remote army settings in the novels. Although few read Adams today, the critic Amanda Jo Pettit praises her "sensitivity to her surroundings and . . . active interest in the issues and people of her day."

Adams, Francis William Lauderdale
(1862–1893) *poet, novelist, journalist*

Francis Adams was born in Malta at a British military outpost to Andrew Leith Adams, a prominent army surgeon, and BERTHA JANE ADAMS, a novelist. Because of his father's career, the family lived in both Ireland and Canada. But at age eight Adams returned to England and attended Shrewsbury (a prestigious boys' school) before studying for two years in Paris (1879–81).

In Paris two important events occurred. First, Adams contracted tuberculosis, a disease that permanently plagued him. Second, he wrote his first novel, *Leicester: An Autobiography* (1885), which recounts Adams's experiences at Shrewsbury. It was republished in 1894 as *A Child of the Age.*

After completing his studies, Adams failed to attain desired appointments to either the English diplomatic service or the Indian civil service. Therefore, he accepted a teaching position at Ventnor College on the Isle of Wight. While at Ventnor, Adams married his first wife, Elizabeth Uttley, and decided to become a writer. In 1884 he moved to Australia, seeking both opportunities as a writer and a milder climate to relieve his steadily worsening health. Adams first wrote for newspapers in Sydney and Brisbane.

During the mid-1880s, Adams developed two central, related concerns as a writer. First, he became an outspoken social critic, championing Australian independence and condemning what he considered the unjust labor practices of capitalism. He addressed these issues in *Australian Essays* and his first volume of poetry, *Poetical Works* (1886). His next volume of poetry, *Songs of the Army of the Night* (1887), fostered his reputation as a spokesman for social change. In the "Proem," Adams proclaims that "the stricken men, the mad brute-beasts, are keeping / No more their places in the ditches or holes" and urges his readers to "rise, and join us."

Second, Adams coupled his distaste for capitalism with an adherence to the cultural philosophy of MATTHEW ARNOLD. He deplored the philistinism of the middle class, and in such novels as *The Australians* (1893) he advocated the infusion of simple, artistic beauty in everyday life.

In 1887 Adams's wife and infant son died. Three years later, after remarrying, Adams returned to England. While suffering from declining health, he wrote a series of articles about Australian life for the *Fortnightly Review*. Suffering from a virulent attack of tuberculosis, he shot and killed himself. The scholar Lucy Frost observes that Adams "influenced a whole generation of idealistic young socialists in Australia, and had a leading role in the development of the Australian labour movement."

aestheticism

The term *aestheticism* refers to a movement that flourished in Europe in the late 19th century. Aestheticism, which promoted the existence of art for the sake of its beauty alone, was a reaction against the utilitarian views of the industrial age. Followers of aestheticism rejected the idea that art should serve a moral, religious, or didactic purpose. Writing about the role of poetry, the English poet ALGERNON CHARLES SWINBURNE declared that "handmaid of religion, exponent of duty, servant of fact, pioneer of morality, she cannot in any way become.... Her business is not to do good on other grounds, but to be good on her own.... Art for art's sake first of all...." The phrase "art for art's sake," coined in 1818 by the French philosopher Victor Cousin, succinctly describes the movement's doctrine.

Aestheticism's early influences came from Germany, specifically in the ideas of the philosopher Immanuel Kant and in the poetry of the German romantics, particularly Johann Wolfgang von Goethe. In England aestheticism was heavily influenced by a long line of poets—from SAMUEL TAYLOR COLERIDGE and JOHN KEATS to art critics such as WALTER PATER and JOHN RUSKIN—and by the artists of the PRE-RAPHAELITE MOVEMENT, all of whom expressed in their work a yearning for ideal beauty. Aestheticism's devotion to art for art's sake was most exemplified, however, by the playwright and novelist OSCAR WILDE, whose masterful wit and extravagant lifestyle defied conventional opinion, and whom many considered to be the leader of the movement. In his essay "The Decay of Lying" (1889), Wilde declared that "Art never expresses anything but itself. It has an independent life, just as thought has and develops purely on its own lines."

Wilde also became the English spokesperson for the French variant of aestheticism, decadence. Decadent writers, such as Charles Baudelaire, Arthur Rimbaud, and J. K. Huysmans, held to the ideal of art for art's sake while exploring themes of perversion, exoticism, and the bizarre in their writings and had a darker and more fatalistic outlook than the aesthetes. Wilde's Dorian Gray is an example of a decadent literary character and is modeled on the hero of Huysmans's novel *À Rebours*.

Works about Aestheticism

Dellamora, Richard. *Masculine Desire: The Sexual Politics of Victorian Aestheticism.* Durham: University of North Carolina Press, 1990.

Johnson, Robert Vincent. *Aestheticism*. New York: Barnes and Noble, 1969.

Schaffer, Talia, and Kathy Alexis Psomiades, eds. *Women and British Aestheticism*. Charlottesville: University Press of Virginia, 2000.

Scheinberg, Cynthia. *Women's Poetry and Religion in Victorian England: Jewish Identity and Christian Culture.* New York: Cambridge University Press, 2002.

Aguilar, Grace (1816–1847) *nonfiction writer, poet, novelist*

Grace Aguilar was born in Hackney, England, to a Sephardic (Spanish) Jewish family. She was taught at home by her parents because her weak health made it impossible for her to attend school.

Aguilar's major nonfiction works examined the nature of her faith, her Jewish identity, and the role of women in Judaism. In *The Spirit of Judaism* (1842) and *The Women of Israel* (1845), she called on women to become students of the Torah, the body of Jewish law. An early feminist and a devout but unconventional Jew, she strongly believed that Jewish women had an important role to play as religious leaders and that they should not be confined to their traditional roles. As she wrote, they have a "mission to perform, not alone as daughters, wives, and mothers, but as witnesses of that faith which first raised, cherished, and defended them, to prove that they have no need of Christianity, or the examples of females in the gospel, to raise them up to an equality with man."

During the 1830s and 1840s, Aguilar also wrote poetry and several domestic novels, including *Home Influence: A Tale for Mothers and Daughters* (1847), the only one to be published in her lifetime. Her other novels were edited and published by her mother after her death and became popular for their intense moral feeling. She died at the age of 31 on a visit to her brother in Frankfurt.

Works about Grace Aguilar

Galchinsky, Michael. *The Origin of the Modern Jewish Woman Writer: Romance and Reform in Victorian England.* Detroit: Wayne State University Press, 1996.

Aikin, Lucy (1781–1864) *children's book writer, poet, historian*

Lucy Aikin was born on November 6, 1781, in Lancashire, northern England, to John Aikin, a physician and author, and Martha Jennings. Her father's sister was the well-known poet and anthologist ANNA LAETITIA BARBAULD. Lucy was educated primarily at home and published her first book, an anthology titled *Poetry for Children*, in 1801. Meanwhile, she produced versions of classic stories such as *Robinson Crusoe* that could be read and understood by young children. *Robinson Crusoe in Words of One Syllable* and *Aesop's Fables in Words of One Syllable* were followed by several others, all published under the pseudonym Mary Godolphin. Aikin did not consider herself a creative writer, but her volume of poetry, *Epistles on Women* (1810), protests eloquently against the frivolity to which male preference has condemned women:

> E'en while the youth, in love and rapture warm,
> Sighs as he hangs upon her beauteous form,
> Careless and cold he views the beauteous mind,
> For virtue, bliss, eternity designed.
> "Banish, my fair," he cries, "those studious looks;
> Oh! What should beauty learn from crabbed books?"

Aikin also wrote popular histories, including *Memoirs of the Court of Queen Elizabeth* (1818), followed four years later by *Memoirs of the Court of James I* (1822) and *Memoir of the Court of Charles I* (1833). She produced biographies of Joseph Addison and of her father; after Barbauld's death in 1825, she edited and published *The Works* of *Anna Laetitia Barbauld, with a Memoir by Lucy Aikin.* Aikin lived part of her life in London, and later moved to Hampstead, on the outskirts of London. She never married.

Ainsworth, William Harrison (1805–1882) novelist, editor

William Harrison Ainsworth was born in Manchester and educated at the Manchester Free School. The son of one of the city's leading attorneys, in 1817 he began training for the law. He also began publishing articles, stories, and poems in such popular magazines as *Edinburgh Magazine, New Monthly Magazine,* and *London Magazine.* In 1822 his first book of verse, *The Maiden's Revenge,* appeared under the pseudonym Cheviot Ticheburn, and he dedicated it to CHARLES LAMB, who became a friend. This early success might have reinforced Ainsworth's preference for a literary life, but he honored his father's wishes, completed his law studies at London's Inns of Court, and was admitted to the Court of King's Bench as a solicitor in 1826. In that same year he published his first novel, *Sir John Chiverton,* written in collaboration with his father's law clerk John Partington Aston, and married Anne Frances "Fanny" Ebers, the daughter of his publisher, John Ebers.

The late 1820s through the 1830s proved pivotal to the direction of Ainsworth's life. *Sir John Chiverton* was an immediate success, drawing the praise of SIR WALTER SCOTT, whose romances had clearly influenced the two young authors. Encouraged by this first critical success, Ainsworth gave up the law by the mid-1830s.

In 1834 Ainsworth published one of his most popular novels, the historical romance *Rookwood.* Similar to Scott's *Bride of Lammermoor* and Nathaniel Hawthorne's *House of the Seven Gables, Rookwood* involves a family struggle over an inheritance when Sir Piers Rookwood dies, leaving two sons—Ranulph (his son by Lady Rookwood) and Luke (his elder, but apparently illegitimate, son by Susan Bradley). Both brothers also compete for the hand of Eleanor Mowbray, who stands to inherit estates from Sir Piers's brother Sir Reginald Rookwood. In a complex plot, Luke seeks to establish his legitimate claim to the estate and the right to marry Eleanor, but he is brought down by his mistreatment of his fiancée Sybil Lovel, whom he had abandoned to pursue Eleanor and his claim to the Rookwood inheritance. The legendary highwayman Dick Turpin is one of the novel's most vivid and engaging characters, even though he is a peripheral one. The scholar Philip Allingham writes that Turpin's "ride on Black Bess from London to York with the minions of the law in constant pursuit and the tragic death of Turpin's faithful mare are the best things in the romance."

Ainsworth's best novel in terms of plot structure and characterization is the NEWGATE CRIME NOVEL and best-seller *Jack Sheppard* (1839). Ainsworth's criminal-hero Jack Sheppard is enticed into a life of crime by Jonathan Wild and is then relentlessly pursued by Wild for years. Unlike Jack, his boyhood friend Thames Darrell chooses virtue over vice. But in the novel's climax, the criminal Jack becomes the hero, saving Thames and his young wife from the seducer Wild. Despite saving Thames, Jack is condemned to the gallows for his many crimes. Poetic justice is served when within seven months of Jack's death Wild, too, is hanged.

As a novelist, Ainsworth was most directly influenced by the historical romances of Walter Scott. However, his skills at plot and character development were more limited than Scott's, and over time his books came to be viewed as contrived and old-fashioned. He had won his public with *Rookwood* and *Jack Shepard,* and continued to enjoy a large audience for *The Tower of London* (1840); *Guy Fawkes* (1841); *Old Saint Paul's* (1841), which contains some of the most vivid description ever written of the plague and Great Fire of London; *The Miser's Daughter* (1842); *Windsor Castle* (1843); and *The Lancashire Witches* (1849), among a lifetime production of almost 40 books. However, by the early 1850s literary tastes had changed and his reputation was in decline. He continued to publish for three more decades, but Ainsworth never again achieved the popular successes of his earlier years.

In 1839 Ainsworth succeeded CHARLES DICKENS as the editor of *Bentley's Miscellany*, a periodical that published essays, stories, and poems, and the first serializations of novels, such as Dickens's *Oliver Twist*. Resigning at the end of 1841, he launched *Ainsworth's Magazine* a few months later. He purchased the *New Monthly Magazine* in 1845 and edited it and *Ainsworth's* at the same time. He continued editing until 1870. His last decade was spent in almost total obscurity. Although his work is seldom read today, as the critic Patrick Kelly observes, Ainsworth was "Like Tennyson and Arnold, [in that] he shares the Victorian preoccupation with finding in the past some clarification of the bewildering present."

A Work about William Harrison Ainsworth
Worth, George J. *William Harrison Ainsworth*. New York: Twayne, 1972.

Alexander, William (1826–1894) *novelist, journalist*

Born in Aberdeenshire, Scotland, William Alexander became a writer purely by accident. His father, William, worked as a tenant farmer in the Garioch Valley, and Alexander initially labored as a shepherd and plowman. But at age 20 an accident resulted in the amputation of his right leg.

During his convalescence, Alexander read voraciously and began writing, eventually winning a prize for an essay that chronicled changes in the agricultural life caused by the rapid expansion of company-owned farms. Alexander combined his natural writing ability with a deep concern for the shifting social landscape of rural Scotland. As a journalist for the *North of Scotland Gazette*, he wrote an essay series, *Sketches of Rural Life in Aberdeenshire*, that offered fictional conversations between a tenant farmer and an urban capitalist and addressed issues such as education, the encroaching railroads and factories, the effect of heredity and environment on the individual, and the preservation of Scottish folk culture. Most important, the dialogue used the local Scots idiom. Alexander believed that such language was necessary to provide a true understanding of rural life.

The local dialect was again prominent in Alexander's first and most memorable novel, *Johnny Gibb of Gushetneuk* (1871). The novel extols Johnny Gibb, a moral, hardworking farmer who "for years—indeed until the bairns [children] grew up to be helpful . . . did every bit of work, out an in, upon the place." The farmer Peter Birse contrasts with Gibb: He is a greedy capitalist and chases success by buying out other farms instead of improving his own. Although Alexander glorified figures such as Gibb, his next major work, a collection of stories, *Life Among My Ain Folk* (1875), sadly suggested that the independent family farmer was disappearing.

Alexander produced many more essays and stories and eventually became editor of the Scottish newspaper *Daily Free Press*. Although some critics believe his abundant use of the local idiom relegates him to the status of a minor rural novelist, Alexander was influential because he incorporated realism into Scottish fiction. Further, he rejected standardized plots, portrayed all classes of society, avoided authorial omniscience, and attempted to explain human behavior. The critic William Donaldson asserts that Alexander is "central to the development of literary culture in Victorian Scotland. His work provides a clear example of the class-relatedness of popular fiction."

Alford, Henry (1810–1871) *poet, editor, hymnist*

Henry Alford was born in Middlesex, where his father, Henry Alford, was a curate of Steeple Ashton in Wiltshire and later of Wraxall near Bristol. Because his mother died during the younger Alford's birth, he lived with various family members. He spent the most time with his uncle,

Reverend Samuel Alford, whose daughter, Fanny, Alford eventually married.

From an early age Alford exhibited an inclination toward the ministry and even wrote sermons and letters to his cousins advising them on their moral conduct. After studying with a number of ministers, he enrolled at Cambridge University in 1829, graduating eighth in his class three years later. He served in several parishes until 1857, when he was appointed dean of Canterbury. While there, he oversaw a major renovation of the cathedral.

In 1845 Alford began editing the Greek (New) Testament. The first volume appeared in 1849; the project was completed in 1861. He also began a commentary upon the Old Testament in 1870. His editorial projects also included volumes of Greek poetry, English descriptive poetry, and the complete works of John Donne.

Alford was a prolific writer, producing lasting contributions both as hymnist and poet. Alford's hymns commemorated both sacramental and natural events. His two most enduring hymns are a baptismal hymn, "In token that thou shalt not fear," and a harvest hymn, "Come, ye thankful people, come." Alford published his first volume of poetry in 1832; the collection was revised and republished several times to include popular poems, such as "The School of the Heart" (1835) and "The Abbot of Muchelnaye" (1841). In 1845 Alford published a final collection of poetry, *The Poetical Works of Henry Alford*. He was friends with ALFRED, LORD TENNYSON and WILLIAM WORDSWORTH, both of whom praised his poems.

Alford's poetry combines his religious background and the aesthetic sensibility of the romantics. For example, in "Lady Mary," Alford describes the Virgin Mary as "the lily in the sun / And fairer yet thou mightest be / Thy youth was not yet begun." Although the poem celebrates Mary's selection as the mother of Christ, Alford cannot conceal a trace of regret for her lost youth. Despite the contemporary respect given to his poetry, Alford is now primarily recognized for his edition of the Greek Testament.

Allen, Charles Grant Blairfindie
(1848–1899) *novelist*

Grant Allen was born near Kingston, Ontario, Canada. His father was a minister and his mother the daughter of a French nobleman. Allen was educated at home as a child. After his family returned to Europe, he attended King Edward's School in Birmingham, England. He married Caroline Anne Bootheway in 1868 and graduated from Oxford University three years later. His wife's health was frail, and Allen held various teaching positions to help pay for her medical care. He was a professor of logic at Queens College in Jamaica for several years, then in 1876 returned to England and began writing for the London *Daily News*.

During the 1880s Allen began publishing his fiction—short stories, such as *Strange Stories* (1884); novels, such as *The Devil's Die* (1888) and his best-known work, *The Woman Who Did* (1895); and popular mysteries, such as *An African Millionaire*. The heroine of one of his mysteries, *Miss Cayley's Adventures,* is one of the earliest female detectives. A versatile writer, Allen also published books of poetry, philosophical essays, and popular science.

Other Work by Grant Allen
Cox, Michael, ed. *Victorian Tales of Mystery and Detection: An Oxford Anthology*. New York: Oxford University Press, 1992.

Allingham, William (1824–1889) *poet*

William Allingham was born in Ballyshannon, Donegal, Ireland, to the merchant, shipowner, and banker William Allingham and his wife Elizabeth. The younger Allingham attended elementary and boarding school in Ireland, then became a clerk in his father's bank in 1838. After working in the bank for a few years, Allingham accepted a job as principal coast officer of customs, holding that post until 1870.

In 1850 Allingham published *Poems,* a collection that includes his most famous poem, "The Fairies," which begins

> *Up the airy mountain*
> *Down the rushy glen,*
> *We daren't go a-hunting,*
> *For fear of little men.*

In 1854 Allingham published his next collection, *Day and Night Songs,* with illustrations by the poet DANTE GABRIEL ROSSETTI and the artist John Everett Millais, both of whom were friends of Allingham (as was ALFRED, LORD TENNYSON). Four years after retiring from the customs office, Allingham married Helen Paterson, a noted painter and illustrator. He continued to write poetry and from 1874 to 1879 was editor of *Fraser's Magazine.*

Many of Allingham's poems are short works that capture the words and feelings of Irish farmers. As the Irish poet William Butler Yeats wrote of him, "[h]e was the poet of little things and little moments."

Other Works by William Allingham

Allingham, H., and Radford D. Allingham, eds. *William Allingham: A Diary, 1824–1889.* New York: Viking, 1985.

Hewitt, John, ed. *The Poems of William Allingham.* London: Oxford University Press, 1967.

A.L.O.E. (A Lady of England)
See TUCKER, CHARLOTTE MARIA.

Arnold, Matthew (1822–1888) *nonfiction writer, poet*

Matthew Arnold was born in Laleham, Middlesex, the son of THOMAS ARNOLD and Mary Penrose Arnold. Thomas Arnold was the headmaster of Rugby School; his educational reforms there made Rugby the model for English public schools in the 19th century. The elder Arnold also was a noted historian. The son was deeply influenced by his father, especially in his attitudes toward social change. Time spent in the beautiful English Lake District also influenced Arnold's future writing. Although he never had the romantic faith in nature that permeates the poetry of WILLIAM WORDSWORTH, he always felt that the natural world had the power to heal some of life's sorrows.

Arnold attended Rugby, where he won a prize for his poem "Alaric at Rome," and Balliol College at Oxford University, where in 1843 he won the Newdigate Prize for his poem "Cromwell." After graduation from Oxford, Arnold returned to Rugby as a teacher of classics.

In the late 1840s he traveled to Europe and, some say, fell in love with a Frenchwoman, who, addressed as Marguerite, is the subject of many of his early lyrical poems that address isolation and loneliness. "To Marguerite—Continued" contains the memorable image of individuals as islands separated from others by "The unplumbed, salt, estranging sea."

In 1851 Arnold was appointed an inspector of schools. For the next 35 years he traveled throughout England and parts of Europe studying and reporting on various educational systems. Although the time Arnold spent on this job might have limited his poetic output, the social conditions he observed influenced many of his later essays. His observations led him to conclude that a democratic society required culture—art, poetry, and philosophy—to better its people, particularly spiritually and morally.

Arnold's first published collection of poetry, *The Strayed Reveller, and Other Poems* (1849), attracted little critical attention, although it contained "The Forsaken Merman," one of his best poems on the inevitable unhappiness that occurs when incompatible beings fall in love. This volume was followed by *Empedocles on Etna, and Other Poems* (1852). The title poem is one of Arnold's most important, recounting the tragedy of a man searching for meaning in a world where the old religious and social values no longer hold. Other volumes followed, including *Poems* (1853), *Poems, Second Series* (1855), *Merope* (1858), and *New Poems* (1867). The latter volume included "Thyrsis," Arnold's moving elegy written on the death of his dear friend ARTHUR HUGH CLOUGH.

Arnold wrote in a variety of poetic forms, including lyric, drama, narrative, and elegy. His poetry reflected the feelings of many intellectuals of the Victorian era who had lost their religious faith and felt alienated from their society, abandoned in the modern world, and cut adrift from the past. Arnold articulates these feelings especially well in these lines from "Stanzas from the Grande Chartreuse," in which the poet describes himself "Wandering between two worlds, one dead / The other powerless to be born."

Arnold's poetry speaks of loss, doubt, and the poet's estrangement and isolation from the everyday world. In the absence of religious faith or an ideal to which humankind can commit, Arnold suggests that stoic resignation may be the only possible attitude toward modern life, which, in "The Scholar-Gypsy," he calls a "strange disease . . . with its sick hurry, its divided aims." All we can do, he says, is "waive all claim to bliss and try to bear."

Arnold's career as a critic began when he was appointed professor of poetry at Oxford in 1857. His first lectures were later collected as *On Translating Homer* (1861) and *Last Words on Translating Homer* (1862). Arnold delivered these lectures in English, thus becoming the first professor not to lecture in Latin. One of his most famous works, *Essays in Criticism,* appeared in 1865. In this work, Arnold criticizes those he calls "Philistines," people who care only about material prosperity and know nothing of the life of the spirit. Arnold suggests that poetry can function as religious faith once did to unify the people of England. He regards criticism as something much broader than mere literary analysis; he sees it as a disinterested and flexible form of thinking about both literature and life.

In *Culture and Anarchy* (1869), Arnold broadens his scope when he proposes that culture, of which poetry is a part, is a cure for unrestrained individualism and materialism. As he had previously done with poetry, he now defends culture as the modern equivalent of religion—as that which allows people to imagine perfection, "the best which has been thought and said in the world." But he points out that "Individual perfection is impossible so long as the rest of mankind are not perfected along with us." Arnold believed that culture, and especially great literature, could unify and ennoble the populace of England and raise up many of the poor and ignorant people he saw on his journeys as a school inspector. He believed that

> The great men of culture are those who have had a passion for . . . carrying from one end of society to the other, the best knowledge, the best ideas of their time; who have laboured to divest knowledge of all that was harsh, uncouth, difficult, abstract, professional, exclusive; to humanize it, to make it efficient outside the clique of the cultivated and the learned, yet still remaining the best knowledge and thought of the time, and true source, therefore, of sweetness and light.

"Sweetness and light" is Arnold's term for a way of thinking inspired by ancient Greek thought, an open-minded, unprejudiced ability to "see the object as in itself it really is."

Arnold's essays on such writers as the French novelist George Sand and the British poets Wordsworth, SHELLEY, BYRON, and KEATS, inspired later generations of literary critics, including the poet T. S. Eliot and the academic writers Harold Bloom and Lionel Trilling. Perhaps more than any other writer, Arnold is representative of the Victorian era in his gentility, his skepticism, and his cautious hope for the future.

Critical Analysis

Arnold's famous poem "Dover Beach" (1867) is set in the seaside town of Dover, notable for its white cliffs overlooking the English Channel. In the opening lines, the poet calls his lover to look out a window toward the flickering lights of the French coast and then toward the "cliffs of

England . . . Glimmering and vast." He tells her to listen to "the grating roar of pebbles" being thrown onto the beach, then drawn back into the sea. He hears the sound

> *Begin, and cease, and then again, begin,*
> *With tremulous cadence slow, and bring*
> *The eternal note of sadness in.*

This note of sadness, the poet says, was also heard by the Greek dramatist Sophocles "long ago." It is "the turbid ebb and flow of human misery."

There was a time, the poet adds, that "the Sea of Faith" was "at the full." But now we hear only "its melancholy, long, withdrawing roar." In these lines Arnold laments the loss of faith in the modern world, a loss that in his essays he often attributes to science's questioning the truth of religious teachings. (Thus, to Arnold, CHARLES DARWIN's theory of evolution argues for a world controlled only by chance rather than divine guidance.) The repetition of long O sounds adds to the sense of mourning and loss conveyed by the poet's images.

In the final stanza the poet urges that he and his lover "be true / To one another," believing that their love is all that is of value left in this sad, modern world. He says that everyday life, which appears to be "beautiful" and "new," offers nothing of value. In truth the lovers are alone

> *on a darkling plain*
> *Swept with confused alarms of struggle and flight,*
> *Where ignorant armies clash by night.*

This final image of chaotic battle is one of the most powerful in Victorian poetry. Stephen Coote in *The Penguin Short History of English Literature* says that these terrifying lines show "a godless Victorian wasteland and . . . a central Victorian moral dilemma." Without faith, many Victorians asked, how shall we live? Arnold asked this question in his poetry and tried to answer it in his prose works. Perhaps culture—the best thoughts of the best people—can give humanity the purpose it craves.

Other Works by Matthew Arnold

Collini, Stefan, ed. *Culture and Anarchy and Other Writings.* New York: Cambridge University Press, 1993.

Shrimpton, Nicholas, ed. *Matthew Arnold.* (Everyman Poetry Library). Boston: Tuttle Publishing, 1998.

Works about Matthew Arnold

Machann, Clinton. *Matthew Arnold: A Literary Life.* New York: St. Martin's Press, 1998.

Pratt, Linda Ray. *Matthew Arnold Revisited.* New York: Twayne, 2000.

Arnold, Thomas (1795–1842) *educator, historian*

The son of a customs inspector on the Isle of Wight whose father died when he was six, Thomas Arnold was educated at first by his aunt; he then attended a local school before enrolling at Winchester, a public (that is, private) school for boys, where he expanded his knowledge of classical languages. At 16 he went to Corpus Christi College at Oxford University, where he remained for eight years, proceeding in 1815 to Oriel College, Oxford, and finally being ordained deacon in 1818; in that year he began his teaching career, preparing students for university entrance. The following 10 years of teaching and his own study (of Roman history particularly) prepared him for the job at which he was to remain until his untimely death.

He became headmaster of Rugby School, and his tenure there was immortalized by THOMAS HUGHES in *Tom Brown's School Days.* Maintaining as headmaster the preeminence of classical languages and literatures, he nonetheless introduced the study of mathematics, modern history, and modern languages into the curriculum. He believed in the unity of knowledge, using principles from one area to shed light on problems in others. He also emphasized sports: The ball game known as rugby originated at the school in 1823. Arnold placed religion at the center of school life and built a chapel on campus. He taught the boys to become men who led integrated lives, combining intellectual, spiritual, physical, and moral qualities in a balanced way. Rugby became a model for other elite boys' schools, whose graduates went on to become judges, statesmen, diplomats, generals, and the leaders of the British Empire.

Arnold himself wrote, in addition to his many sermons, lectures, and abundant letters, a three-volume history of early Rome and a book on the history of the Roman Commonwealth. He was the father of MATTHEW ARNOLD (1822–88), who eulogized him in his poem "Rugby Chapel" and characterized him as "Zealous, beneficent, firm."

A Work about Thomas Arnold
Strachey, Lytton. *Eminent Victorians.* 1918. Reprint. New York: Random House, 1999.

Austen, Jane (1775–1817) novelist

Jane Austen, one of the finest novelists in the English language, was born at Steventon, Hampshire, England, the seventh of the eight children of the Reverend George Austen and his wife, Cassandra. Austen and her only sister, Cassandra, were sent to school for several years, but much of Jane's formative reading was done in her father's library. At age 15 she wrote *The History of England: From the Reign of Henry the Fourth to the Death of Charles the First* (1790), which she signed "by a partial, ignorant, and prejudiced historian."

Austen's fiction was influenced by her reading of 18th-century novelists, including Henry Fielding, Samuel Richardson, Frances Burney, and Maria Edgeworth. In addition to these models, she also read many contrived and emotionally overwrought novels, which she went on to satirize in her own fiction. For instance, "Love and Friendship," a piece of early work unpublished in her lifetime, parodied sentimental novels, and *Northanger Abbey* (1818) satirized the supernatural terrors of the popular gothic form.

Beginning in young adulthood, Austen led a rich social life in London, Southampton, Bath, and other fashionable spots. Through such experiences she developed her humorous perspective on the intrigues of courtship and on the struggles for social status. She also came to sympathize with those people, especially women, whose shaky finances robbed them of the possibility of independence.

Austen published her novels anonymously, but was hardly too shy to address such important contemporary issues as capitalism, slavery, and women's education. However, she focused primarily with wit and irony on the complications of contemporary domestic life. She once described her writings as mere miniatures, painted "on to the little bit (two Inches wide) of Ivory on which I work with so fine a Brush, as produces little effect after much labor." Though this self-effacing statement was long taken to be an apt characterization of Austen's domestic comedies, it may be more in line with the tongue-in-cheek remarks of Elizabeth Bennett, the witty and satirical heroine of Austen's *Pride and Prejudice* (1813).

Austen's contemporaries did not always share her fascination with real-world minutiae. When the Prince Regents librarian suggested that she should write a grand historical novel about the royal family and dedicate it to the prince, Austen wrote back that she could no more write a historical romance than an epic poem, "and if it were indispensable for me to keep it up and never relax into laughing . . . I should be hung before I had finished the first chapter." She dedicated *Emma* to the prince, however.

Critical Analysis

One of the Austen's most important themes is announced in the title of her first novel, *Sense and Sensibility* (1811). Austen's heroines must learn prudence in order to protect their dignity, even if they are powerless to attain their desires. Thus, Marianne Dashwood, a devotee of sensibility, or unfettered emotionalism and romantic affection, nearly dies of a broken heart when the feckless man with whom she has fallen in love marries another for money. Her sensible sister, Elinor, nurses her sister back to health while suppressing her own romantic disappointment. Elinor's dutifulness is rewarded when her beloved finally proposes to her, and her recovered sister marries a devoted, if less than dashing, man.

Pride and Prejudice treats courtship and desire in a more comedic vein, even if the five Bennett sisters' futures hang in the balance. A provision in the will by which Mr. Bennett inherited his property stipulates that it can be inherited only by a male heir, leading to his wife's obsession with marrying off her daughters lest they be left penniless. Elizabeth, the second daughter, is sometimes mortified by her mother's blatant matchmaking, but generally responds with wry humor to the indignities she faces as a woman of the lower gentry. Her irony backfires, however, and is revealed as prejudice when she misreads the reserve of Mr. Darcy as aristocratic pride. In a series of sparkling verbal parries, these two characters exchange witty barbs. Even a simple invitation to dance becomes a contest of wills and wordplay, with Elizabeth telling Darcy, "I have . . . made up my mind to tell you, that I do not want to dance a reel at all—and now despise me if you dare," and Darcy replying ambiguously, "Indeed I do not dare." Eventually, Darcy's kindness toward Elizabeth's younger sister draws Elizabeth and Darcy together.

The title character of *Emma* similarly learns a lesson about pride. However, unlike the Bennett sisters, Emma is financially independent; this independence enables her to cultivate the vices of the powerful: manipulation, meddling, and matchmaking. Emma's efforts to control others' lives are comical, but also potentially disastrous.

By contrast, in *Mansfield Park* (1814) and *Persuasion* (1817) Austen emphasizes the vulnerability of dependent middle-class women. At the age of nine, Fanny Price is sent from her large, humble family to live at Mansfield Park with wealthy relatives, the Bertrams, some of whom treat her harshly. Whereas the lowly Fanny possesses the highest virtue, the unmerited privilege of the Bertram family is suggested not only by the unfeeling actions of some of its members but also by the fact that their wealth comes from a sugar plantation in the West Indies that is worked by slave labor.

When *Persuasion* opens, its heroine, Anne Elliot, has already endured years of dutiful self-renunciation, having earlier broken off an engagement with Captain Frederick Wentworth at the behest of her father, who considered the young naval officer insufficiently wealthy. Anne remains constant in her love for Wentworth, and Austen brilliantly depicts Anne's quiet emotional suffering when they meet years later: Wentworth appears to fall in love with another and decorum prevents Anne from declaring her love.

Anne's psychology is the mirror image of Emma's: This intelligent, attractive, and sensitive character is so accustomed to being denied her desires that happiness surprises her when it is finally within her reach. Austen makes us appreciate Anne's difficulties through an innovation in narrative technique, termed by critics "free indirect discourse." This technique, adopted by later novelists to endow their characters with unprecedented psychological complexity, presents characters' thoughts not through dialogue but by incorporating their idiosyncratic speech patterns into the third-person narration. It created a new narrative stance that mediated between the intimacy of first-person narration and the comprehensiveness and authority of omniscient narration, as when the narrator describes Anne's perception of her ill-treatment by Lady Russell: "She did not blame Lady Russell . . . but she felt that were any young person, in similar circumstances, to apply to her for counsel, they would never receive any of such . . . wretchedness."

There has been extensive speculation among critics about the autobiographical elements of Austen's novels. For instance, Austen's father could not give his daughters much money on which to marry. Further, one of Austen's admirers died before a relationship could develop, she broke off an engagement to a man she did not love, and no other suitors proved desirable. The self-ironizing humor of her letters resembles Elizabeth Bennett's dialogue in *Pride and Prejudice,* although it reveals little about any personal sorrow on which Austen might have drawn for her novels.

Whether or not Austen made art from life, her consummate artistry has ensured that her novels continue to live in readers' imaginations and in the images of film and television adaptations. Feminist critics applaud her depiction of the mental lives of women under socially constrained circumstances. Conservative critics note the triumph of virtue and rationality over impulse in the world Austen creates. Marxist critics often note her frank depiction of economic calculations in marriage and matchmaking decisions. The critic A. Walton Litz writes, "We call Jane Austen the first 'modern' novelist … anticipating the classic form of the nineteenth-century novel, a form that enables the artist to record both the flow of external events and the complexities of personal impressions."

Other Works by Jane Austen

Catharine and Other Writings. New York: Oxford University Press, 1993.
Lady Susan. New York: Schocken Books, 1984.
Sanditon and Other Stories. New York: Alfred A. Knopf, 1996.

Works about Jane Austen

Bloom, Harold, ed. *Jane Austen.* Philadelphia: Chelsea House, 1986.
Handley, Graham. *Jane Austen.* New York: St. Martin's Press, 1992.
Lefroy, Helen. *Jane Austen.* Thrupp, England: Sutton Publishers, 1997.
Shields, Carol. *Jane Austen.* New York: Viking Penguin, 2001.
Spense, John. *Becoming Jane Austen.* London: Continuum, 2007.
Sullivan, Margaret C. *The Jane Austen Handbook: A Sensible Yet Elegant Guide to Her World.* Philadelphia: Quirk Books, 2007.

Austin, Alfred (1835–1913) poet

Alfred Austin was born in Leeds, England, to Joseph Austin, a wool grader, and his wife, Mary, who were Roman Catholic. Austin, who abandoned his parents' religion, graduated with a law degree from London University and practiced as a barrister. However, having published some undistinguished poetry and a forgettable novel, he became convinced that he possessed true literary genius and stopped practicing law in order to pursue literature. Austin worked as a literary critic, political journalist, and for 12 years edited a politically moderate magazine, the *National Review,* all the while writing poorly received sentimental poetry and moralistic novels. He finally gained some popularity with a prose miscellany titled *The Garden That I Love* (1894). Written in diary form and appealing to English sentiment for gardens, it contains this often quoted platitude: "Show me your garden, and I shall tell you what you are."

In 1896, to nearly everyone's astonishment, Austin was named poet laureate, succeeding Alfred, Lord Tennyson. (When Lord Salisbury, the Conservative prime minister who made the appointment, was asked why Austin got the job, he replied, "I don't think anyone else applied for the post.") Shortly after receiving this honor, Austin's reputation was somewhat tarnished by an ode he published in the *Times* praising the Jameson Raid, an ill-conceived attack against the Dutch republic of Transvaal in South Africa made by Sir Leander Starr Jameson. Not only was Austin's ode jingoistic, but the verse was dreadful: "They went across the veldt / As hard as they could pelt." But for truly immortal doggerel his readers had to wait until he wrote these lines on the illness of the Prince of Wales in 1897: "Across the wires the electric message came: / He is no better, he is much the same." The scholar H. B. Charlton ironically notes that Austin's "criticism is profuse in the false attribution to others of precisely those faults which he failed to recognize in himself." Austin's autobiography was published in 1911. He died at his home in Kent two years later.

Aytoun, William Edmondstoune (1813–1865) *poet, novelist*

William Aytoun was born in Scotland on June 23, 1813. He was educated by his mother, Joan Keir, who instilled in her son an appreciation for the ballads and history of Scotland. His father, Roger Aytoun, was a lawyer and a descendant of Sir Robert Aytoun (1570–1638), a Scottish poet and lawyer who had served at the courts of Kings James I and Charles I of England. William Aytoun attended the University of Edinburgh and then, like both his father and his 17th-century ancestor, became both a poet and a lawyer.

In 1832 Aytoun's collection *Poland, Homer, and Other Poems* was published. From 1836 to 1844 he contributed poems to *Blackwood's Magazine*, a literary periodical, whose staff he joined in 1844. A year later, he became a professor at Edinburgh University.

Lays of the Cavaliers (1848), his most popular work, tells the stories of the great heroes of Scotland. The poems are ballad-like narratives of the heroic Scots' exploits:

> *The peasant, as he sees the stream*
> *In winter rolling by*
> *And foaming o'er its channel bed*
> *Between him and the spot*
> *Won by the warriors of the sword*
> *Still calls that deep and dangerous ford*
> *The Passage of the Scot.*

Aytoun's later works include a collection of Scottish ballads, *Ballads of Scotland* (1858), and a novel, *Norman Sinclair* (1861).

Babbage, Charles (1791–1871) *letter writer, mathematician, philosopher*

Charles Babbage was born December 26, 1791, in Devonshire, England, to Benjamin Babbage, a prosperous banker, and Betty Teape. As a child, Babbage suffered from an unidentified illness that made a formal education impossible. He was homeschooled and, although he learned a great deal, he was unprepared for the discipline of formal education.

By 1806 Babbage's health improved and he continued his education at the academy of Rev. Stephen Freeman in Middlesex. During his years at Rev. Freeman's Academy, Babbage came to love mathematics. He took pleasure in reading the Renaissance essayist Francis Bacon, whom he considered the "founder of modern philosophy."

At 16 Babbage demonstrated a mastery of math that was unheard of at his age. In 1810 he entered Cambridge University, where he was disappointed with the level of teaching and scholarship. Retaining the bad habits of his youth, he often worked on projects that had nothing to do with his classes and had trouble following instructions. However, some of Babbage's projects were groundbreaking experiments that included transmitting written messages through aerial wires and the invention of a stomach pump.

Babbage transferred from Trinity College to Peterhouse, from which he received an honorary degree without examination in 1814. That same year he married Georgiana Whitmore, with whom he had eight children. After his wife's death in 1827, Babbage dedicated his life to science and the reformation of social thinking.

During the early part of his career, Babbage was actively involved in several efforts to promote the use of machinery in everyday life. Babbage also tried to invent a calculating machine. He believed that manual calculation would greatly impede the study of science and considered it his mission to eliminate the need for manual calculation. Unfortunately, he could never get his invention to work properly. However, he recorded his various attempts and experiments in his *Memoirs of the Analytical Society* (1813). His biography, *Passages from the Life of a Philosopher* (1864), written by his best friend Harry Buxton, also describes his efforts. Throughout his life, Babbage pursued the restructuring of the English labor force. In his 1834 publication *On the Economy of Machine and Manufacturing,* he highlighted the importance of the division of labor to productivity.

Babbage's son Henry was able to perfect his father's invention of a calculating machine, and Henry attributed the actual invention of the calculating machine to his father. Modern scientists credit Babbage with laying the groundwork for the modern computer. Babbage died in 1871.

Other Works by Charles Babbage

Babbage's Calculating Engines: A Collection of Papers. Los Angeles: Tomash, 1982.

Science and Reform. New York: Cambridge University Press, 1989.

Works about Charles Babbage

Bell, Walter Lyle. *Charles Babbage, Philosopher, Reformer, Inventor: A History of His Contributions to Science.* Corvallis: Oregon State University, 1975.

Buxton, Harry Wilmot. *Memoir of the Life and Labours of the Late Charles Babbage Esq.* Cambridge, Mass.: MIT Press, 1988.

Collier, Bruce. *Charles Babbage and the Engines of Perfection.* New York: Oxford University Press, 1998.

Halacy, Daniel, Stephan. *Charles Babbage: Father of the Computer.* New York: Crowell-Collier Press, 1970.

Bagehot, Walter (1826–1877) nonfiction writer

Walter Bagehot was born in Langport, Somerset, England, to Thomas Watson Bagehot and Edith Stucker Bagehot. He trained to be a lawyer, studied philosophy at University College in London, and worked with his father in shipping and banking.

Bagehot's writings covered a variety of topics, from economics and history to literary criticism. He wrote numerous articles and in 1855 became editor of the *National Review,* a politically and religiously moderate journal of opinion. In 1859 he began editing the political and financial journal the *Economist.* His book *The English Constitution* (1867) is a classic of political science in which Bagehot calls for combining the executive and legislative powers of government.

Bagehot's more theoretical work *Physics and Politics* (1872) is aptly subtitled "Thoughts on the Application of the Principles of 'Natural Selection' and 'Inheritance' to Political Society." Like HERBERT SPENCER, Bagehot attempts to explain societies not in terms of their underlying philosophies but in terms of their relative likelihood of surviving and flourishing. As CHARLES DARWIN did with living things, Bagehot treated societies as inheritors of the past. To him, a society is imperfect and complex, a mixture of time-tested wisdom and obsolete ideas. Because of this view, Bagehot avoids promoting any strict political ideology, writing in *Physics and Politics* that "No nation admits of an abstract definition; all nations are beings of many qualities and many sides." Early indications of Bagehot's tendency to equate reproductive success with cultural excellence can be found in essays, such as his 1856 "Edward Gibbon," in which he says of the British, "The great breeding people had gone out and multiplied; colonies in every clime attest our success; French is the *patois* of Europe; English is the language of the world."

When Bagehot wrote a book on economics, he started from direct observation of the markets in which he worked, rather than with abstractions. In *Lombard Street: A Description of the Money Market* (1873), rather than starting from simple laws of economics, he gives an authoritative, detailed account of English financial systems with recommendations for policy changes that might improve the stability of money markets.

Bagehot's favorite approach to history was through biography, and the posthumous volume *Biographical Studies* (1881) collected his essays on WILLIAM EWART GLADSTONE, William Pitt the Younger, Lord Bolingbroke, Adam Smith, and others. Other posthumous volumes, collected under the title *Literary Studies* (1879–95), featured essays on important writers, including the essay "Wordsworth, Tennyson, and Browning, or Pure, Ornate, and Grotesque Art in English Poetry," in which Bagehot argued that simple, clear poetry, such as that of WILLIAM WORDS-

WORTH, is generally preferable to elaborate, passionate poetry, although the latter can sometimes provide an enlightening negative example of the more monstrous, uncontrolled side of human thought. In his literary essays as in his political essays, Bagehot showed a great interest in the psychological motivations of the agents being studied, expressing a desire to understand the "man behind the writing" when analyzing an author. The historian Jacques Barzun wrote that Bagehot's name was not commonly known after his own era, "But his achievements as a political thinker and a literary critic" were such "that his genius should be as unmistakable as his versatility."

Other Works by Walter Bagehot
Literary Studies: Miscellaneous Essays. Irvine, Calif.: Reprint Services, 1990.
Shakespeare, The Man: An Essay. New York: AMS Press, 2001.

A Work about Walter Bagehot
Irvine, William. *Walter Bagehot.* Hamden, Conn.: Archon Books, 1970.

Baillie, Joanna (1762–1851) *poet, dramatist*

Joanna Baillie was born in Lanarkshire, Scotland, to a family who were descendants of the Scottish patriot Sir William Wallace; Joanna's father was a Presbyterian minister. Joanna moved to London, where her brother had a flourishing medical practice, with her mother and elder sister Agnes in 1784. They established a household in Hampstead that became a well-known site for gatherings of notable literary types of the period. Joanna and Agnes remained in Hampstead for the rest of their long lives.

Baillie demonstrated an early affinity for both the arts and sciences. At boarding school she excelled in music, mathematics, drawing, poetry, and theatrical improvisations. She began her writing career by publishing *Poems, Wherein It Is Attempted to Describe Certain Views of Nature and of Rustic Manners* (1790). The book went virtually unnoticed. In 1798, she published anonymously, to rave reviews, the first volume of *A Series of Plays, In Which It Is Attempted to Delineate the Stronger Passions of the Mind,* familiarly known as *Plays on the Passions.*

The purpose of this work, which Baillie outlined in the prefatory section, "Introductory Discourse," was to provide a dramatic analysis of passion. The three plays included in this first volume each focused on a particular passion: *De Monfort* was a tragedy on hate, *Basil* a tragedy on love, and *The Tryal* a comedy on love. The "Introductory Discourse" itself brings to mind WILLIAM WORDSWORTH's 1800 preface to *Lyrical Ballads,* in its emphasis on the inner workings of the mind as the foundation for art.

In addition, the *Plays on the Passions* suggested a new theory for reviving British drama. Baillie's plays were exemplars for the period, clearly distinct from their predecessors with their simple plots and poetically resonant language. They heightened the psychological dimension of drama, dramatizing the struggles of individuals who were attempting to negotiate the impulses prompted by their passions. Baillie says of her characters, "The chief antagonists they contend with must be the other passions and propensities of the heart, not outward circumstances and events." Baillie's approach would influence writers such as MARY SHELLEY, CHARLOTTE DACRE, and Edgar Allan Poe.

Most critics consider *De Monfort* Baillie's finest work. Janice Patten writes that in De Monfort "Baillie presents a hero consciously motivated by ignoble motives of pride and humiliation, motives which he himself despises; yet possibly subconsciously motivated by a far more powerful drive: incestuous desire." With his intense declamations De Monfort anticipates the Byronic hero:

"It is hate! black, lasting, deadly hate!
Which thus hath driven me forth from kindred peace,

> *From social pleasure, from my native home,*
> *To be a sullen wand'rer on the earth,*
> *Avoiding all men, cursing and accurs'd."*
> (De Monfort 2.2)

De Monfort was produced at Drury Lane in 1800, with the great actors Sarah Siddons and John Philip Kemble in the leading roles, and had a successful run. Baillie went on to publish two more volumes of *Plays on the Passions* and many other plays, nearly 30 in all. Some of them were clearly intended for home reading rather than production, but several were staged and enthusiastically received.

After her death Baillie was largely forgotten, and it is only recently that scholars have called for her work to be studied anew. Some critics feel that Baillie has been neglected because of her gender; however, during her lifetime her identity as a woman did not prevent her from receiving both accolades and harsh reviews from critics. LORD BYRON once remarked that "Women (saving Joanna Baillie) cannot write tragedy"—the exception Byron makes for Baillie, while it betrays Byron's own sexist attitudes toward women and literary production, also testifies to Baillie's ability to compete in a largely male-dominated genre. SIR WALTER SCOTT, who dubbed Baillie "the immortal Joanna," believed her to be Britain's "best dramatic writer since the days of Shakespeare and Massinger."

Other Work by Joanna Baillie
Breen, Jennifer, ed. *The Selected Poems of Joanna Baillie, 1762–1851.* Manchester, England: Manchester University Press, 1999, distributed in U.S. by St. Martin's Press.

Works about Joanna Baillie
Burroughs, Catherine B. *Closet Stages: Joanna Baillie and the Theater Theory of British Romantic Writers.* Philadelphia: University of Pennsylvania Press, 1997.
Patten, Janice E. "Dark Imagination: Poetic Painting in Romantic Drama." The Literary Link. Available online. URL: http://literarylink.com/bailliepg.html. Accessed on July 2, 2008.
Purinton, Marjean D. *Romantic Ideology Unmasked: The Mentally Constructed Tyrannies in Dramas of William Wordsworth, Lord Byron, Percy Shelley, and Joanna Baillie.* Newark: University of Delaware Press, 1994.

Ballantyne, Robert Michael (1825–1894)
novelist

R. M. Ballantyne was born in Edinburgh, Scotland. His father, Alexander Ballantyne, was a newspaper proprietor, and his uncle James printed novels by SIR WALTER SCOTT. In fact, James and Scott were in the printing business together until their company collapsed in 1825, leaving both families in dire financial straits. As a result, at age 16 Ballantyne was apprenticed as a clerk to the Hudson's Bay Company in Canada, where he traded with American Indians for six years. After returning to Scotland, he privately published the diary he had kept, but William Nelson, an Edinburgh publisher, suggested that in order to reach a wider audience Ballantyne should write an adventure book for boys based on his Canadian experiences. In 1865 Ballantyne published *The Young Fur Traders*. He promoted his novel with public lectures; dressed as a trapper in buckskin and toting a gun, his presentations were dramatic crowd-pleasers.

From 1856 on, Ballantyne produced some 30 books for boys, all with upright, intelligent heroes and many illustrated by himself. His most famous novel is *The Coral Island: A Tale of the Pacific Ocean* (1858), in which three boys are shipwrecked on an island and are forced to live off the land and escape sharks, pirates, and cannibals. Critics, always eager to uncover hidden meaning, have interpreted the boys' adventures as those of colonizers and the novel as a thinly disguised endorsement of British imperialism. *Coral Island* influenced ROBERT LOUIS STEVENSON's *Treasure Island,* J. M. Barrie's *Peter Pan,* and William Golding's much darker *Lord of the Flies*.

As the critic Eric Quayle points out, "Ballantyne's stories were among the first to portray boys enjoying real adventures by themselves, away from home and free from parental restraints." Such escape remains the chief attraction of Ballantyne's fiction. Quayle notes that Ballantyne was less interested in characterization and style than in heroic action. Indeed, his nickname was Ballantyne the Brave.

Ballantyne also undertook a series of true-life adventures, for which he did firsthand, often dangerous research on marine rescue in a diving suit, fire fighting, mining, and mail delivery. These experiences led to *The Lifeboat* (1864), *Fighting the Fire* (1867), *Deep Down* (1868), and *Post Haste* (1880). Later, for *Pirate City* (1874), he disguised himself as a Muslim resident of Algiers. He also published an autobiography, *Personal Reminiscences in Book-Making* (1893).

A Work about R. M. Ballantyne

Quayle, Eric. *Ballantyne the Brave: A Victorian Writer and His Family.* London: Rupert Hart-Davis, 1967.

Barbauld, Anna Laetitia (1743–1825)
poet, essayist, literary critic

Anna Laetitia Barbauld, née Aikin, was born in Leicestershire, England, to the Reverend John Aikin and Jane Jennings Aikin. She received her early education from her mother, but later persuaded her father to teach her French, Italian, Latin, and Greek. Her parents were strict, and she sought relief from their discipline in the books in her father's library.

Her father's decision in 1758 to take a position as a tutor at the Warrington Academy, a center for dissenting thought, in Lancashire, had a significant effect on his daughter's life. Warrington provided the stimulating atmosphere that encouraged Anna Aikin's impulse to write—a desire that crystallized in 1773 with the publication of *Poems*. A poem from that collection, "The Mouse's Petition: Found in the Trap where he had been Confin'd all Night," shows her compassionate idealism:

> *Oh! Hear a pensive captive's prayer,*
> *For liberty that sighs:*
> *And never let thine heart be shut*
> *Against the prisoner's cries....*

Poems was a success: It went through four editions that same year. In 1773 Aikin also collaborated with her brother John on *Miscellaneous Pieces in Prose*—the essays it contained won the respect of critics, notably Samuel Johnson.

The following May, Anna Laetitia Aikin married Rochemont Barbauld, a former student at Warrington. They moved to Palgrave, in Suffolk, where they opened a boarding school for boys. Anna Laetitia Barbauld taught history, geography, drama, speech, grammar, and composition to the younger students, and discovered a lack of appropriate books for children. This prompted her to write *Lessons for Children* (1778–79), a series of four books for use with children two to four years old, and *Hymns in Prose for Children* (1781). The latter became so popular that it went through 28 editions and was translated into multiple languages. It is thought to have influenced WILLIAM BLAKE's *Songs of Innocence* and *Songs of Experience* (1794).

Some critics believed that Barbauld's talents were wasted in writing books for children. Her frequent trips to London allowed her to move among many of the literati, including FANNY BURNEY, HANNAH MORE, and WILLIAM WORDSWORTH. The Barbaulds also lived in London for a year after closing their school in 1785 and before moving in 1787 to Hampstead, where Barbauld made friends with JOANNA BAILLIE.

While in Hampstead, Barbauld voiced her opposition to the war with France by publishing political pamphlets. Barbauld's radical tendencies also led her to produce a scathing attack on the slave trade and the British government's complicity in it in her *Epistle to William Wilberforce Esq. On the Rejection of the Bill for Abolishing the Slave Trade* (1791):

> *Cease, Wilberforce, to urge thy generous aim!*
> *Thy Country knows the sin, and stands the shame!*
> . . .
> *She knows, and she persists—Still Afric bleeds,*
> *Unchecked, the human traffic still proceeds . . .*

However, Barbauld did not relinquish her focus on domestic and educational concerns. Collaborating once more with her brother, Barbauld coedited the six-volume *Evenings at Home; or, The Juvenile Budget Opened: Consisting of a Variety of Miscellaneous Pieces for the Instruction and Amusement of Young Persons* (1792–96). Barbauld herself wrote 14 of the 99 pieces.

She continued to write poetry. Her poem "Washing-Day," published in the *Monthly Magazine* in 1797, illustrates her humorous awareness of the drudgery of family life:

> *Come, Muse, and sing the dreaded Washing-Day. . .*
> *. . . Should the skies pour down, adieu to all*
> *Remains of quiet: then expect to hear*
> *Of sad disasters,—dirt and gravel stains*
> *Hard to efface, and loaded lines at once*
> *Snapped short,—and linen horse by dog thrown down,*
> *And all the petty miseries of life.*

Barbauld also did editorial work and wrote literary criticism. Some of her most notable accomplishments include her edition of Samuel Richardson's letters (1804), with a critical biography of the author, and her edition of selected essays from 18th-century periodicals (1804)—the preface to this edition many consider to be her finest piece of literary criticism.

In 1802 Barbauld and her husband left Hampstead for Stoke Newington, where she would live the rest of her life. Soon afterward her husband, who had been mentally unstable for some time, threatened her with a knife. She sent him to London to live under medical supervision, but in 1808, he escaped and drowned himself. Barbauld, grief-stricken, composed a memoir of her husband, and then submerged herself in work. In 1810 she published *The British Novelists* (in 50 volumes), closely followed by *The Female Speaker* (1811).

Critical Analysis

Perhaps Barbauld's most notable literary contribution was the antiwar poem *Eighteen Hundred and Eleven* (1812). Britain was about to plunge into war with the United States, the War of 1812. She warns her country against the arrogance of power, and foresees a time when Britain's civilization will have crumbled:

> *And think'st thou, Britain, still to sit at ease,*
> *An island Queen amidst thy subject seas,*
> *While the vext billows, in their distant roar,*
> *But soothe thy slumbers, and but kiss thy shore?*
> . . .
> *So sing thy flatterers; but, Britain, know,*
> *Thou who hast shared the guilt must share the woe.*
> *Nor distant is the hour . . .*

The controversial poem incited a harsh reaction from the *Quarterly Review* critic John Wilson Croker, who felt that Barbauld's poetic rendering of "the gray ruin and the mouldering stone" of England was a perverse attempt at satire by an intrusive "lady-author." The poem, in the estimation of Croker and others, was nothing short of traitorous. Barbauld appears to have taken this criticism to heart: She stopped writing poetry.

Paula R. Feldman argues that Barbauld's poem, with its description of the fallen state of a nation, anticipates T. S. Eliot's *The Waste Land*. She comments: "As poet, educator, essayist, and critic, she was widely acknowledged to be one of the literary giants of her time."

Other Work by Anna Laetitia Barbauld
The Poems of Anna Laetitia Barbauld. William McCarthy and Elizabeth Kraft, eds. Athens: University of Georgia Press, 1994.

A Work about Anna Laetitia Barbauld
Feldman, Paula R. "Anna Laetitia Barbauld." In *British Women Poets of the Romantic Era: An Anthology.* Edited by Paula Feldman. Baltimore: Johns Hopkins University Press, 1997.

Baring-Gould, Sabine (1834–1924)
novelist, folklorist, travel writer, composer

Sabine Baring-Gould was born in Exeter, in Devon, England. He lived on his family's country estate in Devon until the age of three, when his father took the family on a 13-year tour of Europe. The experience profoundly influenced Baring-Gould, giving him a lifelong fascination with people, places, and the folklore and traditions that shaped them.

Educated at Clare College, Cambridge, Baring-Gould then taught school, where he was remembered for his eccentricities, such as lecturing with a domesticated bat perched on his shoulder. At 30, he took holy orders and was assigned to a mill town in Yorkshire. There he married Grace Taylor, a 16-year-old mill girl. Baring-Gould described their romance in his first novel, *Through Fire and Flame* (1868). In the 48 years of their marriage, the couple raised 13 children. In 1881 Baring-Gould returned to his ancestral estate, where he served as both squire and rector until his death.

Baring-Gould wrote a chapter a day, standing up at a slanted writing desk because his tremendous energy would not allow him to be confined to a chair. A polymath, he wrote more than 100 works—some 30 of them novels—from books of sermons and serious theology to Nordic sagas and tales of the supernatural. His most ambitious work, the 16-volume *Lives of the Saints* (3,600 of them), took him six years to complete. His most celebrated work, the novel *Mehalah* (1880), was said by ALGERNON CHARLES SWINBURNE to be as good as EMILY BRONTË's *Wuthering Heights.* To his own astonishment, however, Baring-Gould was most famous in his own time—and perhaps today as well, for writing the 1865 hymn "Onward, Christian Soldier."

Other Works by Sabine Baring-Gould
A Book of Folklore. Detroit: Singing Tree Press, 1970.
A Book of Werewolves. London: Michael O'Mara Books, 2002.
Curious Myths of the Middle Ages. New York: Crescent Books, 1987.

A Work about Sabine Baring-Gould
Purcell, W. *Onward Christian Soldier.* New York: Longmans, Green, 1957.

Barnes, William (1801–1886) *poet, essayist*

William Barnes, born near Sturminster Newton, in Dorset, to John Barnes and Grace Scott, descended from generations of farmers, all of whom had lived in the same southern county of England. In 1823 he left home to teach school at Mere in Wiltshire, marrying four years later. He returned in 1835 and ran a school while studying for a divinity degree. Ordained in 1848, he became curate for a small parish near Dorchester, where he remained for the rest of his life. A Dorchester neighbor and friend was THOMAS HARDY, who greatly admired Barnes.

Although he wrote also in standard English, the poems that best represent Barnes are in the Dorset dialect. Barnes explained, "It is my mother tongue, and it is . . . the only true speech of the life that I draw." By his use of dialect, Barnes also sought to preserve forgotten words and manners of Dorset. The author of *Tiw: A View of the Roots and Stems of the English as a Teutonic Tongue* (1862), he also wished to keep standard English "pure" of Latin derivatives.

He was nurtured by surroundings that made his love of humanity inseparable from his love of nature. Barnes's poetic aim, like that of ROBERT BURNS, was to give commonplace incidents and ordinary human emotions their due importance.

Poems of Rural Life in the Dorset Dialect (1844) was his first book of poems. "Bob the Fiddler" is typical. On the surface it is a snapshot of "merry Bob," who performs publicly "At Maÿpolen, or feäst, or feäir" (". . . if you'd zee en in his glory, / Jist let en have a fiddle"). However, the poem widens its focus: ". . . when the crowd do leäve his jowl, / They'll all be in the dumps." The last line suggests the hardships of farming, but it also suggests how important Bob—and, by extension, *any* soul—is to the integrity and spiritual functioning of the community to which he belongs. The poem's rhythm, matching the tempo of Bob's fiddle, helps deepen this sense of connection.

A shattering event for Barnes was his wife's death in 1852. "The Wife a-Lost," which appeared in *Poems of Rural Life in the Dorset Dialect, Second Series* (1862), is an especially haunting poem.

A third series of *Poems of Rural Life* appeared in 1863. GERARD MANLEY HOPKINS, himself influenced by Barnes's work, called Barnes "a perfect artist," adding, "it is as if Dorset life . . . had taken flesh and blood in this man."

Other Work by William Barnes
Bradbury, Richard, ed. *Collected Prose Works of William Barnes.* New York: Routledge, 1996.

A Work about William Barnes
Baxter, Lucy E. *Life of William Barnes, Poet and Philologist, by His Daughter.* Temecula, Calif.: Reprint Services, 1992.

Beardsley, Aubrey Vincent (1872–1898)
illustrator, poet

Aubrey Beardsley was born in Brighton, England, to Vincent and Ellen Beardsley. He contracted tuberculosis at age six, and remained fragile and unhealthy for the rest of his life, but he became interested in drawing as a young child. His mother, a piano teacher, encouraged both Beardsley and his sister Mabel (who would become an actress) to develop their precocious talents. Unable to afford art training, Beardsley nevertheless became one of the foremost illustrators in England during the 1890s, as well as a leader in the transition from AESTHETICISM to Decadence. Although influenced by PRE-RAPHAELITES, French poster art, and Japanese woodcuts, his work evolved into a unique art nouveau style of elegant curvilinear black-and-white illustration that often shocked audiences with its sensuality, cruel figures, sinister subjects, and morbidity.

At 18, Beardsley cut into the London art scene and quickly impressed the painter Edward Burne-Jones and OSCAR WILDE with his portfolio. Beardsley's first major project was to illustrate a new edition of Thomas Malory's *Morte D'Arthur,* in 1893. (Compelling as were his knights, fauns, and ladies in billowing costumes, they seldom related directly to Malory's text, evoking instead a general mood of enchantment and mystery.) In 1894, Wilde invited Beardsley to illustrate his banned play *Salomé.* The scandalous drawings made Wilde's play even more notorious and introduced Beardsley to a wide audience. That same year Beardsley became the art editor and illustrator for a quarterly magazine, the *Yellow Book;* then, after being fired because of his association with Wilde, Beardsley helped create the *Savoy,* a magazine that published some of his own poems and a prose parody, "Under the Hill." He continued to illustrate books, but by 1896 he was rapidly succumbing to tuberculosis; he converted to Catholicism, moved to France, and died there at the young age of 25. His friend MAX BEERBOHM summed up his life: "Aubrey Beardsley was famous in his youth, the most gracious gift the gods can bestow. He died, having achieved masterpieces, at an age when normal genius has as yet done little of which it will not be heartily ashamed thereafter."

Other Works by Aubrey Beardsley
Letters of Aubrey Beardsley. Edited by W. G. Good, Henry Maas, et al. London: Associated University Presses, 1975.

Best Works of Aubrey Beardsley. New York: Dover, 1990.

Works about Aubrey Beardsley

Calloway, Stephen. *Aubrey Beardsley.* New York: Harry N. Abrams, 1998.

Sturgis, Matthew. *Aubrey Beardsley: A Biography.* New York: Overlook Press, 1998.

Beddoes, Thomas Lovell (1803–1849)
poet, playwright

Thomas Lovell Beddoes was the son of the scientist and writer Thomas Beddoes, who is said to have brought cadavers home to dissect and who popularized the use of laughing gas to induce euphoria in such bipolar patients as SAMUEL TAYLOR COLERIDGE. Beddoes's mother, Anna, and her sister, the novelist MARIA EDGEWORTH, came from a family that understood and praised imaginative writing. Beddoes began writing his macabre, ghoulish verse at a young age, and while an undergraduate at Oxford, published *The Improvisatore* (1821)—three verse narratives filled with Gothic excess—and a play, *The Brides' Tragedy* (1822), based on a story he had heard about a man who secretly marries, then kills his bride to marry another woman. Critical reception of the play, with its Elizabethan themes of murder and madness, was enthusiastic. But Beddoes, after starting several new plays and failing to finish them, suddenly decided (perhaps because of the early influence of his father) to study anatomy and medicine in Europe. He became a physician, settled in Zurich, Switzerland, and thereafter returned to England only to visit. He also began writing his major life's work, a drama of revenge called *Death's Jest-Book, or, the Fool's Tragedy,* and worked obsessively on it for the rest of his life. Published posthumously in 1850, this play of murder, ghosts, and retribution pays homage to his major influences—Elizabethan and Jacobean tragedy, English and German Gothic tales of terror, and the ROMANTICISM of PERCY BYSSHE SHELLEY. Beddoes labeled his sinister and grotesquely comic writing "florid Gothic." One reviewer for *Blackwood's Magazine* wrote of *Death's Jest-Book,* "In this mad and plotless play there are finer passages than any living dramatist has composed . . . grandeur, tenderness, and a poetry of description totally unequalled." Beddoes contracted a debilitating disease after handling a cadaver and in 1849 committed suicide by poisoning himself with curare.

Works about Thomas Lovell Beddoes

Bradshaw, Michael. *Resurrection Songs: The Poetry of Thomas Lovell Beddoes.* Aldershot, England: Ashgate, 2000.

Donner, H. W. *Thomas Lovell Beddoes.* New York: AMS Press, 1935. Reprinted 1978.

Thompson, James R. *Thomas Lovell Beddoes.* Boston: Twayne, 1985.

Beerbohm, Henry Maximilian (1872–1956)
critic, novelist

Max Beerbohm was born in London to Julius Beerbohm, a prosperous merchant, and his wife, Eliza Draper Beerbohm. He attended Oxford University but never graduated, leaving in 1894 to support himself as a writer.

Beerbohm wrote essays for the literary magazine *Yellow Book,* on a wide range of topics, from literature to the theater. In 1895 Beerbohm published his first book, *The Works of Max Beerbohm,* a collection of seven witty essays on a wide range of topics, as indicated by such titles as "King George the Fourth" and "The Pervasion of Rouge."

Beerbohm was also widely known for his brilliant drawings of such famous people as OSCAR WILDE, WALTER PATER, and DANTE GABRIEL ROSSETTI. During his career, Beerbohm produced an estimated 2,000 of these drawings. As Beerbohm put it, "The most perfect caricature is that which, on a small surface, with the simplest means, most accurately exaggerates, to the highest point, the peculiarities of a human being, at his most characteristic moment in the most beautiful manner."

In 1898 Beerbohm became the theater critic of the *English Saturday Review,* for which he wrote approximately 600 reviews. Virginia Woolf praised Beerbohm as "the prince of his profession," claiming that he "brought personality into literature, not unconsciously and impurely, but so consciously and purely that we do not know whether there is any relation between Max the essayist and Mr Beerbohm the man."

In 1910 Beerbohm married an American actress, Florence Kahn, and a year later published a satirical novel, *Zuleika Dobson,* whose heroine is a beautiful femme fatale who causes havoc when she visits an Oxford college, where all the young men fall in love with her. Although it was well received at the time and is still occasionally read today, it was Beerbohm's only novel. In 1919 he published his other major work, *Seven Men,* a collection of five narrative sketches that mix fictional characters and real people, including Beerbohm himself. In 1936 he began a series of occasional radio talks on topics such as London, music halls, and modern advertising. Beerbohm was knighted in 1939.

Critical Analysis

Max Beerbohm is primarily remembered today for his parodies of contemporary writers in a volume entitled *A Christmas Garland,* in which he pens Christmas stories in the style of Henry James, Rudyard Kipling, H. G. Wells, and a number of other British writers. Beerbohm's immense talent as a parodist is evident in his wicked send-up of James. In a story about two children and their Christmas stockings, he captures perfectly the long, elaborate, comma- and parentheses-studded sentences and the heightened sensibility and self-consciousness of the characters that so distinguish James. Here the narrator notices his and his sister's Christmas stockings and wonders if his sister has already peeked at hers.

> Thus the exact repetition, at the foot of Eva's bed, of the shape pendulous at the foot of *his* was hardly enough to account for the fixity with which he envisaged it, and for which he was to find, some years later, a motive in the (as it turned out) hardly generous fear that Eva had already made the great investigation "on her own." Her very regular breathing presently reassured him that, if she *had* peeped into "her" stocking, she must have done so in sleep.

One of Beerbohm's short stories, "Enoch Soames" (1919) has such a following today that there is even an "Enoch Soames Society" with its own Web site, which celebrates the "work" and "influence" of this fictional poet. Beerbohm's story is a curiously modern, or even postmodern, work whose twists and turns are still turning, in some sense, today. The story combines the idea of time travel with idea of selling one's soul to the devil. Beerbohm names himself as the story's narrator and characterizes himself as a somewhat dim and overly credulous admirer of writers. He meets the self-styled poet, Enoch Soames, who is considered ridiculous and untalented by his contemporaries. Soames, however, comes to believe that he will be revered in the future and sells his soul to the devil for a chance to travel to the reading room of the British Museum on June 3, 1997, to look up all the books that have been written about him and, presumably, revel in his posthumous fame.

Beerbohm meets Soames on his return. The poor fellow has discovered only one reference to him: He is immortalized only as a *fictional* character in a story by Max Beerbohm (the very story we are now reading, of course). Soames goes willingly away with the devil and Beerbohm the character is left to wonder if Soames will reappear in the British Museum in some form when 1997 actually arrives. (Readers "wondered" too, and many showed up at the British Museum on June 3, 1997. Some claimed to have seen a man who looked much as Enoch Soames was described.) Beerbohm also speculates that those who read his story, as opposed to the 20th-century critic whose work Soames finds in the museum in 1997, will know that Soames was "real."

It is hard to imagine that even Jorge Luis Borges, the Argentinian writer who is known for writing stories with similar twists and turns, could have done better than Beerbohm does in "Enoch Soames" in creating so many overlapping layers of reality and fiction. Beerbohm, no doubt, would have enjoyed the fun at the Enoch Soames Web site, where pranksters posing as literary critics lambaste Beerbohm for his supposed jealousy of Soames: "Beerbohm was an unreliable witness, jealous of Soames's dedication to his art and even, perhaps, of the sizeable annuity which enabled him so single-mindedly to court his Muse."

Other Work by Max Beerbohm
Max Beerbohm Caricatures. Edited by John N. Hall. New Haven, Conn.: Yale University Press, 1997.

A Work about Max Beerbohm
Danson, Lawrence. *Max Beerbohm and the Act of Writing.* New York: Oxford University Press, 1991.

Beeton, Isabella (1836–1865) *nonfiction writer*

Isabella Beeton was born in London to Benjamin Mayson, a shopkeeper, and his wife, Elizabeth. She was educated by her parents, and later attended school in Heidelberg, Germany.

In 1856 Isabella married Samuel Orchard Beeton, a successful publisher who specialized in practical nonfiction books, issuing such titles as *Beeton's Book of Garden Management* and *Beeton's Book of Home Pets.* He also published a widely circulated periodical called the *Englishwoman's Domestic Magazine,* for which Isabella began to write on a variety of subjects, especially fashion.

In 1861 Isabella Beeton published *Beeton's Book of Household Management,* parts of which had originally appeared in her husband's magazine. Her book was the first comprehensive guide on how to manage a home, including advice on hiring servants, housekeeping tips, and recipes. By 1868 it had sold more than 2 million copies. Explaining her reason for writing the book, Beeton said, "What moved me, in the first instance, to attempt a work like this, was the discomfort and suffering which I had seen brought upon men and women by household mismanagement. I have always thought that there is no more fruitful source of family discontent than a housewife's badly cooked dinners and untidy ways." In 1865, Beeton died in childbirth.

A Work about Isabella Beeton
Spain, Nancy. *Mrs. Beeton and Her Husband.* London: Collins, 1948.

Bellenden-Clarke, Frances
See GRAND, SARAH.

Belloc, Bessie Rayner Parkes (1829–1925) *journalist, editor*

Bessie Parkes was born into the family of Joseph Parkes and Elizabeth Priestley, liberal political activists and freethinking Unitarians. She became active in the English women's movement, publishing pamphlets such as "Remarks on the Education of Girls" (1856).

In partnership with her friend the feminist writer BARBARA BODICHON, Parkes launched the *English Woman's Journal* in March 1858 and served as its editor until 1862. The scholar Jane Rendall noted that the periodical's "outstanding characteristic . . . is its driving concern with middle-class women's need for occupation and activity. Employment was the key issue of the periodical." The *Journal* also stressed the importance of education for women and encouraged its middle-class readers to aid working-class women to avoid crime and prostitution through religious instruction and job training. According to Rendall, the magazine represented "a 'liberal feminism', rooted in political individualism and political economy," yet Parkes "[i]n recalling the origins of the paper . . . stressed not its radicalism, but its breadth, never excluding diversity of opinion."

After leaving her post as editor, Parkes published her *Journal* articles on women's work in the collection *Essays on Woman's Work* (1865) and joined other activists to form the National Society for Women's Suffrage (1866–67), an organization that was to lead the English women's suffrage movement until 1928. Parkes also distanced herself from the more radical activists in her circle as she embraced the work of the Roman Catholic Sisters of Charity as a more appropriate model for women's action. She had converted to Roman Catholicism in 1864, remaining a devout practitioner until she died.

In 1867, to the dismay and disapproval of family and friends, she married Louis Belloc, an invalid several years her junior, and settled in France. When he died in 1872, Parkes Belloc, who had ceased her feminist activity, returned to England with her children. Her daughter Marie Belloc-Lowndes later became a novelist, and her son, Hilaire Belloc, became not only a noted and prolific writer but also one of Britain's leading antifeminists.

A Work about Bessie Rayner Parkes Belloc
Rendall, Jane. "'A Moral Engine': Feminism, Liberalism and the Englishwoman's Journal." In *Equal or Different: Women's Politics, 1800–1914*, edited by Jane Rendall. Oxford, England: Blackwell, 1987.

Bentham, Jeremy (1748–1832) *philosopher, economist, jurist, political theorist*

Born in London to the prosperous attorney Jeremiah Bentham and his wife, Alicia Grove Bentham, Jeremy Bentham was an avid reader and student of Latin by the age of four. After attending Westminster school, Bentham entered Queen's College, Oxford, at age 12. Upon graduation in 1763, Bentham entered Lincoln's Inn to study law. Although awed by the court proceedings and by the complex expositions of such distinguished speakers as Sir William Blackstone, Bentham perceived the legal system as a whole to be unnecessarily complicated and expensive. To the disappointment of his father, Bentham turned from studying law to critiquing it. In 1776 he published anonymously *A Fragment on Government*, which criticizes Blackstone's opposition to reform and offers an early view of Bentham's own theory of government, which, among other points, promoted a simplified and more equitable legal system. Although Bentham never practiced law, legal reform became his life work.

From 1785 to 1788 Bentham lived in Russia with his brother Samuel. While there, he wrote numerous works on philosophy of law, logic, and political economy, as well as a series of letters on the topics of economics and prison reform, which were published as *Defence of Usury* (1787) and *Panopticon* (1791).

Upon his return to England, Bentham continued to develop his philosophy of law, often discussing his ideas with a circle of friends, among them the philosopher JAMES MILL. In 1789 Bentham published his great work, *An Introduction to the Principles of Morals and Legislation*, in which he defined his philosophy of utilitarianism, which is guided by one central moral principle: "It is the greatest happiness of the greatest number that is the measure of right and wrong." Utilitarianism recognized pain and pleasure as humankind's two governing motives for conduct. It advocated laws that recognized the individual's right to happiness, but not at the expense of the larger community. For example, a bank robbery would bring great happiness for the single robber, but a greater quantity of unhappiness for the many customers of the bank who would lose their savings. Bentham's attempts to quantify human pain and pleasure, and his refusal to take into account issues of morality and religion, earned him the scorn of the popular press. One of his most memorable critics was CHARLES DICKENS, who parodied Bentham's utilitarian rationalism in the character of the fact-obsessed schoolmaster Thomas Gradgrind in *Hard Times*: "A man of realities. A man of facts and calculations. A man who proceeds upon the principle that two and two are four, and nothing over, and who is not to be talked into allowing for anything over."

In his later years, however, Bentham's advice was sought by many leaders throughout Europe, specifically by the two young republics of France and the United States, whose new governments were established on rational principles rather than on tradition. Considered one of the first "philosophical radicals," Bentham greatly influenced political and legal reforms. In 1824 Bentham and JOHN STUART MILL founded the *Westminster Review* as an organ of radical opinion. Legendary in his eccentricities, Bentham directed that his body, after death, was to be dissected and his skeleton dressed in Bentham's usual clothes. Bentham's skeleton is preserved at University College, London.

The Benthamites became a strong political force in England, advocating rational reforms to English institutions. As one of Bentham's biographers, Charles Everett, writes, "The division and organization of the work of governmental departments, the extension of the franchise, the reform of the land laws, the parcel post, a national system of education, the modern police force, the establishment of a permanent civil service based on competitive examinations—all these were, for the most part, the carrying out of plans carefully worked out by Bentham."

Other Work by Jeremy Bentham
A Bentham Reader. Edited by Mary Peter Mack. New York: Pegasus, 1969.

Works about Jeremy Bentham
Dinwiddy, J. R. *Bentham.* New York: Oxford University Press, 1989.
Everett, Charles Warren. *Jeremy Bentham.* London: Weidenfeld & Nicolson, 1966.
Schofield, Philip. *Utility and Democracy: The Political Thought of Jeremy Bentham.* New York: Oxford University Press, 2006.

Besant, Annie Wood (1847–1933)
nonfiction writer

Annie Wood Besant was born in London to William Wood, a businessman, and his wife, Emily. At 19 she married the Reverend Frank Besant, but the marriage failed when she began to question her faith.

Rejecting traditional Christianity while ardently supporting social reform, Besant moved through several philosophical and spiritual stages. In 1874 she joined the Secular Society, where she met Charles Bradlaugh, the editor of the radical paper the *National Reformer.* Invited to join the paper's staff, Besant contributed such articles as "Marriage, As It Was, As It Is, and As It Should Be" (1878) and "The Legalization of Female Slavery in England" (1876). From 1877 to 1887 she served as coeditor with Bradlaugh. In this same period she began a speaking career and quickly came to be regarded as one of Britain's foremost orators. She was the first woman to speak out publicly in support of birth control, and in 1877 she joined Bradlaugh in publishing *The Fruits of Philosophy,* an 1832 treatise on birth control by Charles Knowlton. Arrested and charged with publishing an obscene book, the two were found guilty, but their convictions were overturned on appeal.

Besant's life was transformed in the 1890s when she joined the Theosophical Society, a spiritual movement based on Hindu beliefs in karma and reincarnation, and became its president. Besant moved to India in 1893 to continue her studies in theosophy and also to join the political fight for Indians, then under British rule, to govern themselves. In the last decades of her life, she continued to support women's rights and other progressive causes and wrote and edited works on both theosophy and Indian politics. She died in India.

Other Work by Annie Besant
A Selection of the Social and Political Pamphlets of Annie Besant. Edited by John Saville. New York: August Kelley, 1970.

A Work about Annie Besant
Taylor, Anne. *Annie Besant: A Biography.* New York: Oxford University Press, 1992.

Besant, Sir Walter (1836–1901) *novelist, essayist*

Walter Besant was born in Portsea, England. His father, William Besant, was a merchant, and his mother, Sarah Ediss Besant, was the daughter of an architect. After beginning his education at home, Besant attended both St. Paul's and Stockwell grammar schools. He eventually entered Christ's College, Cambridge, receiving a degree in 1859. He soon accepted an appointment at Royal College on the island of Mauritius, but he declined an offer to head the school in 1867 because he wished to pursue a literary career.

After publishing a series of articles on French literature and political subjects, Besant joined with the editor James Rice to write the serialized novel *Ready-Money Mortiboy: A Matter-of-Fact Story* (1872), a moralistic tale in which the title character's virtue exceeds his greed. The two established a partnership that lasted until Rice's death in 1882. Most notably, the pair wrote annual Christmas stories for the magazine *All the Year Round*. Among these, the most successful, *The Golden Butterfly* (1876), portrays a greedy American millionaire who experiences a Christmas conversion and becomes a philanthropist.

After Rice died, Besant chose to make the East End of London the setting for his fiction. He believed that the lack of cultural and recreational activities, including the theater, opera, and dance halls, was the most oppressive factor in the troubled district. If exposed to these opportunities, he argued, East End residents would overcome such problems as unemployment and crime. Besant's theory represented a significant break from mid-19th-century thought. Other writers, such as BENJAMIN DISRAELI, contended that an unbridgeable gap existed between the English rich and poor, but Besant claimed that individuals possessed the ability to advance socially if they received philanthropic assistance. In recognition of his own philanthropic efforts, Besant was knighted in 1895.

Critical Analysis

Besant's most recognized novel, *All Sorts and Conditions of Men* (1882), illustrates his claim. Angela Messenger, the central character, abandons her life as heiress to a brewery fortune to live in an East End boarding house. She organizes a cooperative of dressmakers, generates work for them by secretly ordering and paying for dresses, provides their meals, and installs a gymnasium and recreation room in their shop.

Messenger also initiates larger changes. Together with Harry Goslett, another expatriate of the upper class, she plans a Palace of Delight, designed to offer free entertainments such as plays, dancing, sports, and music. When the facility opens, Messenger and Goslett marry, she reveals her true identity, and they agree to live permanently in the East End and continue their philanthropic crusade.

Besant intended the novel, first, to motivate the working class to labor harder and to educate themselves and, second, to inspire the rich to donate more generously to charitable causes. Indeed, the novel did have one practical result. In 1841 Thomas Barber Beaumont had willed £12,000 to benefit the East End. The money went unused for 40 years, but spurred by the popularity of Besant's novel, more than £60,000 more was raised and added to Beaumont's in order to build an actual People's Palace, which opened in 1887.

Contemporary critics praised Besant's desire to improve the East End. However, modern critics have failed to applaud Besant's novel. Although his intentions are admirable, Besant mistakenly simplifies the economic and social problems plaguing the East End by crediting them to a lack of entertainment. As the critic John Goode notes, Besant's "catalogue of all that makes the rich happy significantly omits the idea that such things as money, property and leisure might contribute as well."

As Besant's popularity spread, he complemented his novels with essays that advocated better social conditions for the poor. For example, in

Fifty Years Ago (1888), a work celebrating Queen Victoria's reign, he advocates giving the vote to more middle- and working-class people, arguing that democratization will produce a more stable society. Besant also urged the formation of labor unions, denounced child labor, and campaigned for charity.

In his essay "One of Two Millions in East London" (1899), Besant envisions East End workers as bees toiling silently in the hive. But he also personalizes them in the fictional character Liz, who attends a boarding school, works in a jam factory, and raises a family. Because Liz's situation is so detailed and poignant, Besant's essay successfully brought the living conditions of the working poor home for the upper class.

However, this essay again reveals Besant's limitations. Although he supported better working conditions for women, Besant accepted Victorian stereotypes of women and did not believe they had the ability to organize unions or vote competently. Because of such outdated concepts, many modern readers avoid Besant's novels and essays. Yet although he misdiagnosed the cause of poverty in the East End, Besant's enthusiasm and desire to improve the lot of the poor are undeniable. John Goode argues that "Besant [uses] the novel not merely to portray an area of social reality, but also to suggest practical reforms which will transform that reality into an ideal."

A Work about Sir Walter Besant
Howard, David, Jon Lucas, and John Goode, eds. *Traditions and Tolerance in Nineteenth-Century Fiction.* New York: Routledge, 1966.

Bevington, Louisa Sarah (1845–1895) *poet, essayist*
Louisa Bevington was born into a Quaker family, but by the end of her life she was a political anarchist, having made that transition through her reading of evolutionary theory. Her first book of poems, *Key-Notes* (1876), for instance, contains these lines:

> *So we sing of evolution,*
> *·And step strongly on our ways;*
> *And we live through nights in patience*
> *And we learn the worth of days.*

Herbert Spencer, who extended CHARLES DARWIN's evolutionary ideas to what would be called Social Darwinism, admired Bevington's poetry and asked her to write poems and prose articles about evolution; one of the latter appeared in the journal *Mind* in 1879. In 1883 Bevington married Ignatz Guggenberger, but after eight years the couple separated. In the last five years of her life, Bevington wrote poems and articles in socialist and anarchist journals such as the *Torch,* having come to believe that evolution was not a sufficient perspective from which to develop ideas for immediate, direct, and practical social change. She came to believe that violence is justified as a necessary reaction to governmental injustice. Bevington's work has been largely ignored by critics, but her work has been published in *Victorian Women Poets: An Anthology* (1995), whose editors comment that "Bevington's poetry lacks the darker, imaginative recesses of [Christina] Rossetti's, and often sounds, in spite of its secularist goals, more religious and high-minded than hers."

Black, William (1841–1898) *novelist*
William Black was born in Glasgow, Scotland. His father, a successful merchant, sent him to the School of Art at Glasgow, but Black pursued journalism instead of painting. As a teenager he began writing essays for the local Glasgow newspapers.

Some of Black's early articles were on well-known 19th-century English writers and thinkers such as THOMAS CARLYLE and JOHN RUSKIN. His early novel *James Merle* (1864) made little impression.

Black eventually left Glasgow for London, where he began to write for another paper, the *Morning Star*. In 1865 he married Augusta Wenzel, who died in childbirth the following year. Black then went to Europe as a foreign correspondent to cover the so-called Seven Weeks' War, a conflict between Austria and Prussia.

After returning to London, he continued to work as a journalist but also began to have success as a novelist. Three of his books, *A Daughter of Heth* (1871), *The Strange Adventures of a Phaeton* (1872), and *A Princess of Thule* (1873), became especially popular in England. Black set his novels in the Scottish countryside and used a great deal of local color, traditions, and dialect, often setting up a dramatic tension between his rural and his city-bred characters. He was famous for his poetic descriptive passages evoking the landscape of the Western Isles (that is, the Outer Hebrides). OSCAR WILDE, in "The Decay of Lying," flippantly described Black's achievement: "The horses of Mr. William Black's phaeton do not soar towards the sun. They merely frighten the sky at evening into violent chromolithographic effects. On seeing them approach, the peasants take refuge in dialect."

Blackmore, Richard Doddridge
(1825–1900) *novelist*

R. D. Blackmore was born June 7 in Longworth, Berkshire, England. While he was still an infant, his mother, Anne Basset Knight, died of typhus. His father, John Blackmore, an Anglican curate, left Longworth, leaving Richard to be cared for by his aunt. After his father remarried in 1831, Richard went to live with him in Devon. He graduated from Oxford in 1847. Blackmore became a lawyer in 1852, but soon afterward he left the law because of poor health. He became a teacher at Wellesley House Grammar School in Twickenham, near London. In 1854 he published his first volume of poetry, *Poems by Melanter*. Two more, unsuccessful, volumes of poetry followed before he turned to writing novels. His first novel, *Clara Vaughan* (1864), is SENSATION FICTION in the style of WILKIE COLLINS and MARY ELIZABETH BRADDON, set in Corsica. His most famous work, *Lorna Doone*, first appeared in 1869; sales of this edition were limited. However, when a cheap edition appeared in 1870, Blackmore became an overnight sensation. *Lorna Doone* is an adventure story involving highwaymen and swashbuckling cavaliers, but it is also a love story about Lorna Doone, the aristocratic heroine, and John Ridd, "a plain, unlettered man." It is influenced by the Waverley novels of SIR WALTER SCOTT, mixing real and fictional characters in a historical setting, the 17th century. Blackmore published 15 novels, including *The Maid of Sker* (1872), which was based on Blackmore's childhood, and *Perlycross* (1894), a rural adventure tale. The latter remained popular for many years—it was voted favorite novel of Yale's Class of 1906—but today it is considered "children's" rather than "serious" literature.

A Work about Richard Blackmore
Solomon, Harry. *Sir Richard Blackmore*. Boston: Twayne, 1980.

Blake, William (1757–1827) *poet, artist*

William Blake was born in London. He was the son of James Blake, a maker of socks and stockings. At a very young age Blake displayed a talent for drawing, and at age 14 he was apprenticed to an engraver, James Basire. The engraver sent his young apprentice to draw Westminster Abbey and other similar churches, thus introducing Blake to Gothic art and architecture, an experience that had a lasting influence on both Blake's visual art and his poetry.

In 1781 Blake studied briefly at the Royal Academy of Art. When one of his teachers there suggested that he copy the paintings of Rubens rather than those of Michelangelo because Rubens's style was more "finished," Blake responded that that which had never been begun could not be finished. He left the academy to become a professional engraver. While at the academy, Blake had drawn from live models, but at this point he vowed never again to do so. From this time onward, all his drawings were based on ideas from his own fertile imagination. Later in life, Blake proclaimed that "Only imagination is real and imagination is my world."

Although Blake had little formal education in subjects other than art, he read voraciously and taught himself French, Italian, Latin, Greek, and Hebrew. Blake's spirituality may have been influenced by his reading of the Swedish mystic and philosopher Emanuel Swedenborg.

In 1783 Blake's first volume of poems, *Poetical Sketches,* was published. This collection included poems that Blake had written beginning at age 12. In 1789 Blake published a second collection, *Songs of Innocence,* and he also created his own method of printing his books, an idea that he said was given to him by the spirit of his recently deceased younger brother Robert. Blake printed his poems by hand onto copper plates, illustrated each poem with drawings, then hand-colored the prints, making each poem into a visual as well as a literary artwork. Almost all of his later books were published using this technique.

In *Songs of Innocence,* Blake uses musical metrics and simple language to portray the ideal world and the ideal relationship to God. Thus, in "The Divine Image" Blake writes

> *And all must love the human form,*
> *In heathen, Turk, or Jew;*
> *When Mercy, Love, and Pity dwell*
> *There God is dwelling too.*

In *The Book of Thel* (1789), Blake began to shape his mystical vision and personal mythology. Central to Blake's vision are two mythological characters—Urizen ("your reason"), who battles for freedom and human passion, and Orc, who stands for conventional law and morality.

After the publication of *The Book of Thel,* Blake became less interested in pursuing his career as an engraver and more interested in writing and developing his personal mythology. In 1790 he published *The Marriage of Heaven and Hell,* a combination of prose, free verse, and aphorisms (such as "You never know what is enough unless you know what is more than enough") that outline Blake's philosophy of radical freedom and independence. Blake was a proponent of sexual freedom and was opposed to all forms of authority, including political authority. He was a supporter of both the American and French Revolutions.

In 1794 Blake published *Songs of Experience,* a series of poems that contrasts with *Songs of Innocence.* The tone is now dark, cynical, and angry because society has destroyed the ideal world of innocence. For example, in "The Sick Rose" Blake laments

> *O Rose, thou art sick!*
> *The invisible worm,*
> *That flies in the night,*
> *In the howling storm,*
> *Has found out thy bed*
> *Of crimson joy,*
> *And his dark secret love*
> *Does thy life destroy.*

From its first publication onward, *Songs of Experience* has always been published with *Songs of Innocence* under the title *Songs of Innocence and of Experience,* an arrangement that suggests Blake's sense of the duality of human existence.

In *The French Revolution: A Prophesy* (1791), *Visions of the Daughters of Albion* (1793), and *America: A Prophesy* (1793), Blake interprets political events such as the American Revolution in a symbolic manner. Because Blake regarded scientific rationalism, materialism, organized religion, and industrialization as evils that destroyed the natural spontaneity of life, he saw revolutions as symbolic of humanity's struggle to release itself from these bonds. In *America,* for example, while the American Revolution takes place on one plane, Urizen is opposed by Orc on another. These two beings are further developed in *The First Book of Urizen* (1794), *The Song and Book of Los* (1795), *The Book of Ahania* (1795), and

The Four Zoas (1797). Blake's complex symbolism in these works has posed great difficulty for scholars who have tried to interpret them.

The most famous work of Blake's later years was *Jerusalem* (written between 1804 and 1820), in which Blake declares, "I must Create a system, or be enslav'd by another Man's." This poem portrays humanity torn between the forces of imagination and organized religion.

Although many of Blake's contemporaries dismissed him as insane, nothing about how he lived his daily life indicates that he was out of touch with reality, despite the intensity of his poetic vision. However, because his poetry and ideas were so unlike those of his contemporaries, Blake's verse was not widely read or appreciated in his lifetime. It was not until a biography by Alexander Gilcrest was published in 1863 that critics and readers began to take a more serious look at Blake's body of work. As Lord David Cecil says in the introduction to *The Oxford Book of Christian Verse*, Blake "more than any other English poet, more even than Donne or Vaughan ... had the spiritual eye. They have glimpses of the mystic vision; Blake seems to have lived for hours together at the heart of its ineffable light." From a 20th-century perspective, Blake is considered one of the first of the romantic poets (*see* ROMANTICISM).

Critical Analysis

Two of Blake's best known poems serve to highlight his vision of innocence and experience. "The Lamb," from *Songs of Innocence*, exemplifies Blake at his most joyful; "The Tyger," from *Songs of Experience*, reveals the poet at his most dark and puzzling.

At the beginning and end of the first stanza of "The Lamb," the poem's speaker, who is later identified as a child ("I a child & thou a lamb"), asks the question, "Little Lamb, who made thee? / Dost thou know who made thee?" In between the questions, the speaker describes the sweetness and beauty of the lamb's existence in simple, musical, four-beat lines: "by the stream & o'er the mead." In the second stanza, the speaker answers the question he poses in the first, in a manner reminiscent of the question-and-answer format of a catechism. He says the lamb's maker was himself a lamb—that is, Christ, the Agnus Dei, the "Lamb of God."

As with many of Blake's poems of innocence, this one hints at the later poems of experience. Behind the lilting voice of the child lies the fact that Christ is called the lamb because he is a sacrificial victim; he will die on the cross to "take away the sins of the world." He will die, the lamb will die, as will the child-speaker of the poem.

"The Tyger" is Blake's most often anthologized and analyzed poem. Its deceptively simple language seems to hint at unfathomable mysteries lurking behind the poem just as the tiger lurks "in the forests of the night." The central question of the poem is similar to the question in "The Lamb": "What immortal hand or eye/Could frame thy fearful symmetry?" In fact, the poem's speaker asks specifically, "Did he who made the Lamb make thee?" And he wonders if the tiger's maker "smiled his work to see."

Although there are many differing interpretations of what the tiger represents, it is clear that this beast is intended to be an awe-inspiring creature. It is associated with images of fire—"burning bright" and "the fire of thine eyes"—and of fear—"fearful symmetry" and "deadly terrors." Although the tiger is a fearsome creature, it is not evil. It merely follows its nature, just as the lamb does. Both are made by the same hand. If there is evil in the world—war, poverty, enslavement, and repression—Blake suggests these are society's distortion of God's creation.

Other Works by William Blake

The Complete Poetry and Prose of William Blake. Edited by David V. Erdman. New York: Anchor, 1982.

William Blake: The Complete Illuminated Books. London: Thames & Hudson, 2000.

Works about William Blake

Beer, John. *William Blake: A Literary Life.* New York: Palgrave Macmillan, 2007.

Bentley, G. E. *The Stranger from Paradise: A Biography of William Blake.* New Haven, Conn.: Yale University Press, 2001.

Damon, S. Foster. *William Blake: His Philosophy and Symbols.* Whitefish, Mont.: Kessinger, 2006.

Frye, Northrop. *Fearful Symmetry.* Princeton, N.J.: Princeton University Press, 1969.

Hamlyn, Robin, et al. *William Blake.* New York: Harry N. Abrams, 2001.

Blandford, Ann
See EDWARDS, AMELIA.

Blessington, countess of
See GARDINER, MARGUERITE.

Blind, Mathilde (1841–1896) *poet, travel writer*

Mathilde Blind, née Cohen, was born on March 21 in Mannheim, Germany. When she was still a child, her father died and her mother married Karl Blind, a leader of the 1848 revolution in Germany that tried to overthrow the royal governments and replace them with democratically elected ones. After the revolution failed, Karl Blind and his family left for England. Mathilde Blind was educated in London and published her first book of poems in 1867, using the pen name Claude Lake. An ardent feminist and political radical, Blind became widely known for several poems published during the 1880s, including *The Prophecy of St. Oran and Other Poems* (1881) and *The Heather on Fire: A Tale of the Highland Clearances* (1886), both written from her experiences traveling in Scotland. The long poem *The Prophecy of St. Oran* revises a religious legend in order to make a secular point about the modern world:

> *Cast down the crucifix, take up the plough!*
> *Nor waste your breath which is the life in prayer!*
> *Dare to be men, and break your impious vow,*
> *Nor fly from woman as the devil's snare!*

Because of the implied atheism of such lines, the publisher was forced to withdraw the poems from circulation, despite generally enthusiastic critical reviews.

In 1888, Blind published *The Ascent of Man*, a poem about the theory of evolution dedicated to ELIZABETH BARRETT BROWNING. In addition to poetry, Blind wrote a biography of GEORGE ELIOT in 1883. She was also known for her travel writing based on her visits to Italy and Egypt. These books included *Songs and Sonnets* (1893) and *Birds of Passage: Songs of the Orient and Occident* (1895).

Bloomfield, Robert (1766–1823) *poet*

Robert Bloomfield was born to George Bloomfield, a penniless tailor, and Elizabeth Manby on December 3, 1766, in Honington, Suffolk. Before Bloomfield's first birthday, his father died of smallpox, and Elizabeth supported the family by spinning wool.

His mother also ran a small school in the family home. It was here that Bloomfield was educated. His older brother, George, described him as a boy who "could read before he walked."

At the age of 11, Bloomfield was sent to live and work at his uncle's farm. His recollection of this time was the inspiration for his famous poem "The Farmer's Boy." Robert's small frame could not hold up to farmwork, however, and instead he turned to shoemaking in London.

In the cobbler's workshop, Bloomfield was given the task of reading the news to the group. However, because of his relatively meager education, he stumbled over words he was unfamiliar with. His brother, recognizing his zeal to learn, bought him a secondhand dictionary to improve his vocabulary. This led to an improvement in Bloomfield's reading skills, which led to his taking an even greater interest in reading newspapers. By the mid-1780s he was publishing poems in magazines such as the *Gazetteer* and the *London Magazine,* while still working as a shoemaker. In his own writing, Bloomfield decided not to mimic others' language and style but to create his own.

Bloomfield returned to the country because he felt that the countryside was rejuvenating, and this stay reaffirmed his belief. The idea of the country as a healthful and healing place is depicted in many of his poems. However, after two months in the country, Bloomfield returned to London to work as a cobbler. Bloomfield also began to learn to play the violin and wrote to his brother George about this newfound love. Now in his twenties, Bloomfield looked to settling down, and, in December 1790, "he sold his fiddle and got a wife," Mary-Ann Church.

By the time he started to write his most famous poem, "The Farmer's Boy," in 1796, he had two daughters but was barely making ends meet as a cobbler. At first Bloomfield had trouble finding a publisher for his poem. At the time, many publishers would not even consider the work of poor self-educated writers, preferring to publish only the work of the upper classes.

The success of this poem failed to support him and his family, so he still relied heavily on his work as a shoemaker. A second success came when he composed *Rural Tales, Ballads and Songs,* in 1801. However, stomach ulcers and rheumatic fevers plagued him. He was in debt for most of his life and died with more recognition than money.

Other Works by Robert Bloomfield
The Banks of Wye: A Poem in Four Books. London: Longman, 1813.
The Fakenham Ghost: A True Tale. Philadelphia: Johnson & Warner, 1810.

Works about Robert Bloomfield
Lawson, Jonathan. *Robert Bloomfield.* Boston: Twayne Publishers, 1980.
Wickett, William. *The Farmer's Boy: The Story of a Suffolk Poet, Robert Bloomfield, His Life and Poems.* Lavenham, England: Terence Dalton, 1971.

White, Simon. and Keegan, Bridget. Eds. *Robert Bloomfield: Lyric, Class, and the Romantic Canon.* Lewisburg: Bucknell University Press, 2006.

bluestocking writers

The French philosopher Jean-Jacques Rousseau defined a bluestocking as "a woman who will remain a spinster as long as there are sensible men on earth." Derisive as well as affectionate, the term refers to a circle of women who, in mid-18th-century England, held evening receptions to discuss literary and intellectual interests. Following the established example of the French literary salon, these evening conversations served as an informal university, where women exchanged ideas with such celebrated guests as Samuel Johnson, Lord Lyttelton, Horace Walpole, and Sir Joshua Reynolds. The term *bluestocking* derives from Benjamin Stillingfleet's habit of wearing his daytime blue wool stockings to the receptions. Admiral Edward Boscawen is credited with applying *bluestocking* as a collective term for the group of women who hosted the evenings.

The informal group was of considerable size and flourished in London under the vivacious, witty, and learned guidance of Elizabeth Vesey, Elizabeth Montagu, and Frances Boscawen—collectively the "triple crown" of bluestocking hostesses, according to HANNAH MORE in her poem "Bas Bleu." Compared with the French salon hostesses, the bluestockings—although not feminists—opened new paths for the advancement of women in society. Similar to the salons in France, the bluestocking gatherings included men; in contrast, however, the women within the bluestocking circle offered one another mutual support in pursuing their interests, traveling, studying, and writing for publication.

Other Works by the Bluestocking Writers
Carter, Elizabeth. *Memoirs of the Life of Mrs. Elizabeth Carter.* New York: AMS Press, 1974.
Johnson, R. Brimley, ed. *Bluestocking Letters.* New York: Dial Press, 1926.

Kelly, Gary, ed. *Bluestocking Feminism: Writings of the Bluestocking Circle.* Brookfield, Vt.: Pickering & Chatto, 1999.

Montagu, Elizabeth Robinson. *Essay on the Writings and Genius of Shakespeare, Compared with the Greek and French Dramatic Poets.* New York: A. M. Kelley, 1996.

Works about the Bluestocking Writers

Myers, Sylvia Harcstark. *The Bluestocking Circle: Women, Friendship, and the Life of the Mind in Eighteenth-Century England.* New York: Oxford University Press, 1990.

Scott, Walter Sidney. *The Bluestocking Ladies.* London: J. Green, 1947.

Bodichon, Barbara (1827–1891) *nonfiction writer*

Barbara Smith was born in Sussex, England, and raised by her mother, Anne Longden, a milliner. Her father, who was not married to her mother, was the politician Benjamin Leigh Smith. In 1849 Smith attended Bedford Square Ladies' College in London, where she studied art. A year later, she joined her friend Bessie Parkes (later BESSIE RAYNER PARKES BELLOC) on a tour of continental Europe. Defying the conventions of the period, the two women took the trip without a chaperone. In London, Smith met Elizabeth Cady Stanton and Lucretia Mott, leaders of the women's rights movement in America whose ideas deeply influenced her. It was her conversations with Stanton and Mott, in part, that led her to write *A Brief Summary, in Plain Language, of the Most Important Laws Concerning Women* (1854). Smith exposed the laws that forced women to give up their rights when they married and to turn over their property to their husbands.

Smith formed a national movement to change the property ownership laws and in 1856 presented a petition with 26,000 signatures to Parliament. Her efforts would eventually convince Parliament to pass the Married Woman's Property Act.

In 1857 Smith traveled to Algeria, where she met a French physician, Eugène Bodichon, whom she later married. That same year she published a pamphlet, *Women and Work,* that asserted women's need to work and called for the admittance of women into the professions from which they had been excluded. Bodichon wrote, "No human being has the right to be idle. . . . Women must, as children of God, be trained to do some work in the world."

In 1865 Barbara Bodichon helped prepare another petition for Parliament that sought to give women the vote. A year later, she argued for women's suffrage in her publication *Reasons for and against the Enfranchisement of Women.* In 1872 she became the cofounder of Girton College, which was affiliated with Cambridge University but open to women. Throughout her years of social and political activism, Bodichon also painted. Her landscapes were widely exhibited throughout England.

Works about Barbara Bodichon

Herstein, Sheila. *A Mid-Victorian Feminist: Barbara Leigh Smith Bodichon.* New Haven, Conn.: Yale University Press, 1985.

Orr, Clarissa, ed. *Women in the Victorian Art World.* New York: St. Martin's Press, 1995.

Boldrewood, Rolf (Thomas Alexander Browne) (1826–1915) *novelist*

Rolf Boldrewood was born Thomas Alexander Browne in London. His family moved to Australia when he was still a child, and he attended school in Sydney. After leaving school, he went to work in the Australian gold fields. When he was unable to earn enough to support himself, Browne turned to writing, using the pseudonym Rolf Boldrewood. After publishing some early stories in Australian magazines, Boldrewood wrote his first novel, *Ups and Downs* (1878), which was based on his own experiences trying to make a living in Australia. In 1882 he published an adventure novel, *Robbery Under Arms,* which made him popular throughout the country. One of the first writers to feature Australian heroes in his books, he was widely read in his adopted land. His later novels, also set in Australia, included *A Colonial Reformer* (1890) and *A Romance of Canvas Town* (1898).

Booth, Catherine (1829–1890) *nonfiction writer, orator*

Catherine Mumford Booth was born in Ashbourne, England. Her father, John Mumford, was a coach builder and also a Wesleyan lay preacher. Her mother, Sarah Mumford, was fervently religious, and instilled this passion in Catherine while educating her at home. In 1848 Booth joined a sect of Wesleyans known as the Reformers, who advocated a democratic church hierarchy and a revivalist spirit. The Reformers were subsequently expelled from the Wesleyan church. In 1855 Catherine married William Booth, a Reformist preacher.

Catherine Booth gained recognition as a speaker at her husband's services, leading the congregation in prayers. In 1860 she published her first essay, a pamphlet that declared the right of women to preach publicly. After its appearance, Booth regularly delivered the sermons during William's revivals.

In 1877 William Booth formed the Salvation Army. Provided now with a military structure and outlook, the Reformists viewed themselves as soldiers of God, inspired by the Holy Spirit, and engaged in an aggressive battle to save human souls. Although Catherine Booth never held a formal position in the Salvation Army, she was instrumental as a public defender of the movement, especially through a series of essays entitled *Aggressive Christianity* (1880), which urged the salvation of souls through any means: "Save them—pulling them out of the fire. Adapt your measures to your circumstances and to the necessities of the times in which you live."

Booth also remained devoted to the improvement of women's position in the church and society. Writing frequently in *War Cry*, the Salvation Army's periodical, she stressed further participation of women in the ministry, supported institutions to help alcoholic women, and resisted the spread of prostitution.

In 1888 Booth was diagnosed with breast cancer, but for the last two years of her life she continued to advise Salvation Army members. Her efforts earned her the appellation "Mother of the Salvation Army." Her biographer Roger Green praises her ability as a preacher, extolling her "verbal skills, her commitment to the ideas she espoused, and the passion of her delivery. . . . [S]he gave herself in utter abandonment to God and to his work as she perceived it."

A Work about Catherine Booth

Green, Roger J. *Catherine Booth: A Biography of the Cofounder of the Salvation Army*. Grand Rapids, Mich.: Baker Books, 1996.

Booth, Charles (1840–1916) *sociologist*

Charles Booth was born in Liverpool, England, to Charles Booth, a grain merchant, and his wife Emily Fletcher. Educated at the Royal Institution School in Liverpool, Booth left school for the world of business at age 16. At age 22, with his brother Alfred, Booth formed a shipping company that would successfully provide service between Europe and Brazil.

By the time Booth married Mary Macaulay in 1871 he was a successful businessman, well-traveled, and keenly interested in the social issues of the time. His wife's cousin, Beatrice Potter Webb, a social scientist who would later aid Booth in his monumental social investigation, described Booth in her diary: "Conscience, reason, and dutiful affection, are his great qualities. . . . [H]e interests me as a man who has his nature completely under his control, and who has risen out of it, uncynical, vigorous and energetic in mind without egotism."

In 1885 Booth learned that one-fourth of London's population lived in dire poverty. The statistic spurred him to investigate the causes of poverty and the conditions in which people live. With the help of a team of researchers, including

Beatrice Potter Webb, Booth studied London's East End street by street. In 1889 Booth published *Labour and Life of the People,* the result of his research, which indicated that 35 percent—not 25 percent—of London's East End lived in great poverty. This statistic persuaded Booth to expand his investigation to the entire city of London. Over the next 12 years, Booth ran his business during the day and focused on his research and writing in the evenings and weekends, publishing his monumental work, the 17-volume *Life and Labour of the People of London* (1891–1903). The work is organized in three subject areas: poverty, industry, and the influences of religion.

Booth's survey, an original and complex combination of interviews and gathered data of 4,076 cases, contributed to the increased awareness of social problems and to the importance of statistical measurement, which in turn established the basis for decision making in modern social work. Booth believed that government should take responsibility for those living in poverty, argued for the support of the aged, and proposed the introduction of the Old Age Pensions Act of 1908. His other writings include *Old Age Pensions and the Aged Poor* (1899) and *Industrial Unrest and Trade Union Policy* (1914).

A Work about Charles Booth
O'Day, Rosemary, and David Englander. *Mr. Booth's Inquiry: Life and Labour of the People in London Reconsidered.* London: Hambledon, 1993.

Booth, William (1829–1912) *reform writer*
William Booth was born on April 10 near Nottingham in central England to Samuel Booth, a factory owner, and Mary Moss. When he was still a teenager Booth worked in a pawnshop, where he experienced firsthand the conditions of the poor who had to pawn their possessions for money. During the 1840s he joined the Methodist Church and became a preacher, urging people to reform their lives as the best route out of poverty. In 1855 he married Catherine Mumford (*see* BOOTH, CATHERINE); the couple were sent to Manchester—and later to Durham, in northern England—to carry on the work of the Methodist Church.

Booth and his wife grew tired of constantly traveling and settled in London in 1865. There they established a mission for the poor, which eventually became the Salvation Army in 1878. The Salvation Army provided meals as well as spiritual instruction for the poor so they could free themselves from sin. By the 1880s branches of the Salvation Army had formed throughout England as well as in the United States. In 1884 Booth published *Training of Children; or, How to Make the Children into Saints and Soldiers of Jesus Christ.* This book was followed five years later by *The Future of Missions and the Mission of the Future,* and *Holy Living; or, What the Salvation Army Teaches about Sanctification* (1890). In 1890 Booth also published his most famous work, *In Darkest England and the Way Out.* The title, which echoes HENRY MORTON STANLEY's *In Darkest Africa* (1890), announced Booth's intention to argue that the English, urban poor lived in what amounted to heathen colonies devoid of Christian culture. In this book he described the environment of the poor as if it were "darkest Africa," and pointed out that only an organization like the Salvation Army could alleviate poverty through missions that mirrored the missionary work that led to colonization overseas. England too, Booth argued, needed to be "civilized."

A Work about William Booth
Fellows, Lawrence, and Janet Beller. *A Gentle War: The Story of The Salvation Army.* New York: Athenaeum, 1980.

Borrow, George Henry (1803–1881)
nonfiction writer, translator
George Borrow was born in East Dereham, Norfolk, England, to Thomas Borrow, an army captain, and Ann Parfrement, an actress. Borrow attended school in Norwich until age 16 and later apprenticed with a lawyer until 1824.

During this period Borrow also worked with William Taylor, a well-known translator of the German poet Johann Wolfgang von Goethe. By the time Borrow moved to London in 1824, he was proficient in 12 languages, including Gaelic, Welsh, Hebrew, Russian, and Arabic. Borrow eventually found a job with the British and Foreign Bible Society, which asked him to translate the New Testament into Chinese.

Borrow next traveled to Spain, where he served as a missionary handing out Protestant Bibles. He wrote about his Spanish adventures in *The Bible in Spain* (1843), a combination adventure story, Evangelical religious tract, and autobiography. In the preface, Borrow makes claims for his originality: "I was, as I may say, from first to last adrift in Spain, the land of old renown, the land of wonder and mystery, with better opportunities of becoming acquainted with its strange secrets and peculiarities than, perhaps, ever yet were afforded to any individual." While today only a handful of specialists remember Borrow's works, they were runaway best-sellers at the time. A reviewer for the *Examiner* praised *The Bible in Spain,* declaring, "Never was book more legibly impressed with the unmistakable mark of genius."

Over the next 30 years, Borrow continued to publish articles and books on religion, travel, and himself. *Lavengro* (1851) and *The Romany Rye* (1857) comprise a two-part autobiographical novel. Although action-packed, lyrical, and full of romantic reminiscences about his life, these works are marred by Borrow's rabid anti-Catholicism.

Other Work by George Borrow

Wild Wales: Its People, Language, and Scenery. London: Collins, 1977.

Works about George Borrow

Meyers, Robert R. *George Borrow.* Boston: Twayne, 1966.

Williams, David. *A World of His Own: The Double Life of George Borrow.* Oxford: Oxford University Press, 1982.

Boucicault, Dion (Dionysius) (1820?–1890)
playwright, actor

Dion Boucicault was born in Dublin, raised by French Huguenot parents named Boursiquot, educated in Dublin and London, and apprenticed to Dr. Dionysius Lardner, an encyclopedist and Boucicault's putative father. He began acting in and directing school plays. In 1838 he ran away and, under the stage name Lee Moreton, began his dramatic career as actor, director, and playwright. His first major success as a playwright came with his comedy *London Assurance* (1841), a drawing-room farce in a style later associated with OSCAR WILDE, featuring the character Lady Gay Spanker, a fox-hunting harridan and one of Boucicault's most inspired creations. The play had a run of 69 nights at Covent Garden, and as recently as 1997 was revived on Broadway in New York. *London Assurance* announced the beginning of the career of a man who, as his biographer Richard Fawkes puts it, "wrote, adapted or doctored more than 200 plays, many of them highly influential; who made and lost fortunes, was involved in scandal, was considered to be one of the wittiest men of his age . . . and was for fifty years the most important single figure in the theatrical life of both Britain and America." It was Boucicault who said, "None but the brave deserve the fair, and none but the brave can live with some of them."

His professional successes were shadowed early on by personal and financial problems, a pattern that recurred throughout his life. He married a French woman, Anne Guiot, in 1845; was in bankruptcy court in 1847; worked in London and in France until 1848, when his wife died; and was in Insolvent Debtors Court that same year. He continued to be successful as a playwright, however, and began acting under his own name. In 1852 he married the noted actress Agnes Robertson. She sailed for New York in 1853 and he followed shortly thereafter. Boucicault enjoyed a series of successes as his touring company played New York, Boston, Chicago, Philadelphia, Washington, D.C., and other cities. Most of the plays produced were his, and he acted in some of them as well. The couple's stay in the United States saw the birth of three children and Boucicault's successful efforts to help the U.S. Congress pass a copyright law. In 1859 he wrote and produced *The Octoroon,* a play about slavery based on the Louisiana novel *Quadroon* (1856) by Mayne Reid.

The Boucicaults made a triumphant return to London in 1860. *The Colleen Bawn*—the first of three of Boucicault's Irish melodramas that started the trend of what was called "sensation drama," plays with powerful visual effects (real fires, explosions, and so on) and exaggerated, stylized emotion—ran for a record 278 performances. In 1862 the playwright opened his own theater in London, the Theatre Royal, which he mismanaged, causing him to go bankrupt within a year. He and Agnes then successfully worked in Liverpool, in Dublin, and in several London theaters. In London, Boucicault finally teamed with a wealthy partner who leased the famous theater in Covent Garden for his visually spectacular *Babil and Bijou.* Again Boucicault failed financially, and he and Agnes left for New York. The following years saw repeated successes in New York and other American cities, but in 1883 Agnes gave her last American performance. Two years later, Boucicault, having taken the company to San Francisco and then to Australia, married another actress, Louise Thorndyke, apparently without divorcing Agnes. He returned to London in 1886 for a 200-night run of *The Jilt,* after which he returned to the United States. He went broke again in Chicago, then became an acting teacher in New York, where he died poor in 1890.

Boucicault's several periods of poverty should not be considered as failures of his writing, producing, or acting. He simply did not know how to handle money. He was a superb and very popular actor, and his plays brought in huge crowds.

Critical Analysis

Historians of the theater see Boucicault as one of the greatest melodramatists, one whose sure sense of what entertains in the theater influenced several far more "serious" dramatists, particularly GEORGE BERNARD SHAW, Sean O'Casey, and John Millington Synge. In the words of one critic, Boucicault gave Shaw particularly the sense of ". . . how overwhelmingly important the craft of entertainment is for the art of the drama." Shaw himself recommended the study of Boucicault, along with Molière, Ibsen, and other giants of the theater, for young drama critics. In defending his mixture of both the comic and tragic in his plays, O'Casey writes, ". . . it's no new practice—hundreds have done it, including Shakespeare up to Dion Boucicault in, for instance, 'Colleen Bawn' & 'Conn, the Shaughraun.'" For all his personal faults, Boucicault was a man with a social conscience who was deeply concerned with the plight of the poor, particularly the Irish poor. One sees this in the plays mentioned above and in *Arrahna-Pogue* (1864) and *The Rapparee* (1870) as well. In 1876 he went so far as to write Prime Minister DISRAELI in an effort to get Irish political prisoners released from English jails. Despite his years spent abroad, Boucicault considered himself an Irishman: "Nature did me that honour."

Other Work by Dion Boucicault
Selected Plays of Dion Boucicault ed. Andrew Parkin. Washington, D.C.: Catholic University of America Press, 1987.

Works about Dion Boucicault
Fawkes, Richard. *Dion Boucicault: A Biography.* New York: Quartet Books, 1979.
Grene, Nicholas. *The Politics of Irish Drama: Plays in Context from Boucicault to Friel.* Cambridge: Cambridge University Press, 2000.

Bowdler, Thomas (1754–1825) *editor*

Thomas Bowdler is best remembered not for the writing he created but for the writing he concealed. Born in Ashley, Somerset, England, he was the youngest son of a deeply religious lawyer also named Thomas. In adulthood, Bowdler became deeply concerned about the prevalence of the sexually explicit, violent, and sacrilegious in literature, even in Shakespeare, whom he greatly admired. He published a 10-volume *Family Shakespeare* (1807–18) that expurgated about a 10th of Shakespeare's writing—those sections "which cannot with propriety be read aloud in a family," as Bowdler put it. He allowed passages in which characters utter well-intentioned oaths to God to remain, for instance, while removing passages in which characters took God's name in vain. Bowdler argued that when one removes offensive material from a book, one does so "not only without injury but with a manifest advantage . . . to the sense of the passage and to the spirit of the author."

Such censored, or expurgated, versions of classic texts were common at the time, but Bowdler's audacity in editing Shakespeare made him notorious. As the historian Noel Perrin notes, the *Family Shakespeare* "was to become the most famous of all expurgated books, and thirty years later its editor's name turned into a standard verb," *bowdlerize*, which remains a common synonym for *censor* to this day.

Bowles, William Lisle (1762–1850) *poet, nonfiction writer*

William Lisle Bowles is best known for the inspiration he provided to the romantic poets (*see* ROMANTICISM) rather than for his own writings. He was a clergyman, educated at Winchester and at Trinity College, Oxford. He served as the vicar of Bremhill in Wiltshire for more than 45 years. His most famous work, *Fourteen Sonnets* (1789), helped revive the form and influenced the romantic poets SAMUEL TAYLOR COLERIDGE, WILLIAM WORDSWORTH, and ROBERT SOUTHEY to write their longer poems and meditations on nature. Coleridge was, in fact, so inspired by the picturesque sonnets that he wrote out copies of the book to distribute among his friends and composed a sonnet praising Bowles for "mild and manliest melancholy."

In his critical writing, Bowles argued that images drawn from nature and basic human passions gave rise to more important poetical themes than did imagery drawn from artifice or stylized manners of the upper classes. His beliefs led him to publish, in 1806, an edition of the 18th-century poet Alexander Pope, under the title *Strictures on the Life and Writings of Pope*, in which he attacked Pope for being concerned with society, as opposed to nature. LORD BYRON, as well as THOMAS CAMPBELL, voiced support for Pope and wrote pamphlets arguing against Bowles's assertions. This public dialog became known as the "Pope-Bowles controversy."

The scholar John Marston described Bowles's significance as a poet: "His pensive tenderness, delicate fancy, refined taste, and above all his power to harmonize the moods of nature with those of the mind were his chief merits." The following lines from Bowles's "Sonnet V. To the River Tweed" (with its quirky spelling) illustrate Marston's comment:

> *The waving branches that romantick bend*
> *O'er they tall banks, a soothing charm*
>   *bestow.*
> *The murmurs of thy wander'ring wave*
>   *below*
> *Seem to this ear the pity of a friend.*

Braddon, Mary Elizabeth (1837–1915) *novelist, poet*

Mary Elizabeth Braddon was born in London and educated at home. At age 20 she began a brief career as an actress, appearing on stage between 1857 and 1860, but by her mid-20s she had become known as a novelist.

Braddon published her first novel, *Three Times Dead*, in 1861 and used the money she earned from it to help support her mother, who had left Braddon's father. A year later she published her most famous novel, *Lady Audley's Secret*, the story of a woman who tries to keep her lurid past hidden.

Braddon quickly became known as a leading writer of the sensation novel, melodramatic stories that featured mystery, violence, and crime. SENSATION FICTION, which was often published in serial form in magazines, became popular as the middle class became more widely educated and the demand for libraries and periodicals grew. *Lady Audley's Secret* first appeared in a magazine owned by John Maxwell, a publisher whom Braddon lived with and eventually married in 1874. They had six children.

Braddon was extremely prolific. She wrote 20 novels in the decade between 1861 and 1871 and by the end of her career had published 80 books. Among her works were *Eleanor's Victory* (1863), a female detective story, and a historical novel, *Under the Red Flag* (1883). She also wrote plays and poetry.

Other Works by Mary Braddon
Cut by the County. New York: Sensation Press, 2001.
His Darling Sin. New York: Sensation Press, 2001.

A Work about Mary Braddon
Carnell, Jennifer. *The Literary Lives of Mary Elizabeth Braddon.* New York: Sensation Press, 2000.

Bradley, Katherine Harris
See FIELD, MICHAEL.

Bridges, Robert (1844–1930) poet
Robert Bridges was born in Walmer, Kent, England, into the wealthy family of John and Harriet Bridges. He studied medicine at Oxford University and then practiced briefly as a physician until 1882. During that time he began writing poetry, publishing his first collection, the first volume of his work, *Shorter Poems,* in 1873. Bridges wrote, "What led me to poetry was the inexhaustible satisfaction of form, the magic of speech.... [I]t was an art which I hoped to learn." In 1884 he married Mary Monica Waterhouse and from that point on enjoyed a secluded domestic stability, devoting himself to writing and thinking.

Bridges was a prolific writer who published many books of poetry and essays and wrote eight plays. He eventually published five volumes of *Shorter Poems* altogether; the subsequent volumes appeared in 1879, 1880, 1890, and 1894. The long poem *Eros and Psyche* was published in 1895. Bridges also wrote two important studies of British poetry, *Milton's Prosody* (1893) and *John Keats* (1895). An edition of his *Poetical Works,* published in 1912, gained him public recognition, and he was named poet laureate in 1913, succeeding ALFRED AUSTIN. He held the position until his death. Bridges was more concerned with the formal aspects of poetry than with the expression of emotion. According to the poet Robert Hillyer, "Both those who admire and those who dislike the poetry of Bridges agree on one point: that technically he was one of the masters of English verse. His experiments within the tradition are bolder and more informed than most of those outside it."

During his student years at Oxford, Bridges became a good friend of GERARD MANLEY HOPKINS, and he corresponded with Hopkins until the latter's death in 1889. In 1918, 29 years after Hopkins died, Bridges edited his friend's poems for their first publication in book form. It would take 30 years for Hopkins's work to be restored to its original state, and Bridges has been criticized for tampering with the poems. However, without his efforts Hopkins's work might never have been published at all.

Bridges continued to experiment with poetic form and meter and on his 85th birthday published *The Testament of Beauty,* a long, complex poem on the evolution of the human soul, written in what he called "loose alexandrine" lines. He died at his home at Boar's Hill, Oxford, at 96.

Critical Analysis
One poem that seems to embody all of Robert Bridges's strengths—his restraint, precision, and delicacy—is "London Snow," a lyrical look at a London snowfall. The poem is written in quatrains, rhyming *abab*. The rhythm, in keeping

with Bridges's notions of prosody, counts stresses rather than syllables, giving the poem the meter and sound of natural speech. Bridges adds to the richness of the poem by employing alliteration and internal rhyme. In the first stanza, for example, he describes the snow "falling on the city brown,/Stealthily and perpetually settling and loosely lying."

Bridges describes the initial hush the snow brings to the city, again using alliteration and internal rhyme to mimic the muted sounds. Thus, the snow floats down "Silently sifting and veiling road, roof and railing." As the city wakes to the unaccustomed brightness, even the human sounds are "thin and spare" in the freezing air.

In one of the poem's most delightful passages, Bridges describes boys on their way to school gathering up "the crystal manna to freeze/Their tongues with tasting, their hands with snowballing." As conventional as this poem is in many ways, it also has passages like this that are quite modern in their syntax and word choice. Modern-sounding too is Bridges's description of snow-covered trees as "white-mossed wonder[s]."

As the sun comes up and awakes "the stir of the day," doors open and "war is waged with the snow," a phrase that perfectly evokes the feeling of "somber men" as they begin their long trudge to work through mountains of snow. Even these, Bridges says, are "diverted" from their ordinary thoughts "At the sight of the beauty that greets them." "London Snow" is a gem of a poem, an apt product of a poet-laureate.

A Work about Robert Bridges

Phillips, Catherine. *Robert Bridges: A Biography.* New York: Oxford University Press, 1992.

Brontë, Anne (1820–1849) *novelist, poet*

Anne Brontë, born in Thornton, Yorkshire, England, was the youngest daughter of Patrick Brontë, an Anglican clergyman from Ireland, and his English wife, Maria Branwell Brontë. Almost immediately the family moved to Haworth, Yorkshire, where a year later Brontë's mother died. Brontë studied at home and later attended Roe Head School. As children, Brontë and her siblings—EMILY BRONTË, CHARLOTTE BRONTË, and brother Branwell—collaborated on stories about the mythical kingdoms of Gondal and Angria. From these childish beginnings, all three sisters would go on to become major writers.

Beginning in 1839, Brontë worked several years as a governess, while continuing to write numerous poems. In 1846 she and her sisters jointly published a volume of poetry, *Poems,* under the names Currer, Ellis, and Acton Bell, pseudonyms chosen to disguise their gender and identity. Brontë would go on to publish all of her work under her pseudonym. Since her teen years she had written poetry about the mythical Gondal, religion, feminine identity, and especially abandonment and despair. In the midst of loss, however, Brontë retained a sense of hope, as in the poem "Yes Thou Art Gone":

> *Yet though I cannot see thee more*
> *'Tis still a comfort to have seen,*
> *And though my transient life is o'er*
> *'Tis sweet to think that thou hast been.*

The public ignored *Poems,* but a few critics appreciated it. A reviewer for the *Critic* called the volume "genuine poetry" and "a ray of sunshine."

In 1847 her first novel, *Agnes Grey,* appeared. Like her sister Charlotte Brontë's *Jane Eyre, Agnes Grey* is a first-person account of the life of a governess and is based on personal experiences. A year later, Anne Brontë's best-known novel, *The Tenant of Wildfell Hall,* appeared. *Tenant* is a novel in letters that tells the story of Helen Graham, the tenant of the title, who arouses the curiosity of a young man, Gilbert Markham, when she moves to Wildfell Hall with her young son. Gilbert falls in love with her, only to discover that she and her son have fled from her husband, Arthur Huntingdon, a brutal drunkard. At the time, women were not legally permitted to leave their husbands or allowed to have custody of their children. The novel sold well, but was criticized for "dwelling on what is disagreeable," in Joseph Addison's phrase, for its feminist views and harsh realism—the very qualities for which it is beloved today. A year after the publication of her second novel, Brontë died of tuberculosis in the coastal town of Scarborough. Although often overshadowed by the reputations of her two more famous sisters, recently Brontë has begun to be recognized as a major 19th-century talent and *Tenant* as worthy of standing next to her sisters' novels *Jane Eyre* and *Wuthering Heights*.

Critical Analysis

Agnes Grey, while similar in many ways to Charlotte Brontë's *Jane Eyre,* suffers by comparison. *Jane Eyre,* while securely situated in Victorian England, transcends its time and place, with an almost mythic story about a woman's indomitable spirit and fierce sense of her own worth, despite what society may say of her. *Agnes Grey* never quite escapes its place and time and must remain a lesser work.

However, *Agnes Grey* is not without interest or virtue. It is especially powerful in its depiction of the very limited choices open to women without means in Victorian society. Agnes, like Anne Brontë herself, is the daughter of an impoverished cleric who must find a way to help support the family. Sensitive, romantic, and well-educated, Agnes seeks a position as a governess. She hopes to expand her horizons and see a bit more of the world. The world she discovers, unfortunately, is small and hard and humiliating. The families for whom she works treat her as a lesser being, encouraging the children for whom she must care to disregard her as well. At the same time, she is expected to teach the children and enforce discipline. Agnes's task, then, includes the "misery of being charged with the care and direction of a set of mischievous, turbulent rebels, whom … [the] utmost exertions cannot bind to their duty; while, at the same time … [being] responsible for their conduct to a higher power, who exacts … what cannot be achieved without the aid of the superior's more potent authority, which, either from indolence, or the fear of becoming unpopular with the said rebellious gang, the latter refuses to give." It is hard not to see one of her little charges as a serial killer in training, as he proceeds to capture and torture baby birds to death with the encouragement of his father and uncle. At one point Agnes must seize a stolen nest herself and quickly dispatch the babies to keep them from a much worse death.

Contrasted to the families for whom Agnes works is her own family. Hers are loving parents who believe in the importance of education, both academic and moral, and who raise their children to do good, work hard, and show respect. Unlike Agnes, Rosalie Murry, her oldest charge, "had never been perfectly taught the distinction between right and wrong; she had … been suffered from infancy, to tyrannize over nurses, governesses, and servants; she had not been taught to moderate her desires, to control her temper or bridle her will, or to sacrifice her own pleasure for the good of others." These are precisely the lessons Agnes learned in her own poor but ultimately superior household.

While *Agnes Grey* also tells the tale of a romance between Agnes and a young clergyman who shares her values and view of the world, the novel is finally a work of social criticism that compares middle-class values and ideals very unfavorably with the shallow materialism of the upper classes. The servants, in her world, are infinitely superior to their masters.

Works about Anne Brontë
Chitham, Edward. *The Life of Anne Brontë*. Oxford, England: Blackwell, 1991.
Frawley, Maria H. *Anne Brontë*. New York: Twayne, 1996.

Brontë, Charlotte (1816–1855) *novelist*
Born in Yorkshire, England, to Patrick Brontë, an Anglican clergyman from Ireland, and his wife, Maria Branwell Brontë, Charlotte Brontë

was the elder sister of Branwell, EMILY, and ANNE BRONTË. Of the three, she was the most worldly, the only one to marry, and the only one to experience commercial success in her lifetime. In 1820 the family moved to a parsonage in the small town of Haworth, in the moorlands of what is now West Yorkshire. The tuberculosis of her two elder sisters, Maria and Elizabeth, neglected by the boarding school where she and Emily also were enrolled, resulted in their deaths in 1825.

After this, the children were educated at home. Beginning in 1835 Charlotte Brontë taught at Roe Head School. Seven years later, hoping to open a school in Yorkshire, she and Emily both enrolled at Pensionnat Heger, a school in Brussels. In 1844, however, the sisters' plan to open their own school failed. Charlotte Brontë's first novel, *The Professor,* unpublished during her lifetime, drew on her experiences in Brussels.

In 1846 Brontë arranged for the publication of *Poems by Currer, Ellis, and Acton Bell,* which included work by herself and both Emily and Anne. The use of pseudonyms was intended to forestall criticism of their work based on gender, with each pseudonym duplicating the author's real initials. Charlotte Brontë was Currer Bell.

Brontë's first published novel was *Jane Eyre* (1847). The title character is a strong-willed orphan who, working as governess, falls in love with her employer, the imposing, tormented Edward Rochester. Their marriage ceremony is canceled when it is revealed that Rochester is already married, to an insane woman locked up in an attic chamber. Eventually, however, the lovers are able to marry. A major theme is the deprivation of love and its consequences.

A social novel, *Shirley* (1849) portrays a tumultuous time when the introduction of industrialization in the early 19th century threatened the livelihoods of English workmen. Brontë had observed the discontent fermenting in Yorkshire, and included her observations in the book: "Misery generates hate: these sufferers hated the machines which they believed took their bread from them; they hated the buildings which contained those machines; they hated the manufacturers who owned those buildings." Reviewing the novel in the *Edinburgh Review,* G. H. LEWES disclosed that Currer Bell was a woman. By the time *Shirley* appeared, all of Brontë's remaining siblings had died: Emily and Branwell in 1848, and Anne in 1849.

Brontë's last completed novel, *Villette* (1853), offers little detail of the main character's past. The book is based on Brontë's experiences as a teacher in Brussels.

Soon after marrying the Reverend Arthur Bell Nicholls in 1854, Brontë wrote to her friend Ellen Nussey that "[I]t is a solemn and strange and perilous thing for a woman to become a wife." Brontë died less than a year later.

Critical Analysis

The cruelty of Mr. Brocklehurst, who runs Lowood School; the misty night during which Jane Eyre is conveyed to Thornfield, Edward Rochester's estate; Rochester's mysterious torment; the atmosphere of horror inside the mansion; the madwoman in the attic—these Gothic elements in *Jane Eyre,* in concert with the love story (especially with its improbable romantic pairing and edge of desperation) help create a Gothic romance.

In general, critics have disparaged the Gothic genre for its contrivance and shallowness. However, this particular novel contains additional elements that give the result greater depth. For instance, Robert B. Heilman has written, "Jane's strange, fearful symbolic dreams"—in one, a hand instead of the moon emerges from a cloud—"are not mere thrillers but reflect" tensions and emotional states, including her "longing for Rochester after she has left him." Brontë "is plumbing the psyche, not inventing a weird *décor.*"

Some reviewers at the time of the novel's publication, however, had gender, not genre, on their minds. Brontë's pseudonym aroused speculation about her sex. One reviewer, in the *Economist,* even wrote, without irony, that the novel was splendid if written by a man but "odious" if written by a woman. Jane's passion for Rochester offended many reviewers, including Anne Mozley in the *Christian Remembrancer,* who felt that a real-life counterpart of Jane's would be content with her "daily round of simple duties." Mozley found the novel "dangerous."

What kept the novel "dangerous" for three decades, according to her biographer Lyndall Gordon, is its "brazen" narrator, the "indomitable 'I'," Jane herself. Confident and self-reliant, Gordon has written, Jane is "a new kind of woman." We hear composure in her voice, especially when she addresses the reader, as she often does. Recounting her journey from Lowood School to her first employment, for example, Jane says, "A new chapter in a novel is something like a new scene in a play; and when I draw up the curtain this time, reader, you must fancy you see a room in the George Inn at Millcote"—the room where she lodged, which she proceeds to describe. The strength of her voice, as much as the plot, compels the reader to follow her story.

Jane Eyre also inspired another novel that provides an account of Rochester's first wife: Jean Rhys's novel *Wide Sargasso Sea* (1966).

Shirley, Brontë's novel about social conditions in industrial England, differs from its predecessor in more than genre. Brontë's biographer Juliet Barker has summarized these differences: "Unlike *Jane Eyre,* which had been written in the first person and thus had a single point of view, *Shirley* was written in the third person and had a multiplicity of characters, many of whom . . . did nothing to advance or enhance the story. More importantly, there was a significant shift in the book's interest from Caroline Helstone to Shirley Keeldar," giving the novel, as it were, two heroines. As a result, some readers have found the book disjointed and lacking in unity. The critic Helene Moglen, however, has defended the novel against such charges, saying that those who make them fail to connect the novel's various elements, including Brontë's "use of the Luddite riots [by workers destroying industrial property]," "the jaundiced presentation of marriage," and "the impassioned pleas for useful work for women." (Caroline, who is 18, at one point remarks, "I long to have something absorbing and compulsory to fill my head and hands, and to occupy my thoughts.") Moglen argues that in order to understand better "the nature of female oppression," Brontë was searching for connections "between women and the poor and socially dispossessed, between women and unemployed laborers, between women and children."

Lucy Snowe is the impoverished main character and narrator in Brontë's autobiographical *Villette.* According to Moglen, "[Lucy] has already been so hurt by her circumstances that she is unable to talk about her past" and is afraid of feeling and of opening herself up.

Villette is Brontë's most mysterious novel. "It is hard to arrive at clear perceptions and grasp fundamental truths" in the world where Lucy's story occurs, the critic Judith Williams has written, for it is a place "full of ambiguity, illusion, self-deception, deception of others (including us, the readers), spying, surveillance, willful misunderstanding, conjuring tricks, and even black magic." The novel's elusive, at times unfathomable nature is introduced at the outset in a country parish. The aurora borealis inexplicably brings to "neutral, passive" Lucy the "thought" to go to London, its "moving mystery" taking her there as though she were without a will of her own to direct the course of her life. Thus begins the journey that takes Lucy to Villette, a rechristened Brussels, where she teaches school.

One of the major events in Lucy's life is her nervous breakdown, the result of failed attempts at finding love and friendship and the school's oppressive atmosphere, including the headmistress's steady cold eye. It is fellow teacher Paul Emanuel who helps her to recover and patiently coaxes her into a love relationship.

In writing the novel, Brontë may have been trying to better understand her own experiences in Brussels, in part to counter her sense that they were beyond her control. Moglen has written that "[t]he functioning of will, the possibility of choice, the action of 'fate' had become for [Brontë] psychological as well as philosophical problems."

Lucy may have provided the means, then, for working through these problems: during Paul's prolonged absence, instead of pining fruitlessly, Lucy settles into self-sufficiency teaching at the school Paul helped her to start.

Praising "the power and originality of her art," the critic Herbert Read was referring to "psychological observation and analysis" when he wrote, "it is *Villette* . . . that we must recognize as the pioneer of an extension of the province and function of the novelist's art."

Works about Charlotte Brontë
Barker, Juliet. *The Brontës*. New York: St. Martin's Press, 1995.
Gordon, Lyndall. *Charlotte Brontë: A Passionate Life*. New York: W. W. Norton, 1996.
Fraser, Rebecca. *Charlotte Brontë*. New York: Vintage, 2003.
Sellars, Jane. *Charlotte Brontë*. New York: Oxford University Press, 2000.
Smith, Margaret, ed. *Selected Letters of Charlotte Brontë*. New York: Oxford University Press, 2007.

Brontë, Emily (1818–1848) *novelist, poet*
Emily Brontë, whose literary fame derives almost exclusively from her single novel, *Wuthering Heights* (1847), was born in Yorkshire, England, to Patrick Brontë, an Anglican clergyman from Ireland, and Maria Branwell Brontë. Brontë had one younger sibling, ANNE BRONTË, and four older ones: sisters Maria, Elizabeth, and CHARLOTTE BRONTË, and a brother, Patrick Branwell Brontë, called Branwell. The year of Anne's birth, 1820, the family moved when Brontë's father became curate of the church parsonage at Haworth, in what is now the county of West Yorkshire. In 1821 Maria, Brontë's mother, died of cancer. Three years later, Brontë and her older sisters entered Cowan Bridge School, where in 1825 Maria, age 10, and Elizabeth, 9, died of tuberculosis. Patrick Brontë withdrew both Charlotte and Emily from Cowan Bridge and brought them home.

Before their schooling, Emily, Charlotte, and Branwell often invented stories to be acted out—a practice they now resumed. Brontë subsequently collaborated with Anne, the two creating a female-governed fantasy realm, called Gondal, atmospherically modeled on the moorlands where they lived. Reclusive and introverted, Emily perhaps a bit more so than Anne, the two sisters became best friends and confidantes.

Brontë resumed her education in 1835 at Roe Head School, where Charlotte now taught; but, homesick, she stayed only three months. Similarly, ill health brought on by 17-hour workdays forced her withdrawal from teaching, in 1839, after six months. She also cut short a visit to Brussels, where Charlotte was studying in the hope of their starting a school together back home.

By the 1840s the three sisters had written enough poetry to make a book. They hoped to elude reviewers' typical condescension to female writers by using masculine pen names for their combined volume, *Poems by Currer, Ellis, and Acton Bell* (1846). Preserving their initials, Currer Bell was Charlotte, Ellis was Emily, and Acton was Anne. Brontë again used her pseudonym for *Wuthering Heights,* which was published in tandem with a novel by each of her sisters under their pseudonyms. The following year, Brontë, age 30, died of tuberculosis only months after her brother's death of the same disease. Five months later, Anne also succumbed.

Critical Analysis
The little that remains of Brontë's poetry shows a shy person's desire for the resolve needed to face the ordinary world that made her feel uncomfortable. Thus Brontë wrote in "Often Rebuked, Yet Always Back Returning" that she will turn from interior gloom, "the shadowy region," toward nature, "[w]here the gray flocks in ferny glens are feeding, / Where the wild wind blows on the mountainside." These lines reflect the "immense feeling of reality and observation" that the critic and author A. C. Benson attributed to Brontë's verse.

Brontë's novel *Wuthering Heights* is set in Yorkshire; the story begins in the mid-1700s. The protagonist, Heathcliff, is a foundling whom the kindly Mr. Earnshaw takes into his home, sparking a feud between this "gipsy brat," "the dirty, ragged, black-haired child," and Earnshaw's own son, Hindley, who feels replaced in his father's regard. When Heathcliff's benefactor dies, Hindley converts Heathcliff into a workhorse, a servant whom he frequently whips. Humiliated and locked out of the world of privilege that mocks him, Heathcliff grows up bitter. By the time he is 16, his "personal appearance sympathi[z]ed with mental deterioration: he acquired a slouching gait, and ignoble look"; he is "an unreclaimed creature, without refinement, without cultivation: an arid wilderness of furze and whinstone." He is also, as he has been since childhood, in love with Catherine, Hindley's sister. Cathy also feels spiritually connected to him; Heathcliff's wildness echoes something wild in herself. "[H]e's more myself than I am," she has said.

Brontë's novel charts Heathcliff's effect on two families, the Earnshaws and the Lintons, which seemingly unite against Heathcliff when Cathy marries the aristocratic Edgar Linton. Relying on her abiding love for him to make her jealous, Heathcliff takes revenge against Cathy by marrying Linton's sister, Isabella. Even after Cathy dies, he remains obsessed with her for the rest of his life, ruining his own marriage.

One of the themes of the novel is a confusion of family feelings, particularly on Catherine's part. Her heart is initially stirred by someone whose name, given to him by her father, was the name of the brother of hers who died at birth. After Heathcliff has run away and returned, Linton tries to direct his future wife's behavior to what is socially appropriate when he tells her that "the whole household need not witness the sight of your welcoming a runaway servant as a brother." Here, Linton, his soul "as different [from Heathcliff's and Cathy's] as a moonbeam from lightning, or frost from fire," misses the point that Heathcliff and Cathy *are* like brother and sister, and the confusion this engenders because of their other feelings for one another predicts the doom of their romantic relationship. The critic John T. Matthews has written, "What keeps [Cathy and Heathcliff] apart as it attracts them is less the simple facts of class discrepancy, or the conflict of natural appetite and social repression, or the incest prohibition, or the irretrievability of childhood's innocence—less these than the plain unavailability of a form for their bond"—a bond so riddled with ambiguity and contradiction as to suggest the ambivalence both characters feel, a dread encompassing both attraction and revulsion for one another. Matthews continues, "If we subscribe . . . to the simple view that Catherine betrays her heart by marrying Edgar instead of Heathcliff, we ignore the lovers' own unquestioned devotion to *maintaining* the very barriers that keep them apart."

Another theme is the impact of family history as "damage in one generation reproduces damage in the next," according to the critic Stevie Davies, who describes the novel as a "saga of child abuse."

Wuthering Heights does not provide a linear presentation of its story. The servant Nelly's accounts of the bleak history of both the Earnshaw and Linton families are framed by the first-person narrative of Heathcliff's tenant, Mr. Lockwood. The result is a zigzagging course through time that more closely resembles the narration of the 20th century than it does the 19th.

The book was a moral outrage to many contemporary reviewers. In the *Quarterly Review,* for example, Elizabeth Rigby derided its "coarseness of taste," regarding the relationship of the two main characters as "odiously and abominably pagan." But others were ambivalent. Writing in *American Review,* G. W. Peck also found the book "coarse," but added, "if the rank of a work of fiction is to depend solely on its naked imaginative power, then this is one of the greatest novels in the language."

Later critics came to admire the novel. Melvin Watson has called it "a psychological study of an elemental man whose soul is torn between love and hate." Davies has found in it "an original myth of loss, exile, rebirth and return." Lyn Pykett has seen "Catherine's history [as demonstrating] the difficulties of trying to be the heroine's of one's own life in a social and domestic milieu which cannot provide a theatre for heroinism." Beth Newman has written, "Although *Wuthering Heights* ends in cozy domesticity, the gaps in its enunciation express a feminist resistance to the patriarchal order in which its story partially acquiesces." Clearly, the novel has attracted a diverse range of critical approaches, including psychological, mythic, and feminist.

Wuthering Heights has been filmed several times, by directors including by Luis Buñuel (*Abismos de pasión,* 1954) and Jacques Rivette (*Hurlevent,* 1985). Perhaps the most famous film version, though, is William Wyler's (1939), starring Laurence Olivier as Heathcliff.

The critic David Cecil has described Brontë as a visionary, one whose "vision of life does away with the ordinary antithesis between good and evil." For Cecil, Brontë's writing embraces the whole range of human experience, "[t]he storm [as well] as the calm."

Works about Emily Brontë

Barker, Juliet. *The Brontës.* New York: St. Martin's Press, 1995.
Chitham, Edward. *The Birth of* Wuthering Heights: *Emily Brontë at Work.* New York: Palgrave Macmillan, 2001.
Davies, Stevie. *Emily Brontë.* Plymouth, England: Northcote House, 1998.
Stoneman, Patsy, ed. *Wuthering Heights: Emily Brontë.* New York: St. Martin's Press, 1993.
Vine, Steven. *Emily Brontë.* Boston: Twayne, 1998.
Winnifrith, Thomas. *Critical Essays on Emily Brontë.* New York: G. K. Hall, 1997.

Brooke, Emma Frances (1859?–1926)
novelist

Emma Brooke was born in the county of Cheshire, in northern England, and attended Cambridge University. After moving to London, she became an ardent socialist and wrote economic papers describing the dismal working conditions of women. In 1883 she published her first novel, *A Fair Country Maid,* under the pen name E. Fairfax Byrrne. This novel was followed by *Entangled* (1885) and, two years later, *An Heir Without a Heritage.* Her first feminist novel, *A Superfluous Woman* (1894) marked the beginning of her success as a NEW WOMAN novelist. In that novel a young woman dies giving birth because she is neglected by her husband. In Brooke's next novel, *Transition* (1895), a woman named Hora Kemball escapes from her parent's oppressive home to become a socialist in London. Three more new woman novels followed: *Life the Accuser* (1896), *The Confession of Stephen Whapshare* (1898), and *The Engrafted Rose* (1900).

John Sutherland notes that Brooke is militant in her politics and humorous in her daily life. Brooke noted in her *Who's Who* entry that one of her hobbies was "listening to clever people talk."

Brooks, Shirley (Charles William Shirley Brooks) (1816–1874) *journalist, novelist*

Although Brooks started out in the law, he began writing for periodicals and eventually succeeded MARK LEMON as the editor of the British humor magazine *Punch.*

Born in London in 1816, Brooks was the son of William Brooks, an architect, and his wife Elizabeth. At the age of 16, he was apprenticed to this uncle, Charles Sabine, to be trained as a solicitor. Though he studied for five years and passed a required examination in 1838, he evidently never became a solicitor. Brooks was lured away by the desire to write.

Like CHARLES DICKENS, Brooks began his career as a parliamentary reporter, writing summaries of what took place in the House of Commons for the *Morning Chronicle.* In 1853 he was sent on assignment to Russia, Syria, and Egypt. His letters from this trip were published in 1854 as *Russians of the South.*

Throughout his lifetime, Brooks wrote for some of the most prestigious magazines of the day, including *The Illustrated London News.* Brooks also wrote plays, including *The Creole, or Love's Fetters* (1847) and *Daughter of the Stars* (1850); novels, including *Aspen Court: A Story of Our Kind* (1853) and *Gordian Knot* (1859); and even some wickedly comic verse, including a "seize-the-day" love poem that begins, in true post-Darwinian fashion:

> *Miss, I'm a Pensive Protoplasm,*
> *Born in some pre-historic chasm.*
> *I, and my humble fellow men*
> *Are hydrogen, and oxygen,*
> *And nitrogen, and carbon too,*
> *As so is Jane, and so are you.*

He urges his dear love, therefore, not to show too much pride in her pedigree, and he ends:

> *So let us haste in Hymen's bands*
> *To join our protoplasmic hands,*
> *And spend our gay organic life*
> *As happy man and happy wife.*

Brooks is remembered today as one of the best staff writers for *Punch,* which he joined in 1851 and for which he wrote a series of weekly satires of parliamentary debates entitled "The Essence of Parliament." M. H. Spielmann, who wrote a history of the magazine, says that Brooks was "perhaps the most brilliant and useful all-round man who ever wrote for *Punch.*" When the editor, Mark Lemon, died in 1870, Brooks was appointed editor and continued to write for the magazine until his death in 1874.

Broughton, Rhoda (1840–1920) *novelist*

Rhoda Broughton was born to Delves Broughton, a clergyman and the younger son of a baronet, and his wife, Jane Bennett Broughton, in Denbigh, Wales. Her father educated her in Greek, Latin, and English literature. Her first best-seller was written when she was only 22: after being thoroughly bored by a novel she was reading, she decided to write her own. The result was *Not Wisely But Too Well* (1862), which follows the romantic adventures of a young woman in a Welsh seaside town. Broughton's uncle by marriage, JOSEPH SHERIDAN LE FANU, encouraged her to write and helped get her first work published by serializing it in the *Dublin University Magazine,* which he edited.

The publication of *Not Wisely But Too Well* created a sensation for its frank depiction of an intensely passionate heroine, Kate Chester, whom many readers deemed "unladylike." By today's standards, Broughton's novels would not have much shock value; however, during the mid-Victorian period, both the novels and Broughton herself were scandalous: In *Not Wisely But Too Well* Broughton makes passing references to *legs,* a reference that was considered risqué and even distasteful. Broughton's novels presented high-spirited heroines who pursue, relatively freely, romantic liaisons with men of questionable character. Broughton's novels also flirted with taboo subjects, challenging Victorian standards of propriety: "In summer time most women like to have a lover; in winter the fire is lover enough for anyone."

Broughton's next novel and her first major success, *Cometh Up As a Flower* (1867), repeated the subject matter and themes of her first work and was dedicated to Le Fanu. Over the next five decades, Broughton published 25 more novels, all of which went into multiple editions and were very popular with the patrons of circulating libraries. Among her best-known works is *Belinda* (1883), an academic romance set at Oxford. One unique feature of Broughton's style is her use of the present tense for narration, as in this passage from *Red as a Rose Is She* (1870): "Half-an-hour passes, and Mr. Brandon is still in 'the parlour.' It is seven o'clock, and dinner-time. Would you like to know what it is that Mr. Brandon takes so long in saying, and whether it is anything likely to reconcile Miss Craven to the loss of her dinner?"

Broughton's persona almost eclipsed her artistic work. Her charisma won her the respect and friendship of MATTHEW ARNOLD, HENRY JAMES, and MARY CHOLMONDELEY, who described Broughton as having a heart "like a Toledo blade of steel, chased and inlaid with gold." An obituary in *Oxford Magazine* describes Broughton's reputation: "The inquirer of fifty years' hence who wishes to find in fiction a true portrait of the English lady of the later nineteenth century will, if he is wise, go to Rhoda Broughton."

A Work about Rhoda Broughton
Wood, Marilyn. *Rhoda Broughton (1840–1920): Profile of a Novelist.* Stamford, Conn.: Paul Watkins, 1993.

Brown, Thomas Edward (1830–1897)
poet

Thomas Edward Brown, who was to become the national poet of the Isle of Man, was born there on May 5. His mother was Dorothy Thomson Brown. His father, Robert Brown, a minister, educated him at home before sending him to King William's College, where he won a prize for one of his poems. Brown then studied at Oxford (1849–54), becoming, upon his return to the Isle of Man, vice principal of King William's College. After marrying Emilia Stowell in 1857, Brown left King William's to become headmaster of the Crypt School in Gloucester, England. He later left for Clifton College, where he taught for 30 years. Brown began publishing volumes of poetry in 1881 with the release of *Fo'c's'le Yarns; The Doctor and Other Poems* (1887), *Old John* (1893), and *Collected Poems* (1900) followed. Brown was recognized as a comic poet, at times referred to as "the Manx Robert Burns"; most of his poems were written in the Manx dialect. ("Manx" is the proper adjective for the Isle of Man, which is located in the Irish Sea off the northwest coast of England.) His work reveals an effort to salvage a small, Celtic, island culture from the uniformity of a modern, industrial nation. "That so the coming age," he wrote in his first volume of poems, "Lost in the empire mass / . . . May see, as in a glass, / What they held dear." Not much read today, Brown's work has been compared to that of ARTHUR HUGH CLOUGH.

Browne, Thomas Alexander
See BOLDREWOOD, ROLF.

Browning, Elizabeth Barrett (1806–1861)
poet

Elizabeth Barrett was born at Hope End, Durham, Hertfordshire, into the large, wealthy family of Edward Moulton Barrett and Mary Barrett. Her father was a slaveowner who made his fortune on plantations in Jamaica. Elizabeth was the oldest of 11 children. As a child, she had the advantage of being educated more formally than most women during this period, studying Latin and Greek under her brother's tutor and reading history, philosophy, and literature on her own. She grew interested in writing poetry very early. Her father encouraged her writing, and when she was 14 he published her epic poem, *The Battle of Marathon*. She later called this imitation of the 18th-century poet Alexander Pope "Pope's Homer done over again or rather undone." At age 20, in 1826, she wrote *An Essay on Mind; with other poems* and, seven years later, translated Aeschylus's *Prometheus Bound*.

She was often in poor health, having weak lungs, a chronic cough, and a nervous disorder. As a teenager she suffered a spinal injury when she fell off a horse. In 1836 she moved with her family to London, where she withdrew from society and confined herself to her room in their new home at 50 Wimpole Street. She was well enough to write *The Seraphim and Other Poems* in 1838, but that same year her favorite brother drowned and she became even more depressed and introverted.

Her father had never wanted any of his 11 children to marry, especially his favorite, Elizabeth. In her late 30s, Elizabeth Barrett was still living in seclusion in her father's house. She had lost interest in the outside world and was sick without hope of recovering. Her book, *Poems* (1844), contains "A Drama of Exile," which takes up the story of Adam and Eve where John Milton's 17th-century *Paradise Lost* left off. "The Cry of the Children," a heartfelt poem protesting child labor in mines, questions how a loving God can allow such mistreatment of children:

> *Do ye hear the children weeping, O my*
> > *brothers*
> *Ere the sorrow comes with years?*
> *They are leaning their young heads against*
> > *their mothers,*
> *And that cannot stop their tears.*

Another poem from this volume, "Lady Geraldine's Courtship," has a line praising the work of ROBERT BROWNING. Browning saw this poem and immediately became enamored of her poetry. Browning visited her, and they began a courtship and correspondence. In his letters, he declared his love for her poetry and, to her surprise, for her as well. On his visits he brought flowers, gossip from London, and accounts of his travels to Italy. He brightened her dark home and excited her imagination.

They married secretly in 1846, against her father's wishes. With her dog Flush in tow, the couple moved to Europe. They traveled in France before finally settling in Florence, where Elizabeth Barrett Browning remained for the rest of her life. She was 39, and Robert Browning, 33. Her father never forgave her, but through her marriage she experienced a renewed health, happiness, and hope.

When WILLIAM WORDSWORTH died, Elizabeth Barrett Browning was considered for poet laureate. She would have been the first woman to hold the position if it had not gone instead to ALFRED, LORD TENNYSON, a great admirer of her work. In 1849, at the age of 44, she gave birth to a son, Robert Wiedemann Barrett Browning, whom the couple called Pen.

At this time, Barrett Browning was England's most famous female poet and was actually better known than her husband, Robert. Her fame attracted many artistic visitors to their home. She was interested in Italian politics, spiritualism, and the occult. She died in Florence. A year after her death, *Last Poems* appeared.

Critical Analysis

Browning wrote her epic verse novel, *Aurora Leigh*, in 1857. She named the title character after her literary idol GEORGE SAND, whose real name was Aurore Dupin and whom she had been able to meet in Paris in 1852. The poem is about the conflicts of being both a woman and a poet. Barrett Browning knew this conflict well, since traditionally the poet was seen as a male figure. The poem's heroine, the orphaned Aurora, rejects her suitor, her cousin Romney Leigh, because he is condescending and patronizing to her and to her poetry. He tries to win her love with words such as

> *If your sex is weak for art*
> *(And I, who said so, did but honour you*
> *By using truth in courtship), it is strong*
> *For life and duty.*

Aurora goes on to become a struggling writer in London, unheard of for a young, single woman of the period.

> *At least I am a poet in being poor,*
> *Thank God. I wonder if the manuscript*
> *Of my long poem, if 't were sold outright,*
> *Would fetch enough to buy me shoes to go*
> > *Afoot,*

she says. She eventually marries Romney, but only after she has become successful and independent and he blind and homeless.

The plot of *Aurora Leigh* is at times confusing, complicated, and implausible, but critics of the day objected to the poem primarily for its feminist and political themes. In fact, the novel paved the way for many women novelists to write about women's political and creative experience. As the critic Cora Kaplan writes, "*Aurora Leigh* stands behind them as the first and most powerfully sustained literary effort to engage these issues."

Kaplan views Barrett Browning as "primarily a political poet whose subjects were slavery, suppressed nationality (Italy), the plight of the poor and the position of women." Browning's best known and most popular work, however, is *Sonnets from the Portuguese* (1850), a collection of 44 love sonnets. She and her husband wrote alone and did not show each other their work. One day, however, Barrett Browning slipped the sonnets into his pocket, telling him to tear them up if he did not like them. Instead, he called them "the finest sonnets written in any language since Shakespeare's."

The title comes from his nickname for her, "my little Portuguese," because of her olive skin. Although love is the subject of the sonnets, its treatment is not traditional, an expression of male heartbreak and loss. Barrett Browning's sonnets address love from a woman's point of view and in a woman's voice. Further, the poems exuberantly affirm the love between a man and a woman and include the familiar poem that begins, "How do I love thee? Let me count the ways." *Sonnets From the Portuguese* would later inspire CHRISTINA ROSSETTI to write *Monna Innominata* (1882).

Works about Elizabeth Barrett Browning

Boas, Elizabeth Schutz. *Elizabeth Barrett Browning.* Whitefish, Mont.: Kessinger, 2005.

Markus, Julia. *Dared and Done: The Marriage of Elizabeth Barrett and Robert Browning.* New York: Alfred A. Knopf, 1995.

Mermin, Dorothy. *Elizabeth Barrett Browning: The Origins of a New Poetry.* Chicago: University of Chicago Press, 1989.

Stone, Marjorie. *Elizabeth Barrett Browning.* New York: St. Martin's Press, 1995.

Stott, Rebecca, and Simon Avery. *Elizabeth Barrett Browning: Studies in 18th and 19th Century Literature Series.* New York: Longman, 2003.

Browning, Robert (1812–1889) *poet*

Robert Browning was born in Camberwell, southeast London, to Robert Browning, Sr., and Sarah Anna Wiedemann Browning. His father worked as a clerk for the Bank of England. Although he came from a wealthy family, the senior Browning was cut off by his father because of a grand act of defiance: Sent to Jamaica to manage a family estate, he freed all the slaves and distributed the land to them as farms. The younger Browning was influenced by his father's love of learning, his interest in painting, and his habit of reading odd histories and sensational crime stories.

Browning was educated primarily at home and encouraged to read widely in his father's large library. He composed his first book of poems by the time he was 12, later writing his future wife, ELIZABETH BARRETT BROWNING, that "the first composition I was guilty of was something in imitation of [the Irish poet] Ossian . . . , this, however, I thought exceedingly well of, and laid up for posterity under the cushion of a great armchair."

At age 17, Browning asked his father if the family had enough money to allow him to devote himself to "a life of pure culture." When the elder Browning approved the plan, Browning set out to become a poet. Although he published a great many poems and poetic dramas in the succeeding years, he was not counted a popular success until the 1868 publication of *The Ring and the Book*.

In 1833 Browning published his first poem, *Pauline*. In reviewing the poem, JOHN STUART MILL said that Browning had "a more intense and morbid self-consciousness than I ever knew in any sane human being." This criticism made Browning reluctant to reveal his own thoughts and feelings and turned him toward the form he made famous—the dramatic monologue, in which a character's inner nature is revealed through speech to another person. The critic Richard Stoddard said of Browning: "He excels Shakespeare, I think, in the art—if it be art—with which he makes his characters betray what they really are."

Browning's second publication was *Paracelsus* (1835), a poem about the Swiss alchemist, in which Browning explores humanity's quest for spiritual knowledge. This work brought him to the attention of many important writers, including WILLIAM WORDSWORTH, CHARLES DICKENS, and Dickens's biographer, JOHN FORSTER. Forster introduced him to the actor William Macready, who asked Browning to write him a play. Browning wrote several poetic dramas, three of which were produced in the 1830s. The plays were not successful, but they helped him develop his talent for writing dramatic monologues. He became a master of the dramatic monologues, poems spoken entirely by a character, often inadvertently self-revealing.

In 1840 Browning wrote *Sordello,* a poem so obscure that it almost destroyed Browning's career. Critics and the public threw up their hands and declared Browning impossible to understand. From 1841 to 1846 Browning published a series of pamphlets under the title *Bells and Pomegranates* that included many of the poems for which he is known today. Among them was "Pippa Passes," which describes the effects of an innocent factory child on the people who hear her singing as she walks through the town of Asolo. Pippa sings one of Browning's most famous lines, "God's in his heaven and all's right with the world." Other pamphlets included "Porphyria's Lover," in which the demented narrator murders his love; "My Last Duchess," in which the speaker is so brazen and insolent that he admits with impunity to having his late wife killed; and "Soliloquy of the Spanish Cloister," in which a monk reveals his burning hatred and envy of a fellow monk.

In 1844 Browning saw his name in a book of poems by Elizabeth Barrett. Her poem listed those writers from whom Barrett sought inspiration. From Browning, Barrett took "some pomegranate which, if cut deep down the middle, / Shows a heart of blood tinctured of a veined humanity." Browning wrote to Barrett, and the two corresponded for eight months. They met in 1845 and eloped in 1846.

The couple lived in Florence, Italy, for most of their marriage, traveling occasionally to France and England. Their love affair was made famous by Barrett's *Sonnets from the Portuguese* (1850). In 1849 their only child, Robert Wiedemann Barrett Browning (called Pen), was born.

The year of his son's birth, Browning published the long poem *Christmas-Eve and Easter-Day.* In 1851 he brought out his best critical work, "Essay on Shelley," and four years later one of his finest volumes of poetry, *Men and Women.* The latter contained the dramatic monologue "Andrea del Sarto," in which the painter reveals his failure and says, "Ah, but a man's reach should exceed his grasp, / Or what's a heaven for?" Also in the collection was "Fra Lippo Lippi," about the monk-painter who revels so much in life that he is caught by guards in an alley "where sportive ladies leave their doors ajar." Although many readers found Browning's work obscure and unpoetic, his wife's poetry, including the verse novel *Aurora Leigh* (1856), was wildly popular at the time.

When Elizabeth Barrett Browning died in 1861, Browning was distraught. He returned to London, where he edited and published Elizabeth's poetry and essays. The following year, he released two collections of his own poetry, *Collected Poems* and *Selected Poems*. Both were critical and popular successes, as was the 1864 collection *Dramatis Personae*. By 1868, with the publication of *The Ring and the Book,* Browning was among the best-loved and most widely read English poets, second only to ALFRED, LORD TENNYSON. In 1868 Oxford awarded him an honorary master's degree and an honorary fellowship. The Browning Society was formed in 1881, while Browning was still living. Just before he died, he learned that his most recent volume *Asolondo* had been released to excellent reviews.

Browning was ultimately an optimist who believed that human love was the surest evidence of divine love and that knowledge of God could only be arrived at by intuition. Most of the poetry for which Browning is known today, however, is populated by villains whose inner lives are laid bare by Browning's astute psychological insights; they are often people in whom love is missing. His villains are complex and interesting because they are victims of their uncontrolled desires, rather than embodiments of abstract vices. In the chapter devoted to him in *A Literary History of England*, the authors describe Browning as "Shakespearean in his understanding of the weak, the erring, and the self-deceived. His theatre is the human spirit, his great subject, the soul's development."

Critical Analysis

In 1860, at a flea market in Florence, Browning bought *The Old Yellow Book*, a collection of documents about a 1697 murder trial. It told the story of Count Guido Franceschini and four hired killers who murdered Franceschini's wife Pompilia because she had run away from her husband aided by her priest Giuseppe Caponsacchi. From this story emerged Browning's poem of more than 21,000 lines in 12 dramatic monologues, *The Ring and the Book* (1868–69). The "book" refers to the actual book that Browning found, the "ring" refers to the poem itself, created from the poet's imagination. The story is told from many different viewpoints, underscoring the idea that no one individual has the "truth." Each version of the story is a distortion, to a greater or lesser extent.

The most fascinating character is the count, Guido, who tries to avoid being executed by claiming that his actions were justified and, in fact, would improve society:

> *The wholesome household rule in force again,*
> *Husbands once more God's representative,*
> *Wives like the typical Spouse once more,*

Guido even tries to suggest that his suffering is similar to Christ's. But his view is countered by Caponsacchi, who portrays Guido as a "snake, hatched on hill-top by mischance" and Pompilla as a saintly figure, "perfect in whiteness."

After Guido is sentenced to death, he stops pretending to uphold traditional values and reveals his true nature. He complains that society is full of hypocrites, others who are as greedy and unscrupulous as he. He at least acknowledges that he is half wolf and, if he could but "glut the wolf-nature," might "grow into the man again." He insists that in murdering Pompilia he merely "stopped the nuisance" of the weak. Yet when he is taken away to his execution he cries out "Pompilia, will you let them murder me?" words that have led some readers to wonder if he repents.

Other Work by Robert Browning

Loucks, James M., ed. *Robert Browning's Poetry: Authoritative Texts, Criticism.* New York: W. W. Norton, 1980.

Works about Robert Browning

Garrett, Martin. *Elizabeth Barrett Browning and Robert Browning.* British Library Writers' Library Lives Series. Oxford: Oxford University Press, 2002.

Hawlin, Stefan. *Robert Browning: A Sourcebook.* London: Routledge, 2001.

Kennedy, Richard S., and Donald S. Hair. *The Dramatic Imagination of Robert Browning: A Literary Life.* Columbia: University of Missouri Press, 2007.

Martin, Loy D. *Browning's Dramatic Monologues and the Post-Romantic Subject.* Baltimore: Johns Hopkins University Press, 1985.

Roberts, Adam. *Robert Browning Revisited.* Boston: Twayne, 1997.

Ryals, Clyde De L. *The Life of Robert Browning.* London: Blackwell, 1996.

Woolford, John. *Browning the Revisionary.* New York: St. Martin's Press, 1988.

Brunton, Mary (Mary Balfour Brunton)
(1778–1818) *novelist*

Born in the Orkney Islands, off the north coast of Scotland, Mary Brunton was the daughter of an army officer, Colonel Thomas Balfour, and Frances Ligonier Balfour, the niece of the first earl of Ligonier. She was educated at home by her mother, who taught her French, Italian, and German as well as an appreciation for music and literature.

At 20 she married Alexander Brunton, a minister and later professor of oriental languages at Edinburgh University. In Edinburgh, Brunton began to mingle with literary groups and was motivated to start her novel *Self Control*, first in secret and then with the help of her husband.

Self Control (1811) immediately met with great success. Like her didactic novels to follow, it focuses on themes of morality and duty in marriage, reflecting her experiences as a minister's wife with strong views on what she deemed the "appropriate" role of women. Furthermore, she states at the beginning of the novel that she aims "to bear testimony against a maxim as immoral as indelicate, that a reformed rake makes the best husband." Still, she manages to combine her not-so-subtle lessons in morality with an engaging plot (the heroine is abducted and taken on a terrifying journey to the wilds of Canada), lively characters, and a fanciful depiction of the New World. JANE AUSTEN gently criticized *Self Control* as "an excellently meant, elegantly written work, without anything of nature or probability in it." Yet the critic Dale Spender demonstrates, through parallels between Brunton's second novel, *Discipline*, and Austen's *Emma*, that Austen must have learned from her reading of Brunton.

Discipline (1814) continues the theme of prudence in marriage, but treats readers to a more humorous approach and contains vivid scenes of Scottish local color, including balls, auctions, and masquerades. Brunton's last work, *Emmeline*, published posthumously, is a disturbing story of the misery that awaits a woman who foolishly divorces her husband to be with another man.

Emmeline was not yet complete when Brunton died in 1818, after giving birth to a stillborn son. The novel was published posthumously by her husband along with his memoirs of her life that included extracts from some of her lively and humorous letters and journals. Spender remarks that Brunton, with her social commentary, "goes without trepidation into areas where Jane Austen did not tread.... She wanted her novels to be entertaining but she also wanted them to develop and sharpen the intellectual and critical judgment of her readers.... She is one of the mothers of the novel."

A Work about Mary Brunton
Spender, Dale. *Mothers of the Novel: 100 Good Women Writers Before Jane Austen.* London: Pandora, 1986.

Buchanan, Robert Williams (1841–1901)
poet, novelist, playwright

Robert Buchanan was born in Staffordshire, England, to Robert Buchanan, a journalist, and his wife, Margaret. In 1851 the family moved to Glasgow, Scotland, where Buchanan's father became editor of the *Glasgow Herald*. Robert attended elementary school in Glasgow and began writing poetry when he was a boy. He studied at Glasgow University but did not graduate because his father could not afford to pay the tuition.

Instead, at age 19, Buchanan moved to London, where he married Mary Jay. In 1863 he completed a collection of poems called *Undertones*, the first of the many books of poetry, primarily narrative poetry, he would publish during the next 35 years, but he is also known for his scathing reviews of other poets. His attack on the PRE-RAPHAELITES, *The Fleshly School of Poetry and Other Phenomena of the Day* (1872), sparked a notorious controversy. In contrast to his often bitter and satirical critical prose, the poetry is compassionate and tender, often taking the downtrodden as its subject matter.

Buchanan published a novel, *The Shadow of the Sword*, in 1876, then turned to playwriting, which brought him critical and financial success. In 1884 he sailed to the United States to see an American production of his play *Alone in London*. His most popular hit on the London stage was *Sophia*, an adaptation of Henry Fielding's 18th-century comic masterpiece *Tom Jones*, which recounts the mostly amorous adventures of Tom, the rogue-hero. Although Buchanan became wealthy from his writing, he died a poor man after making some disastrous investments.

Other Work by Robert Buchanan
The Complete Poetical Works of Robert Buchanan. New York: AMS Press, 1976.

A Work about Robert Buchanan
Cassidy, John. *Robert W. Buchanan.* Boston: Twayne, 1974.

Buckstone, John Baldwin (1802–1879) playwright, actor

John Buckstone was born on September 14 in Hoxton, England. He was trained for the law but at age 19 joined a provincial theater company, in which he acted for three years as "a low comedian" before making his first London appearance in 1823 in a dramatization of SIR WALTER SCOTT's novel *The Fortunes of Nigel*. Buckstone's first play, *Luke the Labourer,* opened on October 16, 1826, at the Adelphi Theatre in London. Buckstone was subsequently hired to act in his own play, and through the next decade he continued to write plays and act at the Adelphi in the winter and the Haymarket Theatre in the summer. Buckstone acted in the United States from 1840 to 1842, returning to become the featured low comedian at the Haymarket in the latter year. During his years as manager of the Haymarket (1853–76), he worked with many of the best-known actors of the period. By the end of his career, he had written more than 150 plays, mostly farces, including *The Wreck, Victorine, The Dream at Sea,* and *The Forest of Flowers,* performed at the Adelphi, and *Married Life, Rural Felicity, Leap Year,* and *Second Thoughts,* performed at the Haymarket. Of all those plays, Buckstone claimed that "scarcely one was a failure." Buckstone's ghost is said to haunt the Haymarket still.

Bulwer-Lytton, Sir Edward George Earle (1803–1873) novelist, poet, playwright, essayist

The writer of the frequently mocked and famously clichéd opening lines of *Paul Clifford* (1830), "It was a dark and stormy night . . . ," Sir Edward Bulwer-Lytton was both targeted for ridicule and derision and awarded praise, respect, and honors. Although despised as a rouged fop by ALFRED, LORD TENNYSON and as a "silver fork polisher" by WILLIAM MAKEPEACE THACKERAY, he influenced and was admired by CHARLES DICKENS, WILLIAM HARRISON AINSWORTH, GEORGE ELIOT, and ANTHONY TROLLOPE.

Born into the English aristocracy, Bulwer was the youngest son of General William Earle Bulwer and the heiress Elizabeth Barbara Lytton Bulwer. His father died in 1807, and his mother became a powerful, domineering force in his life, a person whom he would rarely oppose. Following her death in 1843, he inherited her family's estate and added her family name, Lytton, to his.

He graduated from Trinity College, Cambridge, in 1826. The next year he married Rosina Doyle Wheeler, for once acting against his mother, who suspended his allowance. The marriage was disastrous, and the couple permanently separated in 1836.

In spite of his tumultuous personal life, he was active in British politics, twice a member of Parliament and serving as secretary of state in Lord Derby's administration. Following the abdication of King Otho of Greece, he was offered the Greek throne, which he declined. He was made a baron in 1866 and elevated to the House of Lords.

From a young age, Bulwer-Lytton was encouraged to write. Two years before entering Cambridge, through his mother's influence, he published a book of Byronic verse, *Ismael: An Oriental Tale, with Other Poems* (1820). At Cambridge he won the Chancellor's Medal for his poem "Sculpture" (negatively reviewed by Thackeray in *Fraser's Magazine*), and published a novel, *Rupert de Linsay* (1825), and a book of verse, *Weeds and Wildflowers* (1826).

Between 1827, the first year of his marriage, and 1836, the year of final separation, he was extraordinarily prolific—in large part to support an extravagant lifestyle—publishing more than one-third of his life's work. He edited the *New Monthly Magazine* (1831–32), produced the two-volume history *England and the English* (1833), and published an edition of *Collected Poems* (1831). By the end of the decade, his plays were being successfully staged by the actor-manager William Macready. Among them were a historical drama, *The Lady of Lyon* (1838), a five-act play in blank verse; *Richelieu* (1839); and a pre-Wildean drawing-room comedy, *Money* (1840).

Bulwer-Lytton is chiefly remembered for his erudite, if somewhat inaccessible, novels of ideas. Although his mannered writing style is full of arcane, footnoted references that often overwhelm present-day readers, Trollope observed that Bulwer-Lytton "was always apt to give his readers the benefit of what he knew. The result has been that very much more than amusement may be obtained from Bulwer's novels."

Critical Analysis

Bulwer-Lytton's first great success was *Pelham* (1828), a SILVER-FORK SCHOOL novel that examines the lives of fops and dandies. His other silver-fork novels include *Ernest Maltravers* (1837) and *Zanoni* (1842), an occult-flavored book well known for an ending similar to that of Dickens's *A Tale of Two Cities*, but published years earlier. He used historical romances to explore the perils of a political career, the meaning of aristocracy, the nature of political leadership, and nationalism, charisma, and ambition. He examined these themes in *The Last Days of Pompeii* (1834), in which the ancient Roman city of the title is destroyed by volcanic eruption. The novel's villainous Egyptian priest Arbaces is the acknowledged antecedent of SIR ARTHUR CONAN DOYLE's evil genius Moriarty. *Rienzi* (1835) is a novel set in medieval Italy. In *The Last of the Barons*, considered his best work in this genre, Bulwer-Lytton argued that medieval feudalism (voluntary commitment to rightful authority) was the foundation of English liberty.

Bulwer-Lytton was also interested in spiritualism and the occult, as seen in *Zanoni, The Haunted and the Haunters* (1842), sometimes described as the best ghost story ever written), and *A Strange Story* (1861). *The Coming Race* (1873), his groundbreaking science fiction novel about a secret subterranean society with advanced technology, anticipates the work of H. G. Wells and Aldous Huxley.

Bulwer-Lytton's belief that crime reveals the truth about human nature led to his preoccupation with the relationship between egoism and villainy. To explore these ideas, he wrote *Paul Clifford* and *Eugene Aram* (1832). Bulwer's daring choice of a murderer-hero for *Eugene Aram*, a historically based psychological crime thriller, caused a sensation and a storm of protest. With these novels, he created the NEWGATE CRIME NOVEL, a genre of fiction critical of the justice system and sympathetic to the outlaw. Named for London's infamous Newgate prison, Bulwer-Lytton's new genre was taken up by other writers: Ainsworth in *Jack Sheppard*, Dickens in *Oliver Twist*, and WILKIE COLLINS in *The Woman in White*.

The British scholar John S. Moore argues that the value of Bulwer-Lytton can be found in the themes he explored: "Lytton's work expresses some of the most significant intellectual currents of the nineteenth century, several of which are far from exhausted. He treated intelligently and interestingly perennial themes of good and evil, of freedom and despotism, egoism and altruism, life affirmation and the power of will."

Works about Edward Bulwer-Lytton

Campbell, James L. *Sir Edward Bulwer-Lytton*. Boston: Twayne, 1986.

Christensen, Allan C. *Edward Bulwer-Lytton: The Fiction of New Regions*. Athens: University of Georgia Press, 1976.

Bulwer-Lytton, Rosina Wheeler (1802–1882) *poet, novelist*

Rosina Wheeler Bulwer-Lytton was born the second daughter of Francis Massy Wheeler, a member of the Irish gentry, and ANNA DOYLE WHEELER, the feminist author, in Ballywire, Ireland. Her alcoholic father, expecting a son, flew into a rage on news of her birth and ignored the child afterward.

In 1818 Rosina fled her unhappy family for London. Shortly after arriving in the capital, she formed friendships with the poet LETITIA LANDON and the scandalous LADY CAROLINE LAMB. She met her future husband, the novelist EDWARD BULWER-LYTTON, in the early 1820s. After a stormy courtship and against the wishes of his mother, they married in 1827. Although they were a popular and fashionable London couple, the marriage proved disastrous. Rosina left the marriage in 1836, humiliated by her husband's public infidelities and unwilling to continue suffering under his violent temper. Rosina was prevented from divorcing Edward, however, because she would not agree to be named the guilty party. She lost custody of her two children and, because her inheritance had gone to him at the time of their marriage, was dependent on an allowance granted by her estranged husband.

Angered by the treatment she received, and in need of money, Rosina began writing. Addressing the legal and social vulnerability of women, her novels include *Cheveley, or, the Man of Honour* (1839)—a thinly disguised, bitter portrait of her husband as a brutish seducer of governesses—and provocative romans à clef and historical novels such as *Bianca Cappello: An Historical Romance* (1843), *The School for Husbands, or, Molière's Life and Times* (1852), *Behind the Scenes* (1854), and *Very Successful!* (1856). Enraged by his wife's novels and her various public efforts to condemn him, Bulwer-Lytton worked to keep publishers from producing her work, withheld her allowance, and prevented her from seeing her children. In 1858 he had her committed to an insane asylum, from which she was released only after a great public outcry. A memoir, *A Blighted Life*, was published under her name in 1880; however, modern scholars doubt that she was the book's author.

Burke, Edmund (1729–1797) *political philosopher, orator*

Edmund Burke was born in Dublin, Ireland, to Richard Burke, an attorney, and Mary Nagle Burke. At the age of six, the sickly Burke was sent by his parents to live in Ballyduff with his maternal uncle, Patrick Nagle. In 1741 Burke was enrolled in a boarding school in Ballintore, where he excelled. He passed entrance exams to Trinity College, Dublin, in 1744.

Burke had a distinguished career at the university, where he founded a debating class and a small miscellany publication, the *Reformer*. He graduated in 1749 with a degree in law. Burke went to London in 1750 to read for the bar, but soon abandoned his legal studies in favor of a career in literature.

In 1756 Burke published *A Vindication of Natural Society: A View of the Miseries and Evils Arising to Mankind* and, a year later, *A Philosophical Enquiry into our Ideas of the Sublime and Beautiful* (1757). *A Vindication,* because of its attack on the established political order, was published anonymously (and indeed was ascribed to another author for years after its publication). In it, Burke writes that "society [is] founded in natural appetites and instincts, and not in any positive institution." To Burke, history is an endless record of deceit and bloodshed, and "political society is justly charged with much the greater part of this destruction."

In *A Philosophical Enquiry,* Burke develops a somewhat complex aesthetic theory. He essentially places different objects, from concrete physical features to more abstract concepts such as courage, into the categories of the beautiful and the sublime. Burke claims that "all works of great labor, expense, and magnificence are sublime," while "beauty is a name I shall apply to all such qualities in things as induce in us a sense of affection and tenderness." Both essays were successful in literary and artistic circles of London, and Burke was encouraged by his publisher to write historical works; however, he concentrated almost solely on political writings.

By the early 1760s Burke had entered the English political scene. In 1759 he became an assistant to William Gerard Hamilton, a well-known parliamentarian. By 1761 Hamilton achieved the important post of chief secretary for Ireland, and Burke accompanied him as a private secretary. Burke remained in Ireland for the duration of Hamilton's tenure, from 1761 to 1764.

Although the job of a private secretary seems insignificant today, Burke seems to have played an important role in Irish politics, particularly during the sessions of the Irish Parliament between 1761 and 1762. Burke attempted to improve significantly the position of the Irish Catholics, against whom the English and Irish Protestants established numerous laws that restricted their political, economic, and social rights. The degree of success and influence of Burke during this period is still debated by historians.

In 1765 Burke's position within the English government rose considerably when he was appointed a private secretary to the marquis of Rockingham, the leader of the Whig, or liberal, party, and elected to Parliament for the borough of Wendover. Burke's great rhetorical skills won him considerable influence among the Whigs, and he gained particular prominence during the parliamentary debate over the political fate of the American colonies. In 1766 Burke adamantly argued for the repeal of the Stamp Act. He showed strong support, however, for the Declaratory Act that affirmed Britain's constitutional right to tax the American colonists without parliamentary representation of the colonists. In his famous later speeches on taxation and on political reconciliation with the colonies, Burke did not abandon that position; instead, he illuminated the imprudence of exercising such theoretical rights.

Critical Analysis

In 1770 Burke published an influential pamphlet, *Thoughts on the Causes of the Present Discontents,* in which he examined the growing political discontent in the American colonies. In this work, Burke was the first political philosopher to argue for the value of political parties in the maintenance of political and social order. Although this idea does not seem revolutionary today, most people in the 18th century believed that political parties were symptoms of dangerous factionalism in the government of the country. Furthermore, Burke publicly called for limitation of crown patronage, an institution that promoted people in the government based on their social standing rather than on merit. As postmaster general in the second administration (1782–83) of Rockingham, he was able to enact some of his proposed reforms.

Although Burke seemingly advocated liberal reforms as a politician and writer, in his later writings he became increasingly conservative. Unlike his position in *A Vindication,* he came to believe that political, social, and religious institutions formed over the centuries represented some kind of natural progression and the best form of government possible. Therefore, he never proposed any political reforms beyond restraints on the powers of the monarch. Indeed, his seminal work, *Reflections on the Revolution in France* (1790), rhapsodically represented the reactionary views of many European conservatives, fearful of democratic and parliamentary reforms:

> Good order is the foundation of all good things. . . . [The common people] must respect that property of which they cannot partake. They must labour to obtain what by labour can be obtained; and when they find, as they commonly do, the success disproportioned to the endeavour, they must be taught their consolation in the final proportions of eternal justice.

As the scholar C. P. Courtney notes, "Burke's reactions to the French Revolution are not quite like those of anyone else in England at that time. He sees it not simply as one of those political upheavals of which history affords so many examples, but as something new and unprecedented." Indeed, Burke describes the revolution as a "monster," "spectre," and "moral earthquake." He views it as a perversion of nature and natural order that flew, as Courtney observes, "in the face of the laws of God."

Burke's words found vocal opposition not only among the works of liberal thinkers such as Thomas Paine and MARY WOLLSTONECRAFT, but also among the ranks of his own party. Burke's pamphlet *Appeal from the New to the Old Whigs* (1791) clearly demonstrated that he favored the conservative Tory positions on most major political issues. Burke had no choice but to break with the Whigs in 1791 after many years of collaboration.

Many literary critics and historians today refer to Edmund Burke as the father of modern conservatism. Although this label is deserved in some respects, Burke instituted many long-lasting political reforms. His views had a tremendous influence on the formation of political thought and institutions in England, France, and the United States years after his death. Himself an Irish Protestant, Burke never failed to criticize the brutal policies of the English administration toward Irish Catholics. Still, as the historian Will Durant observes, "Burke took on the French Revolution as his personal enemy, and in the course of this . . . campaign made a major contribution to political philosophy. . . . In his writings on the French revolution Burke gave a classical expression to a conservative philosophy."

Other Works by Edmund Burke
Pre-Revolutionary Writings. New York: Cambridge University Press, 1993.
The Writings and Speeches of Edmund Burke: Ireland. New York: Oxford University Press, 1992.
The Writings and Speeches of Edmund Burke: The Revolutionary War, 1794–1797. New York: Oxford University Press, 1992.

Works about Edmund Burke
Kirk, Russell. *Edmund Burke: A Genius Reconsidered.* Wilmington, Del.: Intercollegiate Studies Institute, 1997.
O'Brien, Conor Cruise. *The Great Melody: A Thematic Biography and Commented Anthology of Edmund Burke.* Chicago: University of Chicago Press, 1992.
Robinson, Nicholas K. *Edmund Burke: A Life in Caricature.* New Haven, Conn.: Yale University Press, 1996.
White, Stephen K. *Edmund Burke.* Lanham, Md.: Rowman & Littlefield Publishers, 2002.

Burnett, Frances Eliza Hodgson (1849–1924) *short story writer, novelist*

Frances Hodgson, one of five children, was born in Manchester, England, to Edwin Hodgson and his wife, Eliza Bond Hodgson. Her father, who owned a profitable furniture store, died when Burnett was a child. Her mother took over management of the store and supported the children. Burnett's formal education ended at age 16 when the family business failed, and the family emigrated to the United States to live with a relative in Knoxville, Tennessee. Desperate to earn money, Burnett began writing stories for popular magazines. The American magazine *Godey's Lady's Book* purchased two of her stories for $35, and published the first, "Hearts and Diamonds," in 1868. Afterward, her love stories appeared regularly in women's fashion magazines. Her mother died in 1870, but Burnett was able to support the rest of the family with her income from writing. She married Dr. Swan Moses Burnett, an eye specialist, in 1873; had two sons, Lionel and Vivian; and traveled widely (often alone).

Burnett's first novel, *That Lass o'Lowrie's*, was a realistic look at working-class life, with improbable twists and turns of fate that kept readers fascinated. It was printed in monthly segments in *Scribner's* magazine, and was published as a book in 1877. Her success as a writer was a major source of income for her family, and she loved her celebrity status. She received fan mail and held weekly social gatherings that attracted writers, politicians, actors, and many people of high society. Her friends called her Fluffy because of her love of frilly dresses and her curly hair. Her son, Vivian, called dress her greatest "indoor sport."

Burnett continued to produce novels and in 1886 published her most famous and successful book, *Little Lord Fauntleroy*, about Cedric, a young American boy, who discovers is that he is heir to a title of a British earl. Burnett used Vivian as the model for the main character and said she wrote the novel because he wanted her to write more stories for children. Many young boys disliked the book because they thought Cedric was a weakling. Adults, however, loved it for its romantic themes, and the book sold more than 1 million copies, firmly establishing Burnett's reputation as a writer. *Little Lord Fauntleroy* was translated into more than a dozen languages and was later produced as a play.

In 1893 Burnett published *The One I Know Best*, a memoir recounting her youthful struggles, but her eventful life was far from over. Burnett's large income, celebrity, and lengthy travels strained her marriage. She divorced, remarried a man 10 years her junior, became an American citizen, divorced again, and moved to New York.

Through all this, she continued writing. In *A Little Princess* (1905) the heroine, Sara Crewe, an English child who has grown up in India, is brought by her father to a London boarding school. When he dies suddenly, she is reduced to poverty and forced to live in the attic as a servant of the school. Her strength of heart and character support her until once again circumstances radically change. In *The Secret Garden* (1911), the orphaned Mary Lennox, who also grew up in India, comes to live with her uncle and invalid cousin in Yorkshire, where she discovers a secret locked garden.

Both of these novels, with their themes of tragedy and romance, have remained in print since their first appearance. Burnett's writing captures the realism of working-class life while also providing the twists of fate and romantic rags-to-riches developments that readers enjoy.

Burnett also wrote popular novels for adults, mostly about the fashionable social life of the time. *The Shuttle* (1907), for instance, is about an Anglo-American marriage, while *The Head of the House of Coombe* portrays the London social scene prior to World War I.

Burnett lived long enough to attend the opening of the first film of *Little Lord Fauntleroy* in 1921. It would be her last public appearance. She died just a few years later at age 74.

Works about Frances Hodgson Burnett

Carpenter, Angelica Shirley. *In the Garden: Essays in Honor of Frances Hodgson Burnett*. Lanham, Md.: Scarecrow Press, 2006.

Carpenter, Angelica Shirley, and Jean Shirley. *Frances Hodgson Burnett: Beyond the Secret Garden*. Minneapolis: Lerner, 1990.

Thwaite, Ann. *Waiting for the Party: The Life of Frances Hodgson Burnett*. Boston: David R. Godine, 1991.

Burney, Frances (1752–1840) *novelist, diarist*

Fanny Burney, as she was familiarly known, was born in Norfolk, England, to Dr. Charles Burney, a musician and music historian, and Esther Sleepe. Burney's brothers and sisters were so outgoing and talented that the family considered the shy, quiet girl rather stupid. She was eight years old, in fact, before she learned to write. But once she learned, she began, as she later wrote in her diary, "scribbling almost incessantly." From the age of 10, Burney kept a diary, writing about many of the people who frequented her father's house.

After Burney's mother died in 1761, Dr. Burney remarried. His new wife did not approve of writing as a pastime for girls, and she persuaded Burney to burn her early diaries. Thus, the diaries for which Burney is known today span the years 1778 to 1840.

In the same year she resumed her diaries, Burney anonymously published her first novel, *Evelina; or, The History of a Young Lady's Entrance into the World* (1778). But her anonymity did not last long. The novel was an instant success, praised by the writer Dr. Samuel Johnson, the painter Sir Joshua Reynolds, and the political philosopher EDMUND BURKE, and Burney soon confessed to being the author. London society delighted in this witty epistolary novel (a novel made up of letters) about a naive country girl, saddled with boorish relatives, who falls in love with a London lord.

In Burney's second novel, *Cecilia; or, Memoirs of an Heiress* (1782), Cecilia Beverly has been left a large fortune that she will collect only if she can find a man to marry who will give up his own surname and take hers. Complications occur when Cecilia falls in love with the only son of a family extremely proud of its ancient name. Although this novel was well received, it was not as popular as her first. *Cecilia* was more carefully crafted than *Evelina*, but it lacked that novel's spontaneous quality.

In 1786 Burney accepted an appointment as Second Keeper of the Robes to Queen Charlotte, the wife of King George III, a position that brought Burney a salary of £200 a year. Burney held this position for five years, then asked her father to help her petition to resign. She disliked both the dull courtiers and her duties, which entailed standing around for hours at a time at the queen's disposal, folding the queen's clothes, and walking the queen's dog. Her petition was granted, although the queen was amazed that Burney had dared to imply that life away from the court might be preferable to life within its royal confines.

Nevertheless, Burney's request was granted, and she was given a pension of £100 a year. In 1791 she moved with her father to Chelsea, where she met and married Alexandre d'Arblay, a former adjutant general to Lafayette. In 1793, the year of her marriage, Burney published *Brief Reflections Relative to the Emigrant French Clergy*, and in 1794 she gave birth to her only child, a son named after his father. She also wrote several plays, only one of which (*Edwy and Elgiva*) was produced; none were published. In 1796 she published another novel, *Camilla; or, A Picture of Youth*, the romantic adventures of a 17-year-old girl. This work was a popular success, although nothing Burney ever wrote equaled the wit and charm of *Evelina*.

From 1802 to 1812 Burney, her husband, and their son lived in France, where she was made a countess by King Louis XVIII. Burney's least successful novel, *The Wanderer; or, Female Difficulties* (1814) tells the story of a young woman who escapes from Robespierre's reign of terror and lives incognito in England. After Burney's husband died in 1818, she devoted many years to editing her father's memoirs, which appeared in 1832. Her son died of influenza in 1837, and Burney died three years later.

Burney is perhaps as well known today for her diaries and letters, which fill 12 volumes, as for her fiction. The diaries in particular provide a wealth of information about daily life in the 18th century. There has also been a renewed interest in Burney's plays, especially the comedies, which have been compared to the work of the Regency playwright Richard Sheridan.

Critical Analysis

Feminist critics have studied Burney's work from the point of view of the dependence and powerlessness of her female characters. In Burney's world, young, single women are completely dependent on men—fathers, brothers, and suitors. The reputations of these women can be ruined in a moment, making them unmarriageable, and an unmarried woman is an unhappy creature indeed. Thus, feminist critics note the awful narrowness of a woman's world in Burney's novels, and the terrifying vulnerability of their heroines.

Still, Burney has much to offer readers. The critic Walter Allen compared reading about Fanny Burney's youthful heroines as they enter the intimidating world of London high society to "having a mouse's view of the world of cats; the cats are very terrifying, but the mouse's sense of the ridiculous could not have been keener." Influenced by the 18th-century novelists Henry Fielding, Tobias Smollett, and Samuel Richardson, Burney's novels are a charming mix of sentimental fairy tale and pointed social satire. The story of the young girl who learns the hard way about how to conduct herself in high society is embellished with vulgar, low characters whose antics embarrass the heroine nearly to death. Although Burney lacks the psychological insight and sparkling wit of JANE AUSTEN, it is clear that Austen was influenced by Burney. As the scholar Julie Shaffer notes, "Burney's highly popular *Cecilia*, a novel Austen mentions in *Northanger Abbey*, . . . provided the title for Austen's novel [*Pride and Prejudice*] on its last page."

Evelina involves a series of unhappy and often unbelievable coincidences that threaten to unravel the budding romance between the orphaned Evelina and the handsome, charming, and rich Lord Orville. Evelina's father, Lord Belmont, married her mother in secret, and, after the young woman's death, denied that the marriage had taken place. Thus, Evelina is raised an orphan.

On her first trip to London, Evelina meets her maternal grandmother, Madame Duval, and Lord Orville, with whom she falls in love. Because of her youth and her rural upbringing, she makes a series of social mistakes, commenting that "I am too inexperienced and ignorant to conduct myself with propriety in this town, where everything is new to me, and many things are unaccountable and perplexing."

Burney's comic touch is often displayed in the interactions of such characters as Madame Duval, who is frivolous and ill-bred, and Captain Mirvin, a bad-tempered military man who instantly dislikes Madame Duval and takes great pleasure in taunting and insulting her. At one point, Mirvin, pretending to be a highwayman, takes the old lady from the coach, ties her up, and leaves her in a ditch. When she is rescued, she is covered in mud and distraught because she has lost her "curls," without which, she says, she cannot leave her room.

Evelina's newly discovered cousins, the Branghtons, are also the target of Burney's wit. No matter where they go, the Branghtons betray their vulgarity, embarrassing Evelina, usually just as Lord Orville happens by. At one point in the novel, the cousins borrow Lord Orville's carriage by asking for it in Evelina's name (but without her knowledge or permission), then end up damaging it. During another episode, they leave Evelina walking arm in arm with a pair of disreputable women, to be discovered by Lord Orville.

After many more misadventures, a series of improbable coincidences untangle the twisted threads of the plot, and marriages all around return order and sanity to the world of the novel. Although others were to master the comedy of manners, Fanny Burney was among the form's inventors, and her *Evelina* a prime example of the genre.

Other Work by Frances Burney
Troide, Lars E., ed. *The Early Letters and Journals of Fanny Burney.* Vol. II. Montreal: McGill-Queen's University Press, 1991.

Works about Frances Burney
Epstein, Julia. *The Iron Pen of Frances Burney and the Politics of Women's Writing.* Madison: University of Wisconsin Press, 1989.

Harman, Claire. *Fanny Burney: A Biography.* New York: Alfred A. Knopf, 2001.

Burns, James (1808–1871) *publisher*
The Glasgow-educated son of a Presbyterian minister, James Burns had a distinguished publishing career. By 1832 he had settled in London, establishing a bookshop before printing a line of inexpensive, popular books, consisting of some 35 titles, under the trade name Burns's Fireside Library. Such affordable series were becoming common as the demand for "railway literature" (cheap books to read on trains) increased. Burns converted to Roman Catholicism in 1845 and three years later founded the publishing firm of Burns and Oates,

which became the official publisher for the Holy See in England. That same year, Burns published JOHN HENRY NEWMAN's *Loss and Gain*. He also published children's books.

Burns, Robert (1759–1796) *poet*

Robert Burns was the first of seven children born to Agnes and William Burnes, near a small village in the Lowlands of southwestern Scotland. The whole family lived in a two-room cottage on a farm. His father was a hardworking farmer. Although his mother could not read, she and her cousin Betty entertained and educated the children with the many folktales and songs that they knew. Burns (who dropped the letter *e* in his spelling of the family name) would remember that Cousin Betty knew everything there was to know about "devils, ghosts, fairies, brownies, witches, warlocks, spunkies, kelpies, elf-candles, dead-lights, wraiths, apparitions, cantrips, enchanted towers, giants, dragons, and other trumpery." These, he said, "cultivated the latent seeds of poetry."

Burns began his formal schooling at age six. His teacher insisted on correct English rather than colloquial Scots, the dialect of the region, and taught Burns to recite poems by Shakespeare, Milton, Dryden, and Gray. Burns often missed school to help work in the fields, and in his teens he left school altogether, becoming his father's main farm laborer. He continued to educate himself, reading scholarly texts and gathering folk songs and tales. He wrote his first poem when he was 15, for a girl with whom he was in love. Love and poetry became his two favorite pursuits.

When Burns was 19 his family moved to a farm at Lochlie, in southern Scotland. He read everything he could get his hands on, joined a debate team, and became a Freemason. A handsome man with a passion for life and a good sense of humor, he was irresistible to people. When SIR WALTER SCOTT, as a 15-year-old, saw Burns he recalled that the face was "massive" and that "the eye alone indicated the poetical character and temperament. It was large, and of a dark cast, and literally glowed when he spoke with feeling and interest." Burns, however, hid the headaches and heart palpitations that were warning signs of the heart disease that would eventually kill him.

When his father died, bankrupt, in 1784, Burns and his younger brother Gilbert moved to a new farm and continued to work the land. After four years of bad luck, Burns's health was deteriorating. He attempted to escape his troubles by drinking. He had an affair with a servant girl, which resulted in the first of his many illegitimate children.

In 1786 Burns published his first book of poetry, *Poems Chiefly in the Scottish Tradition*. In its preface, Burns deliberately made himself out to be an uneducated peasant. Still, he resented being made to feel he was lower class because of his background and livelihood. In reality, he straddled two worlds, that of the intellectual and that of the hard-working farmer.

That first book, referred to as his Kilmarnock volume after the town in which it was published, was an instant success. It would influence WILLIAM BLAKE in *Songs of Innocence* and *Songs of Experience*, as well as WILLIAM WORDSWORTH and SAMUEL TAYLOR COLERIDGE in *Lyrical Ballads*. It demonstrated Burns's brilliance as a lyricist and thinker.

Two of Burns's admirers secured a job for him as an excise officer, or tax inspector, and rented a farm for him. When this farm failed, he gave up farming completely. By this time he had married his mistress, Jean Armour, and moved his family to the town of Dumfries.

He was commissioned to work on a folk-song anthology for *The Scots Musical Museum* in 1787 and devoted himself to the task of collecting, editing, and publishing Scottish ballads and folk songs. His editorial work on songwriting and original songs are considered among his greatest contributions to poetry. In 1962 the Scots nationalist poet Hugh MacDiarmid wrote, "Burns did a great work when he transmitted, often in refined and vastly improved form, such a great corpus of our traditional song. It was a labor of love." In fact, Burns would secure his place in Scottish literature more quickly and easily than in English. His contributions to English romanticism were acknowledged posthumously.

Burns wrote more than 300 songs and proved to be a master at working new lyrics into existing melodies. He wrote in Scots, the dialect spoken by the peasants of the Scottish Lowlands (that is, southern Scotland), and he restored and revived old forgotten folk songs by changing the lyrics or adding new ones. He labored with a patriotic devotion, refused pay, and insisted on working anonymously. About his work he said, "The rough material of Fine Writing is certainly the gift of Genius, but I as firmly believe that the workmanship is the united effort of Pains, Attention, and repeated Trial." Out of this work came such popular songs as "Auld Lang Syne" (1788) with its haunting, familiar lines:

> *Should auld acquaintance be forgot,*
> *And never brought to min'?*
> *Should auld acquaintance be forgot,*
> *And auld lang syne?*

Later, he worked on the *Select Collection of Original Scottish Airs* (1793–1818).

His ailing heart finally failed him, but even on his deathbed, he continued working on his songs. After he died, Wordsworth paid him this tribute in his poem "At the Grave of Burns": "He has gone / Whose light I hailed when first it shone, / And showed my youth / How verse may build a princely throne / On humble truth." The American writer Ralph Waldo Emerson called Burns "the poet of the poor, anxious, cheerful, working humanity, so had he the language of low life."

Critical Analysis

The verses in *Poems Chiefly in the Scottish Tradition* show many of Burns's poetic strengths, among them his use of Scots dialect. Burns wrote about the people that he knew and loved, and he used their colloquial language. In "The Cotter's Saturday Night," a peasant farmer makes his way home at the end of the day: "November chill blaws loud wi' angry sough; / The short'ning winter-day is near a close; / The miry beasts retreating frae the pleugh." As he approaches home, his children rush out to meet him: "Th' expectant wee things, toddlin', stacher through / To meet their Dad, wi' flichterin' noise an' glee." As James Currie, who introduced Burns's posthumous *Works,* wrote, "The greater part of his earlier poems are written in the dialect of his country, which is obscure, if not unintelligible to Englishmen, and which though it still adheres more or less to the speech of almost every Scotsman, all the polite and ambitious are endeavouring to banish from their tongues as well as their writings."

Humor also played a part in Burns's poetry. Thus, in "To a Louse," the poet spies a louse crawling on a woman's hat and thinks to himself, "Ha! Wh'are ye gaun, ye crowlin' ferlie! / Your impudence protects you sairly!"

Burns often used a stanza consisting of four lines interrupted by two short rhyming lines, as in this first verse from "To a Mouse":

> *Wee, sleekit, cowrin, tim'rous beastie,*
> *O, what a panic's in they breastie!*
> *Thou need na start awa sae hasty*
> *Wi' bickering brattle!*
> *I wad be laith to rin an' chase thee,*
> *Wi' murdering pattle!*

Although scholars call this form a Standard Habbie, after Habbie Simson, a Scottish piper praised by 16th-century poet Robert Semple, the form has also come to be known as the "Burns stanza."

Burns's long 1791 poem *Tam O'Shanter* tells of the humorous and gripping adventures of its title hero who, after a long night of drinking, goes out into a fierce storm, riding his mare Maggie. He stumbles upon a wild deep-woods festival: "Warlocks and witches in a dance: / Nae cotillion, brent new frae France, / But hornpipes, jigs, strathspeys, and reels, / Put life and mettle in their heels." Events get stranger as Tam watches, and he barely escapes with his life, losing his horse. The poem, like Burns's other long poem "The Jolly Beggars" (1785), is full of the garish, lurid folktales of his cousin Betty.

Other Work by Robert Burns
Low, Donald, ed. *Robert Burns*. Boston: Tuttle Publishing, 1997.

Works about Robert Burns
Daiches, David. *Robert Burns and His World*. New York: W. W. Norton, 1978.
McGuirk, Carol. *Robert Burns and the Sentimental Era*. Athens: University of Georgia Press, 1985.
———, ed. *Critical Essays on Robert Burns*. New York: Simon & Schuster, 1998.
McIntyre, Ian. *Dirt and Diety: A Life of Robert Burns*. New York: HarperCollins, 1996.

Burton, Sir Richard Francis (1821–1890)
nonfiction writer, translator

Adventurer, explorer, writer, and master of more than 25 languages, Richard Burton was born in Torquay, Devon, England, to Captain Joseph N. Burton and Mary Baker Burton. The family moved to France when he was five. His gift for languages was apparent early on as he picked up French from his nurses and began studying Latin at three and Greek at four.

Burton returned to England to attend Oxford University, where he began to study Arabic. However, he hated everything else about Oxford and soon left to join the British army in India.

On the four-month voyage to Bombay, Burton began to teach himself Hindustani. He soon passed an examination in the language and became an interpreter; he went on to master several other Asian languages.

Returned to England because of bad health, Burton wrote the first three of his many books, *Goa and the Blue Mountains* (1851), an account of his travels in the area, written for a general British audience; *Sindh and the Races that Inhabit the Valley of the Indus* (1851), an ethnological study, intended for use by civil students in India; and a semi-autobiographical work, *Scinde, or the Unhappy Valley*, in which his real experiences in Sindh are told through dialogue with an invented character. Burton's interest in local folk and their customs served him well the rest of his life as an explorer and ethnographer, but it had as its immediate effect the alienation of some important British superiors who objected to his "going native."

In 1853, disguised as an Afghan, he visited the holy places of Mecca and Medina—places forbidden to non-Muslims. In 1855 he published *A Personal Narrative of a Pilgrimage to Mecca and Medina*, a gripping story of dangerous desert travel culminating in his admission to the holiest place of all, the heavily guarded Kaabah in Mecca: "A blunder, a hasty action, a misjudged word . . . and my bones would have whitened the desert sand." The book sold well, but contemporary reaction to the author was guarded: Not only had the author disguised himself as a Muslim, but he also had performed Muslim rituals with respect and apparent sincerity. Modern critics point out that his open-mindedness toward Islam and his general curiosity about other peoples never disturbed his Victorian belief in the basic superiority of European civilization.

In 1857 Burton and JOHN HANNING SPEKE explored East Africa, searching for the source of the Nile. The expedition was dogged by illness and desertion. They explored Lake Tanganyika, but Burton was too ill to continue on with Speke to another lake they had heard about (now Lake Victoria, the actual source of the Nile). When Speke rejoined him, Burton was skeptical of Speke's claim to have found the source. Their friendship foundered. Speke returned to England ahead of Burton and secured financing to go back and consolidate his claim with a different partner. Burton published *The Lake Regions of Central Africa* (1860), which differed from Speke's book about the journey by focusing on the people instead of the landscape and fauna. He explains his approach thus: "The ethnology of Africa is indeed its most interesting . . . feature.

Everything connected with habits and customs, the moral and religious, the social and commercial state of these new races, is worthy of diligent observation."

He next set off for the United States, where he gathered material for *The City of Saints and Across the Rocky Mountains to California* (1861), a vivid and sardonic account of a journey west from Salt Lake City.

Returning to England, he married Isabel Arundell, a well-born and strong-willed woman. Burton was then posted as consul to Fernando Po (modern Bioko), an island just off the western coast of Africa; the region was thought unsuitable for a woman of Isabel's background, so Burton went alone. From service in Fernando Po he was posted to Santos, Brazil, and this time his wife accompanied him. Five years later Burton became consul in Damascus, Syria, and then in 1873 was posted to Trieste, Italy, where he was to serve until his death.

Burton wrote more than 50 books, in addition to his translations of works from many languages. His curiosity was not restrained by the conventions of his time. In an era when the Society for the Suppression of Vice made fierce use of Parliament's Obscene Publications Act, Burton translated Eastern love manuals such as *The Perfumed Garden of the Shaykh Nefzawi* (1866) and *Vatsayayana: The Kama Sutra* (which he introduced to the Western world). His 16-volume translation of *The Arabian Nights,* titled *The Book of a Thousand Nights and One Night* (1885), contained passages unacceptable to many Victorian ears.

Burton wrote poetry throughout his life, but most of the poetry he published is translations of other poets. His versions of the Portuguese poet Camoëns's epic *Lusiad* and lyric poetry are erudite and were somewhat inaccessible even for Victorian readers because of their archaic vocabulary. He presented his finest poem, *The Kasîdah of Hâjî Abdû el-Yezdî* (1880), as though it were a translation; but in fact it is his own, saturated by Sufi thinking and by his own personal philosophy, distilled in the following stanza:

Do what thy manhood bids thee do,
From none but self expect applause;
He noblest lives and noblest dies,
Who makes and keeps his self-made laws.

Works about Richard Burton

Farwell, Bryon. *Burton: A Biography of Sir Richard Francis Burton.* New York: Viking Penguin, 1988.

Lovell, Mary S. *A Rage to Live: A Biography of Richard and Isabel Burton.* New York: W. W. Norton, 1998.

Butler, Josephine (Josephine Grey Butler) (1828–1906) *nonfiction writer*

Josephine Butler was born in Milfield, Northumberland, England, to John Grey and Hannah Annett Grey. John Grey (a cousin of Earl Grey, the famous parliamentary reformer) was an abolitionist and forceful advocate of social reform who raised his daughter to share his religious and moral beliefs, as well as his abhorrence for injustice.

At age 18 she married George Butler, who later became principal of Liverpool College: He shared her political views and championed her tireless work for women's rights. Butler had decided to devote her life to helping girls and women after she witnessed the accidental death of her only daughter in a fall.

In 1868 she published her first feminist pamphlet, *The Education and Employment of Women,* in which she argues for broader and improved job opportunities for women, noting, "Education was what the slave-owners most dreaded for their slaves, for they knew it to be the sure road to emancipation." In 1869 she wrote and edited essays for *Woman's Work and Woman's Culture,* declaring that while women should have the right to vote, they should not "try to rival men since they had a different part to play in society," mainly caring for and protecting the weak.

Butler is perhaps best known for *Personal Reminiscences of a Great Crusade* (1896), the story of her successful campaign to repeal the Contagious Diseases Act, a one-sided law that placed female prostitutes under police supervision and forced them to endure invasive examinations for sexually transmitted diseases but ignored their male clients. Butler believed that women were forced into prostitution simply because they had no other means of earning an income, and after reflecting on the profound injustices of a society wherein men controlled the sexuality of women, she published *The Hour Before Dawn: An Appeal to Men* (1876), a book that severely criticizes men for hiring prostitutes. Butler also delivered impassioned speeches in her fight against child prostitution and, with the help of Florence Booth of the Salvation Army, induced Parliament to pass a law that raised the age of consent from 13 to 16. Today, the Josephine Butler Society continues her work by advocating a single moral standard for men and women and opposing state regulation of prostitution.

Works about Josephine Butler

Bell, E. Moberly. *Josephine Butler*. London: Constable, 1962.

Jordan, Jane. *Biography of Josephine Butler*. London: John Murray, 2001.

Butler, Samuel (1835–1902) novelist

Samuel Butler was born at Langar Rectory, near Nottingham, England, to Thomas Butler, an Anglican clergyman and a domineering figure who intended his son to follow him into the ministry, and Fanny Worsley Butler. Butler received a traditional education in a conventional public school, but developed a passion for painting and decided to become an artist. After a struggle with his father, who threatened to cut off financial support, in 1854 Butler went to St. John's College, Cambridge University, to study to become a clergyman. Butler was a superb student, particularly of Latin and the classics, but did not consider his education at Cambridge useful. After graduation, he worked in London as an amateur lay assistant to the poor. His experiences among the poor of London completely uprooted his faith in Christian dogma, and in 1859 he rejected the idea of becoming a minister. Thomas Butler reluctantly acquiesced to his son's wish to study art in New Zealand and grudgingly provided £4,200—an immense sum at the time—for the passage.

Between 1860 and 1864, Butler established himself as a successful sheep farmer. He explored the New Zealand back country for possible pastureland, established contacts with several frontiersmen, and made good friends. Butler's first book, *A First Year in Canterbury Settlement* (1863), was essentially a collection of letters to his father, who edited the letters into a lively narrative about life on the frontier and later provided financial support for its publication.

While in New Zealand, Butler read CHARLES DARWIN's *On the Origin of Species*. He became, in his own words, "one of Mr. Darwin's many enthusiastic admirers" and wrote several articles on Darwinism for New Zealand newspapers. In "Darwin among the Machines" (1863), he explores the idea that machines are living creatures competing with humans, while in "Lucubratio Ebria" (1865) he contemplates the possibility of humans evolving by attaching machines to their bodies.

In 1864 Butler returned to England with £8,000 that he had earned through farming and resumed studying painting. Facing health problems, in 1870 he traveled to continental Europe, where he began work on what many critics consider to be his masterpiece, *Erewhon*. Butler published this satiric utopian novel, which incorporates his articles "Darwin among the Machines" and "Lucubratio Ebria," in 1872.

Between 1874 and 1886, an inheritance from his grandfather saved Butler from complete poverty. During these years Butler achieved modest success as a painter—some of his works were exhibited at the Royal Academy—but he did little writing.

Critical Analysis

Erewhon describes an allegorical journey of the narrator, Higgs, through the fantastic land of Erewhon (an anagram of "nowhere"), where every social norm is seemingly turned upside down:

The physically ill people are treated as criminals, while criminals are nurtured as if they were sick. The "colleges of Unreason" of Erewhonians, similar to their European counterparts, aim at providing an education that has no practical value. The students are taught an artificial language that has no conceivable use, and they are rigorously examined in the principles of "unreason" on the grounds that "there is hardly an error into which men may not easily be led if they base their conduct upon reason only." Under this premise, the use of all machines is also forbidden.

Contemporary critical reaction to *Erewhon* was mixed: Some critics praised the work's ingenuity, while others were aghast at its "immorality" and social skepticism. The biographer Lee E. Holt sees the novel as "an account in imaginative form of the freeing experience that Butler's rebellion against his family, his trip to New Zealand, and his reading of Darwin were for him."

Butler's second novel, the posthumously published *The Way of All Flesh* (1902), follows the Pontifex family over five generations and bitterly comments on the hypocrisy of Victorian society. Largely autobiographical, the novel centers on Ernest Pontifex, a conventional young man who suddenly realizes the falseness of the social rules and aspirations forced on him by his teachers and parents. Ernest realizes that

> very few care two straws about truth, or have any confidence that it is righter and better to believe what is true than what is untrue.... [Only a] few ... can be said to believe anything at all; the rest are simply unbelievers in disguise. Perhaps, after all, these last are right. They have numbers and prosperity on their side.

Ernest then scandalously abandons his past convictions on morality, religion, and society. By novel's end, he "is an advanced Radical. His father and grandfather could probably no more understand his state of mind than they could understand Chinese."

Butler succeeds in cracking the public façade of traditional social institutions, such as marriage and parenthood, revealing an underlying dark side of exploitation, fear, and mistrust. Even though cloaked in irony, the novel's questioning and rejection of accepted Victorian values shocked its contemporary readers. "Butler's approach," according to the critic Margaret Ganz, "mutes even as it illuminates ... and ... largely affirms the ... imperative of the ironist—the command that he live sanely and die well by unearthing the truths our mortal unease has attempted to bury."

Butler did not achieve critical recognition during his lifetime, but his keen way of exposing social injustice and corruption rivals that of any modern writer. In 1918 the scholar Orlo Williams wrote that Butler "is one of the few" of the writers of the period following the great Victorians "whose name is little likely to be forgotten by the generations to come."

Works about Samuel Butler

Knoepflmacher, U. C. *Religious Humanism and the Victorian Novel: George Eliot, Walter Pater, and Samuel Butler.* Princeton, N.J.: Princeton University Press, 1965.

Ruby, Peter. *Samuel Butler: A Biography.* Iowa City: University of Iowa Press, 1991.

Shaffer, Elinor. *Erewhons of the Eye: Samuel Butler as Painter, Photographer, and Art Critic.* New York: McPherson Books, 1989.

B. V.
See THOMSON, JAMES.

Byrne, Charlotte
See DACRE, CHARLOTTE BYRNE.

Byron, George Gordon, Lord (1788–1824) poet

Byron is probably as famous for the life he led as for the poetry he wrote. Through both his poetry and his life, he created the figure of the Byronic hero—the melancholy outcast, the bored aristocrat, the world-weary wanderer, who is haunted by his own crimes and the injustice he has suffered at the hands of society. Along with SIR WALTER SCOTT, Byron had a tremendous impact on writers outside of England, influencing the Russian writer Aleksandr Pushkin and the German poet Johann Wolfgang von Goethe, among others. The English philosopher Bertrand Russell once said, "As a myth ... [Byron's] importance, especially on the continent, was enormous."

Byron was born in London. His father was Captain John Byron, nicknamed "Mad Jack," a high-living spendthrift. His mother, John Byron's second wife, Catherine Gordon of Gight, was descended from King James I of Scotland. When John deserted the family soon after Byron's birth, Catherine took her son to live in Aberdeen, Scotland. In 1798, when he was 10 years old, Byron inherited a barony along with a rundown castle.

Byron was born with a club foot, a condition that had a lasting effect on his life. According to MARY SHELLEY, "No action of Lord Byron's life—scarce a line he has written—but was influenced by his personal defect." Certainly he was teased as a youth, and he walked with a pronounced limp as an adult. Worse, his mother, who was notoriously high-strung and fickle, alternated between indulging the boy and insulting him about his deformity.

He entered Cambridge University in 1805, and although he read a great deal, spent much of his time gambling, shooting, boxing, and swimming. While there he met John Edleston, on whom he later based the "Thyrza" poems, written in 1811–12, after Edleston's death. The poems suggest a deep, perhaps romantic, attachment between the two young men.

While still at Cambridge, Byron issued his first volumes of poetry, including *Hours of Idleness* (1807). The poetry was attacked in the *Edinburgh Review*. In 1809 Byron responded with the witty, sharply satirical, sometimes mean-spirited poem *English Bards and Scotch Reviewers*.

In 1811 Byron published the first two cantos of *Childe Harold's Pilgrimage* (1812), a poetic account of his own recent European wanderings and romances. The poem is a virtual compendium of Romantic ideas. Among its most famous lines is Byron's declaration, "I love not Man the less, but Nature more," and his address to the ocean in the fourth canto:

> *Roll on, thou deep and dark blue Ocean—*
> *   roll!*
> *Ten thousand fleets sweep over thee in vain;*
> *Man marks the earth with ruin—his control*
> *Stops with the shore.*

Childe Harold was an instant success and, in addition to the adulation of readers, Byron found himself sought after by many women. Among these was LADY CAROLINE LAMB, who initially said that Byron was "Mad, bad, and dangerous to know," but who later fell madly in love with him—so madly, in fact, that her family had to take her away to Ireland to keep her from him. She is probably the subject of one of Byron's best-known lyrics, "She Walks in Beauty" (1815), which begins "She walks in beauty, like the night / Of cloudless climes and starry skies."

In early 1815 Byron married Anne Isabella Milbanke, who left Byron shortly after the birth of their daughter, claiming that he was engaged in an incestuous relationship with his half-sister Augusta. Anne's allegation remains an open question.

Whatever the truth, Byron stood condemned in the court of public opinion and left England in 1816, never to return. He spent some time in Switzerland with PERCY BYSSHE SHELLEY, whose poetry deeply influenced Byron's own, and Mary Shelley.

From 1816 to 1819 Byron lived in Venice. Here he caroused, rode, and swam, and had at least two love affairs. He also wrote a number of poems, including a canto of *Childe Harold*; *Manfred* (1817), a Gothic drama about an outcast, a villain-hero fallen from greatness; and the first two cantos of his comic masterpiece *Don Juan* (1819).

Byron became heavily involved in Italian politics. He was, according to one critic, a great hater of kings but not truly a lover of the people, his aristocratic roots proving too strong to allow him to be a true democrat. When the Italian forces with which he had allied himself failed, Byron turned to the Greek cause, as the Greeks attempted to free themselves from centuries of Turkish rule. In 1823 he told a friend, "I have a presentiment I shall die in Greece." In 1824 Byron arrived in Missolonghi. As he prepared for battle, amid rumors that he would eventually be crowned king of a democratic Greece, he fell ill and died. His body was returned to England, but his heart was buried in Greece.

Critical Analysis

Byron's reputation as a poet suffered after his death. Although *Don Juan* and *The Vision of Judgement* are indeed excellent satiric verse, parts of them can be difficult for some modern readers because they depend on knowledge of the social and political world in which Byron lived. Still, his vision of ROBERT SOUTHEY, poet laureate of England, reading his poetry to "Devils, Saints, . . . [and] Angels" at the gates of heaven in *The Vision of Judgement* is humorous, even if one does not know the poetry to which the lines refer:

> *He read the first three lines of the contents*
> *But at the fourth, the whole spiritual show*
> *Had vanish'd . . .*
> *The Angels stopp'd their ears and plied their*
>   *pinions;*
> *The Devils ran howling, deafen'd, down to*
>   *Hell.*

This poem was a response to an attack on Byron by Southey in a poem Southey had written to commemorate the death of King George III.

Inspired by the satiric verse of the 18th-century poet Alexander Pope, *Don Juan* has been called the greatest comic poem in English. It uses ottava rima, an eight-line stanza, with a rhyme scheme *ababcc*. This form allowed Byron to move with ease from pathos to farce, using the final couplet to deflate pretentious sentiments developed in the preceding six lines:

> *Juan was taught from out the best editions,*
> *Expurgated by learned men, who place,*
> *Judiciously, from out the schoolboy's vision,*
> *The grosser parts; but fearful to deface*
> *Too much their modest bard by this omission,*
> *And pitying sore his mutilated case,*
> *They only add them in an appendix,*
> *Which saves, in fact, the trouble of an index.*

Don Juan is a picaresque tale detailing the adventures of the innocent title character, who is fatally attractive to women. The narrative thread allows Byron to travel the world and discourse on a variety of subjects, including philosophy, politics, love, manners, and morals. He also mounts several attacks on what he regards as the pretensions of romantic poets such as WILLIAM WORDSWORTH and SAMUEL TAYLOR COLERIDGE. When Don Juan arrives in England as a diplomat from the court of the Russian ruler Catherine the Great, Byron uses this opportunity to satirize the foibles of his native land.

Ultimately, *Don Juan* reflects Byron's own disillusionment and loss of faith in both the social and the cosmic order. According to the scholar George M. Ridenour, the poem represents the myth of the loss of Eden. Yet for Byron, the loss of innocence is not necessarily an evil. According to the critic Elizabeth French Boyd, "*Don Juan*, for all its negations, is fundamentally an affirmative poem. . . . [Byron's] cynicism . . . springs from his ideal of perfection in human nature, which he sees everywhere betrayed by frailty and ignorance."

The sorrow of human mortality and weakness, a major theme of *Don Juan*, is also seen in the last poem Byron wrote, "On This Day I Complete My Thirty-Sixth Year," in which he envisions his own death. Byron's disillusionment with his life and work are clear in the first four stanzas. He is no longer "beloved," and his "days are in the yellow leaf." In the fifth stanza, however, the poet changes his emphasis. If poetry no longer serves, action on behalf of a great cause does. Despairing thoughts, he says, do not belong in Missolonghi, "where glory decks the hero's bier." As his spirit awakens, he sees himself surrounded by "The sword, the banner, and the field." He then asks himself, if he regrets his youth

> ... *why live?*
> *The land of honorable death*
> *Is here:—up to the field, and give*
> *Away thy breath!*

In the final stanza he resolves to "seek out ... a soldiers grave" where he may "take ... [his] rest."

Other Work by Byron

Lord Byron: The Major Works. London: Oxford University Press, 2000.

Works about Byron

Bloom, Harold, ed. *George Gordon, Lord Byron.* Broomall, Penn.: Chelsea House, 1990.

Graham, Peter W. *Lord Byron.* Boston: Twayne, 1998.

MacCarthy, Fiona. *Byron: Life and Legend.* New York: Farrar, Straus & Giroux, 2004.

Caine, T. H. Hall (Sir Thomas Henry Hall Caine) (1853–1931) *novelist*

T. H. Hall Caine was born on May 14 in Runcorn, Cheshire, England, the son of John Caine, a ship's smith. His mother, Sarah Hall Caine, was from the county of Cumberland, in northwest England; this area served as an important regional influence in Caine's novels.

Caine began his career studying architecture, and soon began to write and lecture on the topic. In 1879, he became friends with the poet DANTE GABRIEL ROSSETTI. Rossetti encouraged Caine to give up architectural criticism and concentrate fully on writing novels.

Caine's first novel, *The Shadow of a Crime* (1885), appeared as a serial in the *Liverpool Mercury*. Set in Cumberland during the English Civil War of the 17th century, it reflected Caine's antiroyalist views.

Caine married and settled in the Isle of Man, where Rossetti believed he could find new subject matter for his novels. His next work, a best-seller, was *The Son of Hagar* (1886), and like many of his novels that were to follow, it is full of Manx local color. His next best-seller was *The Deemster* (1887), an intense melodrama involving Manx fishermen and a body dumped at sea that floats ashore. This was followed by *The Bondman* (1890), a historical novel set in Iceland; *The Scapegoat* (1891), set in Morocco, which raised questions about anti-Semitism and the position of women; *The Manxman* (1894), a tormented love triangle involving two Manx fishermen; *The Christian* (1897), whose Manx-born protagonists, the actress Glory Quayle and the clergyman John Storm, experience the sordid life of London; and *The Eternal City* (1901), a love story set in Rome in the second half of the 19th century, for which Caine did meticulous on-site research.

During World War I, Caine quit writing novels to become a correspondent for the *New York Times* and wrote articles urging the United States to join in the war. His efforts earned him a knighthood.

Aside from his numerous novels, Caine also wrote several plays and short stories and two silent film scripts, and edited two books. The self-proclaimed "Shakespeare of the novel" died at his home on the Isle of Man. In her biography, Vivian Allen explores why Caine came to be forgotten after his phenomenal success during his lifetime, and concludes that the answer lies in "his one fatal flaw: he was entirely lacking in a sense of humour."

A Work about T. H. Hall Caine

Allen, Vivien. *Hall Caine: Portrait of a Victorian Romancer.* Sheffield, England: Sheffield Academic Press, 1997.

Caird, Alice Mona (1858–1932) *novelist, essayist*

Little is known about Mona Caird's early life except that she was born on the Isle of Wight and that her father, Hector, was an inventor. She married A. Henryson-Caird in 1877, but it was an unhappy union.

She is chiefly remembered for her essays and NEW WOMAN NOVELS that address the one-sided nature of marriage and economic restraints on women. Responding to the antifeminist writings of ELIZABETH LYNN LINTON, Caird wrote a series of articles on marriage, collected as *The Morality of Marriage and Other Essays* (1891). In such essays as "The Lot of Women Under the Rule of Man," "Motherhood Under Conditions of Dependence," and "Suppression of Variant Types," she took on Linton's conservative view that nature intended women only for marriage and motherhood. Caird argued that women's social inequality was directly linked to marriage, an institution that promoted inequality and the wife's subservient role.

Caird dramatized these issues in her novels. *The Wings of Azreal* (1889) features a tyrannized wife who finally murders her sadistic husband. *The Daughters of Danaus* (1894) (considered her most fully articulated work on the condition of women) tells the story of Hadria, a talented young woman who flees an unhappy marriage to study music but who is forced to return and settle for a conventional life as a middle-class matron. At a wedding, Caird's defeated heroine reflects on the fate awaiting brides:

> "Poor girls. . . . They awake to find they have been living in a Fool's Paradise—a little upholstered corner with stained glass windows and rose-coloured light. They find that suddenly they are expected to place in the centre of their life everything that up to that moment they have scarcely been allowed even to know about. . . . Every instinct, every prejudice must be thrown over. . . . And all . . . with perfect subjection and cheerfulness, on pain of moral avalanches and deluges, and heaven knows what convulsions of conventional nature!"

Caird was also a passionate antivivisectionist. In support of her cause, she wrote *The Savagery of Vivisection* (1894–95), *Some Truths about Vivisection* (1894), and *Legalized Torture* (n.d.).

A Work about Mona Caird

Murphy, Patricia. *Time Is of the Essence: Temporality, Gender, and the New Woman.* Albany: State University of New York Press, 2001.

Cambridge, Ada (Ada Cross) (1844–1926) *poet, novelist*

Ada Cambridge was born in Norfolk, England. She was educated by her parents and lived in Norfolk and Staffordshire until she was in her mid-20s. In 1870 she married the Reverend George Frederick Cross and moved to Australia, where her husband served as a missionary.

Transplanted to the Australian wilderness, Ada Cross began to write. Among her novels depicting life in Australia during the 19th century are *Up the Murray* (1875), her first novel, and *A Mere Chance* (1882). In *A Woman's Friendship* (1889), she documents the social world and customs of 1880s Melbourne, Australia.

Cross, who usually wrote under the name Ada Cambridge, published 28 novels, as well as poetry and short stories. Her poem "Despair," reflecting what must have sometimes been the bleakness of a missionary's life in a remote and wild region of the continent, begins:

> *Alone! Alone! No beacon, far or near!*
> *No chart, no compass, and no anchor stay!*
> *Like melting fog the mirage melts away*
> *In all-surrounding darkness, void and clear.*

Campbell, Thomas (1777–1844) poet, journalist

Thomas Campbell was born in Glasgow, Scotland, to Alexander and Margaret Campbell. Campbell attended the University of Glasgow from 1791 to 1795, distinguishing himself in poetry, the classics, and debate. In 1799 he published a lengthy poem in heroic couplets, *The Pleasures of Hope,* which was quite popular and went through many editions. This poem marks Campbell as a transitional figure between classicism and ROMANTICISM, in that the work combines a balanced and stately form with natural, sentimental elements. Several pithy observations from this poem, including "'Tis distance lends enchantment to the view," have become almost proverbial.

From 1800–01 Campbell traveled abroad and visited a number of German battlefields, including Hohenlinden, which had been the scene of a battle in December 1800. This experience gave rise to several martial poems, including *Ye Mariners of England* and *Hohenlinden,* works for which Campbell is best remembered today. The latter poem ends with a powerful image of a winter battle between Napoleon's French forces and the German defenders:

> Few, few shall part where many meet!
> The snow shall be their winding-sheet,
> And every turf beneath their feet
> Shall be a soldier's sepulchre.

After his return to England, Campbell settled in London and in 1803 began work on his seven-volume biographical-critical work, *Specimens of the British Poets,* completed 16 years later. In 1809 Campbell published *Gertrude of Wyoming,* a poem about American settlers and Native Americans. It is the first long poem by a British poet to be set in America. The "Wyoming" of the title is the name of a valley in Pennsylvania; the state of Wyoming took its name from Campbell's poem.

From 1820 on Campbell wrote little poetry and earned his living primarily as a journalist and editor. He helped found University College, London, for students who could not attend Oxford or Cambridge Universities because of financial or religious reasons. As the Victorian critic G. M. C. Brandes said, in Campbell's "best verse there is a spirit, a swinging march time, and a fire that entitled him, if only for the sake of half-a-dozen short pieces, to a place among great poets."

A Work about Thomas Campbell

Miller, Mary-Ruth. *Thomas Campbell.* Boston: Twayne, 1978.

Canning, George (1770–1827) political essayist, poet

George Canning was born in London. Like his father, George Canning Sr., who was both a lawyer and a poet, Canning pursued both writing and politics. When George was an infant his father died, and his mother, who became an actress to support herself, left George to be raised by an uncle. George attended Eton, where he edited a student magazine called the *Microcosm*. He graduated from Oxford University in 1790, and shortly afterward became a friend of William Pitt the Younger, the English statesman, who helped Canning win election to Parliament in 1794.

From 1799 to 1801 Canning edited the literary and political magazine *The Anti-Jacobin Review* and wrote both poetry and political commentary for it. One of his best-known poems was *The Friend of Humanity and the Knife-Grinder,* a dialogue in which the "Friend of Humanity" is full of pity for the knife-grinder's ragged and oppressed condition—until the knife-grinder mildly suggests that sixpence for a beer would satisfy his rights:

> "I should be glad to drink your Honour's
>   health in
> A pot of beer, if you will give me sixpence;
> But for my part, I never love to meddle
> With politics, sir."
>
> "I give thee sixpence! I will see thee damn'd
>   first—

> Wretch! whom no sense of wrongs can rouse
>   to vengeance—
> Sordid, unfeeling, reprobate, degraded,
> Spiritless outcast!"

In 1800 Canning married Joan Scott, a sister of the duchess of Portland. In 1807, when the duke of Portland became prime minister, Canning was appointed foreign minister. A year later, Canning helped start an influential literary magazine called the *Quarterly Review*. He continued his political career as ambassador to Portugal (1814), later as governor-general of India (1822), and finally as prime minister (1827). In 1823 Canning published his *Collected Poems*. He died in 1827, the same year he was elected prime minister. A book of his collected political speeches was published a year after his death.

Other Work by George Canning
Frere, John Hookhum, ed. *Poetry of the Anti-Jacobin*. New York: Woodstock Books, 1991.

Carlyle, Jane Welsh (1801–1866) *letter writer*

Jane Carlyle was born in Haddington, Scotland, to John Welsh, a medical doctor, and Grace Baillie Welsh. She was educated at home. In 1826 she married the author THOMAS CARLYLE, who later remembered her as protecting him, early on, "from the rude collisions of the world."

Carlyle kept journals, most of which she destroyed, but about 3,000 of her letters survive. Their accomplishment has become emblematic of the untapped potential of other women of her day even more domesticated than she.

Carlyle on the subject of her spouse can be amusing, her wit removing all sense of complaint, as in an 1843 letter to her husband's sister Jane: "Carlyle returned from his travels 'very bilious', and continues very bilious up to this hour."

Other letters, however, admit deeper chords. Three years before their marriage, Jane wrote to Thomas about gender inequity: "[Women] are the weakest portion of the human kind, and nevertheless we have to bear two thirds of the burden of sorrows ... what I would give to be a prime Minister or a Commander in chief!" Eighteen years later, Carlyle returned to the subject in a letter to a woman friend: "We women are naturally so impressible, so imitative! ... Our very self-will, I believe[,] which [men] make such a fuss about, is, after all, only a reflex of their own."

One detects in both letters Carlyle's frustration. One of her closest friendships, with the novelist GERALDINE JEWSBURY, may have been related to this feeling. Theirs might have been, as the critic Norma Clarke suggests, "a relationship between a woman whose identity as a writer became ever stronger as her career progressed, and a woman whose ... writing self had been squeezed into narrowed channels by the demands of her married life."

Through her spouse, Carlyle came to occupy a prominent place in the London literary world, but none of her work was published in her lifetime. Still, according to the critic Morse Peckham, Carlyle is "one of the best letter writers in the language."

Other Work by Jane Welsh Carlyle
Simpson, Alan, and Mary McQueen Simpson, eds. *I Too Am Here: Selections from the Letters of Jane Welsh Carlyle*. New York: Cambridge University Press, 1977.

A Work about Jane Welsh Carlyle
Markus, Julia. *Across an Untried Sea: Discovering Lives Hidden in the Shadow of Convention and Time*. New York: Alfred A. Knopf, 2000.

Carlyle, Thomas (1795–1881) *essayist, social critic, historian*

A towering figure for Victorians, Thomas Carlyle was born in Ecclefechan, Scotland, to Margaret Aitken Carlyle and James Carlyle, a mason and farmer whose background of poverty, philosophy of duty and hard work, and strict Calvinist faith influenced the attitude and direction of his son's writings.

In 1809 Carlyle entered Edinburgh University, where he studied art and began preparing for the ministry, a career path he abandoned in 1817. Five years later, he had a conversion experience that awakened him to a belief in "natural supernaturalism," a visionary sense of the sacred nature of the universe. In 1826 he married; he shared with JANE WELSH CARLYLE, a childless and turbulent, although deeply loving, union. The couple moved to Craigenputtoch in 1828, and to London in 1834. In 1865 Carlyle was elected rector of his alma mater.

Critical Analysis

Carlyle was widely regarded as a national prophet on social, moral, and political matters, although the increasingly sour tone and illiberal nature of some of his views led to the sharp decline of his reputation in the 20th century. Recent reevaluations have somewhat repaired this damage.

Sartor Resartus ("The Tailor Re-tailored") (1836) is a comical autobiographical fiction displaying the convoluted syntax that Carlyle had drawn from his study of German literature and philosophy. Even more unusual is the book's narrative form. The Editor is supposedly putting together fragments by a fictitious German philosopher; hence, the book's secondary title, *The Life and Opinions of Herr Teufelsdröckh*. (*Teufelsdröckh* means "devil's dung"). Some of these "opinions" pertain to Professor Teufelsdröckh's "philosophy of clothes." The professor distinguishes between the "living visible Garment" of Nature and the transcendent reality behind it, and between humanity's material nature and spiritual nature. "'To the eye of vulgar Logic,' remarks Teufelsdröckh, 'what is man? An omnivorous Biped that wears Breeches. To the eye of Pure Reason what is he? A Soul, a Spirit, and divine Apparition. . . .'" (The term *Pure Reason* is taken from the German philosopher Immanuel Kant.)

Throughout the text the Editor pieces together a portrait of Teufelsdröckh's inner struggle. Thus Teufelsdröckh confronts the Everlasting No, moves through the Centre of Indifference, and attains the Everlasting Yea, the basis of a new faith to replace the old one that various forces, such as the profit-and-loss philosophy of utilitarianism (*see* BENTHAM, JEREMY), had conspired to make invalid. In the end the professor rejects despair, turns himself outward to consider great men of history, and finally embraces a philosophy founded on the love of both God and humanity, merging the ideal and the practical. The book's overarching theme, then, is the need for self-motivated spiritual renewal to counter society's crumbling religious foundation.

Carlyle's eccentric masterpiece, which famously describes humans as "tool-using animal[s]" and introduces the term *industrialism,* baffled the British public. Even Carlyle's publisher could not decide whether it was an actual translation. A century later, the American scholar Charles Frederick Harrold wrote, "As a half-mystical rhapsody, strangely composed by turns of fragments of biography, philosophic fantasies, and apocalyptic prose-poetry, [*Sartor*] has been read with despair, indignation, rapture, or bewilderment, but probably never with mere indifference."

The public, as well as critics, embraced Carlyle's next work—*The French Revolution* (1837), the "wild savage Book," as he called it. Instead of a linear account of the history of the French Revolution, Carlyle's is a complicated mix that, according to the critic John D. Rosenberg, reveals that "there were as many different French Revolutions as participants in the event, and its consequences are still unfolding." As Rosenberg describes it, Carlyle, through use of the present tense, makes his reader "eyewitness to a modern Armageddon" affecting the whole of society, from royalty on high to those in the streets, even in small ways that nevertheless seep into people's minds. An example is the following glimpse of fermenting discontent in 1789 Paris: "[C]onsider, while work itself is so scarce, how a man must not only realize money, but stand waiting (if his wife is too weak to wait and struggle) for half-days . . . till he get it changed for dear bad bread!" Carlyle thus applied the concept of *environment,* in its sense of the larger historical and social context, to explain individual actions. His introduction to the Reign of Terror also is morally fierce, dark, and immense: "We are now ... got to that black precipitous Abyss; whither all things have long been tending; where, having now arrived on the giddy verge, they hurl down, in confused ruin; headlong, pellmell, down, down...." The philosopher JOHN STUART MILL, reviewing the book, described it as "an epic poem; and notwithstanding, or even in consequence of this, the truest of histories."

Carlyle's successful 1840 lecture series, revised, became *On Heroes, Hero-Worship and the Heroic in History* (1841). Its underlying theme that "might makes right" led 20th-century critics, notably Eric Bentley, to glean from it the germ of the idea of the Nietzchean "superman" in anticipation even of Adolf Hitler. (Carlyle's histories of leaders, such as *Oliver Cromwell's Letters and Speeches: with Elucidations* [1845] and *History of Friedrich II, of Prussia, Called Frederick the Great* [1865], are also steeped in his notion of the hero.) However, Carlyle's idea of the hero is more complicated than a strongarm dictator. As a transcendentalist (one who seeks beyond the ordinary and usual) he stresses the divine spark in the hero, while as a moralist he emphasizes that the hero as leader is certified by, among other things, his unwavering truthfulness. Hitler would draw confirmation for his political ambition from Carlyle's glorification of the hero and of German culture, but Hitler more closely resembled the false hero Carlyle warns against—a "poor morbid prurient empty man," who, "anxious about his gifts and claims," "cannot walk on quiet paths." "The book that Carlyle actually wrote," Rosenberg has noted, "is not the proto-Nazi tract he is popularly supposed to have written." Carlyle's biographer Simon Heffer writes, "Carlyle sought to prick consciences when he talked of the bankruptcy of an age that denied the existence of great men; for only such men could save a society in moral decline."

In *Past and Present* (1843) Carlyle blames much of this decline on industrial capitalism, which he found cold in its mechanical economic functioning and in the restriction of employer-employee relations to a cash transaction. He regretted the owner's lack of concern for the worker and the worker's lack of reverence for either his own work or the owner. "Cash-payment is not the sole nexus of man with man," Carlyle wrote. "Deep, far deeper than Supply-and-demand, are Laws, Obligations sacred as Man's Life itself." Using the term in its modern sense, Carlyle found workers alienated.

Among those deeply affected by the book was the German socialist FRIEDRICH ENGELS. However, instead of looking ahead to a socialist future, Carlyle looked back to the Middle Ages, a period in which he supposed that a strong leader (again the idea of the hero) often led society wisely and well.

When the 1867 Reform Act expanded voting rights to include workers, all but eliminating royal influence from the nation's governance, Carlyle worried that the upshot would be disorder, and only an illusion of progress for working people—concerns he had expressed in *Latter-Day Pamphlets* (1850). In response to the bill prior to its enactment, he revisited these concerns in the essay "Shooting Niagara: and After?" (1867), a flat, sourly sarcastic work typical of his latter-day disposition: "Certain it is, there is nothing but vulgarity in our People's expectations, resolutions or desires, in this Epoch. It is all a peaceable mouldering or tumbling down from mere rottenness and decay ... there will be nothing found of real or true in the rubbish-heap, but a most true desire of making money easily, and of eating it pleasantly."

The critic LESLIE STEPHEN once described Carlyle as "the beacon-light of the age, according to his disciples—the most delusive of wildfires, according to his adversaries." Carlyle's chosen biographer, his disciple JAMES ANTHONY FROUDE, greased the path for Carlyle's posthumous decline with a sometimes dubious and distasteful four-volume *Carlyle's Life in London* (1882–84), but

Carlyle was largely done in by continuing to write for so long. At his peak, though, he was the prophet he wanted to be, surrounded by disciples, a nation's ear his captive. "A prophet worthy of the name," the critic G. B. Tennyson has written, "must somehow affect people.... And Carlyle did. He changed England in ways more profound than the railway."

Works about Thomas Carlyle

Ashton, Rosemary. *Thomas and Jane Carlyle: Portrait of a Marriage.* London, England: Random House, 2003.

Desauliniers, Mary. *Carlyle and the Economics of Terror.* Montreal: McGill-Queens University Press, 1995.

Heffer, Simon. *Moral Desperado: A Life of Thomas Carlyle.* London: Weidenfeld and Nicolson, 1995.

Kaplan, Fred. *Thomas Carlyle: A Biography.* Berkeley: University of California Press, 1993.

Morrow, John. *Thomas Carlyle.* London: Hambledon & London, 2007.

Carpenter, Edward (1844–1929) *poet, essayist*

Edward Carpenter was born in Brighton, England, one of 10 children of a wealthy navy lieutenant, Charles Carpenter, and his wife, Sophia Wilson Carpenter. Carpenter was educated at Cambridge University.

Abandoning a plan to join the ministry, he instead moved to the town of Millthorpe, where he attempted to live by socialist principles, adopting a sandal-wearing, agrarian way of life, and promoting various causes, such as an end to vivisection and a tolerance of homosexuality. Carpenter himself was openly homosexual, and in his essay "Love's Coming of Age" (1879) he writes of the difficulty of understanding other people's orientations: "In the great ocean, there are so many currents, cold and warm, fresh, and salt, and brackish; and each one thinks that the current in which he lives is the whole ocean." In his poem *Towards Democracy* (1883–1902), published in installments, Carpenter described a quasi-mystical spiritual impulse drawing humanity toward progress and liberation. He acknowledged the influence of his friend the American poet Walt Whitman on the poem, which linked self-love to a universal loving principle at work in the universe. Carpenter also conceded that Whitman was the better poet.

Carpenter was a prolific writer, turning out various books, pamphlets, plays, and short stories, in addition to essays and poetry. His subjects were many, including science, art, religion, economics, sex, politics, pain, and current events. The English novelist E. M. Forster called Carpenter "hard to sum up," and the critic Noel Greig said that Carpenter ranged over many topics without having a great impact in most: "If his name is known at all, it is perhaps for a long poem he wrote—*Towards Democracy*—which is possibly more acknowledged than read."

Other Works by Edward Carpenter

The Drama of Love & Death: A Study of Human Evolution & Transfiguration. Kila, Mont.: Kessinger, 1998.

Intermediate Sex, 1912. Kila, Mont.: Kessinger, 1999.

Carroll, Lewis (Charles Lutwidge Dodgson) (1832–1898) *novelist, poet*

Lewis Carroll, born Charles Lutwidge Dodgson, in Daresbury, England, was the eldest son of Charles Dodgson, a parish curate, and his wife and cousin Frances Jane Lutwidge. After several years at Rugby School, in 1851 Carroll entered Christ Church College, Oxford University, from which he graduated three years later with honors in mathematics. He was appointed a lecturer in mathematics in 1855. To keep this position he had to remain unmarried, as he would his entire life. Although ordained a deacon in 1861, Carroll went no further in preparing for the priesthood, believing he lacked some of the qualities needed to be a priest.

Carroll's two great interests outside mathematics were photography and writing. Carroll was an excellent photographer; ALFRED, LORD TENNYSON and DANTE GABRIEL ROSSETTI were among his adult subjects. In addition, he often photographed children. In 1856 EDMUND YATES, editor of the monthly *Train,* launched the Lewis Carroll pseudonym that the author himself had devised—a Latinized inversion of his first two birth names. Thereafter, the math instructor lived a sort of double life, publishing mathematical treatises and lecturing in math under his own name, while writing satires and children's literature as Lewis Carroll.

Carroll befriended children, especially girls, generally dropping them as acquaintances when they entered adolescence. One of these, the daughter of Oxford dean Henry George Liddell, was Alice Pleasance Liddell, whom Carroll first photographed in 1856, when she was four. Liddell provided the model for Carroll's most enduring character, the child Alice in *Alice's Adventures in Wonderland* (1865) and *Through the Looking-Glass and What Alice Found There* (1871). (When the Mad Hatter asks Alice in the first book what day it is, she answers May 4—Liddell's birthday.) It was on a river outing with Liddell, then 10, and her two sisters that Carroll first conjured the earliest Alice story. Its original printed form was an 1864 Christmas gift to Liddell. Titled *Alice's Adventures under Ground,* it was illustrated by Carroll himself. The expanded version with which we are familiar was illustrated by John Tenniel, whose political cartoons appeared in the magazine *Punch.* Liddell was 18 when Carroll photographed her for the last time.

Alice's Adventures centers on a young girl who, falling asleep in a meadow, dreams a series of adventures involving odd characters, both animal and human, beginning with the agitated, fastidiously dressed White Rabbit, whom she pursues down a rabbit hole. In the book's sequel, *Through the Looking-Glass,* Alice enters the fantasy world through a mirror in her own home. The White Knight she encounters, a pensive bachelor, Carroll may have based on himself.

Three other works are *The Hunting of the Snark* (1876), which relays in humorous verse an ocean journey in pursuit of a mythical creature whose shape and appearance are utterly unknown, *Sylvie and Bruno* (1889) and its sequel, *Sylvie and Bruno Concluded* (1893), novels about two fairy siblings trying to do good in the human world.

Among books that Carroll signed as Dodgson are the scholarly works *Curiosa Mathematica,* parts 1 (1888) and 2 (1893), and *Symbolic Logic* (1896). Dodgson's intense study of logic, begun in 1876, by the early 1880s had taken over much of his time, contributing to his abandonment of lecturing at Oxford and photography.

Critical Analysis

The Alice books are historic in the development of children's literature. Following the lead of CHARLES LAMB, Carroll shifted the aim of such literature from instructing to delighting its audience. Carroll biographer Morton N. Cohen has observed that "children's books after Carroll were less serious, more entertaining, and sounded less like sermons and more like the voices of friends than earlier prototypes."

In *Alice's Adventures in Wonderland,* Alice's dreamed descent takes her from the rabbit hole to a world of "curiouser and curiouser" make-believe that culminates in Alice's confrontation with royalty, the King and Queen of Hearts. Along the way, Alice's size increases and decreases until she hardly knows herself or her environment anymore. She meets various denizens of Wonderland, including the Mad Hatter, the ugly Duchess, and talking animals, such as an inquisitive Caterpillar and the ever-grinning Cheshire Cat. Alice cries to show her sense of frustration at being unable to control things. To compensate for this sense, she can also be rude, as when, contesting the Queen's logic ("Sentence first—verdict afterwards"), she loudly retorts, "Stuff and nonsense!" However, her chief trait is the calm with which she greets all manner of unusual circumstance. She often rationalizes a bizarre event in order to maintain some sense of stability. Thus, for instance, when the Fish-Footman, all the while looking up at the sky rather than at her, tells her that knocking at the door of the Duchess's house will not gain her entry, instead of taking offense at what seems his incivility Alice reasons to herself, "But perhaps he can't help it . . . his eyes are so *very* nearly at the top of his head." The critic Richard Kelly has noted that Alice's "composure is extraordinary," adding that "[a] great deal of the humor found in Alice's encounters with the creatures of Wonderland derives from . . . [her] solemnity."

Intended to delight children rather than to teach them moral lessons and inculcate social values, the book is full of puns and wordplay. For instance, the Mouse's "long and sad tale," which Alice takes to mean "tail," leads to a "concrete poem": a bit of the tale in the shape of a tail on the printed page. The contemporary reviewer writing in the *Guardian,* part of the chorus of praise the book received, found its "nonsense . . . graceful" and "full of humour."

Indeed, Carroll sought to delight adults as well as children. He therefore included a wealth of allusions and satirical references—the mathematician Martin Gardner would track down many in his *Annotated Alice* (1960)—that only adults might catch. When, for instance, Alice complains that she is at the moment only three inches tall, the Caterpillar, who is exactly that size, retorts, "You'll get used to it in time." This is a sly reference to species adaptation—a part of evolutionary theory.

The book's sequel centers on adolescence rather than childhood. "Here we have a real chess game," Morton Cohen has noted, "with chess pieces representing the obstacles the young person encounters and must overcome." "The game of life," Cohen adds, is "more advanced, more adult" than in the first book, and Alice, who is "climbing the social ladder," now "must progress according to [society's] strict rules." Everything she encounters through the looking-glass will be a test. Such, for example, is the poem "Jabberwocky," which clever Alice finds difficult to understand. (She has just demonstrated that cleverness—and congratulated herself on it—by mirror-reversing the poem in order to read it.) Much of the poem's difficulty comes from its use of made-up words, as in the first lines: "'Twas brillig, and the slithy toves / Did gyre and gimble in the wabe." The egg-like Humpty Dumpty explains "brillig" to Alice as "four o'clock in the afternoon—the time when you begin *broiling* dinner," and "slithy" as "lithe and slimy." Like many words in the poem, it is a portmanteau word, one that combines the sound and sense of two familiar words. By way of language as metaphor, then, Alice is confronted by life's challenging conflation of the strange and remotely familiar. The *Illustrated London News* reviewer found the story "quite as rich in humourous whims and fancy" as its "wondrous" predecessor.

Carroll's final outstanding work, *The Hunting of the Snark* (1876), is a nonsensical poem in which various characters pursue an unseen, possibly formless beast representing whatever each person is after: "They sought it with thimbles, they sought it with care; / They pursued it with forks and hope"—that is, with anything at their disposal that might catch it. The book was popular despite mixed reviews, such as the *Athenaeum* reviewer's suggestion that Carroll's goal may have been "to reduce [readers] to idiocy." Later critics have praised the poem; Richard Kelly, for instance, has described it as "Carroll's comic rendering of his fear of disorder and chaos."

Like his most famous creation, Alice, Carroll maintains his composure in the midst of the lunacy that he conjures. "Amid his wildest whimsicalities, his most preposterous inversions of fact and reason," the critic W. Whyte has written, "[Carroll] preserves a singular restraint in his manner. He exhibits a sedateness in absurdity, a precision in inconsequence, which give [his writing] an exquisite incongruity, a delightful piquancy."

Other Work by Lewis Carroll
Lewis Carroll: The Complete, Fully Illustrated Works. New York: Gramercy Books, 1995.

Works about Lewis Carroll

Cohen, Morton N. *Lewis Carroll.* New York: Alfred A. Knopf, 1996.

Collingwood, Stuart Dodgson. *The Life and Letters of Lewis Carroll.* Whitefish, Mont.: Kessinger, 2004.

Leach, Karoline. *In the Shadow of the Dreamchild: A New Understanding of Lewis Carroll.* London: Peter Owen, 1999.

Chambers, Robert (1802–1871) *nonfiction writer, poet, publisher*

Robert Chambers was born in Peebles, Scotland, to James Chambers, a cotton trader, and his wife, Jean Chambers. He developed a love of reading at an early age (of the *Encyclopaedia Britannica,* he said, "I roamed through it like a bee"), and studied in Edinburgh for several years before his family met with financial problems that forced him to leave school.

After working at a series of jobs to help support his family, in 1819 Chambers and his brother William set up a bookstall. Soon after, they formed the publishing house of W. & R. Chambers.

While building his publishing business, Chambers also began to write works about the history and culture of Edinburgh. Titles included *Fires Which Have Occurred in Edinburgh* (1824), *Traditions of Edinburgh* (1825), *Walks in Edinburgh* (1825), and *Popular Rhymes of Scotland* (1826).

In 1829 Chambers married Anne Kirkwood. He continued to write, publishing numerous history and science books, as well as biographies. Some of his more successful books included *History of the British Empire* (1845) and *History of English Language and Literature* (1845). He is best known for his highly controversial book *Vestiges of the Natural History of Creation* (1844), a work that helped popularize the idea of evolution. Published at first anonymously in light of his heterodox views, Chambers's authorship was not verified until 1884, long after his death. Nevertheless, it received praise from many scientists, including CHARLES DARWIN, who rightly saw it as a forerunner to his own work: "In my opinion it has done excellent service in this country in calling attention to the subject [evolution], in removing prejudice, and in thus preparing the ground for the reception of analogous views."

Although Chambers never completed his education as a young man, his lifetime of work earned him an honorary degree from St. Andrews University. Chambers died at St. Andrews in 1871.

Charles, Elizabeth (1828–1896) *novelist*

Elizabeth Charles was born in Tavistock, Devon, England. The only child of John Rundle, an M.P., and his wife, she was tutored at home. She wrote fiction and poetry at an early age.

"Monopoly" (1847), her first published story, was inspired by the moral tales of HARRIET MARTINEAU's *Illustrations of Political Economy,* and suggested that her future writing would treat religious themes. Charles also hinted at the biographical direction her writing would take when she recorded hours of ALFRED, LORD TENNYSON's conversation during an evening he spent with her family at their country home.

In 1851 she married Andrew Paton Charles, a barrister and owner of a soap and candle factory. She continued to write, and in 1863 was offered £400 for what became her most popular and best-known religious novel, *The Chronicles of the Schonberg-Cotta Family,* a narrative of Martin Luther's life as seen through the Cotta children's eyes, with a vivid recreation of the fervor surrounding religious reform and rebellion and the horrors of plague.

Charles published other religious novels, including *The Diary of Mrs. Kitty Trevylyan* (1864), which recounts the times of the Methodist preachers George Whitfield and John Wesley; *Against the Stream* (1873), which pits religious revival against revolution during the Napoleonic era; and *Joan the Maid* (1879), a retelling of the story of Joan of Arc, who declares "there is nothing fruitful but sacrifice."

After the death of her husband, Charles lived off the royalties from her books, became active in several London charities, and in 1885 founded a hospice. During her final years, more than a dozen of her books were published by the Society for the Promotion of Christian Knowledge. Her last book, *Our Seven Homes: Autobiographical Reminiscences* (1896), was published the year that she died.

Cholmondeley, Mary (1859–1925)
novelist

Mary Cholmondeley (pronounced *chumly*) was born in Hodnet, Shropshire, the third of eight children and the eldest daughter of the Reverend Richard Cholmondeley, rector of Hodnet, and Emily Beaumont Cholmondeley. Cholmondeley, who never married and suffered from ill health most of her life, once described herself as "a plain silent country girl, an invalid whom no one cared a straw about." She spent most of her life with her family, helping to raise her siblings after her mother's death when she was 16, and later helping her father with his parochial duties until his retirement in 1896.

Cholmondeley began writing at age 17, and at age 28 published her first novel, *The Danvers Jewels* (1887), a detective story complete with false clues, secret identities, stolen jewels, and a surprise ending. *Sir Charles Danvers* (1889) is a sequel to *The Danvers Jewels*, in which the title character undergoes a moral reformation. The title character of *Diana Tempest* (1893) is a witty woman who searches for a man who will respect her. These works were all serialized in the magazine *Temple Bar*.

Her novel *Red Pottage* (1899) earned Cholmondeley celebrity status; one reviewer called it "the English novel of the year." Sometimes compared to the work of JANE AUSTEN, *Red Pottage* is set in the Victorian upper-class world and depicts love, adultery, betrayal, suicide, and the destruction of a woman novelist's manuscript by an intolerant clergyman. The novel sharply criticizes hypocrisy and the gross subordination of the woman writer in the 19th century.

After *Red Pottage*, Cholmondeley published several more novels and short story collections, none of which received the same critical acclaim. Her last published work, *The Romance of His Life, and Other Romances* (1921), a collection of short stories, returns to her focus on the injustices against women artists. In "The Goldfish," for example, an artist drowns herself after being betrayed by a man who steals her work. Recent critics such as Catherine Rainwater and William Sheick have attempted to resurrect Cholmondeley as a major feminist voice of the turn of the century, praising her "feminist system of human and aesthetic values."

Clare, John (1793–1864) *poet*

John Clare was born at Helpston, Northamptonshire, England. His twin sister died a few weeks after birth, and another sister died in childhood, but his sister Sophy grew to be his companion. The family lived in poverty. Clare's parents could barely read, and he began working the fields and tending the herds at a young age. Early on, he demonstrated a talent for poetry, writing his first verses on his mother's sugar bags. He wrote poems, he said, "for downright pleasure in giving vent to my feelings." At age 13 he witnessed the death of a neighbor farmer, which disturbed him a great deal, and at 16 he fell in love with Mary Joyce, the daughter of a wealthy farmer. The girl's father would not allow them to be together, and the deep disappointment of the loss of his first love tormented him for the rest of his life. Later, he addressed his poems to her, calling Mary his muse and his true wife. As he entered adulthood, Clare enlisted in the militia for a short time, roamed with gypsies, was a vagrant, and continued to write poetry. His earliest influence, because of its celebration of nature, was a book called *The Seasons*, by JAMES THOMSON. Clare's world was the land and his family's farm, and he proved to be a nature poet.

In 1820 Clare published *Poems Descriptive of Rural Life and Scenery*. The book was an instant success, and Clare found himself taken in by intelligent, well-bred society. He was called the "peasant poet" and was held up as an example of someone who became literary and accomplished despite the lack of education and wealth. He is still considered one of the only truly self-educated and accomplished poets of his time. The success of his first book granted him financial stability, and he was able to marry his sweetheart, Martha (Patty) Turner. In London, he met the writer CHARLES LAMB and the poet THOMAS HOOD, and, a few years later, SAMUEL TAYLOR COLERIDGE and THOMAS DE QUINCEY. Clare soon published another book, *The Village Minstrel and Other Poems* (1821).

In spite of these connections and early successes, the "peasant poet" was almost forgotten just a few years later, and Clare was forced to go back to farming. He continued to write, and, in an attempt to resurrect his former success, he even sold his own books door to door. He became overworked and suffered ill health. By now he and his wife had seven children to care for. His book *The Shepherd's Calendar* was published in 1827 and *The Rural Muse* in 1835. Although today they are thought to contain some of his best work, at the time neither book sold.

At age 40 Clare suffered his first bout of insanity, and after struggling with mental illness for many years, he was finally sent to Northampton County Asylum, where he lived for the rest of his life. In the asylum, he was able to go on walks, enjoy his solitude, and write poetry.

He wrote almost 2,000 poems, most of them published long after his death. ARTHUR SYMONS published more of Clare's poetry posthumously, and in 1931 Clare's autobiography was published. A collection of his later work, *The Midsummer Cushion*, appeared in 1979.

In the asylum, he continued to write primarily of nature, which he portrays as purity. As the scholar and critic Michael Schmidt wrote, "His pathos, unheard of elsewhere in English poetry, draws on his sense of the vulnerability of natural things, of the rural order, and, obliquely, his own vulnerability." In his poem "'I Am'" he wrote

> *I long for scenes, where man hath never trod*
> *A place where woman never smiled or wept*
> *There to abide with my Creator, God;*
> *And sleep as I in childhood, sweetly slept,*
> *Untroubling, and untroubled where I lie,*
> *The grass below—above the vaulted sky.*

Critical Analysis

According to the critic Richard Cronin of the University of Glasgow, John Clare "never writes better than when he writes about birds, and in particular about birds' nests." Clare has several such poems, including "The Skylark," "The Nightingale's Nest," and "The Yellowhammer." Clare is an astute observer of nature, and despite his reputation as a peasant poet, his insights are deep and learned. In fact, Cronin speculates that Clare's nest poems represent Clare's dual nature, his existence as a sophisticated poet with his roots, his "nest," embedded in but not precisely part of village life.

"The Yellowhammer" is written in sonnet form, though it does not precisely follow either the Petrarchan or the Shakespearean model, with the "turn" or change in tone, attitude, or idea that is such an important part of the form, occurring at line ten. With a sharp eye for detail, Clare describes the bird's nest, "feathered wi love" yet rudely built near roads where carts carve ruts into the mud. The materials are simple: "Dead grass, horse hair and downey headed bents [reedy grass]/ Tied to dead thistles." Yet the nest is surrounded by the beautiful countryside "where cowslips bloom/And shed over meadows far their sweet perfume." The poem ends with a vision of the yellowhammer building his nest in spring "With yellow breast and head of solid gold." Suddenly the bird's beauty flashes out, in great contrast with his homely nest, like the poet who makes beauty of the stuff of everyday life.

"The Skylark," written in rhyming couplets, evokes a country landscape populated with schoolboys racing to see who might be the first to pluck a newly opened buttercup. They are near the nest of a skylark but do not realize how close it is. The skylark flies "with happy wings/Winnows the air, till in the cloud she sings." The boys cannot imagine such a creature having a lowly nest on the ground "which anything/May come to destroy." They imagine, watching the bird soar and listening to its song, that if they were birds they would "build on nothing but a passing cloud." Yet the nest, "moist with the dews of morn, / Lies safely, with the leveret, in the corn." Again, as simple as the poem is taken at face value, it also seems to have another layer of meaning, again suggesting something about Clare as a poet, soaring above the earth, yet returning to his plain, safe nest.

"The Nightingale's Nest" has a similar theme, but in this poem it is the bird's beautiful song that stands in for the power of the poet. "Her wings would tremble in her ecstasy, and feathers stand on end, as 'twere with joy,/ And mouth wide open to release her heart! Of its out-sobbing songs."

Quite different are the poems Clare wrote after he was locked away in an insane asylum, such as the well-known "'I Am.'" Not surprisingly, nature is virtually gone from this poem. The poet cries out in despair: "I am! Yet what I am not cares or knows." In the last stanza, however, hope and nature creep back in. The poet longs for a return to his childhood and the chance to sleep as he did then: "The grass below—above the vaulted sky." At the same time, this line seems to suggest a longing for the grave.

Other Work by John Clare
The Early Poems of John Clare, 1804–1822. Edited by Eric Robinson and David Powell. New York: Oxford University Press, 1989.
Storey, Mark, ed. *Letters of John Clare.* New York: Oxford University Press, 1997.

A Work about John Clare
Goodridge, John, ed. *The Independent Spirit: John Clare and the Self-Taught Tradition.* Helpston, England: John Clare Society and Margaret Grainger Memorial Trust, 1994.

Clarke, Mary Victoria Cowden Novello
(1809–1898) *critic*

Mary Cowden Clarke, born Novello, was the sister of Alfred Novello, a major British publisher of classical music. In 1828 she married Charles Cowden Clarke, a noted lecturer on drama and Shakespeare's plays.

Mary Cowden Clarke published *The Complete Concordance to Shakespeare,* an alphabetical list of words found in his works, with examples. She completed the enormous task of compiling a concordance of the incomparably rich language in Shakespeare's plays in 1844–45. Her next work was *The Girlhood of Shakespeare's Heroines* (1851–52), in which she imagined the childhoods of famous Shakespearean characters such as Juliet and Ophelia and wrote fictional biographical accounts of them.

Together, the Cowden Clarkes published a series of works on William Shakespeare, including *The Shakespeare Key: Unlocking the Treasures of His Style* (1879). The couple moved to Genoa, Italy, in 1861. In 1878 they published their collections of famous writers whom they had known, including the romantic poet JOHN KEATS and the novelist CHARLES DICKENS. Cowden Clarke also published a biography of her husband in 1887, 10 years after his death, as well as her own autobiography in 1896.

Clarkson, Thomas (1760–1846) *essayist*
Born in Wisbech, Cambridgeshire, England, Thomas Clarkson was the son of John Clarkson, a schoolmaster and curate. While Clarkson was a child, his father died of a disease he contracted while caring for a sick parishioner. This act of self-sacrifice motivated Clarkson throughout his life.

In 1780 Clarkson enrolled at Cambridge University, where five years later he entered a writing contest to answer the question "Is it right to make slaves of others against their will?" His entry, *An Essay on the Slavery and Commerce of the Human Species* (1786), expresses a moral indignation for slavery and refutes the common justifications for its existence by proving that Africans are neither inferior, cursed, nor prisoners of war. Clarkson's essay gained him recognition and ignited his permanent passion for the abolitionist cause.

Clarkson helped found the Society for the Abolition of the Slave Trade and traveled constantly, lobbying politicians to gain support for abolition and compiling evidence to demonstrate the negative effects of slavery. In his next publication, *An Essay on the Impolicy of the Slave Trade* (1788), Clarkson uses this evidence to contend that slavery impedes commerce by restricting the growth of other trades.

After years of ceaseless work, Clarkson collapsed from exhaustion in 1794, but he resumed his efforts in 1805. The abolitionists soon succeeded, and in 1807 Parliament outlawed the slave trade. Clarkson then wrote *The History of the Rise, Progress, and Accomplishment of the Abolition of the Slave Trade* to celebrate the event.

Clarkson soon expanded the abolitionist cause by fighting for an international ban on slave trading and demanding the emancipation of slaves in the British colonies and the United States, arguing that emancipation would be economically advantageous. His popular essay *Thoughts on the Necessity of Improving the Conditions of the Slave* (1823) fueled support for the eventual passage in Britain of the Emancipation Act in 1833. Clarkson spent his remaining years denouncing slavery in the United States. SAMUEL TAYLOR COLERIDGE called him the "moral Steam-Engine, or the Giant with one idea." But Coleridge's praise reveals the reason that Clarkson's writings are no longer widely read: With the abolition of slavery, his essays lost much of their original resonance.

Clive, Caroline ("V.") (1801–1873) *novelist, poet*

Caroline Clive was the second daughter and co-heiress of Edmund Meysey-Wigley, of Shakenhurst, Worcestershire, and his wife, Anna Maria Meysey. Although she was born in London, she spent much of her childhood in Shakenhurst, where she developed polio and became lame. Her first volume of poems was published under the title *IX Poems by V.* (1840). The *V.* stood for "Vigolina," a nickname her husband, the Reverend Archer Clive, had given her. Much of her work was published under this pseudonym. The volume was reviewed favorably in the *Quarterly Review* and elsewhere.

Clive's first novel, *Paul Ferroll* (1855), established her reputation as an author and is what she is remembered for today. The plot of *Paul Ferroll* anticipates the sensation novel (*see* SENSATION FICTION): Its titular hero is a successful writer of "fine fiction," rich, handsome, protective of his servants, and also the murderer of his wife, Anne ("a woman of violent temper and unpopular among her servants"), whom he had married after being rejected by his true love, Elinor. Ferroll goes undetected throughout much of the novel, which enables him to marry Elinor and have a daughter, Janet. However, the truth finally emerges when Ferroll confesses his crime in order to save an innocent suspect. Elinor dies of shock at the revelation. The novel ends as Ferroll escapes with his faithful daughter. Perhaps because Clive felt that she had not achieved a satisfactory resolution in *Paul Ferroll*, she published *Why Paul Ferroll Killed his Wife* (1860), a peculiar kind of "prequel" that retains the former novel's plot structure but changes nearly all of characters' names. It was less critically successful.

Caroline Clive's first published work was a religious tract issued under the pseudonym Paul Ferroll. She published many other volumes of poetry, novels, and short stories before her writing career was cut short; she burned to death when her dress caught fire while she was writing in her room. The critic Charlotte Mitchell summarizes the importance of *Paul Ferroll* in words that could serve for the best of Clive's works: "*Paul Ferroll* is isolated, peculiar, forceful, and memorable: it does not deserve its obscurity." *Paul Ferroll* was reprinted in 1997 by Oxford University Press.

Clough, Arthur Hugh (1819–1861) poet

Arthur Clough (his last name rhymes with *rough*) was born on New Year's Day in Liverpool, England. At age four he moved with his family to the United States, where they spent six years in South Carolina. His father was a cotton merchant, but his mother influenced him more strongly with her religious beliefs. Clough's religious education was furthered when his family returned to England and he was enrolled at Rugby, where he was the favorite student of the headmaster, Dr. THOMAS ARNOLD. Later, he was a bright and active student at Balliol College, Oxford University. There he met fellow student MATTHEW ARNOLD, and the two became lifelong friends. At Oxford, Clough was politically active. He was influenced by the writing of the essayist and thinker THOMAS CARLYLE, and wrote many pamphlets promoting change in education, politics, and economics. He also wrote his first and best-known book, a verse-novel called *The Bothie of Tober-na-Vuolich* (1848). Written in hexameters, it tells the story of a group of students who spend a long vacation in Scotland, and of the love affair one of them has with a shepherd's daughter. Through the dialogue of his characters, Clough addressed the issues that most concerned him, including social class and gender relations.

He had accepted a fellowship at Oxford, but he resigned in 1848 after developing doubts about his religious convictions. Clough's search for truth would inspire his poetry, and his doubt would cloud his career; he was turned down for other academic positions because of it. After giving up the Oxford fellowship, he decided to see the world. He wanted to experience "actual life," he said, from which he felt sheltered as a student at Oxford. He loved to travel and spent time in America, Australia, and Italy. The American essayist and poet Ralph Waldo Emerson, with whom he corresponded, persuaded him to return to the United States. Although Clough spent time there, lecturing and translating, he was not successful, and returned to England after only a year. On his return, in 1853, he married Blanche Smith, a cousin of FLORENCE NIGHTINGALE. He spent the rest of his life working in education.

Some of Clough's contemporaries felt that his writing was inaccessible to most readers. WALTER BAGEHOT, however, commended Clough's conservative, intellectual, upper-class point of view. Today, Clough's work, with its doubt and skepticism, is seen as representative of the spiritual turmoil of the Victorian age.

Most of Clough's work was published posthumously, and most of his poems reveal his spiritual agitation and doubt. Among these writings are "Dipsychus," an unfinished poem consisting of dialogue between the poet and a devilish spirit; *Amours de Voyage*, an epistolary verse-novel about English tourists in Italy, written in 1858; and an unfinished series of tales in verse, modeled on Chaucer's *Canterbury Tales*, called *Mari Magno*. His work is sometimes compared to that of 20th-century writers Ezra Pound and T. S. Eliot, because of its satiric self-introspection. These lines from the close of *Amours de Voyage* illustrate his protagonist Claude's bitter disillusionment with received religious and emotional comforts: "Not as the Scripture says, is, I think, the fact. Ere our death-day, / Faith, I think, does pass, and Love; but Knowledge abideth. / Let us seek Knowledge;—the rest may come and go as it happens." It is tempting to see this as an expression of Clough's own point of view, but, as the scholar Michael Timko points out, Claude is a fictional character, not a mouthpiece; although Clough certainly understood Claude's feelings, his "main purpose ... in this tragic-comedy is the exposé of a self-centered prig unable to realize ... the necessity of striking a balance between theory and practice." In Claude, Clough mocked himself.

Clough died in Florence after an attack of malaria. His lifelong friend Matthew Arnold wrote an elegiac poem, "Thyrsis," to honor him.

Critical Analysis

Much of Clough's poetry is representative of the doubt and ambiguity many Victorians felt about institutionalized religion. Two poems that provide a nice introducton to Clough's take on the subject of religion are "The Latest Decalogue" and "There Is No God, the Wicked Sayeth." These are witty, almost gnomic looks at the hypocrisy of people who call themselves religious. "The Latest Decalogue" is a parody in rhymed couplets of the Ten Commandments, as interpreted by various individuals to their own advantage. Clough notes that the Commandments prohibit the worship of graven images, then adds, "except the currency." Perhaps the most chilling couplet is this: "Thou shalt not kill, but need'st not strive / Officiously to keep alive." It is hard to imagine a more succinct statement of the indifference of Victorian upper classes to the plight of the poor.

"There Is No God, the Wicked Sayeth" begins with a rhymed quatrain that sums up the essential thrust of the poem:

> "There is no God," the wicked Saith,
> "And truly it's a blessing,
> "For what He might have done with us
> It's better only guessing."

Various others express gratitiude at the absence of a god to judge their actions. The tradesman says that it would be funny if God "should take it ill in me/To make a little money." The rich man chooses not to believe because he and his family "Are not in want of victual." However,

> almost everyone when age,
> Disease, or sorrows strike him,
> Inclines to think there is a God,
> Or something very like Him.

Clough deals with some of the same concepts more seriously in some of his sonnets. "That children in their loveliness should die" is akin to the question posed in Dostoyevsky's *The Brothers Karamazov* about how a belief in God can be reconciled with the suffering of children. He says that how children "Should suddenly dissolve and cease to be/Is the extreme of all perplexity." This question has plagued religious doubters for thousands of years.

Other Works by Arthur Clough

Kenney, Anthony, ed. *The Oxford Diaries of Arthur Hugh Clough.* Oxford, England: Oxford University Press, 1990.

Plutarch's Lives. 2 vols. New York: Random House, 2001.

Works about Arthur Clough

Greenberger, Evelyn Barish. *Arthur Hugh Clough: Growth of a Poet's Mind.* Cambridge, Mass.: Harvard University Press, 1970.

Timko, Michael. *Innocent Victorian: The Satiric Poetry of Arthur Hugh Clough.* Athens: University of Ohio Press, 1966.

Waddington, Samuel. *Arthur Hugh Clough (A Monograph).* New York: AMS Press, 1975.

Cobbe, Frances Power (1822–1904)
nonfiction writer

Frances Power Cobbe was born in Dublin, Ireland. Her mother was Frances Conway Cobbe, and her father, Charles Cobbe was a well-to-do Dublin landowner. She was educated primarily at home, where she studied history and literature with private tutors. Although she was raised a Calvinist, Cobbe gradually began to question those religious teachings. She eventually became agnostic, which appalled her father.

Cobbe was a student of the ideas of Theodore Parker, a Boston clergyman and leader of Unitarianism, whose writings she edited after his death. In 1855 she wrote her own book, *Essay on Intuitive Morals*, a consideration of religious teachings and the origins of morality.

In 1858 Cobbe moved to Bristol, England, where she taught at a school for prostitutes and girls who had been in prison. She was part of the antivivisection movement, campaigning against the common use of live animals for scientific research. She was also a strong supporter of the vote for women. Much of her writing is devoted to the suffragist cause. As she wrote in *Why Women Desire the Franchise* (1872), "how the burdens of the poor toilers are to be made less intolerable; how wives are to be protected from brutal husbands . . . may need more than all the men and women in England together may possess. But it is quite certain that if women had heretofore been represented in Parliament, such evils and wrongs would never have reached, unchecked, their present height."

Cobbe believed strongly that women should be able to pursue their own careers to avoid being financially dependent on men. Among her works advocating social change were *The Final Cause of Women* (1869) and *The Scientific Spirit of the Age* (1888). She never married, but lived for 34 years in Bristol with Mary Lloyd.

A Work about Frances Cobbe
Caine, Barbara. *Victorian Feminists.* New York: Oxford University Press, 1997.

Cobbett, William (1763–1835) *nonfiction writer*

William Cobbett was born in Hampshire, England. His father was an innkeeper who had little time to educate William, but the boy learned how to read and taught himself. At age 13 he left home and became a gardener for King George III in Windsor, then later moved to London, where he worked for a lawyer.

Cobbett enlisted in the army soon afterward and was sent to Nova Scotia, where he met Ann Reid, whom he later married. In 1792 Cobbett and his wife moved to America. Writing under the pseudonym Peter Porcupine, he published two magazines, the *Censor* and *Porcupine's Gazette*, in which he supported the position of the Federalist Party led by Alexander Hamilton. He was violently attacked by opposition politicians for the stand he took and, accused of libel, fled back to England.

Cobbett soon started *Cobbett's Political Register*, a weekly newspaper in which he championed liberal causes, such as abolishing beatings as a punishment for soldiers. When his opponents had him arrested, he continued to publish his views from prison.

In 1816 Cobbett's newspaper supported the rights of factory workers, and once again he found himself the object of intense opposition. Cobbett hastily left for the United States and resumed publication of his newspaper. Two years later, he again returned to England, and in 1832 he became a member of Parliament. He ardently supported the rights of workers until his death.

Other Work by William Cobbett
Wilson, David A., ed. *Peter Porcupine in America: Pamphlets on Republicanism and Revolution.* Ithaca, N.Y.: Cornell University Press, 1994.

A Work about William Cobbett
Nattrass, Leonora. *William Cobbett: The Politics of Style.* Cambridge, England: Cambridge University Press, 1995.

Colenso, John William (1814–1883) *nonfiction writer*

John William Colenso was born in Cornwall, England, where his father was a mineral agent. His childhood was a struggle because his father lost a fortune in the Cornish tin mines when Colenso was a boy, and Colenso had to work to pay for his own education. He went to St. John's College, Cambridge, and later worked as a mathematics tutor from 1842 to 1846.

In 1846 Colenso married Sarah Frances Bunyon, became a vicar in Norfolk, and started earning money by writing mathematics textbooks. But his life took a dramatic turn in 1853 when he was appointed the first Anglican bishop of Natal and moved to Africa. He quickly achieved notoriety by advocating African rights, promoting a missionary campaign among the Zulu, translating the New Testament into Zulu, publishing controversial unorthodox treatises, tolerating polygamy, considering the Zulu equal to Christians in God's eyes, and even supporting the Zulu after they defeated British troops at Isandhlwana in 1879.

Colenso's experience of the African landscape made him aware of the vastness of geological time. His new awareness of geology, together with the questions of the Zulus who helped in his translation of the Bible, caused him to examine the Bible critically. When in 1861 he published *Commentary on Romans,* a critical analysis of Saint Paul's epistle, the controversy that followed resulted in his being excommunicated by Bishop Gray, the bishop of Cape Town. A question he asks in *Commentary* makes the difficulty of his position as a missionary and representative of the church poignantly clear: "How is it possible to teach the Zulus to cast off their superstitious belief in witchcraft, if they are required to believe that all the stories of sorcery and demonology which they find in the Bible . . . are infallibly and divinely true?"

London courts reinstated Colenso, but he fearlessly jeopardized his position again by publishing *The Pentateuch and the Book of Joshua Critically Examined,* in which he described the process that brought him to the conclusion that "the Pentateuch . . . cannot personally have been written by Moses . . . and, further, that the (so-called) Mosaic narrative, by whomsoever written, and though imparting to us, as I fully believe it does, revelations of the Divine Will and Character, cannot be regarded as historically true." He went on to displease his superiors further by protesting Natal's banishment of a Zulu chief in 1873 and going to England to argue successfully for the chief's reinstatement. Jonathan Draper stresses "Colenso's emphasis on the value and importance of natural religion, of the universal operation of conscience, and of equality of all races and cultures," and points out that "his teaching encouraged the emergence of a Zulu national identity and cultural revival."

Works about John William Colenso

Hinchliff, Peter B. *John William Colenso.* London: Nelson, 1964.

Landow, George P. "Bishop Colenso and the Literal Truth of the Bible." (Adapted from George P. Landow, *The Aesthetic and Critical Theories of John Ruskin.* Princeton, N.J.: Princeton University Press, 1971.) The Victorian Web. Available online. URL: http://www.victorianweb.org/victorian/religion/colenso.html. Accessed July 3, 2008.

Coleridge, David Hartley (1796–1849)
poet

Born in Bristol, England, Hartley Coleridge was the eldest of the four children of Sara and SAMUEL TAYLOR COLERIDGE. As a child he delighted his parents with his mental agility and creativity, and inspired both his father and WILLIAM WORDSWORTH to write poems about him. His upbringing was somewhat tumultuous. His parents, who had a difficult and loveless marriage, separated in 1806, and for eight years he went without seeing his troubled father. Friends of the family took up a collection to send Coleridge to Oxford University, but he was dismissed in 1820 because of his uncontrolled drinking. He moved to Grasmere in the Lake District, lived with a friend, and submitted poems to periodicals such as *London Magazine* and *Blackwood's.* His poems include such beautiful sonnets as "On Prayer," "To Homer," and "To Shakespeare," with its memorable opening: "The soul of man is larger than the sky, / Deeper than the ocean, or the abysmal dark / of the unfathomed center." His most sustained work, however, is the nonfiction *Biographia Borealis; or, Lives of the Northern Worthies* (1852). He wrote a wicked parody of "Lucy," a famous poem by Wordsworth, that begins, "He lived amidst th' untrodden ways / To Rydal Lake that lead:— / A bard whom there were were none to praise, / And very few to read."

After his death, his collected poems, as well as some essays, were published by his brother Derwent. The scholar Richard Garnett says of Coleridge, "His pure style is admirable for its elegance and perfect adaptation to the matter at hand. His poems . . . are not sufficiently powerful for vivid remembrance and are much too good for oblivion."

Coleridge, Mary Elizabeth (1861–1907)
poet, novelist, essayist

The great-granddaughter of James Coleridge, the brother of SAMUEL TAYLOR COLERIDGE, Mary Elizabeth Coleridge lived in London all her life. Her affluent parents, Mary Anne Jameson Coleridge and the barrister and author Arthur Duke Coleridge, included literary celebrities among their friends. Thus their daughter crossed paths with ALFRED, LORD TENNYSON, ROBERT BROWNING, JOHN RUSKIN, and others. Coleridge traveled widely with her family and spoke and read Hebrew, French, Italian, German, and Greek. When she was in her 20s she started teaching at the Working Women's College and, less formally, in the homes of individual working women. Coleridge never married.

Essays by Coleridge began to appear in 1881 and were collected in *Non Sequitur* (1900). Her first novel was *The Seven Sleepers of Ephesus* (1893), about a secret society in revolutionary Germany. Although it was admired by ROBERT LOUIS STEVENSON, the public perhaps deemed it too fantastical. Her second, though, *The King with Two Faces* (1897), a historical romance, proved popular. Other novels include *The Fiery Dawn* (1901), which, like the others, illustrates Coleridge's belief that history is "chock full of improbabilities," and *The Lady on the Drawing-Room Floor* (1906).

Today, however, Coleridge is most keenly appreciated for her verse, which she began writing at age 13. Content with keeping this work private, she was in her mid-30s when ROBERT BRIDGES was able to convince her to publish the volume *Fancy's Following* (1896). This was one of two books of her poems published in her lifetime; the other was *Fancy's Guerdon* (1897). Both times Coleridge used a pseudonym, Anodos, after the main character in *Phantastes* by GEORGE MACDONALD. *Anodos* is Greek for "on no road." Upon Coleridge's death, *Poems* (1907) appeared, and additional verse taken from her letters and diaries was included in *Gathered Leaves* (1910).

Engaging issues of female identity, her poems are sometimes seen as a step in the transition of women from the domesticity a patriarchal society imposed on them to greater independence and autonomy. In the poem "The Witch," for example, the titular speaker, like the Ancient Mariner a wanderer in a frigid landscape, pleads for shelter: "Oh, lift me over the threshold, and let me in at the door!" The reference to being lifted over the threshold suggests a longing for marriage—more generally, what exists on the other side of the door—but the "witch" comes at the last to represent those women who are married and who are trapped indoors, frustrated in their desire to attain autonomy, respect, and independence.

Another recurrent motif is the mirror. "The Other Side of a Mirror" presents the same drama as "The Witch," only with the two halves of the image on the same side of the door and with the connection between them more plainly drawn. The first line, "I sat before my glass one day," calmly establishes the female speaker's ordinary existence. The face in the mirror, however, reveals the dissatisfaction of this seemingly contented person. This woman, representing multitudes, is "jealous" of the power and authority that men routinely wield and of the freedom they take for granted. She covets "fierce revenge" at the realization that these privileges come at her expense.

Coleridge wrote considerably lighter verse as well. But it is her darker poems that still delight today—enough so, in fact, that Bridges's tribute to her after her death may now strike us as naïve and as missing the point: "[Coleridge] did not write poems . . . because she thought she had valuable moral lessons for well-intentioned people. Her poetry is the irrepressible song of a fancy whose vagaries she would have thought it impertinent to analyze."

Works about Mary Elizabeth Coleridge
Battersby, Christine. "Her Blood and His Mirror: Mary Coleridge, Luce Irigaray and the Female Self," in *Beyond Representation: Philosophy and Poetic Imagination*, edited by Richard Thomas

Eldridge. New York: Cambridge University Press, 1996.

Crisp, Shelley Jean. *The Woman Poet Emerges: The Literary Tradition of Mary Coleridge, Alice Meynell, and Charlotte Mew.* Amherst: University of Massachusetts Press, 1987.

Coleridge, Samuel Taylor (1772–1834)
poet, critic

Samuel Taylor Coleridge was born October 21 in Ottery St. Mary, Devon, England, to John Coleridge, a minister, and his wife, Ann Bowden Coleridge. When Coleridge's father died in 1781, the boy was sent to Christ's Hospital in London, a charity school for the children of clergy. Coleridge excelled in the study of the classics, and, in 1791, entered Cambridge University to continue his studies. During his time at school, Coleridge suffered bouts of rheumatic fever, which troubled him for the rest of his life and may have led to his addiction to opium, which probably began the same year he started college.

While at Cambridge, Coleridge read Thomas Paine, WILLIAM GODWIN, and Voltaire, whose radical political thinking, particularly about individual freedoms and rights, would lead the young man to embrace the principles of the French Revolution. He also read David Hartley, whose *Observations on Man, his Frame, his Duty and his Expectations* (1749) influenced Coleridge's thinking on how the mind worked. He met the poet ROBERT SOUTHEY, and the two planned a sociopolitical movement they dubbed Pantisocracy (or "equal rule for all"). The young poets decided to move to America to establish this new social order. As part of the plan, Coleridge married Sara Fricker, the sister of Southey's fiancée. However, the utopian plan fell apart, and Coleridge found himself married to a woman he did not love.

By 1797 Coleridge had published two volumes of poetry to good reviews. But in that same year, Coleridge met the poet WILLIAM WORDSWORTH and the latter's sister DOROTHY WORDSWORTH. This meeting forever changed the lives of all three, for from it emerged *Lyrical Ballads* (1798), the work that marked the official beginning of ROMANTICISM in England. Wordsworth and Coleridge sought to revolutionize poetry by writing verse that used less conventional poetic language and addressed humanity's relationship to nature.

In this volume Wordsworth wrote poems that gave "the charm of novelty to things of every day," while Coleridge focused on "persons and characters supernatural, or at least romantic." Coleridge's contribution to *Lyrical Ballads* included his most famous poem, "The Rime of the Ancient Mariner." Although Coleridge did not publish them until much later, during this same period he also wrote two other noteworthy poems, "Christabel" and "Kubla Khan." The former, written in ballad form, is a tale of gothic horror, in which the virgin Christabel is pursued by the wicked Geraldine. Coleridge added to "Christabel" in 1800 but never completed the original design.

"Kubla Khan" also remained unfinished. Coleridge claimed that the poem came to him all at once in an opium-induced dream and that, when he sat down to write it, he was interrupted by a visitor from the nearby town of Porlock and was unable to recapture the vision. Beginning with John Livingston Lowe's monumental study of Coleridge's poetry, *The Road to Xanadu* (1927), scholars dismiss this story as a fanciful excuse by the poet for his inability to finish the work. The poem centers on a vision of the palace of the Chinese Emperor Kubla Khan:

> *In Xanadu did Kubla Khan*
> *A stately pleasure dome decree:*
> *Where Alph, the sacred river, ran*
> *Through caverns measureless to man*
> *Down to a sunless sea.*

Most critics agree that Coleridge's fame as a poet rests on these three works, which the biographer Sir Edmund Chambers referred to as "a handful of golden poems." After 1802 Coleridge turned more to philosophy and criticism. His great work of criticism, *Biographia Literaria*

(1817), outlined his ideas on the power of poetry and on his concept of the imagination, which allows the mind to transcend the world perceived by the senses and to discover what lies beyond. Of imagination, Coleridge says, "The primary imagination I hold to be the living power and prime agent of all human perception, and as a repetition in the finite mind of the eternal act of creation in the infinite I AM."

In 1810 a mention by Wordsworth of Coleridge's drug use to a mutual friend led to a quarrel between the two and ended their friendship. In the same year, Coleridge separated from his wife.

In 1816, in an attempt to curb his opium use, Coleridge went to live with the surgeon James Gillman. Gillman's house soon became a center of literary activity as younger writers came to visit Coleridge.

Critical Analysis

When it was first published, "The Rime of the Ancient Mariner" was not well received, and it was some time before this story of a sailor who shoots an albatross and must atone for his act was recognized as among the greatest ballads in English. This mysterious tale of sin and penance has its roots in the biblical tale of Cain and Abel and in the legend of the Wandering Jew. According to Coleridge's own introductory annotation to the work, the poem is about

> How a Ship, having first sailed to the Equator, was driven by Storms to the cold Country towards the South Pole; how the Ancient mariner cruelly and in contempt of the laws of hospitality killed a Sea-bird and how he was followed by many and strange Judgements; and in what manner he came back to his own Country.

But it is the language and striking imagery of the poem that has ensured its place in English literature and that invests the work with its deep and complex symbolism.

As the poem begins, the Ancient Mariner stops a man on his way to a wedding and begins to tell his story. The listener, at first reluctant, finds that he cannot turn away from this gripping tale of sin and penance. The Mariner's ship has been blown to the South Pole where it is trapped by "ice, masthigh." An albatross comes "through the fog . . . As if it had been a Christian soul," and the men hail it "in God's name," because the bird brings with it a "good south wind" that frees the ship. The albatross then accompanies the ship on its journey north until one day, the Ancient Mariner declares, "With my cross-bow / I shot the Albatross." This act appears to be one of pure, unmotivated evil, leading many critics to compare the mariner with Shakespeare's Iago and Milton's Satan. Punishment is immediate. The ship is blown to the equator, where the wind stops and the ship is stranded. The sailors' situation is bleak:

> *Water, water, every where,*
> *And all the boards did shrink;*
> *Water, water every where,*
> *Nor any drop to drink.*
>
> *The very deep did rot: O Christ!*
> *That ever this should be!*
> *Yea, slimy things did crawl with legs*
> *Upon the slimy sea.*

"Instead of the cross," the sailors hang the albatross around the Mariner's neck.

In scenes of incredible descriptive power, the sailors die before the Mariner's eyes. In "agony," the Mariner glances into the sea and notices the beauty of water snakes: "Blue, glossy green, and velvet black . . . every track . . . a flash of golden fire." In a flash of insight he is able to pray, and the albatross falls from his neck. The ship is moved by spirits who return the Mariner to his own "countree," where he finds a hermit who will "shrieve" his soul and "wash away / The Albatross's blood." The mariner again is overcome with "agony" and forced to tell his tale to the hermit. Now, the mariner says, he must wander the earth telling his story to those who "must hear" him. Reluctant as he was to hear the tale, the wedding guest finds himself at the end, "a sadder and a wiser man" for having listened.

Wordsworth called Coleridge "the most wonderful" person he had ever known and celebrated the great power of his intellect when he wrote: "The rapt One, of the godlike forehead, / The heaven-eyed creature." The essayist CHARLES LAMB, a lifelong friend, said of Coleridge that "his face when he repeats his verses hath an ancient glory, an Arch angel a little damaged." As the scholar Russell Noyes observes, Coleridge "influenced his epoch by great original poetry and advanced critical theory."

Other Work by Samuel Taylor Coleridge
Poems and Prose. New York: Random House, 1997.

Works about Samuel Taylor Coleridge
Christie, William. *Samuel Taylor Coleridge: A Literary Life.* New York: Palgrave Macmillan, 2006.
Holmes, Richard. *Coleridge.* New York: HarperCollins, 1998.
Lowe, John Livingston. *The Road to Xanadu: A Study in the Ways of the Imagination.* Boston: Houghton Mifflin, 1927.

Collins, Mortimer (1827–1876) *poet, novelist*

Mortimer Collins was born on June 29 in Plymouth, Devon, on the south coast of southwest England. His father, Francis, was a lawyer, mathematician, and poet. Collins attended private schools and later worked as a private tutor to the children of well-to-do families. He eventually became a mathematics professor at Queen Elizabeth's College on the island of Guernsey in the Channel Islands. He married Susannah Crump in 1849; the couple had one child, a daughter. Collins published his first book of light, humorous poetry, *Idyls and Rhymes,* in 1855, followed by *Summer Songs* (1860). The conclusion of "Winter in Brighton" gives a taste of his style:

If you approve of flirtations, good dinners
Seascapes divine which the merry winds whiten
Nice little saints and still nicer young sinners—
Winter in Brighton!

In 1862 Collins moved his family to the county of Berkshire, northwest of London, where his wife died in 1867. He remarried a year later; his new wife, Frances Cotton, collaborated with him on some of his later works. To support his family, Collins wrote several humorous novels, including *Sweet Anne Page* (1868), a semi-autobiographical novel that one critic deemed "indecorous," and *The Ivory Gate,* whose hero, Collins writes, has "four things to hinder him: his luck, his intellect, his temperament, and his temper," and becomes a novelist for want of anything better. Collins kept a tiring work schedule, writing not only during the day but well into the night. In addition to writing novels, he also contributed witty articles to magazines, including *Punch,* the *Globe,* and the *British Quarterly.*

Collins, William Wilkie (1824–1889) *novelist, short story writer*

Wilkie Collins was born in London to the landscape painter William Collins and his wife, Harriet Geddes Collins. At age 11, Collins was sent to school at the Maida Hill Academy, but he withdrew a year later to spend two years in Italy and France with his parents. Collins said that he learned more from living in Italy than he ever did in school. He returned to school in London, and it was here that he first learned he had a talent for storytelling. The school bully loved stories, and Collins used his gift to stave off beatings. "It was this brute," Collins said, "who first awakened in me, his poor little victim, a power of which but for him I might never have been aware."

Collins left school at age 17 and went to work for a tea merchant. At about the same time, he began writing for publication. In 1843 his first story, "The Last Stage Coachman," in which the narrator dreams of a time when only one horse-drawn stagecoach remains to be replaced by steam-powered vehicles, appeared in the *Illuminated Magazine*. In 1846 Collins began to study law, but although he was admitted to the bar five years later, he never practiced.

In 1848 Collins's first book appeared: *The Memoirs of the Life of William Collins, Esq., R.A.*, a memoir of his father, who had died the previous year. Two years later, Collins published his first novel, *Antonina*, a historical adventure tale set in ancient Rome. *Basil* (1852) is more typical of Collins, with its contemporary setting and its story of seduction and vengeance.

In 1851 Collins was introduced to CHARLES DICKENS by their mutual friend Augustus Egg, a painter. Dickens and Collins became great friends, and many of Collins's most popular novels were serialized by Dickens in his journals *Household Words* and *All the Year Round*. The first story Collins contributed to *Household Words* was "A Terribly Strange Bed" (1852), a Poe-like horror story that is still anthologized today. Two of Collins's best works, *The Woman in White* (1860) and *The Moonstone* (1868), were serialized by Dickens.

Collins and Dickens also worked together in amateur theatricals, with both appearing in 1851 in EDWARD BULWER-LYTTON's play *Not So Bad as We Seem*. For the duo's amateur troupe, Collins also wrote several plays, including *The Frozen Deep* (1856), which is about self-sacrifice on an endangered Arctic expedition and which in 1874 he adapted as a short novel.

Collins and Dickens corresponded extensively and traveled together. They even collaborated on *The Perils of Certain English Prisoners* (1857), a nonfiction work about the Indian mutiny against British imperial rule in India. Many critics feel that Dickens and Collins complemented and influenced each other's work. Dickens was a master of characterization, while Collins was known for his intricate plots. Each learned from the other.

The friendship between the writers was strained by Collins's unorthodox lifestyle and his use of opium. Collins lived openly with a mistress, Carolyn Graves, who was the inspiration for *The Woman in White*. Collins first met Graves while walking with a friend one evening in 1856. He heard a scream from a nearby house, then saw running from the house "the figure of a young and very beautiful woman dressed in flowing white robes that shone in the moonlight." The woman was Graves. They lived together for many years but never married. In 1864 Collins set up the 19-year-old Martha Rudd as his second mistress in a house just a few blocks from where he and Graves lived. Rudd bore Collins three children. Graves left Collins in 1868 to marry, but returned two years later and lived with him for the rest of his life. When Collins died, his will specified in that his property be evenly divided between Graves and Rudd.

Collins became addicted to opium because of painful attacks of rheumatic gout. Sir William Fergusson, a surgeon, claimed that Collins took enough opium every day to kill 12 people. Opium, which figured prominently in many of Collins's novels, notably in *The Moonstone*, eventually eroded his ability to write, and his later novels are disjointed.

Critical Analysis

Wilkie Collins was a prolific writer. In his lifetime he wrote 25 novels, more than 50 short stories, 15 plays, and more than 100 nonfiction pieces. Two works most often read today are *The Woman in White* and *The Moonstone*; each of these established a new genre.

The Woman in White established the formula for SENSATION FICTION, fiction filled with crime, characters harboring dark secrets, and sex. Using multiple narrators—a technique that Collins developed after listening to court testimony—the author tells the lurid tale of the wicked Sir Percival Glyde's attempts to steal the fortune of his wife, the woman in white. As the principal narrator, Walter Hartright, explains to the reader:

No circumstances of importance, from the beginning to the end of the disclosure, shall be related on hearsay evidence.... Thus the story here will be told by more than one pen, as a story of an offence against the laws is told in Court by more than one witness.

This spellbinding tale also allows Collins to discourse on the dangers of marriage, especially for women, who in Victorian England gave over all rights to their husbands. The novel was a tremendous popular success, so much so that it inspired merchandise, much in the manner of today's movies, from Woman in White perfume to Woman in White cloaks. There was even a song, "The Woman in White Waltz." As the scholar John Sutherland notes, "*The Woman in White* remains among the two or three novels of the period which . . . [retain] sheer page-turning readability."

The Moonstone takes its title from a huge yellow diamond stolen from a Hindu temple and presented to Rachel Verinder on her 21st birthday. It is stolen on the very night she receives it, and the rest of the novel tells of the efforts that are made to discover the identity of the thief. The story takes on an exotic tone with the introduction of Indian characters who are trying to restore the stone to its rightful place in the temple.

The Moonstone is widely thought to be the first detective novel: T. S. Eliot called it "the first, the longest, and the best of modern English detective novels." It established many of the conventions of the genre, including the detective who is much more canny than the local police, several plausible suspects, the withholding of key information, multiple viewpoints, twists and turns of plot, and the revelation of the truth before a group of suspects. In *The Moonstone,* as in other novels by Collins, those on the fringes of polite society are portrayed with great sympathy. This is certainly the case with the servant girl Rosanna Spearman, who has the temerity to fall in love with the hero of the story and whose suicide becomes a key to solving the mystery.

The novel is meticulously plotted, and opium plays a large role in its unraveling. As the critic Althea Hayter says, *The Moonstone* "has a Chinese box intricacy; the actions of an opium-dosed man are described by an opium addict who is the invention of a writer heavily dosed with opium." A famous scene in the novel in which Rosanna describes an area of quicksand has all the earmarks of an opium dream: "It looks as if it had hundreds of suffocating people under it—all struggling to get to the surface, and all sinking lower and lower in the dreadful deeps!"

Despite their exotic overtones, Collins's mysteries were enjoyed by his contemporaries because of the familiarity of the people and places in the stories. As HENRY JAMES said, "To Mr. Collins belongs the credit of having introduced into fiction those most mysterious of mysteries, the mysteries which are at our own doors." According to the scholar Julian Thompson, Collins's "rich gifts for characterization and the sustenance of narrative constitute a major part of his appeal. . . . Not the whole of it, however. . . . Collins allows us to glimpse areas of Victorian society usually hidden from fictional consideration."

Other Works by Wilkie Collins
The Haunted Hotel. New York: Dover, 1982.
Thompson, Julian, ed. *The Complete Shorter Fiction.* New York: Carroll & Graf, 1995.

Works about Wilkie Collins
Gasson, Andrew. *Wilkie Collins: An Illustrated Guide.* Oxford: Oxford University Press, 1998.
Nayder, Lillian. *Wilkie Collins.* Boston: Twayne, 1997.
Taylor, Jenny Bourne. *The Cambridge Companion to Wilkie Collins.* Cambridge: Cambridge University Press, 2006.
Thom, Peter. *The Windings of the Labyrinth: Quest and Structure in the Major Novels of Wilkie Collins.* Columbus: Ohio State University Press, 1992.

Condition of England novel
This term refers to a type of novel that flourished in the 1830s and 1840s and that focused on finding solutions to the problems resulting from

industrialization of Great Britain. The phrase "Condition of England" first appeared in *Chartism*, an 1839 pamphlet written by THOMAS CARLYLE. The first chapter, "Condition-of-England Question," begins: "A feeling very generally exists that the condition and disposition of the Working Classes is a rather ominous matter at present; that something ought to be said, something ought to be done, in regard to it." One solution to this question was the Chartist movement, which swept across England at this time, demanding better conditions for factory workers (who often toiled six days a week, 12 hours a day, in unsanitary conditions for little pay) and universal male suffrage. Until nearly the end of the 19th century, only male property owners of a certain income were allowed to vote.

Like the Chartists, Condition of England novelists pointed out the gulf between the rich and poor and proposed a variety of means to reduce it. Among these novelists were BENJAMIN DISRAELI, the author and politician, who wrote *Sybil; or, The Two Nations* (1845). *Sybil* focuses on an aristocrat, Charles Egremont, who conceals his identity in order to get closer to the title character and her father, who are Chartists. Egremont gradually learns through his experiences that England is divided into "two nations," those who have and those who have not: "Two nations; between whom there is no intercourse and no sympathy; who are as ignorant of each other's habits, thoughts, and feelings, as if they were dwelling in different zones, or inhabitants of different planets..."

Other writers who concentrated on social conditions included CHARLOTTE BRONTË in *Shirley* (1849) and CHARLES KINGSLEY in *Alton Locke* (1850). In *Shirley* Brontë focuses on the hardship brought about as skilled craftspeople are replaced by machines, which do the same work faster and cheaper. *Alton Locke* is a fictional autobiography of a working man and poet. Locke, young and idealistic, is drawn to radical political causes, becomes a Chartist, and is eventually imprisoned for it. Detractors of the novel complain that it is little better than propaganda for Kingsley's Christian Socialist beliefs, while its supporters admire his vivid accounts of the conditions of the poor and depiction of the inner workings of radical politics.

In 1848 ELIZABETH GASKELL published *Mary Barton*, which described the living conditions of the poor in Manchester: "You went down one step even from the foul area into the cellar in which a family of human beings lived. It was very dark inside. The window-panes many of them were broken and stuffed with rags..." Originally Gaskell planned to call her novel *John Barton*, after the character of a dispossessed working man who murders a factory owner and becomes a Chartist. Her publisher advised her to retitle the novel after his daughter to lessen the political connotations and enhance the love story. In *Mary Barton*, Gaskell depicts the suffering of the poor of Manchester in a realistic and compassionate light. Her projected solution to the problem of the "two nations" of rich and poor is not violent agitation, like John Barton, but Christian compassion. In 1855 Gaskell wrote another Condition of England novel, *North and South* about a clergyman's daughter who converts a factory owner to Christian charity during a violent strike.

Perhaps the most famous Condition of England novel is CHARLES DICKENS's *Hard Times*. Dickens had exposed the miserable conditions of factory towns, poor houses, and urban slums in such novels as *Oliver Twist* (1837) and *David Copperfield* (1849). *Hard Times*, however, is his most direct and political statement about the lives of factory workers and the class divide in England. Dedicated to Thomas Carlyle, the novel depicts life in the fictional Coketown, based on Manchester. Dickens uses satire to attack what he sees as the ills of society—the reduction of human life to a series of "facts" in the character of the merchant Gradgrind and the heartlessness of industrial capitalism, embodied by Mr. Bounderby the industrialist. Like Gaskell, Dickens advocates Christian charity as an antidote to the suffering and alienation that result from industrialization.

Works about Condition of England Novel
Gallagher, Catherine. *The Industrial Reformation of English Fiction: Social Discourse and Narrative Form, 1832–1867*. Chicago: University of Chicago Press, 1985.
Guy, Josephine. *The Victorian Social Problem Novel: The Market, the Individual, and Communal Life*. New York: St. Martin's Press, 1996.

Cook, Eliza (1818–1889) poet

Eliza Cook was born in London. She was the youngest of 11 children in the family of Joseph Cook, a brass worker, who retired from his business when Cook was nine and moved his family to a small farm near Horsham, in Sussex.

Cook was almost entirely self-taught and, encouraged by her mother, began writing poetry early, publishing her first collection, *Lays of a Wild Harp*, at age 17. One of her most frequently anthologized poems, "The Old Arm-Chair," is a tribute to her mother, who died when Cook was 15. Later set to music by the composer Henry Russell, it contains the lines, "I learnt how much the heart can bear / When I saw her die in that old Arm-chair." Cook wrote sentimental lyrics and messages in rhymed couplets and simple meter to which readers found it easy to relate. Indeed, Cook was extremely popular with the semieducated middle class; women, in particular, appreciated the candor of her work that spoke of lost love and betrayal, and lives of drudgery.

In 1849 Cook established her own magazine, *Eliza Cook's Journal*, a combination of poetry, essays, short fiction, and reviews which she wrote and edited almost single-handedly. It often focused on the difficulties of working women, the need of adequate education for girls, and compassion for unmarried mothers.

Cook also argued for the enactment of a married women's property act and tried to reform women's dress. She herself was often noted for her masculine appearance, with her short hair and tailored shirt and jacket—a look that was considered improper for women at the time.

Although her journal soared in popularity, by 1854 Cook's poor business management and ailing health forced her to cease publication. In 1863, she received a civil list pension of £100 a year and in 1864 published her last book of poetry, *New Echoes, and Other Poems*. Although she had once been touted as a new ROBERT BURNS, in the final years of her life her popularity as a writer rapidly declined. The critic Denise Quirk has noted that in recent years "[h]er often hard-hitting directness has begun to earn her a place among radical social critics of the time."

Cooper, Edith Emma
See FIELD, MICHAEL.

Cooper, Thomas (1805–1892) poet, essayist

Thomas Cooper was born on March 20 in Leicester, in central England. After his father died in 1808, his mother moved the family to the town of Gainesborough, in Lincolnshire, where she supported them by making boxes. Cooper, who taught himself Latin and Greek, became a shoemaker at age 15. He worked at this trade for seven years until a severe illness forced him to abandon it. He became a teacher, then over the next few years held various jobs; he wrote for the Leicestershire *Mercury* and edited a Chartist newspaper, the *Midland Counties Illuminator*. The Chartist movement, which arose in England during the 1830s, protested the brutal working conditions in the factories at the time and demanded universal male suffrage, or the vote for all men, not only those who owned property. In 1843 Cooper was sent to prison for two years for speaking out in support of coal strikers. Afterward, he became a Christian evangelist and taught history for a living while he was writing poetry. In 1845 he published *The Purgatory of Suicides*, a collection of poems, followed by a collection of essays, *Land for the Laborers* (1848). His later works include his autobiography (1872) and *Thoughts at Fourscore* (1885), and another volume of essays.

Corelli, Marie (Mary Mackay) (1855–1924) novelist

Marie Corelli was the daughter of the Scottish poet, lyricist, and essayist Charles Mackay and Mary Ellen Mills, a servant; her parents did not marry until Corelli was four. Her father was the editor of the *Illustrated London News*. Corelli was a gifted pianist and originally intended to pursue a career in music (the name Marie Corelli was a stage name she adopted in anticipation of becoming a concert musician), but her father's dwindling success as a writer forced her to seek a more reliable source of income, and her determination and belief in her writing talent helped her become a published novelist at 31. Ever dramatic and image-conscious, she later declared that she wrote the novel at age 19, and that it was the result of "a strange psychical experience."

The novel, *A Romance of Two Worlds* (1886) (replete with a heroine who encounters reincarnation, "human electricity," cosmic travel, mysticism, psychic events, the revelation of esoteric knowledge, and proposes "to prove . . . the actual existence of the Supernatural"), catered to Victorian fascination with spiritualism and demonstrated Corelli's uncanny ability to write what the public would buy.

Vendetta (1886) depicts a hero who is buried alive but escapes and vows vengeance; *Thelma: A Society Novel* (1887) shows how a Norwegian beauty is rejected by English high society but at last conquers all through love; and *Ardath: The Story of a Dead Self* (1889) features a poet's attempt to regain his prowess through magic, time travel, and the acquisition of hidden secrets of electricity. In 1893 Corelli published *Barabbas: A Dream of the World's Tragedy*, a retelling of the story of the Crucifixion but with an erotic subtext. (Disdained by critics and denounced from pulpits, it simply sold more copies.)

Corelli held such contempt for critics that she had her publisher stop sending her novels to reviewers; they would have to buy their own copies. (She also refused to be photographed, thus allowing her readers to imagine her as a great beauty.) But despite the critics' sniping, she had developed a winning recipe that combined romance, religion, the occult, and social commentary to yield best-sellers. *The Sorrows of Satan* (1895) set a record for sales greater than that of any prior English novel. Corelli used the novel as a vehicle to condemn "loose morality of wealthy women and aristocratic men-about-town." The hero, Geoffrey Tempest is saved from corruption and damnation by Mavis Clare (a thinly disguised version of Corelli) who writes religious novels praising the benefits of proper Christian living and has trained pet dogs to chew up negative reviews.

Corelli also used her books to state her position on various social issues. *The Mighty Atom* (1896) attacked secular education for taking religion out of schools; *The Master Christian* (1900) urged churches to pursue peace; *Temporal Power* (1902) denounced socialism. As for the women's movement, Corelli, who excelled in creating strong female characters, ironically reacted by joining the Anti-Suffrage League. In her article "The Advance of Women" (1905), she maintained that "Woman must learn the chief lesson of successful progress, which is not to copy Man but to carefully preserve her beautiful Unlikeness to him in every possible way, so that, while asserting and gaining intellectual equality with him, she shall gradually arrive at such ascendancy as to prove herself ever the finer and the nobler creature."

At the high point in her career, Corelli earned as much as £10,000 a novel. Many of her books sold more than 100,000 copies each, an impressive number at the time. And although QUEEN VICTORIA, the Prince of Wales, and other worthies read her novels avidly, critics, virtually all male, savaged her work as bizarre, overwritten nonsense. OSCAR WILDE gave the wittiest quip about Corelli when he remarked to the librarian at Reading Jail, "I'm not saying anything against her morals, but judging from her style she ought to be here."

Preferring to remain financially independent, Corelli never married, living instead with her lifelong companion, Bertha Vyvers. In 1901 they moved to Stratford-upon-Avon, where Corelli, who felt that she had a psychic affinity with Shakespeare, bought the house believed to have belonged to Shakespeare's daughter.

Well before her death from heart failure in 1924, Corelli's popularity had peaked. But during the mid-1890s through the first few years of the 20th century, she was, in terms of book sales, the most successful novelist in Britain. Her obituary in the *Daily Telegraph* commented, "She aimed directly at the heart of the people, and gave them as much sentiment and pathos and melodrama—couched in an equally descriptive and exuberant style—as they could possibly desire. Whatever was in her mind came forth with all the turbulence of a river in spate. And the public adored her."

Works about Marie Corelli

Federico, Annette. *Idol of Suburbia: Marie Corelli and Late-Victorian Literary Culture.* Charlottesville: University Press of Virginia, 2000.

Masters, Brian. *Now Barabbas Was a Rotter: The Extraordinary Life of Marie Corelli.* London: Hamilton, 1978.

Ransom, Teresa. *The Mysterious Miss Marie Corelli: Queen of Victorian Bestsellers.* London: Sutton, 1999.

Cowper, William (1731–1800) *poet*

William Cowper (pronounced "cooper") was born at Great Berkhamstead, Hertfordshire, England. His mother, Anne Donne, was a distant relative of the poet John Donne, and his father, John Cowper, was a chaplain to King George II. Cowper's mother died when he was six, and he was sent to a local boarding school, where as a shy and fragile child, he was often bullied by his classmates. From an early age he suffered religious guilt, felt himself to be a sinner, and lived in terror of his soul's eternal damnation. His nervous and deeply melancholy disposition would follow him for the rest of his life. He entered Westminster School, where he was more carefree, and studied the poems of George Herbert, John Milton, and Robert Burns, and translated Greek and Roman classics.

Cowper studied law, was apprenticed to a solicitor, and was called to the bar in 1754. During this time he became engaged to his cousin, Theodora Cowper, but her father opposed the match. In 1763 Cowper's extreme shyness and fits of depression undid him as he prepared for an oral examination to become clerk of the House of Lords. He describes the terror he felt: "They whose spirits are formed like mine, to whom a public exhibition of themselves, on any occasion, is mortal poison, may have some idea of the horrors of my situation." To avoid the examination, he attempted suicide three times and developed delusions and full-blown insanity. Committed to a mental institution, he spent the next year and a half in recovery. Afterward, he moved to the rural town of Huntington and was cared for by the Reverend Morley Unwin and his wife, Mary. When the minister was killed in a horse-riding accident, Cowper and Mary Unwin moved to Olney in Buckinghamshire. There they lived together in a chaste arrangement, and Cowper spent his time writing, gardening, and looking after his pet hares.

Critical Analysis

At Olney, John Newton, the evangelical curate, encouraged Cowper to write 77 devotional poems, called *Olney Hymns* (1779). The poems include such well-known lines as "God moves in a mysterious way," "O, for a closer walk with God," and "Hark, my soul, it is the Lord." These verses were popular and widely read and went through 20 editions between 1779 and 1831. Another Olney friend, Lady Anna Austen, inspired Cowper to write two of his best known poems. "The Diverting History of John Gilpin" (1782) is a humorous ballad of a rider trapped on his runaway horse. *The Task* (1785) is a blank-verse poem in six books of first-person narration that prefigures the romantics and their love of nature: "Nature inanimate employs sweet sounds, / But animated nature sweeter still, / To soothe and satisfy the human ear." *The Task* decries "ambition, avarice, penury" of the city and also satirizes the pretensions of science "in playing tricks with nature, giving laws / To distant worlds and trifling in their own." SAMUEL TAYLOR COLERIDGE liked the "vein of satire which runs through that excellent poem, together with the sombre hue of its religious opinions."

Cowper also wrote many beautiful, personal poems to Mary Unwin, and she encouraged him to write lighter verse. As a result, he published eight gentle satires in 1782; scattered among them are his thoughts on how to write effectively. In "Table Talk" he says of poetry,

> Give me the line that ploughs its stately course,
> Like a proud swan, conquering the stream by force;
> That like some cottage beauty, strikes the heart,
> Quite unindebted to the tricks of art.

In "Conversation" he says,

> A tale should be judicious, clear, succinct;
> The language plain, and incidents well linked.
> Tell not as new what everybody knows,
> And, new or old, still hasten to a close.

Cowper adhered to these guidelines, writing about the joys and sorrows of life in relatively simple language that made him immediately accessible to readers. He said, "In writing, perspicuity is always more than half the battle.... A meaning that does not stare you in the face is as bad as no meaning, because nobody will take the pains to poke for it."

Mary Unwin's unexpected death in 1796 caused Cowper to break down completely, and he never fully recovered. Shortly before he died in 1800, he wrote his gloomy poem "The Castaway," which is based on an account of a sailor being washed overboard and lost. It concludes with these self-pitying lines that bear witness to Cowper's inconsolable condition: "We perished, each alone; / But I beneath a rougher sea, / And whelmed in deeper gulfs than he."

Some critics considered Cowper to have little poetic stature. But as the critic Michael Schmidt says, "In important ways Cowper is original, and the emotional and intellectual range of his poems is wide. A 'milder muse' dominates, but there are reasons for this: Cowper had to court that Muse more intensely than any poet in the language, because for him poetry was a means of talking himself back from the edge...."

Other Works by William Cowper

King, James, and Charles Ryskamp, eds. *William Cowper: Selected Letters.* London: Oxford University Press, 1989.
———. *The Letters and Prose Writings of William Cowper: Prose 1756–1798 and Cumulative Index.* London: Oxford University Press, 1986.

Works about William Cowper

Ella, George Melvin. *William Cowper: The Man of God's Stamp.* Guelph, Canada: Joshua Press, 2001.
Wright, Thomas. *The Life of William Cowper.* Honolulu: University Press of the Pacific, 2005.

Coyne, Joseph Stirling (1803–1868)
playwright, journalist

Joseph Stirling Coyne was born in King's County (now County Offaly), Ireland. His father was a port surveyor in Waterford. He received his education at Dungannon School, and although his family intended him to practice law, he decided to make writing and literature his career.

Coyne experienced success early in his life with publication of his literary articles in Dublin magazines. In 1836 he moved to London where he joined the staff of the *Morning Gazette*, a London newspaper. He continued to contribute to other periodicals, writing for the *Adelphi* and the *Haymarket,* and also becoming the drama critic for the *Sunday Times.* In 1841 he was one of the founders, with MARK LEMON and HENRY MAYHEW, of the humorous magazine *Punch.*

Coyne was also a playwright and served as secretary for the Dramatic Authors' Society. In his lifetime he wrote approximately 55 plays, mostly farces, many of which were adapted from the French. Like the satire he wrote for magazines, Coyne's drama has been reviewed as having "verve, vigor and real humor." His best-known plays include *The Hope of the Family* (1853), *The Secret Agent* (1855), and *The Black Sheep* (1861).

Coyne married Anne Simcockes Comryns, a widow, in 1840. Peter Kavanagh, in his 1946 book *The Irish Theatre*, characterizes Coyne's humor dismissively, saying that it "depends greatly on punning," but all his plays had long runs. *Did You Ever Send Your Wife to Camberwell?* (1846) struck the director Peter Weir as "riotous." Weir mounted a revival in London in 1999.

Other Work by Joseph Stirling Coyne
Booth, Michael R., ed. *The Lights o' London and Other Victorian Plays.* New York: Oxford University Press, 1995.

Crabbe, George (1754–1832) poet
George Crabbe was born in the small coastal town of Aldeburgh, in Suffolk, England, to Mary Loddock and George Crabbe, a schoolmaster, parish clerk, and tax collector. After attending local schools, Crabbe was apprenticed to a pharmacist-surgeon, establishing his own pharmacy in 1775. Disenchanted with medicine, Crabbe abandoned his practice—the vestry had appointed him "surgeon to the poor"—in 1780 to pursue a literary career. (He may have been inspired by the example of his father, who studied literature early on and whose evening readings from John Milton and other poets Crabbe recalled.) The following year, he secured the patronage of the statesman EDMUND BURKE; Burke provided financial support to Crabbe and used his influence to help Crabbe establish himself in the London literary scene. Also that year, Crabbe was ordained as a clergyman.

Crabbe was not a romantic poet. He preferred order to energy, close observation to imagination, satirical cleverness to sincerity; like the 18th-century poet Alexander Pope, he studied humankind. He wrote using heroic couplets, paired end-rhyming lines in iambic pentameter. This was a form that Pope had perfected, among other reasons, to showcase his wit. This example of it in Crabbe, from "The Candidate: To the Authors of The Monthly Review" (1780), dispenses wisdom: "Be not too eager in the arduous Cha[s]e; / Who pants for Triumph seldom wins the Race." Referring to medical quacks selling worthless potions in *The Borough* (1810), Crabbe finds it strange "That Creatures, Nature meant should clean our Streets, / Have purchas'd Lands and Mansions, Parks and Seats." Here, then, Crabbe dispenses witty rebuke.

On the other hand, Crabbe shared with ROBERT BURNS and WILLIAM WORDSWORTH, poets otherwise unlike him, an interest in the poor and those close to the earth. Farmers, clerks, and "Sailors and Lasses" are among his characters. While Crabbe's early poems are imitations of Pope, *The Village* (1783) introduces themes of his own: village life, poverty, and suffering humanity. The poem describes an impoverished land: "Rank weeds, that every art and care defy, / Reign o'er the land and rob the blighted rye." There also is the parish workhouse, whose "walls of mud scarce bear the broken door ... [and] putrid vapours[,] flagging, play."

The Village struck a responsive chord among readers and became instantly popular. The anonymous reviewer in *Gentleman's Magazine*, however, noted that it "treats [its subject] very differently from the ancient and modern writers of pastoral, representing only the dark side of the landscape, the poverty and misery attendant on the peasant." The reviewer could not believe that people lived such disadvantaged lives.

With the 1812 *Tales* Crabbe turned to narrative poetry. Each of the book's 21 sections relates a separate tale, while, taken together, the parts compose a wide-ranging portrait of human nature, including human folly. The title "Procrastination," for example, refers to Rupert, who in setting out in hopes of making his fortune delays too long reuniting with Dinah. When he does return home, he finds that his beloved's feelings for him have been replaced by greed, kindled by the inheritance she received in his absence. Rupert begs forgiveness to no avail as Dinah responds with sardonic chill: "Thou too perhaps art wealthy; but our fate / Still mocks our wishes, wealth is come too late." In "The Lover's Journey," however, it is the journeyer's feelings that change when, thus separated from her, he worries that his beloved back home is being unfaithful to him.

In the *Edinburgh Review*, FRANCIS JEFFREY greeted the *Tales* with condescension and sarcasm, noting "the moral benefit" that "that great proportion of our readers which must necessarily belong to the middling or humbler classes" "may derive" from the tales. However, Crabbe was not primarily preaching or teaching. "With Crabbe," the critic Howard Mills has remarked, "curiosity about people" superceded any didactic impulse "to illustrate ... precepts." Crabbe's interest in both human nature and human beings is the hallmark of his best work. The critic LESLIE STEPHEN wrote, "To define Crabbe's poetry ... [w]e must endow him with that simplicity of character ... which does not disqualify him from seeing a great deal further into his neighbours than they are apt to give him credit for doing."

Works about George Crabbe
Powell, Neil. *George Crabbe: An English Life, 1754–1832*. London: Random House, 2004.
Whitehead, Frank S. *George Crabbe: A Reappraisal*. Selinsgrove, Penn.: Susquehanna University Press, 1995.

Craigie, Pearl Mary (1867–1906) *novelist, playwright*

Pearl Craigie, née Richards, was born in Chelsea, Massachusetts, to the merchant John Morgan Richards and his wife, Laura Arnold Richards. The family moved to England when Craigie was still an infant, and she was educated in private schools there. At age 9, she wrote a story, the "Fountain," that was published in a newspaper. In 1886 she went to Paris to study music and a year later married Reginald Walpole Craigie. She had a son in 1890 but left her husband soon afterward. The breakdown of her marriage seems to have led her to join the Roman Catholic Church in 1892.

Craigie was also writing during this difficult period. Under the pseudonym John Oliver Hobbes, she wrote satirical novels such as *Some Emotions and a Moral* (1891) and *The Sinner's Comedy* (1892), which were followed by a succession of other novels throughout the 1890s. At the turn of the century, Craigie became known as an accomplished playwright. Her 1898 comedy *The Ambassador*, which was the hit of the theatrical season, was quickly followed by *A Repentance* in 1899 and *The Wisdom of the Wise* in 1900.

A Work about Pearl Craigie
Harding, Mildred Davis. *Air-Bird in the Water: The Life and Works of Pearl Craigie*. Madison, N.J.: Fairleigh Dickinson University Press, 1996.

Craik, Mrs. (Dinah Maria Mulock) (1826–1887) *novelist, essayist, short story writer*

Dinah Maria Mulock was born in Stoke on Trent, Staffordshire, England, to Dinah Mellard Mulock, the daughter of a wealthy tanner, and Thomas Mulock, a brash, zealous, and highly opinionated preacher who at one time had written letters to LORD BYRON in an attempt to convert him to Christianity. Because her father had a propensity for getting into debt and was later confined for a time in a lunatic asylum, the family did not have a consistent income, nor did Dinah and her two younger brothers receive a focused or comprehensive education. To combat both of these problems, her mother opened a school in Newcastle where Dinah worked as an assistant. There, she learned that a woman, through her own efforts and resourcefulness, could make money.

When Mulock's maternal grandmother died in 1839, the family inherited enough money to move to London. Mulock took lessons in languages and drawing and, through her parents' friends and acquaintances, met actors and writers. Dinah Mellard Mulock's poor health and Thomas Mulock's inability to avoid encroaching debt ultimately led to the former's death and the latter's insolvency and subsequent abandonment of the family.

Mulock chose to support herself independently through her writing and did not marry until age 40. (Her husband was the Scottish publisher George Lillie Craik, a partner in the firm of Macmillan & Co.) She produced 20 novels, 12 children's books, numerous short stories and essays, four volumes of poetry, and three volumes of travel narratives translated from the French. In addition, she wrote one of the most popular advice books for women during the period, entitled *A Woman's Thoughts about Women* (1857), which offers advice to women on work, aging, and self-reliance.

Critical Analysis

Craik's novels were the most popular of her writings. Many of them went into multiple editions, were pirated in the United States, and were translated into numerous languages. Her most famous novel, a rags-to-riches story, *John Halifax, Gentleman* (1856), appeared in the wake of the optimism produced in 1851 by the Great Exhibition, an event that celebrated British technology, industry, and commerce. *John Halifax, Gentleman* promoted the Protestant work ethic, and reinforced the idea that the virtuous life can lead to both spiritual and material success. Notably, it was one of the first novels to have a tradesman as its hero. He begins the novel poor and industrious—his first words are "Sir, I want work; may I earn a penny?"—and ends a gentleman. As the critic Sally Mitchell notes, "John Halifax himself is a compendium of middle-class virtues. He embodies the holy trinity of economic individualism: self-help, self-denial, and self-control." He is also honest, thrifty, clean, studious, dutiful, moral, family-centered, courageous, prudent—and a teetotaler. In short, the hero undergoes no serious internal conflict; he does not succumb to, or even seem to recognize, temptation.

Craik's other novels take on similar moral issues. *Olive* (1850), for example, deals with a disabled Scotswoman's struggles with physical handicap and parental rejection. It bears more than a passing resemblance to CHARLOTTE BRONTË's *Jane Eyre*. The heroine, Olive, is a strong and appealing character who strives to find self-fulfillment: "I, too, am one of these outcasts; give me then this inner life which is beyond all! Friend, counsel me! master, teach me! Woman as I am, I will dare all things—endure all things. Let me be an artist!"

Craik's work was often used as the standard to which other women writers were held: Reviewers compared the early work of GEORGE ELIOT to Craik's—a comparison that irritated Eliot. While Eliot admired Craik's moral character and her genuine religious feeling, she nevertheless thought that Craik was "a writer who is read only by novel readers, pure and simple, never by people of high culture. A very excellent woman she is, I believe—but we belong to an entirely different order of writers." Craik's response to Eliot's work, though supportive and admiring in many respects, also revealed Craik's objections to Eliot's fictional representations of women. Craik criticized Eliot's decision, in *The Mill on the Floss,* to allow Maggie Tulliver to find resolution to her problems only in "death, welcomed as the solution of all difficulties, the escape from all pain." Although Craik recognized the artistry and skill of Eliot's work, she failed to see its purpose: "Ask, what good will it do?—whether it will lighten any burdened heart, help any perplexed spirit, comfort the sorrowful, succour the tempted, or bring back the erring into the way of peace; and what is the answer? Silence." Her sentiments reveal much about her own beliefs concerning the responsibilities of the novelist; she believed that the novelist should not simply portray reality—the world as it is—but rather illuminate possibilities—the world as it could be.

Her contemporaries agreed. A review in *Victoria Magazine* said of her career that she had "succeeded in what should be the highest aim of the novelist; she has done good."

A Work about Mrs. Craik

Mitchell, Sally. *Dinah Mulock Craik*. Boston: Twayne, 1983.

Cross, Ada

See CAMBRIDGE, ADA.

Crowe, Catherine (Catherine Anne Stevens Crowe) (1800?–1876) novelist, short story writer

Catherine Crowe was born in Borough Green, Kent, England, the daughter of John Stevens. In 1822 she married Lieutenant Colonel John Crowe and moved to Edinburgh, Scotland. The couple had one son.

At times compared to MARY SHELLEY, Crowe enjoyed much success as a writer of supernatural stories. In Edinburgh's medical and scientific circles, she was considered an intellectual; this reputation pleased the emerging author. Between 1841 and 1854, Crowe published five novels, a book of short stories, tales for children, and several other works. *The Night Side of Nature; or, Ghosts and Ghost Seers* (1848) was a two-volume collection of ghost stories and tales of supernatural phenomena. The book was extremely popular in its time, partially because Crowe said the stories were true; the author Richard Garnett described it as "one of the best collections of supernatural stories in our language."

Much like ELIZA COOK, Crowe believed that women were victims of their own economic circumstances and lack of educational opportunities. To counter this, she portrayed strong heroines who overcome the difficulties brought on by circumstances beyond their control. *Lilly Dawson* (1847) portrays a tough-minded middle-class heroine who is forced to become a servant. Crowe wrote other novels featuring women who cross class lines; *Susan Hopley; or Circumstantial Evidence* (1841) is about a servant who discovers that she is the daughter of a colonel.

During the height of her success in the 1840s, Crowe was regarded as a writer for all classes. Many 19th-century readers could relate to her novels because they featured ordinary places and ordinary working people. Her sympathy for the pressures experienced by working-class women made Crowe one of the most popular writers in her time. The novelist Adeline Sergeant (1851–1904), for one, believed that this was Crowe's greatest achievement: "Mrs. Crowe's writings certainly heralded the advent of a new kind of fiction: a kind which has been, perhaps more than any other, characteristic of the early years of the Victorian Age. It is the literature of domestic realism, of homely unromantic characters."

D

Dacre, Charlotte Byrne (1782?–1825)
novelist, poet

Born Charlotte King to Jonathan King, a banker, and his wife, Deborah Lara, both Charlotte and her sister Sophia demonstrated an early literary bent: They published a book of poems, *Trifles of Helicon* (1798), that they dedicated to their father. (Sophia went on to publish four novels under her own name.)

After writing more poems (largely concerned with how love can bring about passion, melancholy, and even nightmares) and submitting them to the newspapers (which were then a popular outlet for poetry), Charlotte began her career as a novelist using the pseudonym Rosa Matilda. Her first novel, *The Confessions of the Nun of St. Omer* (1805), was dedicated to the popular Gothic novelist MATTHEW GREGORY LEWIS. It is a first-person account of the tragic life of a young woman in Italy, filled with stock situations and sentimental hyperbole: "St. Elmer darted from my trembling grasp.—Convulsively I struggled to retain him.... The violence of his tortures had rendered him insensible even to *me*.—I fell enhorrored to the floor." The success of *The Confessions* led to the abandonment of her pseudonym with the publication of *Zofloya; or, The Moor* (1806), a best-seller. Dacre attempted to rival the Gothic sensationalism of Lewis's *The Monk*. Her heroine (or antiheroine, more accurately), Victoria di Loredani, is a murderer and nymphomaniac who offers up her body and soul to a Moor who is really the devil in disguise. Modern feminist critics have praised the novel's reversal of gender expectations and frank depiction of female desire: "In one of those hasty glances which pride alone would permit her to steal, it occurred to her that the figure of the Moor possessed a grace and majesty which she had never before remarked; his face too seemed animated with charms till now unnoticed, and his very dress to have acquired a more splendid, tasteful, and elegant appearance." *The Libertine* (1807) featured another femme fatale as its protagonist. Her last novel was *The Passions* (1811), an epistolary novel which was criticized for its "inflated extravagance of diction." The scholar Ann Jones notes this extravagance, while praising Dacre's depiction of psychology: "[T]hough her novels as totalities are weak, in the very weakness of her obsession with highly-charged emotional scenes she was able to rise at times to an effective portrayal of the disordered mind and to explore the irrational side of human behavior."

Works about Charlotte Dacre
Clery, E. J. *Women's Gothic: From Clara Reeve to Mary Shelley.* Horndon, England: Northcote House, 2000.
Jones, Ann H. *Ideas and Innovations: Best Sellers of Jane Austen's Age.* New York: AMS Press, 1986.

Dallas, Eneas Sweetland (1828–1879)
critic, journalist

Eneas Dallas was born in Jamaica to British parents, John Dallas, a Scottish plantation owner, and Elizabeth Baillie. When Eneas was four, his parents returned to England. After studying philosophy at Edinburgh University, he moved to London, where he became one of the most eminent journalists of his day. In 1852 he published *Poetics: An Essay on Poetry,* an examination of how a poem achieves its aesthetic effects—that is, of how a poem provokes the response it does in the reader. He married Isabella Glyn, an actress, a year later, but their marriage was unhappy and they later divorced. Dallas became a staff writer for the London *Times* and was known for his brilliance and his style. He also contributed biographical pieces, political commentary, and literary criticism to other newspapers, including the *Daily News, Saturday Review,* and *Pall Mall Gazette.* As a critic, he wrote memorable reviews of most of the major Victorian novelists. In 1866, he published *The Gay Science* (a title he borrowed from the 13th-century Troubador love poets), which was another attempt to examine how art affects people. Dallas wanted to identify the cognitive and psychological sources of aesthetic pleasure. As a correspondent in Paris for the London newspapers, he also covered foreign affairs, including the Franco-Prussian War of 1870.

Danby, Frank (Julia Davis Frankau) (1864–1916)
novelist

Julia Davis was born in Ireland. Her father, Hyman Davis, a Jewish artist, moved the family to London when Julia was a child, and she received an education at home. In 1883 she married Arthur Frankau, a wealthy cigar merchant.

Adopting the pseudonym Frank Danby, she began her writing career as a journalist in London. She wrote for the *Saturday Review,* among other publications, and in 1887, with the encouragement of GEORGE MOORE, produced the first of her 14 novels, *Dr. Phillips: A Maida Vale Idyll.* Like many of her subsequent novels, it featured Irish and Jewish characters; but surprisingly, considering her heritage, it was anti-Semitic in its satire of Jews faithful to the "Deity of Gain." It did, however, became a notorious best-seller and stayed in print for 10 years.

A Babe in Bohemia (1889) was Danby's next major work. This novel, which featured seduction, sexually transmitted disease, and a graphic portrayal of violent suicide, disgusted many people and, labeled "unconventional," was banned by circulating libraries. Danby's other satires on Jewish life include *Pigs in Clover* (1902) and *The Sphinx's Lawyer* (1906). Aside from writing novels, Danby also wrote three art history books and cofounded with J. T. Grein the Independent Theatre Society, which produced plays by Henrik Ibsen and GEORGE BERNARD SHAW.

Darwin, Charles (1809–1882)
nonfiction writer, scientist

Charles Darwin was born in Shrewsbury, Shropshire, England, to Robert Darwin, a physician. Darwin's mother, Susannah Wedgwood Darwin, died when he was eight, and Charles's older sisters assumed the responsibility for his upbringing. At age nine, Darwin was enrolled in Shrewsbury School, which its headmaster, the Reverend George Case, made famous throughout England. During his childhood, Charles was a devoted hunter and collector, spending his free time in the fields and woods around Shrewsbury.

At age 16 Darwin left to study medicine at Edinburgh University. He was repulsed by the sight of surgery performed without anesthesia and decided to change careers. Robert Darwin expected Charles to follow in his footsteps and become a physician; however, Charles preferred the career of a clergyman, a respectable profession that allowed plenty of leisure time to study natural history. Darwin left Edinburgh for Cambridge University, where he was befriended by a distinguished biologist, John Stevens Henslow, who encouraged Darwin's interest in zoology and geography, and by geologist Adam Sedgwick.

In 1831 the Royal Navy was preparing the ship *Beagle* for a five-year exploratory voyage to parts of South America and the Pacific Ocean. Henslow strongly recommended Darwin for the unpaid position of ship's naturalist, who was to be responsible for making observations about the geology and biology of the regions to which the ship would travel.

Darwin collected many geological and biological specimens, examined numerous fossils, and made observations of the structure, figures, diversity, and living habits of the different life forms. He also traveled by land through parts of South America.

Darwin began to wonder why similarities existed between landbound species in South America and those of animals found in other parts of the world: The large South American Rhea, for example, looks very much like the African ostrich. However, while surveying the Galapagos Islands off the coast of Ecuador, Darwin was puzzled by the differences that existed between the birds and tortoises on each island, even though those islands were geologically similar to one another. From these and many other observations, Darwin developed a number of hypotheses that later led to the evolutionary theory. As Darwin notes in the opening paragraph of *On the Origin of Species* (1859),

> When on board H.M.S. *Beagle* as naturalist, I was much struck with certain facts in the distribution of the organic beings inhabiting South America, and in the geological relations of the present to the past inhabitants of that continent. These facts ... seemed to throw some light on the origin of species—that mystery of mysteries, as it has been called by one of our greatest philosophers.

Based on his meticulous observations, Darwin concluded that species evolve, with modifications, from other species.

Critical Analysis

On his return to England in 1836, Darwin continued to examine his data and conduct research; however, he waited for years to present his dramatic conclusions. In 1859 Darwin finally published his theories as *On the Origin of Species*. Darwin theorized that, through a process of natural selection, species evolve over time. By natural selection, Darwin meant that some members of a species are better adapted to survive the environmental challenges they face than are others. As Darwin wrote, "favorable variations would tend to be preserved and unfavorable ones to be destroyed. The result would be the formation of a new species." In other words, given enough time, the original species will become a new, separate species as it acquires different characteristics over time as particular adaptations accumulate. In a similar manner, different species facing the same type of environment will actually come to resemble one another. Thus, for example, in deserts, natural selection leads to water-conserving plants.

The effects of *On the Origin of Species* were immediate and widespread. The work contradicted the literal interpretation of the creation story of the Bible, and Darwin and his theory were condemned as anti-Christian. His theories also created a schism in the scientific community: Whereas some scientists, such as T. H. HUXLEY, avidly embraced his theories, others, such as PHILIP HENRY GOSSE, sided with established religion and rejected Darwin's theories outright.

Darwin saw no threat to religion in his work. He himself was not an atheist and always claimed that the evolutionary process was the work of God.

In his concluding words to *On the Origin of Species* he writes that "there is grandeur in this view of life, with its several powers, having originally been breathed by the Creator into a few forms or into one; and that . . . from so simple a beginning endless forms most beautiful and wonderful have been, and are being evolved."

In 1871 Darwin expanded his theories with *The Descent of Man and Selection in Relation to Sex*. In this work he proposed that humans evolved from more primitive species. Darwin also discussed the role of sex in the selection process of evolution and pointed out the evolutionary significance of the physical differences between males and females. This work also stirred up controversy because Darwin openly admitted what was implied in *On the Origin of Species*: Not only were animals subject to natural selection, but so were humans.

Although resistance to the theory of evolution remains to this day, it is accepted by those in the scientific community and many in the religious. Darwin's theory was one of the most significant scientific insights of all time. In the words of Julian Huxley, a follower of Darwin and a fellow scientist, "Darwin's work has enabled us to see the position of man and of our present civilization in a truer light. Man is not a finished product incapable of further progress. He has a long history behind him, and it is a history not of a fall, but of an ascent."

Other Works by Charles Darwin

Brown, Janet, et al., ed. *The Voyage of the Beagle*. New York: Penguin, 1989.
Burlow, Nora, ed. *Autobiography of Charles Darwin, 1809–1882*. New York: W. W. Norton, 1993.
The Expression of the Emotions in Man and Animals. New York: Oxford University Press, 1998.

Works about Charles Darwin

Browne, Janet. *Charles Darwin*. New York: Alfred A. Knopf, 2002.
Browne, E. Janet. *Charles Darwin: The Power of Place*. Princeton, N.J.: Princeton University Press, 2003.
Quammen, David. *The Reluctant Mr. Darwin: An Intimate Portrait of Charles Darwin and the Making of His Theory of Evolution*. New York: Norton, 2007.
Richards, Janet Radcliffe. *Human Nature after Darwin: A Philosophical Introduction*. New York: Routledge, 2001.
Simonton, Dean Keith. *Origins of Genius: Darwinian Perspectives on Creativity*. New York: Oxford University Press, 1999.

Davidson, John (1857–1909) *poet, playwright, novelist*

The son of Helen Crocket Davidson and Alexander Davidson, an evangelical minister, John Davidson was born near Glasgow, Scotland. Struggling with poverty, Davidson's father interrupted his 13-year-old son's schooling and sent him to work. One job, in the chemical laboratory of a sugar refinery in the seaport of Greenock, sparked Davidson's interest in science. This led to a commitment to scientific materialism—a belief system identifying the scientific method, rather than God or faith in God, as the one path to knowledge, and claiming matter and energy as the basic universal components. These beliefs remained at the core of Davidson's philosophy.

After a number of teaching posts, Davidson moved to London in 1889 to pursue a writing career. Recognition arrived with two books of poetry: *Fleet Street Eclogues* (1893) and *Ballads and Songs* (1894). The latter book included one of Davidson's enduring poems, "Thirty Bob a Week," a working-class lament: "It's just the power of some to be a boss, / And the bally power of others to be bossed." Davidson's biographer John Sloan has noted that, pleading his case, Davidson's clerk "[adopts] the argot [idiom] and self-deprecatory tones that belong traditionally to the Cockney costermonger" (that is, the street hawker of produce). In the 20th century T. S. Eliot acknowledged the poem's influence on his own poetry, especially by providing him with an idiom suitable for the "dingy urban images" of the industrial age.

The critic and poet LIONEL JOHNSON wrote in 1895 that "[i]n each poem a situation, an emotion, has been faced and wrestled with and mastered: the solutions are triumphant and satisfying." In "A Ballad of Hell," a poem about double suicide, Davidson introduces a macabre twist by associating Hell with rejoicing and humanity, albeit in an intriguingly qualified way. (The rejoicing, for instance, is "hoarse.")

Now considered among Davidson's best poems, "The Crystal Palace," "The Thames Embankment," "Snow," and "The Wasp" were published in the 20th century. (Some were published posthumously, after Davidson, depressed, professionally isolated and financially struggling, drowned himself.) These poems demonstrate the signature features of his mature work: the minute particularity of his descriptions, the conversational voice, a sometime jaggedness of language, and his inquisitiveness, as in these lines observing a wasp trapped in a train compartment: "She coasted up and down the wood and worked / Her wrath to passion-point again."

Today, Davidson is appreciated most for anticipating modernism, the deliberate break, beginning early in the 20th century, with tradition to pursue subjects, forms, and language that reflected contemporary experience. This limited appreciation is in keeping with the modest nature of Davidson's poetic gifts. The biographer J. Benjamin Townsend describes Davidson's achievement: "An innovator rather than a creator, he adapted familiar lyric forms and traditional myth to contemporary subject matter and a modern message."

Other Work by John Davidson
Sloan, John, ed. *Selected Poems and Prose of John Davidson.* New York: Oxford University Press, 1995.

Works about John Davidson
Halladay, Jean R. *Eight Late Victorian Poets Shaping the Artistic Sensibility of an Age.* Lewiston, N.Y.: Edwin Mellen Press, 1993.

Sloan, John. *John Davidson, First of the Moderns: A Literary Biography.* New York: Oxford University Press, 1997.

Townsend, J. Benjamin. *John Davidson: Poet of Armageddon.* New Haven, Conn.: Yale University Press, 1961.

De Quincey, Thomas (Thomas Quincey) (1785–1859) *essayist*

Thomas De Quincey was born in Manchester, England, the son of a well-to-do linen merchant, Thomas Quincey, and his wife, Elizabeth Penson Quincey. He added the *De* to his name later in life to indicate the Norman-French origin of the family.

An excellent Latin scholar, De Quincey entered Oxford in 1803. There he studied German literature and philosophy and read widely in English literature. In 1807 he moved to the Lake District, in northwest England, to be near the poets WILLIAM WORDSWORTH, ROBERT SOUTHEY, and SAMUEL TAYLOR COLERIDGE. De Quincey was one of the first of Wordsworth's many admirers, but the friendship ended in 1834 when De Quincey published intimate details that angered the poet.

Because of a stomach ailment, De Quincey began taking laudanum. He became addicted to this mixture of alcohol and opium, which was legal and widely available at the time, and used it for the rest of his life.

In 1820 he began his career as a newspaper and magazine writer. He was a prolific writer, best remembered today for *Confessions of an English Opium Eater* (1822), the critical essay "On the Knocking at the Gate in *Macbeth*" (1823), and the bizarrely funny "On Murder Considered as One of the Fine Arts" (1827). The essay on *Macbeth* is deeply influenced by the spirit of ROMANTICISM, in which De Quincey suggests that intuition and emotion are superior to reason in the interpretation of literature. "On Murder" is a satire of the conservative philosopher EDMOND BURKE's notion of the sublime in art. De Quincey is particularly admired for his literary style: for the music of his words, for the careful structure of sentences and paragraphs, and for the use of Greek and Latin expressions when those words expressed more exactly than English what he wanted to say. Although his style is his greatest asset, he is also noted for his psychological insights, his sometimes black humor, his wide-ranging intellect, and his breadth of knowledge.

Critical Analysis

In *Confessions of an English Opium-Eater* De Quincey's purpose is to explain how a "reasonable being" came to "subject himself to such a yoke of misery, voluntarily to incur a captivity so servile, and knowingly to fetter himself with such a seven-fold chain." With his first taste of the drug De Quincey found himself in "the abyss of a divine enjoyment," and he contrasts opium intoxication with that brought about by alcohol: "Whereas wine disorders the mental faculties, opium, on the contrary . . . introduces amongst them the most exquisite order, legislation, and harmony." In describing his early use of opium, De Quincey not only celebrates the euphoric effects of the drug, but also refutes some of the ill effects that others had attributed to it. He notes, for example, that a day of intoxication was widely thought to be followed by a day of depression. In his case, however, "the day succeeding to that on which I allowed myself . . . [to take laudanum] was always a day of unusually good spirits."

In discussing the pains of opium, De Quincey focuses particularly on the period between 1813 and 1819 when he was so enslaved to the drug that to ask him "whether on any particular day he had or had not taken opium" would have been equivalent to asking him "whether his lungs had performed respiration." One of the worst effects for De Quincey, as an intellectual and scholar, was the "sense of incapacity and feebleness" his addiction created:

> The opium-eater loses none of his moral sensibilities or aspirations: he wishes and longs, as earnestly as ever, to realize what he believes possible, and feels to be exacted by duty; but his intellectual apprehension of what is possible infinitely outruns his power, not of execution only, but even of power to attempt. He lies under the weight of incubus and nightmare . . . and cannot even attempt to rise.

Worse than De Quincey's daylight exhaustion, however, were the dreams that haunted his nights, at which time he descended "not metaphorically, but literally . . . into chasms and sunless abysses, depths below depths, from which it seemed hopeless that I could ever re-ascend." De Quincey says that he dreamed about "the minutest incidents of childhood," and he found it terrifying to discover that nothing he had ever experienced had been entirely forgotten, that every moment was indelibly etched somewhere in his brain, concluding that "the dread book of account, which the Scriptures speak of is, in fact, the mind itself."

Nevertheless, even while describing the horror he experienced from his dreams, De Quincey makes them seem at the same time magnificent, rich, sensuous, and seductive—qualities that surely influenced such authors as the American writer Edgar Allan Poe and the French poet Charles Baudelaire to experiment with the drug:

> I was stared at, hooted at, grinned at, chattered at, by monkeys, by paroquets, by cockatoos. I ran into pagodas: and was fixed, for centuries, at the summit, or in secret rooms. . . . I was buried, for a thousand years in stone coffins, with mummies and sphynxes, in narrow chambers at the heart of eternal pyramids.

As the critic Charles Whibley observed, De Quincey "explored the remoter continents of knowledge, and travelled almost as far in the realms of thought as Coleridge himself."

A Work about Thomas De Quincey

Burwich, Frederick. *Thomas De Quincey: Knowledge and Power*. New York: St. Martin's Press, 2001.

De Vere, Aubrey Thomas Hunt
(1814–1902) *poet*

Aubrey Thomas De Vere was born in County Limerick, Ireland, to Sir Aubrey De Vere, a baronet and poet, and Mary Spring Rice De Vere. He studied metaphysics at Trinity College, Dublin. Enamored of WILLIAM WORDSWORTH's poetry since childhood, as an adult De Vere would visit Wordsworth's grave annually until poor health prevented the pilgrimage. SAMUEL TAYLOR COLERIDGE, George Gordon, Lord BYRON, and PERCY BYSSHE SHELLEY also influenced De Vere's work.

De Vere's *The Search after Proserpine* (1843) shows Shelley's influence, as does "Autumnal Ode": ". . . the breeze increases: / The sunset forests, catching sudden fire, / Flash, swell, and sing." FRANCIS THOMPSON found this lyrical aspect De Vere's greatest strength as a poet.

The Irish potato famine of 1846 and the devastation it wrought, especially in the predominantly Catholic west of Ireland, planted the seeds of De Vere's eventual conversion from Protestantism. Reading JOHN HENRY NEWMAN nourished this purpose, as did the intellectual excitement of the OXFORD MOVEMENT. De Vere valued the movement for seeking to restore the spiritual character of the Church of England. In 1851 De Vere converted to Roman Catholicism and, soon after, taught for a while under Father (later Cardinal) Newman at the new Catholic University in Dublin. Pope Pius IX asked De Vere to commemorate his conversion in verse. The result was *May Carols* (1857).

Chronicling Irish history, *The Sisters, Inisfail, and Other Poems* (1861) includes "A Ballad of Athlone." In vivid language, this poem tells of the successful 1691 siege of Athlone by William of Orange's Dutch troops, who were intent on crossing a town bridge in order to defeat the Irish Catholics set on restoring James II to the English throne:

> "Break down the bridge!"—Six warriors rushed
> Through the storm of shot and the storm of shell:
> With late but certain victory flushed
> The grim Dutch gunners eyed them well.
> They wrench'd at the planks 'mid a hail of fire:
> They fell in death, their work half done:
> The bridge stood fast; and nigh and nigher
> The foe swarmed darkly, densely on.

The Tennysonian ring to this poem marks another influence on De Vere. "Lyrical in verse, strong in style, mainly historical in theme, heroic or spiritual in substance, above all, placid," the scholar G. E. Woodbury writes, "[De Vere's poetry] stirs and tranquilizes the soul in the presence of lovely scenes, high actions, and those 'great ideas that man was born to learn.'"

Dickens, Charles (1812–1870) *novelist, editor, journalist*

Charles Dickens has influenced the reading public and popular culture more than any other Victorian writer. Read by an estimated 10 percent of literate Victorians, and read aloud to many more, Dickens's fiction, which inspired myriad imitators, including playwrights, filmmakers, and television producers, continues to pervade the popular imagination.

Born in Portsmouth, Hampshire, England, Dickens was the second of John and Elizabeth Barrow Dickens's eight children. His early years were spent in towns on England's south coast, an area free of industrial development. John Dickens, a clerk in the Naval Pay Office, was frequently in debt. In 1824, shortly after the family moved to London, he was thrown into the Marshalsea prison for debtors, and his family was forced to join him there—except the 12-year-old Charles, who was sent to work in a boot-blacking factory.

Some of Dickens's persistent themes arise from this experience, most notably his concern for the powerlessness of children, such as Oliver Twist, Pip in *Great Expectations* (1861), Jo in *Bleak House* (1853), and Sally Jupe in *Hard Times* (1854). Dickens was so adept at staging the heartrending struggles of his child characters that the periodical featuring installments of *The Old Curiosity Shop* (1841) was flooded with letters from readers when Dickens began to show the novel's beloved Little Nell falling ill. Readers' pleas to spare Nell's life failed, and her affecting death was a literary sensation.

After those few traumatic months at the bootblacking factory, Dickens was rescued by his father and resumed his education. At age 15 he went to work as a clerk in a law office, and by 1834 was a journalist, reporting on Parliament for the *Morning Chronicle.*

In 1833 he started to submit short descriptive essays to magazines, and his literary career began to flourish with a series of pieces in the *Monthly Magazine,* later published in two volumes as *Sketches by Boz* (1836), short pieces describing London scenes and characters and wittily illustrated by the famous artist George Cruikshank. *Sketches* was positively reviewed by George Hogarth, editor of the *Morning Chronicle,* and in 1836 Dickens would marry the editor's eldest daughter, Catherine (Kate). Nine months after their marriage, the Dickenses' first child was born.

Dickens undertook enormous labors to capitalize on his first literary success and support his family. He wrote sequels to *Sketches,* a comic operetta, and began publishing installments, or numbers, of his first novel, *Pickwick Papers.*

The final number of *Pickwick Papers* ran in 1837. The comic exploits and amusing illustrations of its principal characters, Mr. Pickwick, Sam Weller, and the oddball members of the Pickwick Club, doled out in monthly installments, captured the reading public's attention, much as a successful television sitcom would today.

In 1837 the first of 24 installments of *Oliver Twist* appeared. This novel incorporated many elements of the popular NEWGATE CRIME NOVELS, which took crime and the criminals likely to end up in Newgate prison as their theme. Unlike Pickwick's relatively benign London, this novel presents the London Dickens encountered as a reporter—the home of pickpockets, prostitutes, and murderers, in which an innocent orphan has to make his way. This novel earned Dickens a reputation as a social-reform writer because it treated child criminals with sympathy, and attacked the harsh new Poor Law, which sought to eliminate poverty by harassing the poor into working.

The success of this novel enabled the Dickens family to move first into a house on Doughty Street (the only Dickens residence that still survives, now a museum), and then into one on Devonshire Street, both in Bloomsbury. But the family was not happy. By the 1850s Dickens described his marriage as "miserable" and threatened to have Kate incarcerated in a lunatic asylum. In 1856 he began an affair with the actress Ellen Ternan, with whom he probably had a son, and Kate and Charles were legally separated two years later. Eventually Dickens supported three households: one for Kate, one for Ellen, and one for himself.

In 1842, just shy of his 30th birthday, Dickens set off for the United States. He received an enthusiastic welcome, and, at the outset, was as enthusiastic about America as the country was about him. But after months of travel he became disillusioned. Both the travel book *American Notes* (1842) and the novel *Martin Chuzzlewit* (1844) show signs of Dickens's disgust at American slavery and vulgarity.

After a brief hiatus from novel-writing, during which Dickens produced *A Christmas Carol* (1843), along with other short works, he published *Dombey and Son* (1848). In this novel, a man of business must learn to value his devoted daughter—but only after suffering the death of his first wife and his son, his second wife's desertion, and bankruptcy. From this point until 1865, Dickens published a major novel every two to four years.

The autobiographical *David Copperfield* appeared in 1850 and incorporates many episodes of Dickens's life. For instance, David experiences an exaggerated version of Dickens's own factory experience and also has an unhappy marriage, which for Copperfield mercifully ends with the death of his first wife.

Bleak House followed, and, with its intricate plot, dual narrators, biting social criticism, and powerful symbolism, is considered one of the finest novels of the 19th century. *Hard Times* appeared in 1854 and *Little Dorrit* in 1857; both novels address the hardships wrought by capitalism.

All the Year Round, a magazine Dickens founded in 1859, was the outlet for serial publication of his next two novels: *A Tale of Two Cities* (1859) and *Great Expectations* (1861). The opening of the former, "It was the best of times. It was the worst of times," is among the most famous in all of English literature. Dickens's last completed novel, *Our Mutual Friend* (1865), is his most bitter.

Dickens influenced Victorian fiction in his capacity as editor of *Household Words* and *All the Year Round,* publishing works by ELIZABETH GASKELL and WILKIE COLLINS, among others. His predominance was further enhanced by his many public readings.

In 1867 Dickens embarked on another marathon reading tour in America, where he was lionized as a celebrity writer. Despite ill health and exhaustion, he continued to press himself upon his return to England in 1868. He began publishing installments of *The Mystery of Edwin Drood* in 1870, but died of a brain aneurysm before completing the novel. Although he had hoped to be buried near his childhood home, the public sentiment he had so assiduously cultivated for more than 40 years prevailed, and he was laid to rest in Poets' Corner at Westminster Abbey. As Edgar Johnson, one of Dickens's modern biographers, concludes, "the world he created shines with undying life, and the hearts of men still vibrate to his indignant anger, his love, his tears, his glorious laughter, and his triumphant faith in the dignity of man."

Critical Analysis

The word *Dickensian* is now a common adjective. For example, to call a bureaucracy Dickensian is to liken its operation to the interminable, convoluted practices of the Court of Chancery in *Bleak House* (1853), or the Circumlocution Office in *Little Dorrit* (1857). A scheme to aid the poor and their children can be condemned as Dickensian, in order to associate it with the brutal workhouse where Oliver Twist is born or with Mr. Scrooge's heartless recommendation that the poor "die, and decrease the surplus population."

Bleak House, with its huge cast of characters, ranging from the lovable and witty to the evil and grotesque, substantially defined the Dickensian mode of realism. Some critics have faulted the novel for its treatment of women: Esther Summerson, its heroine and one of the two narrators, strikes some as insipid; its "fallen woman," Lady Dedlock, is consigned to a miserable death; and its philanthropic women are ridiculed. It is possible, however, to acknowledge these defects and still appreciate Dickens's accomplishment. Dickens creates a complex vision of the natural bonds among diverse characters and a moving indictment of the institutions and prejudices that deny those bonds, with tragic consequences.

Great Expectations has consistently enjoyed popularity and critical attention. The progress of Pip from hapless orphan to professional man, enabled not by the manipulative Miss Havisham, as he believes, but by the ex-convict Magwitch, is a dark commentary on the rags-to-riches myth. Dickens famously rewrote the ending to soften Estella's rejection of Pip. The story's continuing in appeal is indicated by the many film and TV versions, the most famous being the 1946 movie directed by David Lean. More recently, the late 1990s has seen two new film versions.

In *Our Mutual Friend,* honest human desires are once again sullied by greed and self-interest. Yet, by means of an almost fairy tale–like deception, Dickens allows true love to triumph when the heroine's husband reveals himself to be the man whom she might have married for money, but believed had been drowned. The River Thames, as the repository of drowned bodies and submerged secrets, is the novel's most powerful image.

Other Works by Charles Dickens

Barnaby Rudge. New York: Everyman's Library, 2005
Nicholas Nickleby. New York: Penguin, 1999.

Works about Charles Dickens

Ackroyd, Peter. *Dickens.* New York: HarperCollins, 1990.

Davis, Paul B. *Charles Dickens A to Z: The Essential Reference to His Life and Work.* New York: Facts On File/Checkmark Books, 1999.

Slater, Michael. *Charles Dickens.* Very Interesting People Series. Oxford: Oxford University Press, 2007.

Smiley, Jane. *Charles Dickens.* London: Phoenix, 2003.

Dilke, Lady Emilia Frances (1840–1904)
art historian, short story writer

Emilia Frances Dilke, née Strong, was born on September 2 in Ilfracombe, on the north coast of Devon, in the west of England. Her father, Henry Strong, was an army officer who later became a banker in Oxford. She was educated at home as a child, then in 1859 went to the South Kensington Art School in London. In 1861 she married Mark Pattison, a much older Oxford professor. She hosted literary gatherings in Oxford, and one of her guests was GEORGE ELIOT. Eliot may have had Mrs. Pattison in mind when she created Dorothea in *Middlemarch,* a woman who marries an older man for the brilliance of his mind but suffers disillusionment.

Over the next two decades she wrote books on art history, such as *The Renaissance of Art in France* (1879), published under the name Emilia Pattison. She was also active in the women's suffrage movement and campaigned to improve conditions for women workers. Her husband died in 1884, and the following year she traveled to India. A short time later she married Sir Charles Wentworth Dilke, a well-known British statesman.

Dilke continued to write works on French art history, including *French Painters of the Eighteenth Century* (1889) and *French Architects and Sculptors of the Eighteenth Century* (1900), and also published two eerie story collections, *The Shrine of Death and Other Stories* (1886) and *The Shrine of Love and Other Stories* (1891). She continued her political work, serving as president of the Women's Trade Union League for some 20 years. Her contemporaries saw her as the leading British scholar of French art, but it was her personal celebrity as a speaker and as a friend of intellectuals and politicians that made her an important influence on Victorian society.

A Work about Lady Emilia Dilke

Israel, Kali. *Names and Stories: Emilia Dilke and Victorian Culture.* New York: Oxford University Press, 1999.

Disraeli, Benjamin (1804–1881) *novelist, essayist, statesman*

Benjamin Disraeli was born in London to Isaac D'Israeli, a scholar of independent means, and Maria Basevi D'Israeli. The family was descended from Jewish immigrants, but Disraeli was baptized as a Christian at age 13. He attended Higham Hall School, where he received a traditional classical education. In 1821 Disraeli entered into apprenticeship at a leading law firm in London, where he had a valuable opportunity to meet important political and social figures of his age.

In 1824 Disraeli embarked on a great tour throughout Europe. Upon his return, Disraeli decided to abandon law altogether, and he began speculating in mining shares. The venture failed miserably, and Disraeli found himself in heavy debt. The following year he, along with several investors, attempted to establish a daily newspaper, the *Representative,* which also failed.

After his failure as a businessman, Disraeli turned to writing. His first novel, *Vivian Grey* (1826), was published anonymously. It describes the life of an intelligent, unprincipled, witty young man who endeavors to achieve his goals through bold and impudent behavior, but who, in the end of the novel, is left "knowing himself to be the most unfortunate and unhappy man that ever existed." Although the book was initially well received by reviewers, their opinions quickly reversed once they discovered that the author was a young, middle-class Jew. Despite severe criticism

Disraeli wrote *The Voyage of Captain Popanilla* (1829), an insipid, tedious satire on the Utilitarians, who believed that the best actions are those that bring the most happiness to the most people (see BENTHAM, JEREMY).

In 1830 Disraeli traveled throughout the Mediterranean countries and came back with vivid impressions and ideas for his next novel. *Contarini Fleming* (1832) was "the perfection of English prose," according to Disraeli, and a financial and literary disaster, according to the public taste. Except for its biographical value and insights into the early life of the author, the novel, which is about the travels of a young boy throughout Europe, is rarely read today.

Disraeli is mainly remembered today as a brilliant politician. Between 1832 and 1835 he unsuccessfully sought a seat in the House of Commons, at first as a Radical. In 1835 he joined the Tory Party (shortly thereafter officially called the Conservative Party) but again lost in the elections. However, his witticisms and dramatic public speeches, along with his vindictive and polemical political essays, accorded him wide public recognition. In *A Vindication of the English Constitution in a Letter to a Noble and Learned Lord by Disraeli, the Younger* (1835), Disraeli presented his political ideology. The work essentially praised the traditional institutions of England, including the House of Lords and the landed gentry, and condemned the Whigs (the liberal political party of the time), along with the Utilitarians (radical and liberal political philosophers), for acting against the national interest. Disraeli gained wide recognition from prominent Tories, and continued his political writings in propaganda articles written for the London *Times* and the *Morning Post*. The rhetoric of Disraeli's political pieces was often abusive and fierce. He described the Irish, for instance, as a "wild, reckless, indolent, uncertain, and superstitious race," and "the hired instrument of the Papacy." He was at last elected to Parliament as a Conservative member in 1837. Disraeli also became a distinguished and leading member of Young England, a group that desired an alliance between landed aristocracy and the lower classes against the manufacturers and the new radical groups, such as the Utilitarians.

Disraeli did not turn away from writing novels during his political rise; instead, he used his fiction as a propaganda tool for his Conservative cause. In *Coningsby* (1845) he traces the life of Harry Coningsby, an orphaned nobleman. Its political background depicts the degeneration of both Tory and Whig parties, and inversely, the ascension of Conservative ideology through an alliance of the nobility with the lower classes. In *Sybil; or, The Two Nations* (1845), Disraeli describes the life of the poor factory towns. In the novel, the poor and the rich constitute the two opposing nations in England. Disraeli honestly presents the horrors of industrial revolution: "Naked to the waist, an iron chain fastened to a belt of leather runs between their legs clad in canvas trousers, while on hands and feet an English girl, for twelve, sometimes for sixteen hours a day, hauls and hurries tubs of coals up subterranean roads, dark, precipitous, and plashy; circumstances that seem to have escaped the notice of the Society for the Abolition of Negro Slavery."

Coningsby and *Sybil* were immediate successes, although they antagonized many Tory and Whig politicians alike. *Tancred* (1847), in which Disraeli attempts to reconcile Judaism and Christianity, was ill received by the public. His final novel, *Endymion* (1880), tells of the rise of the twins, Endymion and Myra, in the social world after the impoverishment and death of their father.

Between 1852 and 1876, Disraeli served as one of the leading figures in English government: He was chancellor of the Exchequer three times, twice leader of the opposition in the House of Commons, and for more than eight years (1868, 1874–80) prime minister. Under Disraeli's direction, the government carried out a number of dramatic reforms, including passage of the Reform Bill of 1868 that gave the lower classes more representatives in the House of Commons. On his retirement from politics in 1876, Disraeli was created earl of Beaconsfield.

On learning of Disraeli's death, QUEEN VICTORIA exclaimed, "To England and to the World his loss is immense." As a writer, Disraeli also made a considerable contribution, particularly through exposing the plight of the lower classes. As Christopher Hibbert remarks, "Disraeli was able to present himself as a wise and worldly man of moderation and great common sense, a believer in measures to alleviate the plight of the poorer classes, but above all as the leader of the national party with a concern for the interest of every class and a determination to ensure that the ideals of the Empire were sustained and the greatness of England in the world enhanced."

Critical Analysis

Among the many fictional works written by Benjamin Disraeli are two SILVER-FORK novels (*Vivian Gray* and *The Young Duke*) and three political novels, often referred to as Disraeli's political trilogy (*Coningsby; or, The New Generation, Sybil; or, The Two Nations,* and *Tancred; or, The New Crusade*).

The two silver-fork novels feature Byronic heroes, social outsiders who struggle with flaws in character and education—and some critics believe that both novels are, to some measure, autobiographical. Vivian Grey has neither birth nor fortune to set him apart, but he has confidence in his own abilities. As Disraeli says, "In England, personal distinction is the only passport to the society of the great. Whether this distinction arise from fortune, family, or talent, is immaterial; but certain it is, to enter into high society, a man must either have blood, a million, or a genius." Both of these novels feature thinly disguised portraits of real people, and contemporary readers enjoyed trying to figure out who was who—except, of course, the victims of Disrael's satire such as John Murray—with whom Disraeli founded the newspaper *The Representative* and who is satirized in *Vivian Grey*. Ultimately, Vivian is punished for his overconfidence and becomes the victim of people he thought he had duped.

The Duke tells the story of a wealthy orphan, George Augustus Frederick, Duke of St. James. Overly indulged while growing up, George is nearly destroyed by his selfishness. Unlike Vivian, however, the young duke is saved by the nobility of his own nature and he marries the heroine, May Dacre.

Each of Disraeli's political novels embodies to some extent his political philosophy that it was the duty of the aristocracy to protect the poor. *Coningsby,* the first of the three novels, takes the stance that England's future as a dominant player on the world stage depends on idealistic young politicians. *Sybil* looks at the tremendous gap between the wealthy few in England and the struggling working classes. *Tancred* looks at the relationship between religion and social problems.

Disraeli's strengths as a writer are his sharp wit, his active imagination, and his ability to create characters with a good deal of psychological depth. He tends to be weaker in the construction of plots and his works sometimes ramble. Today, Disraeli's novels are often read in the context of his political philosophy and humanitarian concerns.

Works about Benjamin Disraeli

Feuchtwanger, E. J. *Disraeli.* New York: Oxford University Press, 2000.

Langley, Helen. *Benjamin Disraeli: Scenes from an Extraordinary Life.* Oxford: Bodelean Library, 2005.

Smith, Paul. *Disraeli: A Brief Life.* New York: Cambridge University Press, 1996.

Dixon, Ella Hepworth (1857–1932) *short story writer, novelist, journalist*

Ella Hepworth Dixon was born in London to William Hepworth Dixon, the longtime editor of the *Athenaeum,* and Marian MacMahon Dixon. She was privately educated in Heidelberg, Germany, and attended the London School of Music. She also studied painting in Paris for a short time.

Dixon had intended to become an artist, but was encouraged by her father—who had a progressive attitude and published many women writers—to become a journalist. Dixon had a flair for writing;

her father's literary connections helped launch her career, but it did not take long for Dixon to earn a reputation as a talented writer.

Dixon began writing essays, reviews and short stories, and was published in such London newspapers as the *Daily Mail,* the *Daily Telegraph,* and the *Westminster Gazette,* and in the *Woman's World,* a short-lived publication edited by OSCAR WILDE. Beginning in 1895, Dixon also edited a journal called the *Englishwoman,* which printed articles and stories with a suffragist slant.

In 1892 Dixon published *My Flirtations* under the pseudonym Margaret Wynman. *My Flirtations* is a collection of vignettes narrated by a young woman being romanced by a series of vain, foolish men in her search for a suitable husband. The book received mixed reviews. Two years later, Dixon published her only novel, *The Story of a Modern Woman* (1894). The protagonist of this novel is Mary Erle, an orphan who must make her way in London as an artist and writer. The heroine's progress toward self-determination makes her a characteristic "new woman" of the 1890s (*see* NEW WOMAN NOVEL): "And in all this gaiety of a new-born world only she was to have no part. Henceforward she was to stand alone, to fight the dreary battle of life unaided." The feminist scholar Kate Flint notes, "The radicalism of this novel, unlike the 'new woman' genre as a whole, does not lie in the details of its treatment of sex and marriage, nor in its presentation of an outspoken heroine. Rather, it is a novel which lays bare the relationship between social expectations and women's capacity to achieve self-fulfillment."

Dixon held feminist beliefs and was a strong supporter of the suffragist movement. Through her writing, she encouraged other women to stand up for each other. Because of this, critics classified Dixon as a "New Woman," although she resisted the label. MAX BEERBOHM even used her as the model for the femme fatale and title character of his novel *Zuleika Dobson.*

As I Knew Them (1930), Dixon's last book, was a collection of her reminiscences. Among the friends and associates she recalls are W. B. Yeats, H. G. Wells, May Sinclair, and her former associate and friend, Oscar Wilde. In this work, she portrays herself not as a novelist, but as a journalist whose life was made interesting by the people she knew.

Dixon, Richard Watson (1833–1900) *poet*

Richard Watson Dixon was born in 1833 to Wesleyan minister Dr. James Dixon. He was educated, first, at King Edward's school in Birmingham, then went on to Pembroke College at Oxford. There he participated with WILLIAM MORRIS and the painter Edward Burne-Jones in the Pre-Raphaelite movement.

Dixon was ordained in 1858, and over the years held the post of vicar at Hayton, Cumberland, and Warkworth. In 1899, he received an honorary doctorate in divinity (D.D.) from Oxford University.

Dixon's first two volumes of verse were *Christ's Company* (1861) and *Historical Odes* (1863). He was first widely recognized for *Mano,* a very long historical poem written in terza rima, an Italian verse form that is somewhat difficult to carry off in English. Terza rima is written in three-line stanzas that rhyme *aba, bcb, cdc, ded* and is easier to write in Italian because Italian has more rhyming words than does English. Dante's *Divine Comedy* was written in terza rima.

Mano is the tale of a Norman knight of the tenth century and "Gerbert, the Pope, that doctor high and wise." The narrator, a monk named Fergant, was friend to both men, who came to be at odds with one another. His purpose in telling the tale, he says, is to "vindicate their glory from all foes / And set the truth in order clear and plain." Despite the success of *Mano,* which was praised by the poet ALGERNON SWINBURNE, Dixon was never a widely popular poet, as his work was directed more toward scholars than toward the general public.

In addition to poetry, Dixon wrote *History of the Church of England from the Abolition of the*

Roman Jurisdiction (1878–1902), a six-volume work that covered the period 1529 to 1570. Two of the six volumes were published after Dixon's death.

Dobell, Sydney Thompson (1824–1874)
poet

Sydney Dobell was born in Cranbrook, England, to John Dobell, a wine merchant. He was privately educated and, throughout his life, was generally in bad health and lived reclusively. Dobell became infamous as a poet of the Spasmodic School, a group of writers whose poetry was characterized by formlessness, exaggerated passions, and chaotic, tortured images, such as these from Dobell's poem "Return!": "I quake and yearn, / When Hope's late butterflies, with whispering wings, / Fly in out of the dark, to fall and burn— / Burn in the watchfire of return. . . ."

Dobell, who sometimes wrote under the name Sydney Yendys, often wrote political poems, and in 1850 he published a poem called "The Roman: A Dramatic Poem," which was inspired by his sympathy for Italian nationalism. The poem received favorable critical attention and brought Dobell into contact with politicians and writers who encouraged him to continue writing. In 1853 he published the first part of a sentimental, melodramatic poem called *Balder*. In response, WILLIAM AYTOUN wrote *Firmilian: A Spasmodic Tragedy* (1854), a satire and parody that was so damaging that Dobell left *Balder* unfinished. However, Dobell did publish two collections of poems about the Crimean War: *Sonnets on the War* (1855) and *England in Time of War* (1856). In 1876 a posthumous collection of his essays, *Thoughts on Art, Philosophy and Religion*, described the principles of the Spasmodic School. Edmund Clarence Stedman wrote in 1875, "Sydney Dobell, a man of an eccentric yet poetic disposition, had the faults of both the spasmodic and realistic modes, and these were aggravated by a desire to maintain a separate position of his own."

Dobson, Henry Austin (1840–1921)
biographer, poet, essayist

Born at Plymouth, England, the son of George Dobson, a civil engineer, and his wife, Augusta Harris Dobson, Dobson was educated at Coventry and Beaumaris Grammar School on the Isle of Anglesey before being sent abroad for further study in Strasbourg, France. He entered English government service at 16, in the marine department, remaining an administrator there until his retirement 45 years later in 1901.

Dobson began early to write light poetry, playing with French forms such as the rondeau and the triolet, and published his first volume, *Vignettes in Rhyme*, in 1873. There were several other poets in his unit, leading one of the upper officers in that organization to speak of "certain civil servants who would have been excellent administrators if they had not been indifferent poets." Dobson wrote poetry throughout his life—his *Complete Poetical Works* runs more than 500 pages. But more and more he was drawn to scholarship, reading widely in the history and literature of the 18th century. In 1879 he published his first biography from that period, on the artist William Hogarth. Five biographies of 18th-century writers followed—the last, in 1903, on FANNY BURNEY. By this time Dobson was an acknowledged expert, and he wrote prefaces for and oversaw production of numbers of reprints of works from that period. Dobson was also an indefatigable essayist. A bibliography of his work, published in 1900, before the end of his writing career, runs to 347 pages. But he was capable of being brief, as in "The Paradox of Time": "Time goes, you say? Ah no! / Alas, Time stays, we go."

A Work about Austin Dobson
Dobson, Alban. *Austin Dobson: Some Notes by Alban Dobson, with Chapters by Sir Edmund Gosse and George Saintsbury.* London: Milford, 1928.

Dodgson, Charles Lutwidge
See CARROLL, LEWIS.

domestic novel

Among the most important sociopolitical phenomena of the 19th century was the rise and huge growth of the bourgeoisie, or urban middle class, itself the product of the Industrial Revolution. This created hordes of new and avid readers, as well as new publishers and printing processes to fill their need for literature. These readers were not people of sophisticated tastes, and they enjoyed novels that reflected their lives and concerns. Thus arose the domestic novel, as opposed to the SILVER-FORK novel of fashionable society lives and manners, or the SENSATION novel of crime and suspense.

Domestic novels, more often than not by middle-class female authors, exemplified and preached the virtues of the simple life, hard work, piety and perseverance, and humility, all of which at the end would be rewarded by happiness. The works of MARGARET OLIPHANT and the American writer Emma Southworth are probably the purest examples, but there were literally thousands of books that exhibited enough "domestic" characteristics to fall into this category, including some of the work of FANNY BURNEY, MARIA EDGEWORTH, JANE AUSTEN, ELIZABETH GASKELL, and GEORGE ELIOT. The economics of publishing at the time encouraged writers to produce these novels in three separate volumes, often totalling more than 1,000 pages.

Works about the Domestic Novel

Armstrong, Nancy. *Desire and Domestic Fiction: A Political History of the Novel*. New York: Oxford University Press, 1995.

Cohen, Paula Marantz. *The Daughter's Dilemma: Family Process and the Nineteenth-Century Domestic Novel*. Ann Arbor: University of Michigan Press, 1991.

Douglas, Lord Alfred Bruce (1870–1945)
poet

Lord Alfred Douglas, nicknamed Bosie, was the youngest son of the marquess of Queensbury and his wife, Sybil. Born near Worcester, England, he grew up spoiled, temperamental, reckless, and vindictive, but handsome. He began studying at Magdalen College, Oxford University, but was an undisciplined student and performed badly.

In 1891 he met OSCAR WILDE, and by 1892 the two were inseparable. After Wilde published his play, *Salomé*, in French in 1893, Douglas translated it into English. Under Wilde's influence, Douglas became an accomplished sonneteer. But Douglas, who was more interested in notoriety than in literature, spoke out impulsively and indiscreetly about his relationship with Wilde. His father, enraged by his son's behavior, charged Wilde with homosexuality, which was then illegal. Douglas persuaded Wilde to sue for criminal libel; when the case collapsed, Wilde was imprisoned. Although Douglas spent the rest of his life denying his homosexuality, repudiating Wilde, and engaging in libel suits, he did write a moving sonnet about Wilde called "The Dead Poet" (1901) that contains the lines, "I heard his golden voice and marked him trace / Under the common thing the hidden grace, / And conjure wonder out of emptiness."

Douglas wanted his work to stand on its own rather than to be thought of only as a reflection of Wilde's work. From 1907 to 1910, Douglas edited a magazine called the *Academy*. He published several books of poetry: *The City of the Sorel* (1899), *Sonnets* (1909), *In Excelsis* (1924), and *Lyrics* (1935). In 1929 he brought out *The Autobiography of Douglas*. The critic G. S. Viereck says that "In spite of private quarrels and public scandals, in spite of political feuds and literary vendettas, malice cannot gainsay the vigor of his diction and the loftiness of his lyric vision."

A Work about Lord Alfred Douglas

Murray, Douglas. *Bosie: A Life of Alfred Douglas*. New York: Talk Miramax Books, 2000.

Dowie, Menie Muriel (1867–1945)
novelist

Menie Muriel Dowie was born in Liverpool, England, and educated in Germany and France.

She married Sir Henry Norman, a journalist, in 1891. The couple traveled extensively, and based on her experiences, Dowie published her first novel, *A Girl in the Karpathians* (1891), in which the heroine, dressed like a man, smokes and drinks her way through eastern Europe. The novel received, according to Dowie herself, 400 favorable reviews. As Dowie's first novel suggests, she was interested in women's issues and subsequently wrote both nonfiction and fiction that criticized conventions of femininity; for instance, as the scholar John Sutherland notes, *Women Adventurers* (1893) has a chapter called "Women in Battle." Dowie's most famous novel is *Gallia* (1895), which is still in print. In that novel, the heroine Gallia, structures her life on rational principles, talking openly and frankly about sex and choosing a husband based on his physical and mental attributes instead of the conventions of romance and love. Dowie published other forcefully feminist novels, including *The Crook of the Bough* (1898), as well as a novel about the Boer War, *Love and His Masks* (1901). Because of its revolutionary feminism, Dowie's work has received increasing critical interest, and has been reprinted in anthologies such as *Women's Writing of the Victorian Period: 1837–1901*, edited by Harriet Jump.

Dowling, Richard (Marcus Fall)
(1846–1898) *novelist*

Born in Tipperary, Ireland, Richard Dowling attended elementary school in Limerick, then worked for a trading company in Waterford before moving to Dublin in 1870. Four years later he left for London, where he made his career as a novelist and journalist, publishing some 28 novels under the name of Marcus Fall. Some of the novels are Irish, regional novels, most notably *The Mystery of Killard* (1879), which W. P. Ryan in 1894 noted made "mystery, weirdness, and morbidness . . . attractive half a hundred times." John Sutherland observes that Dowling's view of life in rural Ireland was not particularly cheerful, as evidenced by *Old Corcoran's Money* (1897), "a rather bleak tale of crime and punishment in the small town of 'Ballymore.'" Dowling was also a widely published journalist, having worked for the *Nation* and contributed to *Tinsley's* and the *Cornhill Magazine*. Most of his work is out of print today.

Dowson, Ernest Christopher (1867–1900) *poet*

Ernest Dowson was born in Lee, Kent, to Alfred and Annie Dowson. As a child he traveled abroad with his father, mostly in France, and grew to love French literature. His favorite French writers were Gustave Flaubert, Honoré de Balzac, and Paul Verlaine. He studied at Oxford University in 1886, where he read erotic poets and smoked hashish to induce spectacular dreams, but he had no patience for the life of disciplined academic study and left after one year. He subsequently worked for his father at a dock in London, but spent much of his time writing poetry.

He began to keep company with AUBREY BEARDSLEY, OSCAR WILDE, and W. B. Yeats, and the rest of the group called the Rhymers' Club. They met regularly at the Cheshire Cheese, a pub on Fleet Street, in London, between 1891 and 1894. Although Yeats said the group was sometimes dull, they engaged in discussions on every topic, especially poetry.

Dowson wrote poems for the *Savoy* and the *Yellow Book*. He became good friends with LIONEL JOHNSON, who taught him philosophy and encouraged him to convert to Roman Catholicism. In 1891 Dowson met Adelaide Foltinowicz, the 12-year-old daughter of a restaurant owner. She would become for him the symbol of love and innocence, and was the subject of his despairing love poem "Non Sum Qualis Eram Bonae Sub Regno Cynarae" (more commonly called "Cynara"), which contains the melancholy refrain, "I have been faithful to thee, Cynara! In my fashion."

Other works of Dowson include *Verses* (1896), *Decorations* (1899), and a one-act play, *The Pierrot of the Minute* (1897). *Poetical Works* was published posthumously in 1934 and *Letters* in 1967. Dowson died at 33 of alcoholism and tuberculosis.

Dowson led a wild, dissolute, irregular life, like many other poets of that decade. Yeats called them "the tragic generation," the restless, self-destructive poets of the 1890s. The poet ARTHUR SYMONS said of Dowson, "He had the pure lyric gift."

Doyle, Sir Arthur Conan (1859–1930)
novelist, short story writer

The popular phrase "Elementary, my dear Watson," first recorded in a 1929 film, alludes to the shrewd observations and reasoning of the London detective Sherlock Holmes, as told by his chronicler, John H. Watson, M.D. Although both Holmes and Watson are fictitious, they have become so much a part of the popular culture that countless tourists would regard their first visit to London incomplete had they not tried tracking down Holmes's bachelor quarters at 221B Baker Street. Sherlock-mania has started societies (including the Baker Street Irregulars) and a journal (the *Baker Street Journal*). It has led to countless films, television shows, stories, and novels written by admirers that have given Holmes whole new cases to crack.

Holmes was the creation of Sir Arthur Conan Doyle. Born in Edinburgh, Scotland, to Charles Doyle, a surveyor and artist, and Mary Foley Doyle—both Irish Catholics—Doyle was educated at Jesuit-run schools. In 1877 he began medical studies at Edinburgh University, graduating in 1881 and setting up medical practice in southern England the following year. Doyle had begun to write while in medical school, and the immense popularity of his historical novel *The White Company* (1891) convinced him to give up medicine and write full time. Nine years later, however, during the Second Boer War between Britain and the Boers (descendants of Dutch settlers) in South Africa, Doyle worked again as a doctor. It is largely for this that he was knighted in 1902.

It is for Sherlock Holmes, however, that he is most remembered today. Holmes was based in part on Dr. Joseph Bell, a professor of Doyle's at Edinburgh University, whose keen observation and logical cast of mind had dazzled Doyle. Watson, some have observed, at times resembles Doyle himself. The two characters are introduced to each other in the first Holmes tale, *A Study in Scarlet* (1887).

Most of the Holmes stories originally appeared in the *Strand* magazine. One of the most famous of these, *The Hound of the Baskervilles* (1902), was first serialized there beginning in 1901. The plot involves Sir Charles Baskerville, whose recent death Baskerville's friend Dr. James Mortimer hires Holmes to investigate. During a nighttime walk on his estate, Baskerville may have been chased down by a phantom hound, bringing again to fruition the ancient curse he believed the family to be under. Doyle's journalist friend Bertram Fletcher Robinson's invitation to his home in south Devon introduced Doyle to the moorland atmosphere that is an important element of the story.

Doyle was aware that the fame of the fictional Holmes outdistanced his own. Nearly a decade before *The Hound of the Baskervilles*, Doyle had wearied of the character and dispatched him to his death in the story "The Final Problem" (1893). However, public protests, not to mention financial incentives, succeeded in getting Doyle to resurrect the sleuth several years later.

The most enduring of Doyle's works apart from the Holmes stories is the novel *The Lost World* (1912), in which Professor Challenger's Amazonian expedition uncovers a land where dinosaurs and other prehistoric beasts miraculously survive. In a Darwinian twist, Challenger's own appearance suggests this monstrous world. The narrator, the journalist Edward Malone, writes that "[i]t was his size that took one's breath away.... His head was enormous." Challenger reappears in the sequel, *The Poison Belt* (1913), and in other stories.

In addition to his literary career, Doyle pursued humanitarian causes, exposing, in the nonfictional *The Crime of the Congo* (1909), for instance, the brutal treatment of Belgian Congo natives by trade companies. Also, he fought for 17 years to free Oscar Slater, a German Jew wrongly convicted of a murder; Slater finally was released from prison.

Interested in the occult and the paranormal for a quarter century, Doyle announced his conversion to spiritualism in 1916 and, with his wife, during the next dozen years spread the spiritualist gospel throughout England, Australia, Africa, and the United States.

Critical Analysis

Sherlock Holmes's "continued popularity with all levels of readers," the critic Christopher Clausen has noted, "is all the more striking when one reflects that he is probably the most cerebral protagonist of any importance in English fiction." Doyle, dissatisfied with contemporary fictional detectives who solved crimes too often by sheer luck, wanted him to be acute, logical, and scientific. Holmes, the critic Stephen Knight has written, "stands for science, the exciting new 19th-century force in the public mind." At the very least, he represents the power of reason. The enduring attraction to him also owes something to how Doyle has balanced the character in large and subtle ways. Holmes, who can solve almost any mystery, is himself shrouded in mystery. We know little, for instance, about the education or experience that presumably helped train Holmes's quick mind. Similarly, the control of situations that Holmes's astute crime-solving suggests is balanced by his cocaine addiction and the poor self-mastery this implies. Most important, Doyle succeeds in making Holmes likeable even when Holmes shows negative traits. His delight in his own prowess, for example, is sufficiently contagious to redeem a chilly condescension when in *A Study in Scarlet,* upon being introduced to Watson, he almost instantly declares, "You have been in Afghanistan, I perceive." Holmes later reveals the self-conversation that led to his conclusion:

"Here is a gentleman of a medical type, but with the air of a military man. Clearly an army doctor, then. He has just come from the tropics, for his face is dark, and that is not the natural tint of his skin, for his wrists are fair. He has undergone hardship and sickness, as his haggard face says clearly. His left arm has been injured. He holds it in a stiff and unnatural manner. Where in the tropics could an English army doctor have seen much hardship and got his arm wounded? Clearly in Afghanistan." The whole train of thought did not occupy a second ... and you were astonished.

As is the reader.

This most convoluted murder mystery finds Holmes expressing a theme that also applies to many of his other adventures: "the scarlet thread of murder running through the colourless skein of life," which, says Holmes, it is "our duty ... to unravel ... and expose." The "heap of reddish soil" revealing a freshly dug grave in Utah, of all places, picks up on this theme.

This first Holmes piece wobbles. Doyle's biographer Ronald Pearsall has called *Study* "a [structural] mess, with a center section that is melodrama of the most off-putting kind." The same cannot be said about *The Hound of the Baskervilles* 15 years later. This story, rather than being overelaborated and tangled, is spare and genuinely evocative of something indefinable admitting accents of a universal mystery. The "enormous coal-black hound," with fire bursting from its mouth, its eyes aglow, is a captivating image. Christopher Clausen, moreover, has described the story's Grimpen Mire as a "haunted wasteland," adding, "By the end of the story, the rational mind is back on its throne, and the spectral hound is only a dead dog. But outcome does not erase the impression of horror and unreason that has been so powerfully built up."

Doyle was a prolific writer who believed he would be best remembered for his historical novels, such as *The White Company* and its prequel, *Sir Nigel* (1906). These books, however, are little read today. Instead, Doyle's legacy is the Holmes stories and Holmes himself. Sherlock Holmes, Doyle's biographer Pierre Nordan has remarked, "is generally accepted as the prototype of the detective.... His name has become almost a by-word.... He has been treated like a national hero."

Other Work by Sir Arthur Conan Doyle
The Complete Sherlock Holmes. New York: Bantam, 1998.

Works about Sir Arthur Conan Doyle
Lellenberg, Jon, Daniel Stashower, and Charles Foley. *Arthur Conan Doyle: A Life in Letters.* New York: Penguin, 2007.

Lycett, Andrew. *The Man Who Created Sherlock Holmes: The Life and Times of Sir Arthur Conan Doyle.* New York: Free Press, 2007.

Orel, Harold, ed. *Critical Essays on Sir Arthur Conan Doyle.* New York: G. K. Hall, 1992.

Pascal, Janet B., ed. *Beyond Baker Street.* New York: Oxford University Press, 2000.

Stashower, Daniel. *Teller of Tales: The Life of Arthur Conan Doyle.* New York: Henry Holt, 1999.

Doyle, Sir Francis Hastings (1810–1878)
poet

Francis Hastings Doyle was born near Tadcaster, Yorkshire, in the north of England. His father was an army officer. Doyle, who wrote poetry from the time he was a young man, attended Eton and Oxford University, then became a lawyer in 1837. He was a friend of WILLIAM GLADSTONE, the future prime minister, but political differences estranged them later in life.

At 24 Doyle published his first collection of poems, *Miscellaneous Verses.* Over the next 30 years, he published several more collections of poetry, including *Two Destinies* (1844) and *Return of the Guards* (1866).

Doyle's best-known works are his ballads, such as *The Loss of the Birkenhead,* which describes the sinking of a ship "Caught, without hope, upon a hidden rock." Doyle was also famous for his ballad *The Private of the Buffs,* which praises the courage of a lowly infantry private who dies defending the British Empire:

> *Vain, mightiest fleets of iron framed*
> *Vain, those all-shattering guns;*
> *Unless proud England keep, untamed,*
> *The strong heart of her sons.*
> *So, let his name through Europe ring—*
> *A man of mean estate,*
> *Who died, as firm as Sparta's king,*
> *Because his soul was great.*

In 1867 Doyle became professor of poetry at Oxford. He published his memoirs in 1886. His entry in the 1911 edition of the *Encyclopaedia Britannica* reports, "Doyle's poetry is memorable for certain isolated and spirited pieces in praise of British fortitude."

Drennan, William (1754–1820) *poet, political writer*

William Drennan was born in Belfast, Ireland. His father was William Drennan, a Presbyterian clergyman. He studied medicine at the University of Edinburgh, and received his M.D. in 1778.

In 1779, after practicing medicine for several years in Belfast, Drennan moved to Dublin, where he became involved with the United Irishmen, an organization inspired by the French Revolution and dedicated to the cause of Irish independence from England. One of his most frequently anthologized poems is "The Wake of William Orr" (1797), which commemorates the execution of one of the founders of the United Irishmen for administering an illegal oath:

> *Why cut off in palmy youth?*
> *Truth he spoke, and acted truth—*
> *Countrymen, "Unite!" he cried,*
> *And died—for what his Saviour died.*
>
> *God of Peace, and God of Love,*
> *Let it not thy vengeance move!*

*Let it not thy lightnings draw—
A Nation guillotin'd by law!*

Drennan's political career brought him trouble in 1794 when he and an associate named Rowan wrote a manifesto, the *Address of the United Irishmen to the Volunteers of Ireland*. The two men were arrested and brought to trial. Rowan was fined £500 and sentenced to two years' imprisonment; Drennan (who was actually responsible for the "crime") was acquitted and released.

Drennan married in 1800, and soon after returned to Belfast. Abandoning his political activities, he founded *Belfast Magazine*. Drennan also began writing again; this time, however, instead of publishing controversial political pieces, he chose less inflammatory subjects. Over the years, many of his poems appeared in various periodicals. In 1815, he published *Fugitive Pieces in Verse and Prose*, a collection of poetry.

For all of his work, Drennan is perhaps best known for coining his native land's nickname, "the Emerald Isle," in his poem "Erin to Her Own Tune and Words" (1795).

du Maurier, George (1834–1896) *novelist*

George du Maurier's father, Louis-Mathurin Busson du Maurier, and his mother, Ellen Clarke du Maurier, were living in Paris when George was born, but moved among France, Belgium, and England during his childhood. Du Maurier grew up bilingual in French and English. At his father's urging he enrolled at University College, London, for a scientific education, but he did not do well there. Upon his father's death, du Maurier returned to the Continent to study art. In 1857 he went blind in one eye and had to give up the idea of being a painter, instead turning to black and white drawings, which he began selling to *Punch* magazine in 1860. He found his métier in gently satiric cartoons about English society types, particularly those whose wealth was recently acquired. Not earning enough money as a cartoonist, he began to illustrate books, among them ELIZABETH GASKELL's *North and South*, HENRY JAMES's *Washington Square*, and THOMAS HARDY's *A Laodicean*. He subsequently became fast friends with James, who published an appreciation of du Maurier in his *Partial Portraits* (1888).

It was at James's urging that, well into his 50s, du Maurier began his first novel, *Peter Ibbetson* (1891). The first part of the novel is a lively account of the hero's childhood, an idealized version of du Maurier's own. As an adult, Peter is (blamelessly) driven to murder; in jail, serving a life sentence, he finds that he is able to "dream true"—to have, in his dreams, a romance with the woman he has loved since childhood, Mimsey, who has become an unhappily married duchess in real life but is able to share those dreams. Du Maurier's friends received the novel with delight, but critics were lukewarm and sales were slow.

Du Maurier's second novel, *Trilby* (1894), was an enormous success. Inspired by French novelist Henri Murger's *Scènes de la Vie de Bohème*, it draws on du Maurier's own art student days. The art student Little Billee loves the young model Trilby, but their engagement is destroyed by his mother. Trilby falls under the powerful spell of the evil Svengali, who later mesmerizes—that is, hypnotizes—Trilby so that she becomes an enormously successful singer. In the end, at a concert where Little Billee has come for the first time to hear the famous artist, Svengali dies of a heart attack, and upon his death, Trilby loses her musical ability. She weakens and dies, but not before being reconciled with Little Billee.

The novel was immensely popular, selling hundreds of thousands of copies and coining the term *Svengali* as a name for any person who seems to dominate another. The hat Trilby wore in du Maurier's drawings for the book and in a London stage production of the book became a fashion hit, lending its name to that style of hat. *Peter Ibbetson* experienced a rise in sales because of *Trilby*'s success.

Du Maurier's third novel was *The Martian*, which has autobiographical sections, again combined with an extrasensory element. The central character's mind is possessed by a being from Mars, Martia, who intends to transmit her knowledge to Earth through him; under her influence he begins to write extraordinary books that alter the fate of the world. Du Maurier believed it was his best book, but he died before its publication in 1897, when it was greeted with harsh criticism.

In a tribute to du Maurier's fiction written after his death, William Dean Howells said, "He won the heart, he kindled the fancy, he bewitched the reason; and no one can say just how he did it."

Du Maurier was the grandfather of the popular English 20th-century novelist Daphne du Maurier (1907–89).

Works about George Du Maurier

James, Henry. *Partial Portraits.* Ann Arbor: University of Michigan Press, 1970.

Kelly, Richard Michael. *George du Maurier.* Brookfield, Vt.: Ashgate, 1996.

Ormond, Leonée. *George du Maurier.* Pittsburgh, Penn.: University of Pittsburgh Press, 1969.

Dunne, Mary

See EGERTON, GEORGE.

Eden, Emily (1797–1869) *diarist, novelist*

Emily Eden was born in Westminster, England, in 1797, the daughter of William Eden, first baron of Auckland and a diplomat, and Eleanor Elliot. The family spent a great deal of time traveling, and most of the Emily's siblings were born outside of England.

Eden had a flair for art, and spent her days sketching landscapes and portraits. During her teenage years, she designed the landscape for Eden Farm. Since her brothers were tutored away from home, she constantly wrote to her favorite brother, George, detailing family life.

After her parents' death, George was left in charge of Emily and their younger sister. For financial reasons, they had to move from their family home. Over the years, the girls lived with a number of older sisters and cousins in London. They lived apart from their brother, and Eden was depressed because she missed the rural atmosphere of home.

Eden enjoyed the company of men, but her relationships with them were purely platonic. Her associations included notable members of the British aristocracy and Parliament. In 1806 Eden's brother, George, was promoted to governor and moved to India where his two sisters joined him. In India, Eden established herself as a hostess, using her wit and charm to influence British policy. However, she soon tired of her duties and left Calcutta to explore on her own.

During Eden's travels throughout India, she recorded her impressions in her journals, sketches, paintings, and letters to friends and family. The life she witnessed in India was rife with poverty, sickness, sadness, and death; however, Eden was able to capture India's beauty as she detailed the exotic scenery and culture. Eden returned to England in 1844, and started compiling her letters and journals. However, Eden first published her successful novel, *The Semi-detached House* (1859), a work which was intended to resemble the work of her favorite author, JANE AUSTEN. It details the snobbery and arrogance of the British elite. Her four-volume memoir detailing her life on the Indian subcontinent, *Journals and Correspondence,* was published in 1860.

With the help of her niece, she wrote a second novel, *The Semi-attached Couple* (1860), which tells of a young couple who spent most of the first year of their marriage misunderstanding each other. This was not as successful as Eden's first, and Eden herself claimed not to like it. Emily Eden died in Richmond in 1869.

Other Works by Emily Eden

Miss Eden's Letters. London: Macmillan, 1919.

Up the Country: Letters Written to Her Sister from the Upper Provinces of India. London: Virago Press, 1983.

Works about Emily Eden

Dunbar, Janet. *Golden Interlude: The Edens in India.* London: J. Murray, 1955.

Ghose, Indira. *Women Travelers in Colonial India: The Power of the Female Gaze.* New York: Oxford University Press, 1998.

Edgeworth, Maria (1767–1849) *novelist, nonfiction writer*

Maria Edgeworth was born in Black Bourton, Oxfordshire, England, to Richard Lovell Edgeworth and Anna Maria Elers Edgeworth. Her mother died in childbirth five years later, and Maria formed a close bond with her father, who was an educational theorist, scientist, inventor, writer, and Anglo-Irish landowner.

Edgeworth's first notable original work was her *Letters for Literary Ladies* (1795), in which she defends women's rights to education and argues for their intellectual abilities; however, Edgeworth also advocates that women apply their intellects only in the domestic sphere, not in the public realm of politics. The next year, Edgeworth published *The Parent's Assistant,* a collection of stories and a play for children. Although her stories were moral and instructional like most children's literature of the time, they were more lively and entertaining than previous children's tales and became hugely successful. In 1798, she and her father coauthored *Practical Education.* This important work provided the philosophical rationale behind *Parent's Assistant*: that children are better motivated to learn through pleasure than through fear.

In 1800 Edgeworth tried her hand at novel writing, and met with yet another huge success: *Castle Rackrent.* Critics today consider the novel Edgeworth's masterpiece and the first Irish novel. Initially published anonymously, Edgeworth's comic treatment of Irish provincial life was much admired for its innovative use of an unreliable narrator, Thady M'Quirk, who describes a family of Irish landowners in a colloquial idiom while telling readers as much about himself as his masters: "Having, out of friendship for the family, upon whose estate, praised be Heaven! I and mine have lived rent-free, time out of mind, voluntarily undertaken to publish the Memoirs of the Rackrent Family, I think it my duty to say a few words, in the first place, concerning myself." In his postscript to *Waverley,* SIR WALTER SCOTT acknowledged Edgeworth's *Castle Rackrent* as the artistic inspiration for his novel.

Edgeworth's next novel, *Belinda* (1801), a novel of manners, chronicles a young girl's journey into the adult world and her choice of a marriage partner. In *Belinda,* Edgeworth provides readers with an insightful critique of fashionable society—a critique that would reappear in two later works: "The Modern Griselda" (1805), a satire on women who forgo domestic roles in favor of aspiring to positions among the fashionable elite, and *Tales of Fashionable Life* (1809), a collection of stories that similarly attack bourgeois aspirations toward "fashionable" society and advocate reform through the professionalization of the gentry.

In 1802 Edgeworth traveled through the Midlands of England with her family and then went to Paris, where she and her father were celebrated for their intellectual contributions to the field of education. While in Paris, Edgeworth received a marriage proposal from Abraham Niclas Clewberg-Edelcrantz, a notable Swedish intellectual. She declined, against her father's wishes, but Edelcrantz later inspired the character of Count Altenberg in Edgeworth's 1814 novel *Patronage.* Count Altenberg is the husband of Caroline Percy, who is his intellectual equal and, by Edgeworth's standards, the ideal woman.

Critical Analysis

Patronage describes the contrasting fates of two families: the Percys and the Falconers. While the successful and prosperous Percys are disciplined, independent, and possessed of professional knowledge, the Falconers rely too heavily upon chance and the outdated system of patronage—and thus meet with failure.

Edgeworth's next novel, *Harrington* (1817), is notable for its conscious efforts to represent Jewish characters in a positive light. The novel was inspired by Edgeworth's correspondence with Rachel Mordecai, an American Jew who objected to the stereotypical representations of Jews that Edgeworth had written in previous books.

In *Ormond* (1817), a novel published in the same volume as *Harrington,* the Irish hero journeys to France and England, only to reject the fashionable women of the French court and instead marry an Englishwoman, an act that symbolically suggests the union of the English and Irish gentry. *Ennui* (1809) and *The Absentee* (1812) also address Irish concerns. Both novels explore the problems caused by absentee landlords, who draw income from Irish property but spend most of their time and money in England, and both symbolically resolve the problem by having these landlords return to their Irish estates to set things right. Although Edgeworth is remembered for her contributions to children's literature, her society novels, and her moral tales, her most important contribution to literary history may be her realistic depiction of Irish life.

Other Work by Maria Edgeworth
Helen. London: W. Glaisher, 1924.

A Work about Maria Edgeworth
Butler, Marilyn. *Maria Edgeworth: A Literary Biography.* New York: Oxford University Press, 1982.

Hare, Augustus J. C., ed. *The Life and Letters of Maria Edgeworth.* Gloucester, England: Dodo Press, 2007.

Edwards, Amelia (Ann Blandford) (1831–1892) *novelist, travel writer*

Amelia Edwards was born on June 7 in London, England. Her father was an army officer and later a banker. As a child she was educated at home, but at age 15 she began to study voice with a music teacher.

Edwards was also writing fiction, and her first novel, *My Brother's Wife,* a romantic account of a spurned lover's travels through Europe, was published in 1855. Meanwhile, she was writing stories and music and drama reviews for the *Saturday Review,* the *Morning Post,* and CHARLES DICKENS's *Household Words.* During the 1850s and 1860s she published short stories and novels, often featuring motifs of travel. *Barbara's History* (1864) was her first success, featuring another wandering romantic hero who announces, "I am a citizen of the world—a vagrant by nature—a cosmopolitan at heart. I confess to little of the patriotic spirit, and much of the Bohemian." *Debenham's Vow* (1870), subtitled *A Lady's Captivity Among Chinese Pirates,* similarly features travel.

Today, Edwards is most remembered for her travel writings. In 1873 she traveled to Egypt and became enthusiastic about Egyptology, the study of ancient Egyptian artifacts. She published an account of her journey, *A Thousand Miles up the Nile* (1877), which became a best-seller and the standard work on Egypt for many years. This work describes both contemporary Egyptian society and the monuments of its past. Edwards reports on the destructive effects of visitors to the pyramids: "The tourist carves [the monument] with names and dates, and in some instances with caricatures. . . . Every day, more inscriptions are mutilated—more tombs are rifled—more paintings and sculptures are defaced. . . . When science leads the way, is it wonderful that ignorance should follow?"

After her return from Egypt, Edwards campaigned to stop the destruction she had witnessed. Her efforts eventually led to the founding of the Egypt Exploration Fund in 1882, which preserved Egyptian antiquities. For the remainder of her life Edwards wrote articles about Egyptology and lectured in Europe and the United States.

A Work about Amelia Edwards
Grosskurth, Phyllis, "Amelia Edwards: A Redoubtable Victorian Female." *Review of English Literature.* 6:1 (1965): 80–92.

Egan, Pierce (1772–1849) *journalist, novelist*
Little is known of Pierce Egan's early life. Of his education the *New Yorker* writer A. J. Liebling wrote, "His work affords internal evidence that he was self-educated; if he wasn't he had certainly found a funny schoolmaster." Egan wrote his most famous works during the Regency period (1811–20), when the pleasure-loving prince of Wales ruled on behalf of his incapacitated father, George III, and he wrote for and about the most disreputable elements of that period's society. *Boxiana* (1812) was a collection of pieces he had begun for a sporting magazine, the *Weekly Despatch,* and he published four more volumes in the next 16 years. His essays described the boxing matches, the betting, the fighters, trainers, rich sponsors, and the milieu in which they existed in language ranging from stilted upper-class to Cockney argot.

Egan also wrote *Life in London; or, The Day and Night Scenes of Jerry Hawthorn, Esq. And Corinthian Tom* (1822) a hugely popular work about life on the London streets, told in the vivid slang of the day. It details the adventures of a London dandy, Tom, and his country cousin, Jerry. Egan thoughtfully concludes the work with a slang glossary for the uninitiated, the need for which can be seen from this sentence: He writes, "With my *Tom* and *Jerry*, I try to *'get the best'* of the *coves* in the *East*—and the SWELLS in the West!" *Tom and Jerry; Or, Life in London* had a great success in a musical adaptation for the stage by W. T. MONCRIEFF. CHARLES DICKENS's *The Pickwick Papers* is said to have been influenced by Egan's work.

Egan's son, Pierce Egan the Younger (1814–80), was an illustrator, dramatist, and writer of historical novels; his *Robin Hood and Little John* (1840) began a revival of interest among writers and readers in the legendary hero.

Egerton, George (Mary Chavelita Dunne) (1860–1945) *short story writer, playwright*
Mary Chavelita Dunne, who would write as George Egerton, was born in Melbourne, Australia, to John Dunne, an army captain, and his wife, Isabel George Dunne. At age 15, after her mother died, Dunne left home and began to support herself. She taught school in Germany, worked as a nurse in a London hospital, and lived in Norway, where she learned Norwegian and began translating Norwegian literature into English. In 1891 she married George Egerton Clairmonte and they settled in Cork, Ireland.

Two years later, Dunne published her first book of short stories as George Egerton, a pseudonym she adopted so she could publish stories that were different from the usual romantic and sentimental fiction expected from women. The heroines of her stories exemplified the so-called new woman of the 1890s, who wanted a career and sexual freedom (*see* NEW WOMAN NOVEL).

In 1894 Egerton began writing for the *Yellow Book,* the celebrated and notorious British literary magazine, and in the same year published a second book of short stories, *Discords*. In one story, the heroine defies the conventions of the time when she has a romantic relationship with a poet but never marries him.

In 1895 Dunne and Clairmonte had a son. Six years later the couple divorced, and Dunne married theatrical agent Reginald Golding Bright. She began writing plays, which had less success than her earlier work. After her son was killed in World War I, however, Dunne said she "lost all ambition." Only her last play, *Wild Thyme,* was produced after her son's death.

Other Work by George Egerton
Hammick, Georgina, ed. *Love and Loss: Stories of the Heart.* Boston: Faber & Faber, 1992.

A Work about George Egerton
Ledger, Sally, and Allison Ledger. *The New Woman: Fiction and Feminism at the Fin de Siècle.* Manchester, England: Manchester University Press, 1997.

Eliot, George (Mary Ann Evans) (1819–1880) *novelist, essayist, translator*
George Eliot was born Mary Ann Evans in Warwickshire, England, to a conservative Anglican

family headed by Robert Evans, land agent to a wealthy family, and Christiana Pearson Evans. At school she distinguished herself for her scholarship and her keen interest in Evangelical Christianity. In her young adulthood, influenced by German and English philosophers (including her friend HERBERT SPENCER), she abandoned her childhood beliefs, upsetting her pious father and brother. Among her earliest publications were translations from the German of David Friedrich Strauss's *Das Leben Jesu* (*The Life of Jesus*) (1846), a life of Jesus treating him not as a divinity, but as an ordinary historical personage, and Ludwig Feuerbach's *Essence of Christianity* (1854), which argued that Christianity should be reconceived as a religion of humanity without God.

A believer in the necessity of spreading education, tolerance, and modern medicine in order to foster social progress, Evans often told stories that contrasted the wholesome aspects of rural life in her era with the need to enlighten rural people about modern ideas. In her anonymous essay "Margaret Fuller and Mary Wollstonecraft" (1855), Evans commented upon equality between the sexes and her philosophy of reform in general. She wrote that men sometimes fear educated wives, but "surely, so far as obstinacy is concerned, your unreasoning animal is the most unmanageable of creatures."

Other essays and a stint as editor of the *Westminster Review*, an influential liberal periodical, occupied her early career. In 1858 she turned to fiction, creating her George Eliot pen name for *Scenes from Clerical Life*. This work, popularly and critically praised, included three long stories, among them "The Sad Fortunes of Reverend Amos Barton," which hinted at a theme common in her later work: the tension between idealistic reformers and local reality in the places they seek to reform. One churchwarden in the story, Mr. Bond, says of drab, well-meaning parsons like Barton, "they're too high learnt to have much common sense."

Biographers cite various reasons for Mary Ann Evans's decision to adopt a pen name, but the most convincing follows from her *Westminster Review* essay, "Silly Novels by Lady Novelists" (1856). Written just as she embarked on her own fiction-writing career, this essay attacked the triviality and technical weaknesses of novels by women. Its timing suggests that she adopted a pen name because she feared harming her own reputation as a serious writer by being classified as a "lady novelist." Clearly, George Eliot intended to write more serious and thoughtful fiction than that generally associated with lady novelists. Shortly after the publication of her first novel, *Adam Bede* (1859), the identity of George Eliot was discovered, but she continued to write literature under that name.

Adam Bede convincingly depicts country life while telling the story of a squire who seduces a naïve girl. It also explores the preaching career of Dinah, a character modeled on Eliot's Methodist aunt. Eliot's second novel, *The Mill on the Floss* (1860), tells of Maggie Tulliver, who struggles against middle-class convention, and her estranged brother Tom. This work is thought to have been heavily influenced by Eliot's estrangement from her own brother and father over her loss of religious faith.

In *Silas Marner* (1861), the elderly miser Silas Marner is redeemed by caring for the mysterious foundling left on his doorstep. *Romola* (1863), set in Renaissance Italy, depicts the gradual corruption of the Florentine criminal Tito Melema. Eliot's next novel, *Felix Holt, The Radical* (1866), is a complicated tale of inheritance, mysterious paternity, and political reform efforts set in the time of the 1832 Reform Act, mingling the lives of the activist Felix Holt and the aristocratic Mrs. Transome.

Critics consider *Middlemarch* (1872) Eliot's most nuanced and complex depiction of village life, reform efforts, and family conflict. *Middlemarch* was the climax of her aesthetic and philosophical efforts, although she later wrote *Daniel Deronda* (1876), which concerns Zionism and a loveless marriage inspired by money.

Despite concerns about women's roles in society, Eliot displayed ambivalence toward women's equality. She advocated women's education and wrote about such feminists as MARY WOLLSTONE-

CRAFT and Margaret Fuller; at the same time, she refused to lend enthusiastic support to women's suffrage and insisted on being referred to socially as Mrs. Lewes, adopting the name of her common-law husband, GEORGE HENRY LEWES, who was legally married to another woman. When the feminist BARBARA BODICHON wrote to Eliot, applauding her for her defense of unmarried mothers in *Adam Bede*, the author responded curtly.

Despite George Eliot's complex relationship to Victorian propriety, she was an enormously popular writer, counting even QUEEN VICTORIA among her admirers. Her most appealing characters—such as the preacher Dinah Morris in *Adam Bede;* Dorothea Brooke, the earnest heroine of *Middlemarch;* and Daniel Deronda, who discovers his Jewish heritage and becomes a supporter of Zionism—all struggle with the tensions between ambition and personal desire, on the one hand, and spiritual doubt and social constraints on the other. The view of social reform emerging from their experiences is marked less by utopian revolution than by fitful, compromised, and often painful spiritual battles waged by individuals in the context of powerful historical forces.

As a novelist, essayist, editor, and translator, George Eliot established herself as one of the preeminent literary figures of the 19th century. Her novels were key to the development of realism in the Victorian period and treated broad issues of social reform, philosophy, and history. They also presented psychologically intricate characters involved in complex personal and political situations. In a private letter, Eliot once wrote, "If art does not enlarge men's sympathies, it does nothing morally." Much of her work can be seen as an effort to instill in readers an admiration for thoughtful, caring people and the communities to which they belong. The critic Rosemary Ashton writes that Eliot's novels feature a "subtle probing of human nature that leads many modern critics to regard her as the greatest novelist of the 19th century."

Critical Analysis

Perhaps George Eliot's greatest contribution to realism is her ability to convey through intricate and lengthy plots just how embedded people are in the period in which they happen to be born. In *Middlemarch,* for example, Eliot begins by comparing St. Theresa (1515–82), who reformed the Carmelite Order in the 16th century, with modern women, who fail to achieve heroic deeds not because they lack St. Theresa's talent or zeal, but because they are like cygnets, ugly ducklings, who never find the company of their "oary-footed kind"—that is, other swans, who would acknowledge their worth. Unlike St. Theresa, who lived in an age of unquestioned religious belief, modern women find themselves in a world without a "coherent social faith," shared social values that would guide women toward their vocations.

Still, as *Middlemarch* makes clear, Eliot insists on the value even of the apparently imperfect lives of all her characters, male and female. Dorothea Brooke's hopes of building a utopian rural community and of assisting with the theological scholarship of her first husband, the Reverend Casaubon, come to nothing. Indeed, his young wife's enthusiasm alienates Casaubon, who dies shortly after the marriage.

Still, through her unremarkable life as the wife of her second husband, the political writer Will Ladislaw, and as the mother of their son, Dorothea's impact on the world is "incalculably diffusive." Eliot concludes *Middlemarch* by saying, "that things are not so ill with you and me as they might have been is half owing to the number who lived faithfully a hidden life, and rest in unvisited tombs." Eliot's contributions to realism as a literary technique stem from her efforts to embody this ordinary sense of realistic expectations and to imbue their consequences with enduring significance.

Other Work by George Eliot

Byatt, A. S., and Nicholas Warren, eds. *Selected Essays, Poems, and Other Writings.* London: Penguin, 1990.

Works about George Eliot

Ashton, Rosemary. *George Eliot: A Life*. New York: Penguin, 1998.

Hardy, Barbara. *George Eliot: A Critic's Biography*. London: Continuum, 2006.

Hughes, Kathryn. *George Eliot: The Last Victorian*. New York: Cooper Square Press, 2001.

Levine, George, ed. *The Cambridge Companion to George Eliot*. New York: Cambridge University Press, 2001.

McDonagh, Josephine. *George Eliot*. Jackson: University Press of Mississippi, 1997.

Pangallo, Karen L., ed. *The Critical Response to George Eliot*. Westport, Conn.: Greenwood Press, 1994.

Rignall, John, ed. *Oxford Reader's Companion to George Eliot*. New York: Oxford University Press, 2002.

Ellis, Henry Havelock (1859–1939) *nonfiction writer*

Born in Croydon, Surrey, England, to the merchant sea captain Edward Ellis and the strict, evangelical Susannah Wheatley Ellis, Havelock Ellis was a physician who devoted much of his time to literary essays, science writing, and translations. He also edited the Mermaid Series of Old Dramatists, which brought 17th-century plays to a wider Victorian audience.

But Ellis is best remembered for his writings about sex. Ellis was a popularly recognized authority on psychological and sexual matters who is widely credited with the relaxation of sexual taboos. An associate of other activists and writers who advocated changing sexual mores, such as the birth-control champion and eugenicist Margaret Sanger and the poet-essayist EDWARD CARPENTER, Ellis wrote psychological accounts of sexual practices that many considered deviant at the time. His book *Sexual Inversion* (1897) was an early sympathetic account of homosexuality. Ellis added six more volumes to *Sexual Inversion*, the last appearing in 1928, to form his master work, *Studies in the Psychology of Sex*.

Ellis writes in his autobiography *My Life* (1939) that the concept of evolution led him to look skeptically at heterosexual bonds: "In an instant, as it seemed, the universe was changed for me." Since heterosexual bonds were the result of reproductive instinct, not of logical necessity, he argued, perhaps they need not form the basis for marriage.

In an unsuccessful attempt to put his principles into practice, he married the lesbian activist Edith Lees, hoping to prove that sexual attraction need not be the basis for marriage; however, Lees soon resumed her lesbian relationships and the marriage ended. Ellis was also romantically involved for a time with the feminist novelist OLIVE SCHREINER, but their relationship fell apart as well.

Ellis also wrote *The Criminal* (1890), which describes criminality as a disease to be treated; *Man and Woman* (1894), an analysis of secondary sexual differences and their roots in early childhood development; *The World of Dreams* (1911), quasi-Freudian speculations based on his personal experiences; *The Task of Social Hygiene* (1912), which advocates eugenics; and books of literary and cultural criticism. The scholar Chris Nottingham notes that Ellis remained for decades both an icon of sexual liberation and the target of jokes by people from the novelist Evelyn Waugh to the actor Peter Sellers, making him "an unavoidable point of reference in the study of human sexuality . . . a usable symbol of salacious modernity for a smart young novelist of the 1920s [and for] a comedian of the 1960s."

A Work about Havelock Ellis

Nottingham, Chris. *The Pursuit of Serenity: Havelock Ellis and the New Politics*. Amsterdam: Amsterdam University Press, 1999.

Ellis, Sarah Stickney (1812–1872) *novelist, nonfiction writer*

Sarah Stickney Ellis was born to a Quaker family in England. She was raised on a farm in Yorkshire by her father, William Stickney, and mother, Esther Richardson Stickney, but came to reject her family's Quaker beliefs at a young age and joined the Congregationalists.

In 1833 she published *Pictures of Private Life,* a collection of stories that she advertised as "drawn from the scenes of every-day life." In 1837, she married William Ellis, an author and missionary. United in their beliefs, the couple, who had no children, devoted themselves to working on Christian missions. With the encouragement of her husband, Ellis wrote a series of conduct books that advised women to manage their households and defer to their husbands.

The Women of England: Their Social Duties and Domestic Habits (1839), *The Daughters of England* (1842), *The Mothers of England* (1843), and *The Wives of England* (1843) were very well received in the Victorian period; *The Women of England* went through 20 editions. These guides all advocated submission to male authority, promoting the Victorian ideal of the "Angel in the House," that paragon of feminine domestic piety created by COVENTRY PATMORE.

Not surprisingly, Ellis's work infuriated many feminists in England with statements such as "your position as a woman . . . is, and must be, inferior to his as a man."

Ellis also published a number of novels, most of which supported her antifeminist beliefs. *Home; or, The Iron Rule* (1836) is a cautionary tale warning fathers to employ a firm hand with their children. *Pique* (1850) advocated the submission of women in marriage. Although she did not encourage women to constantly accommodate irresponsible husbands, she did advise them that their best chance at securing happiness was in pleasing their men. Although Ellis's sentiments are distasteful to most modern sensibilities, a few contemporary critics have begun to reassess her contribution to women's writing. Virginia Blain and her coauthors of *The Feminist Companion to Literature in English* suggest that her belief in female solidarity "reveals a strong fellow-feeling for women's domestic trials."

Engels, Friedrich (1820–1895) *political philosopher*

Friedrich Engels was born in Barmen, a neighborhood of the modern-day German city of Wuppertal, to Friedrich Engels and his wife, Elisabeth van Haar Engels. Engels's father ran a bleaching and spinning works in Wuppertal and co-owned a similar factory in Manchester, England.

In 1842 Engels moved to Manchester to supervise the family business. There he found inspiration for his book *The Condition of the Working Class in England* (1845), which laid the foundations of modern sociology, describing the rise of British industrialization and the problems of disease, poor education, crime, sexual abuse, and child labor among the workers. This work attracted the attention of the German political philosopher KARL MARX, whom the wealthier Engels financially supported after Marx moved to England. The two soon collaborated on the book *German Ideology* (1845), which was not published until 1932 and which argues that belief systems are products of the social and economic conditions in which they form.

In 1848 Engels and Marx wrote *The Communist Manifesto,* a landmark socialist work. Published during a year of unsuccessful political revolts in several European cities, the *Manifesto* captured the revolutionaries' sense that the old order of Europe needed to end, along with private property, traditional marriage, and the state.

In 1867 Marx brought out the first volume of his massive work *Das Kapital,* which was an analysis of economic history, which Engels promoted avidly through reviews in newspapers and magazines. After Marx's death in 1883 Engels completed the last two volumes of *Das Kapital* (1885, 1894).

The economic doctrines outlined in *Das Kapital* were accepted by intellectuals and political revolutionaries around the globe for at least a century and included the labor theory of value, according to which things are valuable in proportion to the work put into them, regardless of their use value to others. This theory suggested that workers, not owners, ought to take control of the materials with which they work, by violent revolution if necessary. The historian J. D. Hunley argues that for many critics Engels, like Marx, has become a "scapegoat for all that they dislike in Soviet Marxism," but for others he remains a crucial figure in the history of Western philosophy.

Other Work by Friedrich Engels
The Origin of the Family, Private Property, and the State. New York: International Publishers, 1995.

Works about Friedrich Engels
Arthur, Christopher. *Engels Today: A Centenary Appreciation.* New York: St. Martin's Press, 1996.

Hunley, J. D. *The Life and Thought of Friedrich Engels: A Reinterpretation.* New Haven, Conn.: Yale University Press, 1991.

Equiano, Olaudah (Gustavas Vassa) (1745–1797) *autobiographer*

Olaudah Equiano was born in the Kingdom of Benin in East Africa. His father was a distinguished man in Essaka, the village along the Niger River, and the family had hopes that the son would succeed the father as a judge. Equiano, the youngest child of his father, was, he wrote, "the greatest favourite with [his] mother." His name in the Ibo tribe's language means "one favored, and having a loud voice and well spoken."

When Equiano was 11, he was kidnapped and sold into slavery. In the months after his capture he was transported across the country and sold to several different masters. Eventually, Equiano arrived at the coast, where he was forced aboard a slave ship and transported to Barbados. About two weeks after his arrival in Barbados, Equiano was sent to Virginia, where he was bought and put to work on a plantation. He was then sold to Michael Henry Pascal, a lieutenant in the Royal Navy. After years spent sailing throughout the world with Pascal, Equiano was able to buy his freedom in 1766.

Equiano settled in London, where he became an active member of the movement to abolish slavery in Britain. At age 44 he published the work that was to make him famous, his autobiography *The Interesting Narrative of the Life of Olaudah Equiano, Or Gustavus Vassa* (1789), an immensely popular work that went through nine editions before Equiano's death. The structure and style of Equiano's autobiography influenced many African-American writers who followed him, including Frederick Douglass (ca. 1817–95) and even Malcolm X (1925–65).

Equiano settled in Britain. In 1792 he married Susannah Cullen. The couple had two daughters, Anna Maria and Joanna. Susannah died only four years after their marriage, and Equiano died the next year. Anna Maria died in the same year, leaving only Joanna to inherit her father's estate of £950, an amount which would be worth about £100,000 today.

Critical Analysis

The Interesting Narrative tells the story of Equiano's life, but its real purpose is to demonstrate the essential humanity of people of color and, to some extent, to question the belief that white westerners were "civilized" and black Africans "uncivilized." In the first chapter, in fact, Equiano describes the life and customs of his native village in terms that suggest that the simplicity of that life was superior to life in the great cities to which he had traveled. For example, the food he ate as a child was simple and delicious, "for as yet the natives are unacquainted with those refinements in cookery which debauch the taste." Life in Benin almost suggests an innocent Eden, "where nature is prodigal with her favors" and where the people, "unacquainted with idleness," are highly regarded "for their hardiness, intelligence, integrity, and zeal." Although his people owned slaves, Equiano is quick to note that "with us [slaves] do no more work than other members of the community, even their masters; their food, clothing and lodging were nearly the same as theirs."

From this heaven, Equiano is plunged into hell. In the hold of the slave ship that transports him to Barbados, the stench is "absolutely pestilential" and people are packed so closely that each had scarcely room to turn himself.... This wretched situation was again aggravated by the galling of the chains, now become insupportable.... The shrieks of the women, and the groans of the dying, rendered the whole scene of horror almost inconceivable.

Equiano relates several stories of people who leapt to their deaths rather than endure what passed for life on the slave ships.

The structure and style of *The Interesting Narrative* show the influence of 18th-century adventure novels, such as *Robinson Crusoe*; Protestant captivity narratives, such as *The Captivity of Mary Rowlandson*; and rags-to-riches stories, such as Benjamin Franklin's *Autobiography*. The three-part structure of the story, as Equiano traces his progress from slavery to escape to freedom, parallels the structure of the spiritual autobiography, which moves from sin to conversion to spiritual rebirth. While Equiano uses a conventional form, the details of his story are unique to his own experience first as a slave and then as an African man in a white world.

One important theme of the narrative is the question of identity, symbolized in the various names Equiano is given and must accept. In Virginia he is given two names, Michael and Jacob. Then he receives a third:

> While I was on board this ship, my captain and master named me *Gustavus Vassa*. I ... refused to be called so, and told him as well as I could that I would be called Jacob; but he said I should not, and still called me Gustavus: and when I refused to answer to my new name, which I at first did, it gained me many a cuff; so at length I submitted, and by which I have been known ever since.

Equiano's struggle with his identity prefigures the struggles of generations of enslaved peoples and their descendants. The loss of name, of nation, of freedom seems inevitably to lead to questions about the self. The critic Robert J. Allison points out that "Equiano's book ... reminds us of the lives of millions who did not live to tell their stories."

Works about Olaudah Equiano
Cameron, Ann. *The Kidnapped Prince: The Life of Olaudah Equiano.* New York: Random House, 2000.
Carretta, Vincent. *Equiano, the African: Biography of a Self-Made Man.* New York: Penguin, 2007.

Evans, Matilda Jane (Maud Jeanne Franc) (1827–1886) *novelist*

Matilda Jane Evans was born in Peckham Park, Surrey, located in the south of England. In 1852 she and her husband, a Baptist minister, moved to southern Australia to work as missionaries.

During the 19th century, Baptist women played essential roles in Australia as teachers and missionaries. Evans, who became a deaconess in the Baptist Church, began a school there. She also became a well-known writer, publishing novels under the pseudonym of Maud Jeanne Franc. Her novels usually were serialized in Baptist periodicals before they appeared as books, and many of them, such as *Marian; or, The Light of Someone's Home* (1865), were written especially for teenage readers. In the novels that were meant as moral guides for young readers, such as *Minnie's Mission: An Australian Temperance Tale* (1869), Evans hoped to impart moral lessons by example. In other books, such as *Vermont Vale; or, Home Pictures in Australia* (1866), she tried to present a realistic picture of life in Australia for her readers at home in England.

Ewing, Juliana Horatia (1841–1885)
novelist, short story writer

Juliana Horatia Ewing, née Gatty, was born in Ecclesfield, England. Her father, Alfred Gatty, was vicar of the Ecclesfield parish, and her mother, Margaret, wrote and edited children's stories. When Juliana was young, the family staged plays in their parlor to entertain family and friends.

Juliana frequently wrote and directed these plays, and the family affectionately named her "Aunt Judy." In 1866 Juliana's mother began publishing *Aunt Judy's Magazine,* in which Ewing's first stories appeared. These stories emphasize Ewing's ideal of a blissful family life and stress the importance of a family in a child's development. For instance, in "The Brownies" (1865) two brothers ignore their chores to search for the legendary sprites who, according to legend, help maintain clean households, but when they realize the spirits are mythical, they complete the chores themselves. The boys discover how much their widowed father needs their support, and he realizes that his sons are much more than encumbrances. The story's popularity inspired the Brownie division of the Girl Scouts, which modeled their helpful attitude after the fictional sprites.

In 1867 the young writer married Alexander Ewing, a commissariat in the British army, and traveled with him to Canada. She initially welcomed the chance to experience new places, but soon became homesick. Her health gradually deteriorated, possibly from blood poisoning, and prevented her from joining her husband in his future assignments in Ceylon and Malta.

In 1873, upon the death of her mother, Ewing and her sister Horatia Katherine assumed control of the *Aunt Judy's Magazine.* Ewing also began to publish novels. Like her stories, her novels offer a strikingly realistic portrayal of family life, usually depicting generous women helping those in need. In one of the most popular, *Lob Low-by-the-Fire* (1874), two unmarried sisters adopt a mischievous orphan who eventually flees and joins an army regiment. However, after he completes his service he returns. Ashamed of his previous behavior, he secretly rescues the sisters from financial troubles before revealing his presence.

Some critics dismiss Ewing's novels as formulaic and shallow, but those same books greatly expanded the popularity of Victorian children's fiction. The optimism and compassion of her works influenced writers such as Rudyard Kipling and Mary Molesworth. The critic Judith Plotz notes that Ewing's fiction "dignifies and sanctifies the brief life of a child by embedding that life in the human institution of the family."

Works about Juliana Horatia Ewing

Avery, Gillian. *Mrs. Ewing.* London: Bodley Head, 1961.

McGavran, James Holt, ed. *Romanticism and Children's Literature in Nineteenth-Century England.* Athens: University of Georgia Press, 1991.

F

Faber, William (1814–1863) *poet, religious writer*

Frederick William Faber was born in Yorkshire on June 28. He was educated at Harrow School and graduated from Oxford University in 1836. He began his writing career as a poet, publishing three volumes of poetry that were heavily influenced by his acquaintance WILLIAM WORDSWORTH. In 1839 Faber became a priest in the Anglican Church and was appointed rector of a church in Northamptonshire. During this period the Anglican Church was strongly influenced by the OXFORD MOVEMENT, led by a group of Oxford clerics intent on restoring ritual and also on providing practical social services for the poor. Faber became a Roman Catholic in 1846 and set up a religious community in Staffordshire. A year later he began publishing *Lives of the Modern Saints*. In 1849, Faber established a chapel for the poor in London. He wrote hymns that were sung at the services in the chapel. Over the next few years he wrote 150 hymns, including "Blood is the Price of Heaven":

> Under the olive boughs,
> Falling like ruby beads,
> The blood drops from his brows,
> He bleeds,
> My Saviour bleeds!
> Bleeds.

In addition, Faber published a series of eight religious works, including *All for Jesus* (1853), *Growth in Holiness* (1854), and *Bethlehem* (1860).

Other Work by Frederick Faber

The Blessed Sacrament; Or, the Works and the Ways of God. Rockford, Ill.: Tan Books, 1978.

Farjeon, Benjamin Leopold (1838–1903) *novelist*

Benjamin Farjeon was born and raised in London, where he was sent to a private school by his father, a successful merchant. In 1852 he began writing for a publication called the *Nonconformist*. When he was 17, in rebellion against his family's Jewish religious beliefs, Farjeon left England and sailed for Australia. From there he went to New Zealand, where he became an editor for the *Otago Daily Times*.

Farjeon eventually returned to London in the 1860s and began writing popular novels, the most famous of which was *Grif: A Story of Australian Life* (1866). Among his other works were *Joshua Marvel* (1871), *Love's Victory* (1875), and *Rosemary Lane* (1876).

In 1877 Farjeon married Margaret Jefferson. The couple had five children, among them the writer Eleanor Farjeon, born in 1881, and Joseph Farjeon, a novelist and playwright, born in 1883. During the 1880s and 1890s, Farjeon continued to produce novels and mysteries, such as *For the Defence* (1891) and *The Last Tenant* (1893).

Fawcett, Millicent Garrett (1847–1929)
nonfiction writer, novelist

Millicent Fawcett, née Garrett, was born in Suffolk, England, to Newson Garrett, a successful merchant, and Louise Dunnell. She was educated at boarding school and went to London to stay with her sisters, Elizabeth and Louise.

In 1865 Fawcett attended a speech by John Stuart Mill that proposed equal rights for women. Through Mill she met Henry Fawcett, a member of Parliament, whom she married. Millicent became her husband's secretary, and together they worked to advocate women's rights. Millicent Fawcett also wrote political books for the general reader, such as *Political Economy for Beginners* and *Essays and Lectures on Political Subjects*. She became a member of the London Suffrage Committee in 1868 and three years later helped found Newnham College, Cambridge, for women.

The Fawcetts' support of laws that would protect a woman's right to own property helped accomplish the passage of the Married Women's Property Act in 1882. Two years later, Henry Fawcett died of pleurisy. Millicent Fawcett, however, carried on their political work. As president of the National Union of Women's Suffrage Societies, she was influential in winning the vote for women. After the passage of women's suffrage in 1918, Fawcett wrote an account of the movement, *The Women's Victory* (1920), and a memoir, *What I Remember* (1924). In 1925 she was awarded the Grand Cross, Order of the British Empire, for her work on behalf of women, and was afterward known as Dame Fawcett.

Works about Millicent Fawcett
Caine, Barbara. *Victorian Feminists*. New York: Oxford University Press, 1992.

Rubinstein, David. *A Different World For Women: The Life of Millicent Garrett Fawcett*. Columbus: Ohio State University Press, 1991.

Fenn, George Manville (1831–1909)
novelist, journalist

Although virtually unknown today, in the last decades of the 19th century George Manville Fenn wrote popular historical-adventure stories for boys. He was born in the section of London known as Pimlico to Charles and Louisa Fenn, but family financial troubles forced him to support himself at age 13. He trained as teacher, taught school, then worked as a printer and as a journalist before turning to fiction. He wrote more than a thousand articles for the popular press, including a series in the 1860s on working-class life for the *Star*. He briefly served as the editor of the general interest *Cassell's Magazine* in 1870 and was publisher of *Once a Week* from 1873 to 1879.

In 1864 Fenn published his first short story in *All the Year Round,* and by the 1880s he concentrated full time on writing adventure stories and historical romances for boys. Adventure stories became popular at the end of the 19th century as education became more universally available and literacy spread. Modeled after the historical romances of Sir Walter Scott and Edward Bulwer-Lytton and the adventure tales of Robert Louis Stevenson, the young heroes in these stories demonstrated late-Victorian notions of "manly" behavior.

Another successful writer in this genre was G. A. Henty, whose style Fenn imitated. Henty's influence is apparent in Fenn's novels that relate military history: *The Black Tor: A Tale of the Reign of James I* (1896), *Our Soldier Boy* (1900), *Sweet Mace: A Sussex Legend of the Iron Times* (1885), and *The Young Castellan: A Tale of the English Civil War* (1895). Fenn so admired Henty that he wrote the only book-length biography of the author, *George Alfred Henty: The Story of an Active Life* (1907). Fenn himself was extraordinarily prolific, producing more than 200 novels and short stories for popular magazines such as the *Strand*. Today his work is regarded as representative of outmoded imperialist values.

Ferrier, Susan (1781–1854) *novelist*

Susan Ferrier was born in Edinburgh, Scotland, the youngest of James Ferrier's and Helen Coutts Ferrier's 10 children. Her father was an estate manager and a friend of Sir Walter Scott. She received an education typical for women of her class, with some training in music. She never married, and managed her father's household from the time she was 15 until her father died in his 80s. All the while she observed Edinburgh life, and she recorded her observations in three novels: *Marriage* (1818), *The Inheritance* (1825), and *Destiny* (1831). All three were published anonymously; she did not claim them publicly until they were reissued in 1841.

Marriage is a satiric social comedy about the disappointments of married life, reflected in the careers of Lady Juliana, who elopes with a handsome Scots captain and is appalled to discover the reality of life in a Scottish castle, and of her twin daughters Adelaide, who triumphs in the world's view by captivating an English duke, and Mary, who rejects an advantageous marriage for union with a virtuous Scot. The tedium, superficiality, and restrictions of female life in well-off 19th-century society are humorously conveyed. The main joy of the book is the portrayal of Lady MacLaughlan, a neighbor who greets the new bride, Lady Juliana, with a speech of appraisal: "You really are a pretty creature! . . . but I don't like your eyes; they're too large and too light. . . . Why han't you black eyes? Your mother was an heiress; your father married her for her money, and she married him to be a countess; and so that's the history of their marriage—humph!" The book was an immediate success.

The Inheritance is a more complex novel. The heroine, Gertrude, loses an inheritance and, consequently, the loyalty of the man she thinks she loves, through the revelation of her true birth, but gains another inheritance and the love of a worthier suitor through her virtuous behavior. The testy Uncle Adam Ramsay, who eventually adopts Gertrude, may have been modeled on Ferrier's father. Ferrier describes with affection how Uncle Adam is captured against his will when he happens to open Scott's novel *Guy Mannering*: "Novel-writers he had always conceived to be born idiots, and novel-readers he considered as something lower in the scale of intellect. It was, therefore, with feelings of the deepest humiliation he found himself thus irresistibly carried along."

Ferrier's third and last novel, *Destiny*, was dedicated to Scott. While she was writing it her father died, and the comic spirit that is so lively in the first two books is muted here. The novel centers on the rewards of Christian virtue. True, the heroine, Edith, does marry the good and gentle Malcolm, but this is in a way a subplot: As one of Ferrier's biographers puts it, "Edith's Christian awakening is more important than her marriage." After *Destiny* Ferrier devoted herself to evangelical Christianity and charity work, and wrote no more novels.

A Work about Susan Ferrier

Cullinan, Mary. *Susan Ferrier*. Boston: Twayne, 1984.

Field, Michael (Katherine Harris Bradley) (1846–1914) and Edith Emma Cooper (1862–1913) *poets, playwrights*

Michael Field was considered a promising poet whose work was praised by reviewers until "his" identity was revealed by Robert Browning; shocked to learn that Michael Field was two women, an aunt and niece, reviewers subsequently dismissed their work. Nonetheless, as Michael Field, Katherine Bradley and Edith Cooper went on to write 28 plays, eight volumes of poetry, and 30 journal volumes that chronicled their curious, flamboyant, introspective, and socially engaged daily lives.

Bradley was born in Birmingham, England, and at 16, when her sister fell ill, helped to rear her sister's children. She became especially fond of Edith, whom she educated at home and then accompanied to Bristol University, where they continued to study together. During those years, Bradley had been writing poetry, and she published *The New Minnesinger and Other Poems* (1875) under the pseudonym Arran Leigh (an allusion to Elizabeth Barrett Browning's influential narrative poem *Aurora Leigh*). Bradley's poems were an attempt to capture the "unrecorded life of women," an effort that could characterize much of the work she and Cooper published as Michael Field.

Michael Field's first volume, *Long Ago* (1889), deals with women's passion, extending and elaborating fragments from the classical Greek woman poet, Sappho. Their second volume, *Sight and Sound* (1892), describes the faces and bodies of women as depicted in famous painting; one sonnet in the volume, for example, describes Leonardo's *Mona Lisa*. Their third volume, *Underneath the Bough* (1893), is a collection of love poems written over a number of years. One begins, "It was deep April, and the morn / Shakespeare was born; / The world was on us, pressing sore; / My love and I took hands and swore / Against the world, to be / Poets and lovers evermore." Such lines, written by two women, certainly went against the grain of Victorian public attitudes toward unconventional personal and domestic relationships. But Michael Field flouted convention, celebrating in their poetry "ecstatic joy" in often lush poetic form.

Of Michael Field's plays, 27 tragedies on historical or legendary topics (*Attila, My Attila* [1896], for example) and one masque, only one saw the stage. *A Question of Memory* was produced on October 27, 1893, at the Independent Theatre in London. The other 26 were closet dramas, written to be read, not performed. Michael Field's work received little critical attention after Bradley's and Cooper's deaths, but there are signs of renewed interest in recent books and literary journals.

A Work about Michael Field
Donoghue, Emma. *We Are Michael Field*. Bath, England: Absolute Press, 1998.

Fitzgerald, Edward (1809–1883) *poet, translator*

Edward Fitzgerald was born into the wealthy family of John Fitzgerald at Bredfield, Suffolk, England. He studied at Trinity College, Cambridge, where he became part of the Apostles, a group of friends that included Alfred, Lord Tennyson. After he graduated in 1830, he lived as a reclusive country gentleman, growing flowers, reading literature, and sailing his yacht. He did, however, maintain an active and lively correspondence with Tennyson, Thomas Carlyle, and William Thackeray.

In 1849 Fitzgerald wrote a memoir of Bernard Barton, the Quaker poet who was a friend of Charles Lamb. Fitzgerald also wrote several volumes of verse, including *Euphranor* (1851), a Platonic dialogue about the rebirth of chivalry, and *Polonius: A Collection of Wise Saws and Modern Instances* (1852). His translations of plays by the 17th-century Spanish dramatist Pedro Calderón de la Barca were published as *Six Dramas of Calderón* (1853). In 1856 he published *Salaman and Absal: An Allegory Translated from the Persian of Jami*. Also, in 1856 he married the daughter of his memoir subject Bernard Barton, but the marriage lasted only one year.

Up to that time, none of Fitzgerald's works had sold more than a few copies. His life might have continued in obscurity had he not translated *The Ruba'iya't of Omar Khayyám*, a work by a 12th-century Persian poet that became one of the most popular books of the Victorian period and endures today.

Fitzgerald first read the lengthy poem in 1857, publishing his translation from the Persian anonymously in 1859. Few reviewers noticed the book, and it was soon out of print. But two years later it caught the attention of Dante Gabriel Rossetti and Algernon Swinburne. Their enthusiasm persuaded Fitzgerald to revise his translation, and the new edition became a best-seller. Because of the increased interest and high demand for the *Ruba'iya't,* Fitzgerald considerably revised and polished his stanzas for each edition. Scholars consider his version not so much a translation as an adaptation. Fitzgerald's goal was to capture the mood and the feeling of the verses, and he often used his own imagery to do so. The tone of the *Ruba'iya't,* as it examines the mysteries of life and death, is mocking, bittersweet, and fatalistic, as shown in section 16:

> "The Wordly Hope men set their Hearts
>   upon
> Turns Ashes—or it prospers; and anon,
> Like Snow upon the Desert's dusty Face,
> Lighting a little hour or two—is gone."

Swinburne called the *Ruba'iya't* "that most exquisite English translation, sovereignly faultless in form and color of verse."

Critical Analysis

It is hard today to imagine the profound influence that Edward Fitzgerald's *Ruba'iay't of Omar Khayyám* had for many generations. So familiar and memorable was the work that 43 of its 107 quatrains are quoted *in full* in the *Oxford Dictionary of Quotations.*

Fitzgerald never claimed that his work was a direct translation of the original; in fact, he called it a "transmogrification," and it is fair to say that the work is a rather free interpretation of the original Persian piece, which contained about 1,000 quatrains. Fitzgerald, however, was faithful to the original form. *Ruba'iay't* is the plural form of a Persian word that means "quatrain," and the Persian quatrains rhyme *aaba,* as do Fitzgerald's. Fitzgerald not only picks and chooses among Omar's thousand poems, he also combines quatrains, reorders them, and interprets through his translation. Among the most famous passages in his translation is:

> *A book of Verses underneath the Bough,*
> *A Jug of Wine, a Loaf of Bread—and Thou*
> *Beside me singing in the Wilderness—*
> *Oh, Wilderness were Paradise enow!*

Here is the same passage translated some years later by E. H. Whinfield; it is more accurate than Fitzgerald's, but certainly different in both sound and feeling:

> *In the sweet spring a grassy bank I sought*
> *And thither wine and a fair Houri*
>   *[nymph] brought;*
> *And, though the people call me graceless*
>   *dog,*
> *Gave not to paradise another thought.*

Fitzgerald himself says of Omar, "Having failed of any Providence but Destiny, and any World but this, he set about making the most of it; preferring rather to soothe the Soul through the Senses into Acquiescence with Things as he saw them, than to perplex it with vain disquietude after what they might be." Whether or not this description applies to Omar, it certainly applies to Fitzgerald's poem. It has a fatalistic, yet epicurean outlook—as exemplified in the quatrain quoted above. If "eat, drink, and be merry" is a reductive definition of the philosophy of Epicureanism, it is perhaps not reductive when applied to Fitzgerald's Omar. Here is another quatrain that emphasizes the idea of grasping pleasure while one can:

> *How long, how long, in infinite Pursuit*
> *Of this and that endeavor and dispute?*
> *Better be merry with the fruitful Grape*
> *Than sadden after none, or better, Fruit.*

Fitzgerald's fatalism is revealed in lines such as these:

> *With Earth's first Clay They did the Last*
>   *Man's Knead,*
> *And then of the Last Harvest sow'd the*
>   *seed:*
> *Yea, the first Morning of Creation wrote*
> *What the Last Dawn of Reckoning shall read.*

At the very moment of creation, all was determined, the poet suggests; there's no use battling against fate, and, as one of Fitzgerald's most famous stanzas tells us, nothing one can do to change it:

> *The Moving Finger writes; and, having writ,*
> *Moves on; nor all your Piety nor Wit*
> *Shall lure it back to cancel half a Line,*
> *Nor all your Tears wash out a Word of it.*

Among the lures of Fitzgerald's work at the time of its publication was its exoticism; its language, themes, and outlook were completely opposed to the straitlaced, duty-bound attitudes of most Victorians. While many were scandalized, others regarded the *Ruba'iay't* as a breath of fresh air from the East.

Works about Edward Fitzgerald

Moore, Thomas. *The Life and Death of Lord Edward Fitzgerald.* Whitefish, Mont.: Kessinger, 2007.

Terhune, Alfred McKinley. *The Life of Edward Fitzgerald, Translator of the Ruba'iy't of Omar Khayyám.* Westport, Conn.: Greenwood Publishing Group, 1980.

Fitzgerald, Percy Hetherington (1834–1925) *novelist, biographer*

Percy Fitzgerald was born in County Louth, Ireland. He attended Stonyhurst College in Lancashire, England, and Trinity College, Dublin. Following his graduation from Trinity, he became a lawyer and served as crown prosecutor in northeastern Ireland.

Fitzgerald's fiction first appeared in the *Dublin University Magazine* in 1863, when he was 29. Soon after, Fitzgerald moved to London, where he devoted himself to a career as a writer. He wrote more than 100 books, including biographies, literary studies, histories, and novels. Among his works of fiction were a best-selling novel, *Bella Donna; or, The Cross Before the Names* (1864), *Fairy Alice* (1865), *The Dear Girl* (1868), and *The Middle-Aged Lover* (1876).

In his later years, Fitzgerald turned to works of history and biography. In 1895 he published a two-volume biography of Charles Dickens, who was a friend, followed two years later by a study of the 18th-century Irish playwright William Sheridan, *The Real Sheridan*. He wrote several books about the London stage and biographies of people involved with it. He also sculpted busts of Dickens, in Bath, England, and of the 18th-century writer Samuel Johnson, whose brilliance he admired.

Other Work by Percy Fitzgerald

Bozland: Dickens' Places and People. Ann Arbor, Mich.: Gryphon Books, 1971.

Forster, John (1812–1876) *biographer, historian*

Born to Robert Forster, a butcher, and his wife, Mary, in Newcastle upon Tyne, John Forster moved to London in 1828 to attend University College and study law at the Inner Temple. Choosing journalism over the law, he joined the *True Sun* as drama critic in 1832. He later became editor (1842–43) of the *Foreign Quarterly* and other publications.

Forster was at the center of London's literary life and enjoyed close friendships with Charles Lamb, Thomas Carlyle, Robert Browning, and Alfred, Lord Tennyson. Considered the 19th century's first professional biographer, Forster produced popular works about Daniel Defoe (1860), Oliver Goldsmith (1863), and Jonathan Swift (1875). As a historian, he focused on the English Civil War in *The Statesmen of the Commonwealth of England* (1840) and *Puritan Commonwealth: Lives of the Statesmen of the Commonwealth* (1836–39). An avid collector of books, he amassed a library of more than 18,000 volumes that is now part of the National Art Library of the Victoria and Albert Museum.

Forster's most important association was with Charles Dickens. The two writers were introduced by William Harrison Ainsworth in 1836. Known for his abruptness of manner, Forster was immortalized by Dickens as Podsnap (the epitome of middle-class smugness) in *Our Mutual Friend*, and Forster's rooms at 58 Lincoln's Fields inspired the lawyer Tulkinghorn's residence in *Bleak House*.

From *Pickwick Papers* onward, Forster was an indispensable adviser to Dickens, reviewing manuscripts and proofs of Dickens's writing; advising him on planning, writing, and revising later novels; and providing business and legal guidance. In 1850 he became part-owner of Dickens's periodical *Household Words*. Forster was Dickens's legal adviser following the writer's separation from his wife in the 1850s; the literary executor of the novelist's estate; and his first biographer, with the monumental three-volume *Life of Charles Dickens* (1872–74). Dickens's friend WILKIE COLLINS criticized Forster's biography for its "unbroken continuity of kindly impulses," suggesting that Forster did not present a whole picture of the man. However, as the scholar Philip V. Allingham noted, Forster's knowledge of Dickens . . . was simply greater than that of any other Dickens contemporary. Thus, no matter what biographies . . . will be written in later times, the font of biographical Dickens will continue to be Forster's three-volume *Life*."

A Work about John Forster
Fenstermaker, John J. *John Forster*. Boston: Twayne, 1984.

Franc, Maud Jeanne
See EVANS, MATILDA JANE.

Frankau, Julia Davis
See DANBY, FRANK.

Frere, John Hookham (1769–1846) *poet, translator*

John Frere was born on May 21 in the county of Norfolk, on the east coast of England, to John Frere, a member of Parliament, and Jane Hookham. Frere attended Eton and graduated from Cambridge University in 1792.

In 1797, he joined the staff of *The Anti-Jacobin Review*, a literary and political journal for which Frere and his friend GEORGE CANNING, the author and politician, wrote satire and humorous poetry. Two years later Frere became undersecretary for foreign affairs in the British government, and in 1800 he was sent to Portugal as a diplomat.

Frere also served as ambassador to Spain and Prussia, but he resigned from the diplomatic service after a British expedition he proposed to defend the Spanish peninsula ended in a disastrous defeat by Napoléon. Frere inherited the family estate in 1807. He married Elizabeth Jemima in 1816, and two years later they moved to Malta, where he devoted himself to translating the ancient Greeks and studying Hebrew and Maltese. Frere also composed a long satiric poem with the eccentric title *The Monks and the Giants; Prospectus and Specimen of an Intended National Work, by William and Robert Whistlecraft of Stowmarket in Suffolk, Harness and Collar Makers. Intended to Comprise the Most Interesting Particulars Relating to King Arthur and His Round Table* (1817). LORD BYRON, the romantic poet and a literary hero to many, read *The Monks and the Giants* with pleasure, and wrote that Frere had "no greater admirer." Frere's translations of the work of the ancient Greek poet Theognis and of the plays of Aristophanes, such as *The Frogs*, are considered among the finest in English.

Other Work by John Frere
Canning, George, and John Hookham, eds. *Poetry of The Anti-Jacobin (Revolution and Romanticism, 1789–1834)*. New York: Woodstock Books, 1991.

Froude, James Anthony (1818–1894) *historian, biographer*

James Anthony Froude was the son of Robert Hurrell Froude, rector of Dartington and archdeacon of Totnes in Devon, and Margaret Speddinton Froude. Froude's was an unhappy childhood; he was victimized by older boys at school and began to enjoy life only at Oxford University, from which he graduated in 1840. In 1842 he won the Chancellor's Prize and was elected a fellow of Exeter College.

The religious turmoil incited by the OXFORD MOVEMENT caused Froude to question his own faith. He wrote out his problems in fictional form in a novel, *The Nemesis of Fate* (1849), which depicts a young clergyman in love with a married woman. The scandal caused by the book's publication cost Froude his fellowship. He moved to London and began a career as a writer and editor.

Froude published essays, made many literary friends—including ARTHUR HUGH CLOUGH and CHARLES KINGSLEY—and was the editor of *Fraser's Magazine* from 1860 to 1874. Froude's 12-volume *History of England from the Death of Cardinal Wolsey to the Defeat of the Spanish Armada* (1856–70) made his reputation and ranks along with THOMAS MACAULAY's great *History of England* as a monument of 19th-century historiography.

Froude's history provoked excited reaction both for and against his views, but he was later involved in greater controversy with his handling of the literary remains of his close friend and mentor, THOMAS CARLYLE, and Carlyle's wife, JANE WELSH CARLYLE, both of whom he had known since 1849. As the couple's literary executor, Froude had to decide whether to publish all, some, or none of the material with which he had been entrusted. For years after Froude had published Thomas Carlyle's literary remains as *Reminiscences* (1881), and Jane Carlyle's as *Letters and Memorials* (1883), charges and countercharges were made regarding Froude's frankness, or lack of discretion, in what he allowed to see publication.

Froude's brilliance as a historian, at least, was finally recognized in 1892 when he returned to Oxford as Regius Professor of History. His collected essays, *Short Studies in Great Subjects* (four volumes, 1867–83), reached a large audience. A quotation from his essay "The Times of Erasmus and Luther" gives a suggestion of the sweep of his mind and his awareness of the broad spectrum of humanity:

> In the sciences, the philosopher leads; the rest of us take on trust what he tells us. The spiritual progress of mankind has followed the opposite course. Each forward step has been made first among the people, and the last converts have been among the learned.
>
> The explanation is not far to look for. In the sciences there is no temptation of self-interest to mislead. In matters which affect life and conduct, the interests and prejudices of the cultivated classes are enlisted on the side of the existing order of things, and their better-trained faculties and larger acquirements serve only to find them arguments for believing what they wish to believe.
>
> Simpler men have less to lose; they come more in contact with the realities of life, and they learn wisdom in the experience of suffering.

Works about James Anthony Froude

Dunn, Waldo Hilary. *James Anthony Froude: A Biography.* Oxford, England: Clarendon Press, 1961.

Goetzman, Robert. *James Anthony Froude: A Bibliography of Studies.* New York: Garland, 1977.

Fullerton, Lady Georgiana (1812–1885)
novelist

Georgiana Charlotte Leveson Gower was born in Staffordshire, the youngest daughter of Lord Granville Leveson Gower (later Earl Granville) and Lady Harriet Elizabeth Cavendish (the second daughter of the duke of Devonshire). Georgiana was brought up primarily in Paris, where her father was appointed English ambassador when she was 12 years old. Her mother was a devout Anglican, and she imparted her strong religious feeling to her daughter.

In 1833 in Paris, Georgiana married Alexander George Fullerton, a wealthy heir to estates in Gloucestershire and Ireland and an attaché at the British embassy at Paris. When Lord Granville retired from the embassy in 1841, Lady Georgiana and Alexander Fullerton traveled to France, Italy, and Germany. In 1843, Alexander Fullerton was received into the Church of Rome; three years later, under the mentorship of Father Brownhill, S.J., Lady Georgiana also was received into the Catholic Church. Fullerton's religious affiliations were often represented in her novels, much to some critics' dismay. Her first novel, *Ellen Middleton* (1844), displayed a high Anglican religious bent (belated confession of an accidental killing leads to absolution) that prompted Protestant critics such as Lord Brougham to accuse Fullerton of "rank popery."

Despite some negative reviews from the critics, Fullerton continued writing. *Grantley Manor,* whose plot turns on a secret marriage between a Catholic heroine and a Protestant hero, appeared in 1847, followed by *Lady Bird* (1852) and a historical novel about Charlotte Sophia of Brunswick's murder entitled *Too Strange Not to Be True* (1864). In 1855 Fullerton's only son, whose delicate health had always been a source of worry for her, died; she never recovered fully from the loss. To help assuage her pain, she turned to charity work. She joined the third order of St. Francis in 1856. That same year, Fullerton settled in London, where she would continue to participate in more literary pursuits. She published several novels before her death in 1885 after a sustained illness. Little read today, her work has been characterized in the *Dictionary of National Biography* as having "distinction and charm."

Galt, John (1779–1839) *novelist, poet*

John Galt was born in Irvine, Scotland. His father, also named John Galt, was a sea captain for a West Indies trading company. As a child, Galt was frequently ill, and he spent much time at home listening to his mother, Jean, and her friends exchange stories and gossip. Galt later used these stories to provide realistic descriptions of Scottish village life in his fiction.

In 1803 he began contributing poems to *Scots Magazine,* while supporting himself as a clerk. When a trading company he established in London collapsed, he smuggled goods through Napoléon's Mediterranean blockades to aid the British war effort against France. During these trips, he met GEORGE GORDON, LORD BYRON. The encounter inspired Galt to resume writing. The success of SIR WALTER SCOTT's Waverley novels had generated a new interest in Scottish writers, and Galt soon had several stories accepted by *Blackwood's Magazine.*

The magazine soon began soliciting novels from Galt for serialization. His *Annals of the Parish* (1821) remains the most successful of these. The novel's main character and narrator is Reverend Balwhidder, and each of the book's chapters is devoted to one of the reverend's 50 years as pastor of the Dalmailing parish. Balwhidder's longevity allows Galt to depict changes in Scottish customs and habits. The pastor is a conservative, somewhat dim-witted character, but Galt subtly complements his recollections with other characters' comments. Galt's other notable novel from this period, *The Ayrshire Legatees* (1820), uses an epistolary format. The main character, Dr. Zachariah Pringle, a minister, takes his family to London to claim an inheritance. Their letters home illustrate the contrasts between London and rural Scotland.

That same year, 1820, Galt was appointed as a British representative in Canada. By 1830 he had returned to England, where he spent the last decade of his life writing. His 1830 novel, *Lawrie Todd,* reflects his Canadian experiences. The title character founds two frontier towns and eventually prospers, although he loses two wives and a child to disease.

Galt's novels are most noteworthy for their careful depiction of Scottish life and Scots dialect in the early 19th century. They inspired both the Scottish realism movement and the sentimental fantasies of authors such as J. M. Barrie, the author of *Peter Pan.* The critic Ruth Aldrich notes that Galt's "detailed creation of the world of the

Scottish village and town, his freshness of vocabulary with its homely proverbs and apt figures of speech ... and his unequalled excellence (when he is at his best) of unsentimental tender realism make him a still living novelist."

A Work about John Galt
Aldrich, Ruth I. *John Galt*. Boston: Twayne, 1978.

Gardiner, Marguerite (countess of Blessington) (1790–1849) *novelist, essayist, poet*

The early life of the girl who became the countess of Blessington was not easy. Born Margaret Power to Ellen and Edmund Power in Tipperary, Ireland, she suffered the abuses of an alcoholic father who had fallen on difficult times. Financial pressures prompted Margaret's parents to force her, at 14, to marry Captain Maurice Farmer, who beat her and even locked her up for days without food. She endured his abuses for three months before returning to live with her parents. She then accepted the protection of a succession of men. By 1812 she was living in London near Charles John Gardiner, who in 1816 became the earl of Blessington. The following year, Farmer's death freed Margaret to marry Lord Blessington and become Marguerite Gardiner, countess of Blessington.

With her intelligence, beauty, charm, and wit, she distinguished herself in fashionable London, although she never lived down her disreputable past, and society ladies snubbed her all her life. The Blessingtons were famous for their lavish parties for the literati, all men. Their extravagances, however, soon caught up with them. In an attempt to reduce their expenses, they traveled to the Continent, joined by Alfred, count d'Orsay, a handsome Frenchman whose intimate relationship with the Blessingtons became a source of scandal. In 1823 they settled for a time in Genoa, Italy, where Lady Blessington met LORD BYRON. Other literary intimates were WALTER SAVAGE LANDOR and THOMAS MOORE.

After the sudden death of her husband, Lady Blessington was compelled to pursue a literary career: Lord Blessington had left her deep in debt. She wrote several novels in the SILVER-FORK vein, including *The Two Friends* (1835), *The Victims of Society* (1837), and *Strathern; or, Life at Home and Abroad* (1845). She also edited literary gift books, composed poetry, and wrote two successful travel books, *The Idler in Italy* (1839) and *The Idler in France* (1841), based on her own travel diaries.

Her friendship with Byron provided the material for her best-known work, *Conversations with Lord Byron* (1832). The conversations reported are divided among literary gossip, confessions about Byron's personal life, and general disquisitions about aesthetics and philosophy. They are interspersed with Lady Blessington's sharp and convincing observations about Byron's character, for example: "Byron had two points of ambition—the one to be thought the greatest poet of his day, and the other a nobleman and man of fashion.... This often produced curious anomalies in his conduct and sentiments, and a sort of jealousy of himself in each separate character, that was highly amusing to an observant spectator." Byron scholars still mine the book for information. At the time, some questioned Lady Blessington's veracity, but the book sold well.

However, anxieties over money continued to plague her until her death, from what was most likely a heart attack, at 59. Her obituary in the *Athenaeum* praised her in a way that was dismissive of her literary career: "It would not be difficult to point out ladies of celebrity ... of far superior abilities as authoresses ... but we shall find none who, for an equal length of time, maintained an influence of fascination in literary and fashionable society over the highest intellects."

Gaskell, Elizabeth (1810–1865) *novelist, nonfiction writer, short story writer*

Elizabeth Gaskell excelled at various forms of prose, including the social problem novel, historical novel, and domestic novel, as well as the story and sketch. She also wrote one of the most important biographies of the 19th century, *The Life of Charlotte Brontë* (1857). Her social problem fiction, which graphically exposed factory conditions in her city of Manchester, won praise from CHARLES DICKENS and THOMAS CARLYLE and elicited the anger of factory owners. Her historical fiction displays an insight into other cultures' values and practices. Still, for many years after her death, it was largely for *Cranford* (1853), her witty and apparently benign depiction of village women's lives, that she was remembered. It is only fitting that *Cranford* itself offers a far more biting, feminist, account of women's struggles for autonomy, dignity, and survival than many of its readers have recognized.

The Unitarian tradition of the Stevenson family is crucial to understanding Gaskell's literary vocation. Unitarians, a religious sect dissenting from the Church of England, have long been associated with the ideas of human equality, religious tolerance, and political reform. Many of the leading philanthropists and reformers of the 19th century were Unitarians. Gaskell's father, William Stevenson, was a Unitarian minister, civil servant, and journalist. When her mother, Elizabeth Holland Stevenson, died in 1811, Gaskell was sent from London to live with her beloved Aunt Lumb, in the village of Knutsford in the north of England. Here, Gaskell was surrounded by loving and devout Unitarian women who modeled for her a life of cheerful service, which she would depict in many of her stories and novels.

In 1832 Elizabeth Stevenson married William Gaskell, a Unitarian minister from nearby Manchester. While he led the congregation, Gaskell taught in a school for poor children, visited the sick, and learned first hand of the lives of the working poor. Wife and husband collaborated on a poem, *Sketches Among the Poor,* published in *Blackwood's Magazine* in 1837. When an economic depression threw many people out of work in the 1840s and labor unrest threatened England, MARY HOWITT urged Gaskell to write a novel based on her experience of Manchester's factories that would show owners and politicians the suffering of working people. *Mary Barton* was published in 1848, just as revolutions were sweeping through Europe.

As if *Mary Barton* had not stirred enough controversy, Gaskell's next novel, *Ruth* (1853), tackled an even more sensitive subject. It advocated better treatment for women who were discovered to have had sexual relations outside marriage. Gaskell was stung by the outcry against her novel, but she was praised by feminist reformers.

Gaskell's next work of fiction, *Cranford* (1853), has often been construed as a temporary retreat from political themes. The community of women (all the men who come to the village of Cranford either depart quickly or die) struck readers as quaint, and the lighthearted wit of its narrator contrasts with the urgent tone of Gaskell's first two novels. Yet this novel's examination of what today would be called the "feminization of poverty," brought about by the severe limitations on women's educational and work opportunities, subtly argues its feminist agenda.

Gaskell again employed the novel's power to affect public opinion and improve relations between workers and industrialists in *North and South* (1855), a prime example of the CONDITION OF ENGLAND NOVEL. Like *Mary Barton, North and South* was controversial, but it was a best-selling critical success.

Mary Barton had brought Gaskell to the attention of major editors, including Dickens, who solicited stories from her for their magazines. Many of her stories and novellas treated the lives of struggling women and of the rural life she had come to love in Knutsford. Most notable among them is "Cousin Phillis" (1864), which describes the title character's romantic heartbreak amidst rural tranquility. Of particular significance as well are short works on historical subjects, such as the "moral history" "An Accursed Race" (1855), which tells of the persecuted Cagots people of France, or the novella "Lois the Witch" (1859), set during the Salem, Massachusetts, witch trials of 1691.

In *My Lady Ludlow* (1858), Gaskell combined her interest in communities of women with a historical narrative, framing a tale of aristocrats persecuted during the Reign of Terror following the French Revolution with the story of the titular character, a widow whose gruff and dictatorial manner conceals real compassion for people in need.

Gaskell's only full-scale historical novel is *Sylvia's Lovers* (1863), set in a northern fishing village during the Napoleonic wars. In her last work, *Wives and Daughters* (1866), a domestic novel which she failed to complete before her death, Gaskell took up themes close to her personal experience. Like Gaskell, whose own father married a rather unsympathetic woman after his first wife's death, Molly Gibson endures the breach created between her and her beloved widowed father when he remarries. Before she died, Gaskell managed to sketch out a happy ending, in which the long-suffering Molly finally marries the love of her life.

Gaskell also contributed to feminist literary criticism with her *Life of Charlotte Brontë*. These major literary figures of the north of England met on several occasions and maintained a friendship over many years. When Brontë died in 1855, her father asked Gaskell to write her biography. Gaskell was aware of the toll that running a household and tending to her dying siblings (including her alcoholic brother) had taken on Brontë, who nonetheless managed to achieve literary success. Brontë's circumstances contrasted painfully with Gaskell's own. William Gaskell had always supported his wife's literary labor and refused to exercise his legal right to her earnings. Brontë's death, which came shortly after her marriage and while she was pregnant, seemed the crowning injustice of her life. Gaskell chose to expose the obstacles Brontë had had to overcome; although she was denounced by many of her contemporaries, she opened doors for future scholars investigating the difficulties faced by women writers.

Gaskell not only achieved critical acclaim in her lifetime but also earned a substantial income from her writing. She financed travel with her daughters and was preparing a new family home she had purchased when she died.

Critical Analysis

Mary Barton was informed not only by Gaskell's own experience but also by her reading in economic theory, "Blue Books" reporting Parliamentary investigations into the living and working conditions of factory hands, and reform literature by fellow Unitarians. Gaskell depicted slum housing where raw sewage seeped up into dirt floors and disease was rampant. These disturbing scenes were woven into a romance narrative that portrayed the mill owners as self-absorbed and exploitative (Harry Carson, a mill owner's son, thoughtlessly pursues the working-class heroine, Mary Barton) and argued for class solidarity (Mary Barton finally recognizes her love for her working-class cousin, Jem Wilson, when he is tried for Harry Carson's murder). At the same time, Gaskell cautioned against violent rebellion on the part of the workers. Mary's father, John, is a member of the Chartists who, in 1839, presented to Parliament the "People's Charter," listing demands for political reform. In Gaskell's version of these events, when the workers are sent away without satisfaction, they choose John to murder Harry Carson as retribution. Jem Wilson is nearly convicted of the murder. Mary realizes her father's guilt, and John, a good man who has been driven to violence out of desperation, dies repentant in the arms of the similarly repentant father of Harry Carson. Although 20th-century readers have sometimes found this ending a sentimental betrayal of Gaskell's indictment of industrial capitalism, it was read as incendiary by Manchester mill owners. However, the 20th-century Marxist critic Raymond Williams defended Gaskell by crediting her with creating "structures of feeling" that enable adversaries to understand, if not accept, one another's political position.

The subject matter of *Ruth* assumed particular urgency after the passage of the Poor Law of 1842, which limited the power of poor women to name the fathers of their illegitimate babies, and efforts to assist them became a goal of philanthropists. A major obstacle to change was the common belief that good women might be corrupted simply by knowing of the existence of their "fallen" sisters. Gaskell's story of an orphaned seamstress, seduced and abandoned by a wealthy rake and rescued by a dissenting clergyman who helps her to raise her son, brought a sympathetic portrayal of the fallen woman into the drawing rooms of middle-class women readers.

North and South offers a romance in which Margaret Hale, a clergyman's daughter from the rural south of England, and Mr. Thornton, a mill owner in the industrial north, eventually overcome their mutual antagonism, fall in love, and marry, against the backdrop of a violent strike. Margaret learns that mill owners are not necessarily heartless profit-mongers, and she converts Thornton to her principles of Christian charity.

Works about Elizabeth Gaskell

Matus, Jill L., ed. *The Cambridge Companion to Elizabeth Gaskell.* Cambridge: Cambridge University Press, 2007.

Stoneman, Patsy. *Elizabeth Gaskell.* Bloomington: Indiana University Press, 1987.

Uglow, Jenny S. *Elizabeth Gaskell: A Habit of Stories.* New York: Farrar, Straus & Giroux, 1993.

Gilbert, William Schwenk (1836–1911)
playwright, librettist

W. S. Gilbert was born in London to William Gilbert, a retired naval surgeon, and his wife, Anne Morris Gilbert. At age two, while the family was traveling abroad, Gilbert was kidnapped by Italian brigands and held for ransom; his father was able to get the boy back by paying a ransom of £25. Many years later, Gilbert revisited this event, basing the plot of his comic opera *The Gondoliers* (1889) on the kidnapping of a young prince.

In 1855 Gilbert went to King's College, London. While a student there, he contracted typhoid fever and was sent to France to recuperate. While there, he wrote humorous verse, which, according to Leslie Baily, author of *Gilbert and Sullivan: Their Lives and Times,* was an early indication of Gilbert's sense of humor: "He looked at life through his legs, upside down, which can be both refreshing and amusing." Later, Gilbert's collaborator, the composer Sir Arthur Sullivan, would refer to Gilbert's world as "topsy-turvydom."

Upon graduating, Gilbert took a position as a government clerk, but eventually practiced law. He also wrote humorous verse for the magazine *Fun.* His clever poems, published as *The Bab Ballads*—"Bab" having been his childhood nickname—were extraordinarily successful and eventually provided material for his comic operas. These poems, like Gilbert's comic operas, satirized contemporary society, although the poems were sharper and even vicious at times.

In 1866 Gilbert began writing comic plays. He continued to grow as a playwright and was a successful dramatist by the time he first partnered with Sir Arthur Sullivan, a successful composer and conductor. The two men had met years earlier, but their first collaboration was not until 1871, when Sullivan wrote the music for Gilbert's libretto of *Thespis.* The effort was not a success, in part because it was produced with less than one week of rehearsal. It was only when the operatic impresario Richard D'Oyly Carte persuaded Sullivan to write the music for another Gilbert play that the partnership began to work. The resulting opera was *Trial by Jury* (1875), which ran for 200 performances over the course of two years. The novelty of a British musical that was both intelligent and funny changed forever the history of musical theater. Before Gilbert and Sullivan, the comic opera was vulgar and silly. But *Trial by Jury* initiated a series of musical collaborations that endured for nearly 20 years.

In 1881 D'Oyly Carte built the Savoy Theatre, where the rest of Gilbert and Sullivan's operas were performed under the strict control of Gilbert, who believed that his comic operas should be treated with the utmost seriousness. When George Grossmith, a starring member of the company, played Ko-Ko in *The Mikado* (1885), he experimented during a performance with rolling over completely when pushed by the Mikado. When Gilbert told Grossmith not to repeat the action, Grossmith protested that he got a laugh. Gilbert replied, "So would you if you sat on a pork pie." Gilbert got his way.

Gilbert was just as serious when it came to costume and setting. He believed all the trappings should be as realistic as possible in contrast to the "topsy-turvy" worlds of the plays themselves. For the *Mikado* Gilbert hired a Japanese dancer and a geisha to coach the actors on how to walk and move authentically. Huge sums were spent on stage settings and Japanese silk kimonos, which were worn by the ladies of the chorus without corsets or petticoats—shocking at the time.

The collaboration between Gilbert and Sullivan was frequently on the verge of collapse. Both men felt that their individual work was greater than anything they did together, an idea that posterity rejected. Sullivan wanted to compose serious opera and often resented Gilbert's attempts at unbelievable plots that relied on the use of magic potions. Also, the two men often quarrelled over the relative importance of music over lyric. Still, the relationship endured and produced more than a dozen operas, most of which are still produced today.

Sullivan died in 1900 at the age of 58. Gilbert continued to write plays until his death in 1911. His final work, *Hooligans,* was a gritty and realistic drama. He was knighted in 1907.

Critical Analysis

Gilbert's lyrics are perhaps more famous than the music that accompanies them, something that is seldom true of opera or even of musical comedy. The lyrics are indeed memorable, with their incredible rhymes sometimes extending to several syllables, as in *Pirates of Penzance* (1879), in which Gilbert rhymes "lotta news" with "hypotenuse" in "Modern Major General," a song distinguished by how fast a performer can sing its tongue twisters. (This type of song is known as a patter song.) Much of Gilbert's humor comes from wonderful invented words, such as "matrimonified."

Despite some exotic settings, all of the operas satirize contemporary British society. *Trial by Jury,* about a breach-of-promise lawsuit, sends up the legal system. As the chorus sings, "From bias free of every kind / This trial must be tried," an official of the court describes the plaintiff as "the broken-hearted bride" and her former fiancé as the "ruffianly defendant." In *H.M.S. Pinafore* (1878), the First Lord of the British navy is satirized for his lack of experience: "Stick close to your desks and never go to sea / And you all may be rulers of the Queen's Navee!" In *Patience* (1881) Gilbert mocks the artists of the AESTHETIC MOVEMENT—characters such as OSCAR WILDE, the poet ALGERNON CHARLES SWINBURNE, and the painter James McNeill Whistler. To be part of the group, Gilbert suggested, all one had to do was to "Walk down Piccadilly with a poppy or a lily in your medieval hand"—a line that takes aim at the foppishness and fascination with the past that distinguished these artists.

In *The Mikado,* perhaps the most famous of the operas, although the setting is exotic, the characters are all recognizable as British bureaucrats and politicians. In fact, Pooh-Bah, the Lord High Everything Else, has given his name to every pompous official from that day to this.

The play is set in the Japanese town of Titipu, where the Mikado (emperor) has made flirting a capital crime, so that "all who flirted, leered or winked / (Unless connubially linked) / Should forthwith be beheaded."

Yum-Yum is betrothed to her guardian, Ko-Ko, who is sentenced to death for flirting. Because the town dislikes the law, they release Ko-Ko on bail and make him the Lord High Executioner. Since he is the next in line for decapitation, no one else's head can be removed until he has chopped off his own, so the town feels secure. Ko-Ko assures everyone that if he ever does have to act the part of executioner, he has a "little list" of people Titipu would be better off without. (This song is often updated with contemporary references.)

The town's plan backfires when the Mikado orders them to execute someone. The Mikado's son Nanki-Poo, disguised as a wandering minstrel, volunteers himself because the woman he loves is Ko-Ko's fiancée. Thus, Nanki-Poo no longer wants to live. Arranging a deal so that he can marry Yum-Yum and be allowed to live as her husband for a month, he will leave a widow for Ko-Ko to marry. But there is a problem with this idea: The Mikado's law also requires that the widow of a beheaded man be buried alive.

The plot takes several additional turns until it is sorted out in the end with marriages all around. So ends this satire on British class, family, and romantic relations and their absurd blend of cruel legalism and idealist sentiment.

Other Work by W. S. Gilbert

Haining, Peter, ed. *The Lost Stories of W. S. Gilbert.* New York: Parkwest, 1985.

Works about W. S. Gilbert

Eden, David. *Gilbert and Sullivan: The Creative Conflict.* Cranbury, N.J.: Fairleigh Dickinson University Press, 1986.

Ffinch, Michael. *Gilbert and Sullivan.* North Pomfret, Vt.: Trafalgar Square, 1993.

Fischler, Alan. *Modified Rapture: Comedy in W. S. Gilbert's Savoy Operas.* Charlottesville, Va.: University Press of Virginia, 1991.

Stedman, Jane W. *W. S. Gilbert: A Classic Victorian & His Theatre.* New York: Oxford University Press, 1996.

Gissing, George (1857–1903) *novelist*

George Gissing was born in Yorkshire, England, the son of Thomas Gissing, a pharmacist. At age 15 Gissing won a scholarship to Owens College, Manchester. He fell in love with a young prostitute, Marianne Helen Harrison, for whom he stole money at school. Caught and expelled from college, he left for America, where he published his first short story, "The Sins of the Fathers," in the *Chicago Tribune.*

In 1877 Gissing returned to London and, unable to afford better lodgings, lived in London's slums. Three years later he self-published his first novel, *Workers in the Dawn* (1880), a grim, realistic portrait of the most desperate of London's poverty-stricken multitudes. The novel's call for reform reflects Gissing's brief flirtation with socialism. Eventually he abandoned all thought of reform because, although he continued to write about the poor, he did not believe that their lot could be improved. He made clear distinctions between the "deserving poor," sensitive souls like himself forced to live in poverty, and the lower classes, whom he regarded as beasts who would not benefit from education or better living conditions.

Most of Gissing's 24 novels are set in London, among the lower middle class, who must struggle against the degrading dreariness of life. Thus, in his 1891 novel *New Grub Street,* Edward Reardon is a writer forced to churn out third-rate material in order to survive.

Although humorous events occur in Gissing's novels, his view of life is almost uniformly dark and hopeless. George Orwell observed that Gissing was "the chronicler of vulgarity, squalor, and failure." As a writer Gissing is a naturalist who treats his subjects realistically and who sees people as trapped by both their heredity and environment. Although he occasionally rails against the fates of some of his characters, he usually presents events with little comment: This, he seems to say, is just how things are.

Though subject to the workings of an indifferent universe, Gissing's characters are much more than merely what happens to them. According to Orwell, Gissing was able to "deal sympathetically with several different sets of motives, and makes a credible story out of the collision between them." In none of his works is this collision seen more clearly than in *The Odd Women* (1893), which focuses on the lives of five women who live amid the social pressures of late Victorian England.

In addition to his novels Gissing wrote *Charles Dickens: A Critical Study* (1898), a well-received critical evaluation. However, his reputation rests upon his novels. As Orwell writes, Gissing's strength was his ability to produce "a story which attempts to describe credible human beings, and . . . to show them acting on every day motives and not merely undergoing strings of improbable adventures."

Critical Analysis

Gissing's novels seem much more "modern" than those of many of his contemporaries, in part because of his portrayal of women as complex human beings with the same needs and desires as men. Gissing's female characters, as modern as they seem psychologically, however, exist in late Victorian society which, as Gissing portrays it, is a particularly deadly place for an intelligent, ambitious woman. Gissing's most complicated work dealing with the plight of women in Victorian society is *The Odd Women* (1893). The novel's title refers to unmarried women—women who by choice or circumstance must fend for themselves in a culture where woman's work, outside of homemaking, is particularly brutal and degrading. Women without independent means or husbands to support them had few choices, and women of the middle class—genteel women—had fewer yet. Many were condemned to lives as governesses, maltreated by their charges and their charges' parents alike, underpaid and overworked. Gissing's novel deals with five "odd women," sisters Alice, Virginia, and Monica Madden, and their friends, Mary Barfoot and Rhoda Nunn.

The Maddens are conventional in their approach to the dilemma of how to make a living. Virginia works as a gentlewoman's companion, a kind of genteel servant, while Alice works as a governess. Their younger sister Monica marries a much older and wealthy man to avoid her sisters' fates, but her husband proves to be jealous and brutal. Rhoda Nunn and Mary Barfoot are quite unconventional women—independent, unmarried, and determined to maintain their dignity and freedom. Both are engaged in the business of helping other women to become independent by teaching them how to type. While this may not sound radical to a modern audience, in the Victorian period the position of secretary and the skill of typing were reserved for men. Women like Rhoda and Mary were at pains to convince the world that women could be more adept typists than men—after all, women's nimble fingers had been sewing and knitting for centuries—and had the other abilities needed to do secretarial jobs.

While Gissing's primary focus in the novel is the question of how middle-class women are to live in a patriarchal culture, he complicates the situation considerably by including a romance between Rhoda and Mary's cousin, Everard Barfoot. Both of these characters are independent, intelligent, and unconventional. Yet they are both trapped by the need to control the other, by the myths and fictions about male-female relationships then current in society. Everard wants Rhoda to assent to live with him without benefit of marriage, even though he secretly intends to propose marriage; Rhoda wants Everard to propose, even though she does not want to marry and would not accept the proposal. In this confrontation, Gissing creates the perfect standoff. Everard and Rhoda are interesting, vital, intelligent characters and the reader is led to hope that they can come up with a workable compromise. That they cannot demonstrates how deeply ingrained, even in the most "liberated" people, are the dominant beliefs of their culture.

The novel ends on an ambiguous note of hope. Rhoda holds Monica's baby daughter in her arms. Rhoda and Mary's work on behalf of women is flourishing, and Alice and Virginia are planning hopefully for the future. Yet Rhoda's eyes fill with tears, and the last words of the novel are addressed to Monica's baby, "Poor little child." Social change, Gissing seems to say, cannot come about without suffering and sacrifice, and this particular change—to allow women a measure of social and sexual equality with me—will not happen quickly or easily.

Other Work by George Gissing

The Whirlpool. Boston: Tuttle Publishing, 1997.

Works about George Gissing
Selig, Robert L. *George Gissing*. Boston: Twayne, 1995.

Gladstone, William Ewart (1809–1898)
political writer

William Gladstone was born December 29, 1809, at Liverpool, England, to Sir John Gladstone, a sugar trader in the West Indian and American markets, and Anne Mackenzie Robertson. He was the fourth son and fifth child of the wealthy couple. He went to Eton in 1821, but left there in 1827 and continued his education at Christ Church, Oxford, where he studied the classics and mathematics.

Gladstone's career as politician began early. While still at Oxford, he was elected as the Tory member of Parliament (M.P.) for Newark. Gladstone achieved a double first-class degree in classics and mathematics in 1831; eight years later, he married Catherine Glynne, daughter of Sir Stephen Glynne, the eighth baronet of Hawarden Castle. The couple had eight children, four boys and four girls. Always a proponent of social equality, Gladstone was responsible for the passage of the Railway Bill of 1844, which forced railway companies to transport lower-class travelers for no more than a penny a mile.

By 1868 Gladstone's work as a reformer made him the leader of the Liberal Party. He became Prime Minister in February 1868 and served until 1874. He served as Prime Minister three more times after his first term—from April 1880 to June 1885; from February to July 1886; and from August 1892 to March 1894. When Gladstone was out of office, his political rival Benjamin Disraeli was in, leaving Gladstone the leader of the opposition. Naturally, much of his writing was done during these intervening periods when he was not at 10 Downing Street, the traditional residence of Britain's prime ministers. His first book was *An Inquiry into the Time and Place of Homer in History* (1876), a work that focused on the contributions of the Greeks to Christian culture, and his second was *Bulgarian Horrors and Questions of the East* (1876), which vividly described the massacre and torture of the Bulgarian people by their Turkish rulers and placed the disaster in the context of current historical thinking on historical patterns.

In 1896, at the age of 86, Gladstone gave his final speech, denouncing the massacres of Armenians by the Turks. He died two years later, on May 19, 1898. In his writings, as in his fiery debating style, he remained a champion of the underdog and the downtrodden to the end.

Other Works by William Gladstone
A Chapter of Autobiography. London: J. Murray, 1868.

The Gladstone Diaries. Oxford: Clarendon Press, 1968.

Works about William Gladstone
Archer, Thomas. *William Ewart Gladstone and His Contemporaries: Fifty Years of Social and Political Progress*. London: Blackie, 1883.

Barker, Michael K. *Gladstone and Radicalism: The Reconstruction of Liberal Policy in Britain*. Hassocks, England: Harvester Press, 1975.

Gunsaulus, Frank Wakeley. *William Ewart Gladstone: A Biographical Study*. Philadelphia: Monarch, 1898.

Jagger, Peter J., ed. *Gladstone*. London: Hambledon Press, 1998.

Godwin, William (1756–1836) *political philosopher, novelist*

William Godwin was born in the East Anglia region of England to John Godwin, a minister, and Ann Hull Godwin. Trained at Hoxton Academy near London to be a minister, Godwin ceased to believe in God and became a writer of treatises, essays, and novels. He married the feminist writer MARY WOLLSTONECRAFT; their daughter would marry the poet PERCY BYSSHE SHELLEY and become MARY SHELLEY.

Godwin's most influential works were his political writings. He believed in the "omnipotence of truth"—the idea that if current social institutions were swept away, rational individuals would tend to live in harmony and agreement. In *An Enquiry Concerning Political Justice* (1793), he examines the evils and corruption found in conventional government, proposing as its replacement small, self-sufficient communities. He adds that, when people are no longer accustomed to settling disputes through force, "There will be no war, no crimes, and no administration of justice, . . . and no government. Besides this, there will be neither disease, anguish, . . . nor resentment." Despite his stated desire to end war and violence, Godwin was fanatically pro-Napoléon, seeing the French dictator as a historical, revolutionary force.

In the novel *The Adventures of Caleb Williams; or, Things as They Are* (1794), Godwin attempts to depict and promote his political philosophy. The character of the title learns the unfairness of law when he is hounded and imprisoned by nobleman Ferdinando Falkland, who wishes to protect his own reputation by concealing a murder.

Godwin's *Of Population* (1820) was a reply to THOMAS MALTHUS, who viewed population growth and famine as almost inevitable, while Godwin felt these were a side effect of unequal class relations. Godwin argued against rigid geometric laws and in favor of humanity's ability to fashion its own destiny.

Godwin's collection of essays *Thoughts on Man: His Nature, Productions, and Discoveries* (1831) praised science while condemning authoritarianism. Although today the abolition of private property is usually associated with authoritarian regimes, radical political philosophers in the 19th century often argued that free individuals would voluntarily abandon the institution of private property. Godwin was an early promoter of that view.

Godwin exerted an influence on radical thinkers from KARL MARX to OSCAR WILDE. WILLIAM HAZLITT said, "[H]is name is an abstraction in letters, his works are standard in the history of intellect," and the critic B. J. Tysdahl adds, "Godwin's importance lies not so much in direct influence as in the fact that in him we find early and sensitive reactions to the emotional and intellectual climate in which the Victorians found themselves," treating "problems and themes that were to occupy a new generation."

Other Work by William Godwin

The Anarchist Writings of William Godwin. London: Freedom Press, 1996.

A Work about William Godwin

Woodcock, George. *A Biographical Study*. Montreal: Black Rose Books, 1989.

Gordon, Charles George (1833–1885)
letter writer

Charles Gordon was born January, 28, 1833, the ninth child of Major-General Henry William Gordon, Lieutenant-General of the English regiment at Woolwich Common, England.

Gordon's sister Augusta, ten years his senior, was his closest ally in the family; however, throughout their lives, their close relationship prevented other women from becoming emotionally close to him.

In 1848, Gordon began training at the Royal Military Academy, where he eventually joined the engineering corps. As a military engineer, Gordon could afford to live well, but he did not care much for the life of luxury and so became known as a rather solemn young man. He moved to Pembroke in 1852, where, for the first time, he was able to live alone instead of in military group housing, and he relished the solitude.

In his celebrated letters to Augusta, Gordon complained that he was constantly bored; he longed for action. In 1853 he got what he had hoped for: The Crimean War—between England, France, and the Ottoman Empire on one side and Russia on the other—broke out. In 1854 Gordon was sent to the Crimea (an area on the north coast of the Black Sea) where he was in charge of building winter quarters for the troops.

Gordon's interests were as narrow as his life; he was concerned with little other than religion and his profession. In a letter to his sister, he describes his yearning for death; death was preferable to life, he believed, because he considered the human body vile.

This fatalistic attitude framed Gordon's reaction to the several wars that he fought. In his revealing letters, he constantly referred to himself as "the dead man." He believed he belonged nowhere and was dead to the world. Although he was a soldier, he hated the results of war and constantly worked to raise money to help the desperate and destitute.

Charles Beatty, a soldier in Gordon's regiment, aptly describes him:

> Patriotic admiration would have made him a warlord, but he was a peacemaker... Piety would have made him a pillar of the church, but he was a heretic. Idealists show him as bearing the "white man's burden," but it was the black man's burden which he believed the white man ought to bear... He did not fight against people so much as for principles and... he hated the business of war, even against those who... he was sure... were the vehicles of evil.

After Gordon's death in 1885, many of his letters to Augusta were collected and published.

Other Works by Charles Gordon

Colonel Gordon in Central Africa, 1874–1879. London: T. de La Rue & Co., 1881.
Equatoria under Egyptian Rule. Cairo: Cairo University Press, 1953.
General Gordon's Khartoum Journal. London: W. Kimber, 1961.

Works about Charles Gordon

Abdullah, Achmed. *Dreamers of Empire.* New York: Frederick A. Stokes, 1929.
Strachey, Lytton. *Eminent Victorians.* New York: Garden City Publishing, 1918.

Gordon, Lucie Duff (1821–1869) *travel writer and translator*

Lucie Duff Gordon was born Lucie Austin on June 24, 1821, in London, to Sarah Taylor Austin and John Austin, a jurist. Her mother was an accomplished translator, and Gordon was similarly trained in languages and became a translator as well later in life. This mastery of languages was facilitated by the Austin family's moves to Germany and France during Gordon's childhood. As a child, she also became acquainted with such luminaries as JEREMY BENTHAM, JOHN STUART MILL, Heinrich Heine, and THOMAS CARLYLE. While in France in August 1833, she and her mother witnessed the sinking of the *Amphitrite*, a convict ship, and tried in vain to save those who washed up on shore.

Gordon married Sir Alexander Cornewall Duff Gordon on May 6, 1840, and had four children, one of whom died in infancy. Her household in London became a center for progressive thinkers such as CHARLES DICKENS, WILLIAM THACKERAY, and HARRIET TAYLOR. During the 1840s she earned a reputation as a translator of French and German works, including accounts of travel in the Middle East.

In 1851 Gordon contracted tuberculosis and was forced to seek a dry climate for her health. She settled in South Africa, from where she sent letters vividly describing her daily life that were later published as *Letters from the Cape* (1864), one of two works for which she is best known. The other work, *Letters from Egypt, 1863–1869* (first published in 1865 and expanded in 1875), consists of letters Gordon wrote while living in Luxor, where she moved in 1862. She sympathized with the plight of Egyptian villagers, whose lives were transformed (for the worse, as Gordon saw it) by a program of westernization that included the building of railroads and the Suez Canal. In her writing, Gordon exhibits a great sympathy and admiration for Egyptians while condemning the condescension, mistrust, and exploitative attitude her countrymen displayed toward them.

Gordon succumbed to tuberculosis on July 14, 1869, in Cairo. Although her translations have not survived the scrutiny of years, her letters remain important and informative accounts of the contemporary societies of South Africa and Egypt.

Works about Lucie Duff Gordon

Frank, Katherine. *A Passage to Egypt: The Life of Lucie Duff Gordon.* Boston: Houghton Mifflin, 1994.

Waterfield, Gordon. *Lucie Duff Gordon in England, South Africa and Egypt.* New York: E.P. Dutton & Co., 1937.

Gore, Catherine (Catherine Grace Frances Moody Gore) (1800–1861) *novelist, dramatist*

Catherine Gore rose to popularity in the 1830s with her "fashionable" novels—stories about high-society romance and scandal. Her work was embraced by both the upper-class women she wrote about and the middle-class women who envied the lives of Gore's wealthy characters. She published more than 70 novels in her lifetime.

Born in London, Gore was the daughter of C. Moody, a wine merchant. She was raised in East Retford, Nottinghamshire, where she began writing at an early age. Her first novel, *Theresa Marchmont; or, The Maid of Honour* (1824), a historical romance, was published one year after her marriage to Captain Charles Arthur Gore.

The turning point in her writing career occurred in 1830, with the publication of *Women as They Are; or, Manners of the Day.* Gore moved from depicting the past in the style of Sir Walter Scott to depicting the present in the manner of the silver-fork school of novelists, such as Benjamin Disraeli, who portrayed fashionable society. *Women as They Are* is set among the idle rich, depicting dandies and debutantes in Regency London. King George IV (who died the year it was published) said it was "the best bred and most amusing novel published in my remembrance," and its success placed Gore in the ranks of the major novelists of the day *The Hamiltons; or, The New Era* (1834) adds a new dimension to her "silver-fork" formula by including discussions of contemporary political controversies. *Mrs. Armytage; or, Female Domination* (1836) depicts the consequences of a domineering mother's interference in the lives of her children. *Cecil; or, Adventures of a Coxcomb* (1841) is Gore's most popular novel. It portrays a dandy hero in lively prose: "The leading trait of my character had its origin in the first glimpse I caught of myself, at six months old, in the swing-glass of my mother's dressing room. I looked and became a coxcomb for life!"

Although Gore's silver-fork novels portrayed the lives of the rich, in *The Banker's Wife* (1843) she turned to the darker side of capitalism. This novel tells the story of a corrupt banker who engages in fraud. Ironically, several years after its publication, Gore fell victim to a bank scandal that defrauded her of the £20,000 inheritance that had become her security after her husband's death in 1846.

Gore not only wrote about society's elite, but she also courted their favor, even while ridiculing their follies. She was known for her intelligence and clever personality, and knew such writers as Charles Dickens and William Thackeray. On one occasion, Thackeray even parodied her work.

Although Gore enjoyed her reputation as a popular novelist, she once admitted to her publisher that she had grown rather ashamed of her novels, and once even referred to herself as "a writer of rubbish." She tried her hand at poems and plays, and even wrote a gardening manual. But her other works never received the same acclaim that she had earned with her novels of upper-class manners.

In 1858 Gore's eyesight began to fail and she was forced to quit writing. Upon her death in 1861, the London *Times* praised Gore as "the best novel writer of her class and the wittiest woman of her age."

Other Work by Catherine Gore
Franceschina, John, ed. *Gore on Stage: The Plays of Catherine Gore*. New York: Garland, 1999.

Gosse, Edmund William (1849–1928)
critic, biographer, translator

Edmund Gosse was born in London to Emily Bowes Gosse and the naturalist PHILIP HENRY GOSSE, who was a member of the Plymouth Brethren, a devout group of Christian fundamentalists. Gosse lacked a university education, but in 1865 secured a job as a librarian in the British Museum; this occupation subsidized his career as a writer. A better-paying job as a translator for the Board of Trade enabled Gosse to marry in 1875. In 1879 Gosse met the sculptor Hamo Thornycroft, with whom he formed an intense relationship that lasted until Thornycroft's marriage in 1884. In 1904 Gosse became librarian to the House of Lords, a post he held until 1914. Gosse was knighted in 1925.

Gosse's interest in foreign literature led to his sharing this interest with the British public. In 1893, for example, he wrote an essay on the American poet Walt Whitman. He introduced the Norwegian playwright Henrik Ibsen to the British public, translating *Hedda Gabler* (1891) and *The Master Builder* (1892), and in 1907 publishing *Ibsen*, a biography.

Gosse was friends with many of the writers of his day, among them HENRY JAMES, RUDYARD KIPLING, and GEORGE BERNARD SHAW. He often wrote about literary friends, as he did about ALGERNON CHARLES SWINBURNE in both *Portraits and Sketches* (1912) and the critical biography *The Life of Algernon Charles Swinburne* (1917). These writings about friends contain telling personal details, such as these remarks about Swinburne: "I never heard him complain of a headache or of a toothache," and "As he talked to me, he stood, perfectly rigid, with his arms shivering at his sides, and his little feet tight against each other." However, Gosse's personal acquaintance with Swinburne led him to remain reticent on the significant matter of Swinburne's libertine lifestyle.

Also compromising the value of his work are the numerous factual errors Gosse was prone to make, as he does in *The Life and Letters of John Donne* (1899). In making a point about the 17th-century poet's character, for example, Gosse attributes to his subject an act of a different person, Daniel Donne. In addition to careless research, Gosse speculated on the autobiographical underpinnings of Donne's love poetry. The critic Helen Gardner complained that Gosse "started [literary] criticism on the hopeless quest of deciding which of Donne's poems were written to his wife." Still, the book was lauded in its day, and the book revived interest in Donne. Because of their unreliability, however, even these major works of his, on Swinburne and Donne, have all but vanished from the critical landscape.

One book by Gosse, however, has endured: the anonymously published autobiographical *Father and Son: A Study of Two Temperaments* (1907), which addresses' the central Victorian crisis of religious doubt. Predating Gosse's loss of faith is the crisis that his father, both a scientist and a Christian fundamentalist, underwent in his fierce attempt to reconcile faith and evolutionary theory. (In his book *Omphalos: An Attempt to Untie the Geological Knot*, for example, Philip Gosse argued that God created fossils at the same time he created the world.) Gosse felt that his father, confronting "two theories of physical life, . . . the truth of each incompatible with the other, . . . allowed the turbid volume of superstition to drown the delicate stream of reason." The crisis that visited many Victorians, then, existed in a concentrated form in Gosse's childhood home, and the event helped divide believer and nonbeliever, father and son.

Another theme accounting for the book's abiding interest is the self-division that Gosse describes—"the discovery of an 'other self'" is how critic Masao Miyoshi has put it—a condition Gosse shared with the Irish writer George Russell and the poet William Butler Yeats, among other authors of the day. Also of interest is the book's account of an escape from stifling puritanism to the more liberating world of letters.

The reviewer for the *Athenaeum* called the book "at once a profound and illuminating study in the concrete of the development of a child's mind, and also an historical document of great value." However, the biographer Harold Orel has called the book "self-serving" for giving Gosse the clear advantage in the father-son quarrel that the book recounts. Portraying his father's determined faith as foolish and perhaps intellectually dishonest, Gosse again raises questions about his own trustworthiness. According to Orel, "Gosse is not a completely reliable witness [even] to what he knows."

Gosse's legacy is more than a single book. Due to Gosse's "skill in delineating the personalities of his many friends," the critics Paul F. Matthiesen and Michael Millgate have written, "the study of his career offers one of the best introductions to the literary scene at the end of the [19th] century and the beginning of [the 20th]."

Other Work by Edmund Gosse

Aspects and Impressions. New York: Routledge, 2000.

Works about Edmund Gosse

Mandel, Barrett J. *Full of Life Now.* Princeton, N.J.: Princeton University Press, 1980.

Woolf, James D. *Sir Edmund Gosse.* New York: Twayne, 1972.

Gosse, Philip Henry (1810–1888)
nonfiction writer

Philip Henry Gosse was born in Worcester, England. In 1827 he was sent off as a clerk for a six-year term to Newfoundland, Canada, where, after reading George Adams's *Essays on the Microscope* in 1832, he started collecting insects. In 1838 he traveled to the United States, working as a schoolteacher in Alabama before returning to England in 1839. On the return voyage he wrote *The Canadian Naturalist* (1840), based on his field notes. The book, partly because of a surge of interest in natural history at the time, was well received, but it did not sell well enough to support Gosse, who for the next three years worked as a schoolmaster. In 1843 the Society for Promoting Christian Knowledge (SPCK) commissioned him to write an *Introduction to Zoology* for the general reader. Soon thereafter, the SPCK asked Gosse to write a book on the new ocean fauna that had been discovered by Sir James Ross in the Pacific. The book, entitled simply *The Ocean* (1845), was immensely successful and was reprinted well into the 1880s in England and America.

Gosse was then hired to catalog shells in Jamaica, where he spent the next three years, publishing *Birds of Jamaica* (1847), *Illustrations of Birds of Jamaica* (1849), and *A Naturalist's Sojourn in Jamaica* (1851) upon his return. Those books firmly established his professional reputation, and *Sojourn* sold particularly well. The following sentence provides a sense of Gosse's style in that book: "I gazed around, bewildered and entranced, almost, with the variety of charming objects, all at once appealing for attention; the remembrance of which, protracted as it was through eighteen months' duration, with scarcely any abatement, has given in my habitual feelings, a kind of paradisiacal association with lovely Jamaica." Over the next 10 years Gosse wrote another nine books, culminating in *The Romance of Natural History*, which was reprinted in 13 different editions over the next 30 years.

Gosse was a natural scientist and a Christian, and when evolutionary theory began to challenge the credibility of the Christian Garden of Eden creation myth, Gosse, in "a strange act of wilfulness" according to his son EDMUND GOSSE in *Father and Son* (1907), published *Omphalos: An Attempt to Untie the Geological Knot* (1857). Arguing against evolution, the senior Gosse wrote: "I assume that each organism which the Creator educed was stamped with an indelible specific character, which made it what it was, and distinguished it from everything else, however near or like. I assume that such character has been and is, indelible and immutable; that the characters which distinguish species from species *now,* were as definite at the first instant of their creation as now, and are as distinct now as they were then." In an effort to explain away fossil evidence that showed change within species, Gosse argued that God planted misleading fossils in order to keep mankind humble. That argument, and the book as a whole, was badly received; even Gosse's friends, notably CHARLES KINGSLEY, found the book in the end absurd. Science in the wake of evolutionary theory (CHARLES DARWIN's *On the Origin of Species* was published in 1859) left Gosse behind, and he spent the last years of his life writing theological tracts such as "The Antichrist: Who or What Is He?"

Grand, Sarah (Frances Elizabeth Bellenden Clarke) (1854–1943) *novelist*

Sarah Grand, born Frances Bellenden Clarke in Donaghadee, Ireland, was the daughter of Edward Clarke, an officer in the British navy, and his wife Margaret Bell Sherwood. Grand's father died when she was seven, and her mother moved the family, which included Sarah and two brothers, to Yorkshire. Much of her education occurred at home, and she received only two years of formal education. In 1870 she left school to marry David Chambers McFall, a military surgeon.

In 1888 Grand anonymously published *Ideala*, the first novel of her major trilogy. The title character is a young, intelligent, idealistic woman who struggles against the men in her life to achieve independence. The earnings from this novel allowed Grand to leave her husband and create a new identity for herself as Madame Sarah Grand. In 1893 she published her first novel under this pseudonym, *The Heavenly Twin*. This novel openly discusses the unfair treatment that women endured at the hands of their husbands, depicting a woman, Edity, who contracts syphilis as a result of her husband's infidelity. The novel presents a powerful critique of male oppression, as in the scene where Edith confronts her husband:

"That is why I sent for you all," she was saying feebly—"to tell you, you who represent the arrangement of society which has made it possible for me and my child to be sacrificed in this way. I have nothing more to say to any of you—except"—she sat up in bed suddenly and addressed her husband in scathing tones—"except to you. And what I want to say to you is—Go! go! Father! turn him out of the house. Don't let me ever see that dreadful man again!"

The book was an immediate success and praised by critics such as GEORGE BERNARD SHAW: "A terrible, gifted person, a woman speaking for women, Madame Sarah Grand to wit, has arisen to insist that if the morality of her sex can do without safety-valves, so can the morality of 'the stronger sex,' and to demand that the man shall come to the woman exactly as moral as he insists that she shall come to him."

In *The Heavenly Twins*, Grand coined the term *New Woman* and became the major writer of what came to be called the NEW WOMAN NOVEL.

In 1897 she completed her New Woman trilogy with *The Beth Book*, which draws heavily on her own experiences in an unhappy marriage and on her decision to become independent, to establish her own career, achieve sexual freedom, and win equality with men. Over the next two decades, Grand continued writing novels and collections of short stories. Among the more notable is *The Winged Victory* (1916), which condemns the science of eugenics.

A Work about Sarah Grand

Mangum, Teresa. *Married, Middlebrow, and Militant: Sarah Grand and the New Woman Novel.* Ann Arbor: University of Michigan Press, 1998.

Grant, Anne (1755–1838) *poet*

Anne MacVicar was born on February 21 in Glasgow, Scotland. Her father, Duncan MacVicar, an army officer, took his family to North America, when he was transferred there in 1758. Anne grew up on the American frontier during the French and Indian War, a bloody struggle between France and England for control of North America. After Britain's victory, MacVicar retired to Vermont, then returned to Scotland with his family when Anne was 13. In 1777, Anne married a minister named Grant, with whom she had eight children. When her husband died in 1801, Anne turned to writing to support her family. In 1806 she published a book of poems, *Letters from the Mountains,* which made her widely known throughout Scotland. Two years later, she published another collection, *The Highlands and Other Poems,* and in the same year completed an autobiographical account of her experiences growing up in America, *Memoirs of an American Lady.* The American lady of the title is not Grant herself, but Mrs. Margarita Schuyler, in whose house in Albany, New York, the MacVicar family had stayed. Grant's memories of her girlhood in America were intense, as in this passage about the breaking up of the ice on the Hudson River:

> This noble object of animated greatness, for such it seemed, I never missed; its approach being announced, like a loud and long peal of thunder, the whole population of Albany were down at the river side in a moment; an if it happened, as was often the case, in the morning, there could not be a more grotesque assemblage. No one who had a nightcap on waited to put it off; as for waiting for one's cloak, or gloves, it was a thing out of the question; you caught the thing next you, that could wrap round you, and run. In the way you saw every door left open, and pails, baskets, etc., without number, set down in the street. It was a perfect saturnalia.

In 1810 Grant moved to Edinburgh, where she ran a boardinghouse to supplement her income. Following an injury in 1820, her health declined and she no longer wrote.

A Work about Anne Grant
Bobbe, Dorothie. *The New World Journey of Anne MacVicar.* New York: Putnam, 1971.

Green, Mary Anne Everett (1818–1895)
historian

Mary Anne Everett Green, née Wood, was born in Sheffield, in northern England. Her father, Robert Wood, was a Methodist minister. She was educated at home. In 1841 her family moved to London, and she began doing research in the British Museum.

When Green was still a young woman she began writing history, specializing in the neglected field of women's history. She published *Letters of Royal Ladies of Great Britain,* a collection of original documents, in 1846. That same year she married George Pycock Green, a painter. They lived in Paris for two years.

From 1849 to 1855 Green published *Lives of the Princesses of England,* a collection of biographical sketches. From 1857 until her death Green worked as one of the editors of the *Calendars of State Papers;* she edited 41 volumes that collected public records on the reigns of Elizabeth I, James I, and Charles I, among others. Green combined her intensive editorial work with parenting four children, a son and three daughters, and was a pioneer in scholarship at a time when many libraries placed restrictions on women's admission.

A Work about Mary Anne Green
Bellamy, Joan, et al., eds. *Women, Scholarship and Criticism: Gender and Knowledge, c. 1790–1900.* Manchester, England: Manchester University Press, 2001.

Greenwell, Dora (1821–1882) *poet, essayist*

Dora Greenwell was born at Greenwell Ford, near Durham in northern England. She spent much of her life doing social work with poor families and inmates at Durham prison. In her essays she supported education and meaningful work for women and advocated woman's suffrage.

In 1869, after two collections of earlier work, Greenwell published a book of poems called *Carmina Crucis,* which she described as "roadside songs, with both joy and sorrow in them." She also wrote deeply religious poems, especially later in life, such as *The Soul's Legend* (1873) and *Songs of Salvation* (1873), as well as a collection of religious essays, *The Patience of Hope.* She was a close friend of the poet CHRISTINA ROSSETTI, who was also devout.

In 1874 she wrote the words to the hymn "And Art Thou Come with Us to Dwell," which begins: "And art Thou come with us to dwell / Our Prince, Our Guide, Our Love, Our Lord?"

The American poet John Greenleaf Whittier, one of her contemporaries, wrote of her work, "it bears unmistakable evidence of a realization on the part of the author of the truth that Christianity is not simply historical and traditional, but present and permanent."

Other Work by Dora Greenwell

Cunningham, Valentine, ed. *The Victorians: An Anthology of Poetry and Poetics.* Malden, Mass.: Blackwell, 2000.

Greville, Charles Cavendish Fulke
(1794–1865) *diarist*

Charles Cavendish Fulke Greville was born in Wilbury, Wiltshire, England. His parents, Charles Greville and Lady Charlotte Cavendish Bentinck, were members of the British nobility, and he grew up among the wealthy aristocracy of England. Greville attended Eton, then went to Oxford University in 1810, but did not graduate. Greville spent most of his time as a young man training, racing, and betting on horses. He became manager of the duke of York's racing stables in 1821. In the same year, Greville secured a lifetime position as secretary to the privy council, an advisory board to the British monarch.

Over the next 40 years, Greville kept a diary in which he recorded events during the reigns of King George IV, King William IV, and Queen Victoria. Published between 1874 and 1887 as *The Greville Memoirs,* his journal is a remarkable account by a political insider. It is a detailed record of all that occurred, kept by a man who was close to members of both political parties, the Whigs and the Tories. Greville's lively portraits of the three monarchs, as well as of other political leaders such as the duke of Wellington, are brilliant. His diaries are considered an invaluable source for understanding British political life in the 19th century.

Other Work by Charles Greville

Kronenberger, Louis, ed. *The Great World: Portraits and Scenes from Greville's Memoirs, 1814–1860.* New York: Anchor Books, 1964.

H

Haggard, Henry Rider (1856–1925)
novelist

H. Rider Haggard was a prolific, best-selling author who wrote 55 novels and a dozen nonfiction works. He was the sixth of seven sons born to the barrister William Haggard and his wife, Ella, at West Bradenton Hall, Norfolk, England. He was educated at Ipswich grammar school and by private tutors, and at age 19 went to South Africa as secretary to Sir Henry Bulwer (a nephew of the novelist EDWARD BULWER-LYTTON). Haggard lived in South Africa from 1875 to 1879 and again, with his new bride Mariana Louisa Margitson, from 1880 to 1881. He participated in the British annexation of the Transvaal (1877–1881), served as registrar of its high court, volunteered for missions into the bush, and became knowledgeable about Zulu language, history, and culture before returning home to study law, which he began practicing in 1884.

Haggard, who had published a nonfiction study of South African politics in 1882, was destined to become a writer. When one of his brothers challenged him to write an adventure story to emulate ROBERT LOUIS STEVENSON's *Treasure Island*, Haggard completed *King Solomon's Mines* (1885) in six weeks. The book was an immediate success; it sold 31,000 copies in its first printing and has never been out of print since. (It helped that his friend, ANDREW LANG, reportedly wrote 20 different anonymous reviews praising the novel.)

In *King Solomon's Mines,* a big-game hunter, Allan Quartermain, follows a treasure map and penetrates the unexplored heart of Africa. The sequel, *Allan Quartermain* (1887), follows Quartermain as he canoes down a dangerous river, surviving an attack by giant crabs and rescuing a missionary's daughter from kidnappers, before becoming engulfed in a civil war. *She* (1887), the most popular of Haggard's novels, is an exotic fantasy in which themes of love and death are interwoven. Like its predecessors, this is a quest novel in which Leo Vincey, the last descendant of an ancient race, seeks out the seemingly immortal queen-goddess Ayesha ("She-who-must-be-obeyed") and is recognized by her as the incarnation of a former lover. As the 20th-century American novelist Henry Miller observed, Haggard's mysterious She is "*the* femme fatale," and in these works Haggard established the central conventions of the jungle tale.

The popularity of Haggard's novels is due largely to the many myths embedded in them. Indeed, V. S. Pritchett observes in *The Tale Bear-*

ers, "E. M. Forster once spoke of the novelist sending down a bucket into the unconscious; the author of *She* installed a suction pump. He drained the whole reservoir of the people's secret desires."

Haggard's most productive period was from 1885 to 1890, and by the end of the 1880s he had given up legal practice and was making a living from his writing, earning a considerable sum. Through the Savile Club he came to know other writers, including Sir Arthur Conan Doyle, Sir Edmund Gosse, Henry James, Rudyard Kipling, and H. G. Wells, in addition to Andrew Lang. Like Kipling, with whom he has many affinities, Haggard was an author who became popular overnight but was neither university educated nor particularly literary; he wrote rapidly to formula and rarely revised.

Haggard's early travels gave him a vast reservoir upon which to draw for his African fiction. In later life he traveled abroad again to acquire new material for his work, making several trips to Egypt in order to write the historical adventure *Cleopatra* (1889). Later, he visited Iceland for *Eric Brighteyes* (1891). Based on the Icelandic sagas, *Eric Brighteyes* portrays a medieval Iceland full of witchcraft and heroic battles. Eric and Skallagrim, his companion, engage in heroic exploits to acquire fame. Eric aspires to the hand of the priest's daughter, Gudruda, but is constantly thwarted by her jealous half sister, Swanhild, the daughter of a witch.

Rider Haggard was an expert on the farming and social needs of rural England, addressing these concerns in his nonfiction. He was knighted in 1912 for his services to the Great Britain. His autobiography was published posthumously: *The Days of My Life: An Autobiography of Sir H. Rider Haggard* (1926).

Critical Analysis

For a rollicking good adventure in an exotic location with an overlay of the supernatural, one can hardly do better than a novel by H. Rider Haggard. Among his best and most characteristic stories is his first, *King Solomon's Mines,* which is narrated by Allan Quartermain, the great white hunter who will appear in many subsequent Haggard novels. At the beginning of *King Solomon's Mines,* Quartermain is approached with a proposition by Sir Henry Curtis and his companion, naval captain John Good. Curtis's brother has disappeared in his quest for the legendary diamond mines of King Solomon, and Curtis, who parted with his brother in anger, is desperate to find him and make amends. He asks Quartermain to help him and Good on their journey.

The three adventurers are joined by an imposing and mysterious African named Umbopa, and they set out for the mines, following an ancient map that Quartermain received from a dying Portuguese adventurer. They hunt elephants and other game, cross an arid desert and nearly die of thirst, manage to convince a hostile tribe of natives that they are gods descended from the stars, fight an epic battle, explore and become trapped in the mines, and generally engage in various other acts of derring-do.

Many characteristics distinguish Haggard's adventure stories from later imitators both in novels and film. His characters are well drawn and complicated, unlike the stereotypes one often encounters in such tales. Quartermain, for example, continually characterizes himself as a bit of a coward—an unexpected admission from an adventure hero. He is also something of a philosopher, a man who thinks about truth and the meaning of life. Although the typical tale of adventure focuses almost exclusively on events, Haggard spends a good deal of time describing the beauties of Africa and its exotic landscape. As the group approaches the mountains where Solomon's mines are located, the narrator is enraptured by the beauty of his surroundings: "The landscape lay before us like a map, in which rivers flashed like silver snakes, and Alplike peaks crowned with wildly-twisted snow wreaths rose in solemn grandeur, while over all was the glad sunlight and the wide breath of Nature's happy life."

Haggard was a Victorian colonialist, and he shares some of the racist attitudes of his contemporaries. Quartermain and his cronies are not above posing as gods to fool susceptible natives, for example, and they even predict an eclipse to keep the natives in line. On the other hand, Haggard attributes many fine qualities to his African characters. In describing the bravery of a group of warriors before battle, for example, he says, "Never before had I seen such an absolute devotion to the idea of duty, and such a complete indifference to its bitter fruits."

Haggard's work influenced many later writers, from Edgar Rice Burroughs—the author of the Tarzan novels—to just about anyone else who has ever written about lost civilizations, great white hunters, jungle adventures, or ancient mysteries.

Works about H. Rider Haggard
Katz, Wendy R. *Rider Haggard and the Fiction of Empire: A Critical Study of British Imperial Fiction.* New York: Cambridge University Press, 1988.
Pocock, Tom. *Rider Haggard and the Lost Empire: A Biography.* London: Weidenfeld & Nicholson, 1993.

Hallam, Arthur Henry (1811–1833) *poet, essayist, critic*

Arthur Hallam was born in London to the historian Henry Hallam and his wife Julia Elton. In 1827 the family moved to Italy, where Hallam immersed himself in the poetry of Dante and Petrarch. A year later he returned to England to attend Trinity College, Cambridge, becoming friends with ALFRED TENNYSON. Both were members of the Cambridge Apostles, an exclusive intellectual society, and both competed for many of the same academic prizes, with Hallam winning the college prize for English declamation in 1831.

Hallam began to display symptoms of ill health while still at Cambridge. At age 22, only a year after completing his studies, he suddenly fell ill and died while on a trip to Vienna with his father. At the news of his death, the shocked Tennyson plunged into years of depression from which he would not emerge until the 1850 completion of *In Memoriam,* his monumental poem written in memory of Hallam.

In 1834 the grieving Henry Hallam edited and privately printed *Remains in Verse and Prose of Arthur Henry Hallam,* a collection of poems, essays, and a biographical sketch of his son. The book was not publicly published until 1862. As a poet, Hallam was deeply influenced by the English romantics LORD BYRON, WILLIAM WORDSWORTH, PERCY BYSSHE SHELLEY, and JOHN KEATS. As a critic, he argued for a new theory of poetry that would be based on "the desire for beauty." His 1831 essay "On Some Characteristics of Modern Poetry and on the Lyrical Poems of Alfred Tennyson" was the first to use the term *aesthetic* in the critique of literature, and anticipated what was to become AESTHETICISM half a century later.

Hamilton, Elizabeth (1758–1816) *novelist, nonfiction writer*

Elizabeth Hamilton once wrote that "women cannot escape out of the rubbish in which they may happen to be buried." However, if any woman ever escaped from the misfortunes that were dealt her, it was Hamilton.

Born in Belfast, Ireland, Hamilton was the daughter of Charles Hamilton and Katherine Mackay Hamilton. Upon the death of her father in 1759, Hamilton and her brother and sister were separated, and she was sent to live with an aunt and uncle near Stirling, Scotland. She was educated at a day school but lived a very solitary life. Hamilton began reading novels and writing as a way to escape her loneliness.

A reunion with her brother Charles nearly 20 years later proved to be the turning point in Hamilton's life. She traveled with him, and kept a journal that she published periodically. She assisted Charles, a scholar and historian, with several translations, and in 1785 published an essay on "Anticipation" in the magazine *The Lounger.*

After the sudden death of her brother in 1792, Hamilton experienced her first literary success with the publication of *Translation of the Letters of a Hindoo Rajah*, which satirizes English manners by presenting them from the perspective of a foreigner in the manner of Montesquieu's *Persian Letters* or Oliver Goldsmith's *Citizen of the World*. Her second novel, *Memoirs of Modern Philosophers* (1800), was published anonymously. One of the most famous "anti-Jacobin" novels, *Memoirs* satirized the circle of British radical writers who supported the French Revolution. The novelist Mary Hays is mercilessly parodied as Bridgetina Botherim, an unattractive zealot who throws herself at handsome young men with little success, and the philosopher and novelist WILLIAM GODWIN becomes Mr. Myope in reference to the supposed short-sightedness of his optimism about the perfectibility of human society. The modern philosophers believe that they have discovered the embodiment of their theories among the Hottentots (the Khoikhoi, an indigenous people of southern Africa):

> All our theory realized! Here is a whole nation of philosophers, all as wise as ourselves! All on the high road to perfectibility! All enjoying the proper dignity of man! Things just as they ought! No man working for another! All alike! All equal! No laws! No government!

The scholar Marilyn Butler has called Hamilton "the most amusing of the anti-jacobins."

Hamilton also had a great interest in education. Her book *Letters on the Elementary Principles of Education* (1801) advocated an equal education, both intellectual and moral, for boys and girls. In 1815, she published another book directed at educators, *Hints Addressed to the Patrons and Directors of Public Schools*, which again advocated female education.

Despite her influential nonfiction, Hamilton is perhaps best known for her comic novel *Cottagers of Glenburnie* (1808). The novel is interesting for its early use of Scots dialect, its details of domestic life and work, and for having a disabled heroine, Mrs. Mason. It was especially appealing to middle-class women.

Hamilton never married, and spent much time traveling with her sister. After suffering from poor health for many years, she died suddenly in Harrogate, Yorkshire. *Memoirs of Mrs. Elizabeth Hamilton with Selections from her Correspondence and Unpublished Writings* was published posthumously in 1818. At Hamilton's death, Maria EDGEWORTH praised her as "an original, agreeable, and successful writer of fiction; but her claims to literary reputation as a philosophic, moral, and religious author are of a higher sort, and rest upon works of a more solid and durable nature."

Hardy, Thomas (1840–1928) *novelist, poet*
Thomas Hardy was born in the village of Higher Bockhampton, in Dorset, England, where he continued to spend considerable time throughout his life. His father, Thomas, was a builder and stonemason who passed on to his son not only his talent for architecture but also his love of music. Hardy's mother, Jemima, had been a domestic servant, but she loved to read and instilled in her son a love of literature and local folk tales. Hardy went to a local school for one year, then finished his education in the town of Dorchester, the county seat of Dorset. At age 16 he was apprenticed to an architect.

From 1862 to 1867 Hardy worked as an architect in London. While he was there, he took advantage of many cultural and educational opportunities, studying languages, spending time in museums, and reading on his own. Although from the age of 16 Hardy wanted to be a poet, his first published work was a humorous sketch, entitled "How I Built Myself a House" (1865). Hardy then turned to fiction, because he felt he was more likely to be able to make his living as a novelist than as a poet.

In 1867 ill health forced Hardy to return home to Dorset, where he took work as a restorer of churches. That same year, he began to submit his first novel, *The Poor Man and the Lady*, to publishers—without success. Hardy later destroyed the manuscript. *An Indiscretion in the Life of a Lady*, which is a shortened version of *The Poor Man and the Lady*, was later published serially in *New Quarterly Magazine* and *Harper's Weekly*.

Hardy's second novel, *Under the Greenwood Tree* (1872), partially based on his school years, proved more successful. After the publication of *A Pair of Blue Eyes* (1873), based on his courtship of Emma Lavinia Gifford, and of *Far from the Madding Crowd* (1874), the story of Bathsheba Everdene and the three men who love her, Hardy felt financially secure enough to propose marriage to Emma, whom he had met while restoring a church in St. Juliot, Cornwall. The two were married, somewhat unhappily, for 38 years until Emma's death in 1912.

Between 1874 and 1895, Hardy published many novels, most in serial form. Among them are *The Return of the Native* (1878), *The Mayor of Casterbridge* (1886), *Tess of the D'Urbervilles* (1891), and *Jude the Obscure* (1895). *The Return of the Native* tells the tragic tale of the doomed marriage of the passionate Eustacia Vye to Clym Yeobright—the "native" referred to in the title, recently returned to Egdon Heath from Paris. *The Mayor of Casterbridge* follows the downfall of Michael Henchard, a wealthy and respected man with a dark secret in his past. *Tess of the D'Urbervilles* focuses on a young girl who is seduced, then loses the child that results. She tries to start her life over, but cannot escape the stigma of her past. *Jude the Obscure* details the tragic end of an extramarital affair.

Hardy stopped writing novels in 1895 over the public furor surrounding *Jude the Obscure*. His wife, Emma, objected to his portrayal of marriage and extramarital sex, and it is said that the bishop of Wakefield burned his copy of the novel. Beginning in 1898, Hardy began to publish poetry, some written many years earlier. In all, six volumes of poetry were published, one posthumously, including the verse drama *The Dynasts* (1903). Much of his poetry reflected Hardy's dark view of life. In "A Darkling Thrush," for example, the speaker describes the landscape as he leans upon a gate: "When Frost was spectre-gray, / And Winter's dregs made desolate / The weakening eye of day." Suddenly he hears the song of the thrush, a joyful sound against the dark and drear sky, but the moment does not cure the speaker of his melancholy. Instead, he says the thrush must be singing a song of "Some blessed Hope, whereof he knew / And I was unaware."

After Emma's death in 1912, Hardy hired Florence Dugdale (1879–1937) as his secretary; he married her in 1914. Hardy lived to be 87 years old and, at the time of his death, was considered among the greatest of living authors. He received several honorary doctorates and was awarded the Order of Merit in 1910, and his ashes (except for his heart, which rests in Dorset) were buried in Poet's Corner in Westminster Abbey.

In 1928 the first volume of *The Life of Thomas Hardy* appeared, the second two years later. Although supposedly a biography written by Florence Hardy, this work is actually an autobiography, told in the third person and dictated by Hardy to his wife before his death.

Critical Analysis

Nearly all of Hardy's novels are set in the region of southwest England that Hardy calls Wessex. (Throughout his writing, Hardy gives fictional names to real places.) The novels that are regarded today as among his greatest share many characteristics. The setting becomes almost a character in itself, exerting a powerful influence over the mood and feel of each novel. For example, a rainstorm in *The Return of the Native* takes on symbolic weight as Hardy sets it against the portrait of a vulnerable young woman:

> The noise of the wind over the heath was shrill, and as if it whistled for joy at finding a night so congenial as this. Sometimes the path led her to hollows between thickets of tall and dripping bracken, dead, though not yet prostrate, which enclosed her like a pool. When they were more than usually tall she lifted the baby to the top of her head, that it might be out of the reach of their drenching

fronds. On higher ground, where the wind was brisk and sustained, the rain flew in a level flight without sensible descent, so that it was beyond all power to imagine the remoteness of the point at which it left the bosoms of the clouds.

In his descriptions of nature, Hardy's language rises often to the level of poetry, although his dialogue can sometimes seem stilted.

Hardy's central characters often come from farm families and are portrayed in deft and sympathetic detail; they are victims of a tragic destiny that they can neither understand nor control. For example, the innocent heroine of *Tess of the D'Urbervilles* is destroyed by a cruel seduction, the stigma of which she cannot shake and which love cannot overcome. In many cases, the best plans and highest hopes of Hardy's characters are dashed by tiny coincidences and minor twists of fate; for example, just as Tess finally despairs of her marriage to Angel Clare and moves in with Alex d'Urberville, Angel returns. In many of his novels, Hardy uses rural folk like a Greek chorus, as they watch and comment on the downfall of central characters such as Jude or Tess.

Jude the Obscure was certainly Hardy's most controversial novel. It tells the story of Jude Fawley who, like Hardy's own father, was the village mason. Jude aspires to succeed in life, but while studying in the hope of being admitted to Christminster College, Jude meets the beautiful Arabella Donn, who entices him into marriage by feigning pregnancy. When Arabella leaves him, Jude travels to Christminster (Hardy's fictional equivalent of Oxford) to apply to the university, but his application is rejected by a university official:

> I have read your letter with interest; and, judging from your description of yourself as a working man, I venture to think that you will have a much better chance of success in life by remaining in your own sphere, and sticking to your trade. . . .

Jude's life continues on its downward spiral, as he falls in love with his cousin, Sue Bridehead, who is unhappily married to Jude's former schoolmaster Phillotson. Eventually Sue and Jude divorce their spouses and live together. They have two children, and Jude takes his son by Arabella, nicknamed Father Time, to live with his new family. Ultimately Father Time kills the two younger children and himself "because we are to menny." Consumed with grief and guilt, Sue goes back to Phillotson, and Jude remarries Arabella. In the end, Jude dies, whispering "Let the day perish wherein I was born." In this novel marriage becomes a metaphor for life itself, which Hardy portrays as a prison in which the best are destroyed along with the worst. Society blindly works in conjunction with fate in forcing people to remain in the bonds of marriage even in the face of misery.

In "The Darkling Thrush," discussed previously, Hardy portrays the poet as a seeker, looking out over a dark and forbidding landscape, wishing for joy, meaning, and hope. He can hear the thrush—he can hear the joy and the hope—but it always eludes him. At the cusp of Hardy's poetic career, just as its composition date (December 31, 1900) places it at the cusp of the new century, "Darkling Thrush" records the author's nostalgia for a romantic worldview. His subsequent poetry, notably *The Dynasts* (1904, 1906, 1908), faces squarely the impersonal forces Hardy believed governed human life. Nevertheless, as Tim Armstrong remarks in his introduction to the selected poems, *The Dynasts* "established Hardy as a kind of national laureate . . . selections were dramatized as a morale-boosting play during the war." Donald Davie captures Hardy's modern themes by declaring him "the laureate of engineering."

Critics debate whether Hardy's world is truly tragic—claiming that fate, rather than a flaw of character, destroys his heroes and heroines. But Hardy did not share this definition of tragedy: "The best tragedy—the highest tragedy, in short—is that of the worthy encompassed by the inevitable." That is, Hardy felt that the real tragedy of human existence was that people of great sensitivity and talent are condemned to live in an indifferent universe, without pattern or purpose. Hardy's main characters, people like Tess and Jude, are sensitive souls who are capable of nobility and passion, but who are destroyed by circumstance. It is impossible not to feel a profound sense of loss at their destruction. Hardy paints a dim portrait of life on the moors and heaths of rural England. He challenges both the sexual mores of the Victorian era and the popular religious belief in a benevolent deity. While many Victorians believed in a God who looked after each individual, Hardy saw only a universe indifferent to the actions and hopes of humankind. His view of the world is as hard to take as it is hard to turn away from.

Other Works by Thomas Hardy

Armstrong, Tim, ed. *Thomas Hardy: Selected Poems*. London: Longman, 1993.

Hynes, Samuel, ed. *The Complete Poetical Works of Thomas Hardy*. 5 vols. New York: Oxford University Press, 1982–1995.

A Laodicean; or, The Castle of the De Stancys. New York: Penguin, 1998.

The Woodlanders. New York: Penguin, 1998.

Works about Thomas Hardy

Davie, Donald. *Thomas Hardy and British Poetry*. New York: Oxford University, 1972.

Langbaum, R. W. *Thomas Hardy in Our Time*. New York: St. Martin's Press, 1997.

Pite, Ralph. *Thomas Hardy: The Guarded Life*. New York: Picador, 2007.

Stewart, J. I. M. *Thomas Hardy: A Critical Biography*. New York: Dodd, Mead, 1971.

Tomalin, Claire. *Thomas Hardy*. New York: Penguin, 2007.

Turner, P. D. L. *The Life of Thomas Hardy: A Critical Biography*. Malden, Mass.: Blackwell, 2001.

Harris, Frank (James Thomas Harris)
(1856–1931) *memoirist, editor, short story writer*

Born in Galway, Ireland, the son of a customs shipmaster, Harris lost his mother at age five. He was subsequently educated in Wales. As a young man he traveled widely in the United States and Europe, earning a living in various ways, but by 1882 he was settled in London. Here he began a literary career that drew on material from his previous travels, jobs, and adventures.

Harris became a journal editor in London, working at the *Evening News* (1882–86), the *Fortnightly Review* (1886–94), and the *Saturday Review* (1894–98), where he employed, among others, GEORGE BERNARD SHAW, H. G. WELLS, and MAX BEERBOHM. OSCAR WILDE was a friend, and Harris was one of the few who stood by Wilde during his trials and helped him financially during his final years.

Harris developed a solid literary career as a playwright, short story writer, novelist, and editor, although his arrogance and combative temperament sometimes involved him in controversy. He tended to challenge the staid sexual mores and hypocrisy of his time. Among his writings is a biography of Wilde (1916) that blames the British public for turning on Wilde. It has valuable insights into Wilde's personality, but gives the impression of aggrandizing Harris's own role in Wilde's story.

In 1922 Harris moved to Nice, France, and published the first volume of his four-volume autobiography, *My Life and Loves* (1922–27). The boastful and explicit record of sexual conquests made it necessary schoolboy reading for decades, but the book offended many, including some of his friends, and its truthfulness has been questioned. Shaw remained a friend, and Harris's biography of the playwright (1931) was completed by Shaw himself, after Harris's death, to benefit Harris's estate. Harris died in Nice and was buried there.

Works about Frank Harris

Pearsall, Robert Brainard. *Frank Harris*. Boston: Twayne, 1970.

Pullar, Philippa. *Frank Harris: A Biography*. New York: Simon & Schuster, 1976.

Weintraub, Stanley, ed. *The Playwright and the Pirate: Bernard Shaw and Frank Harris: A Correspondence*. University Park: Pennsylvania State University Press, 1982.

Harris, James Thomas
See HARRIS, FRANK.

Harrison, Frederic (1931–1923) *historian, philosopher, critic*

Frederic Harrison was born in London. He graduated from Oxford University in 1853, becoming a lawyer in 1858. In 1870 Harrison married his cousin, Ethel Harrison, who became his most influential friend and adviser. They had four children. Harrison, who was a professor of international law at the Inns of Court from 1877 to 1889, was elected an alderman of London, serving from 1889 to 1893.

Harrison was the most influential English positivist of the century. Based on the work of Auguste Comte (whom Harrison met in France a few years before Comte's death), positivism claimed that humanity had already moved through a theological and a metaphysical stage and had in the 19th century entered the final, positive stage where humankind, no longer dependent on religion, can base belief only on things that could be scientifically demonstrated to be true. Harrison's first book, *The Meaning of History* (1862), argues that such a positivist view explains how history itself works, with humankind turning increasingly away from priests and toward scientists for guidance.

Harrison published widely in the Victorian periodical press, in such journals as *Contemporary Review* and *Fortnightly Review*, on philosophical, social, historical, and literary topics. He proposed in some of those writings what he called "Neo-Christianity," an effort to fuse Christian ideals of conduct with scientific principles. Harrison believed that great men were the saints of positivism, and to demonstrate that case he wrote a series of biographies of great men: *Oliver Cromwell* (1888), *William the Silent* (1897), *George Washington* (1901), and *John Ruskin* (1902). He also published five volumes of literary essays that discussed a range of authors from the classical (Greek and Roman) to the Victorian periods in terms of positivism.

During his lifetime, Harrison was widely published and respected for his philosophical and practical work; he drafted, for example, the laws that regulated labor-government relations in England in the latter half of the century. Morton Luce in 1923 called Harrison "an un-official Prose Laureate of half a century. He is nearly the last of those great souls who were the glory of our Victorian literature." Today Harrison's name is widely known among scholars of Victorian literature and history.

A Work about Frederic Harrison
Sullivan, Harry. *Frederic Harrison*. Boston: Twayne, 1983.

Harrison, Mary St. Leger Kingsley
See MALET, LUCAS.

Hawker, Robert Stephen (1804–1873) *poet*

R. S. Hawker was born in Plymouth, Devon, on the south coast of western England. His father, Jacob Hawker, was a doctor who later became an Anglican priest. His mother was Jane Elizabeth Hawker.

In 1823, at age 19, he entered Oxford University and married Charlotte I'ans. He won the prestigious Newdigate Prize at Oxford for a poem on Pompeii, which brought him advancement in his studies to become an Anglican priest, because the bishop of Oxford admired it. He became a deacon in 1829 and a priest in 1831. Hawker was appointed vicar of Morwenstow, on a rocky stretch of the north coast of Cornwall in western England, known for its shipwrecks. He restored the church, established a parish school at his own expense, and remained vicar there for the rest of his life. In 1825, Hawker anonymously published perhaps his most famous poem, the "Ballad of Trelawny," sometimes called the Cornish national anthem, with its rousing call to battle:

> *A good sword and a trusty hand!*
> *A merry heart and true!*
> *King James's men shall understand*
> *What Cornish lads can do.*
> *And have they fixed the where and when?*
> *And shall Trelawny die?*
> *Here's twenty thousand Cornish men*
> *Will know the reason why!*

CHARLES DICKENS and SIR WALTER SCOTT both believed that Hawker's poem was an ancient Cornish ballad when it first appeared. In the 1830s and 1840s, Hawker published three volumes of poems, including *Reeds Shaken with the Wind* (1843–44), a collection of mostly religious poems, and *Echoes from Old Cornwall* (1846). Hawker's wife died in 1864, and a year later he married Pauline Anne Kuczyski, who had been a governess. They had three daughters. Among his later works were the long Arthurian poem, *The Quest of the Sangraal: Chant the First* (1864), considered his best, and *Cornish Ballads and Other Poems* (1867), imitations of the ancient ballads in a direct and simple style.

Works about Robert Stephen Hawker

Peters, Robert. *Hawker.* Santa Barbara, Calif.: Unicorn Press, 1984.

Rowse, A. L. "Robert Stephen Hawker of Morwenstow." In *The Little Land of Cornwall.* Gloucester, England: Alan Sutton, 1986.

Haydon, Benjamin Robert (1786–1846)
historical painter, diarist

Benjamin Robert Haydon, the son of a printer and publisher, was born in Plymouth, England. Encouraged by his grammar school teacher and inspired by an Italian bookbinder's descriptions of works by Michelangelo and Raphael, Haydon focused his tremendous energy on painting, portraying events in biblical and classical history. His huge canvases, such as *The Judgment of Solomon*, met with some early success among patrons. In his best-known painting, *Christ's Entry into Jerusalem*, Haydon included in the crowd the faces of his friends JOHN KEATS, WILLIAM WORDSWORTH, CHARLES LAMB, and WILLIAM HAZLITT. Critics, however, including JOHN RUSKIN, found Haydon's work affected and his technical skill mediocre. Nevertheless, Haydon could recognize great art and was one of the first to publicly support the British Museum's purchase of the Elgin Marbles, ancient sculpture that had been removed from the Parthenon in Greece.

Haydon's quarrels with his patrons made for a stormy, frustrating career rife with constant financial troubles, and periodic sentences to debtors' prison. In 1846 Haydon committed suicide, shooting himself in front of one of his large, unfinished paintings.

Haydon is best known by students and scholars of British literature for the keen portraits he drew with his pen rather than brush. In his posthumously published *Autobiography* (1853) and *Diary* (1960–63), Haydon pulls back a curtain on his own life and the lives of his contemporaries in unguarded moments: The most famous account is a description of his "immortal dinner" which contains anecdotes about Keats, and Wordsworth, and especially Lamb, who pretends to be a deranged phrenologist.

Works about Benjamin Robert Haydon

George, Eric. *The Life and Death of Benjamin Robert Haydon, Historical Painter, 1786–1846.* 2nd ed., with additions by Dorothy George. Oxford, England: Clarendon Press, 1967.

Pope, Willard Bissell, ed. *Invisible Friends: The Correspondence of Elizabeth Barrett Browning and Benjamin Robert Haydon.* Cambridge, Mass.: Harvard University Press, 1972.

Hazlitt, William (1778–1830) *critic, essayist*

William Hazlitt, born in Maidstone, Kent, England, was the son of a dissenting, politically radical, Unitarian minister also named William and Grace Loftus Hazlitt. The younger Hazlitt went to a village school in Shropshire and trained for the ministry at the Unitarian New College in Hackney, a borough in north London, but later abandoned the plan.

Encouraged by his friend SAMUEL TAYLOR COLERIDGE, Hazlitt turned instead to philosophy, on which he lectured and wrote. He produced such books as *An Essay on the Principles of Human Action* (1805), a Christian-influenced argument for a secular "principle of disinterestedness" by which people are naturally inclined to sacrifice themselves for the alleviation of others' suffering.

Hazlitt was interested in politics and supported the French Revolution long after his contemporaries—Coleridge, WILLIAM WORDSWORTH, and DOROTHY WORDSWORTH—had turned against it. He regarded their change of heart as a betrayal, and it was a factor in his falling-out with the Wordsworths.

Hazlitt turned his interest in domestic political affairs into a job reporting on the activities of Parliament for the *Morning Chronicle*. He also wrote for the *Examiner*, *New Monthly Magazine*, and *London Magazine*. Some of his essays from this period were collected in the books *Table Talk; or, Original Essays on Men and Manners* (1821–22) and *The Plain Speaker: Opinions on Books, Men, and Things* (1826). These helped establish Hazlitt as a tough, outspoken, and independent-minded critic. Hazlitt had a considerable elitist streak that showed up in all his writing. For instance, in "On the Disadvantages of Intellectual Superiority" (1821), he laments that in teaching modern philosophical notions "Nothing can be more awkward than to intrude with any such far-fetched ideas among the common herd."

Hazlitt addressed history and literature in several volumes. *Characters of Shakespeare's Plays* (1817) cemented his reputation as a serious critic with its analysis of the passions depicted and dramatic tensions created by some of Shakespeare's main characters, while *Lectures on the English Poets* (1818) praises the radical and antiauthoritarian elements of several poets' works and reflects Hazlitt's continued admiration for the French Revolution. *Lectures Chiefly on the Dramatic Literature of the Age of Elizabeth* (1820) was originally delivered as a series of talks at the Surrey Institution and discusses the achievements of several poets in Shakespeare's time. One of his best-known works is *The Spirit of the Age: or, Contemporary Portraits* (1825), combining reprinted essays and new material in an overview of major thinkers of the day, such as JEREMY BENTHAM, Coleridge, Wordsworth, and SIR WALTER SCOTT, with a special emphasis on the liberal tone of the times.

Less successful was Hazlitt's four-volume *Life of Napoleon Buonaparte* (1828–30), an attempt to defend the French emperor, whom Hazlitt, like many other radicals of his day, saw as a heroic destroyer of the old aristocratic order. The book often repeats source material verbatim and recounts historical details such as battles at great length without advancing Hazlitt's argument that Napoleon was not at odds with the liberal spirit of the era.

Hazlitt's *Liber Amoris, or, the New Pygmalion* (1823) depicts a love affair with a landlord's daughter. The scholar Ronald Blythe claims that today's critics agree that although Hazlitt "wrote as marvelously as any essayist," their praise is "eaten through with hesitation," in large part due to his intemperate elitism.

Critical Analysis

The writer J. B. Priestley calls Hazlitt "the supreme genius of Romantic prose" and adds that "his prose rings with courageous expressions of principle and glistens with brilliant passages of critical commentary and analysis." Indeed, Hazlitt's word choice always takes into account both the sounds of words and their sense, and his descriptive passages rival Wordsworth's poetic descriptions of nature. This, for example, is from *An Essay on the Principles of Human Action*:

> If from the top of a long cold barren hill I hear the distant whistle of a thrush which seems to come up from some warm woody shelter

beyond the edge of the hill, this sound coming faint over the rocks with a mingled feeling of strangeness and joy, the idea of the place about me, and the imaginary one beyond will all be combined together in such a manner in my mind as to become inseparable.

One can almost hear the song of the thrush in Hazlitt's words—and he describes perfectly the mystical sense of the infinite that the distant song evokes.

From the beginning, Hazlitt was a supporter of the ideals of the French Revolution, and he continued to support those ideals throughout his life, while other romantics, such as the poets Wordsworth, Coleridge, and Southey, abandoned them. In "On the Feeling of Immortality in Youth" Hazlitt wrote,

It seems to me as if I had set out in life with the French Revolution, and as if all that happened before that were but a dream. Certainly there came to me at that time an extraordinary acceleration of the pulse of being. Youth then was doubly Youth. It was the dawn of a new era; a new impulse that had been given to men's minds and the sun of Liberty rose upon the sun of life in the same day, and both were proud to run their race together. Little did I dream that before long the dawn would be overcast and set once more in the night of despotism.

Although once friendly with Coleridge, Hazlitt attacked him frequently for his change of heart regarding the French Revolution. He writes in *The Spirit of the Age*:

He has nerved his heart and filled his eyes with tears, as he hailed the rising orb of liberty, since quenched in darkness and in blood, and has kindled his affections at the blaze of the French Revolution, and sang for joy, when the towers of the Bastille and the proud places of the insolent and the oppressor fell . . . What has become of all this mighty heap of hope, of thought, of learning and humanity[?] It has ended in swallowing doses of oblivion and in writing paragraphs in the *Courier*. Such and so little is the mind of man!

In addition to political essays, Hazlitt wrote profiles of famous individuals, literary criticism, and philosophical speculation. However, the real joy of reading Hazlitt comes from getting to know the man himself. Not only does he write beautifully, he is also an acute observer of the human comedy and a man who knows himself. In one of his most famous essays, "The Fight," Hazlitt tells of his trip to Hungerford, Berkshire, to watch a boxing match between William Neate and Thomas Hickman. It is a charming story, full of good humor and fun. His trip starts out badly when he incorrectly believes he has missed the Bath mail coach. He berates himself for not taking the time to inquire about it and laments that he "missed it, as I missed everything else, by my own absurdity, in putting the will for the deed, and aiming at ends without employing means." On the way to the fight he meets Tom Turtle, a trainer, who teaches Hazlitt the "whole art of training," which, he tells us, tongue in cheek, "consists in two things, exercise and abstinence, abstinence and exercise, repeated alternatively without end."

At the inn on the evening before the fight, Hazlitt introduces us to an unnamed yeoman who brings himself to Hazlitt's attention by shouting to "a shuffling fellow," "Confound it man, don't be insipid!" He was "a fine fellow, with sense, wit, and spirit, a hearty body and a joyous mind, free-spoken, frank, convivial—one of that true English breed that went with Harry the Fifth to the siege of Harfleur." To Hazlitt, this specimen represents the best of the English spirit. While England as a nation, Hazlitt felt, became stuffy and reactionary in the early years of the nineteenth century, the English people always cherished their liberty and independence.

The writer Somerset Maugham neatly sums up Hazlitt's enduring appeal when he characterizes him as "a solid writer, without pretentiousness, courageous to speak his mind, sensible and plain, with a passion for the arts that was neither gushing nor forced, various, interested in the life about him, ingenious, sufficiently profound for his purposes, but with no affectation of profundity, humorous, sensitive." Moreover, Maugham says, his language was "natural and racy, eloquent when eloquence was needed, easy to read, clear and succinct, neither below the weight of his matter nor with fine phrases trying to give it specious importance." This is high praise indeed.

Works about William Hazlitt

Bloom, Harold, ed. *William Hazlitt.* New York: Chelsea House, 1986.

Cook, Jon. *Hazlitt in Love: A Fatal Attachment.* London: Short Books, 2007.

Lapp, Robert Keith. *Contest for Cultural Authority: Hazlitt, Coleridge, and the Distresses of the Regency.* Detroit, Mich.: Wayne State University Press, 1999.

Priestley, J. B., and R. L. Brett. *William Hazlitt.* Jackson: University Press of Mississippi, 1996.

Hearn, Lafcadio (Yakumo Koizumi)
(1850–1904) *poet, novelist, journalist*

Lafcadio Hearn was born on July 27, 1850, at Leucadia, Santa Maura, one of the Greek Islands in the Ionian Sea. His father was Charles Bush Hearn, an Irish surgeon-major in the British army. His mother, whose name is unknown, was probably Greek. Nevertheless, Hearn always claimed that he was half Asian.

In 1865, in a playground accident at St. Cuthburt's college, he lost the sight in his left eye; over the years the sight in his right eye grew progressively weaker.

In 1869 he moved to the United States, settling in 1871 in Cincinnati, Ohio, where he worked as a reporter for the *Cincinnati Enquirer*. His editor there describes him as having "a soft, shrinking voice" but adds that he was a charming writer with beautiful style and tone. He illegally married an African American woman, Alethea ("Mattie") Foley, which led to his resignation from the *Enquirer*. His crowning achievement as a journalist was his reporting of the Tan-Yard murder case in 1874, in which Hearn depicts the gruesome murder in vivid, sickening detail. This article made his graphic style and unblinking attention to gory particulars, known as the "Vocabulary of the Gruesome," famous. Hearn continued to look unblinkingly at the poor, disadvantaged victims of Cincinnati society and became their scribe.

In 1877 Hearn moved to New Orleans. There he developed a picturesque writing style and also began his study of different cultures, including Creole. During his ten years in New Orleans, he published some translations and wrote editorials for *The Times Democrat*.

In 1887 Hearn moved to Martinique in the French West Indies, where he served as literary contributor for Harper Brothers. He added a sensuous note to his grotesque writing style, which he attributed to the atmosphere of Martinique.

Hearn moved to Japan in April 1890. He was a journalist in the coastal cities of Yokohama, Tokyo, and Kamakura, but his zest for exploration eventually led him to the interior of Japan. He accepted a position as an English teacher in a middle school in Matsue in 1891, where he met Setsuko, the woman who was to become his wife (Hearn married Setsuko despite the fact that he was still married to Mattie Foley, who outlived him). Hearn became a Japanese citizen in 1896, adopting the name Yakumo Koizumi, which means Eight Clouds, before moving again in 1895 to Kumamoto to teach at another middle school.

Hearn went on to become the Dean of the Literary College of Tokyo Imperial University in 1896 and then lecturer of English Literature at the same college. He also taught English literature at Waseda University, Tokyo, Japan. He died in 1904 of a heart attack.

Other Works by Lafcadio Hearn

Barbarous Barbers and Other Stories. Tokyo: The Hokuseido Press, 1939.

Children of the Levee. Lexington: University of Kentucky Press, 1957.

Chita: A Memory of Last Island. Chapel Hill: University of North Carolina Press, 1969.

Works about Lafcadio Hearn

Cott, Johnathan. *Wandering Ghost: The Odyssey of Lafcadio Hearn.* New York: Knopf, 1990.

Murray, Paul. *A Fantastic Journey: The Life and Literature of Lafcadio Hearn.* Japan Library: Kent, United Kingdom, 1993.

Yu, Beongcheon. *An Ape of Gods: The Art and Thought of Lafcadio Hearn.* Detroit: Wayne State University Press, 1964.

Hemans, Felicia Dorothea (1793–1835)
poet

Felicia Dorothea Browne was born in Liverpool, England; her mother, Felicity Dorothea Wagner Browne, was the daughter of the Austrian and Tuscan consul at Liverpool, and her father, George Browne, was an Irish merchant. When the family left Liverpool for financial reasons to settle in northern Wales, whose romantic landscape inspired much of the imagery in Hemans's poetry, Felicia spent much of her time reading. She was educated largely at home—her mother taught her drawing, music, grammar, and French. She did receive, however, some instruction in Latin from a local clergyman, and she taught herself Spanish, Italian, Portuguese, and German. She published her first volume of poetry, simply entitled *Poems,* at age 14, in an effort to earn money for the family.

In 1812 she married Captain Alfred Hemans, an early admirer of her poetry. After six years and five children, the marriage ended. Hemans never spoke of it again. Her marriage years, though not happy, were productive, and Hemans managed to produce three books during this time: *Restoration of the Works of Art to Italy* (1816), *Modern Greece* (1817), and *Translations from Camoens, and Other Poets, with Original Poetry* (1818). Her work drew admiration from PERCY BYSSHE SHELLEY, WILLIAM WORDSWORTH, MATTHEW ARNOLD, and ELIZABETH BARRETT BROWNING, making Hemans, according to Ann Mellor, "the most popular poet in England between 1820 and 1835." In 1821 she wrote *Welsh Melodies,* translations of Welsh poems and historical tales set to music. *Welsh Melodies* remained popular as songs for more than a hundred years.

In 1820 Bishop Reginald Heber, who became a mentor to Hemans, encouraged the poet to try her hand at drama. Hemans greatly admired the plays of JOANNA BAILLIE. She particularly approved of Baillie's female characters, whom Hemans found "so perfectly different from the pretty 'un-idea'd girls,' who seem to form the *beau idéal* of our whole sex in the works of some modern poets." Later the two writers would exchange letters and eventually become friends. Although Hemans's own five-act tragedy, *The Vespers of Palermo,* initially met with little favor, with help from Baillie and SIR WALTER SCOTT (who wrote an epilogue to the play) it became a success. Notably, Hemans's play, a historical drama, featured two strong female characters; the play's underlying thematic concern is the struggle for freedom.

This theme is echoed and explored further in Hemans's poetry. She was particularly concerned with the situation of women. Often her poems describe women's struggles to overcome or simply endure the constraints placed upon them. Although she once remarked, "I utterly disclaim all wish for the post of 'Speaker to the Feminine Literary House of Commons,'" she became a kind of spokesperson for the important issues that women faced during the period. Her most successful book on this theme, *Records of Woman* (1828), is a collection of poems that describes both the triumphs and tragedies of women's lives while providing a subtle critique of the domestic ideal and of patriarchal values (the critique was so subtle that many readers failed to recognize the subversive quality of Hemans's poetry). "The Bride of the Greek Isle," for example, begins with a sweet evocation of the new bride weeping to leave mother, sister, and father for "on earth it must be so, / Thou rearest the lovely to see them go." Such oscillations between hope and defeat may account for the contradictory responses to Hemans's poetry among modern readers.

Other poets (both women and men) recognized the significance of Hemans's literary contribution and paid tribute to their poetic predecessor by eulogizing her in poetry after her death. Letitia Elizabeth Landon's "Stanzas on the Death of Mrs. Hemans," Maria Abdy's "Lines Written on the Death of Mrs. Hemans," Lydia Sigourney's "Monody on Mrs. Hemans," and Elizabeth Barrett Browning's "Felicia Hemans" are notable examples.

Critical Analysis

The popularity of much of Hemans's poetry can be attributed not only to her insightful critique of patriarchal authority, but also to the beauty and clarity of her language and her passionate lyricism, as in these lines from "The Graves of a Household":

The same fond mother bent at night
O'er each fair sleeping brow;
She has each folded flower in sight—
Where are these dreamers now?

Many of her poems, including "The Stately Homes of England," "The Better Land," "The Graves of a Household," "The Treasure of the Deep," and "Casabianca," became standards used in elocution contests in England and America. Schoolchildren were often asked to recite "Casabianca," in particular, perhaps Hemans's most famous poem. With its opening line, "The Boy stood on the burning deck," "Casabianca" is particularly vivid and memorable in its evocation of the beauty and bravery of youth, as a young boy dies in a sea battle that has already killed his father, refusing to leave the post to which his father assigned him.

Hemans also developed a following in America. "The Landing of the Pilgrim Fathers," which appeared in *The Forest Sanctuary* (1829), was a particular favorite because of its celebration of the putative motives for colonization:

Ay, call it holy ground,
The soil where first they trod:
They have left unstained what there they
*   found,—*
Freedom to worship God.

Hemans's poetry became so popular that it inspired many imitators. Her literary influence is unequivocal: She became one of the most widely read poets, on both sides of the Atlantic, of the 19th century. Although Hemans has been remembered mainly because of her vast popularity in the 19th century, and has been dismissed by some as a sentimentalist of only historical interest, critics are beginning to reevaluate her achievement. The scholar Ann Miller writes, for instance, "The recurrent figure of her poetry—the filled circle of the happy family—is repeatedly emptied out, reduced to 'nought,' while patterns of exile, displacement, and the estranged heart come to predominate."

Other Work by Felicia Hemans

Kelly, Gary, ed. *Felicia Hemans: Selected Poems, Prose, and Letters.* Peterborough, Ont.: Broadview Press, 2002.

Works about Felicia Hemans

Sweet, Nanora, and Julie Melnyk, eds. *Felicia Hemans: Reimagining Poetry in the Nineteenth Century.* New York: Palgrave Macmillan, 2001.

Trinder, Peter W. *Mrs. Hemans.* Cardiff: University of Wales Press, 1984.

Henley, William Ernest (1849–1903) *poet, nonfiction writer, dramatist*

W. E. Henley was born into a bookseller's family in Gloucester, England where he went to the Crypt Grammar School. He was self-educated after that, and a lengthy illness gave him opportunity for much reading and experimenting with new forms

Henley, William Ernest

of poetry. This illness, probably a form of tuberculosis, caused Henley to have one foot amputated; in a successful attempt to save the other, Henley spent 20 months during 1873 to 1875 in the Edinburgh Royal Infirmary under the care of the great physician Joseph Lister. "Invictus" was one of his responses to his physical travails; the other was a series of impressionistic poems in free verse, influenced by the American poet Walt Whitman, which were published in 1875 in *Cornhill Magazine* under the title *In Hospital*. During his Edinburgh period he met and became fast friends with another writer affected by tuberculosis, ROBERT LOUIS STEVENSON. Stevenson later revealed that the bluff, hearty and one-legged Henley was the model for his most famous literary character, Long John Silver, in *Treasure Island* (published serially in 1881–82 and in book form in 1883).

A critically well-received poet in his own relatively short lifetime, W. E. Henley is remembered today mainly for "Invictus" (1875). The title is Latin for "unconquered"; the poem was composed during a long period of hospitalization, and since then has been much anthologized. These extracts give a sense of its appeal:

> *Out of the night that covers me*
> *Dark as the pit from pole to pole*
> *I thank whatever gods there be*
> *For my unconquerable soul.*
> * * *
> *I am the master of my fate*
> *I am the captain of my soul.*

Henley was a poet, critic, and editor. He produced far more criticism than poetry. His major gift to posterity, however, is his enthusiastic sponsorship of younger and, at the time, unknown writers. As an editor, he either introduced to the public for the first time, or supported the fledgling efforts of, RUDYARD KIPLING, H. G. Wells, William Butler Yeats, Katharine Tynan, and Kenneth Grahame. He edited journals that also published such writers as Joseph Conrad, GEORGE BERNARD SHAW, and the expatriate American HENRY JAMES. Likewise, he was a staunch supporter of the painter James McNeill Whistler and the sculptor Auguste Rodin. A bust of Henley done by the latter stands today in the National Portrait Gallery, London.

In 1875 Henley moved to London for a literary career. He became editor of the magazine *London*, married Anna Boyle in 1878, and in 1879 became a freelance writer when *London* failed. Two years later he became editor of the *Magazine of Art*, a position he held until 1886. In the meantime, he and Stevenson collaborated in the writing of four plays, but none was particularly successful and they wrote no more. The year 1885 found Henley once more in Edinburgh, where he became editor of the *Scots Observer;* he moved back to London with the magazine when it became the *National Observer,* and continued as editor when it was renamed the *New Review*. During this period he and his friend T. F. Henderson produced the highly regarded centenary edition (1895–96) of the poetry of ROBERT BURNS.

Henley's poetry is sharply different in form, tone, and feeling from that of his immediate predecessors ALFRED, LORD TENNYSON, ROBERT BROWNING, and MATTHEW ARNOLD. He was influenced by the radical forms of Walt Whitman and by forms of the medieval French verse of François Villon. John Milton was another influence, as were the French Parnassians and other mid-19th-century French poets such as Stéphane Mallarmé, Paul Verlaine, and, particularly, Charles Baudelaire. From Baudelaire he took the ideas that poetry can be about even the most sordid of subjects and that there can be a certain beauty in ugliness. His most successful collection is his *London Voluntaries* (1892). Reminiscent of Baudelaire's "Tableaux Parisiens" in *Les Fleurs du Mal,* these poems describe the teeming late-19th-century city and its inhabitants with a clarity and directness unknown in the London descriptions of previous poets. Yet the limited success of these volumes was marred by the death of his beloved child Margaret in 1891, and the poems written after that time do not quite rise to the level of *Voluntaries.*

Works about W. E. Henley
Buckley, Jerome H. *William Ernest Henley.* Princeton, N.J.: Princeton University Press, 1945; reprinted New York: Octagon, 1971.

Flora, Joseph M. *William Ernest Henley.* Boston: Twayne, 1970.

Hichens, Robert Smythe (1864–1950)
novelist

Robert Hichens was born near Canterbury, Kent, in southeast England, to the Reverend Frederick Hichens and Abigail Elizabeth Smythe Hichens. Hichens attended the Royal College of Music in London, where he studied piano and organ. He also studied at the London School of Journalism. Afterward, he wrote short stories for the *Pall Mall Gazette*. In 1894 his most famous novel, *The Green Carnation*, was published. Written with MAX BEERBOHM, it was a comedy about the writer OSCAR WILDE and his circle of friends. In 1904 he published the best-seller *The Garden of Allah*, a story set in the North African desert. Over the next 40 years, Hichens published approximately 40 novels, at the rate of about one a year. One of them, *Bella Donna* (1909), was turned into a play and a movie. He also published poetry, short stories, and plays.

Other Work by Robert Hichens
Child, Lincoln, ed. *Dark Banquet: A Feast of Twelve Great Ghost Stories.* New York: St. Martin's Press, 1985.

Hogg, James (1770–1835) *poet, novelist, short story writer*

Born in Scotland in the parish of Ettrick, Selkirkshire, James Hogg was the son of Robert Hogg, a poor tenant farmer, and Margaret Laidlaw Hogg. Hogg's father went bankrupt when Hogg was six, so Hogg received no formal education, having to work at other local farms for small wages. At 15 he became a shepherd, being hired five years later by a sheep farmer named Laidlaw (a distant cousin of his mother), who shared his small book collection with him. Hogg had at 15 bought a fiddle, taught himself to play it, and begun to write songs of his own to entertain the local girls who sang along with him. He published his first volume of poems, *Scottish Pastorals, Poems, Songs, etc., Mostly Written in the Dialect of the South,* in 1801, which gave him a local reputation as a poet but no national recognition. That changed when he met SIR WALTER SCOTT in 1802.

Inspired by Scott's *Minstrelsy of the Scottish Border* (1802–03), Hogg wrote *The Mountain Bard: Consisting of Ballads and Songs, Founded on Facts and Legendary Tales* (1807), a collection of ballad imitations. He made some money with that publication but lost it in his efforts to establish his own farm. He issued another volume of ballads, *The Forest Minstral; A Selection of Songs, Adopted to the Most Favourite Scottish Airs* (1810). He achieved fame, however, with the success of his long narrative poem *The Queen's Wake: A Legendary Poem* (1813). WILLIAM WORDSWORTH and LORD BYRON both admired the poem, Byron describing Hogg as "a man of great powers and deserving of encouragement." Wordsworth singled out "The Witch of Fife" as the best poem in the volume. The poem chronicles a woman's nighttime adventures in the forest, her story counterpointed by her husband's refrain: "Ye wald better haif been in yer bed at hame / Wi yer diere littil bairnis and me" (you would have been better in your bed at home / with your dear little children and me). As these lines indicate, much of Hogg's poetry is written in rural Scottish dialect and, in ballad form, tells local tales and legends.

After the founding of *Blackwood's Edinburgh Magazine* in 1817, Hogg became a significant contributor, writing stories under the pen name The Ettrick Shepherd (in homage to his origins). His work was featured in the series called Noctes Ambrosianae, which featured the Ettrick Shepherd as a comic, drunken rural genius—both filthy and shrewd. The series ran from 1822 until Hogg's death. Hogg's most famous prose work, however, is the novel *The Private Memoirs and*

Confessions of a Justified Sinner (1824), which is still in print today. The novel, as André Gide put it in his introduction to an edition done in 1947, is about "an 'antinomian'," one who believes that those preelected by God for salvation cannot sin; drunkenness, even murder, which are sins to ordinary men are not evil in one so preordained; the elect can do anything. Gide claims that he was never "so voluptuously tormented by any book."

When Wordsworth learned of Hogg's death, he wrote "Extempore Effusion, Upon the Death of James Hogg." In that poem, Wordsworth links Hogg's death to the passing of a generation of romantic writers, including Walter Scott, CHARLES LAMB, SAMUEL COLERIDGE, and GEORGE CRABBE. Today a serious revival of interest in Hogg's work has begun with the appearance of three volumes of a projected 31-volume collected works of James Hogg, jointly published by the University of Stirling in Scotland and the University of South Carolina.

Other Works by James Hogg

The Brownie of Bodsbeck; and Other Tales. Edinburgh: Blackwood and J. Murray, 1818.
Confessions of a Justified Sinner. Edinburgh: Canongate, 2007.
The Domestic Manners and Private Life of Sir Walter Scott. Glasgow: J. Reid, 1834.

Works about James Hogg

Cortner, Robert Crawford. *James Stephen Hogg: A Biography.* Austin: University of Texas Press, 1959.
Gifford, Douglas. *James Hogg.* Edinburgh: Ramsay Head Press, 1976.

Holcroft, Frances (1778?–1844) *poet, novelist*

Frances Holcroft was the daughter of the writer THOMAS HOLCROFT. She published her first poem, advocating the abolition of slavery, in 1797. Between 1799 and 1803, she lived with her father in Europe and wrote music for his plays. She also translated Italian and Spanish plays into English. Following the death of her father in 1809, Frances Holcroft began writing novels. These included *The Wife and the Lover* (1813), of which, despite the title, a contemporary review reported that the language and moral were "chaste," and also that "The character of Mrs. Tabitha Wormwood, a proud, supercilious sprig of fashion, envious, censorious, and malignant, is well drawn and true to nature." *Fortitude and Frailty* (1817) tells a complicated story of love triangles and the effects of changing fortunes on affections, with a virtuous heroine named Eleanor Fairfax and several comic minor characters.

Holcroft, Thomas (1745–1809) *playwright, novelist*

Thomas Holcroft was born in London, the son of a peddler. Largely self-educated, Holcroft was a stable boy, cobbler, and schoolteacher before he began work in the theater in 1770, first as a prompter in Dublin theaters and then as an actor in various troupes that traveled throughout England. He wrote and produced his first play, *Crisis*, at Drury Lane in 1778. His first novel, *Alwyn; or, The Gentleman Comedian,* based on his experiences as an actor, was published in 1780. A militant atheist and a fervent believer in the individual's capacity for self-improvement, he was drawn into a circle of political and social radicals that included Thomas Paine, John Tooke, WILLIAM GODWIN, and MARY WOLLSTONECRAFT. In 1794 he was arrested and charged with treason for his political activities, but was acquitted and released from the Newgate prison after being held for eight weeks. Plagued by debts, he moved to the Continent in 1799 and spent time in Hamburg, then Paris, before returning to London in 1802. He was married three times. In his last years, his daughter Fanny (Frances) supported him by copying plays, taking dictation, and transcribing letters.

Thomas Holcroft was one of the most ardent of the English radicals who supported the French Revolution. Deeply influenced by the ideas promulgated by it and by his friend William Godwin's radical views, Holcroft used fiction to advocate political and social change. His novels *Anna St. Ives* (1792) and *The Adventures of Hugh Trevor* (1794) reveal the influence of French revolutionary ideas, as does Godwin's polemical novel *Caleb Williams*. Holcroft also used the theater to promote his radical views and to introduce English audiences to theatrical forms popular on the Continent. After a 1784 trip to Paris, where he saw a production of Beaumarchais's *Folle journée: ou, Le mariage de Figaro,* he translated and produced a version for the English stage, *The Follies of the Day* (1784), in which he played the role of Figaro. He introduced to England the melodrama, a sensational theatrical genre developed by French dramatists toward the end of the 18th century in which the main characters were either excessively virtuous or exceptionally evil, with the play *A Tale of Mystery* (1802), his translation of *Coelina, ou l'enfant de mystère* (1800), by the French playwright Guilbert de Pixérécourt (1773–1844). The success of *A Tale of Mystery* helped establish the dominance of melodrama in 19th-century English theater. Among his many other works for the stage are *Duplicity* (1781) which condemns gambling; *The School for Arrogance* (1791); *Love's Frailties* (1794); and *The Deserted Daughter* (1791). His best-known and often revived play is *The Road to Ruin* (1792). A comedy about the rakish young Harry Dornton, who gambles away his small fortune, conveys Holcroft's message with a light touch.

Holcroft's unfinished memoirs were completed by his friend WILLIAM HAZLITT and published in 1816 as *The Life of Thomas Holcroft*.

Other Works by Thomas Holcroft
Memoirs of Bryan Perdue, a Novel. 1805. Reprint, New York: Garland Publishing, 1979.
The Plays of Thomas Holcroft. Edited and with an introduction by Joseph Rosenblum. New York: Garland Publishing, 1980.
Travels from Hamburg, through Westphalia, Holland, and the Netherlands, to Paris. 1804.

Works about Thomas Holcroft
Kelly, Gary. *The English Jacobin Novel, 1780–1805*. New York: Clarendon Press, 1985.
Rosenblum, Joseph. *Thomas Holcroft: Literature and Politics in England in the Age of the French Revolution*. Lewiston, N.Y.: Edwin Mellen Press, 1995.

Hood, Thomas (1799–1845) *poet*

Thomas Hood, the son and namesake of a London bookseller, was educated privately and apprenticed as an engraver. His health grew poor, and he turned to writing. He contributed poetry to the *London Magazine,* through which he met CHARLES LAMB, THOMAS DE QUINCEY, and WILLIAM HAZLITT.

In 1825 he published the humorous and popular *Odes and Addresses to Great People,* a book written in collaboration with his brother-in-law, J. H. Reynolds. Hood had a great flair for humor, and in 1826 and 1827 he published his two-volume book *Whims and Oddities,* containing comic poems that demonstrated his tremendous, albeit sometimes sinister, skill at punning, as shown in this stanza from "Faithless Nelly Gray": "Ben Battle was a soldier bold, / And used to war's alarms; / But a cannon-ball took off his legs, / So he laid down his arms." He often turned to black comedy. His poems are full of undertakers, coffins, and corpses that were always good for a laugh. He also wrote serious poetry, with *The Plea of the Midsummer Fairies* (1827) being influenced by the work of his contemporary, JOHN KEATS. But only Hood's comic writing helped pay the bills. He held a succession of editorial jobs, and in 1830 even started his own magazine, *The Comic Annual,* but found no lasting financial success.

Although he was mainly recognized for his comedy, punning, and wit, some of his serious work became a model for social protest, especially his poem "Song of the Shirt" (1843), which helped inspire legislation to improve factory conditions and child labor laws. The poem, which denounces exploitation of women in the sewing trade, was based on the true story of a seamstress accused of pawning her employer's possessions. She sings

> Work—work—work!
> My labour never flags;
> And what are its wages? A bed of straw,
> A crust of bread—and rags.
> That shatter'd roof—and this naked floor—
> ... And a wall so blank, my shadow I thank
> For sometimes falling there!

The poem was reprinted in the *Times*, printed on broadsheets and cotton handkerchiefs, and was translated into foreign languages. Hood's serious verse, such as the "Song of the Shirt," led the Irish writer Oliver Elton to say of the poet that he was "the truest English poet in the years immediately preceding Tennyson."

Hope, Thomas (1770–1831) *novelist, nonfiction writer*

Thomas Hope was born to English parents in Amsterdam, Holland. His father, John Hope, was a wealthy merchant and art collector living in Amsterdam. Hope studied architecture, then spent eight years sketching and studying architectural ruins in Egypt, Greece, Turkey, Syria, and Spain. In 1796 Hope returned to England, where he became a serious art collector and patron. He had two houses for his collections, one in London and the other on his estate in Surrey, in southern England.

In 1807 Hope published *Household Furniture and Interior Decoration*. This was the first use of the term *interior decoration* to describe methods of designing the inside of a house. The book, which included Hope's drawings of his London home, had a significant influence on the British public's taste in the early 19th century.

Hope married Louisa Beresford in 1806 and had several children with her. In 1819 he anonymously published a picaresque novel, *Anastasius; or, Memoirs of a Greek, written at the Close of the Eighteenth Century*, which was assumed to have been written by the poet LORD BYRON. When Hope revealed that he was the author, one reviewer was amazed that "the man of chairs and tables, the gentleman of sofas" could have written such a stirring romance. Byron wrote to a friend that he wept bitterly when he read *Anastasius*, both because he had not written it and because Hope had. It remained Hope's most famous work. He also wrote *An Historical Essay on Architecture*, with drawings made in Italy and Germany, which was published posthumously in 1835.

Hopkins, Ellice (1836–1904) *reform writer, poet, novelist*

Jane Ellice Hopkins was born to William Hopkins, a mathematics professor at Cambridge University, and Caroline Boys Hopkins. After being educated by her parents, Ellice went to Brighton, England, in 1866 to work at Albion Hill Home, an institution dedicated to improving the lives of prostitutes. She spent four years there, an experience that had a profound influence on her later writing. Hopkins firmly believed that prostitution was the result of poverty and a double standard among men and women regarding sex. In 1876 she published a novel, *Rose Turquand*, a Gothic romance that describes the life of an illegitimate child in Victorian England. That same year she and Bishop Joseph Lightfoot of Durham founded the Ladies Association for the Care of Friendless Girls, which provided job training for single young women. In 1883 Hopkins published *Autumn Swallows: A Book of Lyrics*, which focuses on the theme of the sexual double standard. About the same time, Hopkins started the White Cross Army. This association urged men to "take the pledge" to "treat all women with respect, and endeavor to protect them from wrong and degradation." This also meant that men would not engage in sexual relations before marriage—the same standard expected of women. The women who joined the White Cross Army dedicated themselves to improving the morality of English society. In 1886 Hopkins published a pamphlet titled *True Manliness,* presenting the principles of the White Cross Army. It sold 300,000 copies within a year. She continued publishing pamphlets espousing her principles throughout the 1890s.

Hopkins, Gerard Manley (1844–1889)
poet

Gerard Manley Hopkins was born into the large, prosperous High Anglican family of Manley and Catherine Hopkins in Stratford, Essex, England. Hopkins grew up in the village of Hampstead, on the northern outskirts of London, and was educated at Highgate School, then at Balliol College, Oxford. He distinguished himself as a scholar at Oxford, becoming friends there with ROBERT BRIDGES, WALTER PATER, and JOHN HENRY NEWMAN, who, as Cardinal Newman, received him into the Catholic faith in 1866. Two years later Hopkins became a Jesuit; in 1877, after rigorous study, he was ordained a Jesuit priest. He worked in poor parishes in London, Oxford, Liverpool, and Glasgow until, in 1884, he was appointed professor of classics at University College, Dublin.

When Hopkins became a Jesuit he burned the poems he had written to that date, imposing a vow of silence on himself that he kept for seven years. In 1875, however, his superior encouraged him to write a poem commemorating the recent death of five Franciscan nuns. The result was "The Wreck of the Deutschland," a long, intricately wrought religious ode about the nuns' drowning off the Kentish coast. Following closely an account of the wreck that appeared in the London *Times*—though the wreck itself is only briefly described—Hopkins's poem is in two parts. The first part, comprising 10 eight-line stanzas, recounts Hopkins's own spiritual crisis and suffering, while the second describes the nuns' terror before one of them receives a vision of Christ walking on the waves toward them as they drown. The poem as a whole explores the paradox that salvation comes only through death, the ocean itself representing a powerful double-edged symbol of destruction and salvation.

During his silent years Hopkins kept a poetic journal in which he meticulously recorded observations; from this were quarried some of the startlingly original and beautiful sonnets that burst forth in the late 1870s. Among these are "Spring" and "Hurrahing in Harvest," both 1877. These sonnets are songs of praise.

A later series of poems dates from Hopkins's years of parish work in Oxford. A fine example is the sonnet ("Duns Scotus's Oxford," 1879) in praise of Oxford itself that invokes the university town as "Towery city and branchy between towers."

Finally, there are the "terrible sonnets," poems recording a dark night of the soul, that date from a decade later, when Hopkins lived in Ireland. They include "Carrion Comfort" (1885), "No Worst, There is None" (1885), and "Thou Art Indeed Just, Lord" (1889), the last poem completed a few months before his death. In "No Worst, There is None," Hopkins plumbs the bottomlessness of despair. His opening line derives from Edgar's observation in *King Lear* that "The worst is not, / So long as we can say, 'This is the worst.'" The poet's dark night of the soul is a fall into the abyss: "O the mind, mind has mountains, cliffs of fall / Frightful, sheer, no-man-fathomed."

Hopkins's final years in Ireland were dogged by illness, loneliness, and depression. He died of typhus in Dublin and is buried there in Glasnevin Cemetery. His poems were first published in 1918 by his friend Robert Bridges.

Critical Analysis

Three of Hopkins's 1877 sonnets are among his best work: "God's Grandeur," "Pied Beauty," and "The Windhover." The latter poem was subtitled "To Christ Our Lord" and Hopkins believed it "the best thing I ever wrote." It praises God in the guise of a magnificent kestrel, or falcon, whose very name describes its flight. The enraptured poet sights this bird at dawn, perceiving in its beauty, majesty, and power an emblem of the divine and thus comparing it to a "dauphin" and a "chevalier." The potent train of visual and kinesthetic images Hopkins sets in motion, reinforced by the rocking, hovering rhythms of the kestrel's flight, virtually explode in the sonnet's final lines to reveal, once again, God's glory.

In much of his work, but particularly in "The Windhover," Hopkins reads nature as the Book of the Creation. Every creature or object is charged with the glory of God but also has its own essential, distinctive nature or "inscape," as he called it. The keen observer perceives inscape through what Hopkins terms "instress"—a kind of rapt, intent perception or observation.

"The Windhover" is also often used to demonstrate "sprung rhythm." Hopkins invented sprung rhythm, which he thought closer to actual speech and music than standard verse with a regular number of feet, or syllables, to each line. In musical terms, Hopkins's concept of rhythm counts beats rather than notes per measure. Thus Hopkins's sprung rhythm employs irregular feet of one to four syllables each, the stress generally falling on the first foot, but accommodating any number of unstressed syllables, which Hopkins called "hangers" or "outriders." As he explained in a letter, "One stress makes one foot, no matter how many or few the syllables."

Hopkins's poetry delivers a considerable charge, as seen in "God's Grandeur" and "Pied Beauty." These poems, like most of Hopkins's verse, demand to be read aloud. Their openings are dramatic and arresting: "The world is charged with the grandeur of God" ("God's Grandeur") and "Glory be to God for dappled things" ("Pied Beauty").

His imagery is equally striking. In "God's Grandeur" the metaphors chosen to depict divine splendor, reflected light from a piece of foil or oozing oil, reveal the divine as a radiant force flowing through all of creation. "Pied Beauty," in the five lines of its shortened sestet, normally a six-line ending section of a sonnet, singles out for praise unusual, bicolored, streaked, freckled, and spotted objects in which the poet delights, praising all that is, as Hopkins expresses it, "counter, original, spare, strange."

Diction is original and precise—this is a poet who loves to coin words or give them new meaning. In "Spring and Fall" (1880), for example, Hopkins invents the words "wanwood leafmeal" to describe the mass of pale, sodden leaves found on autumn ground. But his poems are studded with examples of brilliant coinages and ingenious compounds: "dapple-dawn-drawn Falcon" ("The Windhover") and "bell-swarmèd, lark-charmèd, rook-racked, river-rounded" ("Duns Scotus's Oxford").

Acquainted with Welsh verse (*cynghanned,*) Hopkins uses assonance, alliteration, and internal rhyme lavishly, as in these lines from "God's Grandeur": "And all is seared with trade; bleared, smeared with toil; / And wears man's smudge and shares man's smell . . ."

Much of Hopkins's force also derives from Anglo-Saxon rhythms and vocabulary. The rhythm and syntax in his poems are unusual, sometimes contorted, as in the sweeping, hovering, rocking rhythms of "The Windhover":

> *I caught this morning morning's minion,*
> * kingdom of daylight's dapple-dawn-*
> * drawn Falcon, in his riding*
> *Of the rolling level underneath him steady*
> * air, and striding*
> *High there, how he rung upon the rein of a*
> * wimpling wing . . .*

Besides the influence of Anglo-Saxon and Welsh verse, Hopkins's work reflects John Milton in its syntax and JOHN KEATS in its imagery. Hopkins also was influenced by such contemporaries as MATTHEW ARNOLD and CHRISTINA ROSSETTI. His vision and conception of poetry were also shaped by Duns Scotus and St. Ignatius Loyola.

Although Hopkins lived in the Victorian era, he is a modern poet whose poetry rightly belongs to later centuries, not to the 19th. Hopkins was an important influence on others, particularly the poets of the 1930s and beyond—W. H. Auden,

Cecil Day-Lewis, Stephen Spender, Dylan Thomas, and Geoffrey Hill. A poetic pioneer, Hopkins rejuvenated English poetry; his was also a liberating influence. As the critic David Anthony notes, Hopkins "tends to be seen as a 20th-century poet ... because of his enormous influence on contemporary poetry, which was freed by sprung rhythm from the metrical constraints of all that came before."

Other Work by Gerard Manley Hopkins
Gardner, W. H., ed. *Poems and Prose of Gerard Manley Hopkins.* New York: Viking Penguin, 1990.

Works about Gerard Manley Hopkins
Bergonzi, Bernard. *Gerard Manley Hopkins.* New York: Collier Books, 1977.
Lahey, Gerald F. *Gerard Manley Hopkins.* London: Oxford University Press, 1930.
Muller, Jill. *Gerard Manley Hopkins and Victorian Catholicism: A Heart in Hiding.* London: Taylor & Francis, 2007.
Savile, Julie F. *A Queen Chivalry: The Homoerotic Asceticism of Gerard Manley Hopkins.* Charlottesville: University Press of Virginia, 2000.

Housman, Alfred Edward (1859–1936)
poet

A. E. Housman was born to Edward Housman, a solicitor, and his wife, Sarah Williams Housman, near Bromsgrove, Worcestershire, England, a dozen miles or so from the Shropshire border. He had a happy childhood until the death of his mother when he was 12.

Attending St. John's College at Oxford University, Housman was a superior student in classics and philosophy. While there, however, he suffered severe psychological distress as he grew aware of his love for a young man. Consequently, he failed his final exams and received only a "pass" degree. His sexual discovery, combining with the trauma of his mother's death, left Housman isolated, bitter, and unresolved. As the scholar B. Ifor Evans observes, "some deep emotional disturbance affected the whole of his life both as a scholar and a poet."

Housman worked as a clerk in the Patent Office in London for 10 years, during which time he published noteworthy works on Ovid, Horace, and Juvenal. Eventually, his articles caught the attention of other classicists, and he was offered a professorship of Latin at London University in 1892. In 1911 he became the Kennedy Professor of Latin at Cambridge, a position he held until his death. He often complained that his teaching bordered on the elementary because so few of his students had any real aptitude for the classics.

Where Housman's scholarly studies allowed him to be reserved and impersonal—although he could write scathingly about his colleagues' inferior scholarship—his poetry required him to confront his emotions. Indeed, he often wrote verse when he was depressed or ill.

In 1896 he paid for publication of *A Shropshire Lad*. Critics initially ignored the book, but the public responded enthusiastically and turned it into a best-seller. In the 63 poems of this collection, young Shropshire men play, drink, fall in love, enlist, and even murder.

These Shropshire lads do all their living against an idealized countryside that owes much to Housman's knowledge of Greek and Roman pastoral poetry about love among shepherds and shepherdesses, but little to his own experience since, as he admitted, "I never spent much time there." It is a landscape that celebrates human events. In "1887" the very hills commemorate the 50th anniversary of Queen Victoria's reign: "Look left, look right, the hills are bright, / The dales are light between, / Because 'tis fifty years to-night / That God has saved the Queen."

But there is also a dark strain to this pastoral scene. In "On moonlit heath and lonesome bank," sheep graze a hill where "the gallows used to clank" and where "high amongst the glimmering sheep / The dead man stood on air." In "Bredon Hill," a young lover looks forward to his wedding, but instead ends by attending his fiancée's funeral. Still, as William Archer in his

1898 review of *A Shropshire Lad* wrote, "Mr. Housman's melancholy is . . . not to be shaken off, but there is nothing whining about it; rather, it is bracing, invigorating."

In spite of the popularity of his poetry, Housman would publish only two slim volumes in his lifetime, his second being *Last Poems* (1922). Much of his time was spent on scholarship, particularly a five-volume edition of Manilius (1930), a difficult Roman poet of the age of the emperor Tiberius.

A third volume of verse, *More Poems* (1936), appeared after Housman died, and in 1937 his brother, Laurence Housman, wrote a memoir titled *My Brother, A. E. Housman,* which included 18 more poems that had never before been published. Housman, says Evans, "remained a romantic in an age which was aggressively following other ways. He did not much like his contemporaries, either as critics or poets, and he detested their pretentiousness." He is said by one biographer to have been "the most persuasive and perhaps the purest minor poet of his time." Housman is the central character in the 1997 play, *The Invention of Love,* by Tom Stoppard.

Critical Analysis

Running through many of the poems of *A Shropshire Lad* is the dark side of the romantization of youth. If youth is joy, joy fades quickly, and the rest of life is hardly worth living, bringing as it does little but pain. One of the most frequently anthologized of Housman's poems that plays this tune is "To an Athlete Dying Young."

The poem opens with the image of a young athlete being borne through his hometown on the shoulders of his neighbors, everyone cheering his victory. As is often the case with Housman, the verse has a strong rhythm and a regular rhyme, which leads one to expect conventional sentiments, an expectation Housman immediately upsets. In the second stanza, the image is of the same young man in his coffin being carried to his grave. The opening of the next stanza startles even more: "Smart lad, to slip betimes away." Why was the young athlete smart to die?

Eyes the shady night has shut
Cannot see the record cut,
And silence sounds no worse that cheers
After earth has stopped the ears.

Better to die at the height of one's glory than to linger on until someone else beats the record and is the center of the celebration. Lucky young athlete, "Now you will not swell the rout / Of lads that wore their honours out."

The young athlete, Housman says, can place his "fleet foot" on the edge of the grave and use his trophy to "hold the low lintel up."

This poem has always appealed to conflicted young people, with its idealization of the moment of the height of glory. During and after World War I, when so many young men died in the bloom of youth, it seemed almost prophetic.

Other Work by A. E. Housman

The Name and Nature of Poetry: And Other Selected Prose. Edited by John Carter. Chicago: New Amsterdam Books, 1990.

Works about A. E. Housman

Hoagwood, Terence Allan. *A. E. Housman Revisited.* London: Twayne, 1995.

Holden, Alan W., and J. Roy Birch, eds. *A. E. Housman: A Reassessment.* New York: St. Martin's Press, 1999.

Howitt, Mary (1799–1888) *poet, novelist, short story writer, translator*

Mary Howitt, née Botham, was born in Uttoxeter, Staffordshire, England. Her father, Samuel Botham, worked first in the iron industry and then as a land surveyor. The family, devout Quakers, lived an austere and simple life, and Mary later described her childhood as filled with "stillness and isolation." Yet her mother, Ann Wood Botham, encouraged her to read and write poetry, and her education at the Croyden and Sheffield Quaker schools further exposed her to literature.

In 1824 she married a fellow Quaker and poet, WILLIAM HOWITT. The couple established an apothecary shop in Nottingham, but they devoted their efforts to poetry, publishing a small chapbook entitled *The Forest Minstrel* (1823), filled with romantic lyrics celebrating nature. In 1828 their almanac *The Book of the Seasons* was fairly successful. It featured Mary's increasingly complex nature poems.

In 1834 Howitt published her best-known work, the poetry collection *Sketches of Natural History*. These poems develop the genre of romantic animal poems in which the animals embody mysteries of nature normally unfathomable to humans. The poems are also didactic and instruct readers on proper moral conduct. The most famous among these poems is "The Spider and the Fly," in which the spider maliciously ensnares the fly: "'I'm sure you must be weary, dear, with soaring up so high; / Will you rest upon my little bed?' said the Spider to the Fly." The fly initially resists, but ultimately succumbs to the spider's enticements, and Howitt concludes the poem with this undisguised advice: "To idle, silly flattering words, I pray you never give heed; / Unto an evil counsellor, close heart and ear and eye."

In order to be close to the large publishing houses, the Howitts eventually moved nearer to London. Here, Mary Howitt began writing novels and stories. Her most popular book was *Love and Money* (1843), a collection of 13 stories that advises readers how to maintain morality in the face of Victorian materialism. Near the end of her career, Howitt also became a highly successful translator of children's stories and was the first person to offer English editions of Hans Christian Andersen's fairy tales. Howitt was also politically active throughout her life, constantly decrying the negative effects of industrialism on the poor. But she remains best known for her early poetry and its worshipful images of nature. The biographer Amice Lee claims that Howitt's work embodies "the abounding vitality which characterized her all her long life."

A Work about Mary Howitt

Lee, Amice. *Laurels and Rosemary: The Life of William and Mary Howitt.* London: Oxford University Press, 1955.

Howitt, William (1792–1879) *poet, novelist, essayist*

William Howitt was born in Nottingham, England, to mine superintendent Thomas Howitt and his wife, Phebe Tatum Howitt. Both of Howitt's parents were devout Quakers, and their strong belief in social justice and equality powerfully influenced Howitt's later writings. During his boyhood, Howitt spent much time exploring the surrounding countryside, which also became an important literary influence for him.

In 1810 Howitt was apprenticed to a cabinetmaker, and he did some work in GEORGE GORDON, LORD BYRON's residence. Although Byron was not present, the experience inspired Howitt to begin writing poetry. To support himself while writing, he became a pharmacist and opened his own apothecary. In 1821 he married Mary Botham. Motivated by their common affection for romantic poetry, William and MARY HOWITT published a series of poetry chapbooks. Among these, the most notable was *The Forest Minstrel* (1823). The poems are traditional romantic lyrics in which animals and other natural objects assume spiritual qualities. For instance, in Howitt's poem "The Departure of the Swallow," the narrator, unable to find a swallow, associates the departed bird with his own soul: "So the freed spirit flies! / From its surrounding clay / It steals away." The swallow therefore becomes a symbol of freedom from mundane life, and its disappearance and perceived abandonment disturbs the narrator: "'Tis all unknown; / We feel alone / That a void is left below."

The Howitts achieved their greatest joint success with *The Book of the Seasons* (1828), an almanac that combines their romantic poems with essays on farming and other rural subjects and serves as a bridge between ROMANTICISM and a more practical Victorian spirit. As William's career developed, he increasingly wrote prose. His essays preserve memories of his rural upbringing and lament the industrial invasion of the English countryside. His most famous work, *The Rural Life of England* (1838), contends that industrialism oppresses the poor and that government programs designed to help the poor actually benefit the growing manufacturing companies. In later years Howitt advocated political reforms, such as abolition of slavery, voting rights for women, and anti-imperialism. He is best known for his early essays and their ability to depict the topography of the rapidly changing countryside. The biographer Amice Lee notes that "Howitt felt an urgency to write about the so rapidly changing scene, the disappearance of old homes and ways of life . . . all vanishing before the advance of the Industrial Age."

A Work about William Howitt

Lee, Amice. *Laurels and Rosemary: The Life of William and Mary Howitt.* London: Oxford University Press, 1955.

Hudson, William Henry (1841–1922)
novelist, naturalist

W. H. Hudson was born on a cattle ranch in Argentina, where his American parents, Daniel and Katherine Hudson, had immigrated to improve their health. In his teens, he contracted rheumatic fever; it weakened his heart and forced him to abandon ranching. He then turned to bird-watching and to writing, which became a precious means of recording what doctors had warned might be a short life. (In fact, Hudson lived for more than 80 years, wrote a number of books describing birds, and had several species of birds named for him.)

In 1874 Hudson emigrated to Britain, settling in London, and in 1876 he married Emily Wingrave, who was 15 years his senior. Hudson's first collection of stories, all set in South America, was *The Purple Land that England Lost* (1885). In 1887 he published *A Crystal Age*, a utopian novel featuring the demise of sexuality. His books sold poorly, but the influential editor Edward Garnett, admiring the stories in *El Ombu* (1902), encouraged Hudson to continue writing. With *Green Mansions: A Romance of the Tropical Forest* (1904), Hudson gained critical acclaim and a measure of financial security. Set in the Venezuelan rain forest, the novel depicts the romance of Abel Guevez and the mysterious bird-girl, Rima; her death; and Abel's revenge. Remarkable for its haunting natural description, the book may be read as an allegory of society's depredations of nature. It was especially appealing to city-bound readers who had begun to realize that they had forfeited a relationship with forest and primeval wilderness.

In 1905 Hudson published *Hampshire Days,* and, in 1910, *A Shepherd's Life: Impressions of the South Wiltshire Downs,* both books based on his travels through southern England. An autobiography of the author's early years appeared in 1918 entitled *Far Away and Long Ago.* John Galsworthy said of Hudson, "unspoiled unity with Nature pervades all his writing."

Other Work by W. H. Hudson

The Naturalist in La Plata. 1892. Reprint. New York: Dover, 1994.

A Work about W. H. Hudson

Tomalin, Ruth. *W. H. Hudson: A Biography.* London: Oxford University Press, 1984.

Hughes, Thomas (1822–1896) *novelist, nonfiction writer*

Thomas Hughes was born in the village of Uffington, in Berkshire, England, the second of eight children of John Hughes and Margaret Wilkinson Hughes. When Hughes was 11, he was sent to school at Rugby. He studied law at Oxford University and was admitted to the bar in 1848. He had married Fanny Ford, a clergyman's daughter, in 1847; it was their burgeoning family that led Hughes to begin writing.

In 1856 Hughes's oldest son was ready to be sent to school, and Hughes wanted to provide him with guidance and advice. The result was *Tom Brown's School Days* (1857), an evocation of the Rugby Hughes remembered under the leadership of THOMAS ARNOLD, who appears as "the Doctor," the headmaster in the book. Tom Brown enters the school as a small boy, suffers humiliations from bullying, enjoys triumphs in sports, learns to help those weaker than himself, and takes his leave as a strapping 19-year-old, an athletic hero who is able to be friends with his teachers as well as with younger boys. The novel emphasizes all the virtues known as "Victorian": defense of the weak; ruggedness; mental well-being achieved through vigorous physical activity, particularly sports; and devotion to duty, God, and country. Tom Brown is not an intellectual, nor is scholarship glorified in the novel. The emphasis is on moral growth.

Hughes wrote two more novels: *The Scouring of the White Horse; or, The Long Vacation Ramble of a London Clerk* (1859), whose plot takes second place to its accounts of the rural customs of Berkshire; and the sequel to *Tom Brown's School Days, Tom Brown at Oxford* (1861). He also produced periodical essays, biographies, and a defense of muscular Christianity, *The Manliness of Christ* (1879). He was active in the Christian Socialism movement begun by CHARLES KINGSLEY; inspired by these ideas, he became involved in the creation of a utopian community in Tennessee, which he described in his 1881 book *Rugby, Tennessee*.

A Work about Thomas Hughes
Worth, George John. *Thomas Hughes*. Boston: Twayne, 1984.

Hunt, James Henry Leigh (1784–1859)
poet, essayist

Leigh Hunt was born in Southgate, Middlesex, on the outskirts of London. His father, Isaac, was a lawyer and later a clergyman. Hunt, a sickly child, went to elementary school but never attended a university. In 1801, however, Hunt's father financed the publication of Hunt's first volume of poems, *Juvenilia*.

Seven years later Hunt helped establish a newspaper called the *Examiner* with his brother John. A radical paper, it regularly criticized the profane and profligate behavior of the prince regent (later King George IV) and questioned government policy, agitating for the abolition of slavery in the English colonies and fair treatment for the Irish. Hunt and his brother were imprisoned for their radical views but were treated well, being allowed books and visitors with no restrictions; they also continued to write for their journal. The *Examiner* published some of PERCY BYSSHE SHELLEY's and JOHN KEATS's poetry, and Hunt became intimate with both those poets and LORD BYRON.

After his release from prison, Hunt moved to Hampstead, near London, where he became Keats's friend and mentor. In *Lord Byron and Some of His Contemporaries* (1828), Hunt recalls his first meeting with Keats: "I shall never forget the impression made upon me by the exuberant specimens of genuine though young poetry that were laid before me, and the promise of which was seconded by the fine fervid countenance of the writer." Hunt encouraged Keats's more excessive stylistic tendencies, and those very excesses attracted the derision of critics. Shelley, in his shock after Keats's death, blamed a particularly virulent attack on Keats in the *Quarterly Review*, which dubbed Keats's poetry as the "Cockney" school, as the catalyst that led to Keats's fatal illness. Upon meeting Keats, Hunt was moved to write a sonnet that characterizes Keats as destined to fame through Hunt's clear-sighted encouragement, which ends, "As surely as all this, I see, ev'n now, / Young Keats, a flowering laurel on your brow." That sonnet appeared in *Foliage* (1818). Hunt's other volumes of poetry include *The Story of Rimini* (1816), *Hero and Leander, and Bacchus and Ariadne* (1819).

Hunt was in Italy with Byron and Shelley in 1822 when Shelley drowned. Hunt stayed on to produce the journal the *Liberal* with Byron, returning to England in 1825. Despite CHARLES DICKENS's later caricature of Hunt as the impoverished and hypocritical Harold Skimpole in

Bleak House (1853), Hunt was a hardworking writer, publishing numerous volumes of essays and criticism, including *Imagination and Fancy* (1844), his most influential volume, and *Men, Women, and Books* (1847). He also published his *Autobiography* in 1850.

Critical Analysis

The pleasures of reading Leigh Hunt are not the same as those derived from reading the truly great poets; he is, certainly, a minor romantic. However, his best works still stand. They are vivid and finely observed, unpretentious yet well crafted, and, in the case of "The Fish, the Man, and the Spirit," profound and memorable.

This short poem is comprised of three linked sonnets, subtitled "To a Fish," "A Fish Answers," and "The Spirit." The first sonnet imagines a human observing—and criticizing—fish: "You strange, astonished-looking, angle-faced, / Dreary-mouthed, gaping wretches of the sea." The measure of the utter differences between man and fish is exaggerated by the jarring word choice of the human speaker. He calls fish "scaly, slippery, wet, swift, staring wights" and wonders "How do you vary your vile days and nights?"

In the second sonnet, turnabout becomes fair play, and the fish has a few choice words to say on the ugliness of the human form. Humans are "Long-useless-finned, hair, upright, unwet, slow." This is a particularly fine line, containing as it does the hint that humans evolved arms and lungs from fins and gills, as well as the word "unwet," reflecting, as it does, a perfectly fishy view of what humans might call "dry."

The third sonnet takes the long view of the entire debate. The fish, transformed into spirit, now knows that "difference must its use by difference prove, / And in sweet clang, the spheres with music fill." Difference itself is beautiful. The sestet, or last six lines of the poem, play out the contrast between human and fish in terms of their essential beauty: "Man's life is warm, glad, sad, 'twixt loves and graves," but the fish lives "A cold, sweet, silver life, wrapped in round waves, / Quickened with touches of transporting fear." All of the ungainliness of the fish initially perceived is transformed in these final lines to a fleeting beauty.

A Work about Leigh Hunt
Blainey, Ann. *Immortal Boy: A Portrait of Leigh Hunt.* New York: St. Martin's Press, 1985.

Huxley, Thomas Henry (1825–1895)
nonfiction writer

Although T. H. Huxley came from a humble background and did not have the advantage of a university education, by virtue of his substantial intelligence, iron will, and enormous energy he became one of England's preeminent scientists by the time he was 40. When he was born his father, George Huxley, was a poorly paid mathematics teacher in Ealing, near London; his mother, Rachel, was from London. Huxley had only two years of education at his father's school, and at age 13 was apprenticed to a local doctor in Coventry. After two years in Coventry he was apprenticed to a London doctor whose practice was among the poor. Huxley set about teaching himself the standard academic subjects of the day in addition to what he was learning of medicine, and in 1842 won a scholarship to study at Charing Cross Hospital in London.

After three years of medical training, Huxley's finances forced him to leave school and join the crew of the Royal Navy's HMS *Rattlesnake* as assistant surgeon. The *Rattlesnake* was on a voyage of scientific and geographic discovery, and like CHARLES DARWIN on the HMS *Beagle* 15 years earlier, Huxley learned things that radically changed his way of thinking. The first fruit of Huxley's research was the publication in 1859 of *The Oceanic Hydrozoa,* a comprehensive catalogue of the creatures he had studied on the voyage. But the voyage also led to his participation in the discoveries and controversies surrounding the hundreds of fossils being unearthed in England and elsewhere, and forced him to reconsider the historical development of today's living species.

Huxley's continuing research and subsequent publications led him to academic and institutional positions, and to membership in the prestigious Royal Society. In 1859 he formed a friendship and intellectual alliance with Darwin. In Huxley, Darwin saw the aggressive proselytizer of his evolutionist views that Darwin himself, with his introverted personality, never could be. When Darwin's *Origin of Species* was published in 1859, Huxley led his generation in support of the theory of evolution. He became known as "Darwin's bulldog" because of the tenacity with which he argued for some of Darwin's ideas.

By 1860 Huxley had become, among other things, a fervid promoter of scientific education for the working classes and a spellbinding lecturer on scientific subjects. Darwin's *Origin of Species* had only glancingly referred to the necessary impact of evolutionary thinking on our understanding of the origins of human beings. It was Huxley who first spelled out, in *Man's Place in Nature* (1863), the idea that there must be a genetic connection between human beings and "the man-like apes." This work is composed of three relatively short and very readable essays, "On the Natural History of the Man-Like Apes," "On the Relations of Man to the Lower Animals," and "On Some Fossil Remains of Man." It proved immensely popular and established Huxley as the spokesman for a new way of looking at human society. Huxley is at pains to refute the assumption of many that connecting human beings to "lower" animals meant debasing them. "Thoughtful men," he argues, "once escaped from the blinding influences of traditional prejudice, will find in the lowly stock whence man has sprung, the best evidence of the splendour of his capacities; and will discern in his long progress through the Past, a reasonable ground of faith in his attainment of a nobler Future." The hereditary aristocracy and the established church did not approve.

However, English traditional social organization was already slowly giving way to a new order, and Huxley continued to ride the wave of change. In 1869, at the urging of his wife, Nettie, he began collecting his numerous popular essays into a book that would appear as *Lay Sermons* in 1870. These were indeed sermons of the new scientific worldview. While preparing the book and engaging in debate with orthodox churchmen, he devised a new word, *agnostic* (from the Greek for "not knowing"), to describe his position regarding traditional notions of God.

Lay Sermons, with its clear style and brilliant argumentation, secured Huxley's place in the history of English science and English letters. In 1873 Huxley published another collection of essays, *Critiques and Addresses,* as well as a revised edition of his medical textbook on physiology. All the while, Huxley was working tirelessly in the political arena in support of more and better education for all, and particularly for higher scientific education to be more open to those who could profit by it though they might not be able to pay for it. He continued to be a prolific writer of essays, some of which were presented as workingmen's lectures. In the years 1893–94, just before his death, Macmillan published his collected essays in nine volumes. As Huxley's biographer Adrian Desmond puts it, "This man from nowhere had made science fashionable and himself indispensable."

Other Works by T. H. Huxley
Bibby, Cyril, ed. *T. H. Huxley on Education.* Cambridge, England: Cambridge University Press, 1971.
Collected Essays of T. H. Huxley. Bristol, England: Thoemmes Press, 2001.

Works about T. H. Huxley
Desmond, Adrian. *Huxley: From Devil's Disciple to Evolution's High Priest.* Reading, Mass.: Addison-Wesley, 1999.
Paradis, James G. *T. H. Huxley: Man's Place in Nature.* Lincoln: University of Nebraska Press, 1979.
Paradis, James G., and George C. Williams. *Evolution and Ethics: T. H. Huxley's Evolution and Ethics with New Essays on Its Victorian and Sociobiological Context.* Princeton, N.J.: Princeton University Press, 1989.

Inchbald, Elizabeth (1753–1821)
playwright, critic, novelist

Elizabeth Inchbald, née Simpson, was born near Bury St. Edmunds in Suffolk, in the East Anglia region of England. Her father was John Simpson, a farmer, and her mother was Mary Rushbrook Simpson. One of nine children, Elizabeth felt stifled on her parents' farm and at age 18 ran away to London. One of her brothers had already moved there to act in the theater. Elizabeth also wanted to perform, but she had to overcome a childhood stutter to become successful on the stage.

In 1772 she married a well-known actor, Joseph Inchbald, who began to manage her career. Elizabeth appeared in Shakespearean plays with her husband but was never considered an outstanding performer. After her husband died in 1779, Elizabeth realized that her career as an actress might be short-lived. Although there were few women playwrights at the time, she began writing comedies for the stage.

She had attempted some early farces that were ignored, but in 1784 *The Mogul Tale; or, The Descent of the Balloon* was produced. A string of farces and romantic comedies followed, many of them translations and adaptations of French plays, and many with the same theme. Among these plays were *The Midnight Hour* (1887), *Animal Magnetism* (1788), *Young Men and Old Women* (1792), and *Lovers' Vows* (1798).

After a life in the theater as an actress and playwright, Inchbald also became a leading drama critic, the first woman to do so. Her reputation was such that she was asked to write the prefaces to all 25 volumes of *British Theatre*, an authoritative edition of British plays published in 1806. Her novel *A Simple Story*, about a young woman's love for an unattainable priest, was also a literary success. This work was striking for its unusual realism in an era when sentimentality and romance were popular. MARIA EDGEWORTH wrote, "I never read any novel that affected me so strongly, or that so completely possessed me with the belief in the real existence of all the persons it represents." And JULIA KAVANAGH wrote approvingly of the main character, Miss Milner, "She is a new woman, a true one, a very faulty one, introduced for the first time to the world."

Other Work by Elizabeth Inchbald
Women in British Romantic Theatre: Drama, Performance, and Society, 1790–1840. Edited by

Catherine Burroughs. Cambridge, England: Cambridge University Press, 2000.

Ingelow, Jean Orris (1820–1897) *poet, children's writer*

Jean Ingelow was born in Boston, Lincolnshire, in eastern England. Her father was William Ingelow, a successful banker, and her mother was Jean Kilgour Ingelow. She was educated at home by tutors.

In 1863 Ingelow published her first major book of poetry, *Poems,* which went into 30 editions and sold more than 200,000 copies. It caught the attention of notable poets of the time such as ALFRED, LORD TENNYSON and DANTE GABRIEL ROSSETTI. CHRISTINA ROSSETTI thought Ingelow "a formidable rival to most men, and to any woman." The collection included the poem "Songs of Seven," which describes the seven stages of human life. Like much of her poetry, it has a melancholy tone and expresses a pessimistic view of life:

> *I pray you, what is the nest to me,*
> *My empty nest?*
> *And what is the shore where I stood to see*
> *My boat sail down to the west?*
> *Can I call that home where I anchor yet,*
> *Though my good man has sailed?*
> *Can I call that home where my nest was set,*
> *Now all its hope hath failed?*

Ingelow continued to publish poetry, including *A Story of Doom and Other Poems* (1867). The title poem, the longest in the volume, retells the biblical story of Noah and his wife. *The High Tide on the Coast of Lincolnshire* (1883) is a ballad imitation set in the 16th century that uses such archaic spellings as "uppe" and "myne."

Ingelow also wrote children's stories for such periodicals as the *Youth's Magazine* and *Good Words,* and in 1860 published a collection of these stories under the title *Tales of Orris*. In 1869 she published what became her best-known children's story, "Mopsa the Fairy." She followed the lead of LEWIS CARROLL's influential *Alice's Adventures in Wonderland* (1865) in creating an episodic mix of prose and poetry, set in a fantastic world, and free from the overt moralizing that characterized much of Victorian children's literature. "Mopsa the Fairy" relates the adventures of a boy named Jack who travels on the back of an albatross to Fairyland. There, he escorts a kindhearted fairy named Mopsa through a series of often frightening adventures back to her home.

A Work about Jean Ingelow
Peters, Maureen. *Jean Ingelow: Victorian Poetess.* Ipswich: Boydell Press, 1972.

Irish Literary Renaissance (Irish Literary Revival) (ca. 1890–1920)

The Irish Literary Renaissance grew out of a renewed interest by Irish scholars and writers in reviving, creating, and identifying literature that was uniquely Irish. The material at the heart of this movement was based on Irish myths, legends, and folktales about early Irish heroes such as Cuchulain, Fergus, the Sons of Mil, and Fionn MacCoul. The movement also took place against the backdrop of the ever-present desire of the Irish to throw off the yoke of English domination and to establish a national identity. Early works of the movement were STANDISH O'GRADY's two-volume history of Ireland, *The Heroic Period* (1878) and *Cuchullin and His Contemporaries* (1880), and the *Fairy and Folk Tales of the Irish Peasantry* (1888) of William Butler Yeats. Important also was the founding in 1893 of the Gaelic League, an organization whose purpose was the revival of Irish language and literature. Central to the movement's subsequent fame was the establishment of what was to become the Abbey Theatre in Dublin by Yeats, John Millington Synge, and Lady Gregory. Their aim was to promote the creation and production of new Irish drama and to keep alive the repertoire of works already written.

Works about the Irish Literary Renaissance

Watson, George J. *Irish Identity and the Literary Revival.* 2nd ed. Washington, D.C.: Catholic University of America Press, 1994.

Welch, Robert. *The Abbey Theatre, 1899–1999: Form and Pressure.* New York: Oxford University Press, 1999.

Irish Literary Revival

See IRISH LITERARY RENAISSANCE.

Jacobs, William Wymark (1863–1943)
short story writer

W. W. Jacobs was born in Wapping, a district of east London, on the River Thames, known for its docks and warehouses. His father, William Gage Jacobs, was a wharf manager; his mother was Sophia Wymark Jacobs. Jacobs left school at 16, becoming a postal bank clerk. In 1900 he married Agnes Williams, a socialist and suffragette. He, however, remained politically conservative.

Colorful and colloquial, Jacobs's first collection of stories, *Many Cargoes* (1896), proved popular. His fourth financial success in a row, *Sea Urchins* (1898), convinced Jacobs to quit his job to write full-time. Other collections include *Light Freights* (1901) and *Odd Craft* (1904).

Jacobs's stories are drawn from his childhood memories of the docks and from expeditions on coastal steamers undertaken when he was in his 20s. His character the night watchman, a recurrent narrator, was based on an actual longshoreman and oral storyteller named Bob Osborne. Jacobs's stories tend to be humorous and anecdotal. "Bill's Paper Chase" (1902), for instance, observes that "being close with their money is a fault as can seldom be brought ag'in [sailors]," who quickly spend the little money they make. The night watchman describes as a "miser" the one sailor he recalls holding onto his money, and the one time he himself had any he attributes to the hole in his pocket through which the coins entered the lining of his pants. The tale's final image of sailor Bill Hicks is that of a "pore chap" with "'is 'ands in 'is [implictly empty] trousers pockets"—a wistful reminder of poverty lurking beneath the story's rich humor. The writer G. K. Chesterton described Jacobs as "the artistic expression" of "democratic humor"—"the humor of the people."

Jacobs also wrote cautionary horror stories in which characters, as the critic Gary Hoppenstand has written, "become their own worst nightmares, trapped by guilt or doomed by superstition." The most famous is "The Monkey's Paw" (1902). The title object tempts a family trying to bring back to life their son, recently crushed to death in an industrial accident. The paw grants three wishes, but each is fulfilled in an unexpected, even cruel way.

The fluke of "The Monkey's Paw" notwithstanding, it is in his humorous tales that Jacobs's gifts most shine. Jacobs, the author Hugh Greene has written, "was the best humourous writer of [his] time."

A Work about W. W. Jacobs

James, Anthony. *W. W. Jacobs: A Biography.* Knebworth, England: Able Publishing, 1999.

James, George Payne (1799–1860)
novelist, nonfiction writer

George Payne James was born in London. His father was Pinkston James, a doctor who had served as an officer in the Royal Navy. George studied history and poetry and learned some Persian and Arabic, in addition to speaking French and Italian. As a young man he traveled to Europe and fought against the French in the Napoleonic Wars. When he returned to London, he was encouraged by both SIR WALTER SCOTT, whom he admired and imitated, and his friend the American author Washington Irving to pursue a career as a novelist.

In 1829, James published his first historical novel, *Richelieu,* about the 17th-century French cardinal in the court of King Louis XIV. After the success of this work, James was extraordinarily prolific, writing a novel every nine months for the next 18 years. Influenced by Scott, he wrote melodramatic novels that were scrupulously accurate historically, although the characters were unconvincing. Among his many popular historical romances are *Attila* (1873), about the barbarian king; *Agincourt* (1844), about King Henry V's victory over the French in 1415; and *Ticonderoga* (1854), an American drama.

James also wrote popular histories, such as *Memoirs of Great Commanders* (1832), *The Life and Times of Louis the Fourteenth* (1838), and *A History of Chivalry* (1843). James, who married an American, became British consul to Massachusetts in 1850, and to Virginia two years later. In 1856 he was appointed to a similar position in Austria, where he served until his death.

James, Henry (1843–1916) *novelist, short story and travel writer, playwright*

Born in a house just off Washington Square in New York City, Henry was the son of Henry James Sr., a wealthy intellectual. His elder brother William James (1842–1942) became a distinguished philosopher; his sister, Alice James (1848–92), achieved posthumous fame for her *Diary.* The family traveled abroad frequently, accompanied by tutors for appropriate languages and cultures; back in the United States they settled in Newport, Rhode Island, and Henry departed for Harvard Law School at 19. He soon abandoned his law studies, however, and devoted himself to reading novels, particularly those of Honoré de Balzac, who James later asserted was his greatest influence, along with Hawthorne, GEORGE SAND, and GEORGE ELIOT. He also began to write short stories and reviews. This literary apprenticeship was topped off in 1869 by the traditional "Grand Tour" of Europe. It was out of his experience as an upper-class American in upper-class European surroundings that James mined the material for his subsequent great novels. In 1876 James committed himself to permanent residence abroad and moved to London.

His first successful novel, *Roderick Hudson* (1876), is the story of an American sculptor in Rome. The theme of Americans abroad, themselves young, brash, and relatively innocent, faced with the sophistication of their older, more experienced, and even jaded European counterparts, became central to most of James's major works.

In England James had already met some of the most important writers of the time—JOHN RUSKIN, DANTE GABRIEL ROSSETTI, and CHARLES DARWIN among them—and in the late 1870s he came to know ALFRED, LORD TENNYSON, ROBERT BROWNING, and ROBERT LOUIS STEVENSON, as well as the artists James McNeill Whistler (1834–1903) and John Singer Sargent (1856–1925). He became a fixture on the social scene. All the while he was writing novels and travel books, storing up material for his later, greater novels. To this, James's first period, belongs also *Daisy Miller* (1879), the story of a brash and flirtatious American girl whose bold behavior in Rome earns her a reputation as "loose" and who dies there of malaria. Crowning this period is one of his masterpieces, *The Portrait of a Lady* (1881), another tale of an American woman abroad. The same year saw the publication of *Washington Square*, a simply told (for James) story of a wealthy but plain girl caught between a fortune hunter and a cold, dominating father.

James inaugurated his second period with novels concerning those who would rearrange the workings of society and cure what they perceived to be its ills. *The Bostonians* involves a suffragist, who coerces a female evangelist into speaking on behalf of her feminist cause. *The Princess Casamassima* (1884) concerns a British revolutionary who, as part of the class struggle, is set to assassinate a nobleman. The brilliance of James's style and the penetrating analysis of his characters in these works tends to make readers overlook the melodramatic nature of the plots.

James now turned his hand to drama. In 1890 he published *The Tragic Muse*, a novel concerning, among other things, theater and drama, and this perhaps gave him impetus to write his own plays. In 1891 he presented a dramatic version of his novel *The American* (originally published in 1877), and its slight success led him to write more stage works. In 1895 *Guy Domville* was a failure, booed by the audience after its first performance (and replaced at the same theater by the runaway success of Oscar Wilde's *The Importance of Being Earnest*).

James next rethought his entire approach to fiction, turning for a while to purely English society for his material and telling his stories in a style more oblique than that of his earlier work. Perhaps his work with stage drama influenced his choice of subject and method, for the novels of this period are both dramatic and superb. In *The Spoils of Poynton* (1897), Poynton Park and the beautiful antiques it contains become the focus of struggle between a mother and her son's fiancée, and ultimately ruin the relationships of all the characters. *What Maisie Knew* (1897) presents the child Maisie's perspective on the amorous activities of her divorced parents and the other adults in her life. *In the Cage* (1989) has a heroine who, unusually for James, needs to work for her living—as a telegraph clerk, with a wire cage separating her from her customers. *The Turn of the Screw* (1898) is a ghost story about a governess and the mysterious evil that seems to surround her beautiful young charges. In *The Awkward Age* (1899), the main character, Nanda Brookenham, tests and questions the limitations imposed by gender and class in the England of her time.

The beginning of the 20th century marks the beginning of the third and final phase of James's career, and the composition of his three greatest novels: *The Wings of the Dove* (1902), *The Ambassadors* (1903), and *The Golden Bowl* (1904). For his theme he returned to the distinctions between the American character and the European. In 1905 James made a lecture tour of the United States; the fruit of this journey was *The American Scene* (1907). In his last years James worked on a revised collection of his fiction, which began to appear in 1907, with a series of prefaces in which he discussed his ideas about his art. When he died he left two novels unfinished.

Critical Analysis

In *The Wings of the Dove* an American heiress, Millie Theale, knowing that her death is imminent, rents a palazzo in Venice, where she is surrounded by English people. She is tricked by Kate Croy and Merton Densher into leaving Densher a huge sum at her death; although she discovers the deception before dying, her American goodness is such that she leaves him the money anyway. Densher has an attack of conscience and forces Kate to choose between him and money. A contemporary reviewer in the *Times Literary Supplement* wrote, "It is not an easy book to read.... [It] does not make so much for obvious pleasure as for a sort of deep and increasing satisfaction in its admirable workmanship.... It is by reverberation, by allusion, by inference, that we are gradually drawn into the circle of what is, first and last, an elaborated work of art."

The Ambassadors, which James himself felt to be "the best, all 'round, of my productions," is an amusing tale of an older American, Strether, sent as an "ambassador" to Paris (the city where, James says in the preface, a person's "moral scheme does break down") to rescue a young American man, Chadwick Newsome, from the clutches of a worldly Frenchwoman. Sent by the young man's mother, Strether instead falls easily into the carefree French way of life, fails to rescue Newsome, and returns now bereft of even the goodwill of Mrs. Newsome. Again, James presents the clash of worldly-wise Europe and naïve, puritanical America.

James's last completed novel, *The Golden Bowl,* tells the story of the Americans Adam Verver and his daughter Maggie, Maggie's marriage to Amerigo, an Italian prince, and Adam's eventual marriage to Charlotte Stant, an old friend of Maggie's—who is, unbeknownst to Maggie and Adam, Amerigo's lover. Because the characters would have thought it vulgar to discuss explicitly any details of the affair, all is revealed obliquely. Yet the clash of personalities and the two cultures they represent is more than clear as James returns to his constant theme. The golden bowl, first seen in a London curiosity shop where Amerigo and Charlotte are looking for a present for Maggie, is the symbol, with its perfect surface and hidden flaw, of the relationships among the characters. Although Charlotte is drawn to the bowl despite the flaw, the prince cannot consider the idea of presenting Maggie with anything less than perfect—it would be a bad omen for his marriage. The bowl eventually comes into Maggie's possession nonetheless; its shattering marks the end of Maggie's innocence, and the beginning of her ability to assert herself.

James's introspective approach to fiction, convoluted style, and use of the unreliable points of view of his characters instead of an omniscient narrator foreshadow the stream-of-consciousness techniques such 20th-century writers as Marcel Proust, Virginia Woolf, and James Joyce. When they were first published, James's greatest novels sold relatively few copies, particularly when compared to the best-sellers of his day; but his reputation has grown steadily, and today he is easily ranked with Herman Melville, Joseph Conrad, CHARLES DICKENS, and James Joyce. Recent critics such as John Carlos Rowe choose to emphasize less the "difficult," aristocratic, aesthetically demanding James and more the James who explored the boundaries of class and gender. As the scholar Jonathan Freedman remarks, "readers respond vividly to precisely his oddity, his alienation, his (to use James's own sense of the term) queerness: for these, after all, ring with a sense of estrangement that is thoroughly, archetypally modern (if not postmodern). . . . James returns us to familiar territory to see things there we did not think we knew."

Other Works by Henry James

Bayley, John, ed. *Collected Stories.* 2 vols. New York: Everyman's Library, 1999.

Henry James on Culture: Collected Essays on Politics and the American Social Scene. Lincoln: University of Nebraska Press, 1999.

Horne, Philip, ed. *Henry James: A Life in Letters.* New York: Viking Penguin, 1999.

Works about Henry James

Bloom, Harold. *Henry James.* Broomall, Penn.: Chelsea House, 2001.

Brooks, Peter. *Henry James Goes to Paris.* Princeton, N.J.: Princeton University Press, 2007.

Edel, Leon. *Henry James: A Life.* New York: Harper & Row, 1985.

Freedman, Jonathan, ed. *The Cambridge Companion to Henry James.* Manchester, England: Manchester University Press, 2000.

Gard, Roger, ed. *Henry James: The Critical Heritage.* New York: Routledge, 1997.

Novick, Sheldon M. *Henry James: The Mature Master.* New York: Random House, 2007.

———. *Henry James: The Young Master.* New York: Random House, 2007.

Rowe, John Carlos. *The Other Henry James.* Durham, N.C.: Duke University Press, 1998.

Jameson, Anna Brownell (1794–1860) nonfiction writer

Anna Brownell Murphy was born in Dublin, Ireland, to Denis Brownell Murphy, a miniaturist and painter. At age 16 she became a governess in the household of the marquis of Winchester, the first of a series of engagements as governess, before marrying (in 1824) Robert Jameson, a lawyer, with whom she traveled widely. After a trip to Canada in 1836, the couple separated. Jameson described that trip in *Winter Studies and Summer Rambles in Canada* (1838).

She began her writing career much earlier with the publication of *The Diary of an Ennuyee* (1826), a work of fiction, followed by *The Loves of the Poets* (1829), *Celebrated Female Sovereigns* (1831), and *Shakespeare's Heroines* (1832). The last work, subtitled *Characteristics of Women, Moral, Poetical, and Historical*, discusses 225 of Shakespeare's heroines under headings such as "intellect," "passion," "affections," and "history." Jameson called Shakespeare the "Poet of Womankind." That work solidified Jameson's interest in the position of women in English society, an interest that stimulated such later work as *Sisters of Charity, Catholic and Protestant, At Home and Abroad* (1855), which argued for the role of female communities in improving living conditions for what were later called "redundant women" (that is, women with no husbands or acceptable professions) by providing a venue of social service. Her work inspired younger feminists and writers with feminist concerns, including ELIZABETH GASKELL and GEORGE ELIOT (whom she knew and with whom she corresponded), and BARBARA BODICHON, who remarked that Jameson "was to me and to many other young women a guide and companion, ever ready with her sympathy and her experience. The one woman to whom we looked for help and encouragement." The extent of Jameson's sympathy for the position of women is suggested by an 1843 report in the *Athenaeum* on the findings of the Court of the Commissioners on the Employment of Children. In that report, Jameson focused more on the plight of women than on the condition of children, suggesting that middle-class women must be able to earn their living independently.

Although Jameson wrote fiction, criticism, history, theology, travel, social commentary, and biography, she is best known today for her art criticism through such works as *Memoirs of the Early Italian Painters and the Progress of Painting in Italy* (1845), *Memoirs and Essays in Art, Literature, and Social Morals* (n.d.), *Sacred and Legendary Art* (1848), and *Legends of the Madonna* (1852). The last two books, in their concern with developing a historical understanding of Christian symbolism in art, contributed significantly to the Victorian project of the historical study of art, a project that was carried out on many levels. Jameson's friend ROBERT BROWNING, for instance, wrote dramatic monologues based on the lives of Italian Renaissance painters, and WALTER PATER's study of Renaissance painters may be said to have initiated AESTHETICISM, a movement in art and literature that flourished at the end of the century. Jameson is attracting more critical interest today because of the range of her writing, which combines literary, religious, and political interests as part of a larger social vision, and because of the extent of her literary relationships.

A Work about Anna Brownell Jameson
Adams, Kimberly Vanesveld. *Our Lady of Victorian Feminism: The Madonna in the Work of Anna Jameson, Margaret Fuller, and George Eliot.* Athens: Ohio University Press, 2001.

Jefferies, Richard (1848–1887) novelist, essayist, journalist

Richard Jefferies was born at Coate Farm, near Swindon, England. His parents, James and Elisabeth, ran the farm owned by the Jefferies family for generations. The farm had once been sizable, but mismanagement and gradually declining agricultural prices had reduced it to 40 acres. Therefore, Jefferies was intimately familiar with the troubles facing rural English families, and this knowledge shaped his writing.

Jefferies had little formal education after the age of 10. In 1868 he was hired as a local correspondent for the *Wilts and Gloucestershire Standard* to chronicle the increasingly unprofitable status of family-owned farms and describe the tension between the farmers and their hired laborers. Jefferies depicts the laborers as partially barbaric, unable to appreciate the country's beauty and the need to tend the land. Several of these articles were reprinted in the London *Times* in 1872, and his realistic depictions of rural life cemented his literary reputation. Jefferies collected a selection of these articles in *Hodge and His Masters* (1880); together, they condemn agricultural speculation and the disappearance of rural manners.

Jefferies wrote several novels. The earlier ones failed because of their overbearing sentimentality. However, in 1881 he published *Wood Magic*, featuring a young boy, Bevis, who communicates with the family's farm animals. Jefferies portrays nature as a sacred force capable of educating the boy, but he avoids the sentimentalism of his previous novels because Bevis hunts and also mistreats some animals. Furthermore, the animals exhibit unappealing human characteristics. The magpie, Kapchack, who rules the other birds on the farm, is greedy, lascivious, and abusive of the weaker birds. The novel's sequel, *Bevis: The Story of a Boy* (1882), depicts Bevis three years later as he grows increasingly detached from nature.

Jefferies contracted tuberculosis the same year that *Wood Magic* was published. The steadily worsening illness caused Jefferies to move frequently to find a more comfortable location. He resumed writing essays about English rural life. These essays combine his earlier, careful descriptions of natural objects with a reverent approach to nature. In the last collection published during his life, *The Open Air* (1886), Jefferies celebrates nature's regenerative powers, and the essays assume added significance because they express Jefferies's regret at his approaching death. Jefferies is best remembered for this final passionate evocation of nature.

The critic Brian Taylor praises Jefferies's "abilities to exploit language to communicate his joy in the physical world, and few writers have bettered Jefferies in this most difficult of arts."

A Work about Richard Jefferies

Taylor, Brian. *Richard Jefferies*. Boston: Twayne, 1982.

Jeffrey, Francis, Lord (1773–1850)
essayist

Francis Jeffrey was born in Edinburgh, Scotland, the son of George Jeffrey, a legal clerk, and his wife, Henrietta Louden Jeffrey. Jeffrey had a largely classical education at Glasgow College and at Oxford, which he left, overcome with homesickness, after just a year. He attended law lectures at the College of Edinburgh, and in 1794 he was admitted to the Scottish bar. In 1830 he was appointed lord advocate of Scotland (the national attorney general), and four years later he accepted a judgeship in the Court of Sessions (the supreme court), where his father once clerked, becoming Lord Jeffrey.

In 1802 Jeffrey helped found the *Edinburgh Review*, serving as editor from 1803 to 1829, and continuing as a contributor thereafter. "The *Review*," he would explain, "has but two legs to stand on. Literature is no doubt one of them, but its right leg is Politics."

Jeffrey wrote as a Scottish patriot—for instance, when in his review of *Reliques of Robert Burns* (1809) he notes that BURNS's "careless feeling and eccentric genius . . . [have] never found much favour in the eyes of English sense and morality"—and as someone who, the scholar Peter F. Morgan has written, "saw the connection between literature and the state of society." Thus the 1789 French Revolution and its bloody aftermath gave him misgivings about early British romantic poetry, including that of WILLIAM WORDSWORTH. His review of Wordsworth's *Poems in Two Volumes* (1807) contributed to a reversal of Wordsworth's critical reception; and famously beginning "This will never do!," his review of

"The Excursion" (1814) found him decrying the poem's "diluted" version of Wordsworth's style. For Jeffrey, the technical innovation and radical spirit of Wordsworth's verse could conceivably contribute to social breakdowns in Great Britain. Late in life, however, the dread of imminent disorder long since past, Jeffrey favorably compared the quality of romantic poetry to his standard of greatness, that of Elizabethan-age literature.

In his review of a new edition of the 18th-century Irish author Jonathan Swift's *Works* (1816), Jeffrey opines that "[t]he greater part of the wisdom and satire" of *Gulliver's Travels* (1726) is "extremely vulgar and common-place." GEORGE GORDON, LORD BYRON, fared better by Jeffrey's pen. In his 1816 review of *Childe Harold's Pilgrimage, Canto the Third* and *The Prisoner of Chillon and Other Poems,* Jeffrey declares Byron, "in force of diction, and inextinguishable energy of sentiment," the greatest poet among his contemporaries; Jeffrey nevertheless regrets the poetry's "agonizing traces of a wounded and distempered spirit." Four years later, he is freshly ambivalent when reviewing JOHN KEATS's *Endymion* (1818) and *Lamia* (1820): "[B]esides the riot and extravagance of his fancy, the scope and substance of Mr. Keats's poetry is rather too dreamy and abstracted." Still, Jeffrey also describes the poems as "blossoms . . . profuse of sweetness [and rich] in promise."

An unflattering review of THOMAS MOORE's poems (1806) nearly led to a duel between the two. However, they reconciled, and in 1819 Jeffrey anonymously paid Moore's debts.

"[Jeffrey's] *Edinburgh Review,*" THOMAS CARLYLE wrote, "[was] a kind of Delphic Oracle, and Voice of the Inspired, for great majorities of what is called the 'Intelligent Public'; and [Jeffrey] himself [was] regarded universally as a man of consummate penetration."

Jerome, Jerome Klapka (1859–1927)
novelist, journalist, humorist

Jerome K. Jerome, the son of an ironmonger, Jerome C. Jerome, and his wife, Marguerite, was born in Walsall, in the West Midlands region of England, but grew up in London's East End. He was educated at the Marylebone Grammar School until age 14, when his parents died, stranding him in poverty. Jerome worked as a railway clerk, schoolmaster, actor, and journalist. In 1888 Jerome married Henrietta Stanley, who encouraged him to become a full-time writer.

His book *The Idle Thoughts of an Idle Fellow,* comprising 14 reflective, humorous essays on such subjects as "On Being Hard Up," "On Being in Love," and "On Being Idle," appeared in 1896. Its sequel, *The Second Thoughts of an Idle Fellow,* was published two years later. Jerome's humorous classic novel *Three Men in a Boat (to Say Nothing of the Dog)* (1889) is a lighthearted account of the misadventures of three young office workers on a boating holiday on the River Thames. In *Three Men on the Bummel* (1900), the same trio bicycles through the Black Forest in Germany. Jerome's favorite among his works was *Paul Kelver* (1902), a novel whose details closely match those of Jerome's own life as presented in his autobiography, *My Life and Times* (1926). The critic G. B. Burgin observed of Jerome's writing, "The blending of farcical humor with somewhat naïve sentiment, and of pretty descriptive writing with simple philosophizing, suited the taste of the period, and brought Jerome immediate popularity."

Jerome also wrote plays, although his novels are better known. The most popular of these plays is *The Passing of the Third Floor Back* (1907). In this three-part drama, divided into prologue, play, and epilogue, an angelic stranger in a Bloomsbury boardinghouse acts as a catalyst, transforming the other residents from a gallery of rogues into humane beings. (The play was a sensational success in London, toured the United States and Canada, and even was performed in China.)

During World War I, Jerome served as an ambulance driver in France. His later, postwar fiction is more somber, reflective, and religious than the earlier humorous work. Indeed, *My Life and Times* shows a melancholy strain in his temperament: "I can see the humorous side of things and enjoy the fun … but … there seems to me always more sadness than joy in life."

Jerrold, Douglas William (1803–1857)
playwright, journalist

Douglas Jerrold was born in London. His father, Samuel Jerrold, owned a theater and, with his wife, Mary Reid, also acted. As a child, Jerrold too appeared on stage, but he left home at 10 to join the Royal Navy. Deeply upset with the way the officers treated the sailors on board his assigned ship, particularly the practice of flogging, Jerrold left after two years to work as a printer for a newspaper, the *Sunday Monitor*, in London; he later became the *Monitor*'s drama critic.

Jerrold subsequently became a successful playwright, writing mostly melodramas and farces in an effort to free English theater from what he saw as an obsession with French farce. Although his plays—such as the nautical melodrama *Black-Eyed Susan* (1829), which ran for a record 400 performances in its first year on the boards—were financially successful, his greatest fame rests on his work as a journalist. He published many articles on topics of the day, such as government policies toward the working class and the unemployed, hunting laws, and religious hypocrisy, in the periodicals *Athenaeum* and *Blackwood's*, among others. With Mark Lemon, Henry Mayhew, Joseph Stirling Coyne, and John Leech, he helped found the magazine *Punch* in 1841. Writing under the pseudonym Q, he wrote a series of articles that attacked economic inequality in England, reinforcing the reformist work of Mayhew's famous interviews of London workers in his "Labour and the Poor" series. Jerrold also worked as an editor for Charles Dickens's *Daily News*. He became friends with Dickens, Wilkie Collins, and William Makepeace Thackeray. As a playwright, critic, social reformer, and journalist, Jerrold contributed greatly to the literary and political life of his time. His work has not been collected, and he remains an underappreciated figure of the period.

Jewsbury, Geraldine Endsor (1812–1880)
novelist

Geraldine Jewsbury was born in Derbyshire, in northern England. Her father was Thomas Jewsbury, a merchant. From the time she was six, when her mother died, Geraldine was raised by her older sister, Maria Jewsbury.

After her sister married, Geraldine kept house for her father until his death in 1840, then did the same for her brother Frank until 1853, when he married. Their house in Manchester became an intellectual magnet for some of the most prominent writers and thinkers of their time: T. H. Huxley, John Ruskin, Christina Rossetti, and Dante Gabriel Rossetti. In 1841 Jewsbury met Thomas Carlyle, the philosopher, and his wife Jane Welsh Carlyle, who became a lifelong friend.

In 1845 Jewsbury completed her first novel, *Zoe: The History of Two Lives*, which examines religious skepticism. Three years later she published *The Half Sisters* (1848), in which Jewsbury demonstrates the importance of meaningful work in women's lives. She contrasts the story of Alice, who marries a successful manufacturer and then finds herself idle, dependent, and intellectually stifled, with that of Bianca, an actress, who has a satisfying career and financial independence.

Jewsbury's novel *Marian Withers* (1851) examines industrialism and the idea of the self-made man. She had been influenced by the socialist ideas of the Saint Simonian movement, which hoped to change society so that everyone would work and no one could have unfair economic advantages such as inherited wealth or property. Jewsbury also wrote more than 1,600 reviews for the literary magazine *Athenaeum*.

Critical Analysis

Geraldine Jewsbury is best remembered for her long, intimate friendship with Jane Carlyle, wife of Thomas Carlyle. Their letters to each other, numbering in the hundreds, have become a rich source for historical, social, and literary research. However, Jewsbury also wrote five novels in her time that have been neglected by readers and critics for most of the 20th century, but enjoyed a revival in the 1970s when they were reevaluated by feminist critics.

The most highly regarded of these is *The Half-Sisters* (1848). Much like her contemporaries CHARLOTTE BRONTË and GEORGE ELIOT, Jewsbury was concerned with the damaging effects of strict Victorian gender roles on women's lives. It was commonly accepted at the time that men and women were fundamentally different and ought to be accorded different responsibilities and roles in life. Men lived and worked in the public sphere, while women were relegated to the privacy of households.

Jewsbury criticized this arrangement in *The Half-Sisters*. Set in a dreary manufacturing town where the men, exhausted by their labors, return to their homes expecting to be made comfortable by their wives and daughters, the novel follows the strikingly different lives of two half-sisters, Alice and Bianca. Alice's world consists of housework and all the pursuits expected of a middle-class wife, including playing the piano and knowing how to draw, but she finds no spiritual meaning in meeting these expectations. She grows to become deeply dissatisfied, but because of her social conditioning, she never thinks to question her role, much less alter or abandon it.

Bianca, on the other hand, pursues a career as an actress in order to support herself and her destitute mother. Working to support herself gives her strength, and she is free to develop as an individual apart from the empty expectations that stunt Alice's spiritual and emotional growth.

Through these two characters, Jewsbury highlights the destructive nature of the Victorian conception of gender. While Bianca, working in the public sphere as men do, is fulfilled, vibrant, and happy, Alice grows increasingly desperate within the constraints of her life and eventually turns to adultery in an attempt to escape her fate. With this novel, Jewsbury established herself as an ardent critic of the arbitrary limitations faced by women in 19th-century Britain.

A Work about Geraldine Jewsbury

Clarke, Norma. *Ambitious Heights: Writing, Friendship, Love: The Jewsbury Sisters, Felicia Hemans, and Jane Welsh Carlyle.* New York: Routledge, 1990.

Marcus, Sharon. *Between Women: Friendship, Desire, and Marriage in Victorian England.* Princeton, N.J.: Princeton University Press, 2007.

Jewsbury, Maria Jane (1800–1833)
essayist, poet

Maria Jane Jewsbury was born in Derbyshire, in northern England. Her father was Thomas Jewsbury, a well-to-do merchant. After attending elementary school, she was educated at home because her health was fragile. Nevertheless, at age 19, when her mother died, she took over the household and raised her younger sister, GERALDINE JEWSBURY, and three brothers.

At the suggestion of Alaric Watts, the editor of the *Manchester Courier* newspaper, Jewsbury published her first work, *Phantasmagoria; or, Sketches of Life and Character* (1824). It was a mix of poems and prose sketches, many of them satirizing contemporary writers and literary fashions. Jewsbury's next book, written after she was gravely ill and nearly died in 1826, was very different: *Letters to the Young* (1828), based on letters Maria wrote to her sister Geraldine, express her religious beliefs, which had been strengthened during her illness and recovery. A volume of poetry, *Lays of Leisure Hours,* appeared in 1829. It was followed a year later by *The Three Histories: The History of an Enthusiast, the History of a Nonchalant, the History of a Realist,* portraits or considerations of (among other things) religious doubt and the difficulties women writers face. Among Jewsbury's contributions to the literary journal the *Athenaeum* was the first known article on JANE AUSTEN by another woman writer. In 1832, she married the Reverend William Kew Fletcher and went with him to India, where he served as chaplain to the British East India Company. She died the following year, at age 33, of cholera.

A Work about Maria Jane Jewsbury

Clarke, Norma. *Ambitious Heights: Writing, Friendship, Love: The Jewsbury Sisters, Felicia Hemans, and Jane Welsh Carlyle.* New York: Routledge, 1990.

Johnson, Lionel Pigot (1867–1902) *poet, critic*

Lionel Johnson was born in Kent, England, to Captain Victor Johnson and his wife, Catherine, and raised in Wales. He was a serious student at New College, Oxford; after he graduated, he began writing and publishing critical reviews and articles. While living in London and surrounding himself with expensive books, he joined the Rhymers' Club, a literary discussion group whose members included ERNEST DOWSON, ARTHUR SYMONS, and W. B. Yeats. (Yeats quoted Johnson as saying, "When a man is 40, he should have read all the good books in the world, and after that he can be content with a half a dozen.") Johnson would sleep all day and work at night when there were fewer distractions, a habit he had formed after suffering from insomnia.

Johnson wrote reviews to earn money, but he wrote poetry to express his feelings about two subjects. The first was Roman Catholicism, to which he converted in 1891, encouraging his friend Dowson to do the same. The themes of heaven and earth, suffering and deliverance that preoccupied him were reflected in poems, such as "The Dark Angel": "Dark Angel, with thine aching lust / To rid the world of penitence: / Malicious Angel, who still dost / My soul such subtile violence!" "Mystic and Cavalier," a poem in which he confesses to chronic alcoholism, begins "Go from me: I am one of those who fall. / What! hath no cold wind swept your heart at all, / In my sad company? Before the end, / Go from me, dear my friend!"

Johnson's second poetic subject was Ireland, the result of Yeats encouraging him to explore the country. He visited Dublin in 1893, edited the *Irish Home Reading Magazine* in 1894, published *Ireland, with Other Poems* (1897), became a member of the Irish Literary Society of London, and voiced his support for Irish nationalism. Johnson was the one important writer in the IRISH LITERARY RENAISSANCE who was not Irish.

In 1908 Yeats published a posthumous selection of Johnson's poetry, calling it "mystically devotional." Later scholars have criticized Johnson's verse, but claimed that his passion for perfection, his intense scholarship, and his artistic sensibilities showed most highly in his prose.

Johnston, Ellen (1835?–1873) *poet*

Ellen Johnston was born in Hamilton, Scotland, to James Johnston, a stonemason, and Mary Bilsland, a dressmaker. When she was a child, Johnston began working in a factory. When she was 17, she had a daughter out of wedlock. Meanwhile, Johnston had begun writing poetry, and one of her poems appeared in the *Glasgow Examiner* in the early 1850s. Johnston and her daughter later moved to Dundee, Scotland, where she continued working in a factory and writing poetry in her spare time. During the 1860s, Johnston's poems appeared in the *Penny Post*, and in 1867 she published a book of her poetry, *Autobiography, Poems and Songs*. Known as "the Factory Girl," Johnston wrote of the plight of working people trying to find jobs, support their families, and pay for food and housing. One of her most famous poems, "The Last Sark," describes the condition of the Scottish poor in their own voices (*sark* is a Scottish word for *shirt*):

> *This is a funny warld, John, for it's no
>   divided fair,
> And whiles I think some o' the rich have got
>   the puir folks share
> To see us starving here the nicht wi' no ae
>   bless'd bawbee—*

(*Ae* in Scottish dialect means *one*, and a *bawbee* is a copper coin of little value.) Johnston never made enough money writing poetry to support herself, and died in poverty.

Other Work by Ellen Johnston

Kerrigan, Catherine, ed. *An Anthology of Scottish Women Poets.* Edinburgh: Edinburgh University Press, 1991.

A Work about Ellen Johnston

Klaus, H. Gustav. *Factory Girl: Ellen Johnston and Working-Class Poetry in Victorian Scotland.* New York: Peter Lang, 1998.

Jones, Ernest Charles (1819–1869) *poet, novelist, journalist*

Ernest Charles Jones was born in Berlin, Germany, where his Welsh father, Major Charles Jones, was stationed with the hussars, or cavalry. Jones grew up in Germany, writing poetry as a boy, then moved to England at age 19 when his family returned there.

Jones briefly abandoned his law studies to become a journalist, but he resumed them when he married Jane Atherley in 1841. He published his first romantic novel, *The Wood Spirit,* the same year.

In 1846 Jones joined the Chartist movement, which sought to improve conditions for factory workers and supported universal male suffrage, or voting rights for all men, not just property owners. He became editor of a Chartist publication, *Northern Star,* and brought out a very successful collection of political poems called *Chartist Songs* (1846). He championed the working class in ideological poems of bitter humor such as "Song of the Factory-Slave" and "Song of the Poorer Classes":

> Our place we know, we're so very, very low,
> 'Tis down at the landlord's feet;
> We're not too low the grain to grow,
> But too low the bread to eat.

These poems are considered some of his best works. As Jones became more radical, he began to advocate the use of physical force, and he split off from the leaders of the movement who advocated peaceful protest. In 1848 Jones was arrested for sedition, or inciting an insurrection, when he made an impassioned speech in which he proclaimed that the "flag of Chartism will soon be flying over Downing Street" (the prime minister's residence in London). He was sentenced to two years in prison.

During that time he wrote an epic poem, *The Revolt of Hindostan,* which he was said to have written with his blood on the torn-out pages of a prayer book. After leaving prison, Jones started a new Chartist publication, the *People's Paper,* declaring, "A movement that has not the mighty organ of the press at its command is but half a movement. . . ." While running the newspaper, Jones also wrote several novels, including the "fiercely sensational" *The Lass and the Lady* (1855), and poetry. The writer and critic WALTER SAVAGE LANDOR called Jones's collection *The Battle Day and Other Poems* (1855) "noble," saying "Byron would have envied, Scott would have applauded."

Jones, Hannah (1796–1859) *novelist*

Hannah Jones was a prolific and popular novelist. She is sometimes called the queen of the cheap novels because her works were printed in inexpensive editions that were widely read throughout England. Her first novel, *Gretna Green; or, The Elopement of Miss D——with a Gallant Son of Mars: Founded on Recent Facts,* was published in 1820. In 1834, she published *The Gypsy Girl; or, The Heir of Hazell Dell: A Romantic Tale,* followed by *The Gypsy Mother; or, The Miseries of Enforced Marriage* (1835). Most of her novels were issued first in serial form, then collected in single-volume or multivolume editions. However, Jones was not paid much for her works, nor did laws then protect her novels from being copied by other authors. Although her fiction was widely purchased, Jones frequently struggled in poverty. Some of her other novels included *The Ruined Cottage; or, The Farmer's Maid* (1846), *The Shipwrecked Stranger* (1848), and *Katherine Beresford; or, The Shade and Sunshine of a Woman's Life* (1850). Common features of her work included mistaken identity, inheritances going astray, duels, and seduction; misunderstandings usually are resolved in the denouement. Jones recognized that her novels were not great literature but simply light fiction to be enjoyed by the middle and lower classes, who were achieving wider literacy during the 19th century.

Jones, Henry Arthur (1851–1929)
playwright

Henry Arthur Jones was born in Buckinghamshire, in central England. His father was Silvanus Jones, a farmer, and his mother was Elizabeth Stephens. As a boy, he received only an elementary education, then went to work in a drapery shop. He later became a traveling salesman who wrote plays in his spare time. In 1875, Jones married Jane Eliza Seeley; the couple eventually had seven children.

Jones's first play, a comedy called *It's Only Round the Corner,* was produced in 1878. Another comedy, *A Clerical Error,* was staged in 1882 and became a hit. Jones also wrote melodramas, such as *Hearts of Oak* (1879) and *The Silver King* (1882). In 1884 he produced an adaptation of Henrik Ibsen's *A Doll's House* for the London stage, with the title *Breaking a Butterfly.* In the same year he tried his hand with a more serious drama of his own, *Saints and Sinners,* but this work was hooted at in its first performance, and Jones went back to comedy. During the 1880s and 1890s, Jones continued to write plays. *The Case of Rebellious Susan* (1894) is about a "new woman," one of the young British women who wanted to pursue careers and to enjoy more freedom in their personal relationships. In 1896 Jones made another attempt at serious drama with *Michael and His Lost Angel,* about guilt and expiation in a small town, but the reception was discouraging, and Jones turned again to comedy with *The Liars* (1897), about the dangers of flirtation among (titled) married people, and the polite, superficial *Mrs. Dane's Defense* (1900). These were two of his most successful plays. By this time he had become one of the best-known playwrights in London, and had seen more than 50 of his plays produced. In 1906 one of his plays, *The Hypocrites,* was produced in New York, followed by *The Lie* (1914).

A Work about Henry Arthur Jones

Griffin, Penny. *Arthur Wing Pinero and Henry Arthur Jones.* New York: St. Martin's Press, 1991.

K

Kavanagh, Julia (1824–1877) *novelist, nonfiction writer*

Julia Kavanagh was born in Thurles, Ireland, to Morgan Kavanagh, a poet, and Bridget Fitzpatrick Kavanagh. For much of her childhood Kavanagh lived in France—in Paris and in Normandy—where she was educated. When she returned to London at age 20, she began writing. In 1847, she published a book for children titled *The Three Paths*. A year later, she published *Madeleine*, a story about a French peasant girl's "heroic charity and faith" that became extremely popular in England. Her subjects were domestic rather than dramatic, and her typical heroine an independent, capable woman (often French). Kavanagh also published biographies of notable women, such as *Women in France during the Eighteenth Century* (1850), *Women of Christianity Exemplary for Acts of Piety and Charity* (1852), and *English Women of Letters* (1862).

As Kavanagh's fame grew, her father attempted to inflate his own reputation as a writer by claiming to have written some of her books. After his death, Julia Kavanagh cared for her invalid mother while continuing to write novels for young women, such as *Adele* (1858) and *Queen Mab* (1863). She and her mother moved first to Paris and then to Nice, where the author died in 1877. An obituary in the London *Athenaeum* remarked that "her writing was quiet and simple in style, but pure and chaste, and characterized by the same high-toned thought and morality that was part of the author's own nature." In the 20th century her biographical works on women were sought out by feminist writers seeking to recover a female tradition of writing.

Keats, John (1795–1821) *poet*

John Keats, one of the greatest of the English romantic poets and among the best British poets of all time, was born October 31 in London to Thomas and Frances Keats, the owners and operators of a livery stable. In 1804 Thomas fell off a horse and died of his injuries. Only two months later, Frances remarried. Her new husband was a fortune hunter, and she soon left him, but in so doing she gave up her interest in the business. This action, and an unclear will left by Keats's maternal grandfather, resulted in lifelong problems with money for the Keats family.

Shortly before his death, Thomas sent Keats to a progressive school in Enfield, just north of London, run by John Clarke, but the young man's studies were cut short by his mother's death from tuberculosis in 1810. Keats was then apprenticed to a surgeon-apothecary, and began translating Latin poetry.

In 1814, after reading a copy of Edmund Spenser's 16th-century epic poem *The Faerie Queen*, Keats wrote his first poem, "Lines in Imitation of Spenser." Two years later, Keats gave up medicine to write poetry full time, and his first volume of poems was published in 1817. Included was the memorable sonnet "On First Looking into Chapman's Homer," in which Keats compares his sense of discovery on reading George Chapman's English translation (published complete in 1616) of Homer to that of a scientist or an explorer:

> *Then felt I like some watcher of the skies*
> *When a new planet swims into his ken;*
> *Or like stout Cortez when with eagle eyes*
> *He star'd at the Pacific.*

Initially, Keats's poetry was influenced by LEIGH HUNT, the critic, poet, and editor of the liberal journal the *Examiner*. After reading the work of WILLIAM WORDSWORTH and SAMUEL TAYLOR COLERIDGE, however, Keats changed his tone and style from a fashionable romanticized poetry—sentimental, idealized, pastoral—to true ROMANTICISM—philosophical, original, and focused on the imagination as the supreme faculty of the mind.

Keats's first published collection was roundly attacked in the press, and an article in *Blackwood's Magazine* dismissed him as belonging to Hunt's "Cockney school" of poetry, a reference to Keats's humble beginnings and his lack of a university education. PERCY BYSSHE SHELLEY's 1821 elegy for Keats, *Adonais*, blames this cruel response for Keats's early death. In reality, in 1818 Keats began showing signs of tuberculosis, the disease that would kill him.

In the same year, Keats published his long poem *Endymion*, the story of the moon goddess's love for a mortal shepherd, which opens with one of his most famous lines, "A thing of beauty is a joy for ever." Two years later, Keats published his final book of poetry, *Lamia, Isabella, The Eve of St. Agnes, and Other Poems* (1820), which contained much of his greatest poetry. "The Eve of St. Agnes" opens in the dead of winter: "Ah, bitter chill it was! / The owl, for all his feathers, was a-cold." The bitter setting forms a contrast with the richness of young love:

> *Full on this casement [window] shone the*
>   *wintry moon,*
> *And threw warm gules [red] on fair*
> *Madelaine's fair breast,*
> ** * * * * * * * **
> *Rose-bloom fell on her hands, together*
>   *prest,*
> *And on her silver cross soft amethyst.*

Included in the 1820 volume were "Ode to Psyche," "Ode to a Nightingale," "Ode on a Grecian Urn," and "Ode to Melancholy." In these four great poems, Keats explored his vision of truth, and its links to beauty and sadness. Thus at the end of "Grecian Urn" the poet writes: "Beauty is truth, truth beauty,"—that is all / Ye know on earth, and all ye need to know. In "Melancholy," we discover that "Ay, in the very temple of Delight / Veil'd Melancholy has her sovran shrine." In his anthology of romantic poetry and prose, the scholar Russell Noyes writes: "the truth revealed is no mere intellectual abstraction, but a vision of beauty suffused with tenderness and made pensive by the sadness of experience."

In the hope that a warmer climate might help his illness, Keats traveled to Rome, where he died in the arms of his friend the painter Joseph Severn. His tombstone has no name, only the inscription, taken from a 16th-century play by Beaumont and Fletcher, "Here lies one whose name was writ in water."

Critical Analysis

Although Keats never published a theory of poetry, his letters are rich with his ideas, including the concept of "negative capability," which he felt Shakespeare embodied. "*Negative Capability*" occurs, Keats said, in an 1817 letter to his brothers George and Tom, "when a man is capable of being in uncertainties, Mysteries, doubts, without any irritable reaching after fact and reason." Moreover, with "a great poet the sense of Beauty overcomes every other consideration, or rather obliterates all consideration." Such theoretical musing led to some of Keats's finest work, such as "Ode to a Nightingale." Romanticism yearned for the triumph of the imagination and art over mundane reality, and this poem exemplifies both the beauty and the fragility of that dream.

As the poem begins, the poet hears the call of the nightingale as it sings "of summer in full-throated ease," and he wishes he could join the bird—"leave the world unseen / And . . . fade away into the forest dim." In a beautiful image Keats imagines that he might do this with a "draught" of Provençal wine, "a beaker full of the warm South / . . . / With beaded bubbles winking at the brim." Keats emphasizes sound in this poem, using long vowels and alliteration (the repetition of initial sounds) to evoke not only the sound of the nightingale's song but, as with the wine, the sound of tiny bubbles popping.

In the third stanza the poet gives a wider context to the joy he feels in hearing the bird's song. It draws him away from "The weariness, the fever, and the fret" of human reality. There is pure beauty, pure joy in the song of the bird, but human life is impossibly mixed with ugliness and sorrow. In the next stanza the poet realizes that the way for him to participate in the joy and beauty of the bird is not by drinking "but on the viewless wings of Poesy" (poetry).

In his imagination the poet travels with the nightingale through "verdurous glooms and winding mossy ways" to an "embalmed darkness" where he cannot see but where his senses of hearing and smell are nearly overwhelmed with joy. As he listens, the poet wonders if what he is experiencing is like death. He has been so cruelly used by existence that he has long been "half in love with easeful Death." Just at this moment, the poet says, "it seems rich to die" while the bird sings "in such an ecstasy." This is the moment, however, in which the poet's own mortality puts an end to the dream: "I have ears in vain— / To thy high requiem become a sod." He will die, but the "immortal Bird" will not. Clearly as the poem has progressed, the real nightingale has been transformed into a complex symbol of poetry, beauty, art, and song. If the poet must die, Keats tells us, the poem lives on. At the moment of his vision, however, the poet is drawn back into the world. The voice of the nightingale fades and the poet is alone, wondering if he dreamed it all.

For the reader the poem becomes the nightingale that draws each into a realm of perfect joy and beauty for the span of the poem. Then, upon its end, it returns the reader, still mortal but touched by immortality, to the real world. As the critic Clarence DeWitt Thorpe notes of this poem, "opulent imagery, full melody of language, emotion deep, and restrained unite in a poetic harmony as satisfying as it is rare."

Keats began writing poetry seriously when he was 21 and was dead by 25. To Russell Noyes, Keats "placed the highest value on aesthetic experience, reaching toward spiritual consummation through an intuitive vision of truth in beauty. Great poetry for him was a matter of perfect intuitive sympathy with mankind."

Other Work by John Keats
Complete Poems and Selected Letters. New York: Random House, 2001.

Works about John Keats
Blades, John. *John Keats*. New York: Palgrave Macmillan, 2002.

Bloom, Harold, ed. *John Keats*. New York: Chelsea House, 2001.

Motion, Andrew. *Keats*. Chicago: University of Chicago Press, 1999.

Noyes, Russell. *English Romantic Poetry and Prose*. New York: Oxford University Press, 1956.

Vendler, Helen. *The Odes of John Keats*. New York: Belknap Press, 2004.

Wolfson, Susan J. *The Cambridge Companion to Keats.* New York: Cambridge University Press, 2002.

Keble, John (1792–1866) *poet, critic, scholar, clergyman*

John Keble was born in Fairford, Gloucestershire, England, to Sarah Keble and her husband, John Keble, Sr., vicar of St. Aldwyn's Church. Keble graduated from Corpus Christi College, Oxford University, in 1811 with top honors in both classics and mathematics, and was ordained in 1816.

At Oxford, Keble became friends with THOMAS ARNOLD, the future headmaster of Rugby school, and later became godfather to young MATTHEW ARNOLD, who matured into one of Victorian England's most prominent poets and literary critics. At Oxford, Keble began writing the religious poetry that was to bring him wide acclaim and, ultimately a position there as professor of poetry (1831–41).

In 1827, while serving as a curate in Fairford, Keble published anonymously *The Christian Year,* a series of poems tied to the Sundays, feast days, and special services of the Anglican church year and to the Anglican prayer book. Each poem was a meditation on the text for the service of the day. The collection explores such themes as obedience to God's will, acceptance of one's lot in life, and the inevitable doubts that occasionally plague all true believers. One of Keble's best poems concerns the ever recurrent anguish of doubt, or "doubt's galling chain." In "The Sixth Sunday after Epiphany," Keble writes:

> There are, who darkling and alone,
> Would wish the weary night were gone,
> Though dawning morn should only show
> The secret of their unknown woe:
>
> Who pray for sharpest throbs of pain
> To ease them of doubt's galling chain:
> Only disperse the cloud, they cry,
> And if our fate be death, give light and let us die.

The Christian Year spoke to readers of Keble's own time. It went through several editions in Keble's lifetime and sold many thousands of copies.

Keble also is known for having fired the first shot in a religious controversy that was to divide the English Church into verbally warring factions, the OXFORD MOVEMENT. Keble preached a sermon, "National Apostasy," on July 14, 1833, wherein he suggested strongly that the church, or at least its lower clergy, separate themselves from the English government. Keble believed that the government improperly wanted to make religious decisions and policy for the church. This first tract, in what was thus to be called the Tractarian Movement, was immediately followed by others that developed a new but parallel line of thought: The Anglican church should attempt to go back to the far more ritualistic worship services of the 16th and 17th centuries. J. C. Shairp claimed that the Oxford Movement left "two permanent monuments of genius to the Church of England, Newman's sermons and *The Christian Year.*" Keble College at Oxford University was established in 1870 in his memory.

A Work about John Keble

Edgecombe, Rodney Stenning. *Two Poets of the Oxford Movement: John Keble and John Henry Newman.* Madison, N.J.: Fairleigh Dickinson University Press, 1996.

Kemble, Fanny (Frances Anne Kemble) (1809–1893) *nonfiction writer, poet, playwright*

Fanny Kemble's parents were the popular comic actor Charles Kemble and the French actress Marie-Therese deCamp. Fanny Kemble played the role of Juliet in her acting debut in 1829 and received rave reviews. Her acting was so profitable that she paid off her parents' debt on their theater. She soon performed many other roles, including one in *Frances I* (1832), an unsuccessful tragedy that she wrote about the Renaissance French king.

Kemble went on an acting tour in the United States and met a young Philadelphian named Pierce Butler, who was handsome, well educated, and came from a good family. They married in 1834; only then did she discover that he owned a large plantation in Georgia that held 700 slaves. In 1838 he brought Fanny and their two small daughters to the plantation, where she saw for herself the horrors of slavery. As a staunch abolitionist she could not tolerate the plantation. She also supported women's equality, but her husband demanded total obedience. Kemble left her husband in 1845, and when he divorced her in 1849, he gained custody of their daughters. Kemble had to wait years to see them again.

She returned to the stage in England and supported herself mainly through public readings from Shakespeare. She published *Poems* (1844) and *Plays* (1863). She never forgot her experiences in the United States, nor her inside view of slavery. In 1863 she published the books for which she is best known, *Journal of a Residence in America* and *Journal of a Residence on a Georgia Plantation in 1838–39*. When she retired from the stage, she continued writing her memoirs with *Record of a Girlhood* (1878), *Records of Later Life* (1882), and *Further Records* (1890). HENRY JAMES devoted pieces to her in his *Essays in London*. About her he said, "Her rules and her riots, her reservations and her concessions, all her luxuriant theory and all her extravagant practice, her drollery that mocked at her melancholy, her imagination that mocked at her drollery, and her rare forms and personal traditions that mocked a little at everything—these were part of the constant freshness which made those who loved her love her so much."

Other Work by Fanny Kemble

Clinton, Catherine, ed. *Fanny Kemble's Journals*. Cambridge, Mass.: Harvard University Press, 2000.

A Work about Fanny Kemble

Blainey, Ann. *Fanny and Adelaide: The Lives of the Remarkable Kemble Sisters*. Chicago: I. R. Dee, 2001.

Kinglake, Alexander William (1809–1891) *travel writer, historian*

Alexander Kinglake was born in Taunton, Somerset, in the West Country of England, to William Kinglake, a lawyer, and Mary Woodforde Kinglake. Kinglake attended Eton and graduated from Cambridge University in 1832. From 1834 to 1835, Kinglake and his friend John Savile traveled through Europe and the Middle East, visiting Turkey, Cyprus, Egypt, and Palestine. Kinglake's witty account of his travels, titled *Eothen; or, Traces of Travel Brought Home from the East* (1844), is considered a classic work of its kind. The American poet Stanley Kunitz calls it "one of the great ... travel narratives" because of the observations and impressions—the "traces of travel"—that Kinglake records. Kinglake had hoped to enter the army, but his poor eyesight made this impossible. Instead, he became a lawyer in 1837. Although he practiced law during the next 15 years, he spent much of his time traveling. In 1854 he journeyed to the Crimea and witnessed a decisive battle of the Crimean War. He spent four weeks with Lord James Raglan, the commander in chief of the British forces, dining with him and learning about British military strategy. After Lord Raglan's death in 1855, his widow gave Kinglake all of Raglan's papers and asked him to write a history of the Crimean War. Kinglake devoted the next 31 years to the project. His fascination with military history and his perfectionism resulted in a monumental, eight-volume work, *The Invasion of the Crimea* (1863–87).

Kingsley, Charles (1819–1875) *novelist, poet, essayist, clergyman*

Charles Kingsley was born in Holne, Devon, England, to Charles Kingsley, a country vicar, and Mary Lucas Kingsley. Young Charles was an avid student, and composed sermons and poems by the age of four, but was also encouraged to engage in outdoor activities such as hunting and fishing. When Charles was 12, he was sent to a small preparatory school in Bristol where he read Edmund

Spenser's *The Faerie Queene,* Thomas Malory's *Morte d'Arthur,* various works by Rabelais, and the Greek myths and legends.

One of the most important events the young Kingsley experienced was the Bristol Riot of 1831. The agricultural workers organized riots to protest the repressive policies of the government; these riots were brutally suppressed, resulting in many deaths. As a spectator, Kingsley was sickened by the mob violence and formed a strong conviction that uneducated workers must be guided and controlled by the educated and responsible members of the gentry.

In 1842 Kingsley graduated from Cambridge University, was ordained, and was appointed curate of Eversly, a small parish of three scattered villages in Hampshire, in southern England. Kingsley was appalled by the squalid living conditions and poverty faced by the agricultural laborers and their families.

In 1848, to help the working class, Kingsley, along with his close political associates John Malcolm Ludlow and Fredrick Denison Maurice, formed the Christian Socialist movement. The Christian Socialists advocated gradual economic and political reforms based on Christian principles. The group did not favor any radical changes within the structure of the government, nor did it support extending the vote to the working class.

Kingsley began publishing articles under the pseudonym Parson Lot in *Politics for the People,* which was the journal of Christian Socialists and which Kingsley briefly coedited with Ludlow. In 1848 he published three short political essays that advocated the platform of Christian Socialists: "Workmen of England," "The National Gallery," and "Letters to the Chartists." Kingsley also published a highly controversial piece, *Why Should We Fear the Romish Priests?* (1848), in which he argued against granting political power to English Catholics.

After a moderately successful tragedy in verse, *The Saints' Tragedy* (1848), Kingsley produced his first novel, *Yeast* (1848). *Yeast* addressed everyday problems faced by the rural poor, from typhus epidemics to heartless landlords. In his subsequent novel, *Alton Locke* (1850), Kingsley dealt with the problems of the urban workers, depicting the horrors of workhouses, low wages, and substandard living conditions.

In 1853 Kingsley began writing a series of highly successful historical novels. The first of these was *Hypatia,* in which he depicts the conflict between the early Christianity and the pagan philosophies of ancient Alexandria. His most popular and most critically acclaimed novel, *Westward Ho!,* appeared in 1855. The novel, set in Elizabethan England, describes the adventurers who sailed with the famous English captain Sir Francis Drake. In 1866 *Hereward the Wake* told the story of the Norman Conquest from the viewpoint of the Saxon defenders.

In 1859 Kingsley was made a chaplain to QUEEN VICTORIA, and in 1860 he was appointed to the professorship of modern history at Cambridge University, a position that he held for nine years. In 1861 he was assigned an additional duty as a private tutor to the Prince of Wales.

Despite these new jobs, Kingsley continued to write. *The Water-Babies* (1863), a marvelous and enduring tale, was written for children to inspire a love of and reverence for nature. It also promoted CHARLES DARWIN's theories. (Kingsley was one of the first members of the clergy to accept evolution and natural selection.)

Kingsley's religious career culminated when he was made the canon of Westminster in 1873. Kingsley continued to turn out a stream of historical works, religious sermons, and observations as natural historian until his death.

Critical Analysis

Westward Ho! is a swashbuckling adventure story that takes its hero, Amyas Leigh, to the New World in a battle against England's enemy, Spain. The novel ends in a rousing sea battle between the English fleet and the Spanish Armada:

And now begins a fight most fierce and fell.
And fight they did confusedly, and with

variable fortunes.... Never was heard such thundering of ordnance [cannon fire] on both sides, which notwithstanding from the Spaniards flew for the most part over the English without harm. Only Cock, an Englishman ... died with honor in the midst of the enemies in a small ship.

Kingsley's novel is also blatantly anti-Catholic. The novel even advocates violence against Irish Catholics. As the biographer Brenda Colloms notes, Kingsley's "Protestant hero was the kind of honest, overgrown public schoolboy Kingsley felt was the salt of the earth." Despite its anti-Catholicism, *Westward Ho!* remains the most widely read work of Kingsley's adult novels.

Still popular as well is *The Water-Babies,* in which Tom, a young chimney sweep, escapes his brutal employer and falls into a river to be transformed into a water-baby. The transformation is actually a rebirth, with Tom becoming a different creature with no memory of his previous life.

The water-baby Tom meets a number of different creatures in the rivers and seas and learns valuable moral lessons. As many critics have noted, this seemingly simple fairy tale discusses a number of critical social issues, such as education, sanitation, public health, and pollution. Kingsley greatly enjoyed writing for children, and released a collection of educational articles, *Madam How and Lady Why: First Lessons in Earth Lore for Children* (1870).

Even though Kingsley is mostly remembered today for his fiction, he had an indisputable impact as a political thinker. As Brenda Colloms notes, "Much of Kingsley's humanitarian teaching is in his sermons and lectures, which, although obscure to us, were far-reaching and influential both during his life and shortly after his death."

Other Work by Charles Kingsley
Poems of Charles Kingsley. New York: Scholarly Press, 1970.

Works about Charles Kingsley
Colloms, Brenda. *Charles Kingsley: The Lion of Eversley.* New York: Barnes & Noble, 1975.
Stitt, Megan. *Metaphors of Change in the Language of Nineteenth-Century Fiction: Scott, Gaskell, and Kingsley.* New York: Oxford University Press, 1998.
Uffelman, Larry. *Charles Kingsley.* Boston: Twayne, 1979.

Kingsley, Mary Henrietta (1862–1900)
explorer, travel writer

Mary Henrietta Kingsley was born in London to George Kingsley and Mary Bailey Kingsley; she also was a niece of CHARLES KINGSLEY. Her father, a medical doctor, traveled extensively, researching the religions of distant societies. Though largely self-educated in the sciences, Kingsley formally studied German in order to help her father in his research. After her parents' deaths, she disregarded Victorian views concerning a woman's place in society and in 1893 sailed to Africa to conduct research and collect fish specimens for the British Museum. For five months Kingsley traveled alone by cargo ship along the coast of West Africa and inland as far south as the lower Congo River region. Throughout her explorations—no matter how difficult the conditions—Kingsley dressed in a long black wool skirt and long-sleeved white blouse. She credited her attire with saving her from being impaled on a spike after falling into a deep animal pit. On a second trip to West Africa, a year later, Kingsley followed the Ogowe River's tributaries into territory in the Great Forest region previously unmapped by Europeans.

Although Kingsley downplayed her own extraordinary accomplishments and contributions to natural history, she lectured throughout England about her travels. She wrote two lively accounts of her adventures. *Travels in West Africa* (1897) remains her best-known work. Soon after its publication, Kingsley had become a best-selling author, celebrity, and authority on West Africa.

Her peculiar blend of authoritativeness and familiarity made her prose appealing to a wide range of readers: "A few hints as to your mental outfit when starting on this port may be useful. Before starting for West Africa, burn all your notions about sun-myths and worship of the elemental forces." Her other travel narrative, *West African Studies* (1899), was similarly well received. The *Daily Chronicle* predicted its success: "Miss Kingsley's *West African Studies* will take its place among the standard works of West African knowledge." Her final publication, *The Story of West Africa* (1899), is a slim volume that surveys the history of European exploration in the region.

In 1900, while nursing sick prisoners during the Boer War, Kingsley contracted typhoid fever and died in Cape Town, South Africa. At her request, she was buried at sea. Her biographer Katherine Frank characterizes Kingsley as an important feminist role model: "She stepped out of the shadows cast by the men who commanded her to female servitude to become a conqueror of danger, of convention, and of her own unpromising history."

Works about Mary Henrietta Kingsley

Blunt, Alison. *Travel, Gender, and Imperialism: Mary Kingsley and West Africa.* New York: Guilford Press, 1994.

Frank, Katherine. *A Voyager Out: The Life of Mary Kingsley.* Boston: Houghton Mifflin, 1986.

Kingston, William Henry Giles (1814–1880) *children's book writer*

W. H. G. Kingston was born in London. He spent much of his childhood in Oporto, Portugal, where his father was a successful merchant. Kingston took over the business when his father died, but at age 30 he returned to England to devote his time to writing. Most of his books were adventures written for boys; among these are *The Three Midshipmen* (1862), *The Three Lieutenants* (1874), and *The Three Commanders* (1875). He wrote almost 150 books for young people, as well as historical novels and travel books. Kingston was also the editor of the political magazines the *Colonist* and *Colonial Magazine and East India Review.* He was knighted by the Portuguese government for his help in negotiating an important trade treaty. As he was dying in 1880, Kingston asked that a letter be sent out to his young readers, saying that he would no longer be writing books for them.

Kipling, Joseph Rudyard (1865–1936) *poet, novelist, short story writer*

Rudyard Kipling was born in Bombay, India, to John Lockwood Kipling, a sculptor, and Alice MacDonald Kipling, a writer. Raised largely by Indian *amahs*, or nannies, Kipling was fluent in Hindi. Kipling's parents sent him back to England for his education, and during his first few years in England, Kipling lived with family friends. In 1878 he was sent to the United Services College in Devon, a boarding school that prepared young men for entrance into military academies.

Since Kipling's poor eyesight prevented him from pursuing a career in the military, after graduation in 1882 he returned to India, where he worked as a journalist for an English language newspaper. This apprenticeship had a powerful influence on Kipling as a writer. He developed his powers of observation, his eye for detail, and his knowledge of Anglo-Indian society. He began to write poetry and fiction. In 1886 his first collection of poems, *Departmental Ditties,* was published, followed by a collection of short stories, *Plain Tales from the Hills* (1888). Both of these works were very popular and were quickly followed by six additional volumes of short stories about the Indian people and British soldiers and officials stationed in India.

Determined to pursue a career as a writer, Kipling returned to London in 1889 to find that his work had preceded him and that he was already considered by many to be the new CHARLES DICKENS. In 1892 he married the American Caroline Balestier, and in the same year published *Barrack-Room Ballads,* which contained one of his most famous poems, "Gunga Din," the story in verse of a heroic Indian water carrier who accompanies British troops. It contains the famous line, "You're a better man than I am, Gunga Din."

From 1892 to 1896 Kipling lived in Vermont, where his wife owned land. There Kipling wrote *The Jungle Book* (1894) and *The Second Jungle Book* (1895). These are among Kipling's best-loved works for children, telling the story of how the boy Mowgli, raised by wolves, learned "the law of the jungle," which is summed up in the word "Obey!" In 1899 Kipling published another children's book, *Stalky & Co.,* the adventures of boys at a private school.

Kipling's picaresque novel of India, *Kim* (1901), is widely considered to be his finest work. Kim is an orphan boy, the son of an Irish officer stationed in India, who becomes a British spy and whose spiritual growth is guided by a Buddhist monk. This novel, realistic about and sympathetic toward Indian life, is credited with introducing elements of Eastern philosophy to many English readers.

Returning to journalism for a time, Kipling covered the Boer War (1899–1902), a conflict between the British and descendants of Dutch settlers in South Africa. At the war's end he settled in a house he called Bateman's, in Sussex, England.

In 1902 he published his *Just So Stories,* a volume that contains Kipling's myths about how the leopard got his spots, the elephant his trunk, and the camel his hump. *Puck of Pook's Hill* (1906), along with its sequel *Rewards and Fairies* (1910), takes two children on a tour of English history.

In 1907 Kipling became the first British writer to receive the Nobel Prize in literature. The Swedish Academy noted that the prize was given "in consideration of the power of observation, originality of imagination, virility of ideas and remarkable talent for narration which characterize the creations of this world-famous author." In the same year, Kipling received honorary degrees from such distinguished universities as Oxford, Cambridge, and McGill. Kipling counted among his friends HENRY JAMES, H. RIDER HAGGARD, W. E. HENLEY, and Theodore Roosevelt. The start of World War I found Kipling an unquestioning supporter of the conflict, until his son John was killed in combat—a devastating blow to the writer. His short story collections published after the war reflect his reaction to his son's death and to the war itself. Kipling's autobiography, *Something of Myself,* appeared posthumously in 1937.

The great wit OSCAR WILDE described Kipling as "a genius who drops his aspirants [H's]," referring to Kipling's use of cockney dialect in many of his stories and his talent for capturing colloquial speech. The novelist, critic, and Kipling biographer Angus Wilson noted that "Kipling's passionate interest in people and their vocabularies and their crafts is ... the essence of the magic of all his work."

Kipling's poetry was admired by no less a poet and critic than T. S. Eliot, who said that "Kipling's craftsmanship is more reliable than that of some greater poets." Kipling often has been called the unofficial poet laureate of the British people because of his ability to touch their hearts with his verse.

Kipling's reputation suffered after World War I because he had become in the minds of many a symbol of imperialism, colonialism, and "the White Man's Burden," a phrase from his 1899 poem of the same title. Still, much of Kipling's work presented admiring portraits of colonial subjects and often criticized their British rulers.

Critical Analysis

"The Man Who Would Be King" (1888) tells the story of Daniel Dravot and his friend Peachy Carnehan, who decide to become kings over a number of Afghani tribes. More important than the plot is Kipling's choice of narrative strategy. None of the action of the story is directly presented. It is all reflected through a narrator, who like Kipling himself writes for an English-language newspaper in India.

The narrator is traveling "in a railway train upon the road to Mhow from Ajmir" when he meets Peachy Carnehan, "a wanderer and a vagabond." Peachy, who cannot afford to send a telegram, convinces the narrator to give a message to a friend. The narrator does so and briefly encounters a man with "a flaming red beard." One evening many months later when the narrator is working late, he looks up to see these same two men standing before him. Peachy introduces his red-bearded friend as Daniel Dravot. They are, Peachy explains, "going away to be Kings." Their "lunatic" plan is to travel to Kafiristan, "subvert the King and seize his Throne." They have come to the narrator to borrow some books and maps for some primitive research. When they leave the next morning, the narrator is convinced that "they . . . [will] find death, certain and awful death."

Three years later the narrator, again working late, looks up to see "a rag-whipped, whining cripple" whom he recognizes as Carnehan and who tells him that he and Dravot actually did become kings in Kafiristan, fooling the natives into thinking they were deities. But Carnehan's story takes a tragic turn: Dravot decided to marry, even though his subjects warned him that "the daughters of men" should not marry "Gods or Devils." When the terrified virgin he had chosen to wed was brought to him, she bit him on the cheek. He bled, and suddenly Dravot's subjects realized that he was a man, not a God. They attacked, and Carnehan and Dravot tried to escape. However, Dravot was trapped in the middle of a rope bridge, and his enemies cut the ropes. "Old Dan fell," Carnehan tells the narrator, "turning round and round and round . . . till he struck the water, and I could see his body caught on a rock with the gold crown close beside." Carnehan managed to escape. As he finishes telling his story to the narrator, he pulls Dravot's shrunken, withered head from a horsehair bag around his waist. The next day, the narrator finds Carnehan wandering about the town square at noon, singing, and takes him to the local asylum, where he dies.

The narrative strategy Kipling uses gives this tale a sense of tragic inevitability. The newspaper reporter functions almost as the chorus does in Greek tragedy, to warn the hero not to defy the gods, to look with horror on the hero's prideful actions, and to lament his death. Thus the point of view in the story underscores the extent to which power does in fact corrupt. While Kipling believed in empire, he also believed in restraint and the duty owed by the powerful to the powerless. He knew how easy it is to become "drunk with sight of power" ("Recessional," 1897), and "The Man Who Would Be King" serves as a warning against such excess. A memorable film adaptation of the story, directed by John Huston, was released in 1975, with Michael Caine and Sean Connery as Carnehan and Dravot, respectively, and Christopher Plummer as Kipling.

Other Works by Rudyard Kipling

Collected Stories. New York: Alfred A. Knopf, 1996.
Kim. New York: Viking, 1992.
Rudyard Kipling's Complete Verse: Definitive Edition. New York: Anchor, 1989.

Works about Rudyard Kipling

Bloom, Harold, ed. *Rudyard Kipling.* Broomall, Penn.: Chelsea House, 2000.
Gilmour, David. *The Long Recessional: The Imperial Life of Rudyard Kipling.* New York: Farrar, Straus & Giroux, 2003.
Ricketts, Harry. *Rudyard Kipling: A Life.* New York: Carroll & Graf, 2000.

L

Lake Poets

The term *Lake Poets* refers primarily to the romantic poets WILLIAM WORDSWORTH, SAMUEL TAYLOR COLERIDGE, and ROBERT SOUTHEY, who lived in the Lake District of Cumbria in northwest England, a serene rural area surrounded by craggy mountains. (Coleridge was born in Cockermouth, Cumbria, in 1770, and as an adult lived in the Lake District from 1799 until his death in 1850—first at Dove Cottage, in Grasmere (until 1808) and later (1813–50) at Rydal Mount, in Ambleside. Coleridge's time living in the Lake District was relatively brief—a few years at the beginning of the 19th century. Although Southey is considered one of the Lake Poets, it is more because of his friendship with Coleridge and Wordsworth than for subscribing to their particular views and theories of poetry.) The term was first used derisively by FRANCIS JEFFREY, editor of the *Edinburgh Review*, who did not understand or sympathize with Wordsworth's poetry. The prose writers DOROTHY WORDSWORTH, William's sister, and THOMAS DE QUINCEY were influential members of the group that included the Lake Poets.

The essayist and literary critic WILLIAM HAZLITT wryly noted that the landscape influenced writing technique: "Coleridge has told me that he himself liked to compose in walking over uneven ground, or breaking through the straggling branches of a copse-wood; whereas Wordsworth always wrote (if he could) walking up and down a straight gravel-walk, or in some spot where the continuity of his verse met with no collateral interruption."

Works about the Lake Poets

De Quincey, Thomas. *Recollections of the Lakes and the Lake Poets*. Edited by David Wright. New York: Viking Press, 1986.

Jones, Kathleen. *A Passionate Sisterhood: The Sisters, Wives, and Daughters of the Lake Poets*. New York: St. Martin's Press, 2000.

Lamb, Charles (1775–1834) *essayist, poet*

Charles Lamb was the youngest child of John and Elizabeth Lamb. A lonely, skinny, tenderhearted, and imaginative child, he and his sister MARY ANN LAMB were very close. At age seven he entered Christ's Hospital School, where he met his lifelong friend SAMUEL TAYLOR COLERIDGE. At age 15 Lamb became a clerk in the accounting department of the East India Company, where he would work for 33 years.

At age 21 Lamb had a nervous breakdown, during which he suffered severe delusions. Committed to an asylum in 1795–96, he recovered completely and moved home again. The same year as Lamb's recovery, his sister Mary broke under the stress of caring for their invalid parents. In her deluded state, she stabbed their mother to death. Mary was committed to an asylum, and Charles took over the full responsibility of caring for his father. When Mary was released, he cared for her, too. Fearful of passing the family insanity on to children, Lamb never married.

Lamb and his sister shared many interests and were connected with some of London's highest society. They hosted weekly gatherings in their home, attended by the leading writers and artists of England. WILLIAM WORDSWORTH was a good friend, as were WILLIAM HAZLITT and ROBERT SOUTHEY. Lamb's friendship with Coleridge remained strong, and he often critiqued Coleridge's work with an astute and blunt honesty that Hazlitt termed "choice venom."

Lamb loved London—its theaters, its art galleries, and its literary society—and rarely left it. Eventually, however, he and Mary moved to the country for her health.

In 1798 Lamb published a short novel, *A Tale of Rosamund Gray and Old Blind Margaret*, and a book of poems, *Blank Verse*. Four years later came *John Woodvil*, a blank-verse tragedy. Of his poetic talents, Lamb, ever the perceptive critic, admitted that he lacked some quality needed in "the accomplishment of verse." His poetry is generally unspectacular. Still, his "The Old Familiar Faces" (1798) stands out because of its effective and elegant presentation of the sense of loss of family and friends. The poet wonders "Where are they gone, the old familiar faces?" He concludes that "some they have died, and some they have left me, / And some are taken from me; . . . / All, all are gone, the old familiar faces."

It was as an essayist that Lamb truly shone. His best work is in *The Essays of Elia* (1823) and *Last Essays of Elia* (1833). Many of the collected essays appeared in *London Magazine* under the name Elia, a pseudonym that allowed Lamb to write freely. Autobiographical in nature, the essays examine with humor, sometimes with sadness, Lamb's memories of childhood and his experiences with friends and work. Sometimes he borrowed from others, as when he wrote about the office where his older brother John worked. However, Lamb avoided such serious subjects as politics, suffering, and religion. Of Lamb's work, WALTER PATER wrote, "Unoccupied, as he might seem, with great matters, he is in immediate contact with what is real, especially in its caressing littleness, that littleness in which there is much of the whole woeful heart of things, and meets it more than halfway with a perfect understanding of it."

With his characteristic humor Lamb explained in "A Dissertation upon Roast Pig" how a swineherd's son "who being fond of playing with fire, as yonkers of his age commonly are," burned down the family house, killing several pigs living within. In "The Two Races of Men," Lamb explains that "The human species . . . is composed of two distinct races, *the men who borrow,* and *the men who lend.*" The particular emphasis here is on the borrowers of books, "*those* mutilators of collections, spoilers of the symmetry of shelves. . . . [They leave] that foul gap in the bottom shelf facing you, like a great eye-tooth knocked out."

In a more somber tone, the bachelor Lamb writes wistfully of the children he never had in "Dream Children: A Reverie." In this essay, he tells his nonexistent children about their mother, Alice. Then he imagines he sees the woman's face in that of one child. But in the end, "While I stood gazing both the children gradually grew fainter to my view, receding, and still receding, till nothing at last but two mournful features were seen in the uttermost distance, which, without speech, strangely impressed upon me the effects of speech: 'We are not of Alice, nor of thee, nor are we children at all!'" The critic John Mason Brown wrote that Lamb "was big of heart, large of mind, and unique in his endowments. Victim of life though he was, he was never victimized by it. He lived an interior life externally."

Critical Analysis

Charles Lamb ranks with THOMAS BROWNE, Joseph Addison, and Richard Steele as among Britain's greatest essayists; there are even those who rank him with the French master of the genre, Michel de Montaigne. Certainly in honesty, self-awareness, and humor, Lamb ranks with the master.

The Essays of Elia (1823) provides a sense of Lamb's range. Among the most frequently cited essays is the humorous "A Dissertation upon Roast Pig," a work that begins with a dubious story of the origins of cooking—in which a not-very-bright Chinese farmer named Bo-Bo burns down his father's house and accidentally roasts nine suckling pigs—and ends with Lamb's advice not to cook pork with onions. Lamb's style is allusive and may require a trip to a Latin dictionary for some readers, but even without such aids, his enthusiasm and humor shine through, as when he says of roast suckling pig, "Of all the delicacies in the whole *mundus edibilis* [world of food], I will maintain it to be the most delicate—*princeps obsoniorum* [chief of delicacies].... There is no flavour comparable... to that of the crisp, tawny, well-watched, not over-roasted crackling, as it is well called—the very teeth are invited to their share of the pleasure at this banquet in overcoming the coy, brittle resistance." This is, undeniably, mouthwatering prose.

At the other end of the spectrum of Lamb's style and subject matter is "New Year's Eve" in which Lamb reflects on his youth and approaching end. With characteristic self-effacement he portrays his 45-year-old self as "light, vain, humorsome... a stammering buffoon" but begs leave to remember himself as a child, that "'other me' there in the background." In tones reminiscent of Wordsworth's poem "Intimations of Immortality" about the beauty and innocence of childhood, he recalls himself as a child:

> I can cry over its patient small-pox at five, and rougher medicaments. I can lay its poor fevered head upon the sick pillow at Christ's [Lamb's boyhood school], and wake with it in surprise at the gentle posture of maternal tenderness hanging over it, that unknown had watched its sleep. I knew how it shrank from any the least colour of falsehood—God help thee, Elia, how art thou changed?!... I know how honest, how courageous (for a weakling) it was—how religious, how imaginative, how hopeful! From what have I not fallen, if the child I remember was indeed myself...

As is the case with Montaigne, one comes to regard Lamb as a friend, an intimate, who can make one smile, then weep from moment to moment. Lamb's *Essays of Elia* is a classic in the tradition of the personal essay.

Other Work by Charles Lamb
Tales from Shakespeare. With Mary Lamb. New York: Random House, 1999.

Lamb, Lady Caroline (1785–1828)
novelist, poet

Lady Caroline was born Caroline Ponsonby, the only daughter of Frederic Ponsonby, third earl of Bessborough, and his wife Lady Henrietta Spencer. She married William Lamb, second viscount Melbourne, who later became prime minister of Great Britain and confidant to QUEEN VICTORIA. Her fame rests mainly on her passionate and public love affair with the great romantic poet LORD BYRON, who, thinly concealed, became the major protagonist in Lamb's first novel, *Glenarvon* (1816). When she first met Byron, she recorded in her diary that he was "mad, bad and dangerous to know." She herself was eccentric, at times to the point of insanity, and their affair was always tempestuous and occasionally physically violent.

Glenarvon, the novel's hero, is guilty of, among other things, murder, kidnapping, and serial seductions, but nevertheless exhibits those Byronic traits that attracted Lady Caroline (Calantha in the novel) to the poet in the first place. The novel suffers from bad plotting and sketchy characterization. Yet because it revealed gossip, scandal, and the inner workings of very high society (other thinly veiled characters represent, to name just two, Georgiana, the duchess of Devonshire, and Jane Harley, the countess of Oxford), it was momentarily popular. Lamb wrote two other novels, *Graham Hamilton* (1822), an affectionate tribute to her aunt, the duchess of Devonshire; and *Ada Reis* (1823), in which a Byronic hero abducts a young woman whose violent temper resembles the author's own. Critics today see these novels as representing an artistic progress beyond *Glenarvon*, but Lamb had consciously reduced the shock value in them, and they did not sell. She began to write poetry at this time, some of which is accomplished.

Lamb's husband remained loyal to her throughout her pursuit of Byron, and even when the publication of *Glenarvon* jeopardized his political career and his family lobbied for a separation. The couple finally separated formally in 1825, but Lamb remained at her family's country estate, in the company of her father-in-law and her retarded son, and her husband was with her when she died. Her friend SYDNEY OWENSON, Lady Morgan, commented in her memoirs, "She was eloquent, most eloquent, full of ideas, and of graceful expression; but her subject was always herself."

A Work about Lady Caroline Lamb
Blyth, Henry. *Caro: The Fatal Passion*. New York: Coward, McCann & Geohegan, 1972.

Lamb, Mary Ann (1764–1847) *children's author*

Mary Lamb was the older sister of the essayist CHARLES LAMB. As a young woman she cared tenderly for her brother, who was 10 years younger than she, and they grew inseparably close, sharing interests in literature, theater, and the arts.

At age 32 Lamb found herself still unmarried, caring for her ungrateful invalid parents, and trying to support the household with sewing jobs. Laboring under immense stress, she had a severe mental breakdown and stabbed her mother to death. Committed to an institution, she suffered terrible remorse, but came to believe that her mother had forgiven her and began to show signs of recovery. Charles Lamb convinced the court that he could care for her.

When her insanity recurred periodically, Charles would pack a bag for her and they would walk together in tears to the asylum.

Despite her affliction, she and Charles wrote popular children's books. *Tales from Shakespeare* (1807), retelling the plays of Shakespeare in prose, remains popular to this day. Similarly, *The Adventures of Ulysses* (1808) is a prose version of Homer's *Odyssey*. *Mrs. Leicester's School* (1809) is a collection of stories, supposedly told by students at a school about their experiences with church, sea voyages, and supposed village witches.

Landon, Letitia Elizabeth (L.E.L.) (1802–1838) *poet, novelist*

Letitia Landon, also known as L.E.L., was born in London to Catherine Jane Bishop and John Landon, an army agent. Landon was educated at home. Writing poetry since childhood, she was first published in 1820 when William Jerden, a neighbor, became editor of the *Literary Gazette*. Jerden thereafter published her work regularly. Her early work consisted mainly of poems about paintings. In 1824 her father's death left Landon the sole support of her mother and younger brother.

In the 1820s and 1830s Landon was prolific and immensely popular, in part because she shrewdly constructed a persona that avoided the "revolutionary new woman" being espoused in radical romantic circles and hewed instead to a less challenging image of what a female poet should be. The critic Glennis Stephenson has written, "For L.E.L., love, erotic passion, feelings—these are the principles that rule women's lives."

The title poem of *The Improvisatrice and Other Poems* (1824), her second volume of verse—*The*

Fate of Adelaide (1821) preceded it—is based on the Parisian novelist GERMAINE DE STAËL's *Corinne* (1807). It is a deathbed monologue spoken by the anonymous "Improviser," who recounts falling wildly in love with a youth who reciprocated her passion: "There was a charmed note on the wind." He, however, chose to honor a prior arrangement by marrying someone else who, as a result of his not loving her, died. Deprived of him in his absence, upon his return the Improviser also dies after hearing his tale of woe. The man is miserable, but meanwhile the two women who loved him have paid more dearly. The poem suggests that men exercise the control, the power, in love relationships, a reflection of their superior social standing. But some contemporary reviews, exceedingly condescending, missed the point. For example, the reviewer in the *Literary Magnet* wrote that the Improviser "seems to be the very counterpart of [Landon's] sentimental self." Landon's Muse, he concludes, "is always in mourning, and sighs and tears are the food on which she loves to banquet." Such a response may have been the price Landon had to pay for the lavish expression of unrequited female love that helped make the poem popular, but its importance derives from the note sounded on the theme of sexual politics. It is a note Landon's work would continue to sound.

Landon's popularity attracted malice as well as misguided (if generally favorable) reviews. Her status as a successful, independent woman made her a target, and in 1825 published slanders began linking Landon sexually with Jerden. After a period of dormancy, the rumors reappeared in 1834, prompting her to end her engagement to the literary reviewer JOHN FORSTER. Four years later she married George Maclean, but she died soon after, either of one of the epileptic seizures that had long plagued her or of an overdose of the prussic acid (a chemical compound of hydrogen and cyanogen) she was in the habit of taking in order to control these seizures. (In *Ethel Churchill*, 1837, the last of Landon's three novels, Countess Marchmont distils her own prussic acid, keeping it handy for a quick suicide.)

One sign of the impact Landon made on her readers is the large number of poems written for and about her by both men and women. The critics Jerome McGann and Daniel Riess have written, "As the century proceeded . . . [the rite of passage that writing a poem to Landon constituted] became a female devotion. . . . The poems written by Elizabeth Barrett Browning and Christina Rossetti are among their best." This is especially fitting, for it points to a principal part of Landon's legacy linking her with these two and countless other poets later in the century: her persona, which Stephenson has described as "perhaps the first, and certainly one of the most fully developed, examples of the popular Victorian poetess."

Other Work by Letitia Elizabeth Landon

Poetical Works of Letitia Elizabeth Landon. Delmar, N.Y.: Scholars' Facsimiles & Reprints, 1990.

A Work about Letitia Elizabeth Landon

Stephenson, Glennis. *Letitia Landon: The Woman Behind L.E.L.* Manchester, England: Manchester University Press, 1995.

Landor, Walter Savage (1775–1864) *poet, nonfiction writer*

Walter Savage Landor was the eldest son of Walter Landor, a doctor, and Elizabeth Savage Landor. Landor was educated at Rugby School and Trinity College, Oxford. He published *The Poems of Walter Savage Landor* at age 20, having been expelled from Oxford University for discharging a pistol at the windows of some college friends. His brilliance as a student, along with his own prodigious reading, had equipped him for the life he was to lead as a writer for the next 69 years.

As the eldest son of the wealthy Dr. Walter Landor and the heiress Elizabeth Savage, Landor was assured of a substantial income for life and could live where he wanted, write what he wanted, and publish what he wanted. His first volume of verse was classically inspired, including an invocation to the muse and a poem in Latin. For his next work, Landor turned to the classical epic form for *Gebir* (1798). This 1,900-line romance is based on the story of Gebir, who sets out to conquer Egypt but instead falls in love with its queen, Charoba.

Landor published volumes of poetry in 1802 and in 1806. The latter volume, *Simonidea*, contains "Rose Aylmer," his most often-quoted lyric:

> Ah! what avails the sceptred race!
> Ah! what the form divine!
> What every virtue, every grace!
> Rose Aylmer, all were thine.
> Rose Aylmer, whom these wakeful eyes
> May weep but never see,
> A night of memories and of sighs
> I consecrate to thee.

Although this poem earned Landor a small reputation as a lyric poet, critics today ignore his poetry in favor of that of his more progressive contemporaries, WILLIAM WORDSWORTH and SAMUEL TAYLOR COLERIDGE. Even the introduction to a collection of his verse downplays his importance to literary history: "Landor was a minor writer working in the diminishing neoclassical tradition."

Today Landor is best remembered for his prose writings. Beginning in 1824, there appeared the first volume of the work on which Landor's subsequent reputation rests, *Imaginary Conversations*. These are dialogues between historical and literary figures of past ages. Landor had long favored the dramatic form for much of his writing, and these pieces allowed him to express himself to best advantage. These dialogues offered readers an intimate look at familiar figures, providing insight into their characters. The Russian czar Peter the Great, for example, is characterized simply through his orders to his servants: "Away, and bring it: scamper! All equally and alike shall obey and serve me! Harkye! bring the bottle with it: I must cool myself ... and ... harkye! a rasher of bacon on thy life! and some pickled sturgeon, and some krout and caviar, and good strong cheese." The series sold well and was extended to five volumes, ending in 1829.

In the years following *Imaginary Conversations,* Landor continued writing and publishing, but none of his later works achieved the popularity of the *Conversations*. Although his reputation has fallen off significantly since his death, Landor's classical decorum and scholarly erudition have won him admirers in this century. The poet Ezra Pound, for example, claimed that "a set of Landor's collected works will go further towards civilizing a man than any university education now on the market."

Critical Analysis

Although Landor's poetry is not much read today, the six volumes of his *Imaginary Conversations* (1824–29) still give pleasure to many readers. Of the inspiration for *Imaginary Conversations,* Landor said, "When I was younger ... [a]mong the chief pleasures of my life, and among the commonest of my occupations was the bringing before me such heroes and heroines of antiquity, such poets and sages, such of the prosperous and unfortunate as most interested me ... [and e]ngaging them in conversations best suited to their characters." Landor cleverly captures his characters at significant moments in their lives, or allows them to talk at length about subjects dear to their hearts. He includes dialogues between Queen Elizabeth and her minister Lord Robert Cecil, ancient philosophers Epictetus and Seneca, and Diogenes and Plato, American revolutionaries George Washington and Benjamin Franklin. Many of the dialogues are brief, others, such as the discussion between the poet Philip Sidney and his dearest friend Lord Brooke, are wide-ranging and lengthy.

Two of the most interesting of the dialogues are between husbands and wives that occur at crucial moments in history. The first is between Henry VIII and Anne Boleyn shortly after Anne has been convicted of treason and heresy; the setting, though not specified, may be the Tower of

London. Henry is both accusatory and playful with Anne, while she defends her innocence and uses her considerable wit to deflect his accusations. When she sees Henry, she is flustered and blames her confusion on the fact that "it is hardly three months since I miscarried." (Anne miscarried at the end of January and was executed about four months later, on May 19.) Immediately, Henry demands to know who the child's father was, and Anne deflects the question: "The father is yours and mine; he who hath taken him to his own home."

Henry then begins to interrogate Anne on the subject of her supposed adultery; she denies his charges. He asks her how she spent the money he gave her over the previous nine months; she tells him she gave it to the poor. He asks her what she was reading when he arrived, and she tells him she was searching through an "ancient chronicle" for a story of "other young maidens" like herself, who were

> first too happy for exaltation, and after too exalted for happiness, not perchance doomed to die upon a scaffold, by these they ever honoured and served faithfully: that indeed I did not look for nor think of: but my heart was bounding for anyone I could love and pity.

The conversation takes a more serious turn when Henry accuses her again of adultery and heresy; he pretends to accept her claim to know nothing of "the lighter" of the two sins, he says, but what about the "the graver of them"? Anne answers, "Which may it be, my liege?" Henry is aghast that she would equate the two and demands to know, "Are the sins of the body, foul as they are, comparable to those of the soul?" Anne replies that if a person is, in fact, led astray into heresy she believes that "the hand of the Almighty . . . will fall gently on human fallibility." Henry replies, in a speech that perfectly captures his resolve to execute Anne, his continuing love for her, his heartbreak, and his final forgiveness:

Troth, Anne! thou has well sobered me. I came rather warmly and lovingly; but these light ringlets, by the holy rood, shall not shade this shoulder much longer. Nay, do not start; I tap it for the last time, my sweetest. If the Church permitted it, thou shouldst set forth on thy long journey with the Eucharist between thy teeth, however loath.

Landor has fully imagined this scene, with all of its drama, pathos, and ambiguity. He has also done a masterful job at imitating the language and rhythms of 16th-century speech.

Another of Landor's imaginary conversations takes place between Leofric and his wife, Godiva, the afternoon before her famous naked horseback ride to protest her husband's imposition of a heavy tax on the people of Coventry. Godiva asks Leofric to forgive the taxes and he replies "Will I pardon? Yea, Godiva, by the holy rood, will I pardon the city when thou ridest naked at noontide through the streets," the 11th-century equivalent, perhaps, of "When hell freezes over." Godiva, however, decides to take her husband literally and hold him to his oath, although she does not tell him her plans. As they ride into town that evening he notes that some of her hair has come loose: "Take heed thou sit not upon it, lest it anguish thee. Well done! It mingleth now sweetly with the cloth of gold upon the saddle running her and there, as it if had life and faculties and business, and were working thereupon some newer and cunninger advice." Landor here portrays Leofric as giving Godiva not only the idea for the ride but also the method of hiding her nakedness—a very clever reimagination of the prelude to a familiar story.

Lang, Andrew (1844–1912) *poet, novelist, historian, critic*

Andrew Lang was born in the Scottish border town of Selkirk, the eldest son of a sheriff-clerk, John Lang, and his wife, Jane Sellar Lang. He studied classics at St. Andrews and Glasgow Universities and at Oxford University, where he also studied anthropology.

While at university, he began contributing pieces to literary journals, and in 1874 he left Oxford to pursue a career as a man of letters. He quickly became one of the most influential literary critics of his day, contributing articles and reviews to the *Daily News* and *Longman's Magazine*. As a critic, Lang preferred romance, adventure, and fantasy over realism or works that aroused painful emotion. He disliked the novels of THOMAS HARDY and HENRY JAMES, but was a vigorous champion of the works of ROBERT LOUIS STEVENSON, RUDYARD KIPLING, and ARTHUR CONAN DOYLE.

In addition to criticism, Lang wrote novels, poetry, history, and children's literature. His friend, the editor and poet WILLIAM ERNEST HENLEY, who admired Lang's diverse interests and skills, called him "the divine amateur."

Today, Lang is chiefly known for his many contributions to children's literature, particularly for his 12-volume *Fairy Book* series (1889–1910), anthologies of folktales and stories from around the world, including Persian and Greek myths. His research supported his view that myths and folktales were the foundations of literature and that fantasy and imagination were necessary to education and learning. Lang also believed that "Nobody can write a *new* fairy tale; you can only mix up and dress the old stories and put characters into new dresses." His great 12-volume series inspired succeeding generations of writers, among them J. R. R. Tolkien, who recalled that his first childhood encounter with Lang's *Red Fairy Book* (1890) caused him to "desire dragons with a strong desire."

Other Works by Andrew Lang

Custom and Myth. 1884. Reprint. London: Routledge, 1997.
Prince Prigio. 1889. Reprint. Boston: Godine, 1981.

A Work about Andrew Lang

Langstaff, Eleanor De Selms. *Andrew Lang.* Boston: Twayne, 1978.

Lathom, Francis (1777–1832) *novelist, playwright*

Francis Lathom, born in Norwich, in the East Anglia region of England, was believed to be the illegitimate son of a British peer, or titled aristocrat, who seems to have privately supported him. By the 1790s, Lathom was writing plays for the Norwich theater and appearing on stage in some of them. One of his plays, *All in a Battle,* was published in 1795, when he was 18. Three years later, Lathom published his first and most famous novel, *The Midnight Bell,* a Gothic story set in Germany. It was followed by his novel *Men and Manners* in 1799. In 1801 he moved to a farmhouse in Aberdeenshire, Scotland, where he lived for the rest of his life, a local, wealthy eccentric. He produced a steady stream of novels and plays. His play *Holiday Time, or the School Boy's Frolic,* a light farce, opened in 1800, and another comedy, *The Wife of a Million,* in 1802. In that same year, Lathom published a historical romance, *Astonishment!!!,* set during the late 17th century. Among his many other books are a novel in four volumes, *Very Strange but Very True* (1803); an Elizabethan romance, *The Mysterious Freebooter; or, The Days of Queen Bess* (1806); and *Italian Mysteries, or More Secrets than One* (1820), also a romance. Lathom continued writing until 1830, two years before his death.

Lawrence, George Alfred (1827–1876) *novelist*

George Lawrence was born in the county of Essex, near London, to Alfred Lawrence, a clergyman, and Emily Finch Lawrence. He attended Rugby and graduated from Oxford University in 1850. Two years later he became a lawyer, but once he began to write he spent little time practicing law. His first novel, *Guy Livingstone* (1857), is the story of a manly aristocrat, "lean in the flanks like a wolfhound," who is "immoral but never cruel" with women. A huge best-seller, it was the first of a series of "muscular" novels about the exploits of idealized, manly heroes. Two examples are

Sword and Gown (1859), an adventure set in the Crimea, and *Brakespeare* (1868), the story of a freelance soldier in the Hundred Years' War. *Border and Bastille* (1863) is Lawrence's account of his own attempt to fight as a freelance soldier in the American Civil War. He had come to the United States to join the Confederate army, but instead was taken prisoner by the Union army and deported. His later, less popular novels include *Silverland* (1873) and *Hagarene* (1874), a portrait of an amoral adventuress.

Layard, Austen Henry (1817–1894) *travel writer*

Austen Henry Layard was born in Paris. When he was 16, he went to work for his great-uncle, a lawyer, in London, where he spent six years. At age 22, he applied for a position as a civil servant in Ceylon (now Sri Lanka), then part of the British Empire, but decided to set off on a long trip instead. Layard traveled on land through Europe to Turkey and Persia, where he explored on foot and tried to immerse himself in the customs of the native people. The British ambassador in Turkey commissioned him to make archeological explorations of an area that was thought to be the site of Nineveh, the ancient capital (in present-day Iraq) of the Assyrian Empire in the seventh century B.C.

In 1848–49, Layard published the first of two books on his finds, *A Popular Account of Discoveries at Nineveh and Its Remains,* in which he described not only the ancient artifacts he discovered but also his experiences living among the Arabs in the Middle East. The book fascinated the British public and aroused great interest in the archeology and ancient ruins of Mesopotamia. In 1849, Layard served in the British embassy in Constantinople. Three years later, after his return to England, he became a member of Parliament. Layard also served as undersecretary for foreign affairs in the British government. In 1869, he married Mary Evelyn Guest. He wrote a last travel book, *Early Adventures in Persia, Susiana, and Babylonia,* in 1887.

A Work about Austen Layard
Scheller, William. *Amazing Archaeologists and Their Finds.* Minneapolis: Oliver Press, 1994.

Lear, Edward (1812–1888) *poet*

Edward Lear was born in London to Jeremiah Lear, a stockbroker, and his wife, Ann. At age 13, Lear began to earn money by sketching birds, using a coloring method known as Oriental tinting. Two years later, he went to work at the London Zoological Gardens drawing parrots. The first two folios of his first book, *Illustrations of the Family of Psittacidae, or Parrots,* were published in 1831. He also worked for the British Museum, drawing birds for the ornithologist John Gould. As he was sketching in the Zoological Gardens one day, he was approached by the earl of Derby, who had been impressed by Lear's book and requested that Lear draw the birds on his estate. Lear accepted the invitation and lived at the earl's country house, Knowsley Hall, from 1832 to 1836. In addition to drawing the earl's birds and animals, Lear took up landscape painting.

To entertain the earl's children, Lear wrote nonsense verse, much of it in the limerick form—a five-line poem with the rhyme scheme *aabba*. Although Lear did not invent the form, he made it immensely popular. He considered it a form of verse lending itself to limitless variety of rhymes and pictures. One of Lear's most famous is

> *There was an Old Man with a beard,*
> *Who said, It is just as I feared!*
> *Two Owls and a Hen*
> *Four Larks and a Wren*
> *Have all build their nests in my beard!*

Beginning in 1837, Lear lived abroad, visiting England only occasionally. While living in Rome, Lear supported himself by giving drawing lessons. He also published books of sketches, including *Views in Rome and Its Environs* (1841). In 1846 Lear published three books: *Gleanings from the*

Menagerie at Knowlsey, Illustrated Excursions in Italy, and *A Book of Nonsense Verse.*

The last title was a compilation of the poems Lear had written for the earl's children at Knowlsey. It became hugely popular among adults as well as children. In all, Lear published five volumes of nonsense poetry and prose in his lifetime. It is somewhat difficult today to understand the reverence with which he was regarded in his own day by some of England's greatest writers. JOHN RUSKIN placed Lear at the top of his list of greatest authors, and G. K. Chesterton dubbed him "the Father of Nonsense." Many of his contemporaries considered him superior to LEWIS CARROLL, who is read more than Lear today.

Some scholars have speculated that Victorian society, particularly its young, with all its strict rules regarding propriety, needed nonsense in order to be able to experience a sense of freedom. According to the Lear scholar Vivien Noakes, "In the limericks . . . to an extent difficult for us now to imagine, Lear offered children the liberation of unaffected high spirits. . . . In an age when children were loaded with shame, Lear attempted to free them from it." The scholar Clifton Snider evokes the scientific upheavals and religious doubts that tormented Lear's contemporaries, suggesting that "nonsense provided a healthy antidote to Victorian earnestness," and points out the latent sexual content in some of Lear's poetry as, again, an antidote to Victorian prudery.

Lear's limericks, for all their nonsense and silly situations, have overtones of melancholy. His drawings, quickly scribbled pen-and-ink sketches, add to both the humor and pathos of the poems. For instance, Lear's illustration provides an emotional counterpoint to this limerick:

> *There was an Old Man at a Junction*
> *Whose feelings were wrung with*
>   *compunction*
> *When they said, The Train's gone!*
> *He exclaimed, How forlorn!*
> *But remained at the rails of the Junction.*

The illustration shows a man sitting on the rails, mouth wide open, arms upraised. Lear's characters are often outsiders, creatures who are excluded because of some profound difference.

Among Lear's best-known poems is "The Owl and the Pussy Cat," in which the unlikely couple sail to where the bong-tree grows and are married by a piggy-wig. Also popular is "The Jumblies," in which the title characters go to sea in a sieve. In both of these poems, the characters set forth on journeys and end up in a kind of paradise.

Lear spent his last 20 years trying to illustrate all of ALFRED, LORD TENNYSON's works. As his eyesight and health began to deteriorate, however, he realized that he would not be able to finish the project and destroyed all but 30 of the paintings.

Critical Analysis

Edward Lear loved to play with words. He loved to scatter the old ones about in improbable places and to make up startlingly silly new ones. Although he is best known for popularizing the limerick form and for the poem "The Owl and the Pussycat," he may be at his most delightful in some of his prose tales. One, "The Story of the Four Little Children Who Went Round the World," has echoes of "The Owl and the Pussycat" in that the children decide to travel by boat accompanied by a cat. Like the Owl and the Pussycat, they discover a world full of strange and wonderful places, including an island "quite full of veal-cutlets and chocolate-drops, and nothing else."

Lear's use of language, in this story and elsewhere, includes deliberately silly misuses. For example, after one of their many adventures, the children return to the ship to pursue "their voyage with the utmost delight and apathy." After one of the children, Lionel, cheers the others up by standing on one leg and whistling, the children offer him "an earnest token of their sincere and grateful infection."

Lear's word choice is remarkably difficult, given the fact that he wrote primarily for children. For example, Violet, the only girl in the group of four children, puts 260 feathers in her bonnet, "thereby causing it to have a lovely and glittering appearance, highly prepossessing and efficacious." Clearly, Lear chose these words much more for their sound than their sense (or nonsense), and children enjoy the fun even without knowing what the words mean.

Lear also enjoyed making up words. In "The Owl and the Pussycat," the pair eat with a runcible spoon, a word Lear coined. Many years later someone invented an actual utensil, a combination fork and spoon with a sharp edge, and christened it the runcible spoon. In "The Story of the Four Little Children," one member of the boat's crew is a "Quangle-Wangle," and at one point the children return to the boat only to find it clutched in the jaws of a "Seeze Pyder."

The combination of alliteration, malapropism, and made-up words results in a kind of supreme silliness such as occurs when the children visit the country of the Blue-Bottle Fly:

> all the Blue-Bottle-Flies began to buzz at once in a sumptuous and sonorous manner, the melodious and mucilaginous sounds echoing all over the waters, and resounding across the tumultuous tops of the transitory Titmice upon the intervening and verdant mountains, with a serene and sickly suavity only known to the truly virtuous. The Moon was shining slobaciously from the star-bespringled sky, while her light irrigated the smooth and shiny sides and wings and backs of the Blue-Bottle-Flies with a peculiar and trivial splendour, while all nature cheerfully responded to the cerulaean and conspicuous circumstances.

As much as he loved language, Lear almost seems to have loved food more; food is literally everywhere in his writing, and in wonderfully odd combinations. In "The Owl and the Pussycat," the lovers "dine on quince and slices of mince." In "The Story of the Four Little Children," the children devour sole in shrimp sauce right from the ocean, eat hundreds of oranges, beg custard from a mob of white mice, and learn that Blue-Bottle Flies eat "oyster-patties, raspberry vinegar and Russian leather boiled down to a jelly." During their adventures, the children discover a gargantuan cauliflower and a place where they found "nothing at all except some wide and deep pits full of Mulberry Jam." On their return journey, the children have only "four small beans and three pounds of mashed potatoes" left to eat.

Thus, it is not surprising that Lear wrote a piece entitled "Nonsense Cookery" that includes recipes for Amblongus Pie and Crumbobblious Cutlets. The pie recipe concludes, as perhaps many others should, "Serve up in a clean dish, and throw the whole out of the window as fast as possible."

Lear's drawings add yet another layer of silliness to his work. They make the experience of reading him a delight for both eye and ear.

Other Work by Edward Lear
A Book of Nonsense. Everyman's Library. New York: Alfred A. Knopf, 1992.

Works about Edward Lear
Kamen, Gloria. *Edward Lear, King of Nonsense: A Biography.* New York: Atheneum, 1990.
Levi, Peter. *Edward Lear: A Biography.* London: Macmillan, 1995.
Noakes, Vivien. *Edward Lear, 1812–1888.* New York: Harry N. Abrams, 1986.
———. *Edward Lear: The Life of a Wanderer.* London: Sutton, 2006.
Snider, Clifton. "Victorian Trickster: A Jungian Consideration of Edward Lear's Nonsense Verse." Edward Lear: Victorian Trickster. Available online. URL: http://www.csulb.edu/%7Ecsaider/edward.lear.html. Accessed July 3, 2008.

Lee, Harriet (1757–1851) *novelist, playwright*
Harriet Lee was born in London in 1757 to two actors, John and Anna Sophia Lee. When she was a child, her family moved often between London and Bath, where she settled in December 1780 to open a private girls' school at Belvedere House along with her sisters Anna, Charlotte,

and Sophia. Sophia, by then a financially and critically successful playwright, financed the operation. Within a few years, the school became enormously successful itself, providing the Lee sisters with a secure financial foundation.

Inspired by her sister's literary achievements, Lee began publishing her own work in 1786, starting with a five-volume epistolary novel called *The Errors of Innocence,* in which a young woman is trapped in an unhappy marriage because of her decision in a moment of pity to marry a dying man, who speedily recovers. A comedic play, *The New Peerage, or, Our Eyes May Deceive Us,* followed in 1787.

The pursuit of a fruitless romantic relationship consumed Lee's attentions through most of the 1790s, but in 1797 she again published a novel, *Clara Lennox, or, The Distressed Widow.* A play, *The Mysterious Marriage, or, The Heirship of Roselva,* followed in 1789. Also in 1797, Lee published the first two volumes of a collection of novellas that won her the most acclaim: *The Canterbury Tales* (1797–1805). Much like the work of Chaucer from which they take their title, they are a group of stories told by travelers who have fallen in together by accident.

These stories, two of which were contributed by Sophia, were markedly different from the fiction of the time, especially in their pacing, which resembled that of a three-act play. Critics today consider them precursors of the modern short story. One in particular, "The German's Tale: Kruitzer," describes a man without self-control who brings suffering to himself and others; it became so popular it was often reprinted separately, and was the inspiration for the poet LORD BYRON's verse drama *Werner, or, The Inheritance.*

In 1798 Lee was courted by the novelist and philosopher WILLIAM GODWIN, but she refused him because of his disdain for her participation in the Church of England. She published another novel in 1799, *Constantia de Valmont,* which did not meet with much success. The sisters closed the school in 1803, and in 1805 Anna hung herself. Lee did not publish new work after her sister's death, although she did dramatize "Kruitzer" as *The Three Strangers* in 1826.

In later life, Lee continued writing but published nothing; her poems are preserved in the British Library. On August 1, 1851, Lee died of heart failure at her home in Clifton, unmarried and childless.

Lee, Vernon (Violet Paget) (1856–1935)
nonfiction writer, short story writer, novelist, playwright, critic

Vernon Lee was born Violet Paget in Boulogne-sur-Mer, France, the daughter of Henry Hippolyte Ferguson Paget and the English heiress Matilda Adams Lee-Ferguson. The only child of her mother's second marriage, she was brought up on the Continent, moving from place to place with her family before they eventually settled in Florence. Her independent-minded mother was the dominant force in the family and encouraged Lee's interest in the arts and writing. By her early 20s, she began using the pen name Vernon Lee in a bid to have her ideas taken seriously by the male-dominated intelligentsia (reasoning that the name did not indicate whether the writer was a man or woman). Lee never married, but had important, long-lasting friendships with the artists Mary Robinson and Kit Anstruther-Thomson.

Vernon Lee was one of the first writers to be concerned with theories of writing and the writer's relation to the reader, and one of the first female writers concerned with the arts and the study of aesthetics. An important force in late-19th- and early-20th-century artistic and literary circles, Lee earned a reputation for her great intellect and fierce expressions of opinion on all subjects. She began making annual trips to England in 1881 and quickly gained a reputation as a brilliant but combative thinker. HENRY JAMES called her a "tiger-cat" and noted her "monsterous cerebration." Other writers with whom she associated included WALTER PATER, GEORGE BERNARD SHAW, OSCAR WILDE, H. G. Wells, and Edith Wharton.

In her lifetime Lee produced 45 published works, including novels, short stories, plays, and essays on travel, Italian history, music, art, and aesthetics. She was least successful as a novelist. Her satirical attack on the Pre-Raphaelites, *Miss Brown* (1884), was critical of the movement's "art for art's sake" philosophy and its apparent indifference to society and its problems. Perhaps because she made little attempt to disguise the real-life figures on whom she based her characters, Lee managed to offend much of London's literary society. She was stung by her friend Henry James's criticism that the novel was "a deplorable mistake." Lee fared better with her books of travel essays, *Genius Loci: Notes on Places* (1899) and *The Sentimental Traveller: Notes on Places* (1908), which were particularly admired by Aldous Huxley; and with *Ariadne in Mantua* (1903), a play set in Renaissance Italy that examined concepts of love. The feminist critic Vineta Colby writes in *The Singular Anomaly* (1970), that the play "may well epitomize Vernon Lee's achievement: a life dedicated to art, rigorously disciplined and guided not by the 'mere impulse, unreasoning and violent,' of pleasure and the 'forces of nature,' but directed conscientiously toward the 'restraining influences of civilization.'"

For Lee, art was a spiritual, quasireligious experience, and she devoted most of her critical thinking to its examination. Colby notes that "Operating always within her was a kind of puritanical vigilance.... Art is good, not because it is good in itself (though she believed this) but because its effects on us are good. It arouses our better instincts, exhilarates and stimulates us to loftier thought and nobler action." Lee played an important role in the development of theories on literary criticism and influenced critical thinking on aesthetics. Her most significant contributions include studies on Italian history, culture, and the arts, such as *Studies of the Eighteenth Century in Italy* (1880) (a pioneering book that made Lee famous among intellectuals); *Euphorion: Being Studies of the Antique and the Medieval Renaissance* (1884) and *Renaissance Fancies and Studies* (1895); and her writings on aesthetics that include *Belcaro: Being Essays on Sundry Aesthetic Questions* (1881) and *Juvenilia: Being a Second Series of Essays on Sundry Aesthetic Questions* (1887), among other titles. Her essays on writing—"On Style," "On Literary Construction," "Can Writing Be Taught?"—collected in *The Handling of Words, and Other Studies in Literary Psychology* (1923), are noteworthy for their critical analysis of such elements of fiction as structure and technique, and the reader's response to character and language. In *English Criticism of the Novel* (1965), the critic Kenneth Graham argues that Lee's essay "On Literary Construction" was "one of the most remarkable of all late-Victorian pronouncements on the craft of fiction."

"Vernon Lee indeed was more thoroughly committed to art than was any other woman of her generation," writes Colby. In *Renaissance Fancies* Lee explained the source of that commitment: "Art is a much greater and more cosmic thing than the mere expression of man's thoughts or opinions on any one subject.... Art is the expression of man's life, of his mode of being, of his relations with the universe, since it is, in fact, man's unarticulate answer to the universe's unspoken message."

Works about Vernon Lee (Violet Paget)

Colby, Vineta. *The Singular Anomaly: Women Novelists of the Nineteenth Century.* New York: New York University Press, 1970.

———. *Vernon Lee: A Literary Biography.* Charlottesville: University of Virginia Press, 2003.

Gunn, Peter. *Vernon Lee: Violet Paget, 1856–1935.* New York: Oxford University Press, 1964.

Zorn, Christa, Vernon Lee: *Aesthetics, History, and the Victorian Female Intellectual.* Columbus: Ohio University Press, 2003.

Le Fanu, Joseph Sheridan (1814–1873)
novelist, short story writer

Le Fanu was born into the Protestant family of Thomas Le Fanu and his wife, Emma, in Dublin, Ireland, and counted among his ancestors the famous playwright and theater manager Richard Brinsley Sheridan (1751–1816) and the novelist Alicia Le Fanu (1753–1817). When he was 12 his family moved to a small town in County Limerick, but he returned to Dublin to enter Trinity College, from which he graduated in 1837. He studied law and was called to the bar in 1839, but instead of practicing law he chose a literary career. He had published a short story, "The Ghost and the Bone-Setter," in the *Dublin University Magazine* in 1838 and had also written two Irish ballads, "Phaudrig Coohoore" and "Shamus O'Brien." But his early years as a writer were spent mainly as a journalist, working for—and eventually owning—several Dublin papers. He married Susan Bennett in 1844 and was an adoring husband and socially active until her untimely death in 1858, after which he became extremely reclusive and spent his time writing novels and stories with supernatural themes.

It is said that he wrote many of his novels while lying in bed, using whatever scraps of paper came to hand. He was prolific, averaging roughly one novel a year up to 1872. Of his numerous short stories, several are still anthologized. His best-known story, "Carmilla" (1872), is a vampire tale that was a major influence on BRAM STOKER's *Dracula* (1895). Le Fanu captured the eroticism of the vampire legend in his vivid descriptions: "Sometimes there came a sensation as if a hand was drawn softly along my cheek and neck. Sometimes it was as if warm lips kissed me, and longer and more lovingly as they reached my throat, but there the caress fixed itself."

Another of his stories, "Green Tea" (1872), metaphorically presages the work of Sigmund Freud: The pursuing demon, in this case a monkey, does not represent a specific case of wrongdoing but rather a creature from the dark unconscious residing in us all. The poor minister who is pursued cannot attribute his possession by this monkey with the glowing eyes to anything he, the minister, has done, any sin he has committed, but instead simply to evil forces in the universe that strike randomly. Le Fanu seems to be the first writer, in English at least, to introduce as one of his key narrators a German psychiatrist, one Doctor Martin Hesselius. He figures in many of Le Fanu's tales, and the narratives are case histories from the doctor's files. In "Green Tea" the minister tells Hesselius his story, and the latter simply relays it to us. Unfortunately at the last, when the minister needs him the most, he is almost irresponsibly absent. The minister cuts his own throat and is found dead in a pool of blood.

Le Fanu's most famous novel, *Uncle Silas* (1864), uses the conventions of the gothic novel, particularly as practiced by ANN RADCLIFFE, to create a tale of terror set in an English country house. The story is told from the perspective of a young woman to enhance its psychological terror: "I sat without breathing or winking, staring upon the formidable image which with upstretched arm, and the sharp lights and hard shadows thrown upon her corrugated features, looked like a sorceress watching for the effect of a spell."

His biographer Ivan Melada considers Le Fanu not only a popular writer but also a serious thinker, "a master at portraying the obscenity of violence, not just for the sake of sensation but to call attention to the ugliness of violent death as man's ultimate indignity."

Works about Joseph Sheridan Le Fanu
McCormack, W. J. *Sheridan Le Fanu and Victorian Ireland.* New York: Oxford University Press, 1980.
Melada, Ivan. *Sheridan Le Fanu.* Boston: Twayne, 1987.

Le Gallienne, Richard (1866–1947)
novelist, poet, essayist, critic
Richard Le Gallienne was born in Liverpool, England, to Jane Smith Gallienne and her husband, John Gallienne, the manager of a brewery. Richard enrolled in Liverpool College at age nine, but left in 1881 to train to become an accountant. Although his father was a practical man of business, his mother encouraged Le Gal-

lienne's artistic tendencies. Partly as a result of that encouragement, he quickly escaped to London and to the literary life. There he adopted an urban dandy style, added the *Le* to his surname, and began to write poetry. He met the publisher John Lane, who was to give him reviewing jobs and otherwise aid in his career, and associated with AUBREY BEARDSLEY and OSCAR WILDE. He contributed to the aesthetic magazine, the *Yellow Book,* and was a member of the Rhymers' Club, which included W. B. Yeats. His first volume of poetry, *My Ladies' Sonnets* (1887), a collection of mostly love poems, was an immediate success. His next book of poems, *Volumes in Folio* (1889), is a collection of comic love poems about books: "When do I love you most, sweet book of mine? / In strenuous morns when o'er your leaves I pore."

Le Gallienne continued to publish volumes of poetry, novels, and essays for 50 years. Although his works sold well, and Le Gallienne became a literary celebrity, critics were less kind. GEORGE BERNARD SHAW, for example, complained of "a certain commonplaceness and banality of material, which is not altogether compensated by his dainty workmanship" in Le Gallienne's *English Poems* (1892). In 1896 he published his best work, the novel *The Quest of the Golden Girl,* a semi-autobiographical account of a poet in search of the perfect woman. For his novel *Young Lives* (1899), Le Gallienne again drew on his personal experience, basing the character Angel on his first wife Eliza Mildred Lee.

He left England for good in 1903, first for America, and then in 1927 for France, where he died. During his career, as he battled "for solvency and against drink," he wrote newspaper articles, reviews, advertising copy, poems, prose fancies, and whatever he could for whoever would pay him. His memoir, *The Romantic '90s* (1926), is a good portrait of the period. His last work, *From a Paris Scrapbook* (1938), won a prize for the best book written about France by a foreigner. Although his career extended over five decades and 50 books, Le Gallienne is best remembered for his work of the 1890s.

A Work about Richard Le Gallienne
Whittington-Egan, Richard, and Geoffrey Smerdon. *The Quest of the Golden Boy,* London: Union Press 1960.

Lemon, Mark (1809–1870) *playwright, journalist, editor*

Mark Lemon was born in London, the eldest son of Martin Lemon, a London hops merchant, and Alice Collis Lemon. After his father's death in 1817, the 15-year-old Lemon was apprenticed to his uncle, Thomas Collis, a hops merchant in Boston, Lincolnshire, with the expectation that he would continue in the family's brewery trade. However, Lemon was ambitious to become a writer, and by the 1830s he was an established journalist and successful playwright. As a journalist, he contributed stories to various London periodicals—*Illustrated London News, Illuminated Magazine,* and *Household Words*—and was editor of the *London Journal, Family Week,* and *Once a Week.* Lemon also enjoyed success in the theater, writing more than 60 plays during his lifetime, including farce and melodrama. He collaborated with CHARLES DICKENS to write the farce *Mr. Nightingale's Diary* (1851), depicting the bilking of a hypochondriac, and joined Dickens's troupe of performers in staging amateur theatricals.

Mark Lemon is chiefly remembered as the cofounder and editor of *Punch,* the preeminent British humor magazine. In partnership with HENRY MAYHEW, a fellow journalist and playwright, Lemon launched *Punch* in 1841 with an editorial mission to combine humor with political comment in support of liberal causes and to campaign against political and economic injustices. They recruited the self-named Punch Brotherhood, a talented group that included the writers DOUGLAS JERROLD, JOSEPH STIRLING COYNE, THOMAS HOOD, and GILBERT À BECKETT, and the illustrators John Leech, Richard Doyle, and John Tenniel. The "Brotherhood" shared a cynicism about government and a deep concern about the exploitation and suffering of the working poor.

Although the magazine was politically influential, its circulation of 6,000 copies per week was insufficient to make money, and in December 1842 *Punch* was sold to Bradbury & Evans, the London printer and publisher. Lemon was reappointed as editor and Mayhew given the role of "suggester-in-chief." Mayhew's last article for the magazine was published in February 1845. With Mayhew's departure, *Punch* lost its radical edge, and Lemon accepted articles by more conservative writers such as WILLIAM MAKEPEACE THACKERAY, over the protest of Jerrold and other liberal contributors. By the mid-1850s, the originally radical *Punch* had shifted to a more bland, less political content ostensibly to appeal to the more conservative views of Britain's growing middle class. Lemon continued to serve as editor of *Punch* until his death in 1870.

Works about Mark Lemon
Adrian, Arthur A. *Mark Lemon: First Editor of "Punch."* New York: Oxford University Press, 1966.
Fisher, Leona Mae Weaver. *Lemon, Dickens, and Mr. Nightingale's Diary: A Victorian Farce.* Victoria, Canada: University of Victoria, 1988.

Lever, Charles James (1806–1872)
novelist

Charles Lever was born in Dublin, Ireland. His father was a successful architect and his mother was a member of the Irish gentry. Lever entered Trinity College in Dublin at age 16 and graduated in 1827. He traveled to Canada and Germany, then returned to Dublin to study medicine. In 1832 he married Kate Barker, whose editing Lever relied on over the years. In 1839 his first novel, *The Confessions of Harry Lorrequer,* was published. It is a lighthearted account of life in the military, told by the comic hero, an English officer stationed in Ireland. By this time, Lever and his wife were living in Brussels, Belgium, where he was practicing medicine and writing steadily.

In 1841 he published his second novel, *Charles O'Malley,* a similar comical series of adventures. In 1842, now famous as a writer and known for his brilliant portrayals of Irish life, Lever became editor of the *Dublin University Magazine.* He continued writing novels, including *Jack Hinton* (1843), a more serious depiction of English and Irish conflict, and *Tom Burke of Ours* (1844), a novel of the Napoleonic Wars. In 1845, the Levers again left Dublin for Europe; they eventually settled in Florence, Italy. One of Lever's later works is a charming autobiographical portrait of a British family traveling in Europe, *The Dodd Family Abroad* (1854).

A Work about Charles Lever
Haddelsey, Stephen. *Charles Lever: The Lost Victorian.* New York: Oxford University Press, 2001.

Leverson, Ada (1862–1933) *novelist, journalist*

Ada Leverson, née Beddington, was born in London, England, to Samuel and Zillah Beddington, and was educated at home. At age 19 she went against her parents' wishes in marrying Ernest Leverson, a diamond merchant 12 years her senior. The marriage was unhappy but the couple had a daughter, the writer Violet Wyndham.

A relationship with the writer GEORGE MOORE inspired Leverson to try her hand at writing. She contributed clever parodies of the AESTHETES to *Punch* magazine, and stories to the *Yellow Book,* and interviewed MAX BEERBOHM for *Sketch*. In 1892 Leverson met OSCAR WILDE, an association for which she is primarily remembered. Wilde named her the "Sphinx"—a nickname she kept throughout her life—and declared her to be the wittiest woman in the world. Her aphoristic and transgressive humor in fact was quite similar to Wilde's, as demonstrated in a set of "definitions" she published in *Punch*: "*Blasphemy.* Any discussion on religion. *Coquetry.* A manner sometimes assumed by elderly ladies and very young gentlemen. *Cynicism.* Truthfulness..." Leverson became famous for remaining loyal to Wilde during his trial in 1895 and providing a safe refuge for him in her home.

After her husband's business failed and he moved to Canada, Leverson remained in London, where her career as a novelist blossomed. Between 1907 and 1916 she published six novels, comedies of manners detailing life among the Edwardian upper classes. Her novels enjoyed a belated popularity in the 1960s, and in 1962 three of them were published in one volume titled *The Little Ottleys*, so named for the title character of the trilogy, Edith Ottley, a bored but witty married woman. Leverson's biographer Julie Speedie characterizes her novels as "the perfect expression of her personality: frivolous and witty, but with an underlying sense of melancholy."

A Work about Ada Leverson
Speedie, Julie. *Wonderful Sphinx: The Biography of Ada Leverson.* New York: Random House, 1994.

Levy, Amy (1861–1889) *poet*

Amy Levy was born in Clapham (then a suburb of London), England, to Lewis Levy, a stockbroker, and Isabelle Levin, his cousin. In 1876 her family moved to Brighton, where she attended the girls' high school. Levy was the first Jewish student at Newnham College, the women's college at Cambridge University, although she did not graduate. At Newnham Levy decided to pursue writing as a career, at age 18 publishing a letter in the *Jewish Chronicle* on the topic "Jewish Women and Women's Rights." During the next few years she traveled widely. At age 27 Levy committed suicide at her parents' London home, possibly fearing she was sick with syphilis, the disease that had killed her brother, Alfred, and that at the time was misinterpreted as congenital.

Although Levy wrote essays, short stories, and novels, she is primarily read today as a poet. Her first book of poetry was *Xantippe and Other Verse* (1881). "Xantippe" is a dramatic monologue, spoken by the quarrelsome wife of the ancient Greek philosopher Socrates. The dramatic monologue is an often self-serving, inadvertently self-revealing speech addressed to one or more other characters, in this case Xantippe's personal attendants—although in reality Xantippe has no desire to communicate, but only to unburden herself of a catalogue of woes. Xantippe reveals that early in their marriage she opened her heart to Socrates, feeling that they were philosophical soulmates. Given the intimacy and passion of her disclosure, his response, an assumption that her ideas had been borrowed from something she had heard or read, struck her as "cold contempt": "From what high source . . . / Didst [thou] cull the sapient notion of thy words?" How could she countenance this lack of appreciation? After a period of grief and rage, "hope died out." Xantippe's vengeful mission became to make Socrates' life miserable. "Sorely have I sinned," she says, "In all my life." This confession of hers, though, is ironic; her "sin," it would seem, is her being female, the sole reason for her spouse's inability to accept her as an equal. The poem's principal target is the unequal relationship between wife and husband in Levy's own time. According to Richard Garnett, writing in the *Dictionary of National Biography* in 1892, the poem exhibits "a passionate rhetoric and a keen, piercing dialectic."

In 1884 Levy brought out a second volume of poetry, *A Minor Poet and Other Verse*. The title poem is another dramatic monologue. Here, the speaker's subject is suicide—his own. He had made two failed attempts: the first foiled by his friend Tom Leigh, and a second in which the flask of poison slipped from the speaker's hand. The question arises whether Leigh's long lecture to him, in favor of God's design and "the common good," had a hand in his dropping the poison. The speaker addresses the absent Leigh, whose arguments in favor of life he now rebuts. In a fair world, one would not have to contemplate suicide, but the world, the speaker notes, is not fair:

"One man gets meat for two, / The while another hungers." He bids farewell to favorite authors whom he imagines joining on the other side of death. His third suicide attempt succeeds: In an epilogue, Tom Leigh discovers his friend's body. Surely Levy herself is as much this "minor poet" as is the anonymous speaker. She, like him, had her "carping critics," among them the anonymous reviewer in *Jewish World* who derided the poem's "mournful wailing," finding its acceptance of suicide unacceptable, even inconceivable. But time would give Levy a different literary fate from that of the poem's speaker. The scholar Cynthia Scheinberg has noted that Leigh, who represents mainstream society, has the last word in the poem, consigning the words of the dead poet to "historical obscurity."

The majority of Levy's poems are shorter lyrics—heartfelt, though fragile things. In "In a Minor Key," which appeared in the *Minor Poet* volume, she wrote, for instance, "You came—all my pulses burn'd and beat. / . . . You went . . . / The light wax'd dim and the place grew gray."

Feminist critics have embraced Levy; for instance, Isobel Armstrong includes Levy in a discussion of writing "in which an overt sexual politics addresses the institutions and customs which burden women." However, her biographer Linda Hunt Beckman has argued that Levy was not a radical activist. Only rarely, as in "Xantippe," did Levy register protest. Instead, she was an individual minor poet, one who wrote in a minor key, evoking, Beckman writes, "agonized states of mind that are different from those most people ever experience."

Other Work by Amy Levy
New, Melvyn, ed. *The Complete Novels and Selected Writings of Amy Levy*. Gainesville: University Press of Florida, 1993.

A Work about Amy Levy
Beckman, Linda Hunt. *Amy Levy: Her Life and Letters*. Athens: Ohio University Press, 2000.

Lewes, George Henry (1817–1878)
novelist, nonfiction writer, critic

George Henry Lewes was born in London, where his father was an actor and his mother a theater manager. His formal schooling ended at age 16 when he took a job as a clerk. He later studied medicine but abandoned it when he learned that he loathed inflicting pain on patients. From 1838 to 1840 he was in Germany, studying German literature and culture and writing a respected biography of Goethe. Upon his return to London, he began his career as a journalist, becoming that rarity, an intellectual journalist writing on such topics as physiology, psychology, sociology, philosophy, and literary realism. He married Agnes Jervis in 1841, but they separated after he discovered that their fourth child had been fathered by Thornton Hunt (Leigh Hunt's son). As a freethinker, however, Lewes accepted his wife's behavior and supported the three children they had together while continuing to work professionally with Hunt.

Influenced by Goethe, Lewes's first novel, *Ranthorpe* (1845), traces the main character's development of a mature understanding of life and his literary art. *Ranthorpe* is an example of the novel of development (or *Bildungsroman*) that was very popular in the middle of the century. Lewes's second novel, *Rose, Blanche, and Violet* (1848) was written on principles of rigid realism. Though his novels received little notice, nonetheless, Lewes became a highly significant figure in the literary culture of England for two reasons: his superb literary criticism (primarily of the novel) and his role in the development of George Eliot. He encouraged Charlotte Brontë after the publication of her novel *Jane Eyre* (1847), for example, and he reviewed and corresponded with the most important novelists of the period. As the common-law husband of George Eliot, he encouraged her to begin writing fiction, read and discussed all her manuscripts, and worked hard to shield her from criticism. His main contribution to fiction, then, might be said to be his encouragement of a realistic aesthetic in the novel.

Lewes's early interest in physiology remained with him throughout his life. He published *The Physiology of Common Life* (1859–60) and *Studies in Animal Life* (1862) before devoting himself at the end of his life to *Problems of Life and Mind*, which was not completed at his death. With George Eliot's assistance, the work, which is a wide-ranging exploration of the relationship between the mind and body—what today might be called physical psychology—was published posthumously. Lewes remains important as a critic of Victorian literature and as an example of a Victorian intellectual.

A Work about George Henry Lewes

Orell, Harold. *Victorian Literary Critics: George Henry Lewes, Walter Bagehot, Richard Holt Hutton, Leslie Stephen, Andrew Lang, George Saintsbury, and Edmund Gosse.* New York: St. Martin's Press, 1983.

Lewis, Matthew Gregory (Monk) (1775–1818) *novelist, dramatist, memoirist*

Matthew Gregory Lewis, commonly known as "Monk" Lewis, was born in London to Matthew Lewis and Frances Maria Sewell. Although his father served the Deputy-Secretary at War under King George III, the senior Lewis's large income derived from the two large Jamaican plantations he owned. After schooling at Westminster, where he acted in schoolboy plays, Lewis went to Oxford University in 1790, but a year later left for Paris where he began writing a novel and a farce. In 1792 he met Goethe in Germany, and early the next year, having immersed himself in German literature, Gothic and otherwise, he returned to Oxford. By 1794 he had left Oxford again for the post of attaché to the British Embassy in Holland. He served from 1796 to 1802 in the House of Commons.

At The Hague, at age 19, Lewis wrote the work for which he is known, *The Monk*, in less than three months. When it was published anonymously in 1796, it became an immense and immediate success. At least one standard reference work on English literature lists Matthew Lewis not under L, for *Lewis*, but under M, for *Monk*, so associated is his entire reputation with his novel. His was by no means the first gothic novel, a genre begun in 1765 by Horace Walpole and given completed form by ANN RADCLIFFE in the 1790s. *The Monk* is important in the history of the Gothic style, however, because it was the first English novel to emulate the German *schauerroman*, or "shudder novel." The German variant of the Gothic was darker, more violent, and more sensational than its English counterpart, and made much more use of the supernatural.

Lewis's novel involves murder, seduction, rape, incest, ghosts, the devil, torture, and an angry mob attacking a convent, among other horrors. The title character, the monk Ambrosio, begins the novel self-righteous and pure, but a hypocrite at heart. He becomes strangely attracted to one of the new arrivals at his monastery, who turns out to be a woman, Matilda, in disguise. Ambrosio falls under the spell of this woman, and under her influence rapes his sister and strangles his mother. At the end of the novel, Matilda is revealed to be the devil:

> Short-sighted Mortal! Miserable Wretch! Are you not guilty? Are you not infamous in the eyes of Men and Angels. Can such enormous sins be forgiven? Hope you to escape my power? Your fate is already pronounced. The Eternal has abandoned you; Mine you are marked in the book of destiny, and mine you must and shall be!

Following the success of the first edition, Lewis published the next edition under his own name. Authorities were shocked that such a salacious work was written by a member of Parliament, and the attorney general moved to have the novel suppressed. A compromise was reached with the second edition, which omitted the most objectionable passages. Today, of course, it is those very passages for which Lewis's novel is celebrated, and 20th-century editions of *The Monk* reflect its original form. In recent years, critics have become especially interested in Lewis's treatment of sexuality.

In the following years, Lewis wrote numbers of plays, poems, and tales. His play *The Castle Spectre* (1798), another gothic tale, was mounted at the Drury Lane Theatre for an initial run of 47 nights. In 1801, Lewis collaborated with the young WALTER SCOTT, among others, for *Tales of Wonder,* a collection of supernatural ballads, some original and some translations from the German. Lewis's other major work, *Journal of a West India Proprietor,* was published posthumously in 1834. This work describes Lewis's journey to the Jamaican plantations he inherited from his father and which were the source of his affluence. His motives were humanitarian—to improve the condition of the 500 slaves working there—but he was unable to carry out his intended reforms. "Monk" Lewis will always be best remembered for his contribution to the Gothic novel. His biographer Joseph Irwin states that Lewis "brought terror literature to a high state of accomplishment in the approximately 15 years in which he flourished as a writer."

Works about Matthew Gregory Lewis
Irwin, Joseph James. *M. G. "Monk" Lewis.* Boston: Twayne, 1976.
Macdonald, D. L. *Monk Lewis: A Critical Biography.* Toronto: University of Toronto Press, 2000.

Linton, Eliza Lynn (Eliza Lynn) (1822–1898) *novelist, journalist, critic*

Eliza Lynn Linton was the sixth daughter and 12th child of James Lynn, the vicar of Keswick in the English Lake District. Her mother, Charlotte, died when Eliza was five months old. Prevented from attending school by a father who did not approve of education for girls, she taught herself French, German, Spanish, and Italian as well as some Latin and Greek. She moved to London in 1845 determined to become a writer, supporting herself with a small stipend granted by her father and with any writing assignments she could secure from periodicals such as *Household Words*. She published at her own expense her first novel, which was favorably reviewed, *Azeth the Egyptian* (1846), a historical romance based on reading she did in the British Museum. Her second novel, *Amymone: A Romance of the Days of Pericles* (1848), which strongly advocated women's rights, was also favorably reviewed. In 1849 she was offered a salaried staff position at the *Morning Chronicle,* becoming the first Englishwoman to receive a regular salary as a journalist. She wrote more than 80 articles and more than 36 reviews for the *Chronicle* between August 1849 and February 1851. In this same period, she met WALTER SAVAGE LANDOR, who became a mentor and who introduced her into London's literary circles, where she met CHARLES DICKENS, JOHN FORSTER, and GEORGE HENRY LEWES. She appeared well on her way to achieving literary success and financial security.

Her third novel, *Realities,* dedicated to Landor, was published in 1851, but it was a critical and financial failure that marked her turning point as a writer. The novel, documenting the destructive power of patriarchal middle-class mores, was critical of sexual double standards, contemporary divorce laws, and prohibitions against educated women entering male professions. The scholar Andrea Broomfield calls it "one of the most radical, protofeminist novels of her time." The subjects were deemed too radical by publishers and, once again, she had to use her own money to finance publication. In reviewing *Realities,* Lewes said the novel was "a passionate and exaggerated protest against conventions, which failed of its intended effect because it was too exaggerated, too manifestly injust." She never forgave Lewes his tough criticism and bore a lifelong grudge against him and his common-law wife, GEORGE ELIOT. Shortly after the publication of *Realities,* she was humiliated when she was dismissed from her staff position at the *Morning Chronicle.* It would be four years before she would attempt another novel;

and after the punishing failure of *Realities,* she retreated from her support of women's rights.

Between 1852 and 1854 Linton lived in Paris, where she was a correspondent for the *Leader* and also freelanced for periodicals such as Dickens's *Household Words.* Returning to London in 1854, she continued to contribute articles and short stories to various periodicals such as the *English Republic,* where she met her future husband, William James Linton. In her essay "Rights and Wrongs of Women" for the *Republic,* she established her antifeminist credentials writing against the emancipated woman, whom she labeled an "amorphous monster." She married Linton, a widower with seven children, in 1858 and continued to write to support the family. The couple separated in 1865, although they never divorced and she retained her husband's name.

In 1866 Linton was hired as a reviewer and essayist for the *Saturday Review,* an influential conservative periodical that opposed women's rights. Her most controversial and famous piece for the *Review* was the 1868 essay "Girl of the Period," in which she vehemently argued against women's emancipation. Although she was an independent, self-educated, self-supporting woman, Linton attacked the "new woman" as "hard, unloving, mercenary, ambitious, without domestic faculty and devoid of healthy natural instincts," and labeled the movement a "pitiable mistake and a grand national disaster." "Girl of the Period" was issued as a pamphlet in 1868 and reprinted in book form with other essays in 1883. Linton continued her arguments against women's emancipation in subsequent essays such as "The Higher Education of Women" (1885), in which she argued against women's "education carried to excess, and [the] exhausting anxieties of professional life"; and in such novels as *The Atonement of Leam Dundas* (1877), *The One Too Many* (1894), and *In Haste and at Leisure* (1895).

A dedicated agnostic, this daughter of a vicar also used the novel form to attack the hypocrisy of Victorian Christianity in what became her best-known and most widely circulated novel, *The True Story of Joshua Davidson, Christian and Communist* (1872). Her biographer Nancy Fix Anderson notes, "The point of the book was not to advocate communism, but to condemn modern Christianity.... She never really seemed to understand what communism meant.... [S]he did not want to reconstruct society, but merely to strip away the veil of hypocrisy, to make the world more honest, and certainly more caring."

In a career that spanned five decades, Linton produced scores of essays, reviews, and journal articles and published 37 books including novels, collections of short stories and essays, and travel pieces. In 1885 she produced the three-volume novel *The Autobiography of Christopher Kirkland,* whose male protagonist was a thinly veiled autobiographical portrait. Although her views were considered extreme by many observers and often satirized, as Anderson observes: "Eliza's success lay ... in emancipating herself from the dictates of Victorian patriarchy. Imbued with a fighting spirit and inexorable will ... she ... actively shaped the direction of her life, and reached her goals of independence and fame."

A Work about Eliza Lynn Linton
Anderson, Nancy Fix. *Woman Against Women in Victorian England: A Life of Eliza Lynn Linton.* Bloomington: Indiana University Press, 1987.

Little, Janet (1759–1813) *poet*
Janet Little was born in Nether Bogside, Scotland. She never attended school but worked as a chambermaid and acquired the only education she had from books. In 1792 she published her *Poetical Works,* a collection of conventional love poems, as well as more original poems in a distinctive, often colloquial style. In "A Young Lady's Lamentation on the Loss of Her Sister by Marriage," the speaker sadly tells of how she and her sister resisted the blandishments of suitors until her sister "languish'd in the field ... She married was a month ago." The speaker concludes that she herself will continue to defy "man's seducing arts":

The rich, the poor, the proud, the slave,
The fop, the clown, the low, the tall,
The gay, the giddy, or the grave,
I scornfully defy them all.

Little wrote in both English and Scots. Having worked on a dairy farm, she was known as "the Scotch Milkmaid" in literary circles. Little called herself "a crazy scribbling lass." She was almost gleefully defiant of the snobbery a poet of her class and origins (like her countryman ROBERT BURNS) encountered. She wrote in one poem of the "Voracious critics . . . Like eagles, watching for their prey." Many of the poems Little wrote after marrying John Richmond and becoming a stepmother to his five children are religious ones. Even an early poem, "On Happiness," after surveying all the possible sources of happiness in life, reaches the conclusion

All hail, Religion! thou celestial power!
Thy force alone can soothe the anxious breast,
And quite dispel the solitary gloom.

Lockhart, John Gibson (1794–1854)
biographer, novelist

John Lockhart was born in Lanarkshire, in central Scotland, to the Reverend John Lockhart and Elizabeth Gibson Lockhart. A precocious student, he entered the University of Glasgow at age 12, then went to Balliol College at Oxford University. After graduating from Oxford in 1813, he studied law in Edinburgh and became a lawyer in 1816. A year later, however, Lockhart decided to travel to Germany to study literature, which was his first love. When he returned to Scotland, Lockhart began writing political commentary for *Blackwood's Magazine*. In 1820 he married Sophia Scott, the daughter of SIR WALTER SCOTT. Over the next four years Lockhart produced three novels, but it was the biographies to which he turned next that were his most important works. In 1828 he published a biography of the Scottish poet ROBERT BURNS, followed a year later by a history of Napoléon. When Sir Walter Scott died in 1832, he left all of his letters and journals to Lockhart, who used this material as the basis for his memorably vivid portrait of his father-in-law, *The Life of Sir Walter Scott,* published in eight volumes in 1837–38. After the death of his wife in 1837, Lockhart published little else.

Other Works by John Gibson Lockhart
Ancient Spanish Ballads; Historical and Romantic. New York: Wiley and Putnam, 1842.
The History of Matthew Wald. Edinburgh, Scotland: W. Blackwood, 1824.

Works about John Gibson Lockhart
Ballantyne, James. *Refutation of the Misstatements and Calumnies Contained in Mr. Lockhart's Life of Sir Walter Scott, Bart., Respecting the Messrs.* London: Longman, 1838.
Carswell, Donald. *Scott and His Circle.* Garden City, N.Y.: Doubleday, Doran & Company, 1930.

Lyell, Sir Charles (1797–1875)
nonfiction writer, geologist

Sir Charles Lyell was born in Forfar, in the county of Angus, Scotland. His father, also named Charles, was a wealthy landowner as well as a botanist and Italian scholar. The younger Lyell was educated at Oxford University, where he studied mathematics, anthropology, classics, and law. More important, at Oxford Lyell developed his lifelong passion for geology.

Over his long career, Lyell discovered the Ice Ages and popularized the idea of slow geological processes by writing highly influential books about how to deduce Earth's past from its present state. His most important insight, explained in his three-volume *Principles of Geology* (1830–33), was the concept of uniformitarianism. Lyell explained that Earth's surface is the product, not of a handful of cataclysmic or divine events, such as the sudden eruption of mountain ranges out of the ground in a single day, but rather of uniform, gradual processes that have been going on since Earth's formation. Among these formative factors are lava flows, rain, ocean tides, glacier movements, and erosion.

Lyell's research further provided new evidence that Earth is much, much older than the several thousand years that Bishop James Ussher (1581–1656) had claimed based on his interpretation of standard religious accounts of its creation. Lyell explained that he worked backward in time, looking at current geological processes and then stripping away layers of time and sediment to figure out what Earth once looked like. He thus was able to "conduct us gradually from the known to the unknown," as he put it in the first volume of *Principles of Geology*.

The second volume of Lyell's *Principles* presents theories about metamorphic rock and how sedimentary layers near igneous rock reveal the effects of intense heat over time. In the third volume, Lyell suggests using reference fossils, which indicate different time periods, as markers for different geological eras. He dubbed the recent eras the Pleistocene, Older Pliocene, Miocene, and Eocene.

In subsequent editions, he added arguments that many dry regions, including his native Angus, show rock formations—particularly long, groove-like valleys—suggestive of ancient glacial activity similar to that in Scandinavian countries in modern times. In his later *Geological Evidences of the Antiquity of Man* (1863) his analysis of rock strata and human remains found in the rock hinted at a much older point of origin for the human species than had previously been suspected. Here, in the work of one man, were all the founding principles of modern geology. In his scientific paper "Uniformity of Change," Lyell proposed that "[W]e are mere sojourners on the surface of the planet."

In 1848 Lyell was knighted for his scientific achievements and became a baronet. Of Lyell's work, CHARLES DARWIN said, "The greatest merit of the *Principles* was that it altered the whole tone of one's mind, and therefore that, when seeing a thing never seen by Lyell, one yet saw it through his eyes." His biographer, Edward Battersby Bailey, writes of Lyell that he "did more than anyone else to free geology from the authority of tradition.... His enlightened synthesis of geology with archaeology and anthropology has supplied enduring inspiration."

A Work about Sir Charles Lyell

Wilson, Leonard G. *Lyell in America: Transatlantic Geology, 1841–1853*. Baltimore: Johns Hopkins University Press, 1998.

Macaulay, Thomas Babington (1800–1861) *historian, poet, nonfiction writer*

Thomas Macaulay was the precocious son of the well-to-do reformer and philanthropist Zacharay Macaulay; his mother, Selina Macaulay, was the daughter of a Bristol bookseller and had been educated by HANNAH MORE, one of the leading female literary figures of the 18th and early 19th centuries. Born in Leicestershire, in central England, Thomas had a brilliant academic career at Trinity College, Cambridge, where he twice won the Chancellor's Medal for poetry.

While still an undergraduate at Cambridge, Macaulay published poems and essays in the periodical *Knight's Quarterly.* Upon graduating and becoming a fellow of Trinity, he trained for the law, but published essays on literary and historical topics, most notably his essay "Milton" (1825) and "Southey's Colloquies on Society" (1830), in the influential *Edinburgh Review.* These subjects, literary figures of the past, social theory and politics, and the history of England, focused his interest throughout his career. The early writings launched that career by bringing him to the attention of a wealthy sponsor, through whose aid and influence he was elected to Parliament. He took his seat in Parliament just in time to support the Reform Bill of 1832, which substantially enlarged the number of persons who could legally vote.

Macaulay was steeped in the literature of the past, both of classical Greece and Rome and that of England. The great 18th-century English historian Edward Gibbon strongly influenced Macaulay's literary style and approach to history, and SIR WALTER SCOTT's romantic reverence for the English and Scottish past also helped form Macaulay's writing. In addition, in Parliament he became noted for his oratory, developing a manner of public speaking in which elegantly balanced and clear sentences achieved a persuasive effect. An oratorical style, in fact, was evident in Macaulay's early writing, as in the following sentence from "Milton," with its notable brevity and balance: "Hence the vocabulary of an enlightened society is philosophical, that of a half-civilized is poetical."

As the son of an abolitionist and an evangelical, Macaulay wrote against the institution of slavery. He also wanted to make a college education available for English subjects who were not members of the established Church of England. He wrote a series of articles on 17th- and 18th-century English literary figures—John Dryden, Jonathan Swift, and Horace Walpole, for example—in addition to a piece in 1827 on the Italian political theorist Niccolò Machiavelli (1469–1527). Of Machiavelli's books, Macaulay comments that they "were misrepresented by the learned, misconstrued by the ignorant, censured by the church and abused with all the rancour of simulated virtue, by the tools of a base government and the priests of a baser superstition."

Macaulay's essays proved immensely successful. In the meantime he had proceeded with his parliamentary and administrative careers, serving from 1834 to 1838 as a member of the Supreme Council in India, where he introduced educational reforms to improve the quality of English education in India.

Upon his return to England, Macaulay resumed his political career and also immersed himself in the reading of history, both ancient and modern, that was to produce his most notable works. Although not often read today, his poems, *Lays of Ancient Rome* (1842), proved popular and lucrative. They are rhymed retellings of several of the most widely known episodes from Roman history, including those of Horatio at the bridge and the Battle of Lake Regillus. Those poems and others were to be found in school anthologies in England and America well into the 1930s.

While Macaulay was writing the lays and attending to political duties, he was also working on what was to be his masterwork, his *History of England from the Accession of James II*. His intent was to carry the history forward to the Reform Act of 1832, but he got only to the reign of King William III (1689–1702) before he died. The first two volumes appeared in 1849, volumes three and four in 1855. The fifth volume, edited and put together from his manuscript by his sister Hannah, was published posthumously in 1861.

Even critics of the history—and there are many—agree that it is almost compulsively readable by virtue of its organization, subject matter, and above all, style. It has been criticized, however, for its assumption that English middle-class virtues were a standard to be followed by all peoples in all cultures. The following passage demonstrates its appealing style and questionable content: "For the history of our country during the last hundred and sixty years is eminently the history of physical, of moral, and of intellectual improvement. Those who compare the golden age which exists only in their imagination may talk of degeneracy and decay: but no man who is correctly informed as to the past will be disposed to take a morose or desponding view of the present." The constitutional monarchy that resulted from the turmoil of 17th-century English politics was, Macaulay never doubted, the best form of government possible for a modern state and was responsible for England's being the greatest and best of all possible modern states. This confidence in the superiority of the present and the prospect for continual improvement elicited the following response from Lord Melbourne, who became prime minister in 1834: "I wish I was as cocksure of anything as Tom Macaulay is of everything."

Critical Analysis

Although Thomas Macaulay wrote poetry (his *Lays of Ancient Rome* was a best seller), he was more famous in his time for his ambitious *The History of England from the Accession of James II*, an attempt to cover English history from 1685 to 1832. He only lived long enough to complete the history through the year 1702, but the four completed volumes were wildly popular.

The reason for this popularity lies in Macaulay's style. Instead of presenting the facts of history in a dry, roll-call fashion, he chose to make his work as readable as a novel, telling a story that was accurate but also full of lively characters and drama. By portraying historical figures as real people, the *History* also reflected Macaulay's belief in the power of the individual to change society for the better, if given the chance to exercise his or her full potential. This belief was part of the Whig view of history as the march of social progress, which individuals either help or hinder.

Macaulay attempted in his *History* not only to produce a work of lasting value, but also to create a new standard for British historians. He believed that historians had to focus on social history as much as political history, paying attention to popular culture and the changes in its temperament that resulted in the lofty events previous historians had traditionally focused on to the exclusion of descriptions of the everyday life of commoners. Macaulay's vision of the ideal historian also included a tone that combined dispassionate objectivity with the liveliest techniques of the literary arts.

The reaction to the *History* far exceeded Macaulay's modest expectations; the first volume went through several printings in a matter of months after its first appearance in late 1848. To Macaulay's surprise, it was also a great success in the United States and France.

Severe health problems, including a heart attack, prevented Macaulay from achieving his original aim of continuing the *History* through 1832. In the end, only four volumes of this monumental work were completed and published. Though a nationalistic bias is apparent to modern readers, Macaulay's work enjoyed the status of a contemporary classic through the rest of the 19th and part of the 20th centuries.

A Work about Thomas Babington Macaulay

Cruikshank, Margaret. *Thomas Babington Macaulay.* Boston: Twayne, 1978.

Macdonald, George (1824–1905) *novelist, poet, critic, children's book writer*

George Macdonald was born in Aberdeen, Scotland, to George Macdonald, Sr., a struggling farmer, and Helen McKay Macdonald. In 1845 he graduated with an M.A. from King's College in Aberdeen, entering Highbury Theological College, near London, three years later. Without having completed his studies, Macdonald assumed ministerial duties at Trinity Congregation Church in Arundel, Sussex, in southern England, in 1850, preaching universalism, the idea that all souls would eventually be saved.

In response, church deacons cut his salary only months after the birth of his first child, hoping to force the resignation that finally came the next year. A poet since his Aberdeen years, Macdonald then took up writing full time. For four years until her death, the widow of GEORGE GORDON, LORD BYRON, was his patron. Career disappointments followed: In 1865 his candidacy for a teaching post at Edinburgh University failed, and in 1873 a children's magazine he had edited for four years folded. Despite increasing literary fortunes, financial problems dogged Macdonald until the Crown awarded him an annual pension in 1877.

Macdonald wrote fantasy fiction. His taste for fantasy derived from Scottish folklore, medieval and Renaissance allegory (in particular, Edmund Spenser's *The Faerie Queene*), and his reading of such mystics as Jacob Boehme and WILLIAM BLAKE. In turn, Macdonald's fantasies influenced C. S. Lewis and J. R. R. Tolkien.

One of Macdonald's children's fantasies, *At the Back of the North Wind* (1871), takes place in both the real world of Victorian London and the dreamworld of Diamond, a coachman's son, whose imagination takes off from the real world whenever the boy sees the North Wind. The dreamworld thus becomes a seamless extension of the real one, and in fact the story begins in one of Diamond's dreams. One adventure leads him to the North Wind's house. He must step right through her as she sits on her doorstep: "[A]ll grew white about him; and the cold stung him like fire. . . . It was when he reached North Wind's heart that he fainted and fell." Macdonald's style is often transformatively dreamlike.

Macdonald followed this book with *The Princess and the Goblin* (1872), in which children battle the goblins living in a subterranean world. The main character is the eight-year-old Princess Irene, whose "half castle half farmhouse" rests on top of the goblins' domain. Her companion and sometime rescuer is Curdie, a miner's son, who is familiar with the goblins; for instance, he knows that they cannot bear to hear singing. Another of Irene's protectors is her great-grandmother, who gives Irene a magical opal ring. When shown Grandmother's bedroom, Irene sees, hanging, "a lamp as round as a ball, shining as with the brightest moonlight," a majestic bed, and blue walls "spangled all over with what looked like stars of silver," while Curdie, who cannot even see Grandmother, sees "a big bare garret-room . . . a tub, and a heap of musty straw." Both characters, representing both worlds, are necessary allies for combating evil. *The Princess and Curdie* (1883) is a sequel.

Among Macdonald's fantasies for adults are *Phantastes, a Faerie Romance* (1858), about the 21-year-old Anodos, whose adventures in fairyland chart his desire for divine truth, and *Lilith* (1895), in which another other-world journeyer, Mr. Vane, encounters mysteries of human nature, God, and evil, including (according to Macdonald's Christian theology) humanity's fall from grace and subsequent redemption.

Macdonald, many of whose other novels are realistic, saw human experience as a battleground between good and evil. He incorporated sermons into the speech of his characters, some of whom are actual preachers, such as Reverend Walton in the realistic *Annals of a Quiet Neighborhood* (1866) and *The Seaboard Parish* (1868), and some of whom are symbolic, such as the raven, who, when asked the way home by the title character in *Lilith,* answers, "There are . . . many ways. . . . Home is ever so far away in the palm of your hand, and how to get there it is of no use to tell you. But you will get there." The raven presents Macdonald's own view of salvation as the result of God's grace rather than of human endeavor.

In 1898 Macdonald suffered a stroke, lapsing into silence. His death followed his wife Louisa's by three years. The year after Macdonald's death, the author Joseph Johnson wrote, "The essential religiousness of all Mac[d]onald's work distinguishes him from other contemporary novelists. His stories, no less than his sermons, have been, like the oracles of the Prophets of old, burdened with the message of truth."

Other Work by George Macdonald

The Complete Fairy Tales. New York: Viking Penguin, 1999.

Works about George Macdonald

Hein, Rolland. *The Harmony Within: The Spiritual Vision of George Macdonald.* Chicago: Cornerstone Press, 1999.

Raeper, William, ed. *The Gold Thread: Essays on George MacDonald.* Edinburgh University Press, 1990.

Triggs, Kathy. *The Stars and the Stillness: A Portrait of George MacDonald.* Cambridge, England: Lutterworth Press, 2001.

Mackay, Mary
See Corelli, Marie.

Macleod, Fiona
See Sharp, William.

Maginn, William (1793–1842) *poet, journalist*

William Maginn was born in Ireland. The son of a schoolmaster, he graduated from Trinity College, Dublin, at age 14. While attending college, he wrote a poem titled *Eneas Eunuchus*. After college Maginn went back to Cork, where he helped his father run a school. When his father died in 1813, Maginn took over the school himself and ran it for 10 years, while writing articles for *Blackwood's* literary magazine under the pen name R. T. Scott. In 1823 Maginn sold his school and married Ellen Cullen. The couple moved to London, where Maginn began writing poetry for the *Literary Gazette* under the pen name Ensign Morgan O'Doherty, and where his circle of acquaintance included Letitia Landon and William Makepeace Thackeray. Thackeray is said to have been thinking of Maginn when he created the character of Captain Shandon in *Pendennis*. In 1830, Maginn and Hugh Fraser founded *Fraser's Magazine,* which Maginn edited until 1836. The magazine, modeled on *Blackwood's,* published contemporary fiction, literary criticism, and political commentary. Maginn wrote humorous sketches of such famous authors as SIR WALTER SCOTT and THOMAS CARLYLE in his *Gallery of Literary Characters,* which he published in *Fraser's.* Maginn also wrote satiric short stories, such as his widely read "Bob Burke's Duel with Ensign Brady" (1834), and historical novels, including *Stories of Waterloo.*

Maitland, Caroline
See RADFORD, DOLLIE.

Malet, Lucas (Mary St. Leger Kingsley Harrison) (1852–1931) *novelist*

Lucas Malet was born Mary St. Leger Kingsley in Eversley, Hampshire, England. Her father, CHARLES KINGSLEY, was a prominent Anglican minister and writer. (Her cousin MARY HENRIETTA KINGSLEY was also a writer.) Although his daughter studied at the Slade School of Fine Art, Charles Kingsley discouraged her pursuit of a writing career. Instead, he insisted that she marry his former curate, William Harrison, in 1876; the couple had no children.

The marriage was not a happy one, and Kingsley turned increasingly to writing to assuage her unhappiness, as well as to supplement her husband's small salary. To conceal any connection to her well-known father, she assumed the pseudonym Lucas Malet, derived from her grandmother's maiden name and her great-aunt's surname.

Malet's novels describe illicit sexual relations, extreme emotional cruelty, misogyny, and physical deformities, through which Malet exposes the hypocrisies she believed infected the middle class.

Malet's first novel, *Mrs. Lorimer, a Sketch in Black and White* (1882), is loosely autobiographical. The title character escapes her unhappy marriage but later regrets her actions and serves at a charitable institution, where she eventually dies of disease.

Malet received considerable critical recognition for the novel. But much of this praise was retracted after the publication of her next popular novel. *The Wages of Sin: A Novel* (1891) describes the painter Colthurst who initiates an affair with his model, Jenny. The two have an illegitimate child, and Colthurst eventually marries a wealthy, virtuous woman who, through her charitable work, fatefully helps the now consumptive Jenny. The novel was widely read, but many critics condemned the explicit portrayal of Colthurst's relationship with Jenny.

In her most controversial novel, *The History of Sir Richard Calmady: A Romance,* published in 1901, the grossly deformed title character is engaged to an unsuspecting young woman from another noble family, but when she learns of his deformity, she elopes with another man, publicly humiliating Richard. In response, Calmady undertakes a debauched, sexual trip across Europe, but he eventually marries his cousin, Honoria Quentin. Although Malet received letters of gratitude for her sympathetic portrayal of Richard, many critics claimed the novel was grotesque and depraved.

Malet's conversion to Roman Catholicism and her explicit stories steadily eroded her popularity. After her death she was commemorated primarily for her early novels, their carefully developed plots, and her vivid portrayal of late-Victorian society. As the critic Talia Schaffer notes, Malet "was comparable to . . . the other groundbreaking novelists of the turn of the century, but the critics who admired their daring subjects and experimental styles condemned Malet for the same techniques."

Works about Lucas Malet
Schaffer, Talia. *The Forgotten Female Aesthetes.* Charlottesville: University Press of Virginia, 2000.

Schaffer, Talia, and Kathy Alexis Psomiades, eds. *Women and British Aestheticism.* Charlottesville: University Press of Virginia, 1999.

Mallock, William Hurrell (1849–1923)
novelist, nonfiction writer

William Hurrell Mallock was born in Devon, England, to William Mallock, an aristocratic cleric, and Margaret Froude, the daughter of a priest; he was a cousin of the historian J. A. FROUDE. Privately tutored, Mallock grew up sheltered from a world whose scientific, social, and religious tumult he did not discover until he was at Balliol College, Oxford, in the 1860s. His exposure to agnostic instructors and fellow students, however, only served to clarify and fortify his conservative Christian beliefs.

In philosophical nonfiction, Mallock defended Christianity and capitalism while attacking socialism and all other liberal thinking. A major work is his massive *Aristocracy and Evolution* (1898), where, discussing "great men," he praises their accumulation of wealth and the political power this brings them.

Mallock is better known today, however, for two satirical novels. The first, *The New Republic* (1877), is a "conversation novel" in the manner of THOMAS LOVE PEACOCK; party guests, over a few days, discuss religion, social issues, and politics, and try to come up with a blueprint for an ideal society. These characters are based on actual luminaries. In Mr. Rose, for instance, Mallock parodies the essayist WALTER PATER, who wrote approvingly of the idea of art for art's sake. Thus, says Mr. Rose, "[T]here is amongst us a growing number who ... have thrown their whole souls and sympathies into the happier art-ages of the past.... To such men the clamour, the interests, the struggles of our own times, become as meaningless as they really are.... [W]ith a steady and set purpose [they] follow art for the sake of art, beauty for the sake of beauty." Among the guests are parodies also of the poet and social critic MATTHEW ARNOLD and the scientific ethicist THOMAS HENRY HUXLEY. Each of the disguised intellectual leaders, critic Jerome Hamilton Buckley has written, at some point "voice[s] his own earnest credo and in so doing inadvertently betray[s] the folly of his conviction."

Mallock's other satire, *The New Paul and Virginia* (1878), shipwrecks the title characters. The impossibly comfortable island they are washed up on, Robert Lee Wolff has remarked, "put Mallock in a splendid position to assault those who elevated the idea of personal human happiness to the level of a religious tenet." Thus the novel took aim at positivism, a belief system whose highest value is humanity's social progress, rather than faith and morality. Paul, a positivist, ends up miserable in his utopian existence. "To those infatuated with the material and ethical 'progress' of the 19th century," the critic John D. Margolis has written, "the book seemed reactionary and even impious."

It is ironic that an important part of Mallock's legacy is the voice he gave to those of uncertain faith. Mallock's novels, Wolff has noted, "are absorbingly interesting as illustrating the ways in which fiction can be made to reflect the varieties of doubt."

Malthus, Thomas (1766–1834) *political economist*

Thomas Malthus was born into a well-to-do and liberal-thinking family at the family estate near Dorking, in Surrey, in southern England. His father, Daniel, read widely in both contemporary and Continental literature and educated Malthus until he entered Cambridge University. After graduating, Malthus became curate of Albury, in Surrey. In 1805 he was appointed to the post of professor of history and political economy at a college in Haileybury.

His most famous work, and the one that gave to the world the term *Malthusian*, appeared anonymously in 1798 as *An Essay on the Principle of Population as it affects the Future Improvement of Society.* In this work, and in five subsequent and enlarged editions, Malthus argued that an increase in human population would ultimately exceed food supply because sources of food would increase only arithmetically, but population would increase geometrically—that is, at an ever compounding rate. Malthus further argued that only war, famine, pestilence, and the like would postpone the inevitable generalized suffering of overpopulation. Malthus considered overpopulation to be a problem mainly for the lower classes. Consequently, he directs his advice to alleviate misery by marrying late and having fewer children only to the poor. He also objected to government policies, notably the Poor Law, which provided more relief for larger families because, in his view, such relief simply encouraged too many births.

After reading Malthus, CHARLES DARWIN developed the idea of natural selection, which he was careful to apply to nature, not human society. Others did not respond to Malthus so kindly. CHARLES DICKENS's impassioned defense of the poor throughout his fiction may be said to have been inspired by his detestation of Malthus's views. As the biographer and novelist Peter Ackroyd notes, Dickens's character Trotty Veck from the short novel *The Chimes,* who is said to have "no right to exist in the world at all," is a bitter response to Malthus's claim that a poor man "has no business to be where he is. At nature's mighty feast there is no vacant cover for him. She tells him to be gone...." More recently, the noted economist J. K. Galbraith criticized Malthus's point of view as follows: "But among the many who sought to put the poverty of the poor on the shoulders of the poor—or remove it from those of the more affluent—none did so more completely than Malthus."

Works about Thomas Malthus

James, Patricia D. *Population Malthus, His Life and Times.* Boston: Routledge & Kegan Paul, 1979.

Peterson, William. *Malthus: The Founder of Modern Demography.* Edison, N.J.: Transaction Publishers, 1998.

Winch, Donald. *Malthus.* New York: Oxford University Press, 1987.

Mangan, James Clarence (1803–1849)
poet

The great Irish poet James Mangan was born on the colorfully named Fishamble Street in Dublin, Ireland, on May 1, 1803. Mangan was the second child of James Mangan, a grocer, and his wife Catherine Smith. The boy was educated at a Jesuit school in Dublin, but when Mangan's father declared bankruptcy, the 15-year-old had to go to work to support the family.

Mangan worked for seven years as a scrivener (or copyist) in a law office in Dublin. During this time he befriended poet James Tighe. They both wrote riddles and puzzle poems for two Dublin publications, *Grant's Almanac* and the *New Ladies' Almanac.* It was not long before Mangan began writing patriotic poetry; his first such poem, "To My Native Land," was published in 1818 in the *New Ladies' Almanac.* At the time, Ireland was completely dominated by the British, who tried to suppress Catholicism, Irish culture, and the Irish language, Gaelic.

Mangan suffered from severe mood swings and eventually became addicted to opium and alcohol; he also had a morbid fear that he would lose his sanity. In an unfinished autobiography, Mangan claimed to be a completely friendless person. This was not entirely true, but his addictions and other mental problems put a strain on many of his relationships.

In 1826, Mangan took a new position in a solicitor's (attorney's) office, where he was ridiculed by his coworkers because of his odd clothes and behavior. Mangan wore a blonde wig, a witch's conical hat, green goggles, and a long cloak, at a time when cloaks were out of fashion.

Mangan's involvement in the Irish Nationalist movement began about 1830. He joined the Comet Club (which was opposed to tithing—a requirement by the Church of England that everyone pay a portion of their income to the church) at about the same time and contributed poetry to that organization's journal, *The Comet.*

During his lifetime, Mangan published many poems that purported to be translations, primarily from the German, but also from Gaelic, Turkish, Persian, Arabic, and several other languages Mangan did not know. Often he worked from prose translations, but it is now clear that many of his translations were, in fact, original poems that were merely inspired by the originals. Many critics consider Mangan's translations to be much better than the originals from which he worked.

In the late 1830s Mangan began to read poetry written in Gaelic, and published his first translation from the Irish in the *Irish Penny Journal* in 1840. By this time, Mangan appeared worn out and prematurely old because of his drinking. From 1842 to 1846 Mangan worked in the Trinity College Library. A patron described Mangan's odd appearance at the time:

> [His] was an unearthly and ghostly figure in a brown garment (to all appearance) which lasted till the day of his death. The blanched hair was totally unkempt; the corpse-like features still as marble; a large book was in his arms, and all his soul was in the book.

Beginning in 1846, during the height of the Irish potato famine—a period during which a fungus destroyed almost the entire potato crop in Ireland—Mangan became more committed to the cause of Irish nationalism. As the potato was the primary food of most of the Irish people, the famine lead to widespread starvation. A million people died and another million emigrated, reducing the population of Ireland by 25 percent. Much of Mangan's most forceful patriotic poetry, such as "Dark Rosaleen," "A Vision of Connaught in the Thirteenth Century," and "A Warning Voice," was written after 1846 and published in *The Nation*.

Mangan's health declined as his drinking increased. Critic John Mitchel, who wrote the introduction to Mangan's collected poems, has said that at the time there were two Mangans: "one well known to the Muses, the other to the police; one soared through the empyrean [heavens] and sought the stars—the other lay too often in the gutters of Peter Street and Bride Street."

In June 1848 Mangan, after having discharged himself from the hospital, fell into the newly dug foundation of a house and was badly injured. The next year, Mangan, ill and debilitated, caught cholera during an epidemic that ravaged Dublin. Mangan died there on June 20, 1849. Doctors diagnosed the cause of his death not as cholera but as the result of long-term malnutrition.

Mangan suffered the fate of many Irish poets who did not publish in England; he was virtually unknown for many years. He is today regarded as one of Ireland's major poets.

Critical Analysis

Mangan's poetry is both of its time and timeless. He wrote some of the best Irish patriotic poetry of his day, prefiguring Yeats, and crying out against British rule and the destruction of Irish culture. James Joyce celebrated Mangan as a particularly Irish poet, in that "all his poetry remembers wrong and suffering and the aspiration of one who has suffered."

One of Mangan's most famous patriotic poems is "Dark Rosaleen." Although the poem reads at first like a love poem: "O my Dark Rosaleen / Do not sigh, do not weep," it quickly becomes clear that Rosaleen is Ireland, desperate to be saved from British domination:

> O! the Erne [an Irish river] shall run red
>   With redundance of blood,
> The earth shall rock beneath our tread
>   And flames warp hill and wood,
> And gun-peal and slogan cry
>   Wake many a glen serene,
> Ere you shall fade, ere you shall die,
>   My Dark Rosaleen!
>   My own Rosaleen!
> The Judgement Hour must first be nigh,
> Ere you can fade, ere you can die,
>   My Dark Rosaleen!

A characteristic of Mangan's poetry, the use of repetition to create an almost hypnotic effect, can be seen in "Dark Rosaleen."

In another patriotic poem in which Ireland is represented by a woman, "Kathaleen Ny-Houlahan," Mangan looks to Ireland's glorious past, which he contrasts with its diminished present:

> . . . the nobles of our land—
> Long they wander to and fro, proscribed, alas!
>   and banned;
> Feastless, houseless, altarless, they bear the
>   exile's brand.
> But their hope is in the coming-to of
>   Kathaleen Ny-Houlahan.

Another of Mangan's best-known poems, "Siberia," says nothing overt about Ireland at all but portrays metaphorically the plight of Ireland under British rule.

> In Siberia's wastes
>   No tears are shed,
> For they freeze within the brain,
> Nought is felt but dullest pain,
>   Pain acute, yet dead.

Mangan was not merely a patriotic poet. He was also a late romantic who foreshadowed the French *poètes maudite* [accursed poets], such as Charles Baudelaire and Artur Rimbaud—who rejected social norms and often abused drugs and alcohol in search of profound emotional experiences. In "Twenty Golden Years Ago," Mangan cries out against growing old and the "dying of the light"

> Wifeless, friendless, flagonless, alone . . .
> Left with nought to do, except to groan,
> Not a soul to woo, except the Muse—
> O! this, this is hard for me to bear,
> Me, who whilom [in the past] lived so
>   much en haut [in high society],
> Me, who broke all hearts like chinaware
> Twenty golden years ago!

In his fascination with extreme emotional states and death, Mangan is very like his contemporary, Edgar Allan Poe. In one of his most important poems, "The Nameless One," Mangan describes himself as the tortured poet. He says:

> . . . tell how trampled, derided, hated,
>   And worn by weakness, disease, and wrong,
> [The Nameless one] fled for shelter to God,
>   who mated
> His soul with song.

Mangan is also noted for his humor, self-deprecation, and wordplay. Some of his work has even been compared to that of the British comic poet EDWARD LEAR. This is from "Pathetic Hypothetics":

> Even moles . . . are gregarious,
> And cats, when they turn caterwalers;
> Et moi [and me], I like various contrarious
> Assemblies—both punchdrinking brawlers
> And sighers of sighs—both your grinners and
>   grumblers.

A poem that combines many of Mangan's talents is "A Voice of Encouragement—A New Year's Lay," which presents a vivid depiction of the Irish famine. It was written in 1848, just one year before his death. Throughout his career, Mangan experimented with various verse forms, and this poem uses an unusually long line that is crafted to sound like keening, the wail of Irish women mourning, a fitting tribute to the thousands of Irish men and women who died of starvation:

> Friends! The gloom in our land, in our once
>   bright land grows deeper.
> Suffering, even to death, in its horriblest
>   forms, aboundeth;
> Thro' our black harvestless fields, the peasants'
>   faint wail resoundeth.
> Hark to it even now! . . . The nightmare
>   oppressed sleeper
> Gasping and struggling for life, beneath his
>   hideous bestrider,

> *Seeth not, dreeth [dreads] not, sight or terror*
> *   more fearful or ghastly*
> *Than that poor paralysed slave! Want,*
> *   Houslessnesses, Famine, and lastly*
> *Death in a thousand-corpsed grave, that*
> *   momently*
> *   waxeth wider.*

It was only in the 20th century that Mangan's talents have been fully recognized, and many critics see him as modern in his use of language, in his experimentation with poetic form, and in his self-mythologizing—the transformation of the real James Clarence Mangan into the fictional, epic figure of The Poet.

Other Works by James Clarence Mangan

The Collected Works of James Clarence Managan: Poems: 1848–1912. Edited by Rudolph Patrick Holzapfel et al. Dublin: Irish Academic Press, 1997.

The Collected Works of James Clarence Managan: Prose: 1832–1882. Edited by Jacques Chuto et al. Dublin: Irish Academic Press, 2002.

James Clarence Mangan: Selected Writings. Edited by Sean Rider. Dublin: University College Dublin Press, 2004.

Works about James Clarence Mangan

Lloyd, David. *Nationalism and Minor Literature: James Clarence Mangan and the Emergence of Irish Cultural Nationalism.* Berkeley: University of California Press, 1987.

MacCarthy, Anne. *James Clarence Mangan, Edward Walsh, and Nineteenth-Century Irish Literature in English.* Ceredigion, Wales: Edwin Mellen Press, 2000.

Shannon-Managan, Ellen. *James Clarence Mangan: A Biography.* Dublin: Irish Academic Press, 2007.

Marryat, Florence (1838–1899) *novelist*

The daughter of the novelist FREDERICK MARRYAT and his wife Catherine, Florence Marryat followed in her father's footsteps to become a successful author in her own right. Her first novel, *Temper,* was published when she was only 22.

Born in Brighton, on the south coast of England, Marryat was educated at home. She married a soldier, Colonel T. Ross Church, at age 16, and traveled with him to India. The marriage produced eight children, and her time in India inspired several novels, including *"Gup": Sketches of Anglo-Indian Life and Character* (1868).

In 1865 Marryat had her first success with *Love's Conflict,* a novel she wrote while nursing her children through scarlet fever. It is the story of a young wife married to an unbearable older husband.

Marryat was labeled a SENSATION FICTION writer because many of her 90 novels contained plots of steamy romance, sexuality, and family secrets in the manner of such sensation novelists as ELLEN WOOD and MARY ELIZABETH BRADDON. Though criticized for her racy stories, she nonetheless rose to become one of Victorian England's most successful novelists. Some of her more popular titles include *Too Good for Him* (1865), in which a virtuous woman struggles against a dissolute husband; *Petronel* (1870), about a beautiful young woman who falls in love with her older guardian; and *The Nobler Sex* (1892), a disturbing novel of marital abuse and the economic oppression of women.

Marryat was also fascinated with spiritualism and often incorporated it into her writings. *There Is No Death* contains interviews with mediums and accounts of seances. Capitalizing on the popularity of BRAM STOKER's *Dracula* (1895), she also wrote a vampire novel, *Blood of the Vampire* (1897), featuring a sympathetic vampire distraught at having to kill her lovers.

To call Marryat simply a novelist would be underrating her; she was also a successful playwright, public speaker, and biographer. In 1872 she published her father's correspondence in the two-volume book *Life and Letters of Captain Marryat.* She also served as editor of *London Society,* a monthly magazine, between 1872 and 1876. A profile by the Victorian journalist Helen Black illustrates the high reputation of the Marryats in late-Victorian England: "Born of such a gifted father, it is small wonder that the child should have inherited brilliant talents."

A Work about Florence Marryat

Black, Helen C. *Notable Women Authors of the Day.* Glasgow: David Bryce and Son, 1893.

Marryat, Frederick (1792–1848) *novelist*

Frederick Marryat was born in London. He was the second son of Joseph Marryat, a member of Parliament, and his wife, Charlotte Geyer Marryat. As a youth, Marryat made three attempts to run away to sea, but each time was caught and returned home. Finally, at 14, he joined the Royal Navy and, with the rank of midshipman, was assigned to HMS *Impérieuse*, a frigate under the command of Captain Lord Cochrane, earl of Dundonald, who would later appear in fictionalized form as Captain Savage in Marryat's novel *Peter Simple*.

During his career in the navy, Marryat served in the East Indies, the Mediterranean, and along the entire east coast of America, taking part in numerous actions against French and American vessels. He received many honors, including the Royal Humane Society's Gold Medal for saving a life at sea, and at 23 he was promoted to commander. In the peaceful years after the end of the Napoleonic Wars, he began writing as a way to conquer boredom.

Marryat's first novel was *The Naval Officer; or, Scenes and Adventures in the Life of Frank Mildmay* (1829). The plot draws on Marryat's life, depicting, for example, the battle of Trafalgar, and was influenced by the realistic maritime fictions of Daniel Defoe and Tobias Smollett. Marryat earned enough from sales of this work to allow him to resign from the navy in November 1830 to concentrate more fully on writing.

His next novel, *The King's Own* (1830), was followed by a string of other works, including *Newton Forster* (1832) and *Jacob Faithful* (1834). All three of these novels repeat the formula Marryat had established with his first work: focusing on the life of a British sailor, including vivid descriptions of life at sea, and presenting a colorful cast of supporting characters.

Peter Simple (1834), Marryat's first commercial success, tells the story of a British naval officer. It draws on Marryat's experiences at sea, speaking in the peculiar language of sailors: "We made the private signal, which was unanswered, and we cleared for action; the brig making sail on the starboard tack, and we following her—she bearing about two miles on our weather bow."

After he visited the United States in the 1830s, Marryat published a nonfiction work, *Diary in America* (1839), which presented his unfavorable impressions of the country. Before returning to England, Marryat sold the book's American copyright for about $3,000.

In 1841 Marryat published the first of his books for children, *Masterman Ready*. The story is similar to Johann Wyss's *The Swiss Family Robinson*, but in Marryat's novel there is less romanticism and more cold reality as the marooned Seagrave family and their old sailor friend, Masterman Ready, face hostile savages and other perils of a deserted island. Although moral lessons intrude on the action, *Masterman Ready* remained one of the most popular adventure stories for children for many years. *The Settlers in Canada* (1844), another children's book, records the adventures of an English family, the Campbells on the Canadian frontier. *The Children of the New Forest* (1847), another successful book for children, is set in the 17th century during the English Civil War. The book centered on a group of Royalist children hiding and living off the land in the forest. Marryat's treatment of history is unabashedly Royalist at a time when much of Europe was being threatened with revolution, while his attack on 17th-century Parliamentarians indirectly points to their 19th-century successors, the Chartists: "The hatred of these people to anyone above them in rank or property, especially to those of the king's party, which mostly consisted of men of rank and property, was unbounded, and they were merciless and cruel to the highest degree."

In 1848 Marryat's eldest son, Frederick, drowned at sea, and this tragic loss hastened Marryat's own death. His daughter FLORENCE MARRYAT went on to become a successful novelist in her own right, and wrote her father's biography. One of Marryat's greatest champions in the 20th century was the eminent Victorianist Michael Sadleir (1888–1957): "Marryat loved children and knew how to tell stories that they could like and understand. This to-day is undisputed. But that he is equally a novelist for the critical sorely needs reaffirmation."

Other Work by Frederick Marryat

Mr. Midshipman Easy. New York: Henry Holt, 1998.

A Work about Frederick Marryat

Sadleir, Michael. *Excursions in Victorian Bibliography.* London: Chaundy and Cox, 1922.

Marston, Philip Bourke (1850–1887) poet

Philip Marston was born in London to John Westland Marston, a well-known playwright and poet, and Eleanor Potts Marston. He became almost completely blind from scarlet fever at age three and consequently never learned to read. Educated at home by his parents, Marston began to write by dictating to his mother. By the time he was 14 he had composed three volumes of a novel and a book of poems. In 1871 when Marston was 21, the woman he planned to marry, Mary Nesbit, died of tuberculosis. Then, in the late 1870s, he lost both of his sisters within a year of each other.

The losses Marston suffered seem to be reflected in the heaviness and sadness of much of his work. There is a characteristic melancholy even in the love poems. His first collection, *Song-Tide and Other Poems* (1871), expresses his devotion to his fiancée, who died the year it came out. It was followed by *All In All* (1874) and *Wind Voices* (1883). An atheist and skeptic, Marston called his somewhat dark short stories "prose bitters," after the bitter alcoholic drink. After his death at age 37 from a paralytic stroke, some of his stories were collected in a book titled *For a Song's Sake and Other Stories* (1887).

Martin, Sir Theodore (1816–1909)
translator, satirist, biographer

Theodore Martin was born in Edinburgh on September 16, 1816, to a large family that included nine sisters. His father, James, was a successful solicitor. Martin developed an interest in literature while attending Edinburgh University, graduating in 1833. He began practicing law in Edinburgh.

Martin's literary activities began in Edinburgh, however. He edited the *Dramatic Review* with W. H. Logan, contributed to the *Carlton Chronicle* and *Tait's Edinburgh Magazine,* and translated work by François Rabelais. Some of this material was satirical, especially poems written under the pseudonym Bon Gaultier. From 1842 to 1844 he collaborated with W. E. Aytoun on other satires; the poems written as Bon Gaultier were collected in 1845 in *Bon Gaultier's Ballads.*

After moving to London in 1846, Martin began a long and distinguished career as a parliamentary solicitor, shepherding private bills through parliamentary committees and heading the firm of Martin and Leslie. In 1851 Martin married Helen Faucit, an actress for whom he had developed a fascination. His literary output as well as his reputation increased after this. He wrote essays on theater and published translations from German, Italian, and Latin, including work by Horace, Catullus, and Dante. Martin was particularly interested in German poetry, publishing Goethe's *Prometheus* in 1850, the *First Part of 'Faust'* in 1865, and *Second Part* in 1886. In the late 1870s and 1880s, he also translated poems from Heinrich Heine and Friedrich Schiller.

Martin began the work he is best known for in 1866, when QUEEN VICTORIA engaged him to continue *The Life of His Royal Highness the Prince Consort,* a biography of her late husband Prince Albert begun by her private secretary. Martin worked closely with the Queen on the biography, published in five volumes through 1880, when he was knighted. Other biographies of the Lord Chancellor John Singleton Copley (Lord Lyndhurst) and Martin's wife followed in 1883 and 1900, respectively; Helen had died in 1898.

Martin continued to write, primarily articles for magazines and reminiscences of the Queen (*Queen Victoria as I Knew Her,* 1902) that he circulated among his friends, until he died in his country home at Bryntysilio, North Wales, on August 18, 1909.

Martineau, Harriet (1802–1876) *novelist, nonfiction writer*

Harriet Martineau was born in Norwich, England, to a textile manufacturer, Thomas Martineau, and his wife, Elizabeth Martineau. Martineau was essentially self-educated, reading the works of John Milton and William Shakespeare at an early age. At age 12, Harriet acquired a progressive disorder that eventually left her completely deaf.

Martineau's writing career began when her family was financially ruined, and she began writing articles for religious publications, such as the Unitarian periodical the *Monthly Repository.* Although Elizabeth Martineau much preferred to see her daughter at needlework, Martineau finally decided on a career as a writer in 1830, after she won three essay prizes from the *Repository.* In 1832 her *Illustrations of Political Economy* was published. In this series of didactic works, which initially appeared in 24 monthly installments, Martineau demonstrated the workings of basic principles of political and economic philosophy, such as THOMAS MALTHUS's theory of population and JEREMY BENTHAM's greatest happiness principle. She did not aim to originate ideas but to make the ideas of others accessible for the general public. The series appealed to a wide range of readers, from European monarchs and wealthy members of the Parliament to factory workers in England. The series became progressively more populist—too populist for the liking of some European rulers—and Martineau's work was banned in Austria and Russia. (The emperors of both countries found her ideas too dangerous.) Some critics in her own country also reacted negatively. John Wilson Croker, reviewing the installment titled "Weal and Woe in Garvelach," which raised the issue of the benefits of birth control, in the *Quarterly Review,* fulminated against Martineau's "unfeminine and mischievous doctrines on the principles of social welfare.... A woman who thinks child-bearing a *crime against society!* An unmarried woman who declaims against marriage!" Regardless of these reactions, Martineau's reputation as a writer was firmly established, and she finally achieved financial independence.

Between 1836 and 1839 Martineau traveled throughout America, publicly supporting the abolitionist cause to end slavery. In 1837 she published some observations of her trip as *Society in America.* In this work, Martineau scrutinizes the political institutions, economics, and social life in America with respect to the egalitarian principles on which the United States was based, and finds them wanting, especially concerning the status of women. She also provides a candid treatment of the American agricultural system, illuminating the injustices of slavery. The following year, Martineau published *Retrospect of Western Travel* (1838), in which she recounts her personal experiences during the travels throughout America. Both works were widely read and generally received positive reviews.

Critical Analysis

In 1838 Martineau demonstrated her versatility as a writer by publishing the novel *Deerbrook.* The story revolves around Edward Hope, a young doctor; his wife, Hester Ibbotson; and Hester's sister Margaret, with whom Edward is in love. The chain of unrequited love pervades the small village where the action takes place; the denouement resolves problems and finds partnerships for all except the lonely governess.

Martineau's *The Hour and the Man* (1841) is often considered to be her best work of fiction. The novel describes the struggles of Toussaint Louverture (ca. 1744–1803), the Haitian popular hero and revolutionary leader who fought against French colonial rule. Although the novel does not examine the idea of colonialism per se, it vividly describes the horrors and injustices of slavery. Martineau was probably among the first European writers whose central character is not only black, but who also is portrayed positively and heroically. The novel was seen as radical, and was not fully appreciated during Martineau's lifetime.

Between 1839 and 1844 Martineau experienced serious illness, and recounted her suffering in *Life in the Sickroom* (1844). Martineau eventually recovered and was able to travel to Egypt in 1846. She published the accounts of her travels in *Eastern Life, Past and Present* (1848). In a buoyant and spirited style, Martineau describes the vicissitudes of her travels through the exotic lands. Unlike most travel writers of the period, Martineau does not seem to judge the various cultures she encounters, but instead objectively observes various national and cultural customs.

Martineau began working on an extensive autobiography that was published posthumously in 1877. In 1869 she also produced *Biographical Sketches*, in which she recounted her experiences with the famous people that she had met during her lifetime.

By her death in 1877, Harriet Martineau had established herself as a figure of considerable stature in the Victorian literary and political worlds. In her autobiography she recounts her life as "a somewhat remarkable one." In the words of the scholar R. Brimley Johnson, Martineau's "genuine humanity and real moral earnestness give a value to her more personal utterances, which do not lose their charm with the lapse of time."

Works about Harriet Martineau

David, Deirdre. *Intellectual Women and Victorian Patriarchy.* Ithaca, N.Y.: Cornell University Press, 1987.

Logan, Deborah Anna. *The Hour and the Woman: Harriet Martineau's "Somewhat Remarkable" Life.* DeKalb: Northern Illinois University Press, 2002.

Thomas, Gillian. *Harriet Martineau.* Boston: Twayne, 1985.

Marx, Eleanor (1855–1898) *nonfiction writer*

Eleanor Marx was born in London, the daughter of the communist philosopher KARL MARX and Jenny von Westphalen. In 1881 Eleanor Marx met Dr. Edward Aveling, a budding socialist and the editor of *Progress,* a secularist monthly magazine, and when her father died in 1884, Marx entered into a free-love union with the freethinker Aveling. Along with the poet WILLIAM MORRIS and encouraged by Karl Marx's close associate FRIEDRICH ENGELS, the couple in 1885 formed the Socialist League, which declared its mission "revolutionary international socialism." However, the organization's effectiveness was hampered by leftist factiousness. In 1886 Marx became active in the Women's Trade Union League. When Marx discovered that Aveling, to whom she was devoted, had in fact legally married someone else, she committed suicide.

Marx wrote articles on her own, but those written with Aveling are the most widely read. From an 1886 tour of the United States came Marx and Aveling's comprehensive survey *The Working-Class Movement in America* (1891). This work quotes actual laborers whom the authors interviewed in each state, and profiles American labor leaders. The authors conclude that in the United States, the extremes "of poverty and wealth, of exploitation in its active and passive form, are more marked than in Europe." Certainly those they interviewed were eager to share with the authors their discontent as workers, as in this statement from an accountant: "Employers appear to be trying to ascertain how little a working man can subsist upon, rather than to determine what rate of wages will enable them to procure [workers'] wares at the lowest net cost." There is this from a farmer: "I was better off as a slave." From a labor leader the authors find that even the cowboy, an embodiment of American independence, was "as much at the mercy of the capitalist as a New or Old England cotton-operative," his "supposed 'freedom' no more of a reality" than any other American laborer's.

Much of Marx's legacy is as an abiding symbol of humane socialism. According to biographer Ronald Florence, she "believed in Marxism as more than an economic and historical theory. For her it was an ethic, a value system applicable without exception to every aspect of the human experience."

A Work about Eleanor Marx
Stokes, John. *Eleanor Marx, 1855–1898: Life, Work, Contacts.* Brookfield, Vt.: Ashgate, 2000.

Marx, Karl (1818–1883) *nonfiction writer*

Born into a middle-class Prussian family to Heinrich Marx (a lawyer who converted from Judaism to Lutheranism because of state laws limiting the affairs of Jews) and Henriette Presborck, Karl Marx was baptized at age six. He breezed through the requirements of his early education and at 17 was sent to the University of Bonn. He left Bonn for the University of Berlin to study law and philosophy. There he came under the influence of the philosophy of G. F. W. Hegel (1770–1831), who saw history as a "dialectic," or series of oppositions. However, Hegel placed this historical panorama against a mystical background that Marx, increasingly turning away from religion, found unsatisfactory. In his subsequent thinking he combined the dialectic of Hegel with the materialism of the contemporary philosopher Ludwig Feuerbach (1804–72) and "dialectical materialism" was born. In other words, Marx saw history as a process of conflict and resolution that led to new conflict. But while Hegel attributed historical progress to the mystical "geist" or spirit, Marx believed history was grounded on the economic structures of society, leading from primitive communism to feudalism to capitalism and eventually to a new communism.

After finishing his dissertation, in 1842 Marx began his career as an editorial writer and polemicist, contributing to a newly founded liberal paper in Cologne, the *Rheinische Zeitung*. He soon became its editor, and just as soon began offending the authorities with his trenchant criticism of the state and its ways. Within a year he had managed to offend even Czar Nicholas I of Russia, at whose request the paper was shut down.

The next several years marked further developments in Marx's thinking and writing. He had come to believe that the key to the development of future human societies lay in class conflict: One class would fight with another and the resulting synthesis would stabilize for a while until it in turn was attacked. The ultimate and final synthesis would be the triumph of the "proletariat" working class over the bourgeoisie, leading to a classless, communistic society. These ideas are enshrined in Marx's large body of work, the most famous of which is *The Communist Manifesto* (1848) and *Das Kapital* (1867). The former, bearing FRIEDRICH ENGELS's name on it as well as that of Marx, was actually written in Paris by Marx in a deadline-driven haste in 1848 to satisfy the demands of the London-based Communist League. In this work, which famously begins "A spectre is haunting Europe—the spectre of Communism," Marx states that the class struggle will end with the proletariat vanquishing the bourgeoisie, and he outlines what he believes will not work and what must be done to win the battle.

In 1849 Marx moved with his growing family to London, where he was to spend the rest of his life and where he was to write, over the next 34 years, his massive work on history and economics, *Das Kapital*. Although indebted in places to the early English economists Adam Smith and DAVID RICARDO, its inspiration was the frightening consequences of the Industrial Revolution: poverty, death, and disease. The concentration of economic resources (capital) in the hands of a few owners led to the virtual enslavement of the proletariat, who would have to wrest these resources, through whatever means possible, from the bourgeoisie.

Although Marx lived in Victorian London for the last part of his life, his influence on British writers was for the most part delayed until the 20th century, when his works became widely available in English and his ideas infamous because of the Russian Revolution of 1917. He had his disciples among the Victorians, however, most notably the poet WILLIAM MORRIS, who was involved with socialist organizations in Britain and wrote poetry and prose in illustration of his socialist ideals. By the end of the century, Marx's influence became more marked in the works of such writers as GEORGE BERNARD SHAW and GEORGE GISSING.

After World War II, a British school of Marxist literary criticism began to take shape in the north of England. These critics founded their analyses of literature on Marx's dictum in *Contribution to the Critique of Political Economy* (1859): "The totality of these relations of production constitutes the economic structure of society, the real foundation, on which arises a legal and political superstructure and to which correspond definite forms of social consciousness.... It is not the consciousness of men that determines their existence, but their social existence that determines their consciousness." In other words, marxist literary critics analyze the ways in which literary works are determined by, reflect, and distort the economic foundation of society. Among the most famous British Marxist critics are Raymond Williams (1921–88), E. P. Thompson (1924–93) and Terry Eagleton (1943–).

Works about Karl Marx

Blumenberg, Werner. *Karl Marx: An Illustrated History*. New York: Verso Press, 2000.

Skousen, Mark. *The Big Three in Economics: Adam Smith, Karl Marx, and John Maynard Keynes*. New York: M.E. Sharpe, 2007.

Wheen, Francis. *Karl Marx: A Life*. New York: W. W. Norton, 2001.

Maturin, Charles Robert (1780–1824)
novelist, dramatist

Charles Maturin was born in Dublin, Ireland. He graduated from Trinity College, Dublin, in 1800 and became a clergyman. Three years later, Maturin married Henrietta Kingsbury. In 1804 Maturin and his wife settled in Loughrea, Ireland, where he served as a curate, and later moved to Dublin, where he was curate at St. Peter's Church from 1805 until 1824. Meanwhile, Maturin was publishing novels under the pseudonym Dennis Jasper Murphy. In 1807 he published a Gothic thriller called *Fatal Revenge; or, The Family of Montorio*, followed by *The Wild Irish Boy* a year later. Maturin also wrote plays, and in 1816 his drama *Bertram* was produced by the well-known actor Edmund Kean. It became a hit in London. Maturin wrote additional plays, but none was very successful. He continued writing novels, including *Women* in 1818, which describes contemporary life in Ireland, and *Melmoth: The Wanderer* (1820), his most widely read work, about a man who has made a pact with the Devil.

A Work about Charles Robert Maturin

Bloom, Harold, ed. *Classic Horror Writers*. Philadelphia: Chelsea House, 1993.

Mayhew, Henry Philip (1812–1887)
journalist, sociologist, nonfiction writer

Henry Mayhew was born in London to Joshua Mayhew, a lawyer, and Mary Ann Fenn Mayhew. After leaving secondary school early and serving a stint as a naval midshipman, Mayhew turned to journalism and playwriting while still in his teens. Although widely respected for his literary work, especially his documentation of working-class life, Mayhew struggled financially and was deeply in debt when he died.

In 1841 Mayhew and MARK LEMON founded the influential British magazine *Punch,* a weekly filled with political and social satire highlighted by edgy drawings.

In 1849, during a devastating cholera epidemic, Mayhew began writing a series for the *Morning Chronicle* about conditions requiring sanitary reform in poor sections of London. In "A Visit to the Cholera Districts of Bermondsey," for example, Mayhew wrote, "[a]s we passed along the reeking banks . . . [a narrow slip of the water] appeared the colour of strong green tea . . . it was more like watery mud than muddy water; and yet we were assured this was the only water the wretched inhabitants had to drink." Mayhew also addressed the current political economy. The underpaid labor that unregulated industrialists required to maintain their competitive edge, Mayhew felt, is what created poverty, not the overpopulation cited by the weekly *Economist,* which attacked his articles on the subject as "lugubrious."

These pieces formed the basis for Mayhew's *London Labour and the London Poor,* the first three volumes of which appeared in 1851, the fourth in 1862. His interviews with all manner of lower-class people, according to WILLIAM MAKEPEACE THACKERAY, resulted in "a picture of human life" that is "wonderful," "awful," "piteous," "pathetic," "exciting and terrible." A street vendor of baked potatoes, for instance, seems overwhelmed by how hard it is for him to eke out an existence, yet speaks without rancor: "Such a day as this, sir . . . when the fog's like a cloud come down, people [wary of rotting potatoes] looks very shy at my taties . . . money goes one can't tell how, and, 'specially if you drinks a drop, as I do sometimes." A 16-year-old girl's account of what led to her life as a prostitute shows her to be the victim of a more direct cruelty in addition to circumstance: "I am an orphan. When I was 10 I was sent to service as maid. . . . [The wife of my employer] beat me with sticks as well as with hands. I was black and blue, and [after about six months] I ran away." In this massive work, unlike the *Morning Chronicle* articles, the critic Regenia Gagnier has noted, "Mayhew reported the effects of the environment upon the streetfolk without comment."

Mayhew's study of poverty was influential, in particular lending support to social and sanitary reformers, and eventually helping to found the modern science of sociology. In addition, there is his literary merit. Mayhew, the critic John D. Rosenberg has written, "edits, shapes, and intensifies, until we are stunned by the slang beauty and inventiveness of the spoken voices he recreates. . . . Mayhew should be credited with evolving a new art form, a kind of dramatic monologue in prose."

Other Work by Henry Mayhew
Thomas, Donald, ed. *The Victorian Underworld.* New York: New York University Press, 1998.

A Work about Henry Mayhew
Gagnier, Regenia. *Subjectivities: A History of Self-Representation in Britain, 1832–1920.* New York: Oxford University Press, 1991.

Meade, Lillie Thomasina (1844–1914)
novelist

Lillie Meade was born in Cork, Ireland, to the Reverend Richard Thomas Meade. As a child, Meade was educated at home by a governess, and she soon expressed a deep pleasure in storytelling, writing her first novel when she was 15. The London publishing firm Newby guaranteed its publication if Meade could sell 40 copies in advance. She sold 70, and *Ashton Morton,* a story that traces the title character's life from adolescence through old age, was published in 1866. The novel's intelligent, spirited, and affectionate heroine serves as the prototype for many of her later characters.

Meade's father discouraged her writing because he believed that the family's social standing would be damaged if the female members worked and earned money. Therefore, in the early 1870s, Meade moved to London to write and to escape her father's disapproval. Over the next 40 years, she wrote nearly 220 novels.

Initially, her novels portrayed the brutal social conditions of the London poor. Her novel, *Great St. Benedict's* (1876), depicts a hospital established for families who cannot afford private care and where the impoverished patients are either ignored or poorly treated, while the hospital's staff admits middle-class patients who pay bribes for their treatment.

Meade's concern for social issues gradually focused on poor children. Novels such as *The Children's Kingdom* (1878) trace the harmful effects upon children when they move from rural England into the sordid slums of London, but Meade offers hope for her young characters. These early novels emphasize the heavenly rewards children will receive if they maintain a commitment to Christian values.

Meade's fame, however, rests on her girls'-school stories. The most popular, *A World of Girls* (1886), establishes the basic pattern. The young heroine, Hester Thornton, is sent to a private school when her mother dies. There, Hester must choose between the friendship of an alluring, yet morally deficient, student or a quiet, yet honest, student. The school stories address social and emotional problems specific to young women and compel them to make moral decisions. Yet unlike Meade's earlier novels, the characters' decisions are based upon their personalities and values rather than on overt Christian compulsions.

Although some critics dismiss Meade's novels as sentimental and formulaic, she was one of the first novelists to present her stories through a young woman's viewpoint and to write stories intended for an adolescent audience. The critic J. S. Bratton notes that Meade "set up a new pattern of school stories, and also of heroines who are wild and willful."

A Work about Lillie Meade

Bratton, J. S. *The Impact of Victorian Children's Fiction.* Totowa, N.J.: Barnes & Noble, 1981.

Meredith, George (1828–1909) *poet, novelist*

George Meredith was born in Portsmouth, England, to Augustus Urmston Meredith, a tailor and a naval outfitter, and Jane McNammara. Augustus Meredith nourished an idea of social superiority, and young George was not allowed to associate with the children of the tradespeople in the neighborhood. George acquired a nickname of Gentleman George because of his aloofness, physical beauty, and unwillingness to play with the other children.

In 1842 Meredith left England for Germany, where for two years he was a student at a monastery school at Neuwied on the Rhine. The daily contact with the monks who ran the school seemed to soften Meredith's attitude toward life. Furthermore, the students were encouraged to take long hikes and to associate with the townspeople. Meredith's experience at Neuwied eliminated the pretentions of his former days.

In 1846 Meredith returned to England, where he studied with Richard Stephen Charnock for a career in the legal field. Charnock became a mentor to Meredith and introduced him into the artistic and literary circles of London. Meredith soon abandoned his study of law for a literary career and began contributing poems, articles, and translations to a small magazine that circulated in manuscript form in Charnock's circle. Meredith's poems also appeared in *Household Words,* a magazine edited by CHARLES DICKENS and other periodicals as well. In 1851 he published *Poems,* a collection of verse that celebrated nature. The collection received positive reviews but did not sell, and as Meredith paid publication costs himself, he was left in debt.

Meredith turned away from writing poetry for several years and decided to concentrate on prose. In 1855 he published *The Shaving of Shagpat: An*

Arabian Entertainment, an allegorical fantasy highly reminiscent of the *Arabian Nights.* The work was met with indifference by both the critics and the general public. In 1859 Meredith published *The Ordeal of Richard Feverel,* a largely autobiographical novel that remains among his best works. The critics of the day, however, were again unimpressed.

Meredith was able to earn a small income by writing poems for a new weekly magazine, *Once a Week,* and by reading manuscripts submitted to his publisher, Chapman & Hall. He made a number of literary discoveries and was among the first to recognize the talent of THOMAS HARDY.

Meredith's second novel, *Evan Harrington* (1860), is a conventional work about Rose Jocelyn, an independent and frank heroine.

In 1862 Meredith composed *Modern Love,* a poem that recounts a story of love and betrayal and that is one of his most admired works. This poem consists of 50 sections connected by a plot and a complex and intricate matrix of symbols. Each section revolves around a story of infidelity, as a wife betrays her husband with a lover, although it is not clear if the affair has been consummated. Out of revenge, the husband also takes a mistress. Society forces the married couple to put on a façade of marital bliss: "Enamoured of an acting nought can tire, / Each other, like true hypocrites, admire."

Despite the limited success of his previous novels, Meredith continued to write novels throughout the 1860s. He also earned the respect of his peers through critical and journalistic writing. In 1866 he was sent to Italy by the *Morning Post* as a special war correspondent. In 1877 George Meredith delivered a public lecture that later became his famous essay, "The Idea of Comedy and the Uses of Comic Spirit" (1897). The lecture explored such concepts as human progress, gender equality, and comedy in the context of writing fiction. For Meredith, "comedy is a game played to throw reflections upon social life, and it deals with human nature in the drawing-room of civilized men and women, where we have no dust of the struggling outer world, no mire, no violent crashes, to make the correctness of the representations convincing."

In 1879 Meredith published one of his finest novels, *The Egoist,* which revolves around the marital pursuits of Sir Willoughby Patterne, the egoist, as he, along with several other suitors, pursues the charming Miss Middleton. The novel contains ironic, humorous dialogue, as well as a poignant critique of Victorian marriage politics. It is also a study of excessive pride and self-delusion, which Meredith termed egoism and which for salvation must be eliminated and replaced with sanity. For the first time, a Meredith novel was highly acclaimed by the critics and received a wide general readership.

In 1883 Meredith published another volume of poetry, *Poems and Lyrics of the Joy of Earth,* which presented some earlier poems along with some new pieces. Some reviewers complained that Meredith's language and style made the verse obscure. The best of the poems skillfully employ nature imagery. Thus, in these lines from "A Ballad of Past Meridian" (1876), the poet hears a message of life and death in the song of two night birds:

> *Then memory, like the nightjar on the pine,*
> *And sightless hope, a woodlark in night sky,*
> *Joined notes of Death and Life till night's*
>   *decline:*
> *Of Death, of Life, those inwound notes are*
>   *mine.*

Among Meredith's noteworthy later works is his 1885 novel *Diana of the Crossways,* which tells the story of Diana Warwick's unhappy marriage. Diana was reportedly modeled on writer CAROLINE NORTON. Although the book's plot involves political scandal, the novel's main focus is on Diana's search for happiness and independence in a society that the book makes clear unfairly favors men above women.

Critical Analysis

As the scholar Lionel Stevenson observes, "Meredith was interested in motive and environment, in the elusive interplay of one personality upon another." In *The Ordeal of Richard Feverel*, the author finds that interplay between Sir Austin Feverel and his son Richard over the latter's love for a farmer's daughter, whom Sir Austin sees as a social inferior. Pride is the failing of both men.

The novel is both comic and tragic, satiric in its portrayal of Victorian society and heartbreaking in its doomed story of young love. Indeed, the ordeal that Richard endures has elements of both comedy and tragedy. Sir Austin is convinced that the physical and moral decay that he sees among the aristocratic families of his acquaintance can be corrected through sexual restraint, and it is sexual abstinence that he forces on his son.

But above all else, *Ordeal* shows Meredith's fascination with style. Descriptive passages are witty and rich in detail, often reading more like poetry than prose, as in this portrait of Sir Miles Papworth, Sir Austin's political enemy:

> He was a mature specimen of modern England's vaunted race. . . . Prosperous, pigheaded, and just in proportion: bald . . . , corpulent, hearty . . . : a domestic despot, a staunch subject, a fair-dealing father, a foe to innovation and ideas, a devoted worshipper of himself against the world.

Meredith could write in a more direct manner when appropriate. In the following passage, he captures the ominous feeling just before a major storm: "An oppressive slumber hung about the forest branches. In the dells and on the heights was the same dead heat. Here where the brook tinkled it was no cool-lipped sound, but metallic, and without the spirit of water." Equally realistic is Meredith's dialogue, which Stevenson notes "has much the brevity, simplicity, and fragmentary . . . [quality] of actual talk."

Exploring numerous conflicts between the sexes and generations, the psychology of sexual suspicion and suppression, *The Ordeal of Richard Feverel* deeply shocked its Victorian readers. The novel was banned from many lending libraries because of a seduction scene too risqué for Victorian sensibility.

On his 80th birthday Meredith was honored by many notable public figures, among them King Edward VII and President Theodore Roosevelt. Meredith was also awarded the Order of Merit for his contributions to literature. Although even today Meredith is known to scholars and readers of Victorian literature for only two of his 13 novels, *The Egoist* and *The Ordeal of Richard Fervel*, he remains a seminal figure in the history of English literature. As Virginia Woolf asserted in 1928, his novels "must inevitably rise from time to time into view; his work must inevitably be disputed and discussed."

Other Work by George Meredith
The Poems of George Meredith. New Haven, Conn.: Yale University Press, 1978.

Works about George Meredith
Muendel, Renate. *George Meredith*. Boston: Twayne, 1986.
Photiadis, Constantin. *George Meredith: His Life, Genius, and Teaching*. Honolulu: University Press of the Pacific, 2004.
Roberts, Neil. *Meredith and the Novel*. New York: St. Martin's Press, 1997.
Williams, M. Ioan. *Meredith: The Critical Heritage*. New York: Barnes & Noble, 1971.

Merriman, Henry Seton
See SCOTT, HUGH STOWELL.

Mew, Charlotte (1869–1928) *poet, short story writer*
A lifelong resident of London, Charlotte Mew was born to Frederick Mew, an architect, and Anna Kendall Mew. In 1879 Mew entered Gower Street School, where she emulated her literature teacher, Lucy Harrison, by adopting short hair, denoting female independence. By the early 1890s, Mew's brother and one sister had been institutionalized

for mental illness, causing Mew and her sister Anne to determine jointly that they would not marry, lest children of theirs become similarly ill. By 1898, the year her father died, Mew had fallen in love with a woman who did not reciprocate her feelings. A later affair, with the novelist May Sinclair, ended badly. With her mother's death in 1923 came the loss of the trust fund that had financially sustained Mew. Admirers of her work, including THOMAS HARDY, therefore arranged for Mew to receive a government pension. In 1927 Anne died. The next year, Mew committed suicide.

Mew began publishing in the 1890s. Her themes were drawn from her own life. Her poem "The Shade-Catchers" (1921), for instance, expresses her love of children—implicitly, those whom her renunciation of marriage has denied her. Catching shadows, the play that occupies a brother and sister, suggests the children—the "shadows" of themselves—who one day will be theirs: "'I've got one' . . . 'I've got two.' . . . 'Now I've got another.'" Titled after the resting place of her insane brother, who died in 1901, "In Nunhead Cemetery" (1916) is narrated by a male speaker mourning the loss of his fiancée, who died one month short of their appointed wedding. The poem is painful: "Though I am damned for it we two will lie / And burn"—an image that, like the stillborn marriage, suggests the repression that dogged Mew.

Virginia Woolf regarded Mew as the finest female poet of her time. According to the critic Val Warner, Mew's work is "a [cry from the heart] against the meaninglessness of life, if all it means is suffering."

Critical Analysis

The critic Louis Untermeyer compared Mew's poetry to "a cameo cut in steel," referring to the incredible strength of her passions paired with the evident fragility of her technique. As a writer, she has one foot in the Victorian era and one foot firmly planted in the 20th century. Like ROBERT BROWNING, she tended to favor dramatic monologue, but her speaker was seldom a woman, more often a man or boy, and her monologues often had the feel of stream of consciousness, in which events force the speaker along different paths of rembrance. Moreover, Mew's pessimism contrasts deeply with Browning's fundamental optimism. While she sometimes expresses hope in her poetry, the fundamental feeling she conveys is more often of sorrow and longing.

On of her most frequently cited poems is "In Nunhead Cemetery." The speaker of the poem is man who has just attended the funeral of his beloved. Everyone else has left the cemetery, but the speaker says he has "nowhere else to go." It is raining and the speaker is holding in his hand a rose that had been thrown into the grave; he says, "There is something terrible about a flower." At the end of he stanza, it becomes clear what exactly makes the flower terrible: "you do not miss a rose." It is its fragility, the swiftness and ease with which it dies.

The next stanza echoes the first. A child points at the heaped up dirt around the grave and smiles—"This morning after THAT was carried out," THAT referring to the corpse—the lifeless body that has been transmuted from a living thing to an object. The speaker says, "There is something terrible about a child." Without knowing it, the child too is destined to mingle with the heaped dirt, to die and be buried.

In thinking about the child, the speaker remembers that he and his beloved were, only the week before, "like children in the Strand." He credits his love with helping him see things he had never seen before and then imagines he will wake from his dream of her death and "shall see what you see again."

The speaker then seems to resolve to join his beloved in death. "Now I will burn you back, I will burn you through, / Though I am damned for it we two will lie / And burn, here where the starlings fly." Then he realizes, "It would not be you, it would not be you." He remembers how as a child he used to "pray to Christ to keep / Our small souls safe till morning light," but that time of faith and security is gone. "I am scared, I am staying with you to-night- / Put me to sleep."

At the end of the poem the speaker returns to the images of the roses tossed onto the graves; just above the dead, he says, "fields and fields of roses lie—" and, he imagines that if the gravedigger would "dig it all up again they would not die," a foolish, impossible wish on which this elegaic poem ends.

It is easy to see why Thomas Hardy had such an affinity with Mew. She shares with him an unswerving gaze, an ability to stare down the reality of human existence in a world that has lost much of its meaning.

Other Work by Charlotte Mew

Warner, Val, ed. *Collected Poems and Selected Prose.* London: Carcanet, 1998.

A Work about Charlotte Mew

Fitzgerald, Penelope. *Charlotte Mew and Her Friends.* Reading, Mass.: Addison Wesley Longman, 1990.

Meynell, Alice Christiana Thompson
(1847–1922) *poet, essayist*

Alice Christiana Meynell, née Thompson, was born in Barnes, near London, to a moderately wealthy family, and spent most of her childhood in Italy. Her parents kept an artistic, somewhat bohemian household. Thomas Thompson, Meynell's father, educated Meynell and her older sister, Elizabeth, at home; Christiana Weller, Meynell's mother, was a painter and concert pianist. Meynell's early life was marred only by bouts of ill health.

Inspired by the examples of CHRISTINA ROSSETTI and ELIZABETH BARRETT BROWNING, Meynell began writing poetry in childhood. Her first volume, *Preludes* (1875), was a great success. In one poem, "A Song of Derivations," she acknowledges her debt to "past poets," writing, "Voices I have not heard possessed / My own fresh songs." The double meaning disclosed by the syntax—that her songs were possessed (controlled) by these "[v]oices," which themselves originally possessed (in the sense of *contained*) her songs—shows Meynell's gift for concision, as well as her high intelligence.

Thus Walter de la Mare called her one of the few poets "who actually think in verse" and praised her poetry's "serene poise of mind" and "constant refusal to fall captive to caprice of mood and wandering impulse." Subsequent volumes included *Poems* (1893), *Other Poems* (1895), and *Later Poems* (1901).

In 1868 Meynell converted to Roman Catholicism. She was in love with Father Augustus Dignam, the young Jesuit who had prepared her for the conversion and who accepted her into the church. The two continued to correspond for two years. Some of Meynell's early poetry, including "After a Parting" and "Renouncement," is addressed to Dignam. (Both poems were written in 1877, but Meynell made no attempt to publish "Renouncement" for 15 years.) In the first of the two poems, Meynell writes, "Thou dost beset the path to every shrine; / My trembling thoughts discern / Thy goodness in the good for which I pine"; in the second, "the thought of thee waits, hidden yet bright; / But it must never, never come in sight. . . ." Here again there is compressed double meaning: Meynell's thought of her beloved must not come into her own view or into public view. DANTE GABRIEL ROSSETTI declared "Renouncement" one of the three best sonnets ever written by a woman, and renunciation would remain a recurring theme in Meynell's poetry.

Another sonnet in the 1875 volume is the beckoning "My Heart Shall Be Thy Garden" ("Come, my own, / Into my garden . . ."). It, too, was meant for Dignam, but someone else, a London writer, was entranced by it: Wilfred Meynell, another Roman Catholic convert, whom the poet married in 1878. The Meynells had eight children, and they began a joint project, the liberal monthly *Merry England* (1883–95). Several of coeditor Alice Meynell's essays appeared in this publication.

Much of Meynell's subsequent poetry expresses her confident religious faith, sometimes, as in the case of "The Lady Poverty" (1894), in the midst of a modernity out of touch with faith. On two occasions—the deaths of ALFRED, LORD TENNYSON in 1892 and of ALFRED AUSTIN in 1913—she was considered for the post of poet laureate. Only one other woman, Elizabeth Barrett Browning, had been previously considered.

Meynell also was an activist. She worked tirelessly to improve slum conditions and to prevent cruelty to animals. Her kindness was exhibited when she rescued the poet FRANCIS THOMPSON from poverty. The causes with which she is most identified are women's suffrage and the extension of workers' rights to women.

It is, however, as an essayist, rather than as a poet, that Meynell left the deeper mark. Her volumes of collected essays include *The Rhythm of Life* (1893), *The Colour of Life* (1896), *The Spirit of Place* (1899), *Ceres' Runaway* (1909), and *Hearts of Controversy* (1917).

While her poetry provides a restrained record of her religious conviction, a passage such as the following, in which grass is a dynamic metaphor for spirit, more fully conveys Meynell's religious passion: "... the wild summer growth of Rome has a prevailing success and victory. It breaks all bounds, flies to the summits, lodges in the sun, swings in the wind, takes wing to find the remotest ledges, and blooms aloft." Indeed, Meynell's essays often, as here, spring from sharp observation to a broader meditation on life.

Meynell wrote many literary essays—on ROBERT BROWNING, Tennyson, CHARLES DICKENS, and the BRONTËS, among others. She also frequently wrote on the subject of children.

The critic Dixon Scott in 1914 wrote that he could think of no other "prose-tissue" than hers that "presents a surface so free from the faintest falsity or blur, and that clings with so exquisite a closeness and transparency to the rippling body of the swiftly moving thought."

Works about Alice Meynell
Crisp, Shelley Jean. *The Woman Poet Emerges: The Literary Tradition of Mary Coleridge, Alice Meynell, and Charlotte Mew.* Ann Arbor: University of Michigan, 1987.

Halladay, Jean R. *Eight Late Victorian Poets Shaping the Artistic Sensibility of an Age.* Lewiston, N.Y.: Edwin Mellen Press, 1992.

Mill, Harriet Taylor (1807–1858) *nonfiction writer*

Harriet Taylor Mill was born Harriet Hardy in London to a surgeon named Thomas Hardy (no relation to the novelist and poet) and Harriet Hurst Hardy. Her father paid for a good early education, but she was married at age 18 to John Taylor, whom she did not consider an intellectual equal. In the final years of his life, her father grudgingly accepted her friendship with the philosopher JOHN STUART MILL, whom she married after Taylor's death.

With her second marriage, Harriet Mill began to write political essays. In *The Enfranchisement of Women* (1851) she argues that women have been taught to adopt habits that keep them from reaching their full potential. Women, she says, "have been taught to regard their degradation as their honour."

Harriet Taylor Mill, however, is best known for the influence she exerted upon J. S. Mill, both through collaborative writing and through her comments on his work. She is thought to have moderated Mill's laissez-faire economic views, causing him to become more socialistic in later life. That influence is clearest in *The Subjection of Women* (1869), which she cowrote with her husband and which condemns unequal treatment of the sexes because such treatment restricts individual liberty through force. The book argues for the innate equality of the sexes and proposes that women, properly educated, be allowed to compete against men in a state of equality before the law. This work's combination of utilitarian and individualist thinking resembles an untitled essay she wrote in 1832, in which she warned, "Whether it would be religious conformity or social conformity, no matter which the species, the spirit is the same: all kinds agree in this one point, of hostility to individual character." J. S. Mill was so impressed by his wife's thinking that he credited several chapters of his most important works to her influence.

There have been arguments that J. S. Mill exaggerated his wife's brilliance, notably in the book *John Stuart Mill and the Harriet Taylor Myth* (1960) by H. O. Pappe, who concludes: "The wide claims made by [J. S.] Mill's new biographers for Harriet's intellectual ascendancy cannot be substantiated. Her early writings evince her dependence on Mill." However, as the Nobel Prize–winning economist Friedrich Hayek argues, "[E]ven if merely her influence on Mill was as great as he asserts, we should have to think of her as one of the major figures who shaped opinion during the later Victorian era."

Harriet Taylor Mill died in Avignon, France, of tuberculosis.

Other Work by Harriet Taylor Mill

Jacobs, Jo Ellen, and Paula Harms Payne. *The Complete Works of Harriet Taylor Mill.* Bloomington: Indiana University Press, 1998.

Mill, James (1773–1836) *political philosopher*

James Mill was born near Forfar, in the county of Angus, in Scotland, to James Mill, a shoemaker, and his wife, Isabel Fenton Mill, a farmer's daughter. After being educated at Edinburgh University and working as a preacher and tutor, Mill moved to London and became a freelance journalist, publishing essays in *The Anti-Jacobin Review*.

Along with the circle of democratic reformers known as the Philosophical Radicals, which included Mill's mentor JEREMY BENTHAM and the economist DAVID RICARDO, Mill advocated free markets, the reform of the British constitution, and the expansion of the franchise by about 1 million new voters. In such publications as the pamphlet "Commerce Defended" (1807), he denounced tariffs and government-granted monopolies. He defended middle-class as opposed to aristocratic values, writing in his influential essay "Government" (1820) that "There can be no doubt that the middle rank . . . is the chief source of all that has exalted and refined human nature." In addition to his political essays in the *Edinburgh Review*, the *Philanthropist, Encyclopaedia Britannica,* and other venues, Mill wrote a book-length *History of India* (1817), which led to his appointment to India House, Britain's colonial administration for India.

Mill judged legal and ethical rules by a utilitarian standard: their contribution to general human happiness. While educating his son, JOHN STUART MILL, he followed a strict utilitarian philosophy aimed at making the child value socially beneficial behavior, a practice that critics say left the young Mill repressed and always concerned about whether his activities were sufficiently high-minded and self-improving.

Mill and his fellow Philosophical Radicals shifted the terms of political debate in Britain toward utilitarianism (which advocated representative government of elected officials) and were crucial in bringing to passage the franchise-expanding 1832 Reform Law. "Had Mill not appeared on the stage," wrote the 19th-century biographer Alexander Bain, "political thinking at the time of the Reform settlement must have been very inferior."

Other Work by James Mill

Bull, Terence, ed. *James Mill: Political Writings.* Cambridge: Cambridge University Press, 1992.

Mill, John Stuart (1806–1873) *philosopher, nonfiction writer*

John Stuart Mill was born in London to JAMES MILL, an editor, writer, and journalist, and Harriet Burrow Mill. Mill was educated by his father, and this education became legendary. Mill began to learn Greek at age three, and Latin at eight. By the time he was seven he was reading Plato in Greek; by 11 he was reading Newton; by 12 he had tackled a complete course in logic and economics. While he was visiting France for a year at age 14, Mill acquired complete fluency in French. Nor was his education limited to books; Mill's father introduced him to leading progressive intellectuals in England, such as the economist DAVID RICARDO and the father of utilitarianism, JEREMY BENTHAM.

Young Mill was greatly influenced by the utilitarian philosophy of Bentham—which held that the greatest happiness for people is to live morally, that all institutions and actions should be judged morally—and the doctrines of THOMAS MALTHUS, an economist who advocated population control of the masses. He was also influenced by others: SAMUEL TAYLOR COLERIDGE, a major romantic poet and critic; the philosophy of anti-Enlightenment; Gustave d'Eichthal, a socialist follower of the social philosopher Saint-Simon; and Auguste Comte, a "father of sociology."

At age 17 Mill wrote several articles advocating birth control, and was arrested and released on bail after he distributed pamphlets promoting mechanical contraception to the servant girls. This act was judged immoral. During the 1820s, Mill published a number of articles for the *Westminster Review*, the publication of the Utilitarian radicals. Mill acquired a clerical position in India House, the headquarters of the East India Company that protected British interests in India.

Between 1830 and 1831 Mill wrote *Essays on Some Unsettled Questions of Political Economy* (1844), which demonstrated his skill and creativity as a technical economist. In the late 1830s Mill also acquired ownership and became an editor of the *London and Westminster Review*. As an editor, Mill was deeply involved in the pragmatic issues of radical politics, often meeting and organizing radical politicians.

In the meantime, Mill also wrote his own philosophical works. In his seminal *System of Logic* (1843) he proposes two systems for sociological investigation and experimentation: the "physical, or concrete deductive method," and the "inverse deductive, historical method." For Mill, sociology is both mechanical and unpredictable.

In 1848 Mill produced another text of fundamental importance to the social sciences, *Principles of Political Economy*, which went through 32 editions before the end of the 19th century and which dominated the discipline of economics for more than a generation. In this work, Mill airs a number of controversial views that created political and philosophical debate. For instance, he refuses to accept any absolute right to private property in land and opposes the paternalistic treatment of women. Although both works are "now of interest mainly to specialists" primarily because of the developments in psychological and evolutionary studies, as his biographer William Stafford notes, Mill's methodology and reasoning are still of great interest.

In 1851, after her husband's death, Mill married Harriet Taylor (see MILL, HARRIET TAYLOR), whom he had known since 1831. Both Mill and Taylor suffered from tuberculosis, and in 1855 they embarked on a journey to southern Europe in search of relief. Mill often stated that his wife was truly the creative thinker, while his mission was to bring her ideas into the world. In 1851, for instance, Mill published an essay on the "Enfranchisement of Women"; its progressive ideology calls for votes for women, along with an equal access to jobs. Although Mill's name was on the piece to ensure its publication, Harriet wrote it.

In 1858, after the dissolution of the East India Company, Mill was comfortably pensioned off. Later the same year, Harriet unexpectedly died of tuberculosis in Avignon, France. Mill purchased a small house within sight of Harriet's grave in Avignon, where he spent part of each year. His stepdaughter, Helen Taylor, whom he described as "another such prize in the lottery of life," became his constant companion.

Mill turned to active politics and decided to run for election to Parliament as an independent. To promote himself and his views, Mill authorized the People's Edition of his books, a cheap edition for which he received no royalties. Mill won the election and, while serving in the House of Commons, attempted to pass a bill giving women equal voting rights. He also spoke for

Irish land reform and advocated a conciliatory stance toward the Irish, and supported a number of social reforms. He became an active member of the Land Tenure Reform Association, which favored limited nationalization of land.

Critical Analysis

John Stuart Mill championed women's rights not only in voting but also in education and employment. In his essay *The Subjection of Women* (1869) Mill examines the inequalities in marriage and employment laws, and sets forth the social benefits that would emerge from a system that provides women with freedom and equality. Interestingly, he questions the concept of "nature," in terms of differences between men and women, and suggests that the apparent differences may arise from factors such as environment and education. Although most of Mill's writing on women seems a series of truisms today, some of his contemporaries, according to Stafford, "thought that his doctrines about women were just plain wrong: It was obvious to them that women were inferior, mentally as well as physically and that their place was in the home under the authority of their husbands."

Mill's *On Liberty* (1859) was also highly controversial. He identifies liberty with happiness and ultimately with pleasure. Mill argues that all actions that do not harm others should be permitted. He places the highest value on liberty. This essay is perhaps the most widely read work of Mill's today.

Mill's posthumous *Autobiography* (1873) was not favorably received by the contemporary critics. Mill's longtime friend THOMAS CARLYLE, for example, called it an "autobiography of a steam-engine." Today's critics, however, hold a different opinion. In this highly personal book, Mill reports that the education given to him by his father was based on fear and that he wished for a greater opportunity to pursue liberal studies. However, the work is not simply an autobiographical study and lament, but rather, incorporates and includes Mill's philosophical principles. When speaking of Continental philosophers, for example, Mill reveals "that all questions of political institutions are relative, not absolute, and that different stages of human progress not only will have, but ought to have, different institutions."

On his deathbed, Mill said to Helen, "You know I have done my work." Mill was not merely a philosopher, but also a man of action and one of the first advocates of feminism to attempt a serious governmental reform. Mill remains an influential figure of the Western philosophical discourse.

Other Work by John Stuart Mill

Ryan, Alan, ed. *Utilitarianism and Other Essays.* New York: Penguin, 1987.

Works about John Stuart Mill

Baum, Bruce. *Rereading Power and Freedom in J. S. Mill.* Toronto: University of Toronto Press, 2000.
Capaldi, Nicholas. *John Stuart Mill: A Biography.* Cambridge: Cambridge University Press, 2004.
Eisenach, Eldon. *Mill and Moral Character of Liberalism.* Pittsburgh: Pennsylvania State University Press, 1999.
Reeves, Richard. *John Stuart Mill.* Conshohocken, Penn.: Atlantic Books, 2007.
Stafford, William. *John Stuart Mill.* New York: St. Martin's Press, 1999.

Milnes, Richard Monckton (1809–1885)
poet, nonfiction writer

Richard Monckton Milnes was the eldest son of Robert Pemberton Milnes, a member of Parliament for Pontefract, Yorkshire, in northern England, and Henrietta Maria Monckton, a highly trained and accomplished singer. The young Milnes was largely educated by private tutors until he entered Cambridge University, where he met and became close friends with ALFRED TENNYSON. In 1830 he studied in Germany, and in the years following traveled in Europe. When he returned to England, he was elected to the House of Commons in 1837 and later, as Baron Houghton, entered the House of Lords.

In 1833 Milnes published his first work, *Impressions of Greece*. Deeply involved in the study of poetry, particularly that of the romantics, he published in 1838 two volumes of poetry. *Memorials of a Residence on the Continent, and Historical Poems* draws upon his travel experiences, while *Poems of Many Years* deals with such subjects as the death of a friend.

In 1844 Milnes produced *Palm Leaves*, accounts resulting from his visits to the Near East; but his most important work appeared in 1848—*The Life and Letters of John Keats*. This was the first biography of KEATS, who went largely unnoticed in his own time but whose work Milnes greatly admired. It helped to establish Keats's reputation as one of the masters of English poetry. The scholar George Ford calls Milnes's biography "the first attempt to repair the damage wrought [by Keats's reviewers] and to see Keats's character in its true light."

Because of the combined pressure of his work in Parliament and his extraordinarily active social life, Milnes wrote nothing else of great length. He was, however, a steady contributor to literary periodicals of the day, reviewing books and commenting on contemporary issues.

Milnes was the ideal nobleman; born to wealth and power, he nevertheless spent his life according to the ancient dictum *noblesse oblige*, befriending and aiding those less fortunate than he. He promoted the careers of young, unknown, and less well-situated writers.

Critical Analysis

Although not a great poet, Milnes's real greatness lies, many think, in his role as a patron of the arts and a supporter of artists. That is not to say Milnes's poetry is without charm; it has been called "reflective, "Wordsworthian," and "delicate," and many of his ballads were once quite popular.

Often Milnes's reflection revolves around matters of religion. In one particularly nice sonnet, "Because the Few with signal virtue crowned," Milnes wonders why the virtuous are "Sadder and wiser than the rest." The first eight lines, or octet, explores this question and the poet notes that the virtuous may miss the "small delights" that others enjoy. As is usually the case in a Shakespearean sonnet, there is a "turn" or change in tone or direction after the octet. Here, the poet adds that the virtuous few have "special pleasures" that are unknown to those who "have only trod/Life's valley smooth." Indeed, "Man does not live by Joy alone/But by the presence of the power of God."

In a poem of quite different style, Milnes attacks religious hypocrisy. "London Churches" is written in rhyming six-line stanzas. The speaker is standing at a church door, where he sees a woman who is familiar to him. She carries a prayer book with a cross on the cover, "But above the Cross there glistened/A golden Coronet." This is a lady, one used to deference, and the "obsequious beadle" opens the door wide for her. As she walks down the aisle, the poet speculates that "There might be good thoughts in her/For all her evil pride."

Behind this vain woman comes another woman,

> *On whose wan face was graven*
> *Life's hardest discipline,—*
> *The trace of the sad trinity*
> *Of weakness, pain and sin.*

She looks inside the church where the "few freeseats" are crowded. "'God's house holds no poor sinners,'" she says as she creeps away.

These are simple poems with simple messages; still, each is charming in its way and representative of Milnes's work.

Mitford, Mary Russell (1787–1855) *poet, novelist, playwright, essayist*

Mary Russell Mitford was the only child of Dr. George Mitford, a physician, and Mary Russell Mitford. She was a bright child who could read by the age of three. In 1798 she was sent to a girls' school in London. In her five years there she studied French, Italian, and Latin, and won several academic prizes. Her mother had brought a large inheritance to the marriage, but her father's extravagant spending and gambling consumed most of the fortune by the time Mary was six or seven. In 1797, the year before she was sent to school, Mary won a £20,000 lottery prize that was used to pay her father's debts and support the family for several years. Still, the Mitfords were always on the edge of poverty, forced to move several times to accommodate their straitened circumstances. In 1820 the family moved to a small village near Reading (some 40 miles west of London), where Mitford lived for the next 30 years.

George Mitford never gave up his profligate ways, and Mary, who had published several well-received collections of poems and several longer poetic works between 1810 and 1820, turned to writing to solve the family's money problems. She submitted sketches of village life to periodicals such as the *Lady's Magazine* and also tried her hand at drama, with several plays produced between 1823 and 1836. Her most successful play, the romantic historical tragedy *Rienzi* (1828), enjoyed a long run in London and a popular tour in the United States. Her chronicles of village life, *Our Village,* however, established her reputation and made her an international celebrity. Published in five volumes in 1824, 1826, 1828, 1830, and 1832, *Our Village* is, as Mitford explained, "not one connected story, but a series of sketches of country manners, scenery, and character, with some story intermixed, and connected by unity of locality and purpose." Mitford created a genre, the village or local-color novel, that became one of the dominant forms of 19th-century women's literature influencing such writers as ELIZABETH GASKELL, Harriet Beecher Stowe, and Sarah Orne Jewett. To counteract her country isolation, Mitford also maintained a lively correspondence with the writers ELIZABETH BARRETT BROWNING, AMELIA OPIE, CHARLES LAMB, and HARRIET MARTINEAU. Despite her industry and great popularity, Mitford was never free of financial hardship and died impoverished in a tiny cottage near Reading.

Other Work by Mary Russell Mitford
Recollections of a Literary Life; or, Books, Places, and People. New York: AMS Press, 1975.

Works about Mary Russell Mitford
Edwards, Peter David. *Idyllic Realism from Mary Russell Mitford to Hardy.* New York: St. Martin's Press, 1988.
Miller, Betty, ed. *Elizabeth Barrett to Miss Mitford: Unpublished Letters.* New Haven, Conn.: Yale University Press, 1954.
Watson, Vera. *Mary Russell Mitford.* London: Evans Bros., 1949.

Molesworth, Mary Louisa (Mary Louisa Stewart Molesworth) (1839–1921) *novelist, children's writer*

Born in Rotterdam, Holland, Molesworth was the daughter of Charles Augustus Stewart, a merchant, and his wife, Agnes. When Molesworth was two, her family moved to Manchester, England, where she was educated by her mother and later by the novelist ELIZABETH GASKELL. In 1861 she married Richard Molesworth, an officer in the Royal Dragoons. The marriage was unhappy; a head injury left her husband with a violent temper, and two of their seven children died young. In 1879 Molesworth and her husband separated.

The difficult marriage inspired several of Molesworth's early novels, however. Under the pseudonym Ennis Graham (the name of a childhood friend who had died), Molesworth published a three-volume novel titled *Lover and Husband* (1870), a book that warned against the unhappiness marriage can cause. Similar themes appeared in her novels *She Was Young and He Was Old* (1872) and *Not Without Thorns* (1873).

These novels had an audience, but it was not until Molesworth began publishing children's books that she truly found success as a writer. *Tell Me a Story* (1875), a collection of short stories, was followed by some of Molesworth's most enduring children's books, the first of which was *Carrots: Just a Little Boy* (1876), which she based on experience from her own and her children's lives. While *Carrots* drew from real life, in other works Molesworth used elements of fantasy while striving to strengthen children's vocabularies with her writing. *The Cuckoo Clock* (1877), her best-known work, is set in a magic world that the cuckoo from a clock reveals to a young girl named Griselda.

Molesworth continued to write in the 20th century. Aside from her children's books, she also wrote Bible stories, essays, novels, and short stories for adults, but none of these reached the same acclaim as her children's stories. She published more than 100 titles in her lifetime. Although she is no longer popular, critics still regard her as a superb children's writer. The critic R. L. Green praises her as "the Jane Austen of the nursery."

A Work about Mary Louisa Molesworth
Green, Roger Lancelyn. *Mrs. Molesworth.* London: Bodley Head, 1961.

Moncrieff, William Thomas (1794–1857)
playwright, songwriter

William Moncrieff was born in London. He became a clerk in a lawyer's office at age 10 and worked for various London lawyers over the next decade, while also writing songs and plays. Moncrieff's first play, *Moscow, or the Cossack's Daughter,* was produced in 1810, when he was 16. During the next 10 years he turned out a series of plays that were unfailingly entertaining, whether musicals, comedies, or dramas. His comedies *The Dandy Family,* written in 1818, and *Tom and Jerry; or, Life in London,* produced in 1821 (and based on PIERCE EGAN's work of the same name), were huge hits in London. After becoming manager of the Regency Theater in London in the 1820s, Moncrieff continued to be a remarkably prolific playwright, known for his humorous work. He wrote more than 170 plays during his career. By the 1840s, Moncrieff had become completely blind, but he continued to write plays, as well as articles for the *New Monthly Magazine* and the *Sunday Times,* until the 1850s.

Montgomery, James (1771–1854) *poet*

James Montgomery was born in Ayrshire, Scotland. His father, John Montgomery, was the only Moravian minister in Scotland. When the family moved to England, James was sent to a Moravian boarding school in Leeds, in the north of England. While he was at school, his parents both died in Barbados, where they had gone as missionaries. As a student, Montgomery wrote enormous epic poems with such titles as *The World.* The Moravians soon expelled him for writing poems they considered blasphemous, and they apprenticed him to a baker as punishment. In 1787 he ran away. He made his way to Sheffield (some 25 miles south of Leeds), where he became a clerk at the *Sheffield Register,* a politically radical newspaper for which he wrote articles and which he eventually, in 1795, bought.

In the same year, Montgomery published a poem commemorating the anniversary of the fall of the Bastille (July 14, 1789), the event that marked the beginning of the French Revolution, when mobs of Parisians attacked the notorious prison. Montgomery was convicted of libel and imprisoned for printing a piece in support of the revolution, which the English monarchy feared might spread to England. After his release from prison, he published *Prison Amusements* (1796). Two years later he published a series of political essays, titled *The Whisperer,* under the pen name Gabriel Silvertongue. In his time, Montgomery was known as an outspoken journalist and excellent poet. Other volumes of poetry include *The Ocean* (1805) and *The Wanderer of Switzerland* (1806). He also contributed reviews to the *Ecletic Review* and wrote more than 100 hymns during his lifetime.

Montgomery, Robert (1807–1855) *poet*

Robert Montgomery was born in Bath, in the west of England. He was the illegitimate son of a professional theater clown, Robert Gomery, who raised him. Robert later added "Mont" to his father's name to make it sound more impressive. He attended school in Bath and at age 17 started a newspaper, the *Inspector*. Soon after the paper closed, Montgomery began to publish his poems. A long theological poem, *The Omnipresence of the Deity* (1828), written when he was 21, became extremely popular in England and made Montgomery famous. He wrote florid, ponderous poems on religious subjects such as *The Messiah* (1832) and *Satan; or, Intellect Without God* (1830), a poem that became even more widely known than *Deity*. Montgomery put himself through Oxford University with the money he earned from his poetry and graduated in 1833. Two years later, he became an Anglican priest. While serving in Shropshire, Glasgow, and London, Montgomery continued to write poetry, including *Luther: A Poem* (1842), and also wrote on theology. In 1843 he married Rachel Mackenzie, with whom he had one child.

Moore, George Augustus (1852–1933)
novelist, poet, short story writer

George Moore came from a well-to-do landowning Irish family. He was born at the family's estate, Moore Hall, in County Mayo, to George Henry Moore, a member of Parliament, and Mary Blake Moore. Moore's only schooling consisted of six years at St. Mary's Preparatory School in England.

Moore decided in 1873 to move to Paris to become an artist. There he met some of France's leading literary figures, including Émile Zola, and began to write. His first volume of poetry, *Flowers of Passion* (1878), was modeled on Charles Baudelaire's *Flowers of Evil* (1857) and attempted to shock English readers. It was printed with a skull and crossbones on the cover. Although Moore's poetic skill had matured by the time he published *Pagan Poems* (1881), neither volume was well received.

In 1880 Moore returned to London and wrote his first novel, *A Modern Lover* (1883), which was banned from libraries because of its frank depiction of bohemian society. His second novel, *A Mummer's Wife* (1885), established Moore as England's leading naturalistic novelist, following in the style of the naturalist school of the French novelist Émile Zola, whose brutally realistic portraits of lower-class life depicted the Darwinian struggle for existence. It tells of a working-class seamstress who leaves her husband for an actor. She succumbs to alcoholism, killing both herself and her baby. Moralistic critics deplored the subject matter: A critic for the *Academy* proclaimed, "A more repulsive story was probably never written." Today it stands as one of the earliest examples of a realistic depiction of alcoholism.

Moore's next novel, *A Drama in Muslin* (1886), follows the lives of five Irish Catholic girls who have just graduated from a convent school. The central character, Alice Barton, a feminist and Irish nationalist, finally achieves an uneasy peace with the demands of her position in life by marrying and becoming a successful writer.

Other novels followed, including the semi-autobiographical *Confessions of a Young Man* (1888), two volumes of criticism, and numerous articles and short stories. However, Moore's permanent reputation was made with *Esther Waters* (1894), a realistic treatment of the life of a poor London woman who becomes a servant on a country estate, is seduced and then abandoned, and fired by her employer. Moore captures the desperation of Esther's situation: "[A]s Esther was sitting alone, there came within her a great and sudden shock—life seemed to be slipping from her, and she sat for some minutes quite unable to move...." It remains Moore's most highly respected novel.

Moore was the first British writer to use the "stream of consciousness," a literary technique that attempts to capture the reality of human psychology by portraying the rapid movement of thoughts as they pass through a character's mind. *The Lake* (1905), for example, anticipates the psychological experimentation of Virginia Woolf and James Joyce: "The corn was six inches high, and the potatoes were coming into blossom. True, there had been a scarcity of water, but they had had a good summer, thanks be to God, and he thought he had never seen the country looking so beautiful. And he loved this country, this poor Western plain with shapely mountains enclosing the horizon." The critic Anthony Farrow summarizes Moore's achievement: "If George Moore had not lived, English literature in the 20th century would be quite different from what it now is: His influence on other writers has changed the way we think about the novel; and his own work has been of a level of achievement to make it last as long as the English novel will last." He helped to launch the IRISH LITERARY RENAISSANCE and the Irish National Theater.

Critical Analysis

Ethel Waters is a very British take on Émile Zola's greatest novel, *L'Assommoir* (this title, virtually untranslatable, refers to French shops that sold cheap liquor distilled on the premises). In *L'Assommoir*, a Parisian couple is destroyed by alcohol, the characters driven to drink by fate, poverty, and, Zola would suggest, genetics. In Moore's novel the characters struggle, not with alcohol, but with betting on the horses.

Although Moore's work is not nearly so dismal as Zola's, it conveys the same sense of the constraints faced by the poor, and especially poor women, in the 19th century. Their options were few and the consequences of deviation from the straight and narrow could be devastating. The protagonist of Moore's novel is Ethel Waters, a young girl who has been sent from home by a stepfather who no longer wants to support her. Scared, naïve, she leaves home to work as an apprentice cook in a country home. She is seduced and abandoned by the cook's son and sent away by her mistress, who is kind and sympathetic but who cannot allow a fallen woman to remain in her home.

Once her child is born, Ethel must find a way to support him. The best money she can make is as a wet nurse, which means she must pay another to care for her son while she nurses the baby of a middle-class woman who objects to any contact between Ethel and her son.

As is the case in *L'Assommoir*, things eventually begin to look up for Ethel. She ends her tenure as a wet nurse and obtains a better job. Her seducer, William, finds her again. He is now half owner of a pub, and he convinces her to marry him and reunite as a family. They do well for a time, but William is brought low by consumption and gambling, and the couple eventually loses everything. Ethel comes full circle, eventually obtaining a position with the mistress who sent her away when she was pregnant and with her help manages to provide for her son until he enters the army.

It cannot be said that Ethel triumphs, nor does she die in squalor as does Gervaise Macquart, Zola's heroine in *L'Assommoir*. Still, her story is a tragedy, and she the victim of poverty and the constraints placed on women in Victorian England.

A Work about George Moore

Frazier, Adrian. *George Moore, 1852–1933*. New Haven, Conn.: Yale University Press, 2000.

Moore, Thomas (1779–1852) *poet, song writer*

Thomas Moore was born in Dublin, Ireland, to John Moore, a grocer and wine merchant, and his wife, Anastasia, both Roman Catholics. Moore studied at Trinity College, Dublin, where he began writing poetry. After he graduated in 1799, he went to London to study law at the Middle Temple and in 1803 was sent to Bermuda as admiralty registrar. When one of his deputies mishandled funds, Moore was held responsible. He resigned his post, left for Europe in 1819, and did not return to Bermuda until the substantial debt was settled in 1822. Although Moore would go on to financial success, he never stopped worrying about money.

In 1800 Moore published his first book, *Odes of Anacreon Translated into English Verse, with Notes*, whose title gave him the nickname Anacreon Moore. During the next few years he published a collection of his love poems, *The Poetical Works of the Late Thomas Little, Esq.* (1801), and *Epistles, Odes and Other Poems* (1806). A review in the *Edinburgh Review* claiming the work was immoral almost caused Moore to fight a duel over the charge. In 1808 he published a satire, *Corruption and Intolerance: Two Poems with Notes, Addressed to an Englishman by an Irishman*. A chief target of the poem was the Prince Regent, later King George IV, whom Moore believed was unsympathetic toward Ireland. *Corruption and Intolerance*, along with other satires, was collected in *The Twopenny Post Bag* (1813).

Soon, Moore moved on to more profitable endeavors. His friend LORD BYRON encouraged him to use an exotic setting for the long poem *Lalla Rookh* (1817). The book of four narrative poems linked by a tale in prose tells of the adventures of Princess Lalla Rookh, who travels from Delhi to Kashmir to be married to a king. It was widely translated and brought Moore some £3,000, the highest earnings of any British poet for a single poem up to that time.

Despite its initial popularity, *Lalla Rookh* slipped into obscurity, while Moore's most successful and lasting work would be *A Selection of Irish Melodies* (1807–34), a 10-volume series of his songs that earned him the title of Ireland's national lyricist, as well as a good income for the next 25 years. The books' 130 lyrics include "The Last Rose of Summer" ("'Tis the last rose of summer, / Left blooming alone; / All her lovely companions / Are faded and gone") and "Oft, in the Stilly Night" ("Oft, in the stilly night, / Ere Slumber's chain has bound me, / Fond Memory brings the light / Of other days around me").

Moore and Sir John Stevenson set the songs to music, with Moore himself often singing them in public. Already popular in Ireland, Moore now found fame in London social circles because of the songs, many of which painted a sentimental portrait of Ireland and which increased English sympathy for Irish nationalism.

When Byron died in 1824 he left his memoirs with Moore, who, in a controversial act, burned the manuscript, supposedly to protect Byron. He did use some of the material, however, to compile his fine *Letters and Journals of Lord Byron, with Notices of his Life* (1830). Moore also wrote *The Life of Lord Edward Fitzgerald* (1831) and *The History of Ireland* (1835–46), a work whose vast undertaking precipitated the mental breakdown of his final years. He is remembered, as Garnett writes, for reviving the "traditions of the minstrel and the troubadour of the middle ages." For all their sentimentality, Moore's Melodies (as they commonly are called) remain popular and are still sung and recorded today.

Works about Thomas Moore
de Ford, Miriam A. *Thomas Moore*. Boston: Twayne, 1967.
Flannery, James W. *Dear Harp of My Country: The Irish Melodies of Thomas Moore*. Nashville, Tenn.: J. S. Sanders, 1995.

More, Hannah (1745–1833) *poet, novelist, playwright*

Hannah More was born in Harleston, England, to Jacob More, a schoolmaster, and Mary Grace More, the daughter of a farmer. Jacob More, a self-educated man himself, encouraged his daughters to become cultured and learned young women. In 1755 the Mores opened a boarding school for girls in Bristol that was renowned for its rigorous moral and religious education. Hannah More was initially a pupil and later a teacher. The school offered instruction in French, arithmetic, grammar, and needlework. More proved exceptionally proficient in French, Italian, Latin, and Spanish and spent many hours reading the works of William Shakespeare and John Milton.

More wrote five plays, all of which were popular during her lifetime. Her first play, *The Search after Happiness* (1773), was a pastoral drama that she wrote for performance by her female students. It expounded the value of virtue and restraint. By 1787 the play had sold more than 10,000 copies—a considerable number for the 18th century.

Her other plays were tragedies based on classical themes and motifs.

More is mainly remembered today as an influential educator and essayist. She adamantly supported education for women, and the working class yet she also affirmed the secondary role of women within the structure of society. She consistently rejected the liberal ideas of Thomas Paine and MARY WOLLSTONECRAFT, which made her popular among the upper classes.

Hannah More developed a huge following; her significant admirers included the writer Samuel Johnson, the painter Joshua Reynolds, and the actor and playwright David Garrick. She used her popularity for philanthropic endeavors. In the late 1790s and the early 1800s she engaged in public and private projects aimed at educating the poor. Numerous schools opened throughout the country, professing their adherence to More's principles. More spent the last 20 years of her life on a small estate in Clifton, on the outskirts of Bristol, where she continued to write political and educational essays.

In *Strictures of Modern Female Education* (1799) More argued that women should receive an education, not as a foundation of any kind of social or political advancement, but instead to make them more desirable companions for their husbands. An educated female, More argued, would also be able to provide a good education for her children.

In *Thoughts on the Importance of Manners of the Great to General Society* (1788), More proposes a campaign to educate the lower classes in what she deems as appropriate and necessary social protocols. Such a plan would benefit the aristocracy because, according to More, it would make the lower classes more obedient and easily controlled. More's education campaign would have imposed a codified and rigid standard of education upon the masses and further promoted rigid demarcation between the classes.

At the same time More launched an attack on the upper class, questioning its morality and pointing out its failure to meet its social responsibility (by failing to provide a good example) for the lower classes. In *An Estimate of the Religion of the Fashionable World* (1790), More criticizes the secularization of English society and the absence of religious piety among the upper classes. More believed that "Reformation must begin with the great . . . whose example is the fountain whence the vulgar draw their habits, actions, and characters."

Turning from essays to the novel, More used fiction to promote her ideas. *Coelebs in Search of a Wife* describes the quest of Lucilla, a modest and well-educated woman, to find a perfect husband and establish a moral household. Extended dialogues lecture the reader on religion, politics, and education. Coelebs, Lucilla's predestined mate, for example, is instructed by his father-in-law about "the prevailing evils of the day" and the need for emotions to be "curbed by restraint and regulated by religion."

Regardless of the critical debate today, Hannah More made a profound impact—if not on British literature (most of her works were not reprinted during the 20th century), then surely on British society. Her pedagogical principles and ideas have permeated the educational system in England, contributing, to the establishment of the egalitarian public institutions of education. More's ideas about appropriate behavior of females and upper classes have often entered the novels of other 19th-century writers, notably those of JANE AUSTEN. Stricter attitudes toward the kind of education that a person received (proportionate to his or her class status) were largely maintained throughout the Victorian period. In summarizing More's career, her biographer Patricia Demers notes the position of More, restrained by the prevalent ideologies and attitudes of her age, as being "not simply a cold, strange figure of the past." "More," Demers continues, "devoted her long career to one overriding cause: galvanizing women of the middle and upper ranks to act, not as domestic ornaments, but as thinking, engaged, and responsible social beings."

Other Works by Hannah More
Helms, Hal, ed. *Religion of the Heart*. Orleans, Mass.: Paraclete Press, 1993.
Hole, Robert, ed. *Selected Writings of Hannah More*. London: Pickering and Chatto, 1995.

Works about Hannah More
Demers, Patricia. *The World of Hannah More*. Lexington: University of Kentucky Press, 1996.
Ford, Charles Howard. *Hannah More: A Critical Biography*. London: Peter Lang, 1996.

Morgan, Lady
See OWENSON, SYDNEY.

Morier, James Justinian (1780–1849)
satirist, travel writer

James Morier was born in Smyrna, now called Ismir, in Turkey. His father, Isaac Morier, was a merchant employed by a large British trading company in the Middle East. Morier completed his education at Harrow School and in 1807 became a member of the British foreign service. He served in Persia (now Iran) from 1809 to 1816. Morier traveled widely during his years there and in 1812 published an account called *A Journey Through Persia, Armenia, and Asia Minor to Constantinople in the Years 1808 and 1809*. Six years later he published *A Second Journey Through Persia*. By this time, Morier had retired from the foreign service and was living in London, where he married Harriet Greville.

In 1824 he published a satire, *The Adventures of Hajji Baba of Isphahan*. This book, which made him famous, told the story of a Persian barber who not only cut hair but also murdered some of his customers. Although the plot was satirical, Morier tried to give an accurate portrayal of Persian life in the 19th century. In 1828 he published a sequel, *The Adventures of Hajji Baba of Isphahan in England*. Morier also published other novels set in the Middle East, including *Zohrab the Hostage* (1832) and *Ayesha: The Maid of Kars* (1834).

A Work about James Morier
Johnston, Henry McKenzie. *Ottoman and Persian Odysseys: James Morier, Creator of Hajji Baba of Ispahan, and His Brothers*. New York: St. Martin's Press, 1998.

Morris, William (1834–1896) *poet, novelist, translator, philosopher*

William Morris was born in Walthamstow, then a small village north of London, to William Morris, a wealthy businessman, and Emma Shelton Morris. In 1848 Morris entered Marlborough College (a prominent public school) which he left in 1851 after a confrontation with the headmaster. In 1853 he enrolled at Oxford University in preparation for a career in the Anglican Church. While at Oxford, Morris became interested in the arts and literature of the Middle Ages. Despite the protests of his parents, Morris decided to become an architect after his graduation.

In 1855 Morris composed a series of short verses and romances to entertain his friends, and he subsequently helped found the *Oxford and Cambridge Magazine,* which he briefly edited and to which he contributed a number of his own verses. In 1856 Morris's interest shifted to painting instead of architecture after a meeting with DANTE GABRIEL ROSSETTI and other members of the PRE-RAPHAELITE MOVEMENT, which looked to 14th- and 15th-century Italian art for inspiration. Although Morris now largely concentrated on painting, he still continued to compose verse, and in 1858, encouraged by ALGERNON CHARLES SWINBURNE, he published his first collection of poems, *The Defence of Guenevere and Other Poems*. The volume received virtually no critical attention.

Morris shocked his family when he married Jane Burden, the daughter of an Oxford stableman, in 1859. The following year he founded a company that specialized in interior and furniture design that was both beautiful and functional. At first the firm catered to religious institutions, stained glass being its most successful product. Eventually, Morris produced everything from tapestries to wallpaper. One of the firm's lasting legacies was the Morris chair.

Morris's company was based on his love of beautiful objects. He was often outraged at the ugliness brought about by industrialization, from shoddily mass-manufactured merchandise to the grim factory towns that had sprung up all over England. In an effort to halt some of the devastation he saw, he was instrumental in forming the Society for Protection of Ancient Buildings.

In 1867 Morris published his first major poem, *The Life and Death of Jason,* a long narrative poem describing the search for the Golden Fleece by the ancient Greek hero Jason and his companions, the Argonauts. The poem follows Jason through the enchanted wilderness of eastern Europe. The quest is also spiritual and allegorical, as Jason must reject the empty vision of the Earthly Paradise with which he is confronted.

In 1868 Morris, pleasantly surprised by the great success of *The Life and Death of Jason,* published *Earthly Paradise,* a collection of poems on subjects taken from classical and medieval literature. Both works were highly acclaimed for their intricate rhyme and meter, as well as innovative handling of classical images and themes.

In 1871 Morris journeyed to Iceland, a place that became a central, powerful image in his later work. Impressed with the stark landscape of Iceland and the inhabitants' ancient sagas of bravery and adventure, he decided to learn Icelandic. In 1875 Morris published prose translations of the Icelandic sagas, *Three Northern Love Stories.* A year later, he brought out a verse translation as *The Story of Sigurd the Volsung and the Fall of the Niblungs* (1876), the work that he regarded as the pinnacle of his poetic career. As Frederick Kirchhoff, a Morris biographer and critic, notes, "Morris' ability to express the essential tragedy with unflinching stoicism accounts for the remarkable power of the narrative."

In 1881 Morris moved his firm's manufacturing unit to the suburbs of London. Having three years before become an enthusiastic socialist, he attempted to create an environment for the workers consistent with his political beliefs. The workers were paid well and shared in the profits of the firm; the bucolic environment that surrounded the factory was also conducive to their health. Products created under such conditions were expensive. Indeed, Morris's firm catered to the upper classes, among whom the products became fashionable.

By the mid-1880s, Morris had joined the ranks of the Democratic Federation, a moderate socialist group. His political sensibilities estranged many of his old friends. In 1884 Morris was one of the pivotal figures in the formation of the more radical Socialist League, acting in the capacity of the treasurer and as an editor of its organ, *Commonweal.* Morris gave lectures throughout the country and raised funds for the socialist cause. In 1887, along with GEORGE BERNARD SHAW, Morris led thousands of protesting workers, who were dispersed by the police during what became known as the Trafalgar Square Riot, or Bloody Sunday.

Out of Morris's socialist interest came his 1890 *News from Nowhere,* a utopian novel about a future filled with rural socialist communities. The narrator is told:

> our villages . . . [show] no tokens of poverty about them; no tumble down picturesque [buildings]. . . . Such things do not please us, even when they indicate no misery. . . . We like everything trim and clean, and orderly and bright; as people always do.

William Morris was one of the most accomplished people of the Victorian period: he composed poetry, completed magnificent translations, established an original design company (for which he designed everything from type fonts and books, to wallpaper), wrote political and philosophical essays, and greatly contributed to socialist and humanitarian causes. As the biographer Frederick Kirchhoff writes, "To come to know Morris, whatever the avenue of approach, is to find him a 'fact' of one's existence. He becomes, inescapably, a conscience."

Critical Analysis

Morris's distaste for what he called "the dull squalor of civilization" led him to write about past times, in which he supposed romance, beauty, nobility, and courage had existed in greater supply than in the modern world.

In "The Defence of Guenevere" (1858) the title character, King Arthur's queen, stands accused of adultery, although she is innocent of any wrongdoing (at least in Morris's version of the story). Her supposed lover, the knight Lancelot, has escaped. However, in the end, at the risk of his life and safety, he comes to defend her:

> Her cheek grew crimson, as the headlong
>   speed
> Of the roan charger [horse] drew all men to
>   see,
> The knight who came was Lancelot at good
>   need.

In his rendition of the Icelandic saga *The Story of Sigurd the Volsung* Morris retells the legend of Sigurd, or Siegfried. It is a colorful tale, filled with dragons, warrior women, magic, betrayal, jealousy, and revenge. All of this is told in an antiquated style meant to reflect the speech of the period. In the following sequence the Valkyrie Brynhild, who has engineered Sigurd's death because she thought him unfaithful, prepares to kill herself in remorse for her act:

> "Now give me my sword, O maidens,
>   wherwith I sheared the wind,
> * * * * * * * * * * * *
> All sheathed the maidens brought it, and
>   feared the hidden blade,
> But the naked blue-white edges across her
>   knees she laid,
> And spake: "The heaped up riches, the gear
>   my fathers left,
> All dear-bought woven wonders, all rings
>   from battle reft [torn].
> All goods of men desired, now strew them
>   on the floor
> And so share among you, maidens, the gifts
>   of Brynhild's store."

In the last years of his life, Morris published a series of prose romances that also centered on medieval themes of love and honor. In *The Wood beyond the World* (1894) a young man is lured to a witch's land, which he eventually escapes taking an enslaved young woman with him. In *The Well at the World's End* (1896) Ralph, a young prince, seeks out the titular well, whose waters prolong life. Like the Icelandic sagas, these romances are told in a mannered style, supposedly imitating medieval phrasing and vocabulary. Thus *The Wood beyond the World* opens with "there was a young man dwelling in a great and goodly city. . . . He was but of five and twenty winters, a fair-faced man, . . . rather wiser than foolisher than young men are mostly wont."

Other Works by William Morris

The Designs of William Morris. New York: Phaidon Press, 1995.

News from Nowhere and Other Writings. New York: Penguin, 1994.

William Morris on Art and Socialism. Mineola, N.Y.: Dover, 2000.

Works about William Morris

Harvey, Charles. *William Morris: Design and Enterprise in Victorian Britain.* Manchester, England: Manchester University Press, 1991.

Kirchhoff, Frederick. *William Morris.* Boston: Twayne, 1979.

McCarthy, Fiona. *William Morris.* New York: Faber and Faber, 2003.

Thompson, E. P. *William Morris.* New York: Random House, 1977.

Morrison, Arthur (1863–1945) *novelist, short story writer*

Arthur Morrison was born to Jane Cooper and Richard Morrison, an engine fitter, in the East End slums of London, which he would write about as a journalist and a fiction writer. He worked as a clerk in the People's Palace, a charitable institution founded in 1887 by the novelist WALTER BESANT. He moved into journalism, writing for many London papers, including WILLIAM ERNEST HENLEY's *National Observer.*

Stories that Morrison wrote for Henley's weekly were published in 1894 as *Tales of Mean Streets.* The stories are a hard-edged depiction of life in the poverty-ridden East End. His description of the environment demonstrates his style, which the critic P. J. Keating has described as a "compound of realistic observation and quiet despair": "[T]he public houses are always with you; shows, shies [verbal assaults], swings, merry-go-rounds, fried fish stalls, donkeys are packed [close] . . . you may be drunk and disorderly without being locked up,—for the [police] stations won't hold everybody,—and when all else has palled, you may set fire to the turf."

Morrison's first novel, *A Child of the Jago* (1896), portrays "a colony of vermin": "In subterranean basements men and women have swarmed and bred and died like wolves in their lairs." Within this environment, filled with hunger and punctuated with violence, the boy Dicky, exploited by a dealer in stolen goods, is drawn into a life of crime. Morrison's theme is the impact of social environment on human nature. Morrison explained later, "I hoped to bring the conditions of this place within the apprehension of others." Critics praised the novel, although some doubted the accuracy of its portrait of slum life.

A Hole in the Wall (1904), another East End novel, tracks the fate of another boy, Stephen Kemp. Like CHARLES DICKENS's *Bleak House,* this novel is told from first- and third-person points of view. The disruptions in continuity that result from these back-and-forth shifts in perspective reflect the fragmentation of Kemp's life. After his mother dies, Kemp moves in with Grandfather Nat, whose "gap in the right hand where the middle finger had been" symbolizes the harsh effects of slum life. Nothing Morrison subsequently produced, which included supernatural stories and detective fiction, was as highly regarded as his three major works.

The critic Vincent Brome has written, "Descriptions of slums and low life occur in [earlier novels], but Morrison disdained the quaintness of Dickens's slum characters and recoiled from any attempt to romantici[z]e East End lives. He wanted to record the reality."

Morton, John Maddison (1811–1891)
playwright

John Morton was born in Pangbourne, a suburb of London. His father, Thomas Morton, was a playwright. The family lived in England, France, and Germany, where John was educated by his parents at home. From 1832 to 1840, he worked as a clerk at Chelsea Hospital in London while writing plays on the side. His first production, a farce titled *My First Fit of the Gout,* was staged in April 1835. Over the next 15 years, Morton wrote a series of light farces. Most of his works were adaptations of French plays, which became hugely popular on the London stage. His most famous play was *Box and Cox,* which was produced in 1847, and was later made into an operetta with music by Sir Arthur Sullivan. Other plays include *Done on Both Sides* (1847) and *From Village to Court* (1850). By the 1860s, however, the popularity of Morton's farces had waned, and he supported himself by giving readings of his plays. During the last years of his life, when the demand for these readings declined, too, Morton lived in poverty.

Mudie's Circulating Library

During the 19th century, Charles Edward Mudie established a highly successful lending library. Mudie was born in the Chelsea section of London in 1816 and worked as a bookseller before starting the lending library in 1842. For a yearly fee, patrons could borrow as many books as they wanted. Books were delivered by mail.

Mudie figured out that if books were printed in three volumes, he could loan one volume each to three different patrons simultaneously and maximize the return on his books. Mudie bought large quantities of books for his library and insisted that they appear in three separate volumes. Because his orders were so large, the publishers complied, and, as a result, many books were printed as multivolume sets instead of single volumes. In addition, Mudie published a forerunner of the modern best-seller list, which could make or break new authors.

Mudie stocked both fiction and nonfiction, so readers would have a wide variety of books from which to choose. His library continued to be popular until it was gradually replaced later in the 19th century by the public libraries that were established in many English communities.

Muir, John (1838–1914) *naturalist, essayist*

John Muir, founder of the Sierra Club, was born in Dunbar, Scotland, on April 21, 1838, to Daniel Muir and his second wife, Anne. Daniel Muir was a shopkeeper of strong Calvinist convictions and a member of the Campbellite sect (which interpreted scripture literally), who emigrated to American in 1849 in order to be able to practice his religion freely.

The Muir family settled near Milwaukee, Wisconsin, when that city was still a frontier town. Daniel was a strict disciplinarian who required that his children memorize Bible verses daily and forbade them to read fiction or poetry. When Muir was 15, however, he defied his father and began reading books he borrowed from friends. Eventually, his father gave him permission to get up earlier than the rest of the family to read; so intent on reading was Muir that he arose at one A.M. "I had gained five hours," Muir said, "almost half a day! Five hours to myself! . . . I can hardly think of any other event in my life, any discovery I ever made that gave birth to joy so transportingly glorious as the possession of those five frosty hours." Some of his early morning hours were also spent in tinkering and inventing. Among Muir's inventions was an extraordinarily sensitive thermometer and an alarm clock that tipped him out of bed and onto the floor.

In 1860 Muir displayed some of his inventions at the State Fair in Madison, where he met some representatives from the just-founded University of Wisconsin. Despite little formal education, Muir was admitted to the university, where he studied science with Ezra Slocum Carr, who also introduced his young pupil to the writings of WORDSWORTH, Emerson, and Thoreau.

Muir left the university in 1863 and spent the remaining years of the Civil War (1861–65) in Canada, presumably to avoid the draft. When he returned to the United States, he took a job in a machine shop in Indianapolis. There, in 1867, Muir accidentally jabbed himself in his right eye with a file, blinding himself in that eye. He temporarily lost sight in the other eye from sympathetic blindness, and rejoiced when his vision returned. This event, Muir said, changed his life, and he resolved to see as much as he could of the beauties of the land. He left his job and walked a thousand miles from Indianapolis to the Gulf of Mexico. He sailed from there to Cuba, then to Panama—where he made the overland crossing to the Pacific, then up the West Coast to San Francisco, where he disembarked in 1868.

From 1869 to 1873 Muir lived in the Yosemite Valley. As he walked the valley, he came to believe that it had been created by glaciation, an idea that was not popularly accepted at the time. While he lived and studied in Yosemite, Muir was visited by many famous people of the day, including Ralph Waldo Emerson, on Emerson's only trip west of Massachusetts. During this period, Muir studied the plant species of Yosemite and climbed many of the mountains of the Sierra Nevada, including the tallest, Mount Whitney. In 1875 he was stranded atop Mount Shasta for four days in a blizzard, resulting in frostbite and some permanent damage to his feet. Nevertheless, he continued to climb and even ascended Mount Rainier in 1888 when he was 50 years old.

In 1873 Muir began to live during the winters in Oakland, California (he still spent his summers in Yosemite), and to write about some of his experiences. His earliest pieces were descriptions of the beautiful places he visited accompanied by pleas that such places be preserved for future generations to visit.

In 1880, at the age of 42, Muir married Louisa Strentzel and settled with her on a fruit farm in Martinez, California. The couple had two daughters. Muir, a successful farmer, continued to travel whenever he could, visiting Alaska seven times.

It was in Martinez that Muir began to write his books, including *The Mountains of California* (1894), *Our National Parks* (1901), *The Yosemite* (1912), and *The Story of My Boyhood and Youth* (1913). All of his works were autobiographical and replete with exquisite descriptions of nature.

In 1892 Muir founded the Sierra Club and served as its president until his death. Muir, now famous, once camped out in Yosemite with President Theodore Roosevelt, and another time guided President William Howard Taft through the park. He was instrumental in the establishment of Yosemite, Sequoia, Kings Canyon, Grand Canyon, Mount Rainier, and Petrified Forest as National Parks. Muir died of pneumonia in a California hospital in January 1914.

Critical Analysis

John Muir was not merely a nature writer and conservationist, though he was both. He was a writer with a deeply spiritual connection with nature that he wanted to share with others not lucky enough to live in or near the wilderness. In his nature writing, it is easy to see how deeply he was influenced both by romantic poets, such as Wordsworth, and American Transcendentalists, such as Emerson. In Muir's best work, Nature is alive, animate, and an intimate part of life, both human and divine—perhaps even a bridge from humanity to divinity. In *Our National Parks* (1901), Muir begins by prescribing the wilderness as a restorative to "tired, nerve-shaken, over-civilized people." "Going to the mountains," he says, "is going home," and he adds that "wilderness is a necessity; and . . . mountain parks and reservations are useful not only as fountains of timber and irrigating rivers, but as fountains of life." Although a modern ecologist might say that human life and natural life are interdependent, Muir adds a spiritual, almost mystical dimension. Of Yosemite he says

> Nearly all the park is a profound solitude. Yet it is full of charming company, full of God's thoughts, a place of peace and safety amid the most exalted grandeur and eager enthusiastic action, a new song, a place of beginnings abounding in first lessons on life, mountain-building, eternal, invincible, unbreakable order; with sermons in stones, storms, trees, animals brimful of humanity.

Muir invests Nature with charmingly anthropomorphic characteristics. "Every landscape," he says "glows like a countenance hallowed in eternal repose." The dawn starts out rosy, changes to yellow, "then come the level enthusiastic sunbeams pouring across the feathery ridges, touching pine after pine . . . searching every recess, until all are awakened and warmed." Arctic flowers "though lowly in stature, keeping near the frozen ground as if loving it, . . . are bright and cheery, and speak nature's love as plainly as their big relatives of the South." His way of referring to animals is particularly charming:

> A multitude of animal people, intimately related to us, but of whose lives we know almost nothing, are as busy about their own affairs as we are about ours . . . bears are studying winter quarters as they stand thoughtful in open spaces, while the gentle breeze ruffles the long hair on their backs . . . butterflies and bees, apparently with no thought of hard times to come, are hovering above the late-blooming goldenrods, and, with countless other insect folk, are dancing and humming right merrily in the sunbeams and shaking all the air into music.

Muir reserves his greatest praise for Nature. She is "grand," "triumphant," "magnificent," "lofty," "noble." He reserves his greatest disdain for those who destroy nature for profit. "In the noblest forests of the world, the ground, once divinely beautiful, is desolate and repulsive, like a face ravaged by disease." Of the Sierra Reserve he says

> lumbermen are allowed to spoil it at their will, and sheep in uncountable ravenous hordes to trample it and devour every green leaf within reach; while the shepherds, like destroying angels, set innumerable fires, which burn not only the undergrowth of seedlings on which the permanence of the forest depends, but countless thousands of the venerable giants.

In an era before television and movies, Muir's descriptions let those who were unable to travel to the great parks and reserves of the West "see" their awesome beauty:

> Boiling springs and huge deep pools of purest green and azure water, thousands of them, are plashing and heaving in these high, cool mountains as if a fierce furnace fire were burning beneath each one of them; and a hundred geysers, white torrents of boiling water and steam, like inverted waterfalls, are ever and anon rushing up out of the hot, black underworld.

Above all, Muir makes the case for preserving all of this noble beauty from the ravages of commercialism. "God," he says, "has cared for these trees, saved them from drought, disease, avalanches, and a thousand tempests and floods. But he cannot save them from fools." Muir in his life did much to enlighten those fools who failed to understand the importance of preserving Nature.

Other Works by John Muir

My First Summer in the Sierra. New York: Dover, 2004.

Steep Trails. Charleston, S.C.: Bibliobazaar, 2007.

Stikeen: Adventure with a Dog and a Glacier. Minneapolis, Minn.: Tandem Library, 2004.

A Thousand-Mile Walk to the Gulf. New York: Mariner Books, 1998.

Works about John Muir

Erlich, Gretel. *John Muir: Nature's Visionary.* Washington, D.C.: National Geographic, 2000.

Wolfe, Linnie Marsh. *Son of the Wilderness: The Life of John Muir.* Madison: University of Wisconsin Press, 2003.

Mulock, Dinah Maria

See CRAIK, MRS.

Naden, Constance Caroline (1858–1889)
poet

Constance Naden was born in Birmingham, England, to Thomas Naden, an architect, and Caroline Woodhill Naden, who died giving birth to her. Constance was raised by her grandparents and attended a private Unitarian day school. As a girl, she studied languages and philosophy and wrote poetry influenced by her studies. While at Mason College, where she studied science, she also contributed articles to scientific journals. In 1881 Naden published her first collection of poems, *Songs and Sonnets of Springtime*. Six years later, Naden published another volume of poetry, *A Modern Apostle and Other Poems*. Naden was preoccupied with questions of religion and doubt, as in these lines from "The Agnostic's Psalm":

> Oh Thou, who art the life of heaven and earth,
> Eternal Substance of all things that seem;
> Or but the glorious phantom of a dream
> That in the brain of mortal man has birth:
> To know that Thou dost live were little worth,
> Not knowing thee. . . .

She also published two books of essays on philosophical topics. With money inherited from her grandparents, Naden was able to travel throughout the Middle East and to India in 1887. Soon after she returned to England in 1888, she developed a severe illness and died following surgery.

Other Work by Constance Naden
Victorian Women Writers Project. "The Complete Poetical Works of Constance Naden." (1894): A Machine-Readable Transcription. Available online. URL: http://www.indiana.edu/~letrs/vwwp/naden/naden.html. Accessed July 1, 2008.

Nesbit, Edith (1858–1924) *novelist, children's book writer*

E. Nesbit was born in London, the third of four children of Sarah and John Collins Nesbit. Two events in Nesbit's young life influenced her deeply. The first was the death of her father when she was four years old. The second was her sister Mary's illness, which caused the family to spend the next several years moving from place to place in search of the right climate to ease Mary's symptoms.

After Mary's death in November 1871, the family settled at Halstead Hall in Kent, in southeast England. Nesbit and her brothers spent three happy years here. Although she had written poems since she was quite young, Nesbit began writing poetry in earnest at Halstead House. Her mother was impressed enough with her daughter's work that she helped her get her first poem published in the *Sunday Magazine.*

In 1880 Edith Nesbit married the young socialist Hubert Bland. She and her husband were founding members of the Fabian Society, a British political group established in the 1880s, whose goal was the gradual introduction of socialism into British government. Shortly after their marriage, Bland became ill and Nesbit had to write to support the family. In addition to the writing Nesbit did on her own, she collaborated with her husband on many works, writing under the name Fabian Bland in such works as *The Prophet's Mantle* (1885). The two also worked together to edit the Fabian Society's journal, *Today.*

Critical Analysis

Nesbit hoped to be recognized as a poet, but her fame today rests upon the children's books she wrote, beginning with *The Story of the Treasure Seekers* (1899). This novel, which was a great success, told the story of the six Bastable children and their plots and plans to restore the family fortune. Nesbit's children's stories were among the first to portray realistic children. Her characters fight, call each other names, play tricks, get into trouble, and generally act much more like actual children than the paragons of virtue often found in Victorian children's literature. Nesbit was also among the first to avoid overt moralizing and to put contemporary slang into the mouths of her young characters. Here one of her child-narrators speaks directly to the reader:

The best part of books is when things are happening. That is the best part of real things too. This is why I shall not tell you in this story about all the days when nothing happened. You will not catch me saying, "thus the sad days passed slowly by"—or "the years rolled on their weary course"—or "time went on"— because it is silly; of course time goes on—whether you say so or not. So I shall just tell you the nice, interesting parts—and in between you will understand that we had our meals and got up and went to bed, and dull things like that. It would be sickening to write all that down, though of course it happens.

One of Nesbit's most endearing creations is Oswald Bastable, the narrator of *The Story of the Treasure Seekers* (1899) and *The Wouldbegoods: Being the Further Adventures of the Treasure Seekers* (1901). Nesbit portrays Oswald as realistic and intelligent, but still childlike and limited in his perspective. The *Treasure Seekers* reflects Nesbit's own childhood in portraying a large family fallen on hard times. This novel and its sequel provide a forum to showcase some of Nesbit's social concerns. While Nesbit avoids didacticism and moralizing, she does reveal her socialist leanings through her portrayal of middle-class attitudes toward poverty. For example, the children in *The Wouldbegoods* form a club to "do good" but often get into trouble because of their naive misperceptions about the lives of those less privileged, as when they kidnap a baby because they think it is too handsome to belong to a poor couple.

While Nesbit's novels can be sentimental, most are leavened by a lively, humorous style. *The Wouldbegoods,* for example, opens with "Children are like jam: all very well in the proper place, but you can't stand them all over the shop—eh, what?" Later, when one of the characters faints, the narrator describes her as looking "Not at all like fair fainting damsels, who are always of an interesting pallor. She was green, like a cheap oyster on a stall." Nesbit's books are also full of humorous situations as the children get themselves into various scrapes.

Nesbit's next series of books for children began with *Five Children and It* (1902). The characters, based on her own children, encounter a series of fantastic adventures guided by mythical animals, including the Psammead, or Sand-Fairy. *Five Children* was followed in 1904 by *The Phoenix and the Carpet*, in which the children acquire a magic carpet that takes them on a series of adventures, and in 1906 by *The Story of the Amulet,* in which the children gain the ability to travel through time.

For the last book in this series, Nesbit did extensive research at the British Museum, for as the characters travel through ancient cultures in search of the missing half of an amulet, they visit ancient Egypt, Babylonia, and Caesar's Gaul, which Nesbit presents with great historical accuracy. The scholar and author C. S. Lewis said that *The Story of the Amulet* "opened my eyes to antiquity, the 'dark backward and abysm of time.'" Lewis also borrowed the idea of a magic wardrobe from Nesbit, an idea he used as the basis for the first of his Narnia novels.

The Railway Children (1906) is the most frequently reprinted of Nesbit's works for children. This book involves the adventures of three children living near a railway line and was closely based on Nesbit's own childhood experiences at Halstead. Here, as in many of Nesbit's early novels, the story highlights social inequalities and the pain of poverty. The children's father is unjustly taken to prison, and the children and their mother have to move to a small home near a railway line. Roberta, Phyllis, and Peter encounter a series of adventures as they try to help with the family finances and rescue their father. The book was extremely successful in its time and has remained in print, possibly because the children, especially the eldest daughter Roberta, are so well drawn. It twice has been adapted as a film.

Nesbit's next work for children, *The Enchanted Castle* (1907) is the favorite of many critics because of its exquisite plotting and beautiful language. In *The House of Arden: A Story for Children* and *Harding's Luck* Nesbit writes of three children who are able to travel in time. Through their stories, Nesbit paints a picture of an idealized past in rural England in the time of King James I (1603–25).

In 1910, Nesbit published *The Magic City,* in which an orphaned child builds a city of blocks that comes to life. Her last novel for children, *Wet Magic* (1913), involves an undersea world as well as a war that foreshadows the outbreak of World War I in 1914.

Her biographer, Julia Briggs, said that Nesbit helped to reverse the great tradition of children's literature inaugurated by Carroll, Macdonald and Kenneth Grahame, in turning away from their secondary worlds to the tough truths to be won from encounters with things-as-they-are, previously the province of adult novels.

Other Work by E. Nesbit
The Book of Dragons. New York: SeaStar Books, 2001.

A Work about E. Nesbit
Briggs, Julia. *A Woman of Passion: The Life of E. Nesbit, 1858–1924.* New York: Meredith, 1987.

Newbolt, Henry (1862–1938) *novelist, poet*
Henry Newbolt was born in Staffordshire in central England to Henry Francis Newbolt, an Anglican priest, and Emily Stubbs Newbolt. Henry Newbolt graduated from Cambridge University in 1882 and became a lawyer five years later. In 1889 he married Margaret Edina Duckworth. While practicing law, Newbolt began to write. His first novel, *Taken from the Enemy* (1892), is a romance set during the Napoleonic Wars. In 1895 Newbolt published a play, *Mordred,* a tragedy in blank verse based on the King Arthur legend. Newbolt's most famous poem, the nautical ballad "Drake's Drum," appeared in 1896 and was widely read throughout England. Many of his poems glorified England and her history and affirmed people's belief in the greatness of the British Empire. Newbolt published two volumes of rousing, patriotic poems, *Admirals All and Other Verse* (1897) and *The Island Race* (1898), which encouraged all British subjects to support the empire and its queen, VICTORIA. One of his poems contains the

often-quoted lines, "Play up! Play up! And play the game!," urging British soldiers to fight for the empire as they would fight for the school team. By 1899 Newbolt had stopped practicing law and was writing full time. He had become one of the most popular poets in England, whose reputation was surpassed only by RUDYARD KIPLING's. Some of Newbolt's other works include *The Sailing of Long-Ships and Other Poems* (1902), *Songs of Memory and Hope* (1909), and *Poems New and Old* (1912). Newbolt was knighted for his work in 1915. In 1932 he published his memoirs, *My World as in My Time*.

Other Work by Henry Newbolt
Dickinson, Patric, ed. *Selected Poems of Henry Newbolt.* London: Hodder & Stoughton, 1981.

Newgate crime novel

The Newgate Calendar was a list, or calendar, of crimes that had been committed by inmates who were incarcerated in Newgate prison in England. First published in 1773, it continued to appear through the first two decades of the 19th century. *The Newgate Calendar* featured especially lurid and heinous crimes, which appealed to its readers, primarily working-class people who could afford the low price. The *Calendar*'s "true crime" stories not only influenced popular genres such as detective stories, Gothic thrillers, and SENSATION NOVELS, but also inspired a group of novels that were loosely based on actual crimes: EDWARD BULWER-LYTTON's *Paul Clifford*, HARRISON AINSWORTH's *Jack Sheppard,* and CHARLES DICKENS's *Oliver Twist* are among the best known. Although the mass-market Victorian novels called penny dreadfuls had always depicted crime and violence, many people believed that by taking criminals as their subjects, serious writers were condoning the crimes. Bulwer-Lytton, for example, who based his 1846 novel *Lucretia* on an actual poisoner, was attacked because he was thought to sympathize with the heroes of his Newgate novels, both of whom were murderers. Yet despite being morally condemned, such books as *Jack Sheppard* and *Oliver Twist,* first published in serial form, were extremely popular.

A Work about Newgate Crime Novels
Thomas, Donald, and Henry Mayhew. *The Victorian Underworld.* New York: New York University Press, 1998.

Newman, John Henry Cardinal (1801–1890) *essayist, novelist, poet*

John Henry Newman was born in London to John Henry Newman, a banker, and Jemima Foudrinier. Young Newman attended a private boarding school at Ealing that was directed by the renowned Oxford scholar Dr. George Nicholas. A studious child who preferred reading to games, Newman frequently read the Bible along with the works of John Milton, William Shakespeare, and SIR WALTER SCOTT.

In 1816 Newman underwent a dramatic religious conversion and pledged to pursue a life of celibacy and evangelism. He became austere, pious, and conservative, and was vocally anti-Catholic.

In 1817 Newman was admitted to Trinity College, Oxford; he received a full scholarship in 1818, and graduated with honors in 1821. In 1822, ardently supported by prominent members of the faculty, he was elected a fellow at Oriel College, Oxford, where he served at various posts between 1822 and 1825 before his ordination as an Anglican priest in 1825 and in his appointment as the vicar of St. Mary's, the university church, in 1828.

In 1831 Newman embarked on an extensive journey throughout the Mediterranean countries and was particularly impressed with the somber grandeur of Rome. During the trip, Newman composed a number of religious hymns, including the popular "Lead, Kindly Light," in which the devoted speaker begs God for guidance: "Lead, kindly light, amid encircling gloom / Lead Thou me on!"

Newman's position and influence at Oxford steadily increased. His religious convictions, however, characterized by adherence to evangelical or Low Anglicanism, a movement within the Church of England that emphasized the direct relationship of the congregant with God and the Bible, were changing in favor of the hierarchical, conservative principles of High Anglicanism, which favored a greater emphasis on ceremony and ritual and invited congregants to approach God through the mediation of priests. From the pulpit of St. Mary's, Newman preached his religious messages that were later incorporated into the doctrines of the OXFORD MOVEMENT, which was composed of influential clerics and scholars who from 1835 onward argued for supremacy of the Anglican Church (as opposed to the Roman Catholic Church) as the church with direct connection, through apostolic succession, to the apostle Peter and through him to Christ. Newman began *Tracts for the Times* (1833–41), in which his sermons given at St. Mary's were compiled along with essays that provided guidance for the Oxford Movement.

By 1839, at the peak of his influence at Oxford, Newman entered into a second major personal religious crisis. His studies led him to question the teachings of the Church of England, and in 1841 he published the highly controversial *Tract 90*, in which he claimed that the doctrines of High Anglicanism are consistent with Roman Catholic teachings. A year later, Newman placed an advertisement in which he retracted all of his anti-Catholic statements. In 1843 he resigned from his position at St. Mary's; two years later, he converted to Catholicism, and he was ordained a Catholic priest in 1847. Newman brilliantly defended Catholic doctrines, gained the attention of the Pope Leo XIII, and swiftly ascended in the hierarchy of the Catholic Church: He served as a rector of Dublin Catholic University, founded a Catholic school in association with Birmingham Oratory in 1859, and was named cardinal in 1879.

Critical Analysis

Cardinal Newman was one of the most prolific writers of the Victorian period, but today he is mainly remembered for his essays. Of his poetry, only the allegorical *Dream of Gerontius* (1866) is still read. In this poem Gerontius, a man on the verge of death, seeks redemption; after his death, his soul ascends through heaven and is brought into the presence of God. Newman incorporates central Catholic teachings into the poem: "Firmly I believe and truly / God is Three and God is One," states Gerontius. *The Dream of Gerontius* was set to music by Sir Edward Elgar (1857–1934) in 1900; Elgar's version is considered one of the greatest of all English choral works.

Newman's *Apologia Pro Vita Sua* (1864) is considered a masterpiece of religious autobiography. In this work Newman explains the evolution of his religious beliefs: "As I advanced, my view so cleared that instead of speaking any more of the 'Roman Catholics,' I boldly called them Catholics ... [and] I resolved to be received." The work achieved remarkable popularity in England and abroad.

Newman's essays on religion, education, politics, and philosophy were also popular. In the *Grammar of Assent* (1870), Newman expresses his controversial views on the doctrine of papal infallibility. *Idea of a University Defined* (1853) emphasizes that the university "is not a convent, it is not a seminary; it is a place to fit men of the world for the world."

Lytton Strachey described Newman as "a dreamer whose spirit dwelt apart in delectable mountains, an artist whose subtle sense caught, like a shower in the sunshine, the impalpable rainbow of the immaterial world." Upon his death in 1890, Cardinal Newman left a tremendous legacy in literary and religious circles of England. He was loved and respected by both Catholics and non-Catholics alike. He was the first person made honorary fellow by Trinity College, Oxford, and his sermons and tracts are still studied by literary and religious scholars. Today, various religious societies bearing Newman's name exist throughout the world, along with a growing movement for his canonization.

Other Work by Cardinal John Henry Newman
An Essay on the Development of Christian Doctrine. Notre Dame, Ind.: University of Notre Dame Press, 1990.

Works about Cardinal John Henry Newman
Jaki, Stanley. *Newman's Challenge.* Grand Rapids, Mich.: W. B. Eerdman's, 2000.

Martin, Brian. *John Henry Newman: His Life and Work.* New York: Continuum, 2001.

New Woman novel

The "New Woman novel" is a genre of late-19th-century fiction that examined the social, political, and historical events affecting women's lives: a growing class of educated young women seeking new opportunities for employment, the calls for changes in the marriage and property laws, demands for an end to sexual double standards, and a new wave of suffragist agitation. The feminist protagonists of New Woman fiction were educated, self-reliant, adventuresome, and outspoken. The first use of the label was likely in an 1894 article, "The New Aspects of the Woman Question," by the novelist and critic SARAH GRAND. Other New Woman novelists, in addition to Grand, included MONA CAIRD, ELLA HEPWORTH DIXON, AMY LEVY, GEORGE EGERTON, and OLIVE SCHREINER. The New Woman novel also had its detractors. Critics preoccupied with literary aesthetics dismissed the genre as unliterary, calling it "polemical," "pedantic," and "unartistic." ELIZA LYNN LINTON, an antifeminist critic representing the backlash against women's social equality and artistic aspirations, repeatedly attacked the New Woman as unfeminine in a series of articles in the *Saturday Review.* Only a few male writers, such as GEORGE GISSING, were sympathetic in their treatment of the "woman question," as in Gissing's 1893 novel *The Odd Women.*

Works about New Woman Novel
Heilmann, Ann. *New Woman Fiction: Women Writing First-Wave Feminism.* New York: St. Martin's Press, 2000.

Murphy, Patricia. *Time Is of the Essence: Temporality, Gender, and the New Woman.* Albany: State University of New York Press, 2001.

Richardson, Angelique, and Chris Willis, eds. *The New Woman in Fiction and in Fact: Fin de Siècle Feminisms.* New York: Palgrave Macmillan, 2001.

Nightingale, Florence (1820–1910)
nonfiction writer

Although the collected writings of Florence Nightingale, almost exclusively utilitarian in character, run to some 16 printed volumes, she is remembered more for who she was and what she did than for what she wrote.

Born into an upper-class English family in Florence, Italy, where her family was visiting, she showed intellectual precocity and abundant energy as a child. Educated at home, mainly by her father, she mastered the classical languages, Greek and Latin, as well as French, German, and Italian. In addition she studied history, philosophy, and mathematics, but the status of upper-class women of her time gave the brilliant and energetic girl little opportunity to put her education to use.

She later said that when she was 17 God spoke directly to her, stating that she was especially destined to carry out a "mission," the nature of which was not specified. She soon expressed to her parents the desire to become a nurse, something unheard-of for a proper gentlewoman in those days. Nursing was practiced by Catholic and Protestant religious orders, or was a menial task done by untrained, poor women. Over her parents' objection, she visited hospitals in London and in provincial cities and read all the literature available on public health and related matters. She paid particular attention to reports issued by Parliament about widespread illness and disease in the crowded city slums that were spawned by the Industrial Revolution. Throughout her 20s, in addition to her reading, she continued to visit English hospitals and traveled abroad as well, to the countries of western Europe, and to Egypt in 1849–50. There she visited the schools and hospital operated by French nurses of the Roman Catholic order of St. Vincent de Paul, and was impressed by their superiority to their English counterparts. Returning to England via Germany, she spent two weeks at the Institute of Protestant Deaconesses at Kaiserswerth, a visit that was to determine the course of the rest of her life.

Returning to Kaiserswerth in July of 1851, by now age 30 and no longer subject to her parents' objections, she entered the nursing program there, graduating in October. In 1853 her family connections made available to her the superintendency of the London Institution for the Care of Sick Gentlewomen, and she shortly demonstrated the discipline and administrative acumen that was to remake health care in England over the next half century.

In that same year, 1853, Russia attempted to extend its power into Turkey, which led to the Crimean War. England and France entered the conflict in 1854, landing troops in the Crimea in September. Nightingale was asked by her friend and former neighbor Sidney Herbert, secretary of state for war, to take a party of nurses to Turkey, where she was to have complete charge of nursing in all the military hospitals. She and her party arrived at the barrack hospital of Scutari on November 5, 1854, the day the Battle of Inkerman was fought.

A person familiar with modern medical and hospital care cannot imagine what such care was like 150 years ago. The hospitals were crowded and filthy, with wounded and diseased housed together. Indoor plumbing was limited or nonexistent. Neither Nightingale nor any of the doctors were aware that disease and infection were caused by germs (Pasteur's and Koch's discoveries were made 10 to 15 years later and were widely accepted only decades after that), but Nightingale knew that filth was somehow involved. Thus she and her companions scrubbed, cleaned, washed, and bathed ferociously.

Because the Crimean War was the first major conflict to be extensively covered by newspaper reporters and photographers, the details of Nightingale's work were widely reported. In addition to the media coverage of her exploits, she wrote during this period hundreds of letters and made the notes which resulted, in 1858, in the publication of her massive and exhaustive *Notes on Matters Affecting the Health, Efficiency, and Hospital Administration of the British Army*. Returning home in 1856, she once again encountered stubborn opposition to her proposed reforms from the entrenched bureaucracy; yet her fame was such that she was granted an interview with QUEEN VICTORIA, the Prince Consort, and Herbert's successor, Lord Panmure, to plead her case. Upon a subsequent private interview with the queen, a royal commission on army health was appointed; the immediate result was the founding in 1857 of the Army Medical School.

Nightingale became an invalid in that year and for the next 50 years directed health-related activities all over the empire from her bedside, including the establishment in 1860 of the Nightingale School for Nurses. That same year, she published her most famous work, *Notes on Nursing*, and at the request of the Poor Law Board she produced in 1867 *Suggestions for the Improvement of the Nursing Service in Hospitals and on the Methods of Training Nurses for the Sick Poor*. She wrote thousands of letters, papers, and memoranda, and among her correspondents were the highest officials of England, Europe, and India. Her establishment and promulgation of public health and hygiene matters and those pertaining to home and hospital care (particularly of women and the poor), when combined over the ensuing years with the acceptance of the germ theory of disease, were major forces in saving millions of lives.

Nightingale's literary fame today is based on *Cassandra* (1852), which is an impassioned plea for a wider scope of female activity beyond hearth and home. Lytton Strachey, whose chapter on Nightingale in his *Eminent Victorians* (1918) provided the first corrective to the view of Nightingale as merely an angel with a lamp on the battlefield, called it Nightingale's cri de coeur (cry from the heart). It is somewhat surprising, then, that Nightingale opposed the agitation for women's suffrage, but her reasoning was simple. In the words of Myra Stark, "If she [Nightingale] was angered by 'the "Women's Rights" talk about the "want of a field for them" . . . ,' it was evidently because she had already found a field for them." The field of public health, in Nightingale's view, provided scope enough.

Nightingale went blind in 1901 and died in 1910. True to her stern and no-nonsense self, she had refused a state burial in Westminster Abbey.

Works about Florence Nightingale

Dossey, Barbara. *Florence Nightingale: Mystic, Visionary, Healer.* New York: Lippincott Williams & Wilkins, 2000.

Woodham-Smith, Cecil. *Florence Nightingale.* New York: McGraw-Hill, 1951.

North, Christopher (John Wilson)
(1785–1854) *essayist, critic*

Christopher North, the son of John Wilson, a wealthy businessman, and his wife, Margaret Sym Wilson, was born John Wilson in Paisley, Scotland, and educated at Glasgow and Oxford Universities. Following his university years he settled in Edinburgh, where he joined a circle of young Tory lawyers that included his close friend and literary collaborator, JOHN GIBSON LOCKHART.

Wilson published several books of poetry, but real literary success came in 1817 when he took the nom de plume Christopher North and joined the staff of a new periodical, *Blackwood's Edinburgh Magazine*. The publisher William Blackwood launched *Blackwood's* as a Tory (conservative) rival to the Whiggish (liberal) *Edinburgh Review*. The magazine attracted such writers as John Lockhart, JAMES HOGG, and WILLIAM MAGINN. Wilson/North, an ardent Tory, became one of the new magazine's most prolific contributors, writing literary and cultural criticism, light sketches, and political commentary. In 1817, shortly after joining the staff, North and his friend Lockhart published the "Chaldee Manuscript," a biblical parody that was a thinly disguised account of the rivalry between the Edinburgh publishers Blackwood and Constable, the latter the owner of the *Edinburgh Review*. Their prose was so venomous that *Blackwood's* was forced to pay damages, but the notoriety also helped to increase the magazine's circulation and was therefore considered a success. Between 1822 and 1835, North wrote more than half of the sketches for *Blackwood's* popular *Noctes Ambrosianae*, a series of uninhibited, imaginary dialogues on Scottish life set in Ambrose's Tavern, a fictitious Edinburgh pub. Among the many quips credited to North are "Laws were made to be broken" (no. 42, April 1829); and, "Animosities are mortal, but the Humanities live forever." (no. 49, May 1830).

As a critic, North admired LORD BYRON, WILLIAM WORDSWORTH, and WALTER SCOTT, calling them "the three great master-spirits of our day." He could also be a reckless, sometimes cruel, reviewer, and unrelentingly attacked the works of WILLIAM HAZLITT, LEIGH HUNT, and JOHN KEATS (all Londoners of humble origins), joining Lockhart in dismissing their poetry as "the Cockney school of writing." In addition to his contributions to *Blackwood's*, he was the author of three sentimental novels about Scottish life: *Lights and Shadows of Scottish Life* (1822), *The Trials of Margaret Lyndsay* (1823), and *The Foresters* (1825).

Through his Tory political connections, North won the appointment of chair of moral philosophy at Edinburgh University in 1820. Although academically underqualified and dependent on a friend to help write his lectures, North's talent at public speaking attracted generations of student admirers and helped secure his role as one of Edinburgh's literary lions. Unlike most other Scottish writers of his generation, North remained in Edinburgh all his life. Through his columns for *Blackwood's* and his role as "professor," he dominated the city's literary circles until his death in 1854. Roger Morrison comments, "In his longer works his exuberance too quickly went soft or stale, but in the magazine he capitalized on the fragmented and contradictory nature of his knowledge to produce a kind of rhapsodic intellectual play."

Other Work by Christopher North
Alexander, J. H., ed. *The Tavern Sages: Selections from the Noctes Ambrosianae.* Aberdeen, Scotland: Association for Scottish Literary Studies, 1992.

A Work about Christopher North
Morrison, Robert. "*Blackwood's* Berserker: John Wilson and the Language of Extremity." Available online. URL: http://www.erudit.org/revue/ron/2000/v/n20/005951ar.html. Accessed July 1, 2008.

Norton, Caroline Sheridan (1808–1877)
novelist, poet, editor, nonfiction writer

Caroline Sheridan Norton was the second daughter of Tom Sheridan and Caroline Henrietta Callender. Her father, the son of the dramatist Richard Brinsley Sheridan (1751–1816), died when she was young, leaving her mother to raise four sons and three daughters with only a small pension. Given the family's circumstances, it was essential that Caroline and her sisters make the best of their opportunities for marriage. At age 19 and with the prospect of a financially secure union, Caroline Sheridan agreed to marry a man she did not love, George Norton, a Tory member of Parliament.

The marriage proved to be a disaster. She was witty, outgoing, and politically liberal; he was dull, politically conservative, and disliked "cleverness." Within months of the marriage, intent on "teaching her manners," he began beating her. It soon became apparent that Norton had misrepresented his financial circumstances, and the couple was in need of an income. Turning to writing to help support her family, she published two well-received collections of Byronic verse, *The Sorrows of Rosalie: A Tale with Other Poems* (1829) and *The Undying One, and Other Poems* (1830). In each of these volumes, a long title poem is accompanied by short lyric poems. A few lines from Canto I of *The Undying One* give a flavor of Norton's pessimism:

> *There's not a scene on earth so full of lightness*
> *That withering care*
> *Sleeps not beneath the flowers, and turns their brightness*
> *To dark despair!*

In that same year, George Norton lost his seat in Parliament and pressured Caroline to approach her family's friends in the new government for an appointment "suitable to his rank." She wrote to her grandfather's friend, Lord Melbourne, who found Norton an appointment as a magistrate at £1,000 per year. Caroline formed a friendship with this senior politician and, with Norton's knowledge and permission, Melbourne became a frequent visitor to the Norton home. However, the marriage continued to be rocky, with Caroline fleeing her husband's beatings and reluctantly returning for the sake of her three sons. George Norton began to resent Caroline's growing friendship with Lord Melbourne and complained that Melbourne had not done enough for him. Melbourne became prime minister in a Whig government in 1835, and Norton, in a bid to bring down the government, leaked stories to the Tory press suggesting that his wife and the prime minister were having an affair.

Norton barred Caroline from seeing her children and announced that he was suing Melbourne for adultery, charging the prime minister with "alienating his wife's affections." Both Melbourne and Caroline denied any such relationship, but Norton insisted the case be brought to trial in June 1836. Caroline, who had no legal standing separate from her husband, was barred both from attending the proceedings and from testifying on her own behalf. The jury unanimously found in Melbourne's favor, completely exonerating him. Even so, Caroline Norton was branded a scandalous woman and faced notoriety for the rest of her life.

Following the adultery trial, Caroline sought to dissolve the marriage, but was prevented from doing so by English divorce laws. As a married woman, she had no legal standing at all in an English court: "I exist and I suffer; but the law denies my existence." Although she now lived apart from him, George Norton continued to exercise control over her life and over her access to her children. Resolving to fight back, she mounted a campaign to reform the child custody laws, writing a series of persuasive tracts, *Observations on the Natural Claim of a Mother to the Custody of Her Children as Affected by the Common Law Rights of the Father* (1837) and *The Separation of Mother and Child by the Law of Custody of Infants, Considered* (1838). These works resulted in passage of the 1839 Infant Custody Bill, which allowed mothers to appeal for custody of children under seven, and for access to children under 16. Unable to legally free herself from George Norton's physical and financial abuse, Caroline Norton next fought to reform the marriage and divorce laws, laying out her arguments in *English Laws for Women in the Nineteenth Century* (1854), *A Letter to the Queen on Lord Chancellor Cranworth's Marriage and Divorce Bill* (1855), and *A Review of the Divorce Bill of 1856*. She argued that married women must be treated equally under the law and that the same principles of justice must apply to rich and poor, male and female, master and apprentice. With the passage of the Married Woman's Property and Divorce Act in 1857, she succeeded at last. Under the new law, a married woman could inherit and bequeath property, just as single woman could; a married woman could enter into contracts and civil suits on her own behalf; and, if separated from her husband, she could be protected from his claims on her earnings.

During the years that she battled for reform, Caroline Norton published only a few collections of verse and an autobiographical novel about marital conflict, *Stuart of Dunleath* (1851). After the passage of the marriage reform bill, she returned to writing novels, using her experiences fighting for legal and economic independence in *Lost and Saved* (1863), about a separated woman conducting a secret affair in fashionable London—considered her best work—and *Old Sir Douglas* (1867), which, serialized in both Britain and the United States, brought her some financial security.

George Norton, who had steadfastly refused to divorce Caroline, died in 1875. She was at last free. In March 1877, Caroline married a longtime friend, Sir William Stirling-Maxwell, but she died only three months later.

Norton is said to have been the model for GEORGE MEREDITH's heroine in *Diana of the Crossways*. The critic Mary Mark Ockerbloom notes, "Norton saw clearly that her society was one in which women were disadvantaged.... [She] speaks clearly of her life and her experience of marital abuse. Her voice resonates strongly across time: it could be the voice of a friend or relative today."

Critical Analysis

Caroline Norton wrote passionately about many of the issues that concerned educated and liberated women of the 19th century, including child-labor and divorce laws. However, there were few causes that she was more passionate about than child custody. Having lost the custody of her own children, Norton was deeply interested in the passage of the Infant Custody Bill, legislation before Parliament that would grant mothers, against whom adultery had not been proved, custody of children under seven years of age and visitation rights to older children. In 1839 Norton wrote *A Plain Letter to the Lord Chancellor on the Infant*

Custody Bill, a long and closely reasoned argument in favor of the legislation. Because her own divorce and custody case were notorious, and because male writers were taken more seriously than female writers at the time, she wrote under the name Pearce Stevenson.

Before the passage of the bill, divorced women in England had no right to custody of their children. Children belonged to the father, and he could do with them as he pleased. Norton, in her letter, relates a number of well-known cases of the day in which adulterous husbands took children from their mothers and gave them over to the custody of their mistresses or to relatives who had no particular interest in the children. The mothers not only did not have custody; in many instances they were forbidden any contact with their children. Norton even cites situations in which infants at the breast were taken from the mother and turned over to wet nurses.

Norton does not challenge the prevailing notions about the "inferiority" of women or their subordinate status to their husbands. She acknowledges that "To say that a wife should be otherwise than dutiful and obedient to her husband, or that she should be in any way independent of him, would be absurd." She argues not on the platform of equality but rather on the platform of basic human rights. "There is," she says, "a very wide difference between being subject to authority and subject to oppression," and she later characterizes as "ill-advised" women's attempts to "assert their 'equality' with men."

Norton's letter is a carefully reasoned treatise. She outlines six objections to the bill—including the fear that granting mothers custody and visitation would make reconciliations less probable—and addresses each in turn, using logic and counterexamples to overcome each objection. To the idea that allowing mothers custody would increase the chance that a mother would kidnap her children, she scoffs, "Why then should it be supposed that the chances of abduction would be increased by lessening the temptations which lead to it? by increasing the protection afforded in cases of injustice? by making it possible to obtain by fair and equitable means what hitherto could only be achieved by stratagem or violence?"

In addition to using logic and careful agumentation to advocate passage of the bill; Norton also appeals to the emotions with impassioned rhetoric. She notes the absurdity of denying all women custody of their children because of the fear that an occasional unfit mother might gain custody and demands that those who take this stance

> set against the *hazard* of some bad woman obtaining access, the established *certainty*, that bad fathers have wrested their children from blameless wives, to force a disposition of property in their own favour, or to gratify a brutal spirit of vengeance, that to a blameless mother, her diseased and dying child has been refused; that from a blameless mother's care her innocent offspring has been transferred to the home of a wanton.

The great irony in Norton's own life is that after the Infant Custody Bill was made law in 1839, Norton's husband took her children to Scotland, where English law did not apply. When her youngest son fell off a horse and was critically injured, Norton was not immediately notified, and by the time she reached her son's bedside he was dead. Despite her grief, Norton did not cease writing on behalf of women's rights.

A Work about Caroline Norton

Chedzoy, Alan. *A Scandalous Woman: The Story of Caroline Norton.* London: Allison & Busby, 1992.

Ogilvy, Eliza (1822–1912) *poet*

Eliza Anne Ogilvy, née Dick, was born in Perth, Scotland, to Abercromby Dick and Louisa Wintle Dick. In 1843 she married David Ogilvy. Their first child was born a year later, but died in infancy. Ogilvy, who was devastated by the loss of her baby, expressed her grief in her writing, and privately printed a book of poems mourning her daughter. The couple had another child two years later (and eventually had five more). In the same year, Ogilvy published *A Book of Highland Minstrelsy* (1846), a popular collection of poems based on old Scottish legends and history.

From 1848 to 1852 the Ogilvys traveled in Europe and lived in Paris and Italy, where Eliza met the poet ELIZABETH BARRETT BROWNING. In 1851 Ogilvy published *Traditions of Tuscany in Verse,* a book of poems chronicling Italian history and folklore. Her next collection, *Poems of Ten Years, 1846–1855,* includes political poems "written in the passion of the living struggle" and poems on motherhood, such as "Newly Dead and Newly Born," which records a mother's fears of losing a child. Ogilvy's husband died in 1879. She went on to publish poetry for the next 30 years. In 1893 she wrote a memoir of her friend Elizabeth Barrett Browning, whose passionate poetry had influenced her own.

O'Grady, Standish James (1846–1928) *historian, novelist*

Standish O'Grady was born in County Cork, in western Ireland, to Thomas O'Grady, a Protestant clergyman, and Susanna Dowe O'Grady. Standish attended Trinity College in Dublin and became a lawyer in 1872. He had a keen interest in Irish history, however, and soon gave up law to write historical novels and nonfiction.

His *History of Ireland* (1878–80) was widely read and influenced a generation of writers to focus more attention on Ireland's Celtic past. O'Grady published other historical works, including *The Crisis in Ireland* (1882) and *Toryism and the Tory Democracy* (1886). O'Grady's historical novels, many of which are set in the 19th century, include *The Bog of Stars* (1893), *Ulrick the Ready* (1896), and *The Flight of the Eagle* (1897), all stories of Ireland during the age of Queen Elizabeth. O'Grady also drew on the wealth of old Irish legend and myth in novels such as *Red Hugh's Captivity* (1889) and *Finn and His Companions* (1892).

From 1900 to 1906, O'Grady ran the *All Ireland Review,* a literary magazine. He also wrote books for children, as well as dramas such as *Hugh Roe O'Donnell* (1902) and *The Masque of Finn* (1907). O'Grady's depiction of Ireland's heroic age had a strong influence on writers of the IRISH LITERARY RENAISSANCE and fed the growing nationalism among the Irish in the early 20th century.

Oliphant, Laurence (1829–1888) *novelist, journalist, travel writer*

Laurence Oliphant was born in Cape Town, South Africa, the son of a judge, Sir Anthony Oliphant, and his wife Mary Campbell Oliphant. He traveled extensively with his parents as a child and, in a lifetime full of adventures, continued traveling all over the world, especially to areas of military or diplomatic interest. Although he received only a haphazard education, it was sufficient for him to became a barrister and later to serve as secretary to the British diplomat Lord Elgin at posts in Canada (1847), Washington, D.C., (1855), and China and Japan (1857–60). He was a correspondent for the London *Times* during the Crimean War (1853–56) and the Franco-Prussian War (1870–71), and was rumored to have been an adviser to the Italian nationalist leader Giuseppe Garibaldi (1807–82) in the fight for Italian unification. A member of Parliament between 1865 and 1867 and considered a candidate for higher office, Oliphant abandoned politics in 1867 when he became a follower of the American spiritualist Thomas Lake Harris. He spent some time with Harris at a religious community in Salem-on-Erie, New York, but permanently broke with Harris in 1882. He then moved to Palestine to establish a community for Jewish immigrants with his wife, Alice Styleman le Strange, whom he had married in 1872. Alice died in 1886 near Haifa (then part of Syria, now in Israel), and was buried at the foot of Mount Carmel. In 1888, Oliphant married Rosamond Dale Owen, the granddaughter of the socialist Robert Owen. In December of that same year, Oliphant died.

In his full and adventuresome life Oliphant produced a diverse body of work, including travel books—*A Journey to Khatmandu* (1852) and *The Russian Shores of the Black Sea* (1853–54); two novels—*Piccadilly* (1866), satirizing the London social scene, and *Altiora Peto* (1883), about the adventures of a wealthy American girl in Europe; an account of his service with Elgin, *Narrative of the Earl of Elgin's Mission to China and Japan in the Years 1857, '58, '59* (1859); and an autobiography, *Episodes in a Life of Adventure* (1887). His strangest book—supposedly dictated by a spirit through his wife, Alice—was *Sympneumata: Evolutionary Forces Now Active in Man* (1885), which explored mystical concepts of sexuality and divinity. An account of his extraordinary life by his cousin MARGARET OLIPHANT was published in 1891. His obituarist in the *Athenaeum* described him as "A writer more distinguished for his personality than for the intrinsic worth of his literary productions." His biographer Philip Henderson concludes, "Oliphant might have been anything he chose. As it is, one is left with the impression of a life of infinite possibilities run to seed."

Other Work by Laurence Oliphant
Haifa; or, Life in the Holy Land, 1882–1885. Jerusalem: Canaan Publishing, 1976.

Works about Laurence Oliphant
Henderson, Philip. *The Life of Laurence Oliphant: Traveller, Diplomat and Mystic.* London: Robert Hale, 1956.

Taylor, Anne. *Laurence Oliphant, 1829–1888.* New York: Oxford University Press, 1982.

Oliphant, Margaret (1828–1897) *novelist*

Margaret Oliphant, née Wilson, was born in Midlothian, Scotland, to Francis Wilson, a civil servant, and Margaret Oliphant Wilson. She grew up near Edinburgh, Scotland, and began writing as a child. At age 21 she published her first novel, a historical romance called *Passages in the Life of Mrs. Margaret Maitland.* Three years later she married her cousin Francis Oliphant, an artist. After the death of her husband from tuberculosis in 1859, Oliphant became the sole support of their three children. Over the next 40 years she would write almost 100 novels, among them *The Athelings*

(1857), about three children with different talents; *Orphans* (1858); and *Agnes* (1866), the story of a poor widow with three young children. One of her best-known works was a series of seven volumes written between 1863 and 1876, *The Chronicles of Carlingford*, which describes the lives and domestic dramas of the villagers in a small town. With the money she earned from writing, Oliphant sent her two sons to Eton. She also contributed stories and articles to *Blackwood's* and *Cornhill* literary magazines. J. M. Barrie, the author of *Peter Pan*, considered her a master of the short story form. One of her best collections is *Stories of the Seen and Unseen*. Oliphant was one of the most prolific novelists of the Victorian era. Other works include *The Beleaguered City* (1880), *Lady Lindores* (1883), and *Effie Ogilvie* (1886). Oliphant also wrote biographies—including one of her cousin Laurence Oliphant—literary criticism, and a series of travel books. Her autobiography was published in 1899, two years after her death.

Other Works by Margaret Oliphant

Jay, Elisabeth, ed. *The Autobiography of Margaret Oliphant*. New York: AMS Press, 2002.

Minister's Wife. New York: AMS Press, 2002.

Miss Marjoribanks: Chronicles of Carlingford. New York: Penguin, 1989.

Works about Margaret Oliphant

Jay, Elisabeth. *Mrs. Oliphant, A Fiction to Herself: A Literary Life*. New York: Oxford University Press, 1995.

Rubik, Margarete. *The Novels of Mrs. Oliphant: A Subversive View of Traditional Themes*. New York: Peter Lang, 1994.

Trela, T. J. *Margaret Oliphant: Critical Essays on a Gentle Subversive*. Selinsgrove, Penn.: Susquehanna University Press, 1995.

Opie, Amelia Alderson (1769–1853)
novelist, poet

Amelia Alderson Opie was born in Norwich, England, to James Alderson, a physician, and Amelia Briggs. After her mother's death, when Opie was 15, she became mistress of her father's house and entered society. Her father was a political radical, freethinker, and Unitarian. Although she received little formal education, Opie was influenced by her father's beliefs and as a young woman read the works of Jean-Jacques Rousseau, Thomas Paine, and William Godwin. She began making yearly visits to London in the late 1780s and, having met Godwin through her father, was drawn into Godwin's radical circle of thinkers, which included Thomas Holcroft, Elizabeth Inchbald, and Mary Wollstonecraft. Opie formed a close friendship with Wollstonecraft and would later memorialize her in the novel *Adeline Mowbray* (1804).

She married the portrait painter John Opie in 1798 and moved into more fashionable literary and artistic society, playing hostess to the writers William Wordsworth, Lord Byron, Maria Edgeworth, Walter Scott, Lady Caroline Lamb, and Robert Southey, and the artists Joseph Turner, Joshua Reynolds, and Henry Fuseli. Encouraged by her husband, she produced several novels and collections of poetry during her brief marriage to him.

In April 1807 John Opie died and Amelia returned to her father's home in Norwich, where she once again acted as his hostess and ran his household. Dr. Alderson fell ill late in 1820 and was nursed by his daughter until his death five years later. Although raised as a freethinking Unitarian, Opie turned to the Society of Friends (Quakers) for consolation during her father's long illness. In 1825, only a few months after her father's death, she formally converted and, following the tenets of her new faith, gave up her literary pursuits altogether. Her Quakerism imposed a restricted social life, but she continued to maintain friendships with writers such as Harriet Martineau and with Southey, with whom she carried on a lively correspondence. For the remaining 28 years of her life she devoted herself to charitable works and support of social causes such as the antislavery movement. She died at Norwich in 1853.

Critical Analysis

Amelia Opie published her first novel, *The Dangers of Coquetry*, in 1790. The novel, in spite of the radical society she was keeping at the time, was little more than a conventional conduct book aimed at instructing young ladies on proper behavior. It was politely received, but she produced little else until after her marriage to John Opie, who supported her literary ambitions. Her first work after her marriage, *The Father and Daughter* (1801)—the story of a young woman who abandons her widowed father, elopes with her lover, and finally returns home to find her father has gone mad—was widely popular for decades, with translations into French and Portuguese, and was the basis for an opera and two plays. Walter Scott told her that after reading the novel he had cried "more than he ever cried over such things."

In 1804 she published her most significant work, *Adeline Mowbray; or, The Mother and Daughter,* based on the relationship between William Godwin and Mary Wollstonecraft. The heroine, like Wollstonecraft, is freethinking, pure, and full of integrity, but suffers society's censure because of her love of Frederic Glenmurray and her decision to live with him "in honor of her principles." Reflecting the growing conservatism of English society and the backlash against the radicalism of Godwin and Wollstonecraft, *Adeline Mowbray* received mixed reviews. The *Critical Review* found the novel's morals suspect, warning readers "that the effect of [the novel's] morals does not seem to have been consulted . . . we have to object to . . . the fascinating colours thrown over the erroneous virtues of Adeline and Glenmurray." Modern feminist critics celebrate its contribution to the understanding of Mary Wollstonecraft and the never-ending debate about marriage. Dale Spender remarks, "*Adeline Mowbray* exposes many of the hypocrisies associated with marriage and . . . explicitly states the arguments for and against this holy estate—even at the expense of character on occasion."

Opie's other works include the sentimental novels *Valentine's Eve* (1816) and *Madelaine* (1822); the verse collections *Miscellaneous Poems* (1802), *The Warrior's Return* (1808), and *Lays for the Dead* (1833); and a memoir of her husband for the Royal Academy of Art, published in 1809.

As a novelist, Amelia Opie dealt with the same subject matter as her near contemporary JANE AUSTEN, but she lacked Austen's psychological insight. She was satirized as Miss Poppyseed by THOMAS LOVE PEACOCK in his novel *Headlong Hall*. Her own stated purpose in writing—"I like to make people cry, indeed, if I do not do it, all my readers are disappointed"—perhaps illustrates the limitations of her literary ambitions.

Other Work by Amelia Opie

The Works of Mrs. Amelia Opie, Complete in Three Volumes. New York: AMS Press, 1986.

Works about Amelia Opie

Spender, Dale. *Mothers of the Novel: 100 Good Women Writers before Jane Austen.* London: Pandora, 1986.

Ty, Eleanor. *Empowering the Feminine: The Narratives of Mary Robinson, Jane West, and Amelia Opie, 1796–1812.* Toronto: University of Toronto Press, 1998.

O'Shaughnessy, Arthur William Edgar
(1844–1881) *poet*

The Irish-English poet Arthur O'Shaughnessy was born in London to Oscar William and Louisa O'Shaughnessy. Like COVENTRY PATMORE and EDMUND GOSSE, he worked in the British Museum—in his case, the zoological department. This job provided income, but kept him away from his passion, French literature. In 1873 he married Eleanor Marston, sister of the poet PHILIP BOURKE MARSTON. Together they wrote a collection of children's stories, *Toyland* (1875). Their own two children died in infancy, and Eleanor died in 1879. O'Shaughnessy, plagued with frail health since childhood, died two years later.

O'Shaughnessy's work was most influenced by ALGERNON CHARLES SWINBURNE. His first book,

Epic of Women and Other Poems (1870), drew praise from Swinburne and from Dante Gabriel Rossetti, who became O'Shaughnessy's friend. Of this early work, the literary historian Jerome Hamilton Buckley writes, "[it] echoed the melodies of Swinburne transposed with delicacy and tact into the new singer's own minor key."

The Epic of Women surveys five legendary women who "played with men a calculated game," helping to forge events by their influence. The introduction, "Creation," leaves its subject, Eve, unnamed. "The world beheld, and hailed her, form and face," O'Shaughnessy writes; "And ere a man could see her with desire, / [God] looked on her so, and loved her first, / And came upon her in a mist, like fire, / And of her beauty quenched his god-like thirst." Thus, O'Shaughnessy lays the fallen nature of women at masculine feet. Another poem, "The Fountain of Tears," creates an image of beauty out of the grief all humans come to experience: "Very peaceful the place is, and solely / For piteous lamenting and sighing, / And those who come living or dying / Alike from their hopes and their fears."

O'Shaughnessy's "Ode" appeared in his poetry collection *Music and Moonlight* (1874). The poem celebrates the role of poets and often is interpreted as a celebration of the Irish. The first stanza of this poem also introduces the enduring phrase, "movers and shakers." The English composer Sir Edward Elgar (1857–1934) set the poem to music for orchestra, chorus, and mezzo-soprano soloist as *The Music Makers* (1912).

With its sheer love of beauty O'Shaughnessy's poetry suggests AESTHETICISM, the late-19th-century European movement that identified beauty as the sole purpose of art. In O'Shaughnessy's case, Gosse wrote, the result is "soft, tremulous, and rich.... It is flute-music, not strong in quality, nor wide in range, but of a piercing tenderness."

Critical Analysis

O'Shaughnessy is best known for the lovely "Ode from *Music and Moolight*." In this poem and in many of his later works, O'Shaughnessy was influenced by the French symbolist poets, who rejected realism in favor of a world of imagination, a dreamlike universe where they believed deep spiritual truths could be found.

"Ode from *Music and Moonlight*" is a poem about the power of poets and poetry to change the world. Its most famous lines are the first two: "We are the music makers, / And we are the dreamers of dreams." Indeed, the poem itself has a musical quality, using a pronouced rhythm, alliteration, and rhyme to evoke the sweet sound of the poet's songs.

Poetry, however, is not merely the stuff of dreams, O'Shaughnessy says. Poets not only make music and imagine other worlds, but they are also "the movers and shakers / Of the world for ever, it seems." Stories, he says, can build empires and

> *One man with a dream, at pleasure,*
> *Shall go forth and conquer a crown;*
> *And three with a new song's measure*
> *Can trample a kingdom down.*

O'Shaughnessy uses an unconventional form to emphasize the unconventionality of his vision. Although the poem is often printed as having only three stanzas, the original was nine stanzas long. The stanzas are each eight lines long and are rhymed either *abababab / aabbabab*. The third stanza makes a shocking pronouncement—that reality itself is the product of the poetic imagination: "Each age is a dream that is dying, / Or one that is coming to birth." The next stanza drives the point home: "A breath of our inspiration / Is the life of each generation."

O'Shaughnessy brings his poem to a majestic conclusion. He imagines the end of his own era and greets the poets to come:

> *Bring us hither your sun and your summers;*
> *And renew our world as of yore;*
> *You shall teach us your song's new numbers,*
> *And things that we dreamed not before.*

Whereas the poet Percy Bysshe Shelley, in his *Defence of Poetry* (1819), went so far as to characterize poets as the "unacknowledged legislators of the world," O'Shaughnessy goes further: Poets dream the world into existence.

Ouida (Marie Louise de la Ramée)
(1839–1908) *novelist*

Ouida was born in Bury St. Edmund's, a small English town in Suffolk, England, to Louis Ramée, a French schoolmaster and possibly a former secret agent of the French government, and Susan Sutton. (*Ouida* was the young girl's mispronunciation of *Louisa*.) Ramée's part in his daughter's education was to tell her the latest gossip of Paris salons and stories of beautiful princes, gallant counts, wicked politicians, and brave warriors.

In 1857 Ouida moved to London with her mother and grandmother. Looking for a way to make money, she wrote a short story, "Dashwood's Drag," about upper-class doings at a horse-racing track. She then showed the piece to Francis Ainsworth, the family doctor, who recognized Ouida's talent and forwarded her stories to his cousin HARRISON AINSWORTH, an editor with *Bentley's Magazine*. The editor bought Ouida's story, which was published in 1859, along with some 20 other stories over the next four years. Ouida's stories belonged to the genre of SENSATION FICTION, lurid tales that revolved around aristocratic characters who lead immoral but exciting lives.

Ouida's first full-length novel, *Granville de Vigne: A Tale of the Day,* appeared in the *New Monthly Magazine* in installments between 1861 and 1863. The novel, published in book form in 1863 as *Held in Bondage,* was a tremendous success and centers on the adventures of young cavalrymen. The protagonist, Granville de Vigne, marries a wicked lady who turns out to be a bigamist.

More novels followed, the best known of which is *Under Two Flags* (1867). In this novel, the Honorable Bertie Cecil takes the blame for his younger brother's misdeeds and enlists in the French Foreign Legion. All turns out well, but only after much adventure and Bertie's romance with two beautiful women. The novel even has self-sacrifice as the camp follower Cigarette takes the bullets meant for Bertie:

> "Great Heaven! You have given your life for mine!"
>
> The words broke from him in an agony as he held her upward against his heart.... She smiled up in his eyes, while even in that moment, when ... the shots had pierced through from her shoulder to her bosom, a hot scarlet flush came over her cheeks as she felt his touch.

An Ouida novel often contains dashing, high-born heroes, beautiful and flamboyant villainesses who possess innumerable lovers, and modest heroines who remain in the background until the final pages. According to the critic John Sutherland, "Ouida became a favorite author with military readers who liked her ... 'fast' amorality ..., her aura of expensive femininity ..., and her frank worship of the British officer class." Others were less entranced. *Blackwood's Magazine* wrote in 1867 that "we do not feel ourselves capable of noticing ... certain ... very nasty books signed with the name of Ouida."

Ouida also wrote animal stories, of which *A Dog of Flanders* (1872) is the most famous. In this novel, Patrasche, a dog forced to pull a heavy cart for his cruel master, is adopted and cared for by Nello, a gentle peasant boy. This highly sentimental tale describes the subsequent sufferings of the two.

Ouida continued to be a prolific writer, publishing more than a dozen novels and numerous stories for children. At the time of her death, however, her work had ceased to be popular, and she died in poverty.

Many contemporary scholars are rediscovering the greatness of some of Ouida's later works. As a Victorian woman, Ouida was able to achieve an enormous success during her lifetime. As the poet and scholar Wilfrid Scawen Blunt remarked in her obituary, "Though no indiscriminate reader of Ouida's novels, I had and have a high opinion of the best of them as works of genius. In spite of exaggeration and occasional absurdities of detail, I hold them to be the only English novels which can at all be compared with Balzac's as giving a vivid and life-like picture of the larger world of society, women as well as men, they describe."

Works about Ouida

Bigland, Eileen. *Ouida: The Passionate Victorian.* New York: Duell, Sloan & Pearce, 1951.

Gilbert, Pamela. "Ouida and the Other New Woman." In *Victorian Women Writers and the Woman Question,* edited by Nicola Diane Thompson. Cambridge, England: Cambridge University Press, 1999.

Owenson, Sydney (Lady Morgan)

(1776?–1859) *novelist, journalist, poet*

Sydney Owenson was born at sea on the way from Holyhead to Dublin, Ireland, her father's native land. As her father was a roving actor, Owenson spent much of her childhood traveling and, therefore, after the death of her mother in 1789, received little formal education. She became self-taught, and proved to be a voracious reader and a precocious poet. Eventually she became the breadwinner of the family, earning money first as a governess and then a poet, after a long period of unemployment for her father. In her 20s, she turned from poetry to the intensely patriotic Irish novels for which she became known. SIR WALTER SCOTT praised them as "national and picaresque fiction." Owenson published her early novels *The Heiress of Desmond* (1804) and *The Novice of St. Dominick* (1805) while working as a governess. The novel that made her famous, *The Wild Irish Girl* (1806), with an erudite heroine named Glorvina, was both an extremely popular political romance and a serious history of Ireland. It describes the struggles of the Irish people against English rule, as do most of her subsequent novels, or "National Tales," as she called them.

From then on, she was known by her heroine's namesake, "Glorvina." Owenson's popularity rose, and she saw the production of mantles (cloaks) and bodkins (hairpins) fashioned after her well-known heroine. The success of *The Wild Irish Girl* brought Owenson into the highest literary ranks along with writers such as LORD BYRON, PERCY SHELLEY, and THOMAS MOORE.

Owenson's energetic personality, sharp wit, and literary skill made her a favorite among the upper classes. She was so loved that the marquis and marchioness of Abercorn took her under their wing. At their estate she met her future husband, Thomas Charles Morgan, a doctor who was knighted during their engagement for his services. Lady Morgan is described in LEIGH HUNT's poem, "The Bluestocking Revels":

> *And dear Lady Morgan, see, see, when she comes,*
> *With her pulse all beating for freedom like drum,*
> *So Irish, so modish, so mixtish, so wild;*
> *So committing herself as she talks—like a child.*
> *So trim, yet so easy—polite, yet high-hearted,*
> *That truth and she, try all she can, won't be parted. . . .*

Owenson declared in her preface to *O'Donnel: A National Tale* (1814) that she wrote her books to promote "a great national cause, the emancipation of the Catholics of Ireland." She believed it was a novel's job "to inculcate truth" and "possess a moral scope." Politics, she claimed, were simply "morals on a grander scale." Among her novels after the politically provocative *O'Donnel* are *Florence McCarthy: An Irish Tale* (1816) and one of her most widely read books, *The O'Briens and the O'Flahertys: A National Tale* (1827). Both are good examples of her use of the novel to champion her political cause, as she acknowledged: "A novel is specially adapted to enable the advocate of any cause to steal upon the public." Lady Morgan also published travel books and political essays.

Her later works hinted at her disillusionment with the church and Irish politics because they failed to change or improve. Lady Morgan died suddenly at her home on April 16, 1859. Writing until the end, she remained a vital patriotic figure who promoted Irish social reform and the involvement of women in literary and political life.

Critical Analysis

Owenson's works were known for their revolutionary ideas and radical politics, particularly the controversial theme of Irish independence. In *The Wild Irish Girl*, for example, she speaks against the British union, calling for a United Kingdom of Great Britain and Ireland. The heroine, Glorvina, a Gaelic princess, teaches Horatio, the son of an absentee landlord, about the errors of his colonizing ways and the value of Irish culture.

The *Quarterly Review* decried her writings, saying that Owenson, "should exchange her idle raptures for commonsense." For many years thereafter, a writer for the *Quarterly Review* publishing under the pseudonym "John Wilson Croker," continued to comment on her life and criticize her work. The English government allegedly enlisted Croker to destroy Owenson's credibility and reputation because her work was centered on promoting Irish freedom from British tyranny. With her *Wild Irish Girl*, Croker accused her of using her elevated title, Lady Morgan, to mislead and poison the minds of her readers.

Lady Morgan fought back in her four-volume novel, *Florence McCarthy: An Irish Tale*, portraying Croker as the despicable character Conway Townsend Crawley, who is described as "a man formed alike by nature and education to betray that land that gave him birth . . . who would stoop to seek his fortune by effecting the fall of a frail woman, or would strive to advance it by stabbing the character of an honest one—who would crush aspiring merit behind the ambuscade of anonymous security." Their rivalry continued throughout Owenson's life, but Croker, following the publication of *Florence McCarthy*, ignored the repeated rebuttals she issued.

Other Work by Sydney Owenson

Feldman, Paula, and Theresa Kelley, eds. *Romantic Women Writers: Voices and Countervoices.* Hanover, N.H.: University Press of New England, 1995.

A Work about Sydney Owenson

Campbell, Mary. *Lady Morgan: The Life and Times of Sydney Owenson.* London: Pandora, 1988.

Oxford Movement

When King Henry VIII repudiated the Roman Catholic Church in 1534 and established the state religion as Anglican, or English Catholic, and Protestant, he opened the way for several reinterpretations of Christian dogma. At one extreme, some Catholics held onto their beliefs; at the other extreme, some English wanted the church "purified" of all practices and beliefs arising in the church after the fifth century A.D. This led, along with other, political, differences, to the 17th-century English Civil War (1642–48) and the establishment of the Commonwealth (1649–60) by dissenting Protestants. With the Restoration (1660), the Anglican Church became the official state church.

In 1833 at Oxford University, a group of clergymen—who were also professors—reopened the question and expressed a wish to have the Anglican Church return to some of the practices and beliefs associated with Roman Catholicism. Led by JOHN HENRY NEWMAN, who later converted and became a Roman Catholic cardinal, the group publicized their beliefs in a series of tracts (thus the alternative name Tractarians for the group). Included in their number were Edward Pusey, JOHN KEBLE (whose 1833 sermon on the dangers of liberalism in the church set off the whole controversy), and Richard H. Froude. The tracts had wide influence, ignited controversy throughout Britain, and inspired reexamination of medieval history, and the trappings and rituals of the church. Secondary influences of the movement were felt in the works of the PRE-RAPHAELITE MOVEMENT and the works of poets such as ALFRED, LORD TENNYSON.

Works about the Oxford Movement

Crumb, Lawrence N. *The Oxford Movement and Its Leaders*. Lanham, Md.: Scarecrow Press, 1990.

O'Connell, Marvin. *The Oxford Conspirators: A History of the Oxford Movement, 1833–1845*. Lanham, Md.: University Press of America, 2000.

Vaiss, Paul, ed. *From Oxford to the People: Reconsidering Newman and the Oxford Movement*. Harrisburg, Penn.: Morehouse, 1997.

Paget, Violet
See LEE, VERNON.

Paley, William (1743–1805) *nonfiction writer*

William Paley was born in Peterborough, in central England. His father, William, was a minister and headmaster of the Free Grammar School in Giggleswick, in Yorkshire, and Paley attended his father's school. In 1758 he entered Christ's College, Cambridge, to follow his father's profession. Paley later admitted that he wasted his first two years at Cambridge by drinking and gambling, but he renounced these activities after a friend rebuked him. After receiving a master's degree, Paley was ordained in 1767.

In 1785 Paley published his first major work, *The Principles of Moral and Political Philosophy.* The work outlines his moral system, a combination of utilitarianism, in which each object or person's value is determined by the pleasure they provide (*see* BENTHAM, JEREMY), and the will of God. For Paley, God's law is the immutable foundation of morality. Individuals perceive this law through revelation, then use their revelations as guides on how to treat others. Salvation is achieved when individuals act upon their revelations. However, in Paley's view, no specific rules of conduct exist beyond God's original law. Therefore, whatever action appears to achieve the most utilitarian result is the most appropriate. One of the work's most memorable passages defends this principle. Paley depicts a flock of pigeons gathering seeds in a field. Instead of keeping what they gather, the pigeons give their seeds to the weakest pigeon. This pigeon wastes many of the seeds, but Paley argues that its actions are beneficial because the other pigeons learn industry and charity.

Paley's belief in the expediency of actions generated considerable criticism within the Anglican Church, as fellow ministers argued that it undermined fundamental tenets such as the Ten Commandments. Furthermore, some reviewers suggested that Paley had plagiarized his ideas from philosophers such as Immanuel Kant. Paley acknowledged this claim, referring to himself as a synthesizer of ideas rather than as an original writer. In addition, his next major work, *Evidences of Christianity* (1794), rebuked his critics by offering a more conventional history of Christian morality. Today, Paley is praised for his ability to reconcile apparently conflicting philosophies and illuminate their similarities. The critic Victor Nuovo claims that Paley "combined critical historicism with a reverence for Christian antiquity; reason with revelation; [and] mechanism with a new sensibility towards nature and an openness to other more spiritual forces operating within it."

Other Work by William Paley
Nuovo, Victor, ed. *The Works of William Paley.* 6 vols. Bristol, England: Thoemmes Press, 1998.

Palgrave, Francis Turner (1824–1897)
anthologist, poet

Born to wealth and culture as the son of the noted historian Sir Francis Palgrave and his wife, Elizabeth Turner Palgrave, who came from a prominent banking family, Francis Palgrave was exposed to the best in art, music, and literature. He boarded at the exclusive Charterhouse School and then won a scholarship to Balliol College, Oxford. At Oxford, his brilliant circle of friends included the future poet and critic MATTHEW ARNOLD and the poet ARTHUR HUGH CLOUGH. Palgrave worked in teacher training for several years, during which time he became friends with ALFRED TENNYSON, and then embarked on a lifelong career as a member of the government's education department. In subsequent years he published his own poetry, critical essays, and biographies, but he is best known and remembered for his poetry anthology *The Golden Treasury* (1861). Tennyson, it is said, helped him make some of the selections. It was immediately and immensely successful and remained so in its several subsequent editions up until the turn of the century. His success in this anthology, along with criticism of his omissions such as the 17th-century Metaphysical poets, led to revisions, new editions, and companion anthologies such as *The Children's Treasury of English Song* (1875), *Tennyson's Selected Lyrics* (1885), and *Treasury of Sacred Song* (1889). Palgrave's talents were recognized in 1885 by his election to the professorship of poetry at Oxford, a post he held for 10 years. His last published work was a collection of his Oxford lectures, *Landscapes in Poetry,* which appeared in 1897, shortly before his death.

A Work about Francis Palgrave
Palgrave, Gwenllian F. *Francis Turner Palgrave: His Journals and Memories of his Life.* New York: AMS Press, 1971.

Pater, Walter Horatio (1839–1894)
scholar, critic

Walter Pater, one of the finest prose stylists of the 19th century, was born in London to Richard Pater, a doctor, and Maria Hill Pater, and attended King's School in Canterbury before graduating from Oxford University in 1862. He was elected to a fellowship at Brasenose College, Oxford, two years later, and remained in that post for most of his life, living with his two unmarried sisters.

From 1869 to 1873 he contributed articles on Italian artists, such as Michelangelo and Pico della Miradola, to periodicals, publishing them as a group in *Studies in the History of the Renaissance* (1873). That work, which turned away from the Victorian emphasis on the moral value of art, embodied the principles of "art for its own sake." Pater argued for a view of art that considered how the beauty of the work can be perceived fully and individually. In the preface to *Studies in the History of the Renaissance,* for instance, Pater claims that "The objects with which aesthetic criticism deals—music, poetry, artistic and accomplished forms of human life—are indeed receptacles of so many powers or forces: they possess . . . so many virtues or qualities." The question the critic needs to ask, then, is "What is this song or picture, this engaging personality presented in life or in a book, to *me?*" Like the PRE-RAPHAELITES, who influenced him, Pater rejected rules of aesthetic evaluation, claiming that "What is important, then, is not that the critic should possess a correct abstract definition of beauty for the intellect, but a certain kind of temperament, the power of being deeply moved by the presence of beautiful objects." That move, away from principle toward temperament and sensation, startled many of Pater's readers and excited many others. Pater's pronouncements in the conclusion to *Studies—*

among them "Not the fruit of experience, but experience itself, is the end," and "To burn always with this hard, gemlike flame, to maintain this ecstasy, is success in life"—were taken to hedonistic extremes by some of his readers. Feeling misunderstood, Pater suppressed the conclusion in subsequent editions of *Studies*. His position did not imply self-indulgence; on the contrary, according to G. B. Tennyson and Donald Gray, he argued for "a rigorous disciplining of the sensibility to make it receptive to the highest levels of the beautiful." His novel *Marius the Epicurean* (1885) may have been a response to those who embraced and those who criticized *Studies*.

In addition to *Studies* and *Marius the Epicurean*, Pater published essays and other nonfiction prose in *Imaginary Portraits* (1887), *Appreciations* (1889), and *Plato and Platonism* (1893). Pater may be said to have been the unwilling father of AESTHETICISM, which flourished at the end of the century. Arguing that all art should aspire to the condition of music, Pater tried in his prose—through careful attention to sentence rhythm, the melody of phrase, and the sound of individual words—to fulfill that aspiration. Those he influenced most profoundly, notably GERARD MANLEY HOPKINS and OSCAR WILDE, thought he succeeded. All his writing may be said to have affirmed the value of particular artists and poets, for we live, as Pater argues in the chapter "Style" in *Appreciations*, "in a world where after all we must needs make the most of things." Pater spent 1885 to 1893 in London, writing and lecturing, before returning to Oxford, where he died of heart failure.

Critical Analysis

Pater is best remembered for *Marius the Epicurean* (1885), a semiautobiographical novel. The central character, Marius, is clearly modeled on Pater himself, although the setting is Imperial Rome during the reign of Marcus Aurelius (A.D. 161–180). While the reader follows Marius from boyhood through adulthood, there is little action in the tale. Rather, the story is about how Marius develops a philosophy of life, a set of guiding principles that allow him to make reasoned choices and live well.

Pater describes Marius as constitutionally idealistic. After the death of his mother, the boy abandons traditional religion and the belief in an afterlife, but he does not abandon the quest to develop his spirit and intellect fully, to develop an ideal self. Like Pater himself, Marius adopts the philosophy of Epicureanism. He does not subscribe to the popular notion of the philosophy embodied in the phrase, "Eat, drink, and be merry, for tomorrow we may die." Rather, he comes to believe that the best life results from appreciating the beauty and fullness of life itself. As Pater notes, the term the Epicurean is "comprehensive enough to cover pleasures so different in quality, in their causes and effects, as the pleasures of wine and love, of art and science, of religious enthusiasm and political enterprise, and of that taste or curiosity which satisfied itself with long days of serious study."

Marius eventually comes to the court of the philosopher-emperor, Marcus Aurelius, whom he at first admires for his stoic philosophy. However, he is horrified by the emperor's indifference to the suffering of people and animals in the bloody gladiatorial entertainments so beloved of the Roman masses. Marius concludes that the emperor's tolerance of the spectacle is problematic. "There was something," Marius says, "in the bare fact that he could sit patiently through a scene like this, which seem to [him] . . . to mark Aurelius as his inferior now and forever on the question of righteousness; to set them on opposite sides, in some great conflict, of which that difference was but a single presentment." Marius is also distressed by the emperor's stoic indifference to life itself and to what Marius labels "the temper of suicide." Pater says that "Marius, with a soul which must always leap up in loyal gratitude for mere physical sunshine, touching him as it touched the flies in the air" simply could not accept such a "melancholy intellectual attitude."

As he grows older, continuously seeking to learn and grow, Marius begins feel that Epicureanism, by itself, is a philosophy best suited to youth, and he feels a need for something more in his life. He seems to find what he is seeking in the early Christian church. Although he never quite converts, he finds much that appeals to him in this new religion. After attending a mass, Pater tells us, "the natural soul of worship in. . . . [Marius] had at last been satisfied as never before. He felt, as he left that place, that he must hereafter experience often a longing memory, a kind of thirst, for all this over again." He finds in Christianity a deep and abiding sense of humanism, of compassion, love, and what he calls "self-pity"—an understanding of the essential tragedy of the human condition, that we all must suffer and die eventually. Moved by the faith of the Christians he has come to know, Marius sacrifices his own life to save the life of his Christian friend, Cornelius, in a final gesture of love.

Pater worked hard to hone his prose to an exquisite edge, and *Marius the Epicurean* embodies the best of his style. The writing is clear, precise, and carefully balanced. He tells of Marius's determination to develop his prose style:

> He would make of it a serious study, weighing the precise power of every phrase and word, as though it were precious metal, disentangling the later associations and going back to the original and native sense of each, restoring to full significance all its wealth of latent figurative expression, reviving or replacing its outworn or tarnished images.

Pater himself demonstrates this care and sensitivity throughout the novel.

Marius the Epicurean influenced the 19th-century aesthetic movement, and adherents of the movement, such as writer Oscar Wilde and painter DANTE GABRIEL ROSSETTI, lived by Pater's philosophy of living life intensely in the pursuit of ideal beauty.

Works about Walter Pater

Brake, Laurel. *Walter Pater*. Plymouth, England: Northcote House, with British Council, 1994.

Buckler, William E. *Walter Pater: The Critic as Artist of Ideas*. New York: New York University Press, 1987.

Daley, Kenneth. *The Rescue of Romanticism: Walter Pater and John Ruskin*. Athens: Ohio University Press, 2001.

Williams, Carolyn. *Transfigured World: Walter Pater's Aesthetic Historicism*. Ithaca, N.Y.: Cornell University Press, 1990.

Patmore, Coventry (1823–1896) *poet, essayist, critic*

Born to Eliza Robertson Patmore and the writer Peter George Patmore in Woodford, Suffolk, England, Patmore was educated at home until, at age 16, he was sent to school in Paris. In 1846 he became a librarian at the British Museum. Twice widowed, Patmore married three times. His second wife was Marianne Byles, a Roman Catholic convert. Prior to their marriage in 1865, Patmore, an Anglican-raised agnostic, himself converted. His wife's wealth enabled him to write poetry full-time.

The public ignored Patmore's first volume, *Poems of 1844*. Reviews savaged it for being decadent and derivative of ROMANTICISM: The *Blackwood*'s reviewer wrote, "This is the life into which the slime of the [Keatses] and Shelleys of former times had fecundated." Certainly these lines from "The River" suggest the fluctuating cosmos of PERCY BYSSHE SHELLEY's "The Cloud": "The river, late so bright, / Rolls foul and black." However, many poets praised the book, as did novelist EDWARD BULWER-LYTTON for its "luxuriance of fancy," although he placed Patmore among "Poets who are Poets to Poets—not Poets to the Multitude."

The American success of Patmore's third volume of verse, proving contagious, advanced Patmore's public standing at home. *The Angel in the House* consists of two books: "The Betrothal" (1854) and "The Espousals" (1856). Similarly, *The Victories of Love* consists of two books: "Faithful for Ever" (1860) and "The Victories of Love"

(1862). Devastated by the death of his first wife, Emily Andrews, in 1862, Patmore left the story unfinished.

His biographer and great-grandson Derek Patmore has noted that *The Angel in the House* "marks the happiest moments" in Patmore's life. Its main characters are Felix Vaughan, who is Patmore's surrogate, and Honoria Churchill, whom Vaughan loves and courts. Honoria, "all mildness . . . and grace," embodies marriage as sacrament, the love between man and woman that unites them with God. With the poem's title, Patmore had coined a phrase that Victorian England embraced as its expression of ideal womanhood. Honoria takes her cue from Vaughan. "[She] holds me," he says, "'as the weather-vane / Is held by yonder clematis.'"

Each of the segments continuing the poem's story is prefaced with general, philosophical ones on the subject of love. The day's critics dismissed the narrative parts for their mundaneness. EDMUND GOSSE, for instance, referred to "[t]his Laureate of the tea-table, with his humdrum stories of girls that smell of bread and butter"; but he praised the originality of those sections illustrating "the psychology of love." Describing the emotional inequity that a wife may experience despite her best efforts to be sensitive to his needs, Patmore writes about the husband, for example, "[His] each impatient word provokes / Another, not from her, but him."

Most of the poems in *The Unknown Eros* (1877) deal with Patmore's mystical vision of love. In one, "The Azalea," the speaker's beloved has died, and the aroma of "the gold Azalea," with which he identifies the deceased, refreshes his sense of loss after he wakes from a dream of her death. He then discovers her note to him envisioning their reunion: "Parting's well-paid with soon again to meet." The poem illustrates what the critic F. L. Lucas has defined as one of the book's motives: "to prove that married love exists in Heaven," for "Heaven without marriage would have been to Coventry Patmore no Heaven at all."

Critical Analysis

Like many poets, Coventry Patmore developed a theory of poetry and the role of the poet. He believed that the poet's imagination enabled him to look at nature and the things of daily life with a different vision and to see aspects of the divine. In *Principles in Art* (1889) he notes:

> The poet's eye glances from earth to heaven; and his faculty of discerning likeness in difference enables him to express the unknown in terms of the known, so as to confer upon the former a sensible credibility, and to give the latter a truly sacramental dignity.

Thus the poet directs the reader's eye and uses metaphor and other poetic devices to show the reader the truth, which for Patmore is often a religious truth.

This method is clearly demonstrated in Patmore's poem "The Toys," from *The Unknown Eros*. The poem, which uses an irregular rhyme scheme and varying line lengths, is divided into three parts. The first describes a scene between father and son, in which the father, angered at being for the "seventh time disobeyed," strikes his son and sends him away "With hard words and unkissed."

In the second part of the poem, the father, feeling remorseful and afraid that his son's "grief should hinder sleep" visits the boy in his room. He kisses away the sleeping boy's tears and "left others of my own." He weeps because he notices that his son has gathered all his most precious toys "to comfort his sad heart." Patmore does a masterful job of cataloguing the treasures of a typical little boy:

> A box of counters and a red-veined stone,
> A piece of glass abraded by the beach.
> And six or seven shells,
> A bottle with bluebells,
> And two French copper coins, ranged there
>   with careful art

In the final section of the poem, the speaker finds a divine reflection in ordinary things. As he goes to bed that evening, he asks God ("fatherly not less / Than I whom Thou has moulded from the clay") to forgive humankind for its trifling joys and to say of them "I will be sorry for their childishness." Thus does a homely domestic moment, one every parent will recognize, become a metaphor for divine love and forgiveness in Patmore's poetic hand.

A Work about Coventry Patmore
Sussman, Herbert. *Coventry Patmore*. Boston: Twayne, 1981.

Peacock, Thomas Love (1785–1866)
novelist, poet, essayist

The son of Sarah Love and Samuel Peacock, a London glass merchant, Thomas Love Peacock left school at age 12 and never attended university, yet is today considered one of the most scholarly and philosophical novelists of the 19th century. In 1819 he married Jane Gryffydh, with whom he had several children, and joined the East India Company, where he rose to the position of chief examiner and remained with the company until retirement in 1856. Peacock was introduced to PERCY BYSSHE SHELLEY in 1812 and became one of the poet's closest friends, handling his London business affairs and serving as Shelley's executor. In addition to Shelley, Peacock's circle of friends included such other major figures of his day as JOHN STUART MILL, JEREMY BENTHAM, and LEIGH HUNT.

An unsuccessful poet and dramatist, Peacock was nearly 30 when he found a form appropriate for his satirical voice in his philosophical "discussion novels." The novels consist almost entirely of conversations: of Socratic dialogues with little plot or character development. His best-known works include *Nightmare Abbey* (1818), which satirizes the English romantic movement; *Maid Marian* (1822), a cynical account of Robin Hood; and *The Misfortunes of Elphin* (1829), an unconventional interpretation of the Arthurian legends. Many of his satirical books are named after the grand houses in which their characters gather to enjoy one another's company: *Headlong Hall* (1816), *Melincourt* (1817), *Crotchet Castle* (1831), and *Gryll Grange* (1860–61). The critic J. B. Priestley notes that Peacock as satirist "brings fun into the high and dry atmosphere of exposition and debate. His favourite butts are philosophical enthusiasts, especially those who believe that one thing alone will save the world." Peacock's targets included WILLIAM WORDSWORTH and the LAKE POETS, and the political philosophers Jeremy Bentham, THOMAS MALTHUS, and WILLIAM GODWIN.

Peacock's skepticism toward the fashionable in the arts is also found in his critical essays. He questioned the value of poetry in *The Four Stages of Poetry* (1820) and was, in turn, famously rebutted by Shelley in *A Defence of Poetry* (1821, published 1840). Despite their intellectual differences, Peacock was devoted to Shelley and years after the poet's death wrote appreciatively of him in *Memoirs of Shelley* (1858–60).

Peacock continues to be valued by scholars as a satirist who targeted the intellectual excesses and follies of his age. The critic John Mair writes, "He is the first novelist to write purely for an intelligent, highly educated public who would be expected to find amusement in mental rather than physical or emotional contortions. . . . The novels appeal to the curious, humorous, cynical mind, and for that reason are sure of a certain immortality."

Critical Analysis
A crotchet is an odd, whimsical, or stubborn notion. Peacock's novel *Crotchet Castle* is aptly named, because it is populated with residents and guests all of whom pursue their individual crotchets with single-minded fervor. Peacock's novels are not really novels, and his style is quite his own; there is no one else quite like him. There is a smidgeon of plot in each of the novels, but plot is of little importance. While Peacock's people are certainly characters, in one sense of the word, there is no real characterization in his novels. Each character is no more than a mouthpiece for a particular point of view, and the action of the

novel involves discussions, often over dinner, in which the characters' points of view are held up to ridicule. There is little in the way of authorial voice in Peacock; the characters generally end up bringing ridicule upon themselves by the extremism with which they hold their views. As the writer Virginia Woolf put it, in Peacock's fiction, "Instead of being manysided, complicated, elusive, people possess one idiosyncrasy apiece, which crystallizes them into sharp separate characters, colliding briskly when they meet."

In *Crotchet Castle,* many of the characters' names define their crotchets. Mr. Chainmail is an antiquarian, and, as far as he is concerned, everything since the 12th century is merely a falling away from the pinnacle of history. Mr. Toogood is a philanthropist; Mr. Firedamp believes all ills, human and otherwise, are the result of an overabundance of water; Mr. Henbane is a toxicologist who keeps poisoning frogs and cats and reviving them; Mr. Trillo is a musician; Dr. Morbific has been "all over the world to prove that there is no such thing as contagion; and has inoculated himself with plague, yellow fever, and every variety of pestilence, and is still alive to tell the story . . . [He is] a walking phial of wrath, corked full of all infections, and not to be touched without extreme hazard." Other guests include Mr. Scionar, the transcendentalist; Mr. MacQuedy, the Scottish economist; the Reverend Doctor Folliot, a great admirer of all things Greek and a lover of food and drink; Crotchet and his son, Crotchet Junior; and Lady Clarinda and her suitor, Captain Fitzchrome—who seem to be less crotchety than the other characters and serve as nice counterpoints to their obsessiveness.

In one particularly funny scene, Crotchet Junior proposes this question to the group: If they had a large amount of money to spend to "regenerate society," how would they spend it? Mr. Trillo wants to build an opera house. Mr. Scionar wants a sacred space where transcendentalists can "teach the world how to see through a glass darkly." Mr. Trillo counters, "See through an opera glass brightly," and Dr. Folliot caps the exchange with, "See through a wine-glass, full of claret; then you see both darkly and brightly."

Woolf neatly summarizes what it is like to read Peacock. His is a

> world so happily constituted that there is always trout for breakfast, wine in the cellar, and some amusing contretemps, such as the cook setting herself alight and being put out by the footman, to make us laugh—a world where there is nothing more pressing to do than to "glide over the face of the waters, discussing everything and settling nothing."

The pleasures of Peacock are many and sweet and very old-fashioned.

Other Works by Thomas Love Peacock

Almost all of Peacock's works are posted on the Thomas Love Peacock Society Web site. Available online. URL: http://www.thomaslovepeacock.net. Accessed July 3, 2008.

Works about Thomas Love Peacock

Felton, Felix. *Thomas Love Peacock.* London: Allen & Unwin, 1973.

Priestley, J. B. *Thomas Love Peacock.* London: Macmillan, 1966.

Pfeiffer, Emily Jane (1827–1890) *poet*

Emily Pfeiffer, née Davis, was born in Wales. Her father, an army officer, recognized and encouraged her talent for poetry. In 1853, while traveling in Europe, she met and married a successful German merchant, J. E. Pfeiffer. Four years later she published her first poem, a long "imaginative tale" called *Valisneria*. Dissatisfied with her poetry, however, she devoted the next 15 years to studying literature. It was not until 1873 that her second collection of poems, *Gerard's Monument,* appeared; thereafter, she produced a new book of poetry every few years. Her sonnets, which show the influence of Elizabeth Barrett Browning, are considered her best work. Critics praised their delicacy and "moral ardor," which are also characteristic of Browning's poetry. Pfeiffer's books include *Glan Alarch: This Silence and Song* (1877), *Sonnets and Songs* (1880), *Under the Aspens* (1882), and *The Rhyme of the Lady of the Rock and How It Grew* (1884). *The Rhyme of the Lady,* one of her most important works, is a narrative in prose and verse about the difficulties women face as artists. Pfeiffer also wrote a travel book in 1885, *Flying Leaves from East and West,* based on a trip to eastern Europe and Asia. Her husband's death four years later affected her deeply. She published her last book of poems, *Flowers of the Night,* in 1889 and died a year later.

Phillpotts, Eden (1862–1960) novelist, playwright

Eden Phillpotts was born in Rajputana, India, where his father, Captain Henry Phillpotts, was stationed as an officer in the British army. His father died when Phillpotts was a young boy, and his mother took him home to England, where he attended schools in Plymouth. Phillpotts had wanted to become an actor, but, doubting that he had the talent to succeed, he took a job with an insurance company instead. While working there, he began to write novels, including *My Adventure in the Flying Scotsman: A Romance of London and Northwestern Railway Shares* (1888). Two years later, Phillpotts left the insurance company. In 1896 he published *Lying Prophets,* a novel about an artists' colony. *Children of the Mist,* published in 1899, is the story of a peasant who enlists as a soldier, then deserts. Like many of his later rural novels, it is set in Dartmoor, the moorland area in central Devon, which he loved.

Some of his best-known books were mysteries, written under the pen name Harrington Hext. One, *The Red Redmaynes* (1922), features an American detective named Pete Ganns. Phillpotts also published plays, including *The Farmer's Wife,* produced in London in 1924. He continued to write novels as well as poetry until the 1950s.

Pinero, Arthur Wing (1855–1934)
playwright

Arthur Wing Pinero was born in London to the lawyer John Daniel Pinero and his wife, Lucy Davines Pinero. He studied to become a lawyer, but at age 19 abandoned his legal studies to become an actor and joined the company headed by the famous actor and director Henry Irving. Pinero later affectionately drew on his early years in the theater in one of his most famous plays, *Trelawny of the "Wells"* (1898).

After three years with Irving, Pinero wrote his first play, the one-act *£200 a Year* (1877), a light comedy, and was encouraged by its reception to become a full-time playwright. The next few years saw him perfecting his art as a writer of notably well-constructed farces. He began writing for the Royal Court Theatre in London, and in rapid succession produced *The Magistrate* (1885), a farce about a woman who conceals her age; *The Schoolmistress* (1886), a comedy set in a girls' school; and *Dandy Dick* (1887), about a gambling clergyman. All of these works were well received. In addition to farces, Pinero wrote two sentimental dramas—*The Squire* (1881), which deals seriously with bigamy, and the better-known *Sweet Lavender* (1888), a love story involving an illegitimate child. Pinero had a sense that English drama was becoming more substantial. He reworked two serious French plays as *The Iron Master* (1884) and *Mayfair* (1885), and was a great admirer of Norwegian dramatist Henrik Ibsen, whose realistic social plays that challenged the comfortable bourgeois morals and mores of the day appeared in Europe throughout the 1880s.

In 1893 Pinero's decision to turn toward more serious drama resulted in his most famous and controversial work, *The Second Mrs. Tanqueray.* The story is a tragic one of a "woman with a past." The title character foresees her future as "a worn-out creature—broken up, very likely, some time before I ought to be—my hair bright, my eyes dull, my body too thin or too stout, my cheeks raddled and ruddled—a ghost, a wreck, a caricature" and commits suicide. London audiences and the London press were divided in their opinion of the play, with reviews ranging from "A Great Play" to "hideous and squalid." The play was soon translated into French, and was revived several times in 20th-century America. Today it is generally considered Pinero's masterpiece.

Pinero was quick to follow with a succession of "social problem" plays, frequently revolving around women's status in Victorian society. *The Benefit of the Doubt* (1895) involves a divorce suit in which the court gives the alleged "other woman," Mrs. Theo Fraser, "the benefit of the doubt." GEORGE BERNARD SHAW, previously one of Pinero's toughest critics, praised its "higher dramatic pressure" and "closer-knit action."

In 1898 Pinero wrote *The Gay Lord Quex*, a comedy about class differences centering on a manicurist and her sister. His play *Trelawny of the "Wells"*, a romantic comedy about love among a troupe of actors in the 1860s, features memorable comic characters like the curmudgeon Telfer.

Pinero was such a skilled playwright that he was knighted in 1909 by King Edward VII. The glory of his best days might still be accorded him had not another playwright, born just a year later than Pinero, appeared on the scene: George Bernard Shaw. His biographer John Dawick notes Pinero's popularity: "He dominated the British stage for more than a quarter of a century at a time when theatre was more widely popular than it had been since William Shakespeare's day or would be again."

Other Work by Sir Arthur Wing Pinero

Bratton, J. S., ed. *The Magistrate, The Schoolmistress, the Second Mrs. Tanqueray, Trelawny of the "Wells" and Other Plays*. New York: Oxford University Press, 1995.

A Work about Sir Arthur Wing Pinero

Dawick, John. *Pinero: A Theatrical Life*. Niwot: University Press of Colorado, 1993.

Pocock, Isaac (1782–1835) *playwright*

Isaac Pocock was born in Bristol, in western England, to Nicholas Pocock, a painter, and Ann Evans Pocock. After attending art school, Isaac became both a painter and a playwright. In 1807 he received an award for his painting *Murder of St. Thomas à Becket*. In 1808 he wrote his first musical comedy, a farce called *Yes or No,* followed by another musical farce, *Hit or Miss* (1810), which was one of his most successful plays. In 1812 he married Louisa Hime, with whom he had one son. Pocock became widely known for his portraits and historical paintings while he also pursued his writing career. Most of his later works, after his early comedies, are romantic dramas, often with historic subjects as in his paintings. Many of his plays are adaptations of other works, such as *The Robber's Wife* (1829), a romantic drama adapted from the German. He also published *Robinson Crusoe; or, The Bold Buccaneers* (1817), a play based on the novel by Daniel Defoe, and *Rob Roy Macgregor*, a dramatization of one of SIR WALTER SCOTT's popular Waverley novels.

Polwhele, Richard (1760–1838) *poet, historian*

Richard Polwhele was born in Truro, Cornwall, in the southwest of England. By the time he was 12 he was already writing poetry. One of his early poems was published in 1777, the year before he entered Oxford University. Polwhele did not graduate, leaving Oxford to become an Anglican clergyman. In 1782, the year he was ordained, he married Loveday Warren. The couple had three children. After his wife died in 1793, he married Mary Tyrrell.

Polwhele continued to write poetry while he served at various churches in Cornwall and Devon in southwest England. His published works include *The Art of Eloquence* (1785), *Poetic Trifles* (1796), *The Old English Gentleman* (1797), and *The Unsex'd Females: A Poem*. The last was a response to a satirical poem by Thomas James Mathias, who coined the phrase "the unsex'd females" to refer to woman writers such as MARY WOLLSTONECRAFT who stepped outside the bounds of conventional female behavior. Polwhele excoriates Wollstonecraft and many other woman writers of the time by name, and invites his readers to read the work and admire the behavior of HANNAH MORE. ANNA SEWARD wrote a sonnet addressed to him, in support of his approach. Polwhele also published historical works, including his *History of Devonshire*, a work of several volumes written during the 1790s, and a *History of Cornwall* (1803–08). These works are parish-by-parish descriptions of local architecture, property arrangements, etymology of names, and family history, fascinating to local historians today. In 1810 he produced five volumes of poetry. During the 1820s, Polwhele continued to write poetry and local history, including his three-volume *Biographical Sketches of Cornwall* (1831). He also contributed articles to *Gentleman's Magazine* and the *British Critic*.

Porter, Anna Maria (1780–1832) novelist

Anna Porter was born in Durham, in northeast England, to William Porter, an officer in the British army, and Jane Blenkinsop. She attended elementary school in Edinburgh, Scotland, with her older sister, the writer JANE PORTER. Anna began writing when she was 13 and published her first stories in 1797 and 1798. In 1803 she also published a musical, which was produced in London. Her most famous work, *The Hungarian Brothers* (1807), is a three-volume novel about the French Revolution, full of scenes of the "martial glory," as Porter later described it, that she admired. Two years later, *Don Sebastian; or, The House of Braganza*, a romance in four volumes, was published. Many other sprawling romances followed, such as *The Recluse of Norway* (1814) (four volumes), *The Knight of St. John* (1817) (three volumes), and *The Village of Mariendorpt* (1821) (four volumes). Porter was a prolific novelist whose works filled 50 volumes; however, although she had a lively narrative style, the critic George Saintsbury considered her writing to be, at best, "amiable incompetence." Her last novel, *The Barony*, appeared in 1830. Anna Porter died of typhus two years later.

Porter, Jane (1776–1850) novelist

Jane Porter was born in Durham, in northeast England, to William Porter, an officer in the British army, and Jane Blenkinsop. When Porter was three, her father died, and her mother moved the family to Edinburgh. There Jane was educated along with her younger sister, the writer ANNA PORTER, and her brother, Robert. Eventually the family moved to London, where Jane wrote her first novel, *Thaddeus of Warsaw*. A friend who was an editor at Longman publishers liked the novel and published it in 1803. This romance was popular not only in England but also in continental Europe, where it was translated into several other languages. In 1810 Porter published an even more successful novel, *The Scottish Chiefs*, based on the life of the 13th-century Scots patriot William Wallace. The novel was widely read in Europe and America. A few lines give a sense of the drama and violence it contains: "Wallace fought in front, making a dreadful passage through the falling ranks; while the tremendous sweep of his sword, flashing in the intermitting light, warned the survivors where the avenging blade would next descend. A horrid vacuity was made in the lately thronged spot:—it seemed not the slaughter of a mortal arm, but as if the destroying angel himself were there." Porter's next historical novel, *The Pastor's Fireside*, published in 1815, was set during the 17th century. She also began writing plays, including *Switzerland*, a tragedy, which was produced in London in 1819 but which met with little success. Jane and her sister lived with their mother until her death in 1831. They then purchased a new home together in London, where they entertained other writers, including WILLIAM MAGINN.

Praed, Rosa (1851–1935) novelist

Rosa Praed, née Murray-Prior, was born in a remote area of Queensland, Australia, where her father had a small farm. When Rosa was a teenager her family moved to the city of Brisbane, where her father served as postmaster general.

When she was 21 Rosa married Campbell Praed, and they moved to his impoverished farm on an island off the Australian coast. The couple eventually gave up farming, and in 1875 they moved to London, where Rosa began writing novels based on her experiences growing up in Australia. She published *An Australian Heroine* (1880) and *The Romance of a Station* (1889).

In London, Praed became a successful novelist and moved in literary circles with other writers, including Oscar Wilde. Some of her novels, such as *Nadine, The Study of a Woman* (1882), in which a married woman has an affair, were considered scandalous. She also collaborated on a popular series of political novels with Justin McCarthy, an Irish member of Parliament. Praed and her husband, who separated, had four children, all of whom died tragically. One was killed in an automobile accident, another while hunting in Africa, a third committed suicide, and a fourth died insane. Praed turned to spiritualism, the belief that the spirits of the dead can communicate with the living through a medium. In 1899 she began living with a medium, Nancy Harward, who acted as her business manager and secretary. The two women lived together for almost 30 years. During this period, Rosa Praed continued to write novels, including *The Brother of the Shadow* (1901) and *The Insane Root* (1902), which reflect her interest in occultism and reincarnation.

A Work about Rosa Praed
Clarke, Patricia. *Rosa! Rosa! A Life of Rosa Praed, Novelist and Spiritualist.* Melbourne, Australia: Melbourne University Press, 1999.

Pre-Raphaelite movement

The Pre-Raphaelite movement was, properly speaking, not a specific movement at all, but rather a certain commonality of spirit among a group of painters and poets that emerged "officially" in 1848 when the painter and poet Dante Gabriel Rossetti, along with the painters William Holman Hunt and John Everett Millais, formed the Pre-Raphaelite Brotherhood. Believing that "truth to nature" should be the highest goal of art, and feeling that the art of the age was dominated by a rigid conventionality of fixed rules—rules they traced back to the Italian painter Raphael (1483–1520)—the brotherhood advocated a style of painting that, in the words of the scholar Cecil B. Lang, "show[ed] an overmastering concern for proliferated, minute detail as scrupulously defined in background as in foreground." Although the official Pre-Raphaelite Brotherhood disbanded after only four years, the term *Pre-Raphaelite* was applied to the painting and poetry of artists and writers as diverse as the painters Ford Madox Brown and Edward Burne-Jones and the poets Christina Rossetti, William Morris, and Algernon Charles Swinburne.

Championed by John Ruskin, perhaps the greatest art critic of the century, and stimulating curiosity by the enigmatic *PRB* painted near the signatures of their paintings, the Pre-Raphaelites may be said to have transformed English painting and enriched English poetry throughout the century. Some of the most famous Pre-Raphaelite paintings include D. G. Rossetti's *The Blessed Damozel* (also the title of one of his most widely read poems), W. H. Hunt's *The Hireling Shepherd*, and J. E. Millais's *Ophelia*. Although very different in composition and texture, the paintings have in common a brilliancy of color and striking attention to detail. The poems are equally striking, as in these lines from Rossetti's "The Blessed Damozel":

> *And still she bowed herself and stooped*
> *Out of the circling charm;*
> *Until her bosom must have made*
> *The bar she leaned on warm,*
> *And the lilies lay as if asleep*
> *Along her bended arm.*

Pre-Raphaelitism "did much," according to the scholar Jerome Buckley, "to establish the autonomy of art and the independence of the artist from didactic purpose and sectarian demand; it made clear the importance of the vivid detail and the symbolic overtone of the sharp perception; and by its stress on the quality rather than the variety of experience it ultimately did more than a little to quicken the aesthetic sensibility of a whole culture."

Works about the Pre-Raphaelite Movement

Buckley, Jerome H., ed. *The Pre-Raphaelites: An Anthology.* Chicago: Academy Chicago, 1986.

Lang, Cecil B., ed. *The Pre-Raphaelites and Their Circle.* 2nd ed. Chicago: University of Chicago Press, 1975.

Wood, Christopher. *The Pre-Raphaelites.* New York: Seven Dials, 2001.

Prince, Mary (1788–1833) nonfiction writer

Mary Prince was the first woman to write about her experiences in slavery. In her narrative, *The History of Mary Prince: A West Indian Slave, Related by Herself* (1831), she described the brutal treatment she received as a slave in Bermuda. She wrote of her owner's wife that "she caused me to know the exact difference between the smart of the rope, [and] the cart-whip . . . when applied to my naked body by her own cruel hand. And there was scarcely any punishment more dreadful than the blows I received on my face and head from her hard heavy fist. She was a fearful woman, and a savage mistress to her slaves." In 1826, Prince married Daniel James, a free black man. When her master discovered the marriage, Prince was whipped severely. She and her husband wanted to buy her freedom, but her owners refused. Finally, on a trip to England with them, she escaped. Slavery had been abolished in Britain by that time, so she was now free. The British Anti-Slavery Society helped publish her book. After its publication, her former owners sued her publishers for libel, but lost. Her book was reissued in the 1990s by the University of Michigan Press.

Probyn, May (1856?–1909?) novelist, poet

Few details exist about May Probyn's early life. In 1878 she published an adventure novel, *Once!* *Twice! Thrice! and Away!,* and during the 1880s her short stories and poetry appeared in periodicals such as *MacMillan's Magazine* and *Month.* Many of her poems are about the condition, or predicament, of women. *A Ballade of Lovers,* for example, talks about the greater sexual freedom that men have. Poems such as "Masquerading, I. Before," and "Masquerading II. After" describe the bittersweet nature of love, especially for women—but not without humor, as in "Love In Mayfair":

> *I must tell you, my dear,*
> *I'm in love with him vastly!*
> *Twenty thousand a year,*
> *I must tell you, my dear! He will soon be a*
>   *peer*
> *And such diamonds!—and, lastly,*
> *I must tell you, my dear,*
> *I'm in love with him, vastly!*

Probyn became a Roman Catholic in the 1880s. Her last poems, in a book titled *Pansies* (1895), describe her strong religious feelings.

Procter, Adelaide Anne (1825–1864) poet

Raised in a literary household where family friends included WILLIAM WORDSWORTH, WILLIAM HAZLITT, and CHARLES DICKENS, Adelaide Anne Procter became a published poet at age 18. She received much encouragement as a child and developed a love for poetry at an early age; Dickens once wrote that she "carried about a notepaper album of favorite poems as another child would have toted a doll."

Procter was born in London to the poet Bryan Waller Procter (who wrote under the pseudonym Barry Cornwall) and his wife, Anne Skepper Procter, who held a regular literary salon in their home. Educated at home in the typical fashion of a proper young lady, she became fluent in French, Italian, and German, and mastered playing the piano and drawing.

In 1843 she published her first poem, "Ministering Angels," in *Health's Book of Beauty.* In 1853 she began sending Dickens, then editor of *Household Words,* poems under the pseudonym Mary Berwick (she did not want him to be influenced by his friendship with her father), which he praised and published. Procter's poems became so popular that they were later collected and issued in two volumes, titled *Legends and Lyrics* (1858, 1861). Many of the poems were inspired by Procter's recent conversion to Roman Catholicism and featured images of convents, cathedrals, and angels. Her poem "A Lost Chord," set to music by Sir Arthur Sullivan, became a popular hymn.

Procter was also an influential figure in the early feminist movement. She served as secretary for the Society for Promoting the Employment of Women, and many of her poems appeared in the *English Woman's Journal,* a magazine established in 1858 as a vehicle for promoting feminist issues. Her poems "A Warning" and "A Parting" both warn women against relying upon men for financial security and respect. In "A Woman's Question," she courageously states, "Whatever on my heart may fall—remember, I *would* risk it all!" Procter herself never married.

In 1861 Procter edited *Victoria Regia,* a volume of prose and poetry printed and bound by women at Victoria Press. In 1862 she published her last volume of poetry, *A Chaplet of Verses,* the proceeds of which were donated to a Catholic charity for women and children. That same year, Procter fell ill with tuberculosis. After 15 months in bed, she died at home. Dickens wrote a preface for the posthumous reissue of *Legends and Lyrics* (1866). Although he praised her talents as a poet, the preface contained no mention of her work as a feminist. In contrast, recent feminist scholars such as Cheri Lin Larsen Hoeckley have noted "the simultaneous sexual, political, and economic depths that frequently complicate her work."

Pusey, Edward Bouverie (1800–1882)
clergyman, theologian

Edward Bouverie Pusey was born on August 22, 1800, in the village of Pusey (Oxfordshire), to the aristocrats and landowners Philip Pusey and Lady Lucy Sherard. His early education took place at a preparatory school in Surrey under the guidance of clergyman Richard Roberts. When he was 12 he attended Eton College, then left for Christ Church, Oxford, in 1819. After graduating in 1822, he won an Oriel fellowship and began attending the lectures of Charles Lloyd, regius professor of divinity. Heavily influenced by Lloyd's fear of the threat posed to Christian doctrine by the new German rationalist approach to biblical scholarship, Pusey attended the universities of Berlin, Bonn, and Göttingen from 1826 to 1827, studying theology, Hebrew, Arabic, and German.

In 1828 Pusey married Maria Catherine Barker, was ordained as a deacon and then a priest, and became regius professor of Hebrew at Oxford as well as canon of Christ Church. Starting in 1833, Pusey became closely associated with the OXFORD MOVEMENT (or Tractarianism), which sought to revive the Catholic inheritance of the Church of England. That year he authored a tract advocating fasting, and because he signed it (other such tracts had all been published anonymously), the movement became popularly known as Puseyism. Along with the originators of the Oxford Movement, the clergymen JOHN KEBLE and JOHN HENRY NEWMAN (whom Pusey had met at Oriel College), Pusey continued to publish *Tracts for the Times,* arguing for the adoption of Roman Catholic practices and theological stances.

From the mid-1830s until his death, Pusey also presided over an ambitious and highly influential literary project, the *Library of Fathers of the Holy Catholic Church, Anterior to the Division of East and West.* This was a collection of works by church fathers, including St. Augustine, most of which were translated into English for the first time.

The Oxford Movement began to flag in the 1840s. Pusey assumed leadership when Newman withdrew from the movement in 1841, and was suspended from preaching for two years because of his 1843 sermon, "The Holy Eucharist: A Comfort to the Penitent," in which he advocated the doctrine of the Real Presence, a Catholic belief considered heretical by Anglicans.

For the rest of his life, Pusey wrote and preached tirelessly against rationalism. He was deeply hurt by the perception that he was anything but loyal to the Church of England, which he sought to strengthen through reform. In one of his last major works, the *Eirenicon* (1865–70), he sought to pave the way for reuniting the Church of England with the Roman Church, but his proposals resulted in nothing but great controversy. However, the main body of his work, especially his sermons, forever changed the character of the Anglican church by increasing the importance of the eucharist, liturgy, and ritual. He died on September 16, 1882, in Ascot Priory, Berkshire.

Other Works by Edward Pusey

The Entire Absolution of the Penitent: A Sermon, Mostly Preached before the University. 1846. Reprint, Boston: Elibron, 2001.

"The Rule of Faith." Sermon, 1851.

Works about Edward Pusey

Faught, C. Brad. *The Oxford Movement: A Thematic History of the Tractarians and Their Times.* University Park: Pennsylvania State University Press, 2004.

Liddon, Henry Parry, and John O. Johnston, ed. *Life of Edward Pusey: Doctor of Divinity, Canon of Christ Church, Regius Professor of Hebrew in the University of Oxford.* Vol. 1, *1800–1836*. Whitefish, Mont.: Kessinger, 2007.

Quiller-Couch, Sir Arthur Thomas (Q)
(1863–1944) *novelist, essayist, short story writer, critic*

The son of a medical doctor, Thomas Quiller-Couch, and his wife, Mary Ford Quiller-Couch, Arthur Quiller-Couch was born in Bodmin, Cornwall, and educated at Newton Abbot and Clifton Colleges before entering Oxford University, where he wrote parodies for *Oxford Magazine* and began using the pseudonym Q. He published his first novel, *Dead Man's Rock* (1887), a romance. Moving to London in the same year he began to write for periodicals (particularly the *Speaker*, of which he became assistant editor). Until 1892 he did journalistic work in London, contributing essays and short stories (one per week) to the *Speaker* as well as other periodicals, and writing novels. Love of the sea led him to move in 1892 to Fowey (pronounced "foy"), a small port town on the south coast of Cornwall, and his wife's home town, where he lived in a large house overlooking the scenic Fowey River estuary. He remained there until his death except for periods when he lectured at Cambridge University, where he was appointed the first King Edward VII Professor of English Literature in 1912. His most enduring work is *The Oxford Book of English Verse* (1900), which sold more than half a million copies over the next 44 years, and *The Oxford Book of English Ballads* (1910). Collections of his extremely popular Cambridge lectures are *On the Art of Writing* (1916) and *On the Art of Reading* (1920). As a professor of English literature he insisted that his students write. He said, "Literature is not a mere science, to be studied; but an art to be practiced." He set the example with his prodigious output. Quiller-Couch's editor Frederick Brittain says, "His chief contribution to letters was his style—neat, colorful, apparently effortless, accurate without being pedantic, and distinguished by a clarity and conciseness that were natural to him and were reinforced by his early classical training."

Other Work by Arthur Quiller-Couch
Q Anthology, compiled and edited by Frederick Brittain. London: J. M. Dent, 1948.

Works about Arthur Quiller-Couch
Brittain, Frederick. *Arthur Quiller-Couch: A Biographical Study of Q.* New York: Macmillan, 1948.
Hanff, Helene. *Q's Legacy.* New York: Viking, 1986.
Rowse, A. L. *Quiller-Couch: A Portrait of "Q".* London: Methuen, 1988.

Quincey, Thomas
See DE QUINCEY, THOMAS.

R

Radcliffe, Ann (1764–1823) *novelist*

Ann Radcliffe, née Ward, was born in London to Ann Oates Ward and William Ward, the owner of a hat store. When she was still a child, the family moved to Bath, where her father ran a store for the Wedgwood china company. At age 23 she married William Radcliffe, a writer. He became editor of a newspaper, the *Gazetteer,* and later owned the *English Chronicle.* In 1789 Radcliffe published her first novel, *The Castles of Athlin and Dunbayne.* Subtitled *A Highland Story,* the novel takes place in medieval Scotland, focusing on the inhabitants of two castles that are connected by a secret passage. The next year she published *A Sicilian Romance,* but her first major success did not come until *The Romance of the Forest* (1791). This introduced a heroine named Adeline, who is based on Radcliffe herself. As the titles of these novels suggest, Radcliffe modeled her novels on the medieval romance, featuring characters placed in extreme situations, struggles of good and evil, and supernatural occurrences. She modernized this tradition, however, by providing rational explanations for all seemingly supernatural mysteries.

Her most successful novel, *The Mysteries of Udolpho,* appeared in 1794. It was an overnight sensation and inspired a wave of overt imitations with titles like *The Monk of Udolpho.* JANE AUSTEN parodied this craze in her novel *Northanger Abbey* (written in 1798–99 but not published until 1818). Austen's heroine, Catherine Morland, is so consumed by gothic fiction that she loses touch with reality, imagining the country house she visits to be the Castle of Udolpho.

A Journey Made in the Summer of 1794 draws on Radcliffe's travels in Holland with her husband. Radcliffe published one more novel, *The Italian* (1797), then unaccountably stopped writing.

Her Gothic thrillers influenced a large number of authors both directly and indirectly, including MARY SHELLEY, EMILY BRONTË, and WILKIE COLLINS. Her novels achieved both critical and popular success in her own time and today. WALTER SCOTT called her "a mighty magician" and "the first poetess of romantic fiction." Today she is most appreciated for her picturesque landscape descriptions, her depiction of feminine psychology, and her influence on gothic, mystery, and horror fiction.

Critical Analysis

The Mysteries of Udolpho, while not the first gothic novel (that honor goes to Horace Walpole's *Castle of Otranto,* 1764), is certainly the first to possess all of the elements of what the genre would eventually become: a combination of the romance with the horror story, which includes a lovely, vulnerable heroine; a dashing hero; a malevolent villain; an ancient, Gothic castle; deep, dark family secrets; and elements of the supernatural. The novel was an immediate popular success in its day and has spawned hundreds of imitators over the centuries.

The heroine of *The Mysteries of Udolpho* is Emily St. Aubert, and it is hardly possible to imagine a more perfect young lady of her time. She has been well brought up by her parents, away from the corrupting influence of the big city, in a beautiful, secluded villa in Gascony. She is well-educated, talented as a poet and musician, religious and deeply moral, and has learned from her parents always to keep her sentiments in check, to balance feeling with reason. Fully the first third of the novel is dedicated to portraying Emily as a connoisseur of both the beautiful and the sublime. Beautiful landscapes—meadows and forests—evoke feelings of joy and happiness in the young lady; sublime landscapes—towering mountains, precipices, thundering waterfalls—evoke appropriate feelings of awe, wonder, and even fear. Her emotions are always at the forefront; she is delicate, sensitive, subject at times to melancholy, but equally capable of tender joys.

Due to a series of unfortunate circumstances, she finds herself trapped in an ancient Gothic castle in the Italian Alps, captive of the evil Count Montoni, who is determined to sell her in marriage to the highest bidder. While she is there, she stumbles upon successive horrors and what may even be supernatural occurrences. She and the reader are subjected to gloom, death, and decay, groans and lamentations from unknown sources, mysterious music that seems to come from nowhere, secret passageways, dungeons, and all the paraphernalia that we now associate with the gothic novel.

Interestingly, Radcliffe has situated her novel right at the fulcrum of the transition from superstition to enlightment. Her evil characters are medieval in their behavior and outlook, seeming to have stepped from the pages of a feudal romance; while her admirable characters are figures of the Age of Reason, free of superstition, rational—yet capable of the experiencing delicious shudders of fear when confronted with events that may be supernatural. While reason wins out in the end, the real fun is in the fear.

Works about Ann Radcliffe

Miles, Robert. *Ann Radcliffe: The Great Enchantress.* New York: Manchester University Press, 1995.

Norton, Ricter. *Mistress of Udolpho: The Life of Ann Radcliffe.* Leicester, England: Leicester University Press, 1999.

Rogers, Deborah. *Ann Radcliffe: A Bio-Bibliography.* Westport, Conn.: Greenwood Press, 1996.

Radcliffe, Mary Ann (c. 1746–c. 1810)
nonfiction writer

Although she disapproved of being compared with MARY WOLLSTONECRAFT, Mary Ann Radcliffe was a significant figure in the early feminist movement.

Born in Scotland, Radcliffe was the only child of a Roman Catholic mother and a much older Anglican father who died when Radcliffe was two. At age 15, she secretly married a man more than 20 years her senior, Joseph Radcliffe, with whom she had eight children. Her husband was a poor provider, and Radcliffe was forced to find work to support her family. She took jobs as a housekeeper, governess, and shopkeeper, and managed to put her sons through school. In 1781, Radcliffe separated from her husband.

Although her publisher tried to pass her off as the popular gothic novelist ANN RADCLIFFE, Mary Ann Radcliffe is best known for her feminist works. Her most popular book, *The Female Advocate; or, An Attempt to Recover the Rights of Women from Male Usurpation* (1799), was written in response to her own bitterness and frustration at her husband's neglect and financial irresponsibility. Radical for its time, it condemned economic oppression and made clear that the lack of job opportunities for women forced them into prostitution to earn money. The book also warns women against rushing into marriage.

Radford, Dollie (Caroline Maitland) (1858–1920) poet

Dollie Radford was born Caroline Maitland in Worchester, England, and educated at Queens College in London. But other details of her youth are sparse because no biographies of her life exist, and later in her life Radford was extremely hesitant to discuss her past.

In 1883 she married the poet Ernest Radford, an original member of the Rhymers' Club, a poetical group that included William Butler Yeats, ERNEST DOWSON, LIONEL JOHNSON, and ARTHUR SYMONS. The group stimulated Radford, and her first poems appeared shortly after her marriage. First collected in *A Light Load* (1891), her verses rely heavily upon romantic images of nature and love. For Radford, nature possesses a purity that shapes human emotions. For example, in "Ah, Bring It Not," the narrator urges her potential lover to bring her a token of love "through the summer land, / Through the sweet fragrance of the flowers." The token, endowed with nature's beauty, will make the narrator "fair to see; / And beautiful, through all the years."

Contemporary critics praised such verses for their beautiful images and lyrical qualities. Yet they also questioned Radford's ability to write more emotionally complex poems. Such doubts were unfounded: Even Radford's early poems suggest that trivial romantic situations are no longer suitable for poetry. For instance, "Ah, Bring It Not" concludes with a surprising pronouncement. Although the narrator requests her lover's token, she orders him not to request "the answering gift of mine," but be "content to pass to-day / Empty away."

Radford's increasing concern for female independence characterizes her later poetry. Additionally, Radford's second major collection of poetry, *Songs and Other Verses* (1895), reveals the strains her marriage suffered as Ernest Radford developed a mental illness. The narrators search for passionate love and reject the Victorian ideal of meek femininity. For instance, "October" recounts the narrator's unreciprocated desire: "In my great joy I craved so much, / My life lay trembling at your hand." After a year passes, the man responds by taking her hand, but now her feelings have changed: "A thousand years have passed away, / Since last year—when I loved you so." The narrator no longer wants, or needs, the man's affection.

Radford's poetry, although no longer widely read, is significant because she defied conventional Victorian notions of female behavior. As the critic LeeAnne Richardson notes, Radford tried "to naturalize previously unacceptable behavior by women, and to re-envision—through the power of song and the power of nature—the relations between men and women."

A Work about Dollie Radford

Richardson, LeeAnne Marie. "Naturally Radical: The Subversive Poetics of Dollie Radford." Available online. URL: http://muse.jhu.edu/journals/victorian_poetry/v038/38./richardson.html. Accessed July 3, 2008.

Ramée, Marie Louise de la

See OUIDA.

Reade, Charles (1814–1884) novelist, playwright

Charles Reade was born to Anna Marie Scott-Waring and John Reade on the Reade family estate at Ipsden in Oxfordshire, England. The seventh of 11 children, he was for the most part educated at home until he won a scholarship to Oxford University in 1831. Becoming a successful scholar, Reade was offered a lifelong fellowship with attached stipend under the condition that he be ordained and remain unmarried. Reade never did marry, and he kept his fellowship residence throughout his life.

Had Reade lived in the Renaissance, he would have been called "a man of many parts." As a musician he played the violin well; as a businessman he was a dealer in violins; he was a lawyer (although he never practiced law); he was a college official; he studied medicine; he managed theaters and produced plays; and he wrote short stories, letters, pamphlets concerning social issues, and 40 plays and 14 novels over a period of some 20 years.

He began writing in 1851, adapting Tobias Smollett's *Peregrine Pickle* for the stage. This began a lifelong habit of turning novels into plays, or vice versa. He rewrote his next play, *Masks and Faces,* as the novel *Peg Woffington,* with a beautiful actress as the title character. A year later Reade met his own beautiful actress, Laura Seymour, and they lived together until her death in 1871.

Much of Reade's work directly or indirectly was concerned for the plight of those less fortunate than he. This led to a decades-long struggle against the many social evils besetting a country in the throes of huge societal readjustments brought on by the Industrial Revolution. His next novel, *Christie Johnstone* (1853), was an attack on the horrors of the prison system and the cruel treatment of prisoners. He based another novel, *It Is Never Too Late to Mend* (1856), which attacked the prison system, partly on a play he had written in 1853, *Gold!,* set in an Australian gold district. Although George Orwell found Reade's work interesting merely for the abundance of technical details, he said of the hero of *Foul Play* (1868), "He is hero, saint, scholar, gentleman, athlete, pugilist, navigator, physiologist, botanist, blacksmith and carpenter . . . , the sort of compendium of all the talents that Reade honestly imagined to be the normal product of an English university."

In 1861 Reade published the novel generally considered to be his best, *The Cloister and the Hearth,* which is still widely read; in 1863 came *Hard Cash,* a novel vehemently attacking abuses in private insane asylums. In 1866 he published the novel *Griffith Gaunt; or, Jealousy,* which, because of its explicit treatment of sexual themes and infidelity, became a lightning rod for Victorian moralists and led to lawsuits and a somewhat scandalous reputation for Reade.

Critics, however, point out that the themes of chastity, celibacy, and sexual frustration attendant upon priestly vows had always figured, although partly hidden, in his novels and plays. *The Cloister and the Hearth,* a historical novel about Gerard Eliassoen, the father of the great Renaissance scholar Erasmus, details at length the sufferings endured by Gerard and his true love, Margaret Brandt, as they fight against fleshly temptations. Reade describes the enforced celibacy of the clergy as "an invention truly devilish."

All the while that Reade was producing his many novels, he was busy in the theater, not only as a playwright but also as a producer-manager whose innovations, in props and staging particularly, established patterns of stagecraft that exist today. He brought the real outside world into the theater; instead of painted renditions of mountains, mills, tools, furniture, and the like, he had the real thing, including explosions. Combined with this physical realism were the treatments of real and current social evils and problems. In 1865 he presented *It Is Never Too Late to Mend,* a dramatized version of his earlier novel, which shocked theatergoers and critics with its explicit representation of prison cells and inhumane prison conditions. In the play *Free Labour* (1870), an attack on the strong-arm tactics of trade unionists, there is a real forge, complete with anvil and bellows. While the use of these effects in this "social" drama caused some critics to rank Reade as one of the fathers of the modern theater's engagement with political and cultural life, more recent critical opinion suggests that he primarily was aiming for sensational effects to bring paying customers into the theater, not trying to appeal to the audience's political conscience.

Whatever the case, just as THOMAS CARLYLE believed that the lives of "great Men" and "heroes" should serve as exemplars, Reade, the anti-Carlylean, made the case for the nobility of the common man in his daily struggles for survival and moral rectitude in a hostile and predatory world. In the end, however, Reade's place in literature was secured by *The Cloister and the Hearth,* the novel that the scholar Avrom Fleishman has called "the first and best-known" late-Victorian historical novel.

Critical Analysis

Although Reade is best remembered today for *The Cloister and the Hearth,* his 1856 novel, *It Is Never Too Late to Mend,* may be a better measure of both his strengths and weaknesses as a writer. This is a spawling tale that ranges from the cozy English countryside to the Australian goldfields and contains dozens of characters who in true Victorian fashion are either very, very good or very, very bad. The subject matter of the work shuttles between the machinations of a complex villain, Squire John Meadows, who is in love with the hero's fiancée, the horrors of the Victorian prison system, the rigors of the Australian outback, and the trials and tribulations of a Jewish moneylender. The novel is fascinating in each of its many parts, but it ultimately feels like two or even three separate stories. One fears they will never come back together and, indeed, the ending of the novel has a hurried and almost desperate feel.

Perhaps the most fascinating portion of the novel is that dealing with the prison system. It is here that Reade's propensity to do large quantities of research is evident, and he paints a portrait of cruelty that the great reformer CHARLES DICKENS himself might have envied. The prison Reade describes is a reformed prison, not a place of dirt and squalor but of clean, bright, efficient inhumanity and torture. The system at this particular prison is referred to as "separate and silent," in which the prisoners are housed separately, kept from speaking to one another, and are forced to wear visors so that they cannot even see one another's faces. The idea behind such a program is to prevent the hardened criminals from infecting the minds of those newer to a life of crime. However, the psychological and spiritual damage of such isolation is immense, especially on the younger prisoners. Those sentenced to hard labor are put to turning a handle that moves a machine that does nothing, and the prison warden can make the weight heavier and heavier. In fact, the punishment for not doing enough rotations in the time allotted is more weight and less food, which of course leads to failure. Failure results to confinement in a dreadful apparatus that Reade describes as akin to crucifixion and strangulation at the same time, with which the guards bring prisoners over and over to the brink of death, only to revive them. Reade writes about the treatment of prisoners with white-hot outrage. The warden, he says,

> kept one poor lad without any food at all from Saturday morning till Sunday at twelve o'clock and made him work; and for his Sunday dinner gave the famished wretch six ounces of bread and a can of water. He strapped one prisoner up in the pillory for twenty-four hours, and directed him to be fed in it. The prisoner had a short neck, and the cruel collar would not let him eat, so that the tortures of Tantalus were added to crucifixion. The earnest beast put a child of eleven years old into a strait-waistcoat for three days, then kept him three days on bread and water, and robbed him of his bed and his gas for fourteen days.... When ... a prisoner was robbed of his bed, he was robbed of the means of keeping himself warm as well as of that rest without which life soon comes to a full stop.

Reade makes the fundamental humanity of this characters clear, despite whatever it is they have done to end up in prison. They are human beings, he says emphatically, and they are entitled to humane treatment.

One of the several heroes of *It Is Never Too Late to Mend* is the Reverend Eden, the cleric who is assigned to the prison and manages to hoist the warden on his own petard, using the rule book against a man who claims that he is only following the rules. Eden works hard to reform the soul of one of the prisoners, Tom Robinson, who has despaired of his belief in God as a result of his treatment. Eden is an almost Christlike figure who insists on being placed in solitary confinement and trying out the apparatus of torture so that he can speak with authority about the effects of each of these punishments.

It Is Never Too Late to Mend suffers from Victorian sentimentality and is quite overwritten in places. Still, it is also a fervent prayer for humane treatment, and a rousing good story.

Works about Charles Reade

Elwin, Malcolm. *Charles Reade.* London: Jonathan Cape, 1931. Reprint, New York: Russell & Russell, 1969.

Smith, Elton E. *Charles Reade.* Boston: Twayne, 1976.

Reynolds, George William MacArthur
(1814–1879) *novelist, journalist*

G. W. M. Reynolds was born in Sandwich, Kent, in southeast England, the son of George Reynolds, a captain in the Royal Navy. Intending to continue in the family tradition of military service, Reynolds entered the Royal Military College at Sandhurst in 1828 but left after only two years to pursue a writing career.

Reynolds directed his writing energy toward a rising new audience for stories: the working poor. Unlike the genteel, middle-class readers of WILLIAM AINSWORTH, EDWARD BULWER-LYTTON, or CHARLES DICKENS, Reynolds wrote specifically for a growing urban working-class readership and was one of the most prolific contributors to the cheap serial periodicals whose offices were clustered around London's Salisbury Square. By 1846 he had been appointed editor of the *London Journal,* a mass-circulation periodical aimed at a working-class audience, and in the same year he launched his own periodical, *Reynolds' Miscellany,* a penny weekly magazine of sensational stories and poems. In addition to contributing to the mass-circulation periodicals, Reynolds was also one of the most successful producers of serialized "penny dreadful" fiction, cheaply printed novels of mystery, adventure, and crime without any literary pretentions, and hence "dreadful," that sold for a penny. He was also guilty, as were many of his penny dreadful writing colleagues, of plagiarizing the popular stories of Dickens, using such titles as *Pickwick Abroad* (1839), *Pickwick Married* (1841), and *Master Timothy's Book-Case* (1842).

His *Mysteries of London,* based on the French author Eugene Sue's *Les Mystères du Paris* (1842–43), was one of the most widely circulated fictional works of the 1840s. His Regency romance *The Mysteries of the Court of London* was serialized from 1849 to 1856. The scholar Barbara Gates notes that "Mysteries literature of this sort viewed the great 19th-century cities of Paris and London as tropes for life, as dark mazes of secrecy and corruption, menacingly unpredictable and ultimately unknowable," and that Reynolds appealed to his dispossessed readers by confirming their mistrust of the powerful, "painting the upper classes as deceitful and responsible for the mysteries of London." His other best-selling penny dreadfuls include *The Soldier's Wife,* published in 1852, with 60,000 copies sold the first day of publication, and *The Bronze Soldier,* published in 1854, with the first two installments selling 100,000 copies each.

Reynolds's interest in his working-class audience ran in tandem with his support of the Chartist political agenda. Taking its name from the 1838 People's Charter drafted by the radical William Lovett, Chartism campaigned for an end to economic and political subservience through parliamentary reform. Reynolds was active in the movement during the 1840s. The Chartists petitioned Parliament in 1839, 1842, and 1848 with six fundamental demands: universal male suffrage, equal electoral districts, a secret ballot, annual elections, the abolition of the requirement that members of Parliament be property owners, and that all members of Parliament be paid for their service in office. Their petitions were resoundingly rejected each time. After 1848 the movement splintered and was no longer an organized political force. Many of the demands made by the Chartists, however, were eventually met by Parliament in the repeal of the Corn Laws and the Reform Acts of 1867 and 1884.

Reynolds remained dedicated to his political ideals and continued to campaign for the working class. On May 5, 1850, he launched the *Reynolds's Weekly Newspaper,* declaring in a front page editorial of the first edition that his paper would be "devoted to the cause of freedom and in the interests of the enslaved masses." He added that the paper would "prove not only a staunch, fearless, and uncompromising friend of popular principles, but likewise a complete and faithful chronicle of all domestic, foreign, and colonial events of interest or value." The paper, which combined sensationalism with crusading support of working-class political issues, was a success, especially in the north of England. By 1870 *Reynolds's Weekly Newspaper* had a circulation of 350,000 a week. Reynolds served as its publisher-editor until his death in 1879, when he was succeeded by his brother Edward. By the turn of the century, *Reynolds's Newspaper* had become the Sunday paper voice of the Liberal Party. In the 20th century, after being acquired by the National Co-operative Press, the renamed *Reynolds News and Sunday Citizen* stayed true to its founder's principles as the Sunday paper voice of the British Labour Party. The *Sunday Citizen* was published until 1967.

The critic Robert Mighall credits Reynolds with creating a genre through his extreme worldview: "By focusing almost entirely on corrupt aristocrats and vicious criminals, and by largely excluding representatives of the middle classes... Reynolds... effectively achieves the transformation necessary for an Urban Gothic fiction."

A Work about W. M. Reynolds

Mighall, Robert. *A Geography of Victorian Gothic Fiction: Mapping History's Nightmares.* New York: Oxford University Press, 2000.

Ricardo, David (1772–1823) *economist*

David Ricardo was a leader in the establishment of English primacy in economic theory in the early 19th century. He was born to a wealthy Jewish member of the London stock exchange, Abraham Ricardo, and his wife, Abigail, but broke with his family when he became a Unitarian and married a Quaker. On his own at age 21, his brilliance in business matters earned him a fortune in only five years—his worth at his death some 25 years later was estimated to be, in today's money, $100 million. He purchased an estate called Gatcombe Park, in Gloucestershire, and retired there to pursue his interests and studies in chemistry, geology, mathematics and, above all, economics. In 1817 he published *The Principles of Political Economy and Taxation,* a work that built upon the economic insights of Adam Smith and that has brought him enduring fame. The most influential of the several theories put forward in that book was "the iron law of wages," which grimly asserts that wages for labor tend naturally to sink to the lowest level necessary for laborers' subsistence.

Among those who later sought to refute this thesis, through whatever means necessary, was KARL MARX. Ricardo also first promulgated the labor theory of value, which proposes that a manufactured item's worth is closely related to the amount of labor necessary to produce it. Marx later turned this capitalistic tenet into a cornerstone of his anti-capitalist economic philosophy in *Capital.* The scholar Mark Blaug points out this central irony of Ricardo's legacy: "that most bourgeois of all bourgeois economists [Ricardo] stands before us as the unwitting founding father of Marxian economics."

Works about David Ricardo

Henderson, John P., and John B. Davis. *The Life and Economics of David Ricardo.* New York: Springer, 1997.

Hollander, J. H. *David Ricardo: A Centenary Estimate.* Baltimore: Johns Hopkins University Press, 1960. Reprint, New York: AMS Press, 1982.

Riddell, Charlotte (Charlotte Elizabeth Lawson Cowan Riddell) (1832–1906)
novelist

Charlotte Riddell, née Lawson, was born in Carrickfergus, County Antrim, Ireland. Her father, James Lawson, was high sheriff of County Antrim, and the family lived comfortably until his death in 1852. After his death, Lawson cared for her ailing mother, Ellen, and in 1856 moved to London where she hoped to make a living as a writer.

Her first two novels went largely unnoticed, but her third, *The Moors and the Fens* (1858, published under the pseudonym F. G. Trafford), in which the heroine is a writer, became a success.

In 1857 she married Joseph Hadley Riddell. His job as a civil engineer provided her with insight into the City (London's business and financial district), the setting for many of her novels. Her most popular City novel was *George Geith of Fen Court* (1864), in which a minister abandons his wife, takes up accounting in the City, becomes a bigamist, and fathers an illegitimate child. The novel was adapted into a successful play. Riddell did not apologize for choosing the City as a setting for her novels, noting, "Every other class has found some writer to tell its tale."

Her husband's poor management of money forced Riddell to write prolifically. In her lifetime, she published nearly 50 novels and collections of short stories, including tales of the supernatural. *Weird Stories*, published in 1884 and considered one of Riddell's most accomplished works, combines mystery and romance with haunted-house settings and capitalizes on the Victorian fascination with spiritualism.

In 1901 Riddell became the first writer to receive a pension from the Society of Authors. Her reputation as a writer of supernatural fiction endures. The critic James Campbell states in *Supernatural Fiction Writers: Fantasy and Horror* that Charlotte Riddell was "the best writer of supernatural tales in the Victorian era."

Other Work by Charlotte Riddell
The Collected Ghost Stories of Mrs. J. H. Riddell. New York: Dover, 1977.

Ritchie, Anne Thackeray (1837–1919)
novelist, short story writer, essayist

Born in London, Anne Thackeray Ritchie was the daughter of WILLIAM MAKEPEACE THACKERAY and his wife, Isabella Shawe Thackeray. When she was three, her mother became mentally ill and was permanently hospitalized. Eventually, Anne Thackeray married her cousin Richmond Ritchie and had two children.

Her father's fame ensured Ritchie an early introduction to London's literary circle. In 1863 William Thackeray, as editor of *Cornhill Magazine*, serialized his daughter's first novel, *The Story of Elizabeth*. In this work, the title character flees her home after her mother both undermines her engagement to Sir John Dampier and marries a pastor, who abuses Elizabeth. After suffering multiple misfortunes, Elizabeth is finally reunited with Dampier. HENRY JAMES would later praise the novel for its ability to capture impressionistic moments of feeling.

Elizabeth also presents the first of many absent or ineffective maternal characters to be found in Ritchie's fiction, reflecting the loss of her own mother. Thus, in *Old Kensington* (1873), Ritchie's best-known novel, the main character, Dorothea Vanborough, lives with her stern aunt because her father has died and her mother has deserted her. Searching for emotional stability, Dorothea mistakenly agrees to marry the bland Robert Henley, but after Henley ends the engagement, she ultimately marries the more appealing Frank Raban. In this novel, Ritchie again displays her ability to capture vividly her characters' emotions.

Throughout her life, Anne cultivated the literary relationships that her father began. She befriended ALFRED, LORD TENNYSON, LEWIS CARROLL, ROBERT BROWNING, and ELIZABETH BARRETT BROWNING, and wrote essays on many of these figures. In the 1890s Ritchie wrote the introductions to a new collected edition of her father's novels. They provide insightful pictures of his life and offer valuable details about the composition of each novel. Ritchie is most commonly praised for her careful depictions of Victorian life, and modern critics echo James's original praise. Virginia Woolf claimed that Ritchie's novels "offer us a world unlike any other when we are setting out upon one of our voyages of the imagination."

A Work about Anne Thackeray Ritchie

Gérin, Winifred. *Anne Thackeray Ritchie*. New York: Oxford University Press, 1981.

Robertson, Thomas William (1829–1871) *playwright*

Thomas Robertson was born in Newark-on-Trent, Nottinghamshire, in central England, to the actors Margharette Elisabetta Marinus and William Robertson. His formal schooling was sporadic. Robertson made his stage debut at age five, and by 16 he was writing and acting regularly. When he was 19, Robertson moved to London, where he subsidized his playwriting by working as an actor, stage manager, and drama critic. *A Night's Adventure* (1851) was his first play. Robertson became successful in 1865, with the production of his comedy *Society*. Newly rich, the Chodds are trying, as John Chodd, Sr., himself puts it, "to wriggle [themselves] into [s]ociety." It is a bumbling endeavor, but Robertson contrasts their lack of breeding with the snobbery of the high society Lady Ptarmigant. Chodd, Jr., ends by rejecting "blue blood" in favor of blood of "the natural colour."

Caste (1867) revisits the theme of class, with all ending happily when the families of an aristocratic officer and the actress he has married set aside class differences to unite behind the couple. In this play and others, Robertson dealt with social issues, most often from a conservative viewpoint. Thus in *Caste* he makes the activist Eccles so "detestable," as the critic Maynard Savin has noted, that the character discloses Robertson's own opposition to "the thrust of the working class towards suffrage and unionism." Eccles's self-serving whining helps make him distasteful: "Once proud and prosperous, [I am] now poor and lowly . . . [and] driven to seek work and not to find it."

Robertson's plays were generally popular with audiences, but their lack of grandeur, their drawing-room domesticity, led many critics to deride them as "teacup-and-saucer drama." H. Barton Baker, for instance, dismissed them as "domestic and commonplace" and requiring of actors only the "tame emotions of everyday existence." However, the relative naturalness of Robertson's dialogue is part of what made the plays popular. Robertson's romantic dialogue in particular could be tender and charming, as in the following lines from *Caste*: "Wouldn't you have loved me better if I'd been a lady?" "You *are* a lady—you're my wife."

Robertson's plays are rarely read or performed today. His importance has nothing to do with either their style or content. Instead, his legacy is the innovations, introduced at the Olympic Theatre in London in the 1930s, that Robertson adapted, bringing a new realism to theater. One of these is the box or drawing-room set. His highly detailed stage directions also contributed to this realism. "Robertson," critic Raymond Williams has written, "invented stage-management, and indeed invented the modern figure of the producer or director, impressing an overall atmosphere and effect."

Robinson, Mary (1758–1800) *poet, playwright*

Mary Darby was born in Bristol, in western England. Her father, the captain of a whaling ship, abandoned his family and left for America when she was a child. Mary's mother sent her to school in Chelsea (a district of London), where she first became interested in writing poetry. Mary's beauty attracted the attention of David Garrick (1717–79), the famous British actor and producer, who asked her to appear in Shakespeare's *King Lear*. Before beginning an acting career, however, Mary married Thomas Robinson in 1774, at age 16, and gave birth to a daughter. Soon after their baby was born, her husband went bankrupt, and the family was sent to debtors' prison. While imprisoned with her husband and baby, Robinson wrote poetry, some of which was published in 1775.

After her release, she began her career in the theater, acting in many productions in 1777 and 1778. The Prince of Wales, the future King George IV, attended a performance and was smitten by Robinson. After a brief affair with him, Mary went to Paris, where she became friends with Marie Antoinette, the French queen who would soon be overthrown and beheaded during the French Revolution. Robinson returned to London, then in 1784 became partially paralyzed due to complications of pregnancy and had to give up her career on stage. It was then that she turned her full attention to writing. Her *Poems* (1791) was published with the help of a subscription list of 600 people, including those of many of the nobility, headed by the Prince of Wales. *Sappho and Phaon* (1796) is a sonnet sequence about unrequited love, which Robinson imagines the ancient Greek poet Sappho suffered. The penultimate sonnet welcomes the return of reason:

> So shall this glowing, palpitating soul,
> Welcome returning Reason's placid beam,
> While o'er my breast the waves Lethean roll,
> To calm rebellious Fancy's fev'rish dream;
> Then shall my Lyre disdain love's dread control,
> And loftier passions, prompt the loftier theme!

In another vein is humorous commentary in the poem "Female Fashions of 1799":

> *Cravats like towels, thick and broad,*
> *Long tippets made of bear-skin,*
> *Muffs that a RUSSIAN might applaud,*
> *And rouge to spoil a fair skin.*
>
> *Such is CAPRICE! but, lovely kind*
> *Oh! let each mental feature*
> *Proclaim the labour of the mind,*
> *And leave your charms to NATURE.*

The poetry collection *The False Friend* followed in 1799, and *Lyrical Tales* and *The Mistletoe* in 1800, the year she died.

Robinson did better financially with her prose works. Several novels combined Gothic elements with enough biographical hints to titillate a public fascinated by the persona of the beautiful, crippled actress. She also wrote a work of social criticism, *A Letter to the Women of England, on the Injustice of Mental Subordination* (1799), in which she argued for the right of women to initiate divorce.

Robinson's daughter published her mother's memoirs in 1801, and a collection of poems, the *Poetical Works of the Late Mrs. Mary Robinson*, appeared in 1806.

Other Works by Mary Robinson

Barros, Carolyn A., and Johanna M. Smith, eds. *Life-Writings by British Women, 1660–1815: An Anthology.* Boston: Northeastern University Press, 2000.

Pascoe, Judith, ed. *Mary Robinson: Selected Poems.* Boulder, Colo.: Broadview Press, 2000.

A Work about Mary Robinson

Bass, Robert D. *The Green Dragoon: The Lives of Banastre Tarleton and Mary Robinson.* New York: Henry Holt, 1957.

Roche, Maria Regina (1764?–1845)
novelist

Maria Dalton was born in Waterford, in southern Ireland. Her father, Blundell Dalton, was a captain in the British army. In 1789, Maria published her first novel, *The Vicar of Lansdowne*, followed in 1793 by *The Maid of Hamlet*. Both were Gothic romances. In 1794 she married Ambrose Roche and left Ireland for England with him. Two years later Maria Roche published the novel that made her famous, *The Children of the Abbey*. JANE AUSTEN refers to it in *Emma* as one of Harriet Smith's favorite novels, which suggests that Austen might not have thought highly of it. Roche continued to write Gothic romances in the same vein, combining mystery and sentimentality, for the next 25 years. Among her other novels are *The Nocturnal Visit* (1800), *The Discarded Son; or, The Haunt of the Banditti* (1807), and *The Munster Cottage Boy* (1819). In her later years, after her husband's death in 1829, Roche wrote little, and the popularity of her novels began to wane.

Other Work by Regina Roche
Clermont: A Tale. London: Folio, 1968.

Rolfe, Frederick William (Baron Corvo)
(1860–1913) *novelist, poet*

Frederick Rolfe was born in London. Little is known about his early education, but in 1878 he began teaching at various elementary schools. In 1880 he composed a poem to honor the memory of one of his students who had drowned; titled *Tarcissus: The Boy Martyr of Rome*, it was privately printed. Rolfe converted to Roman Catholicism in his 20s and hoped to enter the priesthood. He attended St. Mary's College near Birmingham, England, but was expelled for spending too much time painting. From there, he went to Rome and attended Scots College, but was again expelled, this time for writing poetry.

During the 1890s his poems began to be published in various magazines, such as the *Yellow Book*. Rolfe moved to Hampshire, in southern England, where he called himself Baron Corvo, one of several pen names he used as a poet. At the same time, Rolfe was painting seriously and had become a photographer, having briefly worked as a photographer's assistant in Aberdeen, Scotland. In 1895 he published *Stories Toto Told Me*, which drew on his experiences in Italy. In 1901, *In His Own Image*, another collection of his Italian stories, appeared. The book that is considered his masterpiece was *Hadrian VII* (1904), which one scholar calls "magnificently paranoid." The story of a writer who gets himself elected pope, the novel reflects Rolfe's lifelong bitterness against Rome after his unsuccessful attempt to become a priest. He spent the last years of his life almost destitute in Venice yet still going by the title Baron. Rolfe and his work inspired Peter Luke's 1969 play *Hadrian VII*.

Works about Frederick Rolfe
Benkovitz, Miriam. *Frederick Rolfe, Baron Corvo: A Biography.* New York: Putnam, 1977.
Symons, A. J. A. *The Quest for Corvo: An Experiment in Biography.* Harmondsworth, England: Penguin Books, 1940.

romanticism
Romanticism is both a general term for the literature of the late 18th and early 19th centuries and a specific term for an artistic movement in literature, music and art. The romantic movement is characterized by a belief in the power of the imagination, a celebration of nature, and a fascination with the supernatural and the exotic as a reaction against the rational thought and scientific principles of the 18th-century Age of Reason. WILLIAM WORDSWORTH, SAMUEL TAYLOR COLERIDGE, and WILLIAM BLAKE constitute the first generation of English romantic poets. While Blake's visionary illuminated volumes were produced in such small quantities that he went largely unrecognized in his day, Wordsworth and Coleridge were major literary figures and close friends. Their collaborative volume *Lyrical Ballads* (1798) is often considered the inaugural document of English romanticism. In such contributions as "The Rime of the Ancient Mariner," Coleridge explores religious and philosophical concepts through fantastic, haunting narratives. In contrast, Wordsworth's contribu-

tions, such as "The Thorn" and "We Are Seven," tell stories of the common people of northern England in "the real language of men," as he claims in his preface.

The second generation of romantic poets, most notably PERCY BYSSHE SHELLEY, GEORGE GORDON, LORD BYRON, and JOHN KEATS, were deeply influenced by the first generation but also rebelled against them. Shelley and Byron in particular were troubled by Wordsworth and Coleridge's renunciation of their own earlier idealistic political beliefs. In their poetry, both Shelley and Byron were deeply concerned with social reform. Shelley went so far as to declare that "Poets are the unacknowledged legislators of the world," because they exercise our imaginations, a faculty necessary for empathy and ethical behavior. Byron's poetry, such as *Childe Harold's Pilgrimage* and *Manfred,* epitomized another feature of aristocratic romanticism—the power of the individual, the romantic hero. Byron's dark, troubled, solitary protagonists, modeled on himself, inspired a literary type, the "Byronic hero." Later Byronic heroes include CHARLOTTE BRONTË's Edward Rochester in *Jane Eyre* and EMILY BRONTË's Heathcliff in *Wuthering Heights.* Keats's poetry, in contrast to Byron's and Shelley's, is less concerned with political issues. Instead, he focuses on themes of aesthetics, melancholy, and illness. Other major second-generation romantic poets include ANNA LETITIA BARBAULD and FELICIA HEMANS.

Among prose genres, the Gothic novel perhaps best embodies the spirit of romanticism. Gothic authors such as M. G. LEWIS and ANN RADCLIFFE wrote thrilling supernatural tales set in exotic locations, emphasizing the power of the irrational and the beauty of nature. One of the best Gothic novels is MARY SHELLEY's *Frankenstein; or, The Modern Prometheus* (1818). The title character is an 18th-century scientist and man of reason. He discovers a way to create life and fashions a man of his own making. The man becomes monster, however, and turns against his creator. In its exploration of the limits of reason and human knowledge, its depiction of exotic locales such as the Arctic and the Alps, and its dark, troubled creator-hero, Shelley's *Frankenstein* epitomizes the romantic spirit.

Works about Romanticism
Berlin, Isaiah. *The Roots of Romanticism.* Princeton, N.J.: Princeton University Press, 2001.
Gaull, Marilyn. *English Romanticism: The Human Context.* New York: W. W. Norton, 1988.
Wu, Duncan. *Romanticism: An Anthology.* Cambridge, Mass.: Blackwell, 2000.

Rossetti, Christina (1830–1894) *poet*

Christina Rossetti was born in London to Gabriele Rossetti, an Italian expatriate, and his wife, Frances Polidori Rossetti. Her older brother was the painter and poet DANTE GABRIEL ROSSETTI.

Rossetti was educated at home by her mother, who was once a governess. Rossetti spent portions of her childhood at the country home of her maternal grandfather, but lived most of her life in London. Except for poems privately printed by her grandfather, the first publication of Rossetti's poetry was in the *Germ.* This magazine, cofounded by her brother, promoted the PRE-RAPHAELITE MOVEMENT, an artistic and literary school that supposedly took its inspiration from 14th- and 15th-century Italian art. Altogether, Rossetti contributed seven poems to the *Germ.* Among these was "Dream Land" (1850), a meditation on the death of a young woman:

> *She cannot feel the rain*
> *Upon her hand.*
> * * * * *
> *Sleep that no pain shall wake;*
> *Night that no morn shall break.*

This early poetry has a clarity and simplicity that was in tune with the aims of the Pre-Raphaelites.

When she was young, Rossetti was passionate and easy to anger. Her brother William said she was "vivacious and open to pleasurable impressions, and during girlhood, one might readily have supposed that she would develop into a woman of expansive heart, fond of society and diversions, and taking part in them of more than average brilliancy." But during her adolescence Rossetti suffered illnesses and was once diagnosed, as her biographer Jan Marsh reports, with "a religious mania, bordering on insanity." When she recovered, she was quieter and more introspective than she had been before.

While no longer exhibiting signs of religious mania, Rossetti remained an extremely devout Christian, so much so that she refused to marry two men with whom she was in love because of their religious beliefs, or lack thereof. In 1848 Rossetti became engaged to the Pre-Raphaelite painter James Collinson. Collinson had converted from Roman Catholicism to Anglicanism at Rossetti's request, but when he reconverted to Catholicism in 1850, she broke off the engagement. She later fell in love with Charles Bagot Cayley, a translator of Dante, but refused to marry him because he was not a Christian. She continued to love Cayley and remained friends with him throughout her life. Much of Rossetti's poetry deals with the theme of lost love, and her feelings for Cayley figure in several poems.

In Rossetti's first volume of poetry, *The Goblin Market and Other Poems* (1862), the title poem is considered among her best. Full of sensuous imagery, the poem tells the story of two sisters, Lizzie and Laura, and their encounter with goblins. They are tempted by the goblins'

> *Apples and quinces,*
> *Lemons and oranges,*
> *Plump unpecked cherries-*
> *Melons and raspberries,*
> *Bloom-down-cheeked peaches,*
> *Swart-headed mulberries,*
> *Wild free-born cranberries,*
> *Crab-apples, dewberries,*
> *Pine-apples, blackberries,*
> *Apricots, strawberries—*
> *All ripe together*
> *In summer weather—*

Laura succumbs to the temptation and Lizzie tries to save her. The poem is unquestionably erotic in its descriptions, but it also offers a religious interpretation. The critic Marian Shalkhauser says that "Lizzie . . . is the symbol of Christ; Laura represents Adam-Eve and consequently all of mankind." The richness of the poem has inspired a multitude of different interpretations, ranging from Freudian to feminist.

In 1866 Rossetti published a second volume of her work, titled *The Prince's Progress and Other Poems,* followed by a volume of short stories in 1870. In addition to two more volumes of poetry for adults, *A Pageant and Other Poems* (1881) and *Verses* (1893), Rossetti wrote a volume of poems for children, *Sing-Song: A Nursery Rhyme Book* (1872, enlarged 1893) and several volumes of devotional material.

In 1871 Rossetti was diagnosed with a thyroid dysfunction that left her an invalid and distorted her appearance. She seldom left the house in her later years, but continued to write and revise her work.

Critical Analysis

Of Christina Rossetti, Virginia Woolf wrote, "Death, oblivion, and rest lap round your songs with their dark wave. And then, incongruously, a sound of scurrying and laughter is heard. . . . For you were not a pure saint by any means. You pulled legs; you tweaked noses. You were at war with all humbug and pretence." As Woolf notes, Rossetti often yearned for death in her poetry, and she wrote frequently about lost love and the unfulfilled life. But, as Woolf further observes, there is a playful character to Rossetti's verse as well.

Many of Rossetti's poems are deeply religious, and she has been compared to 17th-century poets such as John Donne. Although she was mystical in her thinking, her poetry is never obscure. Rossetti is known for the incredible melodiousness of her work.

Rossetti was appreciated in her own day and was even considered for the post of poet laureate of England. Her reputation remains high, in large part due to her sonnets. In sonnet 11 of her sonnet sequence *Monna Innominata*, the poet writes of the depth of her love for another:

> *Many in aftertimes will say of you*
> *"He Loved her"–while of me what will they*
>   *say?*
> *Not that I loved you more than just in play*
> *For fashion sake as idle women do.*
> * * * * * * * * *
> *I charge you at the Judgment [day] make it*
>   *plain*
> *My love of you was life and not a breath.*

Love, like religion, was a major theme of Rossetti's. In one of her love poems, "A Birthday," she develops the idea that she is reborn into love when her lover arrives. She describes her joy at his approach in rich pictorial terms:

> *My heart is like an apple-tree*
> *Whose boughs are bent with thickset fruit;*
> *My heart is like a rainbow shell*
> *That paddles in a halcyon sea;*

The music of these lines complements the richness of the visual imagery. To greet her lover she imagines herself on an elaborate dais, richly draped with "silk and down," hung "with vair and purple dyes," and carved "in doves and pomegranates, / And peacocks with a hundred eyes." When her lover arrives, it is the birthday of her life.

At the other end of the spectrum of Rossetti's poetry is "When I Am Dead, My Dearest." Here, as in many of her darker poems, Rossetti seems to long for death. She tells her lover "To sing no sad songs for me," but simply to "remember" her. Though Christian in her belief, Rossetti here and in many of her poems envisions death not as eternal bliss but as a kind of limbo, a time to rest from the hardships and trials of life. When she is gone, she says,

> *I shall not see the shadows,*
> *I shall not feel the rain;*
> *I shall not hear the nightingale*
> *Sing on, as if in pain.*

Like the work of the American poet Emily Dickinson, Rossetti's work is prized for the honesty and depth of her feelings and the clarity and simplicity of expression. As the critic ARTHUR SYMONS observes, "a power of seeing finely beyond the scope of ordinary vision; that, in a few words, is the note of . . . Rossetti's genius, and it brings with it . . . [a] power of expressing subtle . . . conceptions; always clearly, always simply."

Other Work by Christina Rossetti
Grump, R. W., and Betty S. Flowers, eds. *The Complete Poems.* New York: Penguin, 2001.

Works about Christina Rossetti
Kent, David A., ed. *The Achievement of Christina Rossetti.* Ithaca, N.Y.: Cornell University Press, 1989.
Marsh, Jan. *Christina Rossetti: A Writer's Life.* New York: Viking, 1995.
Palazzo, Lynda. *Christina Rossetti's Feminist Theology.* New York: Palgrave Macmillan, 2002.

Rossetti, Dante Gabriel (1828–1882)
poet, artist

Gabriel Charles Dante Rossetti was one of four children born to Gabriele Rossetti, an Italian expatriate, and Frances Polidori Rossetti. Rossetti, who later rearranged his name to emphasize his intellectual connection to Dante (the author of *The Divine Comedy*), was the older brother of poet CHRISTINA ROSSETTI.

From his earliest years, Rossetti showed an interest in and talent for both writing and painting. From 1836 to 1843 Rossetti attended King's College School in London. From there he went to Cary's Art Academy to prepare for entrance into the Royal Academy, the most prestigious art school in England at the time. He was accepted into the Royal Academy but left after a year because he disliked both the methods of instruction and the pace. He studied for a time under Ford Madox Brown, who nurtured Rossetti's interest in medievalism. In 1848, along with John Everett Millais, Holman Hunt, and others, Rossetti founded a school of painting called the Pre-Raphaelite Brotherhood. The young painters of the PRE-RAPHAELITE MOVEMENT wanted to return to what they perceived to be the style of painting in 14th- and 15th-century Italy, before the time of the painter Raphael—hence the name. They felt that the Renaissance artist had manipulated the subject of his art to correspond to his idea of beauty, and they preferred to focus more on the inherent beauty of the subject. The members of the Pre-Raphaelite Brotherhood became known for their use of mythological, biblical, and medieval subjects and for the depth and brilliance of color in their work. They also redefined the Victorian notion of female beauty by painting women who were tall and frail-looking. The Brotherhood also founded a journal in 1849, originally called the *Germ*, in which Rossetti's early poetry was published. Among Rossetti's poems of this period were "The Blessed Damozel," which envisions a woman in heaven longing for the lover she left behind; "My Sister's Sleep," which portrays the death of a baby on Christmas Eve; and "Jenny," whose title character is a young prostitute.

One of the Pre-Raphaelites' most popular models was ELIZABETH SIDDAL, who is best known as Ophelia (from *Hamlet*) in Millais's painting of the drowned girl, *Ophelia* (1851–52). Rossetti painted her many times, fell in love, and became engaged to her in 1851. A number of factors, including her ill health, prevented their marriage for many years. The couple was finally married in 1860, but because of her illness, which may have been tuberculosis, Siddal became addicted to laudanum, of which she took a fatal overdose in 1862.

Throughout his career, Rossetti alternated between painting and poetry. From 1850 to 1860 he focused largely on the former, but in 1861 he published a collection of translations titled *The Early Italian Poets*. His work on this book inspired him to write again, and he began to collect and revise his early poetry and write new poems. When Siddal died, however, Rossetti's grief was so great that he buried the poems with her.

After Siddal's death, Rossetti moved to a house in the Chelsea district of London where he collected a menagerie of exotic animals. In the late 1860s Rossetti returned to writing. Many of his new poems were sonnets about his paintings, including "Soul's Beauty" (1866), "Body's Beauty" (1866), and "Venus Verticordia" (1868). Some of these poems Rossetti actually inscribed on the frames of his paintings. His major work from this era is an autobiographical sonnet sequence titled *The House of Life* (1870) about the intense love between a man and a woman. In an opening verse, Rossetti explains his concept of the sonnet:

> *A Sonnet is a moment's monument,*
> *Memorial from the Soul's eternity*
> *To one dead deathless hour. . . .*
> *. . .*
> *A Sonnet is a coin; its face reveals*
> *The Soul.*

Rossetti decided to publish a book of poems that included his sonnets along with his early poetry. He convinced some friends to exhume Siddal's body to recover the poetry. They did so, and Rossetti then copied the poems and burned the original manuscript. The result of this effort was *Poems* (1870). The book was well received, but in 1871 a hostile review by ROBERT BUCHANAN titled "The Fleshly School of Poetry" criticized Rossetti for the overt sexuality of the work. Rossetti replied with a long essay titled "The Stealthy School of Criticism."

Rossetti returned to painting and did not write poetry again until the last years of the 1870s. During this period he seldom went out during the day and tried to treat his growing depression and insomnia with doses of alcohol and chloral hydrate. In 1872 he attempted suicide by swallowing a bottle of laudanum.

For many years Rossetti had been in love with Jane Morris, the wife of fellow Pre-Raphaelite

WILLIAM MORRIS. For a time Rossetti lived with the Morrises in their home at Kelmscott, in Oxfordshire, and when he returned to poetry in the late 1870s much of his work was inspired by his feelings for Jane.

Beginning in 1879 Rossetti wrote several ballads, including "The White Ship" (1880) and "The King's Tragedy" (1881). "The White Ship" tells the story of the drowning of the son of England's King Henry I during an invasion of France:

> "Your son and all his fellowship
> Lie low in the sea with the White Ship."
>
> King Henry fell as a man struck dead.

"The King's Tragedy" is the tale of Catherine Douglas, a young woman who tries to save the life of Scotland's King James I by standing between him and his assassins—and is probably the origin of the phrase "Katy, bar the door."

Rossetti continued to paint and also decided to publish a new edition of *Poems* and a new volume titled *Ballads and Sonnets,* both in 1881. He was in the habit of revising his work repeatedly, and left several different versions of many of his major poems. After the publication of these two volumes, Rossetti traveled to the Lake District in the hope of improving his health, but died there of kidney failure.

Critical Analysis

A favorite of many readers is "Jenny," a dramatic monologue, certainly influenced by ROBERT BROWNING, which begins with the often-quoted lines, "Lazy laughing languid Jenny, / Fond of a kiss and fond of a guinea." Jenny is a young prostitute whom the speaker describes in terms that recall the rich and sensual ideal of female beauty portrayed in Rossetti's paintings:

> *Why Jenny, as I watch you there,—*
> *Your silk ungirdled and unlac'd*
> *And warm sweets open to the waist,*
> *All golden in the lamplight's gleam,—*
> *You know not what a book you seem,*
> *Half-read by lightning in a dream!*

As the speaker watches Jenny resting sleepily on his knee, he muses on what must have been her innocent childhood: "When she would lie in fields and look / Along the ground through the blown grass, / And wonder where the city was." He then envisions an awful future when she will "stare along the streets alone." The speaker has spent time with prostitutes before this evening, but this is evidently the first time he has thought about what the woman's life must have been and will be.

The speaker comes to realize that Jenny is no different from his beloved sister Nell, who is also "fond of fun / and fond of dress, and change, and praise." This conclusion flies in the face of the Victorian view of women as either angels or fallen women. As Jenny finally drifts off, he notices that she sleeps

> *Just as another woman sleeps!*
> *Enough to throw one's thoughts in heaps*
> *Of doubt and horror,—what to say*
> *Or think,—this awful secret sway,*
> *The potter's power over the clay!*
> *Of the same lump (it has been said)*
> *For honour and dishonour made,*
> *Two sister vessels.*

The difference between Jenny and pure women, he concludes, is the "toad within the stone"—the sexual desire of men:

> *Yet, Jenny, looking long at you.*
> *The woman almost fades from view.*
> *A cipher of man's changeless sum*
> *Of lust, past, present, and to come,*
> *Is left.*

To what extent Rossetti intended the speaker's sudden insight to be tinged with irony is unclear, but critics from JOHN RUSKIN to modern feminists have regarded this narrator as deeply flawed.

They emphasize his bourgeois tendency to place women in separate spheres and his part in the exploitation of women like Jenny.

The writer of Rossetti's obituary in the London *Times* notes that Rossetti was "as pictorial a poet as he was a poetic painter," and his painting and poetry do share many qualities. There is a richness of sensual, visual detail in his poetry that is in tune with the brilliant color and depth of his painting. Indeed, Rossetti said that "color and meter . . . are the true patents of nobility in painting and poetry, taking precedence of all intellectual claims." Of Rossetti the scholar Edmund Clarence Stedman writes that "throughout his poetry we discern a finesse, a regard for detail, and a knowledge of color and sound. . . . His verse is . . . [composed] of tenderness, emotional ecstasy, and poetic fire."

Other Work by Dante Gabriel Rossetti
Marsh Jan, ed. *Dante Gabriel Rossetti: The Collected Writings.* Chicago: New Amsterdam Books, 2000.

Works about Dante Gabriel Rossetti
Ash, Russell. *Dante Gabriel Rossetti.* New York: Harry N. Abrams, 1995.

Keane, Robert N. *Dante Gabriel Rossetti: The Poet As Craftsman.* New York: Peter Lang, 2002.

McGann, Jerome. *Dante Gabriel Rossetti and the Game that Must Be Lost.* New Haven, Conn.: Yale University Press, 2000.

Riede, David G. *Dante Gabriel Rossetti and the Limits of Victorian Vision.* Ithaca, N.Y.: Cornell University Press, 1983.

Rowlands, John
See STANLEY, HENRY MORTON.

Ruskin, John (1819–1900) *social critic, art critic, nonfiction writer*

One of the great Victorian thinkers and social reformers, and a draftsman and art critic, John Ruskin was born in London to first cousins Margaret Cox and John James Ruskin, a Scottish wine merchant. Ruskin was educated at home until age 15. In 1837 he entered Christ Church College, Oxford, where he studied architecture, geology, mathematics, and painting, and from which he graduated in 1842.

In 1840 Ruskin met the person he regarded as his "earthly master," the painter J. W. M. Turner, about whom he wrote to a friend shortly after, "He seems to have seen everything, remembered everything, spiritualized everything in the visible world."

Reserving the highest praise for Turner in its eclectic survey, the first of five volumes of Ruskin's *Modern Painters* appeared in 1843. However, the full work bounded beyond Turner; for instance, volume 2 aimed to introduce to the British public two schools of Italian painting, those of the 15th-century Florentine Fra Angelico and the 16th-century Venetian Tintoretto. Regardless of which painters he discussed, Ruskin attempted to define, as much for himself as his readers, what constituted beauty in painting. The completed work established Ruskin as Britain's leading aesthetician and art critic.

Ruskin believed that art had claimed a spiritual basis and should ennoble humanity. The title of *The Seven Lamps of Architecture* (1849), a work written during his 10-year hiatus between volumes 2 and 3 of *Modern Painters,* refers to the Christian virtues that he felt architecture should embody: sacrifice, truth, power, beauty, life, memory, and obedience.

The three volumes of *The Stones of Venice* (1851–53) are a detailed study of Venice and its architecture. One of its principal themes, in Ruskin's own words, is "the relation of the art of Venice to her moral temper . . . and that of the life of the workman to his work." As a result of the book's influence, Venetian Gothic infiltrated British architecture.

Among Ruskin's most important works outside the field of art criticism, *Unto This Last* (1860) began a trilogy—the other two books being *Munera Pulveris* (1862) and *Time and*

Tide (1867)—on the topic of political economy. Finding that the pursuit of wealth in England's mercantile economy overwhelms humane considerations by sustaining and advancing poverty, Ruskin describes as an outcome what the next century would widely term "alienation": the isolation from society of the individual, especially the unskilled, laborer.

Ruskin started teaching in 1854 at the newly founded socialist Working Men's College. Once seemingly headed for the ministry, he abandoned Protestantism in 1858. In 1869 he began teaching fine arts at Oxford. Committed to ecology, two years later he founded the Guild of St. George, still in existence, whose work included reclaiming wasteland, creating botanical gardens, building art schools and museums and, even back then, discouraging energy waste in industry.

Critical Analysis

Believing that art should be creative and imaginative rather than imitative, and greatly preferring Turner's "organic," dynamic landscapes to the ordered, "geometric" landscape painting of the past, Ruskin wrote as a Romantic for whom nature is holy and sunlight divine. Ruskin believed that Turner's paintings, aspiring to celebrate nature's infinite variety, constituted an act of devotion that enabled Turner to penetrate appearances and reveal nature's spirit. Ruskin biographer W. G. Collingwood has written, "by beginning with the observed facts of nature—truths, he called them—and the practice (not the precept) of great artists . . . [he] created a perfectly new school of criticism." Ruskin's close analysis of Turner's painting of water seems to merge with the artist's own creative activity: "Turner [is] the only painter who [has] ever represented the surface of calm or the *force* of agitated water. He obtains this expression of force in falling or running water by fearless and full rendering of its forms. He never loses himself and his subject in the splash of the fall, his presence of mind never fails as he goes down; he does not blind us with the spray, or veil the countenance of his fall with its own drapery."

Ruskin's biographer Tim Hilton has written that *Modern Painters* "revealed to Ruskin his power as a writer."

Contemporary reviews of Ruskin's work were highly favorable, although *Blackwood's Magazine,* hostile to Turner's painting, was indignant that Ruskin favored contemporary artists over past ones. The *Globe* called the book "the work of a poet," and *Artists' and Amateurs' Magazine* declared it "by far the most intelligent, philosophic and comprehensive [current] work on the subject of Art."

Ruskin's theme of truth to nature led in volume 3 (1856) to one of his most famous formulations, that of what he called the "pathetic fallacy," which in literature is the false assigning to nature of human feelings and traits. (The sea's "cruel, crawling foam" is an example Ruskin gives.) Pathetic fallacy, then, is the misguided attempt to see nature in one's own terms rather than in nature's terms. Ruskin's mission to do the latter would remain one of guiding motives of his life.

According to Ruskin's biographer Joan Abse, *The Seven Lamps of Architecture* "was inspired by the passionate attachment Ruskin had conceived for medieval architecture and his desire to explain to his contemporaries the elements that made it so wonderful." Architecture, Ruskin wrote in this book, "so disposes and adorns the edifices raised by man, for whatever uses, that the sight of them may contribute to his mental health, power and pleasure." He also thought that great buildings are not calculated but are instead drawn from nature and its infinite variety. Their "variations are not mere blunders, or carelessness," he wrote in the chapter "The Lamp of Life," "but the result of a fixed scorn . . . of accuracy in measurements; and, in most cases, I believe, of a determined resolution to work out an effective symmetry by variations as subtle as those of Nature." Poet ALICE MEYNELL praised the work's "invincible vitality."

Recent critics such as C. Stephen Finley and Michael Wheeler, however, find evangelical Christianity instead of nature Ruskin's guiding force in *Seven Lamps.* Another critic, Gill Chitty, finds in a comparison of *Modern Painters I* and *Seven Lamps* Ruskin's shift of allegiance from present to past. Referring to architecture as "the most precious of inheritances, that of past ages," Ruskin in "The Lamp of Memory" exhorts the reader not to modify or otherwise damage old buildings, for "[t]hey are not ours . . . [but] belong partly to those who built them, and partly to all the generations of mankind who are to follow us."

"The Nature of Gothic" appears in volume 2 (1853) of *The Stones of Venice*. The most widely read of all of Ruskin's writings, this chapter is grounded in what the critic Jeffrey L. Spear has called "the mid-19th-century . . . association between Gothic and raw nature." Contrasting the architecture of the Christian era to that of ancient Greece and Assyria, where the workmen were slaves, Ruskin writes, "Go forth again to gaze upon the old cathedral front . . . [and] examine once more those [sculpted] ugly goblins, and formless monsters, and stern statues, anatomiless and rigid; but do not mock at them, for they are signs of the life and liberty of every workman who struck the stone." While granting that "Ruskin was idealizing the situation of the workman in medieval times, forgetting that many of them spent their lives in gruelling physical labour," Abse closes in on the work's crucial importance: "[I]n a world in which the necessities of the machine and the market held sway, Ruskin put man squarely back at the center." She continues: "[T]he key to [the Gothic style, Ruskin] believed, lay in its expressiveness . . . [This] could not be ordained or planned; [this] sprang from the workmen who built the architecture with their own hands, crudely, imperfectly perhaps, but endowing it with the spirit of life."

The poet WILLIAM MORRIS, Ruskin's disciple, called "The Nature of Gothic" the most compelling part of Ruskin's masterpiece, "one of the very few and inevitable utterances of the century."

"Ruskin's genius," the critic John D. Rosenberg has written, "was a unique fusion of the capacity to see with the amazed eyes of a child and to reason with a mind as swift and penetrating as any that England has produced."

Other Works by John Ruskin
Complete Works of John Ruskin. New York: Classic Books, 2001.
Rosenberg, John D., ed. *The Genius of John Ruskin*. Charlottesville: University Press of Virginia, 1998.

Works about John Ruskin
Abse, Joan. *John Ruskin: The Passionate Moralist*. New York: Quarter Books, 1980.
Batchelor, John. *John Ruskin: A Life*. New York: Carroll & Graf, 2000.
Birch, Dinah, ed. *Ruskin and the Dawn of the Modern*. Oxford, England: Oxford University Press, Clarendon Press, 1999.
Chitty, Gill. "A Great Entail" in *Ruskin and Environment: The Storm-Cloud of the Nineteenth Century*. Edited by Michael Wheeler. Manchester, England: Manchester University Press, 1995.
Hilton, Tim. *John Ruskin*. New Haven, Conn.: Yale University Press, 2002.
Nicholls, Peter, and Giovanni Cianci. *Ruskin and Modernism*. London: Macmillan, 2001.

Rutherford, Mark
See WHITE, WILLIAM HALE.

Saintsbury, George (1845–1933) *literary scholar, historian, critic, journalist*

George Edward Bateman Saintsbury was born on October 23, 1845, in Southampton. His father, George Saintsbury, was the superintendent of Southampton docks, and his mother was Elizabeth Wright. His family moved to London in 1850 when his father became secretary of the East India and China Association. The younger Saintsbury attended King's College School and Merton College, Oxford, leaving in 1868 when he could not obtain a fellowship. In the same year, he married Emily Fenn King, with whom he had two sons.

Saintsbury became schoolmaster of Manchester grammar school, then Elizabeth College, Guernsey. He began writing literary reviews during this time, and after serving as headmaster of Elgin Educational Institute in Moray, Scotland, from 1874 to 1876, he returned to London to begin a literary career.

Saintsbury's first successes were a series of articles on French literature, particularly contemporary novelists, printed in the *Fortnightly Review* as well as the *Encyclopaedia Britannica* (to which he contributed 35 biographies as well as the article on French literature). An essay on Baudelaire that appeared in the *Fortnightly Review* in 1875 drew the attention of the literary world, and is widely considered to be his first significant work. He also wrote a *Short History of French Literature* in 1881. His interests shifted to English literature by the end of the 1880s, when he published his *History of Elizabethan Literature* (1887). By the 1890s he was highly regarded by the reading public, mostly for the broad reading and incisive opinions he displayed in his essays, collected in *Essays in English Literature, 1780–1860* (1890, 1895) and *Miscellaneous Essays* (1892). During this time, he was also a prolific journalist, writing for the *Pall Mall Gazette* and *Saturday Review* among many other journals; he also served as assistant editor of the latter from 1883 to 1894.

In 1895 Saintsbury was appointed to the regius chair of rhetoric and English literature at the University of Edinburgh, a position he would hold for twenty years. He produced a flood of critical works, most notably *A Short History of English Literature* (1898), *A History of English Prosody from the Twelfth Century to the Present Day* (1906–10), and 21 chapters of the *Cambridge History of English Literature* (1907–16). One of his most characteristic works was *A History of Criticism and Literary Taste in Europe from the Earliest Texts to the Present Day* (1900–04). In this work, Saintsbury provided one of the first comprehensive surveys of literary theory and criticism extending back to Greek commentators.

After retiring from his chair in 1915, he moved briefly to Southampton, then settled in Bath, and continued to write substantial and well-received books, including *History of the French Novel* (1917–19) and *Notes on a Cellar-Book* (1920), a book that inspired the formation of a dining society, the Saintsbury Club, in 1931. (In addition to his literary interests, Saintsbury was a connoisseur of wine.)

In addition to his more substantial critical works, Saintsbury also wrote a number of volumes for popular series on individual subjects, including *Dryden* (1881), *Marlborough* (1885), *Manchester* (1887), and *Lord Derby* (1892). He edited and wrote introductions for collections of works by SIR WALTER SCOTT (1897) and MATTHEW ARNOLD (1899), and the plays of John Dryden (1904) and Thomas Shadwell (1912).

In his later years, he was lavished with awards, including election as a fellow of the British Academy and an honorary fellowship to his alma mater, Merton College, Oxford (both in 1911). The breadth of his literary knowledge as much as his engaging, even conversational style of criticism made him one of the most influential English critics of the early 20th century.

Saintsbury died on January 28, 1933, in his Bath home, and was buried in the cemetery of Southampton.

Critical Analysis

Aside from his prolific output in journalism and literary history, George Saintsbury is best known for perfecting a style of criticism often described as the conversational school. Hallmarks of this style include an engaging tone, substantial scholarly knowledge that is not overwhelming in its presentation, and an offering of the critic's personal reaction to works under discussion as a way of demonstrating their value. In adopting this style, Saintsbury aimed to stimulate the reader and make the act of reading criticism pleasurable and even exciting in the manner of reading a well-written novel.

This style can be found in virtually all of his critical works, including those like *The English Novel* (1913) that were groundbreaking studies in their own right. In an early passage from this work, Saintsbury discusses early romances, including *Beowulf*, as precursors to the modern novel:

> *Beowulf* itself consists of one first-rate story and one second-rate but not despicable tale, hitched together more or less anyhow. The second, with good points, is, for us, negligible: the first is a "yarn" of the primest character. One may look back to the *Odyssey* itself without finding anything so good, except the adventures of the Golden Ass which had all the story-work of two mightiest literatures behind them. As literature on the other hand, *Beowulf* may be overpraised: it has been so frequently. But let anybody with the slightest faculty of "conveyance" tell the first part of the story to a tolerably receptive audience, and he will not doubt (unless he is fool enough to set the effect down to his own gifts and graces) about its excellence as such. There is character—not much, but enough to make it more than a mere story of adventure—and adventure enough for anything; there is by no means ineffectual speech—even dialogue—of a kind: and there is some effective and picturesque description.

Saintsbury tempers authoritative assessments of the value of *Beowulf* as well as its constituent elements with an intimate tone. The critical practice of offering one's subjective experience of a work as the primary evidence supporting one's evaluation of it was already old in Saintsbury's time. However, he adapted this approach by phrasing his evaluations in a style accessible to a general literate audience, rather than solely to one composed of other literary specialists. The Saintsbury touch won him a large and devoted audience.

Its impact did not end with the general public, however. Critics for generations to come emulated Saintsbury's style, a combination of the congenial and the erudite in which the critic's highly refined personal taste was the final arbiter of literary worth. Even today, a century later, echoes of this approach can be seen in the work of prominent critics throughout the anglophone literary world.

Saintsbury is less remembered for his evaluations of literature in sweeping surveys such as *The English Novel* and *A History of Criticism* (1900–04); since he never formulated a coherent philosophy of literature, such studies tended to lack a unifying framework. Today, his best work is considered his studies of individual works or authors. In both cases, his boundless enthusiasm for his subject is still vividly evident in his prose.

Works about George Saintsbury

Jones, Dorothy Richardson. *"King of Critics": George Saintsbury, 1845–1933, Critic, Journalist, Historian, Professor.* Ann Arbor: University of Michigan Press, 1992.

Leuba, Walter. *George Saintsbury.* New York: Twayne Publishers, 1967.

Waddell, Helen. *George Saintsbury: An Appreciation.* Cambridge: Cambridge University Press, 1946.

Sand, George (Amandine-Aurore-Lucille Dupin) (1804–1876) *novelist*

One of the most important influences on Victorian novelists, especially women writers, was the French novelist George Sand. Among the more notable authors indebted to Sand's revolutionary, feminist, and sentimental novels are CHARLOTTE and EMILY BRONTË, JANE CARLYLE, GERALDINE JEWSBURY, and GEORGE ELIOT (who chose her masculine pseudonym as an homage to Sand). The poet ELIZABETH BARRETT BROWNING pays tribute to Sand in "To George Sand. A Desire," which begins:

> *Thou large-brained woman and large-hearted man,*
> *Self-called George Sand! whose soul, amid the lions*
> *Of thy tumultuous senses, moans defiance*
> *And answers roar for roar, as spirits can.*

Sand's novels, such as *Indiana* (1832), *Valentine* (1832), and *Lélia* (1832), provoked controversy because of her socialist politics and her questioning of preconceived notions of gendered identity. Equally scandalous to Victorian sensibilities were Sand's numerous love affairs with prominent men such as Alfred de Musset and Frédéric Chopin.

Although Victorian novelists domesticated the more rebellious aspects of Sand's novels to suit English standards of morality, her feminism, passion, and blend of realism and sentimentality played a crucial part in the shaping of such classic Victorian novels as *Wuthering Heights, Jane Eyre,* and *The Mill on the Floss.* The critic Patricia Thomson contends that Sand is "the missing link between the earlier 19th-century writers and those of the Victorian period."

Critical Analysis

George Sand's *Indiana*, her first work written independently, is, in some measure, a political novel, in that it protests how the Napoleonic Code deals with the rights of married women. The heroine, Indiana Delmare, has been forced by her brutal father to marry a much older man, Colonel Delmare. She is very young, very naïve, and very miserable. Like many of her contemporaries, she has read romantic fiction and longs for real, romantic love, which her old and old-fashioned husband cannot and will not provide. Sand refuses to portray Delmare as a bad man; he is who he is and does not intend to be cruel to his wife; it is their incompatability in age, tastes, and sensibility that is at fault. However, Indiana comes to hate her husband and the awful situation in which she finds herself.

When the handsome and charming Raymon de Ramière comes on the scene, Indiana falls madly in love. At first, thinking of her social position, Indiana keeps her feelings for Raymon to herself. However, she eventually declares her love for him, though she resists his sexual overtures. Divorce is not an option for her; her only choices are to keep de Ramière at arm's length or to abandon her husband and accept the condemnation of society. She is too sweet and too romantic to consider an affair.

De Ramière is reminiscent of other rakes in French literature, and especially of the Viscount de Valmont in *Les Liaisons Dangereuses,* in that the moment Indiana begins to return his love, he loses interest in her. Not realizing this, Indiana eventually does leave her husband and come to de Ramière, only to find that he has already married another. She has "risked everything" for him—and he no longer cares at all for her.

Feminists have long argued over whether or not *Indiana* is a feminist work. If one looks at the character of Indiana herself, it would be hard to conclude that it is. She is not strong or independent, and the novel's ending seems to suggest that it is not the institution of marriage itself that is problematic—the only difficulty is in whom one marries. Still, the overall impact of the novel is undeniably feminist and on several occasions Indiana herself rises to the level of a role model, particularly when she tells her husband

> I know I am the slave and you're the lord. The law of the land has made you my master. You can tie up my body, bind my hands, control my actions. You have the right of the stronger, and society confirms you in it. But over my will, Monsieur, you have no power. God alone can bend and subdue it . . . [and] if you don't control a woman's will, your power over her is a mockery.

Later she tells her husband, "I am prepared to help you and follow you because that is what I intend. You can condemn me but I shall never obey anyone but myself."

Indiana never quite lives up to the independence and boldness she achieves in this scene, but it is impossible not to sympathize with her and to despise the social system that so traps and smothers her. It also is easy to imagine that she might have been quite a different person had she been educated to think for herself and accustomed to freedom. Sand does not make much of these ideas in the novel, but they are implicit in her treatment of her heroine.

Other Works by George Sand
The Castle of Pictures and Other Stories: A Grandmother's Tales. Holly Erskine Hirko, trans. New York: Feminist Press at the City University of New York, 1994.
Horace. Zack Rogow, trans. San Francisco: Mercury House, 1995.

Works about George Sand
Eisler, Benita. *Naked in the Marketplace: The Lives of George Sand.* Berkeley, Calif.: Counterpoint, 2006.
Harlan, Elizabeth. *George Sand.* New Haven, Conn.: Yale University Press, 2004.
Jack, Belinda Elizabeth. *George Sand: A Woman's Life Writ Large.* New York: Vintage Books, 2001.
Massardier-Kenney, Francoise. *Gender in the Fiction of George Sand.* Atlanta, Ga.: Rodopi, 2000.

Schreiner, Olive Emilie Albertina
(1855–1920) *novelist, essayist, short story writer*

Olive Schreiner was born at Wittebergen, a Wesleyan mission station near Cape Town, South Africa, to the evangelical missionaries Gottlob Schreiner, a German Lutheran, and Rebecca Lyndall, an English Methodist. In 1867 family bankruptcy found Schreiner moving in with three of her older siblings in Cradock, South Africa, where one, Theo, ran a school. She subsequently went to England to train to be a nurse, but found herself unsuitable for medical work and in 1881 turned to writing. Schreiner had a brief love affair in 1884 with the author HAVELOCK ELLIS, and they remained lifelong friends. In 1889, inspired by the plans of Cecil Rhodes, the prime minister of the

Cape Colony, to annex South Africa for Britain, Schreiner returned home, settling in Matjesfontein. In 1894 she married Samuel Cronwright, a farmer, and moved with him to Kimberley and then to Johannesburg, hoping to find relief from her asthma and weakening heart. A member of the Women's Enfranchisement League, Schreiner resigned in 1908 when she realized that the group would not pursue black female suffrage. During World War I, in which the Union of South Africa participated on the side of the Allies, Schreiner supported conscientious objectors to the fighting.

Schreiner's most enduring work, first published under a pseudonym, Ralph Iron, is the semi-autobiographical *The Story of an African Farm* (1883). The novel, like EMILY BRONTË's *Wuthering Heights* (1847), traces the damaged lives of characters who are introduced as children: in particular, Lyndall, an orphaned English girl whose rapid loss of religious faith mirrors Schreiner's, and Waldo, the son of the devout German manager of the African farm where they both live, whose loss of faith is slower in coming.

The novel addresses many important issues, from evolution to feminism. Schreiner attempts to reconcile the new evolutionary science with the old faith, and to analyze the relations of the sexes—for instance, how women cope with the absence of recognized gender equality. One strategy, as critic Joyce Avrech Berkman has noted, is the use of "the most powerful instrument at [women's] disposal, their sexual powers, to guarantee their survival and self-respect." Lyndall, addressing Waldo and men in general, says, "We are not to study law, nor science, nor art, so we study you [in order to manipulate men]."

Schreiner's book-length essay *Women and Labour* (1911) addresses differences between the sexes regarding work and other matters. Regarding work, she noted, men were expected to perform whereas women, entitled to "sex parasitism," that is, being subsidized by male labor, were not.

Schreiner further explored the problems facing women in *From Man to Man* (1926), which remained unfinished at her death. The main character is Rebekah, and a major focus is her unequal marriage: her husband Frank is routinely absent (on outings with male friends, business trips, adultery) and is inattentive at home, failing to participate in raising their children.

Schreiner's choice of a masculine pen name suggests that she might have held the bias that she sought to sidestep. However, as biographers Ruth First and Ann Scott have noted, "Too much can be made of [Schreiner's] internal conflicts and too little of the constraints imposed on her by the times in which she lived. She took gigantic leaps—away from religion into freethinking; away from colonial racism and segregationist white politics to advocacy of the African cause [of political independence]; out of the suffocating limits imposed upon women and into the exploration of female psychology and sexuality."

Critical Analysis

Olive Schreiner's *The Story of an African Farm* (1883) is an odd little book, part novel, part polemic, part philosophical treatise. The first half of the work focuses on the childhoods of the three main characters, Lyndall, Em, and Waldo, all orphans. Em is the stepdaughter of Tant' Sannie, a Boer or Dutch woman; Lyndall is her cousin, and Waldo is the son of the farm's German overseer.

The novel evokes life on a South African farm in the 1850s and 1860s. Black servants do the heavy work. Ostriches roam the farmland. Old Boer customs and language dominate the scene, as does the straitlaced Protestant morality of the Dutch settlers. Em is a sweet child but ordinary in her abilities and expectations. She will live much as her stepmother does and unquestioningly accepts the conventional way of life in her world. Lyndall is different. She is desperate for life and experience and cannot wait to leave the farm, to travel, and to learn. Waldo is a dreamer and seeker of spiritual and religious truth.

The peace of the farm is fractured by the arrival of an unscrupulous Irish con man, Bonaparte Blenkins. Smooth talking but cruel, Blenkins manages to make Tant' Sannie believe that he is in love with her. He schemes to drive Waldo's father, Otto, from the farm, but Otto dies on the night before his departure. He charms Waldo into showing him his invention, a mechanical sheep shearer, then stomps on the model and destroys it. Before Blenkins can carry out his plan to marry Tant' Sannie and take over the farm, however, his fiancée overhears him making love to her young niece and sends him away in disgrace. With the villain's comic demise, the cast of characters find their old way of life restored.

The next part of the novel is a long, discursive interlude in which Shreiner describes a falling away from religious belief. The chapter entitled "Times and Seasons" describes Waldo's quest for understanding, but it is written as the story of all humans who lose faith.

> Now we have no God. We have had two: the old God that our fathers handed down to us, that we hated and never liked; the new one that we made for ourselves, that we loved; but now he has flitted away from us, and we see what he was made of—the shadows of our highest ideal, crowned and throned. Now we have no God.

The next chapter, entitled "Waldo's Stranger," is a long parable told to Waldo by a stranger, a parable intended to portray a life in search of truth in a world without religious faith.

After these chapters, the novel picks up some years later. Em is grown and is engaged to a young neighbor, Gregory Rose. Lyndall returns from her years in boarding school. Rather than show through her actions how Lyndall has grown and changed, Shreiner chooses to have her reveal herself to Waldo in a very long disquisition—sometimes impassioned, sometimes bitter—in which she outlines the difficulty of being a woman—an intelligent and ambitious woman—in a patriarchal society. She asks Waldo if he would like to be a woman. He immediately answers "no." She laughs and says she would give 50 pounds to the first man who ever says yes to her question. "It is delightful to be a woman; but every man thanks the Lord devoutly that he isn't one."

Lyndall is portrayed as a feminist, but Schreiner also portrays her as cold, calculating, and devoid of human feeling. Perhaps Schreiner paints Lyndall in this fashion to suggest that her clear-eyed understanding of her position leaves her no other option, but for many readers, Lyndall is difficult to like or identify with.

The Story of an African Farm essentially stops being a novel for a long stretch in the middle and only picks up any semblance of a story toward the end. The characters seem less like real people than mouthpieces for Schreiner's feminism and religious views. Many modern critics note another problem with the work: While Schreiner is outraged at the treatment of women, she seems not to notice the treatment of native people by colonial settlers. Indeed, in one of her diatribes, Lyndall points to a black man and wonders if his bones will one day be in a museum as "a vestige of one link that spanned between the dog and the white man." There are several other instances in which she discusses blacks as if they were not quite human.

A controversial work in its own time, *The Story of an African Farm* offended many people because of its feminism and criticism of traditional religion. It is still controversial because of its failure to recognize the clear parallels between women in a patriarchal society and native peoples under colonial rule.

Works about Olive Schreiner

Berkman, Joyce Avrech. *The Healing Imagination of Olive Schreiner*. Ann Arbor: University of Michigan Press, 1993.

First, Ruth, and Ann Scott. *Olive Schreiner: Beyond South African Colonialism*. Piscataway, N.J.: Rutgers University Press, 1991.

Scott, Hugh Stowell (Henry Seton Merriman) (1862–1903) *novelist*

Hugh Scott was born in Newcastle upon Tyne in northeast England. He traveled with his parents to Scotland and Germany, where he attended elementary schools. At age 18, Scott left school and went to work at a large insurance company in London. He disliked the work, but his parents frowned on his ambition to become a professional writer. Nevertheless, he wrote in his spare time and began to publish his writings under the pen name Henry Seton Merriman. In 1888 he published his first novel, *Young Mistley,* followed a year later by *The Phantom Future,* a portrait of bohemian students and artists. He married Ethel Frances Hall in 1889. Three years later, with the publication of *From One Generation to Another,* a study of revenge, he was able to leave the insurance company and earn his living as a writer.

Scott became one of the most successful romantic novelists in England, known for fast-paced, exciting narratives set in foreign lands such as India, Corsica, and Russia. In 1894, he published *With Edged Tools,* a violent account of slave trading in West Africa, followed a year later by *The Grey Lady,* the story of a boy who goes to sea with the Royal Navy. His best-known work, *The Sowers* (1896), is a portrait of the 19th-century Russian nihilists, who advocated the use of terrorism and assassination to overthrow the government. Scott died at age 41; in his essay "Through the Magic Door" (1919), ARTHUR CONAN DOYLE grouped him with ROBERT LOUIS STEVENSON and the great ROMANTIC poets as creative geniuses who died too young.

Scott, Sir Walter (1771–1832) *novelist, poet*

Walter Scott was born in Edinburgh, Scotland to Walter Scott, a lawyer, and Anne Rutherford Scott. As a child, Scott developed an illness that was probably polio, and he remained lame throughout his life. During his childhood, he listened to Scots ballads and tales, many of them told to him by his grandfather. He attended school in Edinburgh and then enrolled at Edinburgh University, but left the university without graduating. In 1792 he became a lawyer, and five years later he married Charlotte Carpenter.

Scott began his literary career as an editor. In 1802 he published his first major work, *The Minstrelsy of the Scottish Border,* an annotated collection of folk ballads he had collected by traveling around Scotland. His work as a ballad collector inspired his first major original work, *The Lay of the Last Minstrel* (1805). This long narrative poem is set in 16th-century Scotland and is based on an actual battle between the Scots and the English. Scott claims in his preface that his goal was "the description of scenery and manners" instead of "a combined and regular narrative." His assessment of his first work holds true for all his fiction and poetry—his descriptive powers are unmatched, while his plots are loose. *Lay* was an instant sensation. Inspired by his success, Scott continued to publish poetry for the next decade while continuing his activities as a lawyer, amateur historian, editor of the works of John Dryden, Jonathan Swift, and Daniel Defoe, and head of a growing family. *Marmion* (1806) was his next major poem, followed by *The Lady of the Lake* (1810). For these and other poems Scott repeated the formula of the *Lay*: a long narrative poem, modeled on medieval ballad and romance, set in the past and depicting thrilling events from Scottish history. His poetry did much to increase Scottish pride and a sense of national identity, as in these famous lines from *The Lay of the Last Minstrel*:

> *Breathes there the man, with soul so dead,*
> *Who never to himself hath said,*
> *This is my own, my native land?*

The success of these poems made Scott the most famous and highly-paid poet of the British Isles. He turned down the post of poet laureate, recommending his friend ROBERT SOUTHEY instead. But by the early 1810s, LORD BYRON's newfound fame threatened to eclipse Scott's.

Perhaps for this reason, Scott turned to fiction in 1814. He initially published his novels anonymously, because writing novels was not considered a respectable pursuit for a gentleman and lawyer, while poetry was. In 1814, his first novel,

Waverley, appeared. After this, each subsequent novel was published under the name "The Author of Waverley," and they were collectively called the Waverley Novels. Scott did not officially reveal his authorship until 1826, even though most readers suspected it.

Waverley deals with the attempted Jacobite rebellion of 1745. The Jacobites were supporters of King James II (1633–1701), who was forced from the throne in 1688 because of his Catholic faith, and James's exiled heirs. In 1745 supporters of James's son James Stuart (1688–1766; the Old Pretender), led by James II's grandson Charles Edward Stuart (1720–88; Bonnie Prince Charlie, the Young Pretender), landed in Scotland from France in an ultimately unsuccessful attempt to regain the English throne. Into these real events, Scott inserts the fictional Edward Waverley, who "wavers" between sides in the conflict. JANE AUSTEN, for one, recognized the hand of the poet Scott in the anonymous novel: "Walter Scott has no business to write novels, especially good ones.—It is not fair.—He has Fame and Profit enough as a Poet, and should not be taking the bread out of other people's mouths.—I do not like him, and do not mean to like *Waverley* if I can help it—but I fear I must."

After *Waverley* came *Guy Mannering* (1815), set in 1770s Scotland and featuring a cast of colorful characters including smugglers and gypsies. Scott's next novel, *The Antiquary* (1816), introduced one of his favorite and most memorable characters, Jonathan Oldbuck. Oldbuck, the antiquary of the title, neglects his family in favor of his collections of books and artifacts. Scott based his caricature of an absentminded collector and scholar partially on himself.

He returned to serious historical subjects for his next novels, *Old Mortality* (1816), *Rob Roy* (1817), *The Heart of Mid-Lothian* (1818), and *The Bride of Lammermoor* (1819). The series of novels beginning with *Waverley,* collectively known as "the Scotch novels," is generally considered Scott's finest work. Set in 17th- and 18th-century Scotland, these novels depict colorful and eccentric characters, blend fact and fiction, and deal with Scotland's transition from medieval anarchy to a modern-day commercial society. In 1818 Scott was made a baronet in recognition of his contribution to poetry.

During this time, Scott began a labor of love, the creation of his estate at Abbotsford, near the small town of Melrose, Scotland. He had purchased property in the Scottish Borders in 1812 and spent much of his life transforming a simple farm into a mock-medieval castle, filling it with historical artifacts such as suits of armor, battle-axes, and relics of famous Scots such as Rob Roy (1671–1734) and Mary, Queen of Scots (1542–87). He raced to produce more of the increasingly popular Waverley novels, sometimes writing as many as three a year, to fund his renovations.

In 1819 Scott expanded the range of his subject matter in *Ivanhoe.* The novel is set in England instead of Scotland and in the 12th century instead of more recent times. This tale of Normans and Saxons, featuring historical characters like King Richard I (Richard the Lionhearted) and Robin Hood, remains his most popular work. Several other novels from this period focus on monarchs, including *Kenilworth* (1821), about Queen Elizabeth I; *The Fortunes of Nigel* (1822), about King James I; and *Quentin Durward* (1822), about King Louis XI of France. Scott returned to the topic of Jacobitism and drew on incidents from his youth for *Redgauntlet,* his best novel of the 1820s.

Although Scott had become a wealthy man from his works, a printing firm he co-owned went bankrupt in 1825. He was forced to work even harder to pay off his creditors. The novels published after this crash show signs of haste and carelessness. More lucrative was Scott's publishing of a "Magnum Opus" edition of his novels. For this edition he commissioned new illustrations and added prefaces and historical and critical notes. The profits from this venture paid off his debts, but the intense strain of so much activity weakened his health and led to his death in 1832.

Critical Analysis

Although he was immensely successful as a poet, Scott is remembered mainly for his fiction. He was the most popular novelist of his day, selling more copies than any novelist had previously done. His influence upon the succeeding generation of novelists cannot be overestimated. CHARLES DICKENS, GEORGE ELIOT, and WILLIAM MAKEPEACE THACKERAY all tried their hand at the Scott model of historical fiction and emulated his descriptive powers and representations of social complexity. By the end of the 19th century, however, Scott's popularity waned. His realistic, descriptive style, genial tone, and simplistic characters no longer appealed to the modernists, who demanded ethical ambiguities and linguistic experimentation. The Waverley novels were relegated to the status of children's literature. A new generation of readers and critics has begun to rediscover the richness of Scott's historical fiction. Although Scott has never lacked for readers, especially in Scotland, his sophisticated analyses of social change have attracted new appreciation.

Although it has long been assumed that Scott "invented" the historical novel, recent scholars have demonstrated Scott's reliance on previous novelists, especially women writers like Sophia Lee, MARIA EDGEWORTH, and SYDNEY OWENSON. If he was not the first, however, he was certainly the most successful historical novelist of his time, and helped to define one of the most enduringly popular literary genres. He also depicted the richness of everyday life in another era to a greater degree than his predecessors. His background as a collector and historian gave him a fine sense of historical detail in scene, setting, and language.

Three issues of concern to recent critics of the Waverley Novels have been nationalism, gender, and historical development. *Rob Roy* provides a good example of Scott's creation of a romantic image of Scotland. Although the narrator of the novel is the Englishman Francis Osbaldistone, its center of interest is the legendary Highland outlaw Rob Roy. Osbaldistone does not suspect the Jacobite conspiracies being planned under his nose and does little to engage the reader. Rob Roy, on the other hand, performs heroic rescues and daring escapes and leads his clan in battle. Scott's sympathetic treatment of the Highland clans helped establish a romantic myth of the Highlanders who had been forced off their land in a program of "clearances." Scott's nationalism is not of the militant variety but the armchair nostalgia of a comfortable Lowlander.

Scott creates one of the greatest 19th-century heroines in *The Heart of Mid-Lothian*. Jeanie Deans, based on the real-life Helen Walker, is a poor Scottish woman who walks from Edinburgh to London to save her sister from execution. Her sister Effie is accused under an arcane and unjust law of murdering her child. Jeanie explains her purpose in an unlearned dialect: "'If I were anes at Lunnon,' said Jeanie, in exculpation, 'I am amaist sure I could get means to speak to the queen about my sister's life.'" Despite her lack of schooling, Jeanie displays the greatest degree of moral rectitude of any character in Scott's novels.

Finally, in all his novels Scott balances nostalgia for the past with optimism about the future. *Ivanhoe* illustrates this tension. On the one hand, it is a nostalgic romanticization of the Middle Ages, depicting chivalry, sieges, and jolly outlaws. On the other, Scott emphasizes the brutality of the past—the cruel strictures against the Jews, the mistreatment of women, and the presence of slavery among the freedom-loving Saxons. After one of his more extended treatments of a medieval tournament, Scott recollects himself: "Thus ended the memorable field of Ashby-de-la-Zouche, one of the most gallantly contested tournaments of that age. For although only four knights, including one who was smothered by the heat of his armour, had died upon the field, yet upwards of thirty were desperately wounded, four or five of whom never recovered." The balance of progress and nostalgia, romanticism and realism, description and action, and fact and fiction in Scott's best novels has challenged readers from his time to our own.

Works about Sir Walter Scott
Johnson, Edgar. *Sir Walter Scott: The Great Unknown.* New York: Macmillan, 1970.
Sutherland, J. A. *Life of Walter Scott: A Critical Biography.* London: Blackwell, 1995.

sensation fiction

Sensation fiction became popular in England in the early 1860s and was referred to at the time as "sensation mania." Blending elements of the Gothic and romantic novel and domestic realism—mixing themes such as bigamy, kidnapping, stolen identities, sexual excess, and hereditary insanity, for instance, with middle-class domestic settings, the tranquility of rural life, and the ordinary world of the professions in London—the sensation novel, as one reviewer in the *Quarterly Review* wrote, "aims at electrifying the nerves of the reader."

Sensation novels are driven primarily by plot, a fact lamented by ANTHONY TROLLOPE in his *Autobiography* (1883) in criticizing WILKIE COLLINS, whose *The Woman in White* (1860) is considered a prime example of the genre. In that novel, Laura Fairlie marries Sir Percival Glyde, who kidnaps Ann Catherick, his wife's physical double, who is suffering from a fatal disease; he then imprisons his wife in an insane asylum under a false name and installs the fatally ill Ann as his wife. When Ann dies, Sir Percival inherits Laura's estate. After numerous twists and turns involving Count Fosco, the rotund, genial Italian villain, and Walter Hartright, the lean, steady English hero, the truth is revealed.

The theme of mistaken identity in Collins surfaces again in MARY ELIZABETH BRADDON's *Lady Audley's Secret* (1862), probably the most widely read sensation novel ever. The central character leaves her husband, steals someone else's identity, marries Sir Michael Audley, attempts to kill her first husband by pushing him down a well when he finds her, and is committed to an asylum in France at the end of the novel, having been judged to be suffering from a "taint in the blood," meaning hereditary insanity. Sensation novels deployed many melodramatic qualities in their plots and characters, so it is no surprise that many of the novels were dramatized, including *Lady Audley's Secret*. As recently as 1996, the Victorian dramatization of ELLEN WOOD's *East Lynne* (1861), a novel in which the female heroine is driven from her home, returning years later disfigured from an injury and in disguise to take care of her own children as a governess, played to packed houses at the Greenwich Theatre outside of London. In her study of the sensation novel, Winifred Hughes explains the popularity of sensation fiction as follows: "In a self-styled 'age of analysis and criticism,' of rational and scientific explanation, the missing dimension of transcendence was liable to take on strange and twisted forms." Scholars and students today are still intrigued by those forms.

A Work about Sensation Fiction
Hughes, Winifred. *The Maniac in the Cellar: Sensation Novels of the 1860s.* Princeton, N.J.: Princeton University Press, 1980.

Seward, Anna (1747–1809) *poet*

Anna Seward, the daughter of a minister, Thomas Seward, and his wife, Elizabeth, spent most of her life in Lichfield, Staffordshire, England, where, because of her poetry, she was called "the swan of Lichfield." She became a member of a literary group that included William Hayley (1745–1820), a poet best remembered as a benefactor of WILLIAM BLAKE, Erasmus Darwin (1731–1802), a poet, philosopher, and social reformer, who encouraged her to write poetry, and Richard Lovell Edgeworth (1744–1817), an educational reformer. In 1784 she wrote a long sentimental poem, *Louisa*, which gained attention because very few women were publishing poetry at the time.

When Seward was about 15, a young girl named Honora Sneyd came to live with the Seward family and stayed with them for 13 years. Seward developed a passionate love for Honora, nine years her junior. When Honora married,

Seward was heartbroken, and when Honora died seven years later, Seward mourned her for the rest of her life. Many of her poems address her grief, as in these lines from "Elegy": "I write, Honora, on the sparkling sand!— / The envious waves forbid the trace to stay: / Honora's name again adorns the strand! / Again the waters bear their prize away."

Seward continued to develop close friendships with women. In the late 1790s she became friends with the so-called Ladies of Llangollen, two women who had eloped and set up house together in Llangollen, Wales. In their honor Seward wrote the long poem *Llangollen Vale,* explaining how she admired them.

When Seward died, she bequeathed her poetry to Sir Walter Scott, with whom she had corresponded. He published the poems with a memoir in 1810. Six volumes of her letters were published in 1811. She was known for her elegies, her commemorative poems, and her love poems.

Other Work by Anna Seward
The Swan of Lichfield. Edited, with a short biography and preface, by Hesketh Pearson. London: Namish Hamilton, 1936.

Sewell, Anna (1820–1878) *novelist*

Anna Sewell was raised in a family of strict Norfolk Quakers. Her father, Isaac, was a bank manager, and her mother, Mary, wrote poetry and stories for children. At age 14 Sewell injured both ankles; she was lame for the rest of her life. "My ankles are twisted like the leg of the wagonhorse who fell on the frozen cobbles last year and had to be shot," she wrote in her diary.

Over the years, she kept a journal and dabbled at painting. In the 1860s she began the Working Man's Evening Institute in Norfolk, where she taught classes to local miners and laborers. At 50 she began writing her only novel, *Black Beauty* (1877), subtitled *The Autobiography of a Horse, Translated from the Original Equine.* The book's purpose, she wrote in a letter to a friend, was to inspire "kindness, sympathy, and an understanding treatment of horses."

Black Beauty, the horse, narrates his own story, detailing his many changes in ownership, his adventures and mishaps, and how he was treated. He says, "We horses do not mind hard work if we are treated reasonably; and I am sure there are many driven by quite poor men who had a happier life than I had when I used to go in the Countess of W——'s carriage, with my silver-mounted harness and high feeding."

Black Beauty drew attention to many of the cruel practices of the day. It showed how many horses died of exhaustion from having to pull overloaded wagons. One of its chief targets was the bearing rein, which prevented the free movement of the horse's head. The bearing rein was supposed to make the horse look elegant, but the horse was unable to breathe properly and often died of respiratory complications.

The most famous of all Victorian animal novels, *Black Beauty* sold 100,000 copies in its first year, has never been out of print, and has been made into at least seven films. Dying three months after its publication, Sewell did not live to see how her work improved the treatment of horses. The use of bearing reins ended within 20 years, as did many other of the abuses detailed in the book. During Sewell's funeral, her mother insisted that the bearing reins worn by the horses in the procession be removed.

A Work about Anna Sewell
Chitty, Susan. *The Woman Who Wrote* Black Beauty: *A Life of Anna Sewell.* London: Hodder & Stoughton, 1971.

Sewell, Elizabeth Missing (1815–1906)
novelist, children's and religious writer

Elizabeth Missing Sewell was born on the Isle of Wight, England, the seventh of 12 children of Thomas Sewell, a solicitor, and Jane Edwards Sewell. Her mother sent Elizabeth to school at age four. She attended school for 10 years, her education serving her well when she was forced to help support her family after her father's death in 1842. Bank failures pushed the family into debt and her five older brothers—three Oxford University fellows, a government official, and a solicitor—all proved lacking in good business judgment. It fell to Elizabeth to repay the family's debts, and she turned to writing and teaching to support the family. In 1852 she opened a school for girls in a house she owned in Bonchurch, Isle of Wight. In 1866, Sewell established the St. Boniface Diocesan School for girls in Ventor, Isle of Wight, where she served as headmistress until her death in 1906.

Sewell is known for her educational manuals, children's history, and devotional literature, but her best work is found in the novels *Amy Herbert* (1844) and *Margaret Percival* (1847), both of which illustrate Oxford Movement doctrines and provide spiritual guidance for adolescent girls; and in her autobiographical novel *The Experience of Life* (1853) in which her protagonist, Aunt Sally, stresses the need for female education and teaches her nieces the importance of financial independence and emotional self-reliance. In these works she skillfully explores the two themes that were central to her life: the High Church tenets of the Oxford Movement and the position of unmarried women in Victorian society (as well as the education of all women).

In *A Literature of Their Own: British Women Novelists from Brontë to Lessing*, the scholar Elaine Showalter describes Sewell's approach: "Sewell regarded self-control and dutifulness as good disciplines for women who could not expect much support if they rebelled; she felt there was no point in their uselessly dispelling their energies. But she saw no reason for them to abandon their intellectual independence. Her theory of education was intended to produce freedom, originality, and reasoning ability. . . . Her women are as thoughtful, devout, and responsible as any clergyman could be, but they are also more realistic. . . . [They are] practical women concerned with the daily needs of the people around them."

A Work about Elizabeth Missing Sewell

Showalter, Elaine. *A Literature of Their Own: British Women Novelists from Brontë to Lessing.* Princeton, N.J.: Princeton University Press, 1977.

Sharp, William (Fiona Macleod) (1855–1905) *novelist, essayist, poet*

The son of David Galbraith Sharp, a merchant, and Katherine Brooks Sharp, a diplomat's daughter, William Sharp was born in Paisley, Scotland. At age nine, Sharp ran away from boarding school three times. Later he would write, "I think I sailed up every loch, fjord, and inlet in the Western Highlands and Isles." His restless adolescence led, at age 18, to a "truant" adventure when, during the summer, he joined a band of gypsies wandering through the western Highlands. His restlessness was not a phase; the discipline that his father did his best to impose barely held the boy in check.

When three summers later Sharp's father unexpectedly died, the 20-year-old broke free. Sharp never returned to complete his education at the University of Glasgow. Instead, he went to Australia and toured the bush country. It is not known whether Sharp, exhausted from schoolwork, was sent to Australia in order to recuperate or whether he went because he had threatened his mother that he would contract tuberculosis if he were not sent. On his return home a year later—he had also visited the South Seas—his journeys continued unabated. Sharp moved to London, where he was befriended by Dante Gabriel Rossetti, and traveled to Rome and throughout Italy, where he studied art. He moved on to France, Canada, the United States, Germany, North Africa, and Greece, all the while supporting himself as a writer. An early work was his *Life of Rossetti,* published in 1882, the year of the painter-poet's death.

In 1884, in Paris, where he was working as an art critic, Sharp married a cousin, Elizabeth Sharp, who after his death would write *William Sharp: A Memoir* (1910–12). In this work, she quotes a friend, perhaps fictitious, who described her husband as "a Viking in build, a Scandinavian in cast of mind, a Celt in heart and spirit."

Sharp published several books under his own name, among them *Romantic Ballads and Poems of Phantasy* (1888), the novels *The Gypsy Christ* (1895) and *Children of To-Morrow* (1889), and the essay collection *Literary Geography* (1904). Sharp's poetry is not much remembered today, but "The White Peacock" (1891) contains dreamily sensual symbolism: "Dim on the cream-white are blue adumbrations, / Shadows so pale in their delicate blueness / That visions they seem as of vanishing violets. . . ." The two novels are of particular interest. Each projects onto the characters the author's own sense of his divided Celtic and Scandinavian heritage.

Sharp signed another portion of his work with the pseudonym Fiona Macleod, borrowed partly from Seumas Macleod, an old fisherman he knew as a child. For Sharp, the old man was an embodiment of the nature that intoxicated him. Sharp's widow would write, "The three influences that taught [Sharp] most in childhood were the wind, the woods, and the sea."

For Fiona Macleod, Sharp would imagine a whole, detailed life, including a love affair with himself. This alter ego expressed inner visions, connected to ancestral memories and steeped in fantasy and fable, allegory and transcendentalism, and Celtic mysticism and folklore. Becoming Macleod resulted in writing that was more beautiful and compelling than what "William Sharp" produced. Sharp claimed he wrote as Macleod while in trances; his handwriting became "feminine" when he did so. For a time, even his closest friends believed that "Fiona Macleod" was a separate person. Only after Sharp's death did the reading public learn the truth.

Macleod broke into print with the publication of *Pharais* (1894). Under this alias, Sharp wrote *From the Hills of Dreams* (1896), *The House of Usna* (1900), and *Winged Destiny* (1904).

With their stirring ancient echoes, many of Macleod's poems bewitch and haunt. For example, in "Oona of the Dark Eyes and the Crying of Wind" (1895), the poet writes:

> *Congal, thou . . . shalt lie*
> *Still and white*
> *. . . And rise no more to any Field of*
>   *Spears,*
> *But, under the brown leaf,*
> *Remember grief*
> *And the old, salt, bitter tears.*

The implied linkage here of tears and blood belongs to a strain in Macleod's poetry that the critic Flavia Alaya characterizes as "the past's so often spectral presence—as though a dead hand were laying its weight upon the efforts of life to refresh itself."

Sharp's pseudonyms multiplied. In 1892 he founded the *Pagan Review,* in which essays and stories of his appeared under a wide range of domestic and foreign names. Sharp was, in fact, the journal's sole contributor.

These personae bear the stamp of the dramatic monologues of ROBERT BROWNING and of Browning's own influence on Sharp, who met the older poet through Rossetti. Beginning in 1888, Sharp became acquainted, too, with the young William Butler Yeats, who would come to address the world through his own "mask." Masao Miyoshi, a critic of Victorian literature, suggests that Sharp's "impersonations" were an "extraordinary" manifestation of late Victorian role-playing and destructive opposition of selves, familiar in the work of many of Sharp's literary contemporaries. Not everyone would agree. We may even detect the boast of a compatriot in Yeats's claim after Sharp's death, "He never told one anything that was true."

Other Work by Fiona Macleod/William Sharp
Where the Forest Murmurs: Nature Essays. North Stratford, N.H.: Ayer Co. Publishers, 1906.

A Work about William Sharp
Meyers, Terry L. *Sexual Tensions of William Sharp: A Study of the Birth of Fiona Macleod.* New York: Peter Lang, 1996.

Shaw, George Bernard (1856–1950)
playwright, critic

George Bernard Shaw was born in Dublin, Ireland, to George Carr Shaw, a merchant, and his wife, Elizabeth. Shaw was mostly educated at home, with brief stints of formal education. In 1876 he moved to London, where he found work as a music critic and wrote five unsuccessful novels.

At age 26 Shaw became a socialist and a member of the Fabian Society, an organization devoted to bringing about socialism in Britain by gradual means rather than through revolution. Shaw became a speaker for the society and lectured extensively.

Shaw was increasingly attracted to literature that criticized Victorian society. The plays he would later write were influenced by the satiric writings of SAMUEL BUTLER and the works of the Norwegian dramatist Henrik Ibsen, whose realistic plays attacked middle-class convention. In 1891 Shaw published *The Quintessence of Ibsenism*, a critical study of Ibsen's work. Later, from 1895 to 1898, Shaw mercilessly attacked the sentimental and romantic fare that populated much of the British stage.

Shaw's first play, *Widowers' Houses* (1892), was a drama about the evils perpetrated by slum landlords. *Mrs. Warren's Profession* (1893) was banned from the British stage because its subject is prostitution. In *Arms and the Man* (1894), Shaw aired his antiwar views through the comic dialogue of a soldier who carries chocolate instead of bullets. Shaw's first commercially successful play was *Candida* (1897), the story of an odd threesome, a love triangle among a minister, his wife, and an 18-year-old poet.

In 1898 Shaw collected for publication the plays he had written up to that time, under the title *Plays Pleasant and Unpleasant*. This volume includes the first of his many prefaces, in which he attacks censorship and discusses his themes and his theories of human existence. Shaw believed that humans could, through individual acts of will, evolve into something better. People could do so by tapping into an underlying principle of existence, the "Life Force."

Shaw wrote more than 50 plays. In 1901 he published *Three Plays for Puritans*, which includes two of his best plays: *The Devil's Disciple*, in which an American Revolutionary War soldier is frustrated in his attempts to become a hero, and *Caesar and Cleopatra*, in which a 16-year-old Cleopatra is instructed in the ways of the world by Julius Caesar. *Man and Superman* (1903) looks at love and marriage as it explores how the Life Force operates in ordinary life (the play is so long that its third act, the dream-sequence, *Don Juan in Hell*, is a full-length play in itself). *John Bull's Other Island* (1904) is a condemnation of English policies in Ireland; *The Doctor's Dilemma* (1906) targets both physicians and artists; *Major Barbara* (1907) attacks what Shaw saw as evangelical hypocrisy; *Androcles and the Lion* (1912), set in the early days of Christianity, explores the nature of religion; and *Pygmalion* (1913), his most popular and best-known play, examines the nature of social class.

After World War I, Shaw wrote a sequence of five comic one-act plays, published as *Back to Methuselah* (1921), outlining his philosophy of creative evolution, a progressive concept of spiritual growth. Shaw rejected traditional morality and believed that humankind could continue to grow spiritually apart from conventional religion. What religious people call evil, according to Shaw, is merely a series of mistakes in the progress toward spiritual perfection.

In *Saint Joan* (1923) Shaw presents Joan of Arc as the embodiment of the Life Force, who as Shaw said, is "crushed between those mighty forces, the church and the law." In the play's epilogue, Shaw suggests that even 400 years later most people still would be unable to tell the difference between a saint and a heretic.

Although Shaw continued to write plays in his later years, he focused more of his attention on political works. His *Intelligent Woman's Guide to Socialism, Capitalism, Sovietism, and Fascism* (1928)—written in response to his sister-in-law's questions—is a lively discussion of various economic theories.

Critical Analysis

Shaw believed that drama should, in the words of the ancient poet Horace, "delight and instruct," and his plays are unashamedly didactic. Unlike many didactic writers, however, Shaw could be devastatingly witty, and many of his one-liners are enshrined in books of quotations: "Lack of money is the root of all evil"; "Patriotism is your conviction that this country is superior to all others because you were born in it"; "He who can, does. He who cannot, teaches"; and "England and America are two countries divided by a common language."

This wit overshadows even Shaw's faults. There is, for example, no question that many of his characters are mere straw men, set up to be knocked down. But these one-dimensional characters often speak (or are spoken to) with such incisive wit that it hardly matters what else they lack. As the writer G. K. Chesterton once remarked about Shaw's failings, "Shaw is like the Venus de Milo: all that there is of him is admirable."

Wit is the hallmark of *Pygmalion,* Shaw's attack on the artificiality of class distinctions in Britain. Professor Henry Higgins believes that he can teach Eliza Doolittle, a cockney flower girl, to be a lady by changing her pronunciation. He finds to his dismay that he also ought to have focused some of his attention on topics for conversation. On her first outing dressed as a lady, Liza tells her newfound friends, in upper-class tones, that her aunt was too tough to die of the flu:

> Why should she die of influenza? She come through diphtheria right enough the year before.... Fairly blue with it, she was. They all thought she was dead; but my father he kept ladling gin down her throat til she came to so sudden that she bit the bowl off the spoon.

Higgins tells the group that this is the new slang and hustles Eliza home for more lessons in polite conversation. But even that is not the key. Eventually Eliza observes that "the difference between a lady and a flower girl is not how she behaves, but how she's treated."

Also typically Shavian is Eliza's father, Alfred P. Doolittle. Higgins first meets Doolittle when the older man comes to try to collect a little money in exchange for his daughter, believing Eliza to be a "kept woman." When Higgins calls his bluff, Doolittle admits he is one of the "undeserving poor" but points out that his needs are just as great "as the most deserving widow's that ever got money out of six different charities in one week for the death of the same husband." He adds:

> What is middle class morality? Just an excuse for never giving me anything.... I'm playing straight with you. I aint pretending to be deserving.... I mean to go on being undeserving.

In one of the play's central ironies, Higgins is so impressed with Doolittle's unconventionality that he writes an article calling him one of the world's most original moralists; Higgins's act eventually leads to Doolittle's social advancement. Along with his respectability, Doolittle is forced to give up all his unconventionality; he even has to go so far as to marry his mistress.

For those who know *Pygmalion* only through the musical adaptation *My Fair Lady* (1956), it is important to note that the original is sharper and less romantic. For example, the ending of the musical suggests that Eliza and Higgins will have a "happily-ever-after" future, but Shaw leaves the ending of the play open and, in his epilogue, points out that Eliza, as an embodiment of the Life Force, could never live in harmony with Higgins.

As with all of Shaw's plays, the intention of *Pygmalion* was to make the audience look at itself. "I must warn my readers," Shaw once wrote, "that my attacks are directed against themselves, not against my stage figures." Thus, as the audience laughs, its members are forced to question their smug complacencies.

In 1925 Shaw won the Nobel Prize in literature. Shaw's plays succeed and remain popular because of his craftsmanship. According to the scholar Robert Warnock, Shaw's "ample genius found room for a superb art of characterization, plot development, and even poetic expression that converted the comedy of ideas into exciting theatre."

Other Work by George Bernard Shaw

Plays by George Bernard Shaw. New York: New American Library, 1989.

Works about George Bernard Shaw

Holroyd, Michael. *George Bernard Shaw: The One-Volume Definitive Edition.* New York: Random House, 1997.

Innes, C. D., ed. *The Cambridge Companion to George Bernard Shaw.* New York: Cambridge University Press, 1998.

Shelley, Mary Wollstonecraft

(1797–1851) *novelist*

Mary Wollstonecraft Shelley was born in London to the anarchist philosopher WILLIAM GODWIN and the feminist philosopher MARY WOLLSTONECRAFT. Her mother died shortly after her birth and she received no formal education but was tutored by her father, benefiting from his vast library and the frequent visits by his circle of writer friends, which included WILLIAM WORDSWORTH, CHARLES LAMB, SAMUEL TAYLOR COLERIDGE, and WILLIAM HAZLITT. She would go on to marry the romantic poet PERCY BYSSHE SHELLEY and befriend GEORGE GORDON, LORD BYRON as well.

Mary's romance with the married Percy began in 1814 and the two eloped to the Continent, but they did not marry until Percy's first wife committed suicide in 1816. The same year, Byron suggested that he and the Shelleys, who were staying in Switzerland near Lake Geneva, should each write a ghost story. In response to the challenge Mary Shelley wrote *Frankenstein; or, The Modern Prometheus* (1818).

Shelley then produced a conventional novel about Renaissance Italy, entitled *Valperga* (1823). Her next novel, *The Last Man* (1826), returned to the fantastic, as she detailed the adventures of a survivor of a world disaster. Shelley also wrote or edited biographies, essays, short stories, and poetry collections, as well as a popular collection of travel essays, *Rambles in Germany and Italy, in 1840, 1842, and 1843* (1844).

Critical Analysis

In *Frankenstein,* Mary Shelley's most famous work, the daring but reckless scientist Frankenstein assembles a creature from pieces of dead bodies and gives it life. The creature is without a family and without a real past, but has an adult intellect and a few texts by which to form its impressions of the world. Among his reading is John Milton's *Paradise Lost* and Johann Wolfgang von Goethe's *The Sorrows of Young Werther.*

Initially well-intentioned but angered by his isolation from the rest of civilization and his eventual abandonment by Frankenstein, the creature ultimately turns on his creator and the two die in a frozen wasteland. Frankenstein's final words show that although his experiment failed horribly, he has not lost his belief in scientific experimentation: "I myself have been blasted in these hopes, yet another may succeed."

Frankenstein is remembered mainly today as a cautionary tale about the limits of science and the risks of playing God, and as such has been the inspiration for countless later science fiction works, from H. G. Wells's *The Food of the Gods* (1904) to Michael Crichton's *Jurassic Park* (1990). However, Shelley's novel was likely influenced by her hopes and fears for ROMANTICISM, the literary movement of which she and her friends were a part. Unlike proponents of Enlightenment science, Shelley was conscious of the possibility for tragic disaster whenever ambitious men asserted their infallibility. She made the point that experiments can go horribly awry, whether in science, poetry, or politics.

It is no coincidence that the creature, much like some of Shelley's contemporaries, clings to a few emotionally charged favorite literary works and is heartbroken when the world does not share his sensitivity. The creature comes to see in Werther a soul that feels as intensely as he does, while eventually finding in the Satan of *Paradise Lost* a rebel, like himself, doomed to struggle against his own creator and to be banished from civilization.

In some sense Shelley's novel can be taken as a conservative warning about the risks of romanticism, similar to the 18th-century writer EDMUND BURKE's metaphor for the risks of the French Revolution: remaking the world from scratch, warned Burke, was like trying to improve a human being by dismembering him and reassembling the corpse. On the other hand, Shelley's later novel *Lodore* (1835) is often interpreted as a defense of her husband and his romantic sensibilities.

Shelley was also a pioneer of apocalyptic science fiction. In her novel *The Last Man,* she depicts the destruction of humanity by a plague at the end of the 21st century. The Percy-inspired figure of Adrian, earl of Windsor, believes that the plague will vanish when nations are liberated, ending poverty. He is a romantic idealist but cannot find a mate, attracts few followers, and dies. The sole survivor is a shepherd boy in Rome. This novel's premise, too, has since recurred many times in such science fiction novels as Brian Aldiss's *Greybeard* (1964) and J. G. Ballard's *The Crystal World* (1966) and in such films as *No Blade of Grass* (1970) and *The Omega Man* (1971). For Shelley, the lone survivor of worldwide disaster is her version of the romantic conception of the noble savage, as initially inspired by the French philosopher Jean Jacques Rousseau.

Lodore, too, involves a lonely, noble savage of sorts, a girl named Ethel who is torn between life in London and life in the wilderness of Illinois with her father. Unlike Rousseau, Shelley seems to have understood that someone stripped of civilization, living in a state of nature, could become either noble or unpredictable and monstrous, as could a radical philosopher or artist.

Because of her handling of these themes, Shelley must be thought of as a writer participating in the major philosophical and cultural dialogues of her day, not merely as a footnote to genre fiction. The biographer Emily Sunstein calls Shelley "an important Romantic who survived into the Victorian age . . . a major literary figure of the first half of the 19th century."

Other Works by Mary Shelley

Feldman, Paula R., ed. *The Journals of Mary Shelley, 1814–1844.* Baltimore: Johns Hopkins University Press, 1995.

Maurice; or, The Fisher's Cot. New York: Alfred A. Knopf, 1998.

Robin, Charles E., ed. *Collected Tales and Stories.* Baltimore: John Hopkins University Press, 1990.

Works about Mary Shelley

Hoobler, Dorothy, and Thomas Hoobler. *The Monsters: Mary Shelley and the Curse of Frankenstein.* Boston: Back Bay Books, 2007.

Sunstein, Emily. *Mary Shelley: Romance and Reality.* Boston: Little, Brown, 1989.

Williams, John. *Mary Shelley: A Literary Life.* New York: St. Martin's Press, 2000.

Shelley, Percy Bysshe (1792–1822) *poet*

Percy Bysshe Shelley was born at his family's country estate near Horsham, Sussex, in the south of England, the first child of Timothy Shelley, a recently unseated member of Parliament, later a baronet, and his wife, Elizabeth Pilfold Shelley. From his earliest years, Shelley was a brilliant child who could recite Latin verses at age six. The idyll of his youth on a large country property, surrounded by adoring sisters, ended abruptly at the age of 10, when he was sent away to school at the Syon House Academy in Brentford, near London. According to a cousin, Tom Medwin, Shelley was tormented by his fellow students, making these years "a perfect hell" for the delicate boy. While he was at Syon, Shelley devoured Gothic novels and was fascinated by new scientific discoveries. Home on vacation, Shelley involved his sisters in his experiments, once attempting to cure chilblains with electricity.

From 1804 to 1810, Shelley attended Eton, where his schoolmates dubbed him "Mad Shelley" (partly because he was absentminded) and (because of his unconventional ideas) "the Eton Atheist." After Eton, Shelley entered University College, Oxford.

From his youth, Shelley was a visionary and a reformer; at first, he hoped science would transform the world. Later he was to believe that poetry might, calling poets "the unacknowledged legislators of the world" in his *A Defence of Poetry* (1821).

While still in his teens, Shelley began to publish fiction and poetry, including two conventional and uninspired Gothic novels, *Zastrozzi* (1810) and *St. Irvyne* (1811), as well as a book of poetry written with his sister Elizabeth, *Original Poetry by Victor and Cazire* (1810). He and his friend Thomas Jefferson Hogg were expelled from Eton for publishing and disseminating a pamphlet, *The Necessity of Athiesm* (1811). This short work is not as inflammatory as the title makes it sound; rather, it is a very logical debunking, from a rationalist perspective, of arguments in favor of a belief in God. In the end, Shelley calls himself an atheist, "thro' deficiency of proof." Influenced by the writings of the peripatetic revolutionary Thomas Paine, the French philosopher Jean-Marie Condorcet, and the British philosopher WILLIAM GODWIN, Shelley evolved a liberal philosophy that opposed monarchy, matrimony, and most other established institutions, all of which he believed interfered with the ability of individuals to improve their political, social, and spiritual existence. Although intellectually and temperamentally a revolutionary, Shelley did not advocate violence as a method of effecting change.

Despite his opposition to the institution of matrimony, Shelley married Harriet Westbrook in 1811, when she was 16 and he 19. Disowned by his father for his radical ideas and for marrying beneath his station, Shelley led a nomadic existence for the next few years, moving his household frequently to avoid creditors. He and Harriet spent some time in Ireland, distributing pamphlets that urged the Irish people to work toward freedom without resorting to violence. He also spent time in Wales, where he witnessed the terrible living conditions of laborers there. In 1813, Shelley summarized his visionary political philosophy in *Queen Mab*. In this poem, the maiden Ianthe meets the fairy Queen Mab, who verbally attacks monarchy, marriage, established religion, commerce, and warfare. After Shelley's death, *Queen Mab* was reprinted many times and became a bible for youthful radicals.

Shelley's marriage began to fall apart after the birth of his daughter Eliza Ianthe in 1813. His correspondence with William Godwin led to Shelley's becoming a frequent guest in the Godwin household, where he fell in love with the daughter of Godwin and the feminist MARY WOLLSTONECRAFT, Mary (see SHELLEY, MARY WOLLSTONECRAFT). Shelley left Harriet in 1814, just before the birth of their second child, and ran off to Europe with Mary. In this same year, Shelley wrote *Alastor,* the tale of a poet's search for the Platonic ideal, and Mary gave birth to their son William. With GEORGE GORDON, LORD BYRON, the Shelleys spent that summer at Lake Geneva.

At the end of this summer in Switzerland, Shelley wrote "Hymn to Intellectual Beauty" (1816), now considered his first great poem, modeled on the odes of WILLIAM WORDSWORTH and SAMUEL TAYLOR COLERIDGE. The speaker invokes Beauty, the "unseen Power" that "consecrates . . . human thoughts . . . [and] forms." During the same summer, before returning to England, Shelley took Mary and his stepsister Claire to the Swiss Alps, where he wrote "Mont Blanc." In this poem he portrays nature as "remote, serene, inaccessible," not as the source of comfort that the elder romantics had seen it.

On their return to England, Shelley and Mary were devastated by the suicide of Mary's half sister, Fanny Imlay. Then, in November, Harriet drowned herself. Shelley, though still opposed to the institution of marriage, wed Mary, partly in a failed effort to gain custody of his two children by Harriet.

In 1818 Shelley left England, never to return. He lived the rest of his life in Italy, where he wrote his most mature poetry. In the same year he wrote *Julian and Maddalo*, which gives poetic form to his relationship with Byron. In 1819 he wrote what many critics consider his masterpiece, *Prometheus Unbound*, a retelling in dramatic verse of the ancient Greek myth about the Titan who angered his fellow gods by bringing fire to mankind. Shelley reenvisioned the story because he could not accept the idea that Prometheus, the great savior of humanity, could ever become reconciled to Jupiter, "the Oppressor of mankind." The reconciliation he allows in the poem is not a reconciliation under authority, but a universal harmony of nature. Earth is a character in the drama and speaks these words in act 3 in response to Prometheus's leadership:

> . . . I hear, I feel;
> Thy lips are on me, and thy touch runs
>   down
> Even to the adamantine central gloom
> Along these marble nerves; 't is life, 't is joy,
> And, through my withered, old, and icy
>   frame
> The warmth of an immortal youth shoots
>   down
> Circling. Henceforth the many children fair
> Folded in my sustaining arms; all plants,
> And creeping forms, and insects
>   rainbow-winged,
> And birds, and beasts, and fish, and human
>   shapes,
> Which drew disease and pain from my wan
>   bosom,
> Draining the poison of despair, shall take
> And interchange sweet nutriment . . .

In the same year he wrote "Ode Written in Dejection, near Naples" (1819), which perhaps reflects Shelley's disenchantment with his marriage. In 1819 his favorite son, William, died. Between 1819 and 1822, Shelley wrote some of his best known works, including "Ode to the West Wind" (1819); "The Masque of Anarchy" (1819), Shelley's response to a massacre of more than 400 peaceful demonstrators advocating parliamentary reform; and "Adonais" (1822), his elegy on the death of JOHN KEATS, one of the greatest elegies in the English language, second only to Milton's "Lycidas." It explores not only grief but grief's place in the pattern of existence:

> Alas! that all we lov'd of him should be,
> But for our grief, as if it had not been,
> And grief itself be mortal!

Shelley had often used the image of the boat in his poetry to portray the soul of the poet, traveling to realms of thought and imagination. Thus, it was especially ironic that he drowned in a storm while sailing off the coast of Italy.

Critical Analysis

To many, Shelley is the epitome of the romantic poet for both his work and the unconventional life he led. He was fundamentally a reformer who believed that social strictures, conventions, and institutions prevented humankind from reaching its full potential. When he could no longer believe in the possibility of reforming society by political action, Shelley put all his reformist passion into his poetry and critical works. He believed in the power of the imagination to lead one toward the ideals of love and sympathy and in the power of love to create moral perfection.

Shelley was a master of his craft. In particular, his "Ode to the West Wind" demonstrates his ability to write impassioned verse within the strictures of the complicated terza rima. The rhyme scheme, used by Dante in *The Divine Comedy* (*aba, bcb, cdc, efe, ff*) is much more difficult in English than in Italian, because English has fewer rhyming words.

In the first three stanzas of "Ode to the West Wind," the poet invokes the "Wild West Wind," which symbolizes the destructive, death-bringing power of nature, as well as nature's ability to renew life. The wind holds power over earth, sky, and sea. It rips the leaves from the trees and hurls rain, hail, and fire from the sky. It wakes the sleeping Mediterranean at the end of the summer, cleaving the seas "into chasms."

In the fourth stanza, the poet wishes to be infused by the spirit of the wind, to be a "dead leaf" borne on the breath of the wind, to be a "swift cloud to fly" with the wind, to be "a wave to pant beneath" the power of the wind. In the best-known lines in the poem, Shelley contrasts his wish for immortality and power with his earth-bound, uninspired suffering: "Oh, lift me as a wave, a leaf, a cloud! / I fall upon the thorns of life! I bleed!"

In the final stanza, Shelley begs the wind to inspire his poetry, to "make me thy lyre," to infuse him with its immortal strength: "Be thou, Spirit fierce, / My Spirit! Be thou me impetuous one!"

And he asks that his poetry receive the power of the wind: "Drive my dead thoughts over the universe / Like withered leaves to quicken a new birth."

This hope reflects Shelley's belief in the power of poetry and of the imagination to change the world, to reform, to revolutionize. Shelley envisions his words as being like "ashes and sparks" that the wind will kindle into a fire over the sleeping earth. The poem ends on a note of hope: "If Winter comes, can Spring be far behind?" Shelley envisions a kind of immortality through his poetry, and from his despair comes beauty, truth, and hope.

Other Works by Percy Bysshe Shelley

The Complete Poems of Percy Bysshe Shelley. Modern Library Series. New York: Random House, 1994.
Shelley's Poetry and Prose. Edited by Donald H. Reiman. New York: W. W. Norton, 1990.

Works about Percy Bysshe Shelley

Bieri, James. *Percy Bysshe Shelley: A Biography.* Baltimore: Johns Hopkins University Press, 2008.

Cooperman, Robert. *In the Household of Percy Bysshe Shelley.* Gainesville: University Press of Florida, 1993.
Duff, David. *Romance and Revolution: Shelley and the Politics of a Genre.* New York: Cambridge University Press, 1994.
Tomalin, Claire. *Shelley and His World.* New York: Scribner, 1980.

Sherwood, Mary (Mary Martha Butt Sherwood) (1775–1851) *novelist*

The daughter of a Church of England clergyman, George Butt, and his wife, Martha, Mary Sherwood was born in Stanford-on-Tene near Worcester, England. Her religious upbringing became the backbone of her writing career. She published her first stories, religious tales for her Sunday school students, in 1802.

In 1803 she married her cousin Henry Sherwood, an army officer, and in 1805 traveled with him to India, where his regiment was posted. There she became active in charities and began work on her most famous novel, *The History of the Fairchild Family* (1818). The novel, as Sherwood explains on the title page, is "calculated to show the importance and effects of religious education," and went through 14 editions between 1818 and 1842.

Sherwood wrote a number of novels, mainly for children, trying to convert Indians to Christianity. Examples include the extraordinarily popular *Little Henry and His Bearer* (1814) and *The Indian Pilgrim* (1815).

In 1816, Sherwood and her husband returned to England with their five children and three adopted orphans. She continued her charitable work, as well as her didactic writing for children. In 1830 she began to study Hebrew in order to write a biblical dictionary, which she completed shortly before her death in Twickenham, near London, in 1851. The work was never published.

Although it is largely unread today, Sherwood's work played an influential role for children in Victorian society.

Shorthouse, Joseph Henry (1834–1903)
novelist

Joseph Shorthouse was born in Birmingham, in central England. His father was a successful manufacturer, and, after finishing grade school, Joseph went to work in the family business as a chemist. Shorthouse had little interest in manufacturing and hoped to enter politics, but he was afflicted with a severe stutter that made public speaking impossible. Instead, he pursued another serious interest—writing. His first novel, *John Inglesant*, was privately printed in 1880 in an edition of 100 copies, and it was only after MARY WARD saw it and brought it to the attention of her editors that it was published, in 1881, to great acclaim. The story is set in 17th-century England, during the Civil War in which the Puritans, led by Oliver Cromwell, opposed King Charles I. Two years later, Shorthouse published another novel, *The Little Schoolmaster Mark*, followed by *Sir Percival* (1886) and *The Teacher of the Violin* (1888). His last novel was *Lady Falaise* (1891). None of these novels, however, had the wide success of *John Inglesant*.

A Work about Joseph Shorthouse
Wagner, F. J. *J. H. Shorthouse*. Boston: Twayne, 1979.

Siddal Rossetti, Elizabeth Eleanor (1829–1862) *poet, artist, model*

Elizabeth Siddal was born in London, where her father was an ironmonger. She had little formal schooling, but learned dressmaking, and was working in a hat shop when she was "discovered" by the painter William Howell Deverell in 1849, the beginning of the PRE-RAPHAELITE MOVEMENT. Siddal was tall and stately, with luxurious golden red hair and features that embodied the remote, otherworldly beauty revered by the Pre-Raphaelites. Artists seeking models were soon interested in her, including DANTE GABRIEL ROSSETTI, one of the founding members of the Pre-Raphaelite Brotherhood. She sparked Rossetti's creative genius, and he not only painted her but also fell in love. They were engaged for years before finally marrying in 1860. A year later she gave birth to a stillborn daughter. Her health and spirits declined, and she committed suicide with an overdose of laudanum. Rossetti, deeply mourning her death, put a manuscript of his poems into her coffin, but in 1869 had her body exhumed to recover it.

Aside from modeling, Siddal painted watercolors and wrote poems describing lost love, betrayal, and death. These lines from "Dead Love" are representative of her style and tone: "Oh never weep for love that's dead / Since love is seldom true / But changes his fashion from blue to red, / From brightest red to blue, / And love was born to an early death / And is so seldom true." Manuscripts of her poems are housed at Oxford University, and were not published until 1978.

silver-fork school

The silver-fork school of novel writing was popular between 1825 and 1850. These novelists provided admiring, often uncritical portraits of the aristocracy and others considered to be members of fashionable society. Writers associated with this school include Thomas Henry Lister (1800–42), Plumer Ward (1765–1846), Theodore Hook (1788–1841), CATHERINE GORE, SUSAN FERRIER, BENJAMIN DISRAELI, and EDWARD BULWER-LYTTON. WILLIAM MAKEPEACE THACKERAY's *Vanity Fair* is considered the single great book of the school, although Thackeray was critical of much of the genre's accepted character and plot devices. By the 1850s, the fashionable novel had declined in popularity as the realism of CHARLES DICKENS and GEORGE ELIOT gained the public's favor. After mid-century, OUIDA was one of the few novelists who still embraced the plots, heroes, and fashionable settings of this style of fiction.

Even at the height of its popularity, the silver-fork school was the target of criticism and derision. In his 1827 essay "The Dandy School," WILLIAM HAZLITT attacked the narrow superficiality of such novels, which he believed encouraged the "admiration of the folly, caprice, insolence, and affectation of a certain class." Thackeray parodied the titled ladies and fashionable life portrayed in these novels with his story "Lords and Liveries" in *Mr. Punch's Prize Novelists* (1847). However, Bulwer-Lytton, whose *Pelham* is a frequently cited example of the genre, believed that the silver-fork novels paradoxically exposed "the falsehood, the hypocrisy, the arrogance and the vulgar insolence of patrician life."

A Work about the Silver-Fork School
Adburgham, Alison. *Silver Fork Society: Fashionable Life and Literature from 1814 to 1840.* London: Constable, 1983.

Skene, Felicia Mary (1821–1899) poet, novelist

Felicia Skene was born in Aix-en-Provence in southern France, to Scottish parents, Jane and James Skene. She attended school in Paris, then moved to Greece with her family in 1838. She published her first collection of poems, *Isles of Greece and Other Poems,* five years later. During the early 1850s, she worked with FLORENCE NIGHTINGALE to train nurses to serve in the Crimean War. Skene dedicated herself to various philanthropic causes, such as prison reform and improving conditions in the slums, which are the subjects of many of her novels. Her novel *Hidden Depths* (1866), based on her work with women in prison, describes poor young women in Oxford who out of desperation turned to prostitution. Skene began her decades-long campaign for more humane treatment of prisoners in the 1850s, after becoming an official prison visitor. *Scenes from a Silent World* (1889), which exposed the prison conditions she sought to reform, is considered her best work for its portraits of prisoners. Skene herself considered the religious convictions she expressed in *Through the Shadows: A Test of Truth* (1888) (written under the pseudonym Erskine Moir) to be her most important statement.

Smedley, Menella Bute (1815?–1880?) novelist, poet

Menella Smedley was born in Great Marlow, Buckinghamshire, in central England. She was educated at home by her father (a clergyman) and mother. She and her younger brother, Francis Edward Smedley, both grew up to be writers, and he later became editor of *Cruikshank's Magazine.* Smedley's first novel, published in 1849, was *The Maiden Aunt,* followed by *The Use of Sunshine* two years later. Her plots, which were sentimental and pious, were intended to serve as moral examples. Unlike her poetry, which one critic described as "noble and delicate in feeling," Smedley's moralistic novels and stories offered lessons but little literary value. A collection of her poems, many of them written for children, was published in 1868. Smedley, who never married and was childless, devoted herself to charitable work to improve the education of orphans and paupers. Her last important work was a report on this topic, *Boarding Out and Pauper Schools,* published in 1875, five years before her death.

Smiles, Samuel (1812–1904) biographer, nonfiction writer

Samuel Smiles did not have, as so many Victorian writers did, the benefit of a university education in classics. Smiles was one of 11 children born to Samuel Smiles, a paper maker and merchant, and Janet Wilson Smiles in Haddington, Scotland. He received an elementary education, but at age 14 he was apprenticed to a family medical practice. When one of the doctors moved to Scotland three years later, taking young Smiles with him, Smiles attended medical classes at the University of Edinburgh. He graduated in 1832, returned to Haddington and began to practice.

The practice of medicine was neither as lucrative nor as intellectually stimulating and demanding as it is today, and Smiles's desire for a better life led him to begin lecturing and writing, mainly on medicine and health-related subjects. After six years of this work, he was not satisfied with his life or prospects, so he headed for Europe, where he spent the summer on a walking tour of the Low Countries and northern Germany. Returning to England in the fall of 1838, he answered a newspaper advertisement for an editorial position; in November 1838 he became editor of the *Leeds Times* in northern England. This ended the preparatory phase of his career. He was 26 years old and embarked on a new career as a liberal, if not radical, crusading newspaper editor.

For four years, he struggled for the causes of franchise extension (the extension of voting rights), the economic and intellectual development of the working classes, and the repeal of the Corn Laws, which kept the price of bread artificially high. In 1842 Smiles resigned his editorship and set up as a freelance writer and lecturer. He wrote, among other things, guidebooks and histories, including *History of Ireland and the Irish People Under the Government of England* (1844). Then in 1845 George Stephenson, the inventor of the locomotive, invited him into the railroad business, where he was to remain for more than 20 years. New railroad-line construction and the railroad business were booming during that period and Smiles was continually elevated in importance, ending up as secretary to the South Eastern Railway, in London. He officially retired from that position in 1866, devoting himself for the rest of his life to lecturing, writing, and promoting the welfare of the common man. This welfare, however, he saw ultimately resulting from what today have become identifying features of Victorianism, including character, duty, will, along with earnestness, hard work, and thrift. One might add to that a sort of "noblesse oblige," a commitment on the part of those who have prospered by exercising those virtues to helping develop them in the downtrodden.

Throughout his early career in journalism and middle career as a railroad executive, Smiles developed the idea of exemplars, outstanding examples of the many men of his time who, by exercising the appropriate virtues, rose from poverty or near poverty to great prosperity and renown. For Smiles personally, the nearest and best example was George Stephenson, whose biography Smiles wrote in 1857. Enormously successful, Smiles's biography of Stephenson determined the course of the rest of his career. He had earlier written *Self-Help, with Illustrations of Character and Conduct*, but could not find a publisher for it until 1859, after the success of the Stephenson biography. *Self-Help* was an even greater success; it sold more than 150,000 copies in the next 30 years and was translated into all the major European languages as well as Arabic and Japanese. Such sales, according to the historian Asa Briggs, "far exceeded those of the great 19th-century novels." Smiles intended the book to teach by example; each of the 13 chapters (with such titles as "Application and Perseverance") illustrate the main point by offering examples of men who have succeeded through the application of the central principles of the chapter. As Smiles writes in the chapter called "Self-Help: National and Individual," "Help from without is often enfeebling in its effects, but help from within invariably invigorates." Sections of *Self-Help* are still anthologized today.

The decade of the 1860s saw his retirement from the railroad and the publication of the three-volume *Lives of the Engineers: Industrial Biography, Iron Workers and Tool Makers,* and *Lives of Boulton and Watt*. In the 1870s, Smiles turned his attention to Victorian virtues and exemplars thereof: first *Character,* then *Thrift,* then *Duty,* and finally in the 1880s *Life and Labour*. His later years saw steady activity and several books, but none was ever as popular as those extolling the virtue of the men who, while making their way in the world, also built the British Empire.

A Work about Samuel Smiles
Briggs, Asa. "Samuel Smiles and the Gospel of Work." In *Victorian People*. Chicago: University of Chicago Press, 1972.

Smith, Alexander (1830–1867) *poet, essayist*
Alexander Smith was born in Kilmarnock, Scotland, to Peter Smith, a lace pattern designer, and

Helen Murray Smith. Alexander received his early education in Glasgow, Scotland, then trained in his father's trade. In his time off, however, Smith wrote poetry. Two of his early poems appeared in the *Critic* and *Eclectic Review* in the early 1850s. In 1853 he published his first book of poems, *A Life Drama*, which was well received. ARTHUR CLOUGH praised the "real flesh and blood" of his work. Smith decided to leave the factory and move to London to become a full-time writer. He met GEORGE HENRY LEWES, the essayist, who encouraged Smith in his literary career. After the success of his first book, however, he was unable to make a living as a poet. In 1854 he began working as a secretary at the University of Edinburgh and writing poetry in the evenings. In 1857 he published his second book, *City Poems*, but it met with little success. That same year he married Flora Macdonald, from the Isle of Skye, off the western Scottish coast. Smith turned from poetry to a book of essays, *Dreamthorp*, in 1863, and two autobiographical novels, *Alfred Hagart's Household* and its sequel, *Miss Oona McQuarrie*. These were followed by *A Summer in Skye*, a travel book, in 1865. Smith died of typhoid fever two years later.

Smith, Charlotte (1749–1806) *novelist, poet*

Charlotte Turner was born in London to Nicholas Turner, a wealthy landowner, and Anna Towers Turner. She was sent away to school at age six, after her mother died, and she had no formal schooling after age 12. At 16, she married Benjamin Smith, a merchant, who was an extravagant man with a weakness for wild business schemes. After years of financial struggle, the couple and their seven children were sent to debtors' prison in 1782. Upon their release, Charlotte attempted to make money from the sonnets she had been writing privately for years. Her first book of poems, *Elegiac Sonnets and Other Poems*, was published in 1784. The critic and writer LEIGH HUNT described her poems as "natural and touching." She and her husband finally separated in the late 1780s and Charlotte turned to novel writing. In 1788 she published *Emmeline; or, The Orphan of the Castle*, which was an overwhelming commercial and literary success. SIR WALTER SCOTT said that the characters in this "tale of love and passion" were "sketched with a firmness of pencil and liveliness of colouring which belong to the highest branch of fictitious narrative." Smith wrote a novel a year during the 1790s, including *The Old Manor House* (1793), which Scott considered her best book. In 1804 she published her last work, *Conversations Introducing Poetry*, a book of poems about nature, such as "The Ladybird" and "The Snail," for parents to read with their children.

Other Work by Charlotte Smith
Curran, Stuart, ed. *The Poems of Charlotte Smith.* New York: Oxford University Press, 1993.

Smith, Sarah
See STRETTON, HESBA.

Smith, Sydney (1771–1845) *pamphleteer, polemicist, literary critic*

Sydney Smith, the second son of Robert Smith and Maria Olier Smith, was born in Woodford, Essex, England. Smith entered Oxford University in 1789, leaving in 1794 to become curate in the tiny town of Netheravon, Wiltshire.

In 1798 Smith became a tutor in Edinburgh, Scotland, where he and others founded the *Edinburgh Review*, which became Britain's most popular journal of arts and letters. As a reviewer, Smith displayed his unique wit, a combination of sarcasm, satire, irony, and exaggeration that was to make him, among other things, one of QUEEN VICTORIA's favorite humor writers. For example, in his attack on Chancellor of the Exchequer Spencer Perceval's fears of Catholic emancipation, Smith noted that those fears "must be considered as more ambiguous proofs of the sanity and vigour of his understanding."

For the *Review* Smith wrote on various subjects both temporal and ecclesiastical, literary and polemical. In 1807, having honed his skills, Smith began to produce the series on which his fame rests, *Peter Plymley's Letters*. Published initially as a series of 10 short pamphlets (1807–08), the work was published in book form in 1808. Because of its serious attacks, which were perhaps actionable as libel or even treason under the existing laws, on the Tory government's anti-Catholic policies, Smith vigorously denied authorship. His major point was that the laws against Roman Catholics, particularly Irish Catholics, were absurd. He suggested that such laws, which among other things prevented Catholics from serving in England's military, might even encourage the Irish to welcome an invasion from France. *Peter Plymley's Letters* were reprinted 16 times by the end of 1808.

Although Smith continued to argue for Catholic emancipation until 1829, when the Roman Catholic Relief Act, which removed many political and educational handicaps, was passed, he took on other issues as well. He campaigned for an end to slavery, which was abolished in the English colonies in 1830; for better treatment of the mentally ill; for humane treatment of the poor; and for the rights of women. As he grew older, however, Smith became more conservative.

A Work about Sydney Smith

Virgin, Peter. *Sydney Smith*. New York: HarperCollins, 1994.

Southey, Robert (1774–1843) *poet, dramatist, essayist*

Robert Southey was born in Bristol, England. His father, also named Robert, an impoverished linen draper, eventually declared bankruptcy, and the family was forced to send the two-year-old Robert to live with Elizabeth Tyler, the older half sister of his mother, Margaret Hill Southey. Although Southey's aunt was domineering and overbearing, she greatly contributed to his intellectual development, encouraging his interest in reading and often taking him to the theater. By age eight, deeply impressed by the works of Shakespeare, Southey began to write poetry and plays.

In 1788 Southey was admitted to Westminster school, where he demonstrated great promise. While at Westminster, he became an avid supporter of the ideals promoted by the French Revolution, and became fascinated with such Continental writers as Voltaire and Johann Wolfgang von Goethe. Southey was eventually expelled from Westminster for writing an article denouncing flogging.

In 1792 Southey entered Oxford University, but he left in 1793 to pursue his personal interests. Southey returned to his family in Bristol, and was horrified by their financial destitution. After the death of Southey's father, his mother ran a boarding house to support the family. While in Bristol, Southey met Edith Fricker, a young woman from a poor background, with whom he fell in love. Aunt Tyler, dismayed by Southey's relationship with the Fricker family, cut off all financial assistance, prohibiting the possibility of his return to Oxford.

Prior to leaving Oxford, Southey became friends with SAMUEL TAYLOR COLERIDGE. The two had common interests in philosophy and politics as well as literature. In 1794, inspired by the principles of the French Revolution, Coleridge, Southey, and several others planned to found a utopian group, the Pantisocracy (meaning "equal rule of all"), for which they attempted to raise money by writing dramatic and political pieces. In 1794 Southey wrote *Wat Tyler*, a play based on the peasants' revolt of 1381, in which he expressed his political views. Southey could not find a publisher willing to print the play. In 1796 he published *Joan of Arc: An Epic Poem*, a work of radical political sentiment. It was well-received among the liberal circles of England. The utopian scheme he and Coleridge had planned, however, was never realized.

In 1795 Southey married Edith Fricker, while Coleridge married Edith's sister, Sara. Between 1796 and 1803 Southey traveled to Spain and Portugal. His travels left an immense impression on the young author and began his transformation from liberal to conservative. His *Letters from Spain and Portugal*, published in 1797 to some success, contain many translations of poetry. His *Poems* also appeared in 1797; one of these, "The Battle of Blenheim," is today his best-known work. The poem describes a conversation between two children and their grandfather, who witnessed the "famous victory" of 1704 in his youth but is quite unable to give a coherent answer to their request to "tell us all about the war, / And what they fought each other for." Every detail the grandfather relates seems senseless and horrifying to the clear-eyed children, but the refrain comes around again as the final line of each stanza:

> "But what good came of it at last?"
> Quoth little Peterkin.
> "Why that I cannot tell," said he,
> "But 'twas a famous victory."

In 1803 the Southeys and the Coleridges settled together near Keswick in the Lake District. However, the relationship between Southey and Coleridge quickly deteriorated. Coleridge eventually left Sarah, and Southey was forced to support both families. Fortunately for Southey, Charles Wynn, an old friend from Oxford, set up an annuity for him in return for Southey's work in Wynn's law office. Southey worked on law during the day, but continued to write poetry and prose at night.

Southey wrote prolifically over the next several years, turning out poetry, history, criticism, and political writings. In 1801 he published *Thalaba the Destroyer*, a work that centered on an Arabian fantasy and that brought him financial success. *Madoc* (1804), a fantastical epic poem about a 12th-century Welsh prince who travels to the New World and defeats the Aztecs, was also favorably received by the critics, although sales were disappointing. In 1810 Southey completed his longest work, *The Curse of Kahama*, an epic set in India. Kehama is a tyrant who may be compared to Napoléon, and he fails in his endeavors in the end; Britain was at war with Napoléon at the time, and its message of hope was welcome:

> *Faith was their comfort, Faith their stay;*
> *They trusted woe would pass away,*
> *And Tyranny would sink subdued,*
> *And Evil yield to Good.*

During this period Southey abandoned his radical political views, becoming an outspoken member of the conservative Tory Party, and regular contributor to the influential, conservative journal *Quarterly Review*. Indeed, he even supported censorship of subversive writing, publicly criticizing the poetry of the more liberal LORD BYRON.

In 1813 Southey was appointed Britain's poet laureate. A year later, he published a historical poem, *Roderick, the Last of the Goths*, which Southey considered his best work. It concerns the adventures of the former king of Spain, Roderick, in his efforts to subdue the Moors who have conquered his kingdom. Much of the poem concerns Roderick's penance for the sins that have brought about the Moors' ascendancy, and his struggle to achieve the wisdom of knowing that earthly power is not the ultimate good. His mother, Rusilla, speaks these words:

> *. . . even on earth*
> *There is a praise above the monarch's fame,*
> *A higher, holier, more enduring praise,*
> *And this will yet be thine!*

In 1829 Southey was offered a baronetcy and a seat in the Parliament, which he declined. Southey spent the remainder of his career editing the works of WILLIAM COWPER and writing prose works such as *The Life of Nelson* (1813).

Southey was ridiculed by many of his contemporaries, but nonetheless retained the admiration of both Coleridge and WILLIAM WORDSWORTH. Southey left a mixed legacy. Some greatly admired his works, while others considered them pretentious and mediocre.

Although forgotten by critics for many decades, many of Southey's works are being rediscovered and appreciated today. During his own lifetime, his status as the poetic genius was unsurpassed. His biographer Kenneth Curry speaks of "his truly amazing facility in composing verses and his unwillingness to give his poems the kind of ruthless revision and rewriting which they demanded," and speculates that Southey chose mental health above creative fire.

Critical Analysis

In his day, Robert Southey was the most prominent of the romantic LAKE POETS, although today he is the least well known. He distinguished himself from his romantic peers by his prolific output of both poetry and prose, writing everything from epics, ballads, odes, and plays to histories, biographies, fiction, travelogues, and a barely classifiable collection of miscellaneous reviews, articles, and political documents, most of them produced after he assumed the post of poet laureate in 1813. A remarkably versatile writer, his onetime friend and collaborator Samuel Taylor Coleridge called him a "complete man of letters."

Indeed, his collections of personal correspondence, journals, and autobiographical writings are his most enduring. Today, Southey is chiefly remembered for his prose works rather than for his poetry, which is largely regarded as examples of the florid tradition other romantic poets were trying to escape. His prose, on the other hand, was pointed, clean, vigorous, and precise. It helped set a new standard for journalistic writing in Britain. Interestingly, his development as a prose writer paralleled a dramatic shift in his political views, from a revolutionary, republican stance to a pro-establishment, thoroughly Tory one.

This shift can be seen as early as his first popular prose work, *Letters Written During a Short Residence in Spain and Portugal* (1797), penned while he lived in Iberia from December 1795 to May 1796. In this work he vividly describes filthy living conditions, decries Catholic superstition, and praises his native England. The work is a combination of descriptions, anecdotes, translations, poems, and essays, and though Southey demonstrates a fine command of detail, the tone of the entire work is decidedly pitched toward comparing England favorably with these countries. The success of this work helped launch his career as a prose writer.

This work was followed 10 years later by a similar one, entitled *Letters from England* (1807). Southey tried to make the work as encyclopedic as possible, including, in his words, "all that I know and much of what I think" of England at the time. Again, this book is a collection of essays about contemporary England, written from the perspective of a Spanish Catholic visitor. Using a fictional narrator allows Southey to achieve some critical distance from his subject; this device helped ensure the work's success by adding a degree of knowing charm to the satirical, humorous, and, at times, politically charged work.

After returning to England in 1796, he began writing reviews for various publications, including the *Critical Review* starting in 1798. In a particularly infamous review, he dismisses Wordsworth and Coleridge's *Lyrical Ballads,* today celebrated as one of the most influential and innovative romantic works. During this period of journalistic activity, he developed what would become his characteristically lucid prose style. It was also during this period that he formed the political views that would dominate his subsequent writings until the end of his days; while essentially conservative in nature, these also incorporated occasional liberal notions. These views made him increasingly embattled as time wore on, especially after he was made poet laureate in 1813, as his critics lamented the demise of his youthful revolutionary fervor.

In 1813 he also published one of the books for which he is still remembered, *The Life of Nelson*. This enormously popular work continues to be read today, and stands as a touchstone of the kind of engaging, precise writing Southey was capable of but rarely achieved in other works. Many of the latter are now criticized as lacking historical perspective and restraint, often striking the modern reader as needlessly verbose.

Another significant work of Southey's was his mammoth *History of Brazil,* on which he concentrated between 1810 and 1819. A multivolume work of more than 2,300 pages crammed with an exhausting amount of detail, it was the first accurate and comprehensive history of Brazil, although it is so stiflingly overloaded with description that it has since been supplanted by more concise works.

Unfortunately, although he contributed significantly to the development of a more direct, lucid prose style, Southey did not produce many prose works of great insight or genius, at least according to most critics. As a literary figure, he played a decisive role in the early romantic movement and restored dignity, vitality, and purpose to the post of poet laureate (which had languished under uninspired poets for some time), but his own poetry has since been eclipsed by that of his Lake Poet peers.

Other Work by Robert Southey
Five Romantic Plays, 1796–1821. New York: Oxford University Press, 2000.

Works about Robert Southey
Curry, Kenneth. *Southey.* Boston: Routledge, 1975.
Speck, W. A. *Robert Southey: Entire Man of Letters.* New Haven, Conn.: Yale University Press, 2006.
Storey, Mark. *Robert Southey: A Life.* New York: Oxford University Press, 1997.

Speke, John Hanning (1827–1864)
explorer, nonfiction writer

John Hanning Speke was born in Devon, in western England. At age 17, Speke left to serve in the British army in India, which was then part of the British Empire. After 10 years' service, he left Calcutta and headed south to explore central equatorial Africa. He joined an expedition to Somali country, led by the explorer RICHARD BURTON, but had to return to England when he was badly wounded during an attack on their camp by local tribesmen. Speke went back to Africa in 1856 on a second expedition with Burton to search for the source of the Nile. After being told of three inland lakes by an Arab trader, Burton and Speke split up to explore.

In 1858, after traveling through the harsh terrain of central Africa, Speke became the first European to reach what he correctly believed to be the Nile's source, a lake he named in honor of QUEEN VICTORIA. Burton disputed Speke's claim that this lake was the river's source. Two years later Speke returned to Africa on his own expedition to confirm his discovery. Although he was unable to travel the entire length of the river because of the tribal warfare and hostility he encountered, Speke triumphantly announced to the Royal Geographical Society that he had traced the Nile to its source. His *Journal of the Discovery of the Source of the Nile* was eagerly and widely read as soon as it was published in 1863. Speke wrote, "Here at last I stood on the brink of the Nile! Most beautiful was the scene, nothing could surpass it." A year later he published a second volume of his account, *What Led to the Discovery of the Source of the Nile.* In 1864, on the day he was scheduled to debate Burton, who had attacked his theory, Speke died after shooting himself, apparently by accident, while hunting.

A Work about John Hanning Speke
Harrison, William. *Burton and Speke.* New York: St. Martin's Press, 1982.

Spencer, Herbert (1820–1903) *philosopher, sociologist*

Herbert Spencer was born in Derby, England, to William George Spencer, a schoolmaster and secretary of the Derby Philosophical Society, and Harriet Holmes Spencer. The younger Spencer turned down an offer to go to Cambridge University, preferring to study through self-directed reading instead. He trained to be a railway civil engineer but turned to journalism and philosophy and became a close friend of GEORGE ELIOT and an assistant editor of the *Economist*.

Fusing the twin Victorian concepts of biological evolution and social progress, Spencer argued that societies, too, undergo a sort of weeding-out process, with those that avoid violence and embrace individual freedom tending to flourish and those that regulate and control people tending to fail. Spencer coined the term "survival of the fittest," usually associated now with the biological evolutionary theories of CHARLES DARWIN. Indeed, Spencer was often condemned in the 20th century as an advocate of what came to be called Social Darwinism, the belief that whoever triumphs in social struggles, by whatever means, deserves victory and has the right to oppress the weak. This view is almost the exact opposite of Spencer's own as articulated in *Social Statics* (1851), *The Synthetic Philosophy* (1862–96), and *The Man versus the State* (1884).

Like many progressive thinkers of his day, Spencer hoped to see the government gradually wither away as humanity learned to live in peace. One chapter of *Social Statics*, "The Right to Ignore the State," defends such a right. Unlike such thinkers as KARL MARX, however, Spencer hoped to see a system of private property maintained. Further, he often warned of the absurdity and danger of letting politicians rule the rest of society. Criticizing government economic planners in *The Principles of Sociology* (1876–96), he wrote, "A fly seated on the surface of the body has about as good a conception of its internal structure as one of these schemers has of the social organization in which he is embedded." Spencer preferred laissez-faire capitalism, in which individuals make economic decisions without direction from a central authority. Decades after the release of *Social Statics*, the work was mentioned in a U.S. Supreme Court decision as an example of laissez-faire capitalist thinking that the Court would not wish to take as its legal philosophy when making regulatory decisions.

Spencer also addressed the physical sciences in such volumes as *The Principles of Biology* (1864–67), *The Classification of the Sciences* (1864), and *Factors of Organic Evolution* (1887), as well as psychology in *Principles of Psychology* (1855). The critic Hugh Elliot writes, "no one who wishes to understand the thought of the 19th century can neglect him … he helped to popularize evolutionary ideas; in politics he represented, if he did not lead, a body of opinion which had great influence in its day."

A Work about Herbert Spencer

Taylor, Michael, ed. *Herbert Spencer and the Limits of the State*. Bristol, England: Thoemmes, 1997.

Speranza

See WILDE, JANE FRANCESCA.

Staël, Madame de (Louise Germaine Necker, baronne de Staël-Holstein)

(1776–1817) *philosopher, novelist, playwright*

After GEORGE SAND, Germaine de Staël was probably the most important foreign influence on British women's writing in the first half of the 19th century. Born to wealthy and accomplished Swiss parents in Paris—her father was finance minister to King Louis XVI and her brilliant mother almost married the great English historian Edward Gibbon—she grew up attending her mother's salons, meeting the leading writers, artists, and intellectuals of the day. Later her own salons were to become more brilliant even than her mother's. At age 20 she made a marriage of convenience with Baron Erik de Staël-Holstein, the Swedish ambassador to France. In 1789 the French Revolution began; she remained in Paris during its early tumultuous years, and began an affair with the very important minister of Louis XVI, Louis de Narbonne. In 1793 he fled for England and she followed. She returned to Paris in 1794, began an affair with Benjamin Constant, a novelist and politician, and both of them for a short while were good friends with Napoléon.

Staël wrote plays, philosophical treatises, and literary criticism throughout her life. Her influence in England, however, was felt most profoundly with her two novels, *Delphine* (1802) and *Corinne* (1807). She was a feminist, having famously stated, "The more I see of men the more I like dogs." Her novels vividly illustrated her feminist beliefs. Her first novel, *Delphine,* is a sentimental love story that begins with two rivals for the same man. It is notable for its complex characterization of the heroine, Delphine, a strong, impulsive, emotional woman. She falls victim to the strictures of a male-dominated society, and commits suicide at the end of the novel.

The heroine of Staël's other novel, *Corinne,* is an even more compelling character. Half English, half Italian, Corinne is an actress, poet, and feminist. In her first appearance in the novel she is almost deified: "Her bearing as she rode by was noble and modest: she was visibly pleased to be admired, but her joy was suffused with a timidity that seemed to beg indulgence for her triumph. . . . She seemed at once a priestess of Apollo making her way toward the Temple of the Sun, and a woman perfectly simple in the ordinary relationships of life."

English feminist writers such as SYDNEY OWENSON, CHARLOTTE BRONTË, and GEORGE ELIOT embraced Staël's feminist heroines and emulated them in their own works. The character of the poet Corinne was also an important model for female poets such as FELICIA HEMANS and especially ELIZABETH BARRETT BROWNING. Browning modeled the heroine of her *Aurora Leigh* directly on Corinne and said, "*Corinne* is an immortal book, and deserves to be read three score and ten times—that is once every year in the age of man." The critic Karyna Szmurlo has noted the growing interest in Staël's novels: "Over the last two decades American academia has shown unprecedented interest in Staël's novel. No longer dismissed as a weak exemplar of the genre, *Corinne* is now acknowledged as the productive reply of a woman writer to the feminine condition."

Works about Madame de Staël
Fairweather, Maria. *Madame de Staël.* New York: Carroll & Graf, 2006.
Herold, J. Christopher. *Mistress to an Age: A Life of Madame de Staël.* New York: Grove, 2002.
Wilkes, Joanne. *Lord Byron and Madame de Staël: Born for Opposition.* London: Ashgate, 1999.

Stanley, Henry Morton (John Rowlands)
(1841–1904) *essayist*

Henry Morton Stanley was born in Denbigh, Wales. He was the illegitimate child of an alcoholic farmer, John Rowlands, after whom he was originally named, and Elizabeth Parry, a butcher's daughter. Rejected by the Parry family, Stanley ended up in the St. Asaph Union Workhouse. Later, in his posthumously published autobiography (1909), Stanley would write a fictionalized account of this childhood.

In 1858 he enlisted as a sailor aboard a ship bound for New Orleans. There, he met Henry Hope Stanley, who eventually helped him gain a comfortable clerkship in a wholesale company. Grateful for Stanley's fatherly generosity, Stanley renamed himself after the merchant.

In 1865 Stanley convinced the editor of the *Missouri Democrat* to hire him as a western correspondent. His articles describing the Native American tribes of the Great Plains interested James Gordon Bennett, the editor of the *New York Herald,* and he soon hired Stanley. Bennett eventually assigned Stanley to find Dr. David Livingstone, the Scottish explorer who had been missing in central Africa for three years. The resulting journey ensured Stanley's fame and produced his famous statement—"Dr. Livingstone, I presume"—when he finally found the British explorer.

Stanley published his experiences in *How I Found Livingstone* (1872). The volume is frequently wordy, full of clichés, and pretentious. In places, descriptions of the African landscape are bombastic and sometimes incomprehensible because Stanley relies upon Victorian stereotypes of nature. For example, he describes an "undulating plain, lovely with its coat of green verdure, with its boundaries of noble woods." Yet Stanley also offered stunning, vivid descriptions of the customs, manners, and dress of the African people.

Because Livingstone remained in Africa, some critics doubted the truth of Stanley's account, even claiming that letters Livingstone had sent back with Stanley were forgeries. To refute these accusations, Stanley planned a second expedition. Begun in 1874, the expedition lasted three years as Stanley became the first European explorer to cross the entire continent, trace the shapes of Lakes Victoria and Tanganyika, and prove that the Lualaba River was a tributary of the Congo and not the Nile. He recounted his journey in *Through the Dark Continent* (1878). Despite his famous encounter with Livingstone, this second expedition remains his most significant—and dubious—act because it opened central Africa to European colonization and exploitation. The biographer Ian Anstruther praises Stanley's journalistic skills, claiming that he had "a clear and vivid style, and when he wrote without inhibition . . . he could bring the dullest subjects to life."

Works about Henry Morton Stanley

Bierman, John. *Dark Safari: The Life Behind the Legend of Henry Morton Stanley.* New York: Alfred A. Knopf, 1991.

Jeal, Tim. *Stanley: The Impossible Life of Africa's Greatest Explorer.* New Haven, Conn.: Yale University Press, 2007.

Newman, James. L. *Imperial Footprints: Henry Morton Stanley's African Journeys.* Dulles, Va.: Potomac Books, 2006.

Stannard, Henrietta Vaughan (1856–1911) *novelist, short story writer*

Henrietta Vaughan was born in York, in northern England. Her father was an officer in the Royal Artillery who later became an Anglican priest. The descendant of three generations of soldiers, Henrietta began writing stories about life in the military before she was 20. Her early stories were published in the *Family Herald* under the pen name Violet Whyte, but she adopted the pseudonym John Strange Winter for her first collection, *Cavalry Life* (1881), when her publisher suggested that military stories would "stand a better chance as the work of a man." Three years later, she married Arthur Stannard. In 1885 she published her best-known work, the military novel *Bootles' Baby: A Story of the Scarlet Lancers.* Over the next decade the novel sold 2 million copies. Stannard published a sequel, *Bootles' Children,* three years later. The critic JOHN RUSKIN praised Stannard's "faithful rendering of the character of the British soldier." It was not until 1889, when her books had become enormously popular, that her readers discovered that she was a woman.

Steel, Flora Annie (Flora Annie Webster Steel) (1847–1929) *novelist*

Nicknamed "the female RUDYARD KIPLING," Flora Annie Steel is best remembered as a writer and advocate for the women and children of India. Of her more than 30 novels, more than half were concerned with Indian life.

Born in Harrow, England, to George and Isabella Webster, and raised in Scotland, Steel received no formal education. She married Henry William Steel at age 20, and within a day of the ceremony, Steel and her new husband, a district officer with the Indian Civil Service, departed for the Punjab, in India. For more than 20 years, Steel devoted herself to the people of India. She acted as a medical adviser and fought for improvements in education and housing. She set up numerous schools for children, and became an advocate for Indian women.

Steel's writing career began with a collection of short stories about her experiences in India, although only one of the stories was published before she left the country in 1889. The novels that followed were written mainly as an attempt to "educate the British about the culture and customs of the East." Her most famous novel, *On the Face of the Waters* (1896), uses the Indian Mutiny of 1858 and the siege of Delhi as settings to reveal complex relationships among the English and their Indian subjects. The critic E. M. Bell notes that it is "written with faithful accuracy and complete impartiality." Other novels inspired by her time in India include *Miss Stuart's Legacy* (1893); *The Potter's Thumb* (1894), whose title is an allusion to fate and destiny, from the Indian saying, "The potter's thumb has slipped; the pot will crack in the firing"; *Red Rowans* (1895); and *Hosts of the Lord* (1900). Her book of Indian folktales, *Tales of the Punjab* (1894), was illustrated by Kipling's father. In 1887 she also wrote *The Complete Indian Cook and Housekeeper*, a guide intended to help young English brides coming to India.

Steel was also a supporter of the suffragist movement. She made many speeches on behalf of the suffragists, and many of her later writings reflected her views. Her last novel, *The Curse of Eve* (1929), advocated birth control for women. Steel's autobiography, *The Garden of Fidelity*, (1929), was published posthumously. A London reviewer for an 1897 issue of the *Spectator* said, "While her [Steel's] only rival in this field of fiction is Mr. Kipling, her work is marked by an even subtler appreciation of the Oriental standpoint—both ethical and religious—a more exhaustive acquaintance with native life in its domestic and indoor aspects, and a deeper sense of the moral responsibilities attaching to our rule in the East."

A Work about Flora Annie Steel

Powell, Lady Violet Georgiana. *Flora Annie Steel: Novelist of India*. London: Heinemann, 1981.

Stephen, Leslie (1832–1904) *critic, biographer*

Born in London to Jane Venn and the historian and government official Sir James Stephen, Leslie Stephen was educated at Eton and at Cambridge University. Ordained in 1855, he withdrew from holy orders in 1862, announcing his sympathy with the religious doubts of his age. ("I do not the less believe in morality," he later remarked.) Stephen then turned to journalism. In 1867 he married Harriet Thackeray, the daughter of the novelist WILLIAM MAKEPEACE THACKERAY. Harriet died eight years later, and in 1878 Stephen married Julia Jackson Duckworth. Among the couple's children were the painter Vanessa Bell (1879–1961) and the novelist and critic Virginia Woolf.

From 1871 to 1882 Stephen edited *Cornhill Magazine*, a genteel upper-middle-class monthly that helped launch during his tenure such emerging authors as HENRY JAMES, THOMAS HARDY, and ROBERT LOUIS STEVENSON. In addition, Stephen himself contributed numerous critical literary pieces later collected in *Hours in a Library* (1892).

His essay "An Agnostic's Apology" (1876) helped popularize the term *agnostic* (literally "not knowing," referring to someone who has doubts regarding the existence of God but who does not necessarily deny that existence), coined by T. H. HUXLEY six years earlier. Stephen writes that God's existence is unknowable: "No honest man will deny in private that every ultimate problem is wrapped in the profoundest mystery... We are a company of ignorant beings, feeling our way through mists and darkness,... dimly discerning light enough for our daily needs, but hopelessly differing whenever we attempt to describe the ultimate origin or end of our paths." Stephen's collection bearing its title (1893) includes this essay.

The same year as the essay appeared, Stephen published his book *History of English Thought in the Eighteenth Century*. It argues that the changing currency of ideas is indebted not only to individual thinkers but also to shifts in social conditions that pave the way for the acceptability of their ideas. Receptivity to the ideas of the philosopher David Hume, for example, that sought to detach morality from what Hume regarded as its false basis in religion, for example, was enhanced by the rise of agnosticism that preceded them. Stephen dissects the thought of a vast number of individuals, EDMUND BURKE and WILLIAM PALEY among them. He also addresses numerous topics, such as deism, the belief that true religion reveals natural law with which the Creator in no way interferes. Well received, the book marked an important step forward in Stephen's career. A reviewer, Mark Pattison, wrote in *Fortnightly*, "The mere list of books read over by the author, many of them not easy reading, is formidable enough in itself. The mastery of the material evinced is proof of a capacity for continuous and comprehensive thinking." A century later, Stephen's biographer Noel Annan would be most impressed by Stephen's attribution of different modes of thought to different social classes. Stephen's *The English Utilitarians* (1900) applies the same complex view of the way ideas take hold to certain thinkers of Stephen's own century, JOHN STUART MILL and THOMAS CARLYLE among them.

In 1882 Stephen began the monumental job of editing (along with Sidney Lee) the first 26 volumes of the *Dictionary of National Biography*, writing 378 entries himself. Typically, Stephen's entries are long and no-nonsense. The entry on poet WILLIAM WORDSWORTH, for example, explains that "[Lucy, in the 'Lucy poems'] has been taken for a real person.... Nothing, however, is known to suggest that there was any such person." (Also no-nonsense are the publishing arrangements that Stephen details, including the sum of money each contributor received.) All the work Stephen edited, in addition to his own writing, reflects what Annan has called "Stephen's greatest rule": "that each life was to be readable, a biography in itself, not a compendium of sources or a disquisition by a scholar on disputed points." The *Dictionary* thus became the standard for such works.

Before starting on the *Dictionary*, Stephen predicted "[it] will be a very heavy bit of work." The project indeed savaged Stephen's health, leading in 1888 to a nervous breakdown, but it also was the primary reason he was knighted in 1902.

The *Dictionary* indeed remains the principal legacy of the writer whom scholar Crane Brinton has described as a "historian of ideas" and "sociologist of knowledge" and who was mainly concerned "with the range of the behavior of man as a ... *political animal*."

Other Works by Leslie Stephen

English Literature and Society in the Eighteenth Century. Ford Lectures, 1903. London: Duckworth & Co., 1904.
Hours in a Library. New York: Putnam, 1904.
Sir Leslie Stephen's Mausoleum Book. Oxford: Clarendon, 1977.
Studies of a Biographer. New York: G.P. Putnam's Sons, 1902.

Works about Leslie Stephen

Annan, Noel Gilroy. *Leslie Stephen: The Godless Victorian.* Chicago: University of Chicago Press, 1990.
Maitland, Frederic William. *The Life and Letters of Leslie Stephen.* Honolulu: University Press of the Pacific, 2003.
Matthew, H. C. G. *Leslie Stephen and the New Dictionary of National Biography.* New York: Cambridge University Press, 1997.

Stevenson, Robert Louis Balfour

(1850–1894) *novelist, nonfiction writer, poet*

Robert Louis Stevenson is one of the most enduring writers of popular fiction, especially works of adventure and horror. Born in Edinburgh, Scotland, to engineer Thomas Stevenson and Isabella Balfour Stevenson, he was frustrated by the straitlaced professionals, mostly engineers, with whom he and his family associated. (His father and other forebears had designed and built numerous lighthouses around the Scottish coast.) He resisted his father's insistence that he follow the family profession and become a civil engineer, although for a time it appeared he would become a lawyer. Instead, motivated partly by the lifelong respiratory illness that would later kill him, he left Edinburgh for the French Riviera in 1873, planning to become a writer. His first major works were descriptions of his travels in Europe, *An Inland Voyage* (1878) and *Travels with a Donkey* (1879).

In 1879 Stevenson followed Fanny Vandegrift Osbourne, with whom he was in love, to America, crossing the ocean and the North American continent in difficult conditions to join her in California. He recorded that journey in *Across the Plains* (1892) and *The Amateur Emigrant* (1895).

Stevenson married Osbourne, and they honeymooned in a deserted miner's cabin on a California mountain. Again, Stevenson turned life into art by recording the honeymoon in *The Silverado Squatters* (1883).

The couple moved to Scotland and eventually continued on to southern France because of Stevenson's renewed health problems, and during this period he produced a collection of essays, *Virginibus Puerisque* (1881), and a book of poetry, *A Child's Garden of Verses* (1885), which is distinctly Victorian in its depiction of a staid, distant adult world and a childhood world of sadness, illness, and immobility alleviated by fanciful daydreaming. However, Stevenson's best-known poem was not written for children: "Requiem" (1887) describes a gravesite and ends with the famous lines, "Home is the sailor, home from the sea, / And the hunter home from the hill."

During this period Stevenson wrote one of his best-known works, *Treasure Island* (1883), which tells the rousing adventure of the boy Jim Hawkins, Long John Silver, Old Pew, and a host of colorful characters in search of hidden pirate loot. The book opens with Jim's recollection of the day when his father's inn was visited by a mysterious pirate who chanted the disturbing sea song, "Fifteen men on The Dead Man's Chest—Yo-ho-ho, and a bottle of rum!" Jim is soon caught up in a violent battle between pirate factions over the buried treasure.

For a short time Stevenson lived in Bournemouth, England, where he befriended HENRY JAMES, a somewhat unlikely union of one of the 19th century's best-known adventure writers with one of its most intellectual and subtle realists.

Two of Stevenson's best novels appeared in 1886: *Kidnapped,* a tale of revolution gone wrong, and *The Strange Case of Dr. Jekyll and Mr. Hyde,* a psychological thriller. In *Kidnapped*, David Balfour, an adolescent living in the Scottish Lowlands in 1751, is orphaned and sold to slave traders. He survives a shipwreck, and flees across the Highlands with his friend, Alan Breck. Both characters are more fully realized psychologically than the sometimes cartoonish figures in *Treasure Island*, earning *Kidnapped* a greater critical reputation.

In 1887 Stevenson again left England for the United States, where he wrote *The Master of Ballantrae* (1889), about the bitter rivalry of two Scottish brothers, the somewhat bland Henry Durrisdeer and his wild and daring brother James. They clash and even duel against the backdrop of the 1745 Jacobite Rebellion and a trip to colonial America.

After finishing this novel, Stevenson traveled the South Seas. He felt the climate there was perfect for his health. As if living out one of his adventure stories, he settled on the island of Samoa, where he lived with his wife, mother, and stepchildren in the fashion of a tribal chief. He wrote nonfiction books inspired by the region, including *A Footnote to History* (1892), which was an argument against European meddling in the affairs of the native rulers of Samoa, and *In the South Seas* (1896), admired for the social realism and attention to history and politics in its description of the region.

During this time, Stevenson also wrote *The Beach of Falesá* (1892), *David Balfour* (1893), and *The Ebb-Tide* (1894). He died before finishing his novel *Weir of Hermiston* (1896), one of several works concerning his native Scotland. *Weir of Hermiston* also has a trace in it of Stevenson's old conflict with his family and neighbors in his youth, as it depicts a clash in the Scottish Lowlands between an authoritarian judge and his rebellious son.

Critical Analysis

Stevenson was fascinated by dark characters, such as pirates and violent revolutionaries, and this fascination shaped *The Strange Case of Dr. Jekyll and Mr. Hyde*. Dr. Jekyll, dwelling in reserved Victorian society, decides to probe the dark side of human nature, creating a chemical that transforms him into the violent Mr. Hyde. At first, the transformation is exciting and revealing, but it soon becomes uncontrollable and Hyde's depravity increases. Jekyll leaves behind a "Statement" in which he tries to describe his story in the language of good and evil instead of the detached speech of science: "Strange as my circumstances were, the terms of this debate are as old and as commonplace as man."

Like Edgar Allan Poe, Stevenson evokes the distance between a horrified narrator and his actions. The popular story influenced many later science fiction stories, such as Paddy Chayefsky's novel (and later movie) *Altered States* (1978) and the comic book hero the Incredible Hulk, in which a scientist releases a more primitive, darker side of himself.

The story of Jekyll and Hyde tapped into the Victorian fascination with crime and violence (themes of Dostoyevsky that Stephenson may have borrowed). Although the period was relatively peaceful, Victorians feared abnormal behavior, especially by murderers, and were avid consumers of tales of urban violence and depravity, such as the Jack-the-Ripper crimes. The mild-mannered Jekyll transforming into the beast Hyde, who commits murders in dark alleys, was a character perfect for the times.

Critics debate whether to view Stevenson as a truly great writer or merely an effective teller of exciting tales. The scholar Saxe Commins noted that Stevenson had become such a legendary character during his lifetime that it was difficult to judge his work apart from his real-life notoriety. Commins wrote that Stevenson was at various points a moralizer, a courageous invalid, a bohemian, a teller of violent tales, a sentimentalist, a dissenter from Calvinism, a vagrant aesthete, a casual adherent of Leo Tolstoy's idealistic politics, and finally almost a feudal chieftain in Samoa. "During the later of the 44 years of his lifetime, Robert Louis Stevenson became a world legend," writes Commins. Decades later, "Shorn of the romantic attitudes assumed by and for him, he still retains a generous share of his reputation."

But for a time many critics looked upon Stevenson as an overrated, unsophisticated writer. The scholar Paul Maxiner, however, believes that the public's admiration of Stevenson produced this critical backlash, with both attitudes obscuring Stevenson's real achievements: "The view [of critics] . . . was a reaction against the uncritical adulation of him." For much of the 20th century, argues Maxiner, "he was on the whole better received by general readers, and practising writers, than by literary critics," but the time has come to "restore to his writings some of the 'supremacy and mystery' Henry James and other figures of his stature found in them." Nevertheless, thanks to the many film adaptations of his works, Stevenson has earned an enduring place in popular culture; his stories and characters are known to many who have never read him.

Other Work by Robert Louis Stevenson
Neider, Charles, ed. *The Complete Short Stories of Robert Louis Stevenson, with a Selection of the Best Short Novels*. Cambridge, Mass.: Da Capo, 1998.

Works about Robert Louis Stevenson
Buckton, Oliver S. *Cruising with Robert Louis Stevenson: Travel, Narrative, and the Colonial Body*. Columbus: Ohio University Press, 2007.

Callow, Philip. *Louis: A Life of Robert Louis Stevenson*. Chicago: Ivan R. Dee, 2001.

Stoker, Abraham (Bram) (1847–1912)
novelist, short story writer

Bram Stoker was born in Clontarf, a suburb of Dublin, Ireland. His father Abraham Stoker, was a civil servant who worked at nearby Dublin Castle, and his mother, Charlotte Thornley, was an excellent storyteller from Sligo, in the west of Ireland, who regaled her children with frightening tales of her own childhood, as well as with Irish ghost stories and myths.

Stoker may have heard more than his fair share of stories because he was bedridden for most of his early childhood. Unable to walk until he was seven years old, Stoker had to be carried from room to room by his mother and was unable to join his brothers and sisters in outdoor play. According to his biographer Barbara Belford, "Stoker's interest in the theater, the gothic tradition, in the preternatural" began during the years he was ill.

Stoker recovered from his illness at age seven, and grew strong and tall. He enrolled in Trinity College, Dublin, in 1863.

As a young man, Stoker had gone to the theater with his father, and he continued to attend plays throughout his college days. In 1867, he first saw the actor Henry Irving perform in Richard Sheridan's *The Rivals*. By 1871, the next time he saw Irving perform, Stoker was working as a civil servant. Chagrined to find that there were no reviews of Irving's performance in the local papers, Stoker volunteered to be an unpaid drama critic for the *Evening Mail*. For the next five years, Stoker spent as much time as he could in the theater and backstage, writing reviews, meeting actors, and learning about lighting and stage sets and other technical aspects of the theater.

Stoker began to write stories in addition to his reviews. His first published story, "The Crystal Cup," appeared in *London Society* in 1872, followed in 1875 by three stories serialized in *The Shamrock*. Stoker's early stories tended to be standard romances replete with Gothic houses and villains. Stoker also published a nonfiction work in 1879, *The Duties of Clerks in Petty Sessions in Ireland*, in which he codified the duties of his own job.

In 1876, after reading Stoker's review of his performance as Hamlet, Irving invited Stoker to dine with him. The two men became instant friends. A year later, Irving told Stoker that he planned to lease the Lyceum theater in London and that he wanted Stoker to manage his business affairs. Stoker enthusiastically accepted the offer.

Before he left for London, Stoker married Florence Balcombe—known as one of the most beautiful women in Ireland—who had also been courted by Stoker's friend OSCAR WILDE.

From 1877 to Irving's death in 1905, Stoker worked tirelessly for this very demanding and not very grateful taskmaster. He rewrote plays, managed accounts, designed sets, and wrote—he estimated after Irving's death—more than a half million letters for the actor. To serve Irving, Stoker neglected his wife and was seldom home to help raise his son, Noel.

As busy as he was while working for Irving, Stoker still found time to write. His first collection of stories, *Under the Sunset*, was published in 1882 and his first novel, *The Snake's Pass*, an adventure story with an Irish setting, was published in 1890. Stoker usually wrote very quickly, but *Dracula* (1897), his most famous work, and the only one still read today, took six years to complete. Reviews of *Dracula* were generally positive—except for Irving's, who listened to a reading of parts of the novel and told Stoker it was "dreadful." Following the publication of *Dracula*, Stoker published a romantic novel, *Miss Betty*, which was not well reviewed.

Irving died in 1905, and the following year Stoker published *Personal Reminiscences of Henry Irving* (1906), which Belford describes as "two volumes of unobjective idolatry." For the next six years, Stoker continued to write both fiction and nonfiction. His most popular work, after *Dracula*, was *The Lair of the White Worm* (1911). This novel, about a female vampire who must find virgins to satisfy a huge white worm that hides beneath her country house, was made into a masterpiece of film kitsch by Ken Russell in 1988. It was Stoker's last novel.

Critical Analysis

There had been tales of vampires before Stoker's *Dracula*, but none of the previous efforts made the lasting impression that Stoker's did. Much of the popularity of the work can be attributed to its numerous screen versions, beginning in 1922 with the German-made *Nosferatu,* which many critics believe is the best and most imaginative retelling of the story. The best-known version is probably the 1931 *Dracula,* directed by Tod Browning and staring Bela Lugosi.

Stoker's tale, written in letters and diary entries, begins as a mysterious creature is draining Lucy Westenra of her blood. Dr. Van Helsing must try to determine the culprit. Once the guilty party is discovered, the novel becomes an adventure story, with a band of friends out to stop the evil Count Dracula by any means possible. The novel ends with a chase halfway across Europe, as the Count evades his adversaries and nearly makes it back to his castle and to safety.

Much of the writing in *Dracula* is overwrought; characterization, except for Dracula and the insect-eating Renfield, is uninspired; and Stoker's attempts at dialect, especially that of Professor Van Helsing, are embarrassing.

What has fascinated readers about the novel is the universality of its story and the suggestiveness of its symbolism. The struggle between good and evil as presented in *Dracula* has been compared to the story of Dr. Faustus, that of the flying Dutchman, and COLERIDGE's "Rime of the Ancient Mariner." Clearly part of the story's appeal is in the nearly overwhelming evil the Count represents. For a time it does not appear that the band of puny humans determined to stop him will succeed; his evil is too powerful, too cunning, too pervasive.

Another part of the novel's appeal, at least to its original Victorian audiences, is the religious element of the story. In an era when scientific discoveries challenged traditional religious beliefs, Stoker's novel allied science and religion. His chief detective, Abraham Van Helsing, is a scientist who uses research and reasoning to figure out why Lucy Westenra dies. But the scientist uses the cross and the Communion wafer in his battle to defeat the monster.

Most modern readers and interpreters, however, have focused on the obvious sexual symbolism that pervades the novel. University of Florida Professor James Twitchell has called *Dracula* "sex without genitalia, sex without confusion, sex without responsibility, sex without guilt, sex without love—better yet, sex without mention." Although sex is not overt in the novel, it is a constant undercurrent. The male vampire attacks women in their sleep by penetrating them with his fangs. When women become vampires, they become sexual predators; even the lovely, innocent Lucy becomes an inflamed seductress. And vampires can only be killed by having stakes or swords, phallic symbols, driven through their hearts. These powerful elements of Stoker's story have inspired a whole genre of vampire fiction, most notably the novels of Anne Rice.

Works about Bram Stoker

Belford, Barbara. *Bram Stoker: A Biography of the Author of Dracula.* New York: Alfred A. Knopf, 1996.

———. *Bram Stoker and the Man Who Was Dracula.* New York: Da Capo, 2002.

Whitelaw, Nancy. *Bram Stoker: Author of Dracula.* Greensboro, N.C.: Morgan Reynolds, 1998.

Stone, Elizabeth (1803–1881?) novelist

Elizabeth Wheeler was born in Manchester, at that time a newly industrial city, in northern England. Her father, John Wheeler, was the editor of the *Manchester Chronicle.* She began her career as a novelist with *William Langshawe, The Cotton Lord* (1842), an indictment of the cotton manufacturing industry. The novel exposes the harshness of life in the cotton mills. The plot includes the seduction of a young girl and the murder of a union member. Her next novel, *The Young Milliner,* published in 1843, describes the tragic death of a young factory worker. The heroine is an orphan who dies of exhaustion working in a mill that is trying to meet the demand for fabric for new dresses for the social season. Stone addresses her book to the "Fashionable ladies," who are, as she says, "individually kind and good" but "collectively the cause of infinite misery to the young and unprotected of their own sex." Both books are considered CONDITION OF ENGLAND NOVELS.

Strauss, David Friedrich (1808–1874)
theological writer

Enormously influential on British intellectuals, the German theologian David Friedrich Strauss was born in Ludwigsburg, in southwest Germany, and began his formal studies in classics and theology at the evangelical seminary at Blaubeuren when he was 13. Four years later, in 1825, he entered the University of Tübingen, from which he graduated with honors five years later, and he thereupon became assistant for nine months to a local pastor. His pastoral career ended, however, when he accepted a post as a high school teacher in Maulbronn, where he taught Hebrew, Latin, and history. All the while he entertained doubts of a philosophical and theological nature, and he hoped to settle them by study with the philosophers Schleiermacher and Hegel at Berlin. Strauss attended only a few lectures by Hegel before the philosopher died of cholera, but he came strongly under the influence of Hegel's many followers and was likewise influenced by Schleiermacher's lectures on the life of Jesus.

In 1832 Strauss returned to Tübingen as lecturer in logic, Plato, the histories and philosophy and ethics, and there began work on the book which was to have enormous impact on British and European thought in the 19th century, *The Life of Jesus*. The book was translated into English in 1846 by Mary Ann Evans, who would go on to write novels as GEORGE ELIOT. *The Life of Jesus* reflected the inquiring spirit of the 18th-century Enlightenment and the influence of the burgeoning spirit of scientific investigation in England, which culminated in 1859 with CHARLES DARWIN's *On the Origin of Species*. Strauss subjects the New Testament, the four gospels in particular, to objective scholarly investigation. Strauss's conclusions were, among others, that Christ performed no miracles and was not in the traditional sense "divine" at all, but was only the figure upon whom ancient biblical writers had pinned their hopes for a predicted messiah. In short, he argued that the traditional Christ was a mythic figure rather than a supernaturally divine one.

Stretton, Hesba (Sarah Smith) (1832–1911) *novelist, short story writer*

Hesba Stretton was born Sarah Smith in Shropshire, in western England near Wales, to Benjamin Smith, a bookseller, and Ann Bakewell Smith. Sarah read widely from the books that her father sold and began publishing her own stories when she was in her 30s. Feeling that Sarah Smith was too common a name, she changed it to Hesba Stretton. *Fern's Hollow*, published in 1864, was the first of her stories about a child's religious experience, a subject she returned to again and again. *Jessica's First Prayer* (1867) is another evangelical, or religiously inspirational, story about a little girl living in the slums of an industrial city who is adopted by a miser and comes to believe in Christ. It sold more than 1.5 million copies, was translated into many languages, and made Stretton famous almost overnight. The lives of the poor formed a major theme in all of Stretton's writing. Having lived in poor parts of Manchester and London herself, she had firsthand knowledge of the nature of her characters' lives. Her later novels, such as *In Prison and Out* (1879) and *Through a Needle's Eye* (1879), are darker. Many reflect her increasing concern about child abuse, which, in 1884, led her to help establish the London Society for the Prevention of Cruelty to Children.

Strickland, Agnes (1796–1874) *poet, historian*

Agnes Strickland was born in London to Thomas Strickland, manager of the Greenland shipping docks, and his wife, Elizabeth Homer Strickland. Strickland, along with her siblings, was educated by her parents and encouraged to write. Her father's poor business decisions left his family nearly destitute on his death in 1818. To ease the family's financial difficulties, Strickland began to write professionally.

Initially, Strickland wrote poetry, but even her most popular collection, *The Seven Ages of Women, and Other Poems* (1827), sold poorly; it was overly romantic and melodramatic. The same year, while visiting a cousin, she met SIR WALTER SCOTT. After their encounter, Strickland turned to prose and began collaborating with her sister Elizabeth.

The two sisters first wrote a series of children's books, culminating with the publication of *Historical Tales of Illustrious British Children* in 1833. The popularity of this work sparked the sisters' interest in British history, and the two initiated a massive project titled *Lives of the Queens of England*. This broad historical study was divided into 12 volumes, the first two published in 1840, the last in 1848. The Stricklands gained access to the state archives, visited the private libraries of numerous noble families, and even received QUEEN VICTORIA's official blessing. Consequently, the work is amazingly thorough and is filled with documentary and anecdotal information.

Because Elizabeth Strickland feared public recognition, she refused to have her name appear on the work. Therefore, although the sisters evenly divided the writing and although Elizabeth oversaw the publishing contracts, Agnes is the work's sole credited writer.

Agnes Strickland did produce two significant works of her own. She edited the *Letters of Mary, Queen of Scots* (1843) and wrote *Lives of the Queens of Scotland and English Princesses* (1859). Strickland's accomplishments earned her a civil pension in 1870, and the popularity of *Lives of the Queens of England* extended well into the 20th century. Current historians frequently criticize her clear bias for Mary, Queen of Scots and her unhidden prejudice against Tory politicians. Still, Strickland and her sister were the first historians to include domestic details and to provide an accurate depiction of everyday life in the English court. The critic Miriam Burstein notes that Strickland's "sentimentality was . . . one of the most positive elements of her project, promising as it did to personalize historical inquiry."

A Work about Agnes Strickland
Burstein, Miriam Elizabeth. "The Reduced Pretensions of the Historic Muse: Agnes Strickland and the Commerce of Women's History." *The Journal of Narrative Technique* 28, 3 (Fall 1998): 219–42.

Surtees, Robert Smith (1805–1864)
novelist

Robert Smith Surtees was a keen observer and appreciator of eccentric human beings, whom he depicted with enthusiasm and care in his eight novels. His father, Anthony Surtees, was a country squire whose marriage to Alice Blackett produced nine children; Robert, born in Durham in the north of England, was the second son. Surtees served as an apprentice to a lawyer in Newcastle upon Tyne in northeast England. When both his older brother and his father died, he inherited his father's estate.

Surtees had begun to write anonymously essays for the periodical *Sporting Magazine* and became its hunting correspondent. Later, he established the *New Sporting Magazine* and published a nonfiction work, *The Horseman's Manual* (1831).

Surtees invented the unforgettable character, Mr. John Jorrocks, London Cockney, and wrote a series of hunting sketches involving him. These were gathered together and published in 1838 as *Jorrocks's Jaunts and Jollities*. With *Handley Cross* (1843), Surtees extended his Jorrocks sketches into a full length novel, focusing on the character's hunting adventures. Considered his best work, *Handley Cross* presents an array of comic sportsmen.

Hillingdon Hall (1845) presents an interesting portrait of a Victorian gentleman farmer. In this work Jorrocks moves to the country to become a "scientific" farmer, attempting to improve his estate through new methods of agriculture. One measure of his comic difficulties is his confusing the two plants, the pineapple and the pine tree.

Surtees is best remembered for his Jorrocks tales, but his most successful novel at the time was *Mr. Sponge's Sporting Tour* (1853), starring the crooked Soapy Sponge, a man who "hates work and . . . despises poverty" and tours English estates cheating his hosts and hunting. RUDYARD KIPLING described the world of Surtees's novels as "a heavy-eating, hard-drinking hell of horse-copers, swindlers, matchmaking mothers, economically dependent virgins selling themselves unblushingly for cash and lands, Jews, tradesmen, and an ill-considered spawn of Dickens-and-horsedung characters."

Swinburne, Algernon Charles (1837–1909) *poet, playwright, novelist, critic*

Algernon Charles Swinburne was born in London to the aristocratic family of Admiral Charles Swinburne and his wife, Lady Jane Henrietta Swinburne. He spent his childhood in comfort and privilege. After attending Eton school, he entered Balliot College, Oxford, at age 19. At Oxford he met fellow students DANTE GABRIEL ROSSETTI, WILLIAM MORRIS, and Edward Burne-Jones, all of whom would become leading figures in the PRE-RAPHAELITE MOVEMENT. Spoiled and precocious, Swinburne hated school and never received a degree. Still, he mastered Greek and Latin, French and Italian, and poetic form.

After leaving Oxford he went to London, where he became involved in the Pre-Raphaelite movement and also met such poets as ROBERT BROWNING and MATTHEW ARNOLD. For a time he shared an apartment with Rossetti and GEORGE MEREDITH.

In 1860 Swinburne published his first plays, *Rosamund* and *The Queen Mother*, historical tragedies that he dedicated to his friend Rossetti. Next came *Atalanta in Calydon* (1865). Set in ancient Greece, this verse drama, which takes its form from classical Greek plays, tells the tragic story of the lovers Meleager and Altalanta. It made Swinburne famous, and of this play, JOHN RUSKIN wrote, it was "the grandest thing ever done by a youth—though he is a demoniac [sic] youth." Also in 1865 Swinburne published *Chastelard* (1865), the first part of a trilogy about Mary, Queen of Scots; it eventually was followed by the sequels *Bothwell* (1874) and *Mary Stuart* (1881).

In 1866 Swinburne published *Poems and Ballads*, a book that brought him fame. His poetry also stirred up controversy. The poems were attacked for their sensuality, eroticism, and anti-Christian sentiments because of lines like the following from "Laus Veneris" ("Praise of Venus"):

> *Alas, Lord, surely thou art great and fair.*
> *But, lo, her wonderfully woven hair!*
> *And thou didst heal us with they piteous*
> * kiss;*
> *But see now, Lord, her mouth is lovelier.*

The theme of Swinburne's ballads is love, often love that ends in tragedy or crimes of passion. Swinburne often links love to pain and death as in "A Ballad of Burdens,": "What pain could get between my face and hers? / What new sweet thing would love not relish worse? / Unless, perhaps, white death had kissed me there, / Kissing her hair?"

Above all else, Swinburne's verse is metrically dazzling. His rhythmic patterns highlight the beautiful sound of the words. T. S. Eliot wrote, "Only a man of genius could dwell so exclusively and consistently among words as Swinburne."

For the next decade Swinburne wrote fiercely and prolifically. After he met the Italian exile Giuseppe Mazzini, he published political poems in *Songs of Two Nations* (1867) and *Songs before Sunrise* (1871) that sympathetically portrayed the struggle of Italy. *Under the Microscope* (1872) was a defense of his friend Rossetti against attack in Robert Buchanan's essay "The Fleshly School of Poetry." Swinburne would continue to use his fame to defend and champion the work of Dante Gabriel and his sister CHRISTINA ROSSETTI, whose poetry he greatly admired. He wrote another Greek drama, *Erechtheus* (1876), and *Poems and Ballads: Second Series* (1876). The latter included an elegy, "Ave

Atque Vale" ("Hail and Farewell"), to the French poet Charles Baudelaire, of whom Swinburne wrote, "Now all strange hours and all strange loves are over . . . / Hast thou found place at the great knees and feet / Of some pale Titan-woman like a lover . . . / Where the wet hill-winds weep?" During this time Swinburne also wrote an erotic novel, influenced by the Marquis de Sade, called *Love's Cross-Currents: A Year's Letters* (1877).

By his mid-40s Swinburne was an alcoholic, in poor health, and past the peak of his career. In 1879 a good friend of his, THEODORE WATTS-DUNTON, took him to his suburban home in Putney, where he watched over Swinburne and guarded his health in the relatively quiet and conventional setting and where Swinburne continued to write poetry and criticism until he died.

Of Swinburne, ALFRED, LORD TENNYSON, an admirer, said, "He is a reed through which all things blow into music." Indeed, Swinburne's poetry was an eclectic mix. His great affinity for the Pre-Raphaelites and his admiration for JOHN KEATS led to his ideas of beauty and love, which were further refined when he read WILLIAM BLAKE. His preoccupation with death and with the idea of beauty as pain were influenced by his study of Baudelaire. All of these elements came together in what EDMUND GOSSE called "an extraordinary exhilaration . . . something uplifted, extravagant." As the scholar M. H. Abrams wrote, Swinburne's poetry defies "traditional analysis and oblige[s] us to reconsider the variety of ways in which poetry may achieve its effects."

Critical Analysis

T. S. Eliot once said of Swinburne's poetry: "the tumultuous outcry of adjectives, the headstrong rush of undisciplined sentences, are the index to the impatience and perhaps laziness of a disorderly mind." Critic Jerome J. McCann sees some of the same qualities in Swinburne's poetry but regards them more positively: "His poetry tends not to move in a direction like a path, but to accumulate additions, like coral. . . . His propensity is toward forms which do not so much move forward as they spin off from a center, accumulating all the while what can be a bewildering variety of figures and images."

One of Swinburne's finest early poems, "The Triumph of Time," a lament for a lost love, reveals both his strengths and his excesses. It is a very long poem, nearly 400 lines, written in ottava rima—an Italian form of eight lines in iambic pentameter, usually rhyming *abababcc*. In this poem, however, Swinburne uses a more complex rhyme scheme, *ababccba*.

In the first stanza, the poet sets the scene; he is standing by the sea, about to part from the one he loves, and resolving "to say no word that a man might say/Whose whole life's love goes down in a day." When follows then, is not a speech to the beloved but a kind of interior monologue, the poet's lament to himself. The love that is lost, he says. was godlike in its beauty and intensity; the lovers were once "One splendid spirit." This time is gone, however, and now the landscape seems as blighted as the poet's soul:

> *The low downs lean to the sea; the stream,*
> *One loose thin pulseless tremulous vein,*
> *Rapid and vivid and dumb as a dream,*
> *Works downward, sick of the sun and the rain;*

As the poet explores his heartbreak, his description of his pain—so detailed and lovingly portrayed—provides insight into Swinburne's own sadomasochistic tendencies. He says he would have done anything his beloved asked, to live or to die for her. These, he says,

> *were the thoughts that stung.*
> *The dreams that smote with a keener dart*
> *Than shafts of love or arrows of death;*
> *These were but as fire is, dust, or breath,*
> *Or poisonous foam on the tender tongue*
> *Of the little snakes that eat my heart.*

In addition to its complex stanzaic form and rhyme scheme, "The Triumph of Time" showcases Swinburne's use of alliteration and internal rhyme. The poem is rich with repeated sounds, piling rhyme upon rhyme, echo upon echo. He says he wishes he and his lover were dead, "Clasped and clothed in the cloven clay," and he compares his thoughts to dead things

> *wrecked and whirled*
> *Round and round in a gulf of the sea;*
> *And still through the sound and the*
> *straining stream*
> *Through coil and chafe, they gleam in a*
> *dream*
> *The bright fine lips so cruelly curled,*
> *And strange swift eyes where the soul*
> *sits free.*

After his long lament for lost love, the poet turns again to the sea, and looks at it anew, as the "great sweet mother" who may set his soul free. He recalls the story of Tristan and Isolde:

> *There lived a singer in France of old*
> *By the tideless dolorous midland sea*
> *In a land of sand and ruin and gold*
> *There shone one woman, and none but*
> *she.*

He tells of Tristan's death and exclaims, "O brother, the gods were good to you" because he died with his beloved's lips upon his. The poet renounces the world, says he will never again take pleasure in the scent of roses or the sound of sweet tunes. War and passion will be nothing to him. "The stars that sing and the loves that thunder / The music burning at heart like wine? . . . These things are over, and no more mine."

The poem ends with the poet's declaration that he will never make these complaints to his beloved on earth, but, he wonders, "in heaven / If I cry to you then, will you hear or know?" The only thing rescued from this shipwreck of love and loss, Swinburne suggests, is his poem. The song lives on, even the singer and the love have died. His is not an original thought, of course. Many poets have said as much. However, Swinburne's form and the language are distinctive and the poem clearly shows the promise of a fine young poet that never matured.

Other Work by Algernon Charles Swinburne
Lang, Cecil Y., ed. *The Swinburne Letters,* 6 vols. New Haven, Conn.: Yale University Press, 1959.

A Work about Algernon Charles Swinburne
Thomas, Donald Serrell. *Swinburne: The Poet in His World.* Chicago: Ivan R. Dee, 1999.

Symonds, John Addington (1840–1893)
poet, biographer, art historian

John Addington Symonds was born in Bristol, England, to John Symonds and his wife, Harriet Sykes. He studied at Balliol College, Oxford, where he won the prestigious Newdigate Prize for poetry, and where he became increasingly aware that he was gay. He also developed tuberculosis. He married in 1864 perhaps in an attempt to deny his homosexuality.

Symonds's major works of this period were scholarly studies of Dante (1872) and Greek poets (1873) and a biography of PERCY BYSSHE SHELLEY (1878). Over the next few years Symonds wrote poetry, collected in the privately published *Verses* (1871).

Beginning in 1880 Symonds wrote the sonnet sequences *New and Old* (1880), *Anima Figura* (1882), and *Vagabundulis Libellus* (1884). The subject of each is homosexual love, whose meaning is hidden in coded phrases such as "unutterable things," "valley of vain desire," and "the impossible." Critical response ranged from indifference to ridicule. After 1884 Symonds abandoned poetry.

Meanwhile, Symonds labored on his life's work, the seven-volume *The Renaissance in Italy* (1875–86), a sweeping, detailed history covering every aspect of 13th- and 14th-century Italian culture. Symonds wrote prolifically over the next few years, producing two biographies of Renaissance artists, *The Life of Cellini* (1888) and *The Life of Michelangelo Buonarroti* (1892). He also was one of the first British admirers of the American poet Walt Whitman and in 1893 wrote a study of Whitman. In addition, Symonds published *A Problem in Greek Ethics* (1883) and *A Problem in Modern Ethics* (1891), two of the first serious works ever to address on homosexuality, and anonymously offered his own life history to HAVELOCK ELLIS for the latter's *Sexual Inversion*.

Symons, Arthur William (1865–1945)
poet, critic

Arthur Symons was born in Milford Haven, Wales, to Cornish parents, the Reverend Mark Symons and his wife, Lydia Pascoe Symons. He was educated privately and became fluent in French and Italian.

Moving to London, he joined the Rhymers' Club, a literary discussion group that included ERNEST DOWSON, LIONEL JOHNSON, and OSCAR WILDE. In 1895 he shared an apartment with W. B. Yeats, and the two became close friends. In the 1890s Symons contributed poems to the London literary journal *Yellow Book,* and in 1896 he was asked to edit its successor, the *Savoy.* He agreed to do so on the condition that AUBREY BEARDSLEY, whom he had heard of but never met, be art editor. Later, Symons wrote a biography of Beardsley (1898), as well as of Ernest Dowson (1905).

Symons was able, unlike many of his contemporaries, to remain sober. In fact, Yeats once jokingly said to him, "Symons, if we had felt a tendency to excess, we would be better poets." In keeping with the spirit of the decade, however, Symons had affairs with women, none of whom captured his heart.

Symons published four books of his own poetry: *Days and Nights* (1889), *Silhouettes* (1892), *London Nights* (1895), and *Images of Good and Evil* (1899). His verse had all the elements of the 1890s: dark, interior rooms; music halls; and dancing girls, much like those that appeared in Beardsley's drawings. Thus, in "Emmy" (1892) Symons wrote,

> There, in the midst of the villainous
>   dancing hall,
> Leaning across the table, over the beer,
> While the music maddened the whirling
>   skirts of the ball,
> As the midnight hour drew near,
>
> There with the women, haggard,
>   painted, and old,
> One fresh bud in a garland withered and
>   stale,
> She, with her innocent voice and her clear
>   eyes, told
> Tale after shameless tale.

Symons's most important work, however, is *The Symbolist Movement in Literature* (1899), in which he introduced French Symbolism to English-speaking readers. Of this book, T. S. Eliot would later write, "I myself owe Mr. Symons a great debt; but for having read his book I should not, in the year 1908, have heard of Laforgue or Rimbaud; I should probably not have begun to read Verlaine . . . So the Symons book is one of those which have affected the course of my life." Symons also translated the French poetry of Charles Baudelaire, and wrote a 1920 biography of the French poet.

Symons wrote many other critical works, such as *An Introduction to the Study of Robert Browning* (1886), *William Blake* (1907), and *Studies in Elizabethan Drama* (1920). In 1908 he suffered a severe mental breakdown, which he described in *Confessions* (1930). Of Symons, the critic B. Ifor Evans observes, in *English Poetry of the Later Nineteenth Century* (1933), "his most pungent verse remained in those lyrics of the nineties" and "it is as a critic that he will probably be best remembered."

Critical Analysis

Arthur Symons's poetry, deeply influenced by the French symbolists, and particularly by Charles

Baudelaire and Paul Verlaine, is vivid in its imagery, deeply erotic, and dark. His eroticism was not appreciated by many of his contemporaries. Here, for example, are the words of a critic writing for the *Pall Mall Gazette* in 1895:

> Mr. Arthur Symons is a very dirty-minded man, and his mind is reflected in the puddle of his bad verses. It may be that there are other dirty-minded men who will rejoice in the jingle that records the squalid and inexpensive amours of Mr. Symons, but our faith jumps to the hope that such men are not.

Symons was regarded as "dirty minded" because he dared to write about lovemaking itself and even about making love to prostitutes. In *Poetica Erotica* (1921), for example, a number of the poems are fairly explicit in their descriptions of Symons's desires and sexual activity. Symons—like his fellow turn-of-the-century decadent poets who rejected conventional morality—shocked many who did not feel sexuality was a fit subject for poetry. "I Know Your Lips Are Bought" is a sonnet about Symons's unrequited love for a prostitute. Merely by using the sonnet form, the preeminent form of love poetry since the Renaissance, Symons intends to shock.

Symons's poem is a Shakespearean sonnet, divided into three quatrains with a final couplet; the rhyme scheme is *aabb ccdd eeff gg*. In the first quatrain, Symons tells his beloved that he knows her lips "are bought like any fruit," and that her "kisses toll for love that dies." He has no hope that she will love him or repay the love he feels for her.

In the second quatrain, the poet admits that he is "degraded" for his beloved's sake and that she takes little heed of him; "my shame will not so much as make/Your glory, or be reckoned in the debt/Of memories, you are mindful to forget."

In the third quatrain, he sums up, "All this I know" and yet, he says, he comes "Delighted to my daily martyrdom." In the final couplet, he likens himself to one who begs for "the broken crumbs that from your table fall" even though he knows that the crumbs fall "freely" in her "indifference, on all."

Another of Symons's poems about lovemaking, "White Heliotrope," uses the symbolist technique of synesthesia, in which one sense evokes another. Baudelaire uses synesthesia in his poem "Correspondances":

> *There are perfumes fresh like the skin of*
> *   infants*
> *Sweet like oboes, green like prairies,*
> *—And others corrupted, rich and*
> *   triumphant*
>
> *That have the expanse of infinite things,*
> *Like ambergris, musk, balsam and incense,*
> *Which sing the ecstasies of the mind and*
> *   senses*

In "White Heliotrope," Symons creates a vivid impressionistic portrait of a room that suggests a night of frenzied lovemaking:

> *The feverish room and that white bed,*
> *The tumbled skirts upon a chair,*
> *The novel flung half-open where*
> *Hat, hair pins, puffs, and paints are spread;*

He continues his description and in the final quatrain sums up all the details in a single word, "This," which he says he will see vividly if "Ever again my handkerchief/Is scented with White Heliotrope." The lover's perfume will forever call up the sights, sounds, and emotions of that night.

T

Taylor, Helen (1831–1907) *editor, political writer*

Helen Taylor was born to John and Harriet Taylor on July 27, 1831, in London. John Taylor died in 1849, and Harriet Taylor married JOHN STUART MILL in 1851. Taylor herself had little formal education, though she traveled widely with her mother throughout Europe. She joined an acting troupe in northeast England and worked under an assumed name (at her mother's behest) until Harriet Taylor's death in 1858.

Taylor assisted her stepfather in pursuing women's suffrage, writing many letters for him and even convincing him to change his positions on certain issues. Taylor was instrumental in drafting the Ladies' Petition on suffrage that Mill presented to the House of Commons in 1866. She also acted as chief correspondent between Mill and petition organizers. Later that year, the *Westminster Review* published her influential article "The Claim of Englishwomen to the Suffrage Constitutionally Considered."

Taylor edited the works of Mill's disciple Henry Thomas Buckle in the late 1860s, and after Mill died in 1873, she also completed and published his *Autobiography, Three Essays on Religion: Nature, the Utility of Religion and Theism, Chapters on Socialism,* and the final volume of *Dissertations and Discussions.* Her subsequent writings were all in defense of a variety of political and social issues she came to champion, including free and universal education, reform of industrial schools, Irish home rule, and the abolition of fox hunting. Her leadership on committees and in associations devoted to these causes was significant, although her literary production was never large.

She died in Torquay, Devon, on January 29, 1907. Today she is remembered as an outspoken activist who helped catalyze a number of reform movements, particularly the fight for suffrage.

Another Work by Helen Taylor

Sexual Equality: A John Stuart Mill, Harriet Taylor Mill, and Helen Taylor Reader. Edited by Ann P. Robson. Toronto: University of Toronto Press, 1994.

Taylor, Philip Meadows (1808–1876) *novelist*

Philip Taylor was born in Liverpool, England. His father was a merchant who went bankrupt, forcing Philip to work as a clerk in a merchant's office when he was still a child to help support the family.

At age 15, he went to Bombay, India, to work for an English trader. Unhappy with the job, he enlisted in the army of the Indian ruler of Bombay. During his service as an adjutant in the army, he investigated a secret society of criminals called Thuggis, who practiced terrorism and assassination. (The English-language word *thug* derives from the Hindi word for this society.) Taylor went home to England on furlough in 1840 and was married, then returned to India as a correspondent for the London *Times*. His experience in Indian affairs convinced the ruler of Shorapore to appoint him as regent, putting him in charge of the government until her son was old enough to rule. He eventually was named commissioner of Shorapore, India, when it became a British territory.

In novels such as *Confessions of a Thug* (1839) and *Tippos Sultaun* (1840), Taylor chronicled the history of India from the 17th century to the colonial era during which he lived. Taylor's novels are not only "picturesque, brilliant, and lively," as the critic and poet Stanley Kunitz describes them, but also are historically accurate and present a view of Indian society that is remarkably objective and free of racism. After Taylor returned to London in 1860 he continued to write novels about India, including *A Mahratta Tale* (1863), as well as a nonfiction work, *A Student's Manual of the History of India* (1870).

A Work about Philip Meadows Taylor

Brantlinger, Patrick. Introduction to *Confessions of a Thug*. New York: Oxford University Press, 1998.

Taylor, Sir Henry (1800–1886) poet

Henry Taylor was born on October 18, 1800, at Bishop Middleham, Durham. His father, George Taylor, farmed and studied classical literature, while his mother, Eleanor Ashworth, died before he was two years old. His father educated Taylor at home, though he was not a particularly promising student.

In 1814 he went to sea as a midshipman, serving in the Americas during the War of 1812. He returned to his father's house in 1814 and read extensively, then took a position in the Treasury until 1820, when his branch was consolidated with another within the department. For the next three years, he lived in his father's house again and read widely, also studying Latin, Greek, and Italian. During this time, he began to write poetry as well.

In 1822 Taylor began publishing literary essays in the *Quarterly Review* and *London Magazine*. He moved to London the next year to attempt to make a literary living. He met WILLIAM WORDSWORTH, SAMUEL TAYLOR COLERIDGE, and other important literary figures. He was appointed to a clerkship in the Colonial Office in 1824, and the following year he advanced to senior clerk for the Caribbean colonies.

Taylor used his experience in public service to write *The Statesman* (1836), an ironic work of practical advice that many at the time considered too cynical, though today it is regarded as a minor classic. He married Theodosia Alice Spring Rice in 1839 and settled into a happy home life, eventually having five children.

During his career in the Colonial Office, he continued writing poetry, publishing a volume of lyric poems as well as five long verse dramas. Though most of his poetry did not long survive him, the best regarded of his works was *Philip Van Artevelde* (1834), a verse drama taking place in 14th-century Flanders that was written in a restrained style, against the fashion of the day. His complete poetic works were printed in 1877–88.

Although he considered himself a poet first and foremost, Taylor achieved the most lasting fame through his prose, including *The Statesman* and his *Autobiography 1800–75* (1885), which has proved an important source of historical information on the Colonial Office as well as the colonial Caribbean. Henry Taylor was knighted in 1869 for his service in the Colonial Office, and died on March 27, 1886, in London.

Other Works by Henry Taylor
Isaac Comnenus: A Play. London: J. Murray, 1827.
Poems. London: Edward Moxon, 1845.
St. Clement's Eve: A Play. London: Chapman and Hall, 1862.
The Virgin Widow: A Play. London: Longman, Brown, Green, and Longmans, 1850.

A Work about Henry Taylor
Braham, Olive Fern. *The Dramas of Sir Henry Taylor.* Ithaca, N.Y.: Cornell University, 1927.

Temple, Frederick (1821–1902) essayist

Frederick Temple was born to Octavius and Dorcas Temple on November 30, 1821, on Santa Maura, an Ionian Island. In 1830, his family returned to Devon, England, in order to farm. His father died in 1834 in Sierra Leone, having been appointed governor there after he failed at farming. Temple was raised and educated by his mother until he was old enough to attend school; he became enduringly close to her as a result.

He was such an extraordinary student at Blundell's School, Tiverton, that he won a scholarship to enter Balliol College, Oxford, in 1839. There he obtained a double first-class in classics and mathematics in 1842. He was appointed a lecturer in mathematics and logic the same year, and elected fellow of Balliol afterward, then junior dean in 1845. He was ordained an Anglican priest in 1847.

Temple's work and writings during the 1850s and 1860s centered on educational reform at Oxford and Rugby School, where he served as a progressive and inspiring headmaster from 1857 to 1869. In 1869, he was offered and accepted the bishophric for the see of Exeter. An essay of his, "The Education of the World," was the first of seven to appear in a 1860 volume entitled *Essays and Reviews*, which generated much controversy due to the scientific challenges it posed to Christian doctrine. Though Temple's essay was harmless in this regard, he was vilified along with his associates, but only withdrew his essay in 1870.

Throughout the 1870s, he worked to reform and expand the secondary school system in the see, putting his liberal views into practice with great success. He married Beatrice Blanche in 1876 and became the bishop of London in 1885, where he pushed through further educational reforms and championed temperance in sermons; in 1884 he also delivered a series of lectures ("The Relations Between Religion and Science") in which he affirmed scientific findings, particularly in the theory of evolution, declaring that they did not contradict religious teachings. In 1897, in failing health, he became the archbishop of Canterbury.

That year, Temple and the archbishop of York issued a response to Pope Leo XIII's bull, known as the *Apostolicae Curae*, declaring Anglican Orders invalid. Two years later, the two archbishops issued the Lambeth Opinions, declaring that the liturgical use of incense and lights in procession were "neither enjoined nor permitted" in the Anglican Church. Both of these documents were primarily written by Temple, and they helped shape and support doctrines of the Anglican Church in the 20th century.

Frederick Temple died on December 23, 1902. Many of his sermons and other public talks were published during his lifetime, contributing greatly to the social reform movements, particularly in elementary and secondary education, that marked the latter half of the 19th century.

Works about Frederick Temple
Hinchliff, Peter Bingham. *Frederick Temple, Archbishop of Canterbury: A Life.* New York: Clarendon, 1998.
Wolf, William J., John B. Booty, and Owen, C. Thomas. *The Spirit of Anglicanism: Hooker, Maurice, Temple.* Wilton, Conn.: Morehouse-Barlow. 1979.

Tennyson, Alfred, Lord (first baron Tennyson) (1809–1892) poet

Alfred, Lord Tennyson was born in Somersby, Lincolnshire, England, to George Tennyson, a clergyman, and his wife, Elizabeth Fytche Tennyson. Tennyson attended grammar school until age 11, from which point he was tutored by his father until he was ready to attend university. In 1827 Tennyson enrolled at Trinity College, Cambridge, where he met ARTHUR HALLAM, a brilliant student who became his dearest friend. Tennyson disliked Cambridge and so perhaps was not unwilling to leave in 1831 when his father died and the family could no longer afford his tuition. Before he left, however, Tennyson was awarded the Chancellor's Medal for English verse.

Tennyson's first three published volumes of poetry, *Poems by Two Brothers* (1827, with his brother CHARLES TENNYSON TURNER), *Poems Chiefly Lyrical* (1830), and *Poems* (1833), were neither popular nor critical successes. Nevertheless, *Poems* contains several poems that are today recognized as among Tennysons's best. "The Lady of Shalott," set in the world of King Arthur, tells the tragic story of a woman who is condemned to look at the world only through a mirror. This poem was the subject of several paintings by several artists of the PRE-RAPHAELITE MOVEMENT. "Oenone," which has its roots in Greek mythology, is the story of the nymph Oenone's tragic love for Paris. "The Lotos-Eaters" is inspired by an episode in the *Odyssey,* in which some of the men of the Greek hero Odysseus eat the lotus flower and lose their desire to return home:

> *Most weary seemed the sea, weary the oar,*
> *Weary the wandering fields of barren foam.*
> *Then someone said, "We will return no*
>   *more";*
> *And all at once they sang, "Our island*
>   *home*
> *Is far beyond the wave; we will no longer*
>   *roam.*

In 1833 Arthur Hallam died. Tennyson described his emotions in vivid terms: "I suffered what seemed to me to shatter all my life so that I desired to die rather than to live." So overcome by grief was Tennyson that he wrote no poetry for 10 years, but would detail his grief in his magnificent long poem *In Memoriam* (1850).

In 1842 Tennyson found critical and popular success with the publication of an enlarged two-volume edition of *Poems*. Three years later, he was recommended for and received a government pension, which eased his financial worries. But the year 1850 was, perhaps, the high point of Tennyson's life. First, he was financially secure enough to marry. Second, as a result of WILLIAM WORDSWORTH's death, Tennyson was appointed to succeed Wordsworth as poet laureate of England. Third, Tennyson published one of his greatest works, *In Memoriam* (1850), a series of more than 100 meditations on death that he dedicated to the memory of Hallam. The meditations begin with the grim fear that the universe is a soulless machine, in which "the stars . . . blindly run." But the poet works through his grief and finds comfort:

> *That God, which ever lives and loves,*
> *One God, one law, one element,*
> *And far-off divine event,*
> *To which the whole creation moves.*

Tennyson's first poem after his selection as poet laureate was a failure; "Ode on the Death of the Duke of Wellington" (1852) was unpopular because of its unusual meter and because of some of the political opinions it expressed. But *Idylls of the King* (1859), a series of poems about King Arthur, won Tennyson widespread admiration. QUEEN VICTORIA's consort, Prince Albert, greatly admired this poem. Aware of this, Tennyson, at Albert's death in 1861, incorporated an ode to him into the *Idylls*.

In the 1870s Tennyson turned away from poetry to concentrate his effort on drama. Between 1875 and 1892 he wrote six verse dramas, none of which was successful. In 1884 Queen Victoria granted him the title of baron; Tennyson was the first poet so honored solely on the basis of his writing.

Critical Analysis

Tennyson's work is often filled with striking images, as in these lines from "The Lady of Shalott":

> *Willows whiten, aspens quiver,*
> *Little breezes dusk and shiver*
> *Through the wave that runs for ever*
> *By the island in the river*
> *Flowing down to Camelot.*
> *Four grey walls, and four grey towers,*
> *Overlook a space of flowers,*
> *And the silent isle imbowers*
> *The Lady of Shalott.*

The beauty of the imagery paired with the beauty of the sound lends this poem a dreamy and magical air.

In his own day Tennyson was popular not only because of the lyricism of his poetry but also because his themes struck a chord with many Victorian readers. His tendency to look backward to a heroic past in many of his poems reflected the ambiguity of the Victorian attitude toward progress. Although many of his poems were melancholy and focused on mortality, Tennyson's worldview nevertheless embodied a fundamental optimism and faith in the human spirit.

"Ulysses" (1842) is a poem first and foremost about the human spirit. This dramatic monologue begins with Ulysses as an old man reflecting on his current situation. He calls himself an "idle king," and laments that all that seems left to him is to "mete and dole / Unequal laws unto a savage race." But he knows himself too well to live out his life in this tedious and ordinary way: "I cannot rest from travel," he says. "I will drink / Life to the lees." Ulysses' greatness of spirit is reflected in his appetites: he has suffered, he has rejoiced, he has fought, he has sailed "Thro' scudding drifts the rainy Hyades." Yet he wants more, "Life piled on life / Were all too little." He wants to "follow knowledge like a sinking star / Beyond the utmost bound of human thought." Ulysses does not wish to wait for death; he wishes to travel forth and seize both the rest of his life and his death as he has all else, with courage and gusto. He believes that there is still work for him to do, something of "noble note . . . not unbecoming men that strove with Gods."

Ulysses decides to leave the governance of the land to his son Telemachus and sail forth "beyond the sunset, and the baths / Of all the western stars, until I die." In the final, and most famous, line, Ulysses determines "To strive, to seek, to find, and not to yield." The rhythm of this line has been often and justly praised. The single-syllable, heavily stressed words sound like marching feet, but the final phrase, "and not to yield," gains emphasis from the change in rhythm.

Another of Tennyson's most famous poems, "The Charge of the Light Brigade" (1854) deals with the courage of "six hundred men" who rode into "the valley of death" during the Crimean War, in which Britain fought Russia. Theirs was, essentially, a suicide mission. "Someone had blundered," but the men charged anyway:

> *Theirs not to make reply,*
> *Theirs not to reason why,*
> *Theirs but to do and die.*

Tennyson often wrote about death, but never with so much hope of something better to follow, as in a late poem, which he asked to be placed at the end of all future editions of his poetry, "Crossing the Bar" (1889). Here, contemplating his own death, Tennyson takes a hopeful, Christian view:

> *For though from out our bourne of time*
> *   and place*
> *The flood may bear me far,*
> *I hope to see my Pilot face to face*
> *When I have crost the bar.*

As T. S. Eliot observed of Tennyson, "whatever he sets out to do, he succeeds in doing. . . . *In Memoriam* . . . [is] given form by the greatest lyrical resourcefulness that a poet has ever shown. . . . Tennyson is the great master of metric."

Works by Alfred, Lord Tennyson

Hill, Robert W., Jr., ed. *Tennyson's Poetry: Authoritative Texts, Context, Criticism.* New York: W.W. Norton, 1999.

Idylls of the King. New York: Penguin, 1989.

Works about Alfred, Lord Tennyson

Markos, Louis A. *Pressing Forward: Alfred, Lord Tennyson and the Victorian Age.* Ave Maria, Fla.: Sapienta Press of Ave Maria University, 2007.

Page, Norman. *Tennyson: An Illustrated Life.* Chicago: New Amsterdam Books, 1990.

Shaw, D. David. *Alfred, Lord Tennyson: The Poet in an Age of Theory.* New York: Twayne, 1997.

Walters, J. Cuming. *Tennyson: Poet, Philosopher, Idealist: Studies of the Life, Work, and Teaching of the Poet Laureate.* Columbia, Mo.: Athena University Press, 2004.

Thackeray, William Makepeace (1811–1863) *novelist, journalist*

William Makepeace Thackeray, author of *Vanity Fair* (1847–48), remains one of the leading figures of Victorian literature. Thackeray was born to English parents in Calcutta, India, where his father, Richmond, was an important civil servant. When Richmond Thackeray died in 1815, his son was sent to England to be educated, while his mother, Anne, remained in India and remarried. (Thackeray drew on his painful years at the prestigious Charterhouse boarding school in *Vanity Fair*, which denounces the sadistic discipline and arid teaching methods that characterized such institutions.) Thackeray went on to Trinity College, Cambridge, where he was a greater social than intellectual success, meeting ALFRED TENNYSON and EDWARD FITZGERALD but leaving without a degree. After a tour of Europe that included an introduction to the famous German romantic writer Johann Wolfgang von Goethe, Thackeray returned to England to pursue the social life of a well-to-do young man and try his hand at studying law.

An investment in a newspaper, which he came to edit, was Thackeray's first experience with the literary life. When the paper failed and his inheritance was lost through the collapse of an Indian bank, Thackeray launched a career as a professional writer, contributing to *Fraser's Magazine*, the *Morning Chronicle*, and the esteemed satirical journal *Punch*. In 1836 he married Isabella Shawe, who later suffered from mental illnesses and was eventually confined to an asylum.

From the mid-1830s through mid-1840s Thackeray under various pen names produced satires and comic pieces, including *Catherine* (1839–40), a parody of NEWGATE CRIME NOVELS, and *The Book of Snobs* (1846–47), which was reprinted in *Punch*. The latter chronicles the adventures of "Mr. Snob," as he encounters characters who exhibit an amusing variety of snobbish behaviors. Thackeray also wrote travel literature about Paris, London, and Cairo.

With *Vanity Fair*, published in installments in 1846 and 1847, Thackeray became a popular success. Whereas Thackeray's earlier writings were not as well received by critics or readers as CHARLES DICKENS's first major publications, *Vanity Fair* established Thackeray as Dickens's major rival. With his next novel, *Pendennis* (1849–50), Thackeray went head-to-head with Dickens, whose *David Copperfield* was appearing simultaneously. Like Dickens's novel, Thackeray's was semiautobiographical.

The composition of *Pendennis* was interrupted for several months while Thackeray recovered from cholera. But during that period he also composed *Rebecca and Rowena*, a revision of SIR WALTER SCOTT's novel of the Middle Ages, *Ivanhoe*. In Thackeray's version Ivanhoe ends up not with the conventional fairy-tale heroine, Rowena, but with the more exotic and adventuresome Jewish woman, Rebecca. In his next novel, *The History of Henry Esmond* (1852), Thackeray would further demonstrate his skills as a historical novelist, this time choosing an 18th-century setting.

In 1852 Thackeray undertook a tour of America, lecturing on English humorists, including the 18th-century satirists Jonathan Swift and Lawrence Sterne. Disturbed by slavery, Thackeray nonetheless generally reported a positive impression of the United States.

Upon his return Thackeray began publishing in installments another novel, *The Newcomes* (1852–53), narrated by Arthur Pendennis. The Newcomes are a family of social climbers, whom Thackeray satirizes.

Thackeray returned to his own passion, history, with his next novel, a revision of an earlier periodical series, now titled *The Memoir of Barry Lyndon* (1856). This novel, like *Henry Esmond,* is set in the 18th century. Lyndon, the despicable character who narrates the novel, is a paid soldier in various armies, tries to make his fortune by marriage, but after treating his wife cruelly, dies in prison. After an unsuccessful run for Parliament, Thackeray next turned to an American subject in *The Virginians* (1857–58). This novel takes up where *Henry Esmond* left off, in colonial New England. Its principal characters are Henry Esmond's two grandsons, who fight on opposing sides in the American Revolution.

By the 1850s Thackeray's rivalry with Dickens had blossomed into vigorous, though amicable, literary disputes carried on in the periodical press. However, an all-out feud erupted when Thackeray publicly mentioned Dickens's affair with the actress Ellen Ternan. In 1860 Thackeray was offered an opportunity that would allow him to challenge Dickens on another front. Dickens influenced literary tastes and authors' careers as a periodical editor. Now, however, Thackeray became an editor as well of the newly founded *Cornhill Magazine,* aimed at a somewhat more sophisticated audience than were Dickens's periodicals. Quickly *Cornhill* achieved record circulation figures, and the two editor-novelists competed for work by the best authors of the day, while enjoying mass-circulation outlets for their own writing. In the end, Thackeray published only one novel in *Cornhill*—*The Adventures of Philip* (1861–62)—before resigning his editorship. The early numbers of *Denis Duval* (1864), which Thackeray failed to complete before his death, were published posthumously in *Cornhill.* But he was able to see into print in the magazine *The Story of Elizabeth,* the first novel by his daughter, ANNE THACKERAY RITCHIE.

Despite Isabella Thackeray's illness and his own intense work habits, Thackeray managed to be a good parent, as Anne Thackeray Ritchie testified in biographical introductions to her father's works. He had also been a friend of many writers, including ELIZABETH BARRETT BROWNING and CHARLOTTE BRONTË. Thackeray died suddenly on Christmas Eve, 1863, and although he was not buried in Westminster Abbey, as Dickens would be, he was mourned by thousands.

Thackeray's works hearken back to earlier fictional modes but also anticipate some postmodern literary techniques. The critic James Phelan argues that Thackeray's narrative voices are "characteristically complex" and reward attention from "rhetorical and feminist perspectives [which] usefully complicate our responses to Thackeray's achievement." Whatever the fluctuations in literary tastes, appreciative readers of Thackeray can concur with Anne Thackeray Ritchie, writing in her 1910 introduction to *Vanity Fair,* that he has earned "rest after effort, the immense happiness of good work achieved."

Critical Analysis

Showing signs of its author's experience as a journalist, *Vanity Fair* is filled with historical references and topical satires. Thackeray's Victorian masterpiece came just on the other side of the watershed constituted by such novels as *Jane Eyre* (published in the same year) and *David Copperfield* (1850). These novels created a taste for more complex characterization and coherent plotting and by contrast *Vanity Fair* can seem old-fashioned. Its setting during the early decades of the 19th century intensifies this impression. Furthermore, compared with the sentimental response Dickens elicited for his characters, Thackeray's stance in his "Novel Without a Hero," as *Vanity Fair* is subtitled, may appear unfeelingly satirical. However, the novel includes such unforgettable characters as the cynically opportunistic Becky Sharp and the faithful Captain Dobbin. Indeed, Thackeray's unsentimental attacks on social climbing, romantic delusions, and commercial calculation anticipate the satires of such 20th-century novelists as Kingsley Amis or Fay Weldon. The novel also reveals a good deal about Victorian England and its empire. Finally, Thackeray provided his own wonderful comic illustrations for this novel, as well as others.

If *Vanity Fair* seems old-fashioned to readers who have been introduced to Victorian fiction through Dickens or GEORGE ELIOT, *Henry Esmond* is self-consciously so. It is set in the early 18th century and includes such historical personages as the founders of the *Spectator,* Joseph Addison and Richard Steele. Addison and Steele created literary journalism, and although they are minor characters in the novel, Thackeray's satirical and urbane literary voice is modeled on their style. Even in the format of its publication—a three-volume bound edition, instead of the Victorian format of installments followed by a complete volume—*Henry Esmond* announced its affiliation with an earlier era and a waning sensibility. The novel is a remarkable feat of historical imagination, not merely placing a fictional story within a historical context, but reproducing 18th-century figures of speech and employing scrupulously accurate historical detail. In this respect *Henry Esmond* recalls some of the great literary forgeries, such as the epic poems of Ossian, an 18th-century creation by James Macpherson (1736–96) that purported to be a medieval text.

In *The Newcomes* only one of the three Newcome sons exhibits a passion for anything except money and prestige, with the other two marrying to enhance their social standing. Yet even the sorts of romantic desires for true love and a happy family, ultimately indulged in most of Dickens's plots, are wholly thwarted here, even when a son of the next generation chooses his wife to please his honorable father. Virtue is not, in Thackeray's world, rewarded with happiness.

Works about William Makepeace Thackeray
Bloom, Harold, ed. *William Makepeace Thackeray.* New York: Chelsea House, 1987.
Harden, Edgar F. *Thackeray the Writer.* New York: St. Martin's Press, 2000.
Monsarrat, Ann. *An Uneasy Victorian: Thackeray the Man.* New York: Dodd, Mead, 1980.
Taylor, D. J. *Thackeray: The Life of a Literary Man.* New York: Carroll & Graf, 2001.

Thompson, Francis (1859–1907) poet

Francis Thompson was born into the Roman Catholic family of Charles Thompson and his wife, Mary Morton Thompson, in Preston, Lancashire, England. To please his father, after studying at Ushaw College, he enrolled at Owens College, Manchester, to study medicine, but he failed the final exams three times in six years, and at 25 he moved to London.

Impoverished, homeless, and addicted to opium, he scribbled poems on the back of sugar packaging. Eventually he submitted a few poems and an essay to a magazine called *Merry England,* whose editors, the poet ALICE MEYNELL and her husband Wilfred, took an interest in Thompson. Thompson became close to the Meynells, who found him a place to live. Under their tutelage, he published critical articles in the literary magazines the *Academy* and the *Athenaeum* and made friends with other writers.

Thompson published three books of poetry: *Poems* (1893), which he dedicated to the Meynells; *Sister Songs* (1895); and *New Poems* (1897). Of his verse, ARTHUR SYMONS wrote that "The spectacle of him was an enchantment; he passed like a wild vagabond of the mind, dazzling our sight. . . . He had no message." The 1893 "Making of Viola" certainly dazzles with "Spin, daughter Mary, spin, / Twirl your wheel with silver din" and "Weave, hands angelical, / Weave a wool of flesh to pall."

Thompson's most famous and most thoughtful poem is "The Hound of Heaven" (1893). Dealing with the often antagonistic relationship between man and God, the poem opens with a fearful soul in flight from God, just like a rabbit runs from a hound:

> *I fled Him, down the nights and down the days;*
> *I fled Him, down the arches of the years;*
> *I fled Him, down the labyrinthine ways*
> *Of my own mind.*

In the end the hound corners the soul, but not to offer death, rather divine love, saying: "Whom wilt thou find to love . . . thee? / Save Me, save only Me!"

Thompson died of opium addiction and tuberculosis before he was 50. The critic B. Ifor Evans writes, "In judging Thompson one is driven to judge him by the standard of the great writers, Donne, Crashaw, Coleridge, Shelley. Such were his models . . . and sometimes, though rarely, he has an original quality, not unlike that of the masters he imitated."

Critical Analysis

Both a devout Catholic and a drug addict, Francis Thompson was a figure with many contradictions, and this extended to his poetry and its reception. For one thing, although he is often classified as a minor poet, some critics argue that he is, in fact, the greatest Roman Catholic poet of post-Reformation Britain, a designation that most would apply instead to GERARD MANLEY HOPKINS. For another, although he turned to his deep faith and Catholic education for inspiration in most of his poetry, he also developed striking imagery and themes that reached beyond Catholic symbolism to create a unique vision.

Thompson's poetry is considered excessively ornate by today's standards; he relies on dense, highly elaborate metaphors in many of his works, most of which deal with religious experiences and spiritual suffering. While his favored form is the ode, the loftiness of his tone frequently gives his work an almost epic feel. More than anything, Thompson's poems come across as deeply felt and lyrical, in contrast with the more intellectual, reserved, and ironic verse that came to dominate the British scene in the decades following his death. Because of this change in tastes, Thompson's work has been neglected for many years.

Nevertheless, several of Thompson's poems are generally if not universally acknowledged to be great. "The Hound of Heaven" is the most highly regarded of these; it describes the harrowing chase the human soul experiences in life, pursued by a divine force that is revealed as Love, though it is also meant to be understood as God. The lack of identifying titles in the poem, however, makes the spiritual experience it depicts universal rather than specifically Christian, as does the poem's overarching metaphor of a divine love hunting the spirit.

Pursued by the Hound of Heaven the speaker, exhausted, offers images of his own ruin: "I stand amid the dust o' the mounded years—/ My mangled youth lies dead beneath the heap. / My days have crackled and gone up in smoke, / Have puffed and burst as sun-starts on a stream." He confronts his pursuer about the necessity of death ("Ah! must Thou char the wood ere Thou canst limn [draw] with it?" and, later, ". . . must Thy harvest-fields / Be dunged with rotten death?") before he realizes the transformative, unconditional love of the divine "hound," finding that this love was all along synonymous with self-love of the deepest kind.

When the poem first appeared in the July 1890 issue of *Merry England,* it helped solidify Thompson's reputation as a significant poet. It was included in his first collection, *Poems,* in 1893. Another of his poems, "In No Strange Land," perhaps the last he wrote and certainly one that stands in stark contrast with "The Hound of Heaven," expresses a similar notion of the closeness and ubiquity of divine love: "The drift of pinions, would we hearken, / Beats at our own clay-shuttered doors." At the poem's end, the speaker exhorts his soul, "my daughter," to heed this message, to see Jesus Christ walking on the water, "Not of Genesareth, but Thames!" The images in this much shorter poem (it consists of six strictly-rhymed quatrains) are deftly controlled and better harmonized than those in Thompson's earlier works.

Today, many critics agree that Thompson's greatest poetic gift was his ability to produce original images, some of them worthy of major poets such as TENNYSON, KEATS, and Shakespeare, but that Thompson lacked the discipline and ear to employ these to their greatest potential. Also, although it is proper not to forget that in his time Thompson was an influential leader among Catholic poets, his work ultimately does not evince the same inventiveness of language and sound as that of his contemporary, Hopkins. Nevertheless, some critics argue that Thompson's body of work is more impressive and worthy of attention than the critical consensus has so far deemed.

Thomson, James (Bysshe Vanolis) (B. V.)
(1834–1882) *poet, essayist*

Born to Sarah Kennedy and James Thomson, a sailor in the merchant service, in Port Glasgow, Scotland, James Thomson was an orphan by age eight. (His father lived 10 more years, but was completely paralyzed from a stroke.) The Royal Caledonian Asylum, a school for children of the Scottish poor, was Thomson's home for the next eight years. In 1852, working as a teacher's assistant in Ireland, Thomson became engaged to the 13-year-old Matilda Weller, who soon died. In 1854 he enlisted as an army schoolmaster. Following several teaching assignments, he was demoted and in 1862 was discharged from the army owing to alcoholism. For the next 20 years he subsidized his writing with a variety of jobs, mostly secretarial.

Thomson wrote under the pseudonym Bysshe Vanolis, or B.V., in honor of two romantics: the English poet PERCY BYSSHE SHELLEY, and the Prussian Saxon (German) poet and novelist Novalis (the pseudonym of Friedrich Leopold, Baron von Hardenberg).

The loss of his fiancée and his father in the same year deepened Thomson's pessimism. Moreover, Thomson was an atheist; he had lost his faith in part because of the death of his mother, a devoutly religious person.

Thomson's masterpiece, *The City of Dreadful Night*, first appeared in the workers' weekly *National Reformer* (1874) and again in *The City of Dreadful Night and Other Poems* (1880). Recalling the harsh prophetic tone and contemporary commentary of ALFRED, LORD TENNYSON's *Maud* 10 years earlier, the poem negates Victorian optimism and faith in human progress, offering instead a vision of spiritual bankruptcy amidst dehumanizing urban growth and urban consciousness: "The City is of Night, but not of Sleep; / . . . The pitiless hours like years and ages creep, / A night seems termless hell. . . ."

Prefacing the poem are lines from Giacomo Leopardi, the early-19th-century Italian poet, whose pessimism appealed to Thomson. Leopardi believed that misery is the only human certainty. Nearly a half century after Thomson's death, G. H. Gerould called *The City of Dreadful Night* "the most faithful and magnificent expression of the spirit of despair in all modern poetry."

Other work by James Thomson
The Poetical Works of James Thomson, Vol. I. Temecula, Calif.: Reprint Services Corp., 1992.

Works about James Thomson
Paolucci, Henry. *James Thomson's the City of Dreadful Night: A Study of the Cultural Resources of Its Author and a Reappraisal of the Poem*. Bergenfield, N.J.: Griffon House, 2000.

Singh, Gurdit. *Visions of James Thomson ("B.V."): An Exploration*. Boston: Brill Academic, 1980.

Tighe, Mary (1772–1810) *poet*

Mary Tighe, née Blachford, was born in Dublin, Ireland, to William Blachford, a clergyman, and Theodosia Tighe Blachford. Mary's father died when she was a child, and her mother educated her at home. In 1793 Mary married her cousin, Henry Tighe. Two years later she wrote the poem that made her a celebrated poet in England: *Psyche; or, The Legend of Love*. Based on the story of Psyche and Cupid from Greek mythology, it is an allegory of Love and the Soul. The poem is written in elegant Spenserian stanzas, the form the 16th-century poet Edmund Spenser invented for his famous allegory *The Faerie Queene*. Tighe's work, with its poetic language and deep feeling, is thought to have been a major influence on early romantic poetry. Many critics have observed similarities between Tighe's imagery and that of JOHN KEATS, who admired her work.

In 1803 Tighe developed tuberculosis, which was incurable at the time. The manuscript of *Psyche* had been privately circulated among friends, poets, and other readers for a decade, but it was not published until 1805. It was so remarkably successful that she was able to donate money from her earnings to build an addition to an orphanage. The poem remained popular throughout much of the 19th century. Tighe died at age 37. A collection of her other poems and "wild" Irish ballads was published in 1811, a year after her death.

Other Work by Mary Tighe

Psyche, with Other Poems. New York: Woodstock Books, 1992.

Todhunter, John (1839–1916) *poet, playwright*

John Todhunter was born in Dublin, Ireland. He studied medicine for five years at Trinity College in Dublin, graduating in 1867. He continued his studies in Vienna and returned home to open a medical practice. In 1870 he married Katherine Ball. By 1872, however, partly because of the success of his essay "A Theory of the Beautiful," published in that year, Todhunter had decided to abandon medicine and become a professor of English literature in Dublin. In 1875 he moved to London, where he helped found the Irish Literary Society. Following the death of his first wife, Todhunter married Dora Louise Digby in 1879, with whom he had three children.

During the 1870s, Todhunter began publishing poetry, including *Laurella and Other Poems* (1876) and *Alcestis* (1879). His poetry is consciously full of Irish themes and rhythms, as in "Maureen":

> O, you plant the pain in my heart with
>   your wistful eyes,
> Girl of my choice, Maureen!
> Will you drive me mad for the kisses your
>   shy, sweet mouth denies,
> Maureen?

His poem "Golgotha" reflects the Victorian pain over the loss of confidence in religious faith, when the poet, addressing Christ on the cross, asks, "Thou didst bear the sins of mortals, / Who shall bear the sins of God?" Other volumes include *Forest Songs and Other Poems* (1881) and *The Banshee and Other Poems* (1888). Todhunter also wrote plays, such as *Helena in Troas*, produced in London in 1886 with the great Herbert Beerbohm-Tree in the lead; *A Sicilian Idyll* (1890); and *The Black Cat* (1893). He is thought to have influenced the dramatic work of his friend William Butler Yeats.

Tonna, Charlotte Elizabeth (1790–1846) *novelist*

Charlotte Browne was born in Norwich, in eastern England. Her father, Michael Browne, was an Anglican clergyman. At age 23 she married George Phelan, a British army officer, but after 11 years of marriage the couple separated. Following her husband's death in 1837, she married Lewis Tonna, a writer, in 1841. Beginning in the 1820s, Charlotte wrote novels that addressed social problems in an effort to bring about reform. Her book *The System* (1827), for example, is about the evils of slavery. She deplored many of the consequences of industrialization and the moral decay that she believed it had caused. Her best-known novel, *Helen Fleetwood: Tale of Factories* (1841), told the story of a family forced to move from the country to a manufacturing town. Its depiction of the harsh conditions of 19th-century factories was influential in passing the 1844 Factory Act, which limited women's workdays to 12 hours. Other novels in which Tonna especially protested oppressive working conditions for women include *Perils of the Nation* (1843) and *The Wrongs of Woman* (1843–44). Tonna also wrote religious-historical novels, such as *The Rockite* (1829), and worked as an evangelical editor for the *Christian Lady's Magazine* and the *Protestant Magazine*. Her political and religious convictions, which fueled the social-protest fiction she wrote, were fervent and extreme. Harriet Beecher Stowe described her as "a woman of strong mind and powerful feeling."

Trelawney, Edward John (1792–1881)
memoirist

Edward Trelawney was born in London to Charles Trelawney, a poverty-stricken officer in the Coldstream Guards, and Mary Hawkins, whose main attraction, her son later said, was her money. Trelawney was indifferently educated and his father sent him to sea at age 12 as a midshipman. Six years and 10 different ships later, Trelawney was discharged with no money and no prospects. Over the next several years Trelawney educated himself by reading voraciously, particularly of the works of LORD BYRON. Traveling on the Continent, he eventually became a friend to Byron and PERCY BYSSHE SHELLEY.

Upon Trelawney's return to England, he turned to writing. In 1831 he published *Adventures of a Younger Son,* supposedly an account of his adventures in Europe. Although he presented the work as a memoir, Trelawney borrowed incidents for the work from the lives of friends and from books in order to make his story more romantic, exciting, and self-aggrandizing. He recounts a series of adventures in which he inevitably emerges as the hero: "Suspecting, which was the case, that the chief was waiting for a reinforcement to attack us, and fearing, from the rising commotion without-outside, they had already arrived, and would, whilst my men were under the paralysing effect of the poison, rush in and butcher us, or fire the huts, and slaughter us as we attempted to escape, I drew a pistol, sprang up, and attempted to gain the entrance."

In 1858 Trelawney brought out *Recollections of the Last Days of Shelley and Byron,* which was revised and expanded as *Records of Byron, Shelley and the Author* (1878). Neither version is considered by most literary historians to be either good or accurate. The critic William St. Clair, for example, complains, "To the historian or biographer, Trelawney is an intensely irritating figure because of his uncomfortable habit of telling lies about everything he did." Despite their dubious claims to truth, Trelawney's memoirs make for fascinating reading. As a recent biographer, David Crane, writes, "the more he is discredited as a chronicler of his own deeds, the more distinctly he is seen as an imaginative artist of compelling power."

A Work about Edward Trelawney
Crane, David. *Lord Byron's Jackal.* London: HarperCollins, 1998.

Trimmer, Sarah Kirby (1741–1811)
children's book writer, educational writer

Sarah Trimmer, née Kirby, was born in Ipswich, Essex, in southern England, to John Kirby, an artist, and Sarah Bull. At age 21 she married James Trimmer, a brickmaker. They had 12 children, all of whom she educated at home. Trimmer, who began writing stories for her own children, was one of the first and most prolific children's authors. In the 1780s she published lessons (in narrative form) in English history, Roman history, and biblical history, which became classics. Her guides for teaching at home, such as *An Easy Introduction to the Knowledge of Nature and Reading Holy Scriptures* (1780), were extremely popular and were used well into the 19th century. Her most famous children's book was the *Fabulous Histories* (1786)—(sometimes known as *The History of the Robins*)—which promoted kindness to animals.

Its story of a group of children who care for a nest of baby robins was intended to teach by example. Trimmer established Sunday schools for poor children and dedicated herself to their education. She began the *Family Magazine,* for which she wrote more exemplary tales (stories that are meant to set a moral example), such as *The Servant's Friend* (1787) and *The Two Farmers* (1787). From 1802 until 1806 she also published the *Guardian of Education,* a periodical that provided critiques of children's books for parents.

Trollope, Anthony (1815–1882) *novelist*

Anthony Trollope was one of the most prolific of the many prolific Victorian novelists, author of 47 novels, an autobiography, and many other works, who wrote five pages a day while working for the Post Office from 1834 to 1867. Trollope was born in London to Thomas Anthony, a failed barrister, and FRANCES (née Milton) TROLLOPE, who took to writing in order to keep her family out of debtors' prison. Trollope was educated at a series of schools, including Harrow and Winchester, where he was intimidated by his wealthier and more sophisticated schoolmates.

Trollope secured a low-level clerkship with the Post Office in 1834 and worked in London until 1841, when he was transferred to Ireland. There, among other things, he developed a lifelong passion for fox hunting, which he would endeavor to incorporate into each of his novels. After marrying Rose Heseltine in 1844, he began work on a series of novels, including *The Macdermots of Ballycloran* (1847) and *The Kellys and the O'Kellys* (1848), that addressed the causes of Irish suffering.

The first of his so-called Barchester novels, *The Warden* (1855), was begun on a Post Office assignment to the west of England. *The Chronicles of Barsetshire* would eventually include three novels: *The Warden, Barchester Towers* (1857), and *The Last Chronicle of Barset* (1867). Another novel in a related vein was *Framley Parsonage,* which began serialization under WILLIAM THACKERAY's editorship of the *Cornhill* magazine in 1860. These novels trace the lives of a constellation of largely clerical characters and their families within a fictional western England village.

These were not the only novels Trollope was writing in the 1850s and 1860s, nor was novel writing Trollope's only occupation. Steadily promoted into administrative positions, he undertook many other trips for the Post Office, including visits to Egypt and the West Indies. In 1859 he settled his family in Waltham Cross, just outside London. In 1861 his literary success earned him election to the Garrick Club, where CHARLES DICKENS, Thackeray, and other famous writers and theater celebrities were members. The popularity of his novels led to solicitations from editors and publishers, and he enjoyed financial security and a wide circle of friends, including GEORGE ELIOT.

Trollope considered his 1862 novel *Orley Farm* to be his best because of its carefully constructed plot. In two separate trials, a woman is acquitted of a crime the juries believe she has actually committed.

In 1864 Trollope embarked on his Palliser novels, a six-novel series treating the relationships between private, family life and Parliamentary politics. The most brilliant creation of the Palliser novels, Lady Glencora Palliser, sparkles in several novels with her fiery independence, youthful enthusiasms, and, eventually, mature charm. The novels in the series are *Can You Forgive Her?* (1864), *Phineas Finn* (1869), *The Eustace Diamonds* (1873), *Phineas Redux* (1874), *The Prime Minister* (1876), and *The Duke's Children* (1880).

From 1876 to 1880 Trollope took a break from the Palliser series, but not from novel writing. Among the many additional novels he wrote in these years, the standout is *The Way We Live Now* (1875). Although Victorian readers were surprised by its bitter satire, many modern critics consider it to be Trollope's finest novel.

Between the last Palliser novel in 1880 and his death in 1882 Trollope finished 10 more novels, four of which were published posthumously, plus several other literary works. Another posthumously published work was Trollope's autobiography, an absorbing chronicle of the life of an author and public servant. Along with this considerable literary legacy, Trollope invented the pillar box—the British post box—a design still used today.

Critical Analysis

Along with their send-ups of pompous, scheming, and unctuous clergymen and their family members, the Barchester novels also offer depictions of honorable (generally humble) people, notably the much-abused warden of the first novel, Mr. Harding. In *The Warden* (1855) Trollope satirizes the reforming press, a theme he would pursue in the Palliser novels. John Bold solicits the aid of his newspaper friends to expose as an example of corruption in the Church of England a small income bestowed on Mr. Harding to tend to some poor men in a hospital. The gentle Mr. Harding finds himself caught between Bold and the conservative Archdeacon Grantly, his son-in-law. Like most reform schemes in Trollope's novels, this one causes the maximum damage, with no benefits: Mr. Harding loses his position, the poor men he cared for are left untended, and the hospital falls into ruins. *The Last Chronicle of Barset* again treats the theme of wrongful accusation, this time against the curate, Josiah Crawley, who is suspected of having stolen a check. The bishop's wife, Mrs. Proudie, a domineering figure in the series, publicly condemns Crawley, but before she can do permanent damage she dies of a heart attack.

Orley Farm addresses a contrasting case, wherein Lady Mason, actually guilty of a crime, is twice acquitted. Lady Mason's forged addendum to her husband's will left one farm to their son, while the original will had left all his property to the son of his first marriage. Trollope makes clear that the defense lawyer in the second trial, and probably the judge and jury as well, believe Lady Mason to be guilty, but they acquit her anyway. The motives of the jury are left a mystery, but Trollope's narrator confesses his sympathy for this character of his own creation, despite her illegal acts.

The Palliser novels weave parliamentary politics, money, and love into a complex web of characters' desires and disappointments. Like the Barchester novels, these volumes balance probing satire with models of faithfulness and integrity. In the first book, *Can You Forgive Her?* (1864), Alice Vavasor rejects a solid but unromantic suitor in favor of her dashing cousin. She realizes her mistake when she becomes aware of the cousin's unscrupulous behavior, which includes a bid for Parliament motivated only by a desire for money.

The next novel in the series, *Phineas Finn* (1869), introduces another notable character, drawn from Trollope's experience in Ireland. Phineas Finn manages to get himself elected to Parliament from his native Ireland. His motives are hardly altruistic and he exhibits considerable political naïveté, but in the course of this novel and *Phineas Redux* (1874), he grows into one of the series' most admirable and appealing figures. This novel also develops the character of Plantagenet Palliser, the aristocrat whom Glencora is forced to marry instead of her ne'er-do-well first love. Here, he is a dutiful cabinet minister, by turns fascinated and shocked by his beautiful and willful wife. In the course of the series, he, too, is allowed to grow on the reader, as he grows on Lady Glencora. Eventually, he becomes prime minister of England, but power sits awkwardly on this quiet man of principle.

In *Phineas Redux* Trollope features another stunning female character, the exotic Madame Max Goesler, as well as one of his most repulsive creations, the unscrupulous journalist Quintus Slide. Phineas is accused of murder, and the same firm that defended Lady Mason defends him. Although the lawyer Chaffenbrass wrongly believes Phineas to be guilty, he wins acquittal anyway, no thanks to Slide, who engages in a smear campaign against the hero. Phineas survives his ordeal to retain his seat in Parliament and to marry Madame Max.

Finally, with its theme of the pervasive corruption of human values by the profit motive, *The Way We Live Now,* one of Trollope's last novels, is the one present-day readers are likely to find most realistic. Like today's grim satires on stockbrokers, corporate executives, and people on the make, such as David Mamet's *Glengarry Glen Ross* (1984) or Tom Wolfe's *Bonfire of the Vanities* (1987), Trollope's novel presents a world in which money compromises everyone's ideals. Lady Carbury, whose financial difficulties have driven her to authorship, is thought by some critics to refer to Frances Trollope. At the center of the novel is the fraudulent financier Melmotte, a villain whose greed and duplicity would seem pathological were it not for his pathetic recognition that his power derives from nothing more substantial than the paper on which his worthless stocks and contracts are printed. When his schemes are exposed and he faces ruin, he kills himself.

Works about Anthony Trollope

Glendinning, Victoria. *Anthony Trollope*. New York: Alfred A. Knopf, 1993.

Hall, N. John. *Trollope: A Biography*. New York: Oxford University Press, 1991.

Super, R. H. *The Chronicler of Barsetshire: A Life of Anthony Trollope*. Ann Arbor: University of Michigan Press, 1988.

Trollope, Frances Milton (1779–1863)
novelist, travel writer

Frances "Fanny" Trollope, née Milton, was born near Bristol, England, to William Milton, a clergyman, and Frances Gresley, who died when Fanny was a child. She was educated at home by her father in languages, the arts, and the classics. After her father remarried, Fanny moved to London to serve as her brother Henry's housekeeper. In 1809, when she was almost 30, Fanny surprised her family by marrying Thomas Anthony Trollope, a lawyer. She had seven children in eight years—four sons and three daughters—among them the journalist THOMAS TROLLOPE and the novelist ANTHONY TROLLOPE. Her husband failed as a lawyer in London and as a farmer in Harrow, and after 18 years of marriage the Trollopes were on the brink of bankruptcy. In 1827, hoping to salvage the family's finances, Trollope and her husband sailed with their three youngest children to America, where they helped to found the utopian community of New Hope in Memphis, Tennessee. But New Hope was a failure, and after three years the family returned to London. Turning to writing as means of paying off her husband's debts Fanny Trollope, at 52, became the sole supporter of her family. She was an indefatigable writer, producing 114 books, including 34 novels, in her lifetime. Following the deaths of her husband in 1835 and her daughter Cecilia in 1838, Trollope settled in Florence, Italy, where she lived and continued to write until her death in 1863.

Trollope launched her writing career with an enormously successful travel book and portrait of a culture, *Domestic Manners of the Americans* (1832). Central to the book was her belief that the "the lamentable insignificance of the American woman" was the result not of economic necessity, but of a male hostility toward women that lurked just below the surface. Although upsetting to many American readers, her witty and somewhat critical portrait of the young nation ("I certainly believe the women of America to be the handsomest in the world, but as surely do I believe that they are the least attractive") was an immediate success in Britain and went through many editions in Britain and the Continent, as well as in America. Mark Twain was among those who admired the book, saying that *Domestic Manners* was "accurate enough to be called photography." Other similar travel books followed: *Belgium and Western Germany in 1833* (1834), *Paris and the Parisians* (1835), *Vienna and the Austrians* (1838), and *A Visit to Italy* (1842).

Although her travel books were a great success, the burden of moving her household to research each project caused her to turn to novel writing, work that would allow her to settle in one place. Her first successful novel, *The Vicar of Wrexhill* (1837), caused a sensation because its satire was considered too pointed for a lady. It sold well, and Trollope was paid £600 for her next novel, *The Widow Barnaby*. The new book's central character, Martha Barnaby, bears a resemblance to Trollope herself, but seen in a refreshingly unflattering light: Martha is energetic, ambitious, and crass. The reviewer for the London *Times* wrote, "Her vulgarity is sublime. Imaginary personage though she be, everybody who has read her memoirs must have a real interest in her.... Such a jovial, handsome, hideous, ogling, bustling monster of a woman as maid, wife, and widow, was never, as we can recollect, before brought upon the scene." Two sequels followed: *The Widow Married* (1840) and *The Barnabys in America* (1843).

Concerned with social reform, Trollope wrote several social problem novels. *The Life and Adventures of Jonathan Whitlaw* (1836) reflected her strong revulsion against American slavery in the story of a cruel overseer. Published 15 years before *Uncle Tom's Cabin*, Trollope's book anticipated the themes of Harriet Beecher Stowe's popular novel. *The Vicar of Wrexhill* (1837) attacked the unfortunate effects of evangelical excesses on women. Trollope argued for reform of child labor laws, including a 10-hour workday, in *Michael Armstrong, the Factory Boy* (1839). She joined her contemporaries CHARLES DICKENS (in *Oliver Twist*) and THOMAS CARLYLE (in *Past and Present*) in criticizing the New Poor Law in *Jessie Phillips: A Tale of the Present Day* (1843). Unlike Dickens and Carlyle, however, Trollope dealt directly in *Jesse Phillips* with the dire consequences of the New Poor Law's bastardy clauses, which effectively barred unmarried destitute mothers from claiming support from their babies' fathers. She was criticized for having "sinned grievously against good taste and decorum." In later works, such as *The Three Cousins* (1847), *The Lottery of Marriage: A Novel* (1849), and *The Young Heiress: A Novel* (1853), strong, independent-minded female protagonists are often in conflict with tyrannical fathers or weak husbands. Her last novel, *Fashionable Life; or, Paris and London* (1856), seemed to resolve the torments of her earlier female protagonists, offering instead the story of a community of women living together in harmony, peace, and cooperation.

Trollope was one of the most admired writers of her day. Her biographer Pamela Neville-Sington quotes a contemporary reviewer on Trollope's achievement: "Her people . . . talk as real men and women talk. . . . Hence they make upon the mind and the memory the same impressions as are made by personages whom we have known. They do not pass away with the closing of the book, as is usual with the characters to whom we are introduced in ordinary novels, but they form a part of the crowd of recollections that continually recur in after life, and as vividly as any of the forms that memory cherishes."

Works about Frances Trollope

Ayres, Brenda. *Frances Trollope and the Novel of Social Change.* Westport, Conn.: Greenwood Press, 2001.

Ellis, Linda A. *Frances Trollope's America.* New York: Peter Lang, 1993.

Heineman, Helen. *Three Victorians in the New World: Interpretations of the New World in the Works of Frances Trollope, Charles Dickens, and Anthony Trollope.* New York: Peter Lang, 1992.

Neville-Sington, Pamela. *Fanny Trollope: The Life and Adventures of a Clever Woman.* New York: Viking, 1998.

Ransom, Teresa. *Fanny Trollope: A Remarkable Life.* New York: St. Martin's Press, 1995.

Trollope, Thomas Adolphus (1810–1892) *novelist, essayist*

Thomas Trollope was born in London to FRANCES TROLLOPE and Thomas Anthony Trollope. His mother, Frances, began writing in her 50s to support the family and became well known as a novelist. His brother ANTHONY TROLLOPE was one of the great British novelists of the 19th century. As a teenager, Thomas Trollope spent three years in the United States with his parents and traveled throughout the country. After graduating from Oxford University in 1835, he became a teacher in Birmingham, England. After his father's death, however, he accompanied his mother on a trip to Italy and settled with her in Florence, where he decided to become a journalist. He married Theodosia Garrow, an essayist, in 1848, and their home in Florence became a literary gathering place for British writers such as ELIZABETH BARRETT BROWNING, CHARLES DICKENS, GEORGE ELIOT, and GEORGE HENRY LEWES. Trollope contributed to Dickens's *Household Words* and was the Italian correspondent for the London *Standard,* among other English newspapers. His books included travel books, such as *Impressions of a Wanderer in Italy, Switzerland, France, and Spain* (1850); histories, such as *A Decade of Italian Women* (1859); and novels, such as *Beppo the Conscript* (1864). His wife died in 1865, and a year later he married Frances Eleanor Ternan, also a writer. Thomas had neither his mother's commercial success nor his brother's literary talent, but he was an extremely disciplined writer who produced a steady stream of articles as a journalist and an estimated 60 books.

Tucker, Charlotte Maria (A.L.O.E., A Lady of England) (1821–1893) *novelist, short story writer*

Charlotte Maria Tucker, born in London to a senior civil servant, was educated largely at home. She became a prolific writer of novels and short stories for children, sometimes set in foreign locales, such as Italy and India (where she went as a missionary at age 54), in addition to her native England. Her works, which had strong fantasy elements, include *Wings and Stings* (1855), *Old Friends with New Faces* (1858), *The Giant Killer* (1868), and *The Story of a Needle* (1868).

In Tucker's popular first novel, *The Rambles of a Rat* (1854), the hero-narrator rat travels throughout the human city in which he lives, meeting runaway children, hamsters, and rat-hating sailors, along with his friend and fellow rat, Whiskerandos. In the end they settle in London, resolving to avoid adventures: "We loved adventures and getting out of them; and in some ways we are useful to the world . . . and our skins are useful to men. But Whiskerandos and I don't mean that our skins shall be useful for a long time."

Tucker drew upon the stories and atmosphere of India for her books *A Wreath of Indian Stories* (1876), *Pomegranates from the Punjab* (1878), and *Hours with Orientals* (1881). She combined history and religious tales in *Stories from the History of the Jews* (1872) and *A Life of Luther* (1873).

Turner, Charles Tennyson (1808–1879) *poet*

The older brother of ALFRED, LORD TENNYSON, Turner was born Charles Tennyson in Lincolnshire, England, where his father, George Clayton Tennyson, was rector of Somersby. His mother was Elizabeth Fytche. Turner grew up in genteel poverty. He began writing poetry at an early age. His first published volume, *Poems by Two Brothers* (1827), included poems by himself, Alfred, and a third brother, Frederick. Turner entered Cambridge University in 1828. In 1830 his first collection of sonnets appeared. Following his ordination in 1834, Turner became curate at Tealby, where he became addicted to opium. A year later, his paternal grandmother's brother Sam Turner died, bringing him an inheritance—this precipitated the name change—and a new, more rewarding post as vicar of Grasby. The following year, Turner married Louisa Sellwood, who suffered a nervous breakdown from the strain of curing her spouse of his drug habit. (Her sister, Emily, would marry Alfred Tennyson.) Other volumes of Turner's poems, almost exclusively sonnets, appeared in 1864, 1868, 1873, and (posthumously) 1880.

While much of Turner's poetry arises from his parish duties, he is finest at observing nature. For Turner, nature helps humanity to focus on God, as in "On the Eclipse of the Moon of October 1865" (1866): "One little noise of life remained—I heard / The train pause in the distance, then rush by, / Brawling and hushing, like some busy fly / That murmurs and then settles; nothing stirred /

Beside." Here, nature appears to purge the industrial age of its noisy distractions so that God remains accessible.

"The Steam Threshing Machine" (1868), a pair of sonnets respectively subtitled "With the Straw Carrier" and "Continued," expresses a similar contest, but between nature's purity and industry's smoke instead of silence and noise. The threshing machine, "the mighty engine," is "like a god," not, however, the god that modernity may take it to be. But nature is given precedence by its connection with the supernatural: ". . . ever rising on its mystic stair / . . . The straw of harvest . . . / Climbed, and fell over, in the murky air." Turner's work justifies the critic A. H. Japp's claim that it is marked by "simplicity, grace, and occasional sustained beauty of phrase."

Other Work by Charles Tennyson Turner

Pinion, Frank B., ed. *The Collected Sonnets of Charles Tennyson Turner.* New York: St. Martin's Press, 1988.

V

"V."
See CLIVE, CAROLINE.

Vanolis, Bysshe
See THOMSON, JAMES.

Vassa, Gustavas
See EQUIANO, OLAUDAH.

Victoria, queen of Great Britain, empress of India (1817–1901) diarist, letter writer

Because she reigned for 64 years and presided over England's greatest years as a world power, Victoria and the British Empire have been exhaustively studied and written about by historians. Yet, history aside, as a person Victoria lives for contemporary readers far more vividly than does any other monarch of her time because of her writings.

When she was born in 1819 her father, the duke of Kent, called her a "pocket Hercules," and although she never grew to physically imposing size, her will and stamina never flagged, despite the early death of her beloved husband Albert and the rigors of giving birth to nine children in 17 years. When she was born she was fifth in line to the throne, and thus was accorded little more education than any other well-bred girl of the time. She was exposed to a ladylike curriculum of reading, writing, and arithmetic, piano lessons, history (particularly church history), some Latin, and manners, but little else. She never developed into the intellectual marvel that England's other great queen, Elizabeth I, became, but she was a powerful symbol and exemplar of the virtues we have come to call Victorian. She sought and delighted in an early marriage to a man whom she adored almost beyond measure, and she bore him children whom she equally loved. Her loving qualities, as well as her literary style, are exemplified by the letter she wrote, two days after Albert's death, to her oldest daughter, the crown princess of Prussia:

> I will do all I can to follow out all his [Albert's] wishes—to live for you and for my duties. But how I, who leant on him for all and everything—without whom I did nothing, moved not a finger, arranged not a print or photograph, didn't put on a gown or bonnet if he didn't approve it shall be able to go on,

to live, to move, to help myself in difficult moments? . . . try to feel and think that I am living on with him, and that his pure and perfect spirit is guiding and leading me and inspiring me!

Her journals and letters comprise some 60 million words. At age 13 she began to keep a daily diary, in which she continued to write until the end of her life. She also turned out thousands of letters to friends, relatives, and other political figures. In addition, she wrote voluminously in her official political capacity—notes, memoranda, annotations, and the like regarding the affairs of her country, its government, and her subjects. As a constitutional monarch she could affect the affairs of government very little by direct order, yet she nevertheless wrote her opinions about such matters as free trade, religious tolerance, and constitutional government and never failed to let her prime ministers and counselors know exactly where she stood on issues of both great and small importance. At times, particularly when the prime minister and his followers were not to her liking, her intrusions into affairs of state did not have the effect that she wished. But she evidently enjoyed a good relationship with BENJAMIN DISRAELI when he was prime minister. One of her early 20th-century biographers, Lytton Strachey, describes such a situation: "When the cabinet met, the Prime Minister [Gladstone] . . . would open the proceedings by reading aloud the letters which he had received from the Queen upon the questions of the hour. . . . Not a single comment, of any kind, was ever hazarded; and, after a fitting pause, the Cabinet proceeded with the business of the day."

Yet her writings in general have elicited praise for their genuineness, innocence, and straightforwardness. "Undoubtedly," Strachey writes, "it was through her writings that she touched the heart of her public." Her writings are those of a queen, it is true, but also those of a loving wife, doting mother, and a woman who famously said, at age 12 when she was informed of the likelihood of her becoming queen, "I will be good."

Other than two volumes of her journals written on her vacations in the Scottish Highlands, no bound volumes of her writings were published in her lifetime. The journal left out almost all mention of affairs of state and politics, emphasizing, in the words of Adrienne Munich, "simple family pleasures," as in the following description from the journal of Victoria's and Albert's dress at a Torch Light Ball: "I wore a white bonnet, a gray watered silk, and (according to Highland fashion) my plaid scarf over my shoulder, and Albert his Highland dress, which he wears every evening." Because of such a self-presentation in her published journals and because of the volume of her correspondence and the number of those to whom she wrote, her personality was widely known and lovingly respected.

Other Work by Queen Victoria
Hibbert, Christopher, ed. *Queen Victoria in Her Letters and Journals: A Selection.* New York: Viking Penguin, 1985.

Works about Queen Victoria
Hibbert, Christopher. *Queen Victoria: A Personal History.* New York: Basic Books, 2001.
Munich, Adrienne. *Queen Victoria's Secrets.* New York: Columbia University Press, 1996.

Walford, Lucy (1845–1915) *novelist*

Lucy Colquhoun was born in Portobello, near Edinburgh, Scotland, to John Colquhoun, a well-off author and former army officer, and Frances Fuller-Maitland. She was educated at home by governesses and was an avid reader as a child. Lucy claimed that reading JANE AUSTEN's novels had an "abiding influence" over all her own "future efforts" as a writer. In 1869 she married Alfred Walford. The couple had seven children, but Lucy Walford still managed to write stories, which were published in the literary magazine *Blackwood's*. In 1874 she finished her first novel, *Mr. Smith, a Part of His Life*, a light domestic comedy that was a favorite of QUEEN VICTORIA's. Other novels followed, such as *The History of a Week* (1886), the story of three young girls, and humorous works such as *The Havoc of a Smile* (1890) and *The Mischief of Monica* (1892). She also became the London correspondent for the *New York Critic* and wrote for various magazines. Walford's autobiography, *Recollections of a Scottish Novelist*, was published in 1910.

Warburton, Eliot (1810–1852) *novelist, travel writer, historian*

Eliot Warburton was born in Galway, Ireland, to George Warburton and Anna Acton Warburton. After graduating from Cambridge University in 1833 he studied law, but he spent most of his life traveling and writing. He was a friend of ALEXANDER KINGLAKE, and Kinglake wrote his Middle Eastern travel book, *Eothen* (published anonymously in 1844), as a conversation with Warburton. Perhaps inspired by Kinglake, Warburton traveled throughout the Middle East in 1843 and wrote accounts of the places he visited for the *Dublin University Magazine*. In 1845 his articles were published as a book, *The Crescent and the Cross; or, Romance and Realities of Eastern Travel*, which became extremely popular for its vivid depictions of life in the Middle East. Warburton married Matilda Jane Grove in 1848, and the couple had two sons. Meanwhile, Warburton turned to history. A work about the followers of King Charles I during the English Civil War, *The Memoirs of Prince Rupert and The Cavaliers, with Their Private Correspondence*, appeared in 1849. A year later he published a novel about Ireland in the 17th century titled *Reginald Hastings: A Tale of the Troubles* (1849). In 1851 he edited the literary *Memoirs of Horace Walpole and His Contemporaries*. The following year, Warburton died when the ship on which he was traveling to Central America caught fire shortly after leaving England.

Ward, Mary (1851–1920) *novelist*

Mary Ward, née Arnold, was the granddaughter of Thomas Arnold, famed headmaster of Rugby, and the daughter of his second son, Thomas Arnold, a teacher, and Julia Sorrel Arnold. She was also the niece of Matthew Arnold, the poet, literary critic, and education reformer. Ward was sent to boarding school, where she entertained her schoolmates by spinning stories about knights and their ladies.

When Ward's father took a position at Oxford University she began a program of self-education, mainly in Spanish language and history. In 1872 she married an Oxford tutor, Humphry Ward, with whom she had three children.

Ward and her husband soon moved to London, where he became a literary critic and she met, among other notables, Henry James, who encouraged her to write novels. Her first major success, and the work for which she is known today, was *Robert Elsmere* (1888). William Gladstone, the four-time prime minister of Great Britain, wrote a lengthy and positive review of the work in the periodical *Nineteenth Century* titled "Robert Elsmere and the Battle of Belief."

The "battle" of Gladstone's title refers to the questioning of religious beliefs, church doctrine, and the truth and authority of the Bible among intellectuals. Robert Elsmere, an earnest young cleric and Oxford graduate, is married to Catherine Leyburn, herself an intellectual. Possessed of a comfortable living, Robert comes to doubt that merely performing his comfortable and conventional pastoral duties is true to the spirit of Christianity; he gives up his post, moves to the slums of London's East End, and sets up a commune where he works toward improving the lot of the poor. Elsmere's religious crisis is the central concern of the novel: "As to religious belief, everything was a chaos. What might be to him the ultimate forms and condition of thought, the tired mind was quite incapable of divining."

Robert Elsmere established Ward as the leading female novelist of her time and, although none of her subsequent books was to garner comparable critical acclaim, her prolific energy allowed her to produce some 16 novels over the next 32 years, in addition to works of propaganda done in aid of Anglo-American unity against the Germans during World War I. Her later novels include *Helbeck of Bannisdale* (1898), the story of the love between a devout Catholic and a freethinking intellectual, and *Tressady* (1896), which argues in favor of improving working conditions in factories.

Despite being a leading female thinker of her age, Ward opposed women's suffrage and was a founder of the Anti-Suffrage League movement. She was active in founding a settlement house as well as childcare centers for the offspring of poor working mothers. Although her novels have fallen out of favor and out of print, Ward's biographer John Sutherland notes her earlier importance: "By 1905 Mrs. Humphry Ward could plausibly claim to be the most famous living novelist in the world."

A Work about Mary Ward
Sutherland, John. *Mrs. Humphry Ward: Eminent Victorian/Pre-Eminent Edwardian.* New York: Oxford University Press, 1990.

Watson, John William (1858–1935) *poet*

William Watson was born just outside Leeds, in the north of England, to Dorothy Robinson and John Watson, a shopkeeper. In 1861 the family moved to Liverpool, where Watson was privately tutored. By 1876 he was contributing to the weekly magazine the *Argus*.

Watson's first book of poems was *The Prince's Quest* (1880). Although the title poem is more of a stylistic exercise than a deeply felt piece ("... grass / Grew now where once the flowers, and hard by / A many-throated fountain had run dry"), it shows the influence of Lord Byron and Percy Bysshe Shelley, as well as of John Keats, Dante Gabriel Rossetti, Alfred, Lord Tennyson, and Matthew Arnold.

Beginning in 1881, Watson suffered several nervous breakdowns. His poem "World-Strangeness" (1881) conveys the emotional distress that dogged him: "In this house with starry dome . . . / Shall I never feel at home, / Never wholly be at ease?" William Butler Yeats responded sympathetically to this "expression of a sensitive nature and of its trouble over the riddle of things, a nature that is refined, inquiring, subtle—everything but believing."

Watson's next major poem attracted scant notice until it reappeared as the title poem of the book *Wordsworth's Grave* (1890) three years after its initial publication. Written 37 years after WILLIAM WORDSWORTH's death, the poem, Watson's biographer Jean Moorcroft Wilson has noted, "is unlike most English elegies in giving no sense of immediate loss, either public or private . . . [or] any meditation on death." Instead, it focuses on poetry and poets. Esteeming Wordsworth's wholesomeness and latter-day calm ("Men turned to thee and found—not blast and blaze, / Tumult of tottering heavens, but peace on earth"), Watson contrasts Wordsworth's "lofty song of lowly weal and dole" to the "empty music" of CHARLES ALGERNON SWINBURNE and other "idly tuneful" contemporaries. A reviewer, Grant Allen, found the piece "delicately-finished . . . not hysterical or overwrought, after the common modern fashion, not involved or enigmatical, but subdued, terse, graceful . . . and clear as crystal." Watson's career took off.

Occasioned by Tennyson's death, "Lachrymae Musarum" (1892) is, in its portrayal of a grieving nation, a more traditional elegy: "With wandering sighs of forest and of wave / Mingles the murmur of a people's grief / For him. . . ." "England, My Mother" (1892) and "Ode on the Day of the Coronation of King Edward VII" (1902) also helped establish Watson's reputation as a national poet. In 1917 he was knighted.

Watson is little read today. As the critic John Churton Collins has noted, Watson's work has "limited and unambitious range, . . . comparatively few notes, . . . persistent threnody [lamentations], . . . joyless agnosticism, . . . [and] thin and uncertain ethic."

Watts-Dunton, Theodore (1832–1914)
poet and novelist

Theodore Watts-Dunton was born Walter Theodore Watts in St. Ives, Huntingdonshire, on October 12, 1832, to John King Watts and Susannah Dunton. (He added his mother's surname to his own in 1896.) He attended Cambridge, where he studied literature and science; he also spent a good deal of time outdoors.

Watts-Dunton became a solicitor like his father and practiced law in London, where his brother introduced him to primarily Pre-Raphaelite circles of poets and artists which included DANTE GABRIEL ROSSETTI, A. C. SWINBURNE, and GEORGE BORROW. Watts-Dunton soon gave up law and began writing criticism for the *Examiner* in 1874, as well as poetry, contributed anonymously, for *Anthenaeum* in 1876. Many of his poems explored the life of gypsies, who had fascinated Watts-Dunton since his childhood; most of these poems were collected in *The Coming of Love* in 1897, which failed to garner critical acclaim, although the poems published in *Anthenaeum* were widely admired when they first appeared. Watts-Dunton himself described them as "too formless to have other than an ephemeral life."

Watts-Dunton did score a popular success in 1898 with his novel *Aylwin,* in which he blended Celtic mysticism, a talent for scenic description, and gypsy characters of the kind appearing in his poetry in a romantic story of lovers separated by a gnostic curse.

More than for his literary efforts, however, Watts-Dunton is notable for his critical work. He wrote a highly regarded article on Poetry for the ninth edition of the *Encyclopaedia Britannica* in 1885, and in 1916 published *Old Familiar Faces,* a book of literary sketches of artists he knew that also contained an essay encapsulating his view of poetry, "The Renascence of Wonder in English Poetry." In it, he defends the romantic movement and criticizes materialism.

Watts-Dunton was a devoted friend as well as critic, using his articles to promote the careers of poets such as GEORGE MEREDITH. He was particularly supportive of Swinburne, for whom he acted as de facto literary agent as well as host from 1879 until Swinburne's death in 1909. His support of Swinburne was criticized for its apparent stifling effect on the poet's work, but Watts-Dunton convinced his friend to give up drinking, thus prolonging his life and lifting him out of the misery in which he had been mired since 1877.

Watts-Dunton married Clara Jane Reich in 1905, but they had no children. On June 6, 1914, he died at the Pines, his quiet home in Putney.

Other Works by Theodore Watts-Dunton

Christmas at the Mermaid. London: John Lane, 1902.
Henry Thoreau and Other Children of the Open Air. Cedar Rapids, Iowa: The Torch Press, 1910.
Vesprie Towers: A Novel. London: John Lane, 1917.

Works about Theodore Watts-Dunton

Douglas, James. *Theodore Watts-Dunton: Poet, Novelist, Critic.* New York: Haskell House Publishers, 1973.
Hake, Thomas, Arthur Compton-Rickett, and Clara Watts-Dunton. *The Life and Letters of Theodore Watts-Dunton.* New York: G.P. Putnam's Sons, 1916.
Panter-Downes, Mollie. *At the Pines: Swinburne and Watts-Dunton in Putney.* London: Hamilton, 1971.

Webster, Augusta (1837–1894) *poet, playwright*

Augusta Webster, née Davies, was born in the county of Dorset, in southwest England, to George Davies, a vice admiral in the navy, and Julia Hume. She was educated at the Cambridge School of Art and also studied in Paris and Geneva, Switzerland. Her first book of poetry, *Blanche Lisle and Other Poems,* was published in 1860 under the pen name Cecil Home. In 1863 she married Thomas Webster, a law professor at Cambridge University. They had one child. Webster wrote poems, plays, and essays, many on women's issues. She was also an accomplished translator of ancient Greek classics, publishing *The Prometheus Bound of Aeschylus* (1866) and *The Medea of Euripides* (1868). In 1866 she completed *Dramatic Studies,* a collection of dramatic monologues in blank verse, each in the voice of a different character, which were modeled on ROBERT BROWNING's famous poem *My Last Duchess.* A strong feminist, Webster was especially committed to women's suffrage and education. Many of her poems, such as *By the Looking Glass* (1866), about a spinster, "Woman enough to feel what it means / To be a woman and not be fair," and the more controversial *A Castaway* (1870), about a prostitute, comment on women's place in Victorian society. The realism and power of these works offended some of her contemporaries, but CHRISTINA ROSSETTI, among others, admired and imitated her. Webster also wrote plays, such as *Disguises* (1879) and her drama *The Sentence* (1887), about the Roman emperor Caligula, but her most lasting work is her poetry. One of her best-known poems is *The Snow Waste* (1866) from her *Dramatic Studies,* an intense work preoccupied with hate and death, which concludes:

> And those strange dead were borne along with him,
> As though they were himself. So they passed on
> And far away along the dreadful waste
> I heard the droning murmur of his words
> But knew not what they bore. And when they died
> In distance all things slept in one great hush,
> The plain of snow and the unchanging sky.

Other Work by Augusta Webster

Sutphin, Christine, ed. *Augusta Webster: Portraits and Other Poems.* Peterborough, Ontario: Broadview Press, 2000.

Wells, Charles Jeremiah (ca. 1800–1879)
poet

Charles Jeremiah Wells was born in approximately 1800 to James Turner and Jane Wells. His place of birth is obscure, but was probably London. He attended Cowden Clarke's school in Edmonton, where he befriended JOHN KEATS as well as Keats's brother, Tom, before leaving school and becoming apprenticed to a solicitor.

He was part of the Keats circle for several years until John discovered that Wells had played a cruel prank on his brother just prior to Tom's death in 1818. Adopting a highly poeticized style that borrowed heavily from Keats's early work, Wells had written love letters to Tom from a fictional Amena Bellafila; when Tom discovered the truth, he was heartbroken. Keats considered this to have exacerbated his brother's illness and hastened his death, and from 1818 on, Wells was barred from the Keats social circle, and in his correspondence Keats referred to him as "that degraded Wells."

Wells began working as a solicitor and published a collection of stories modeled on Giovanni Boccaccio (*Stories after Nature*) anonymously in 1822 and a dramatic poem (*Joseph and His Brethren: A Scriptural Drama*) under the name H. L. Howard in 1823. Neither work generated any excitement or even much notice. Wells married Emily Jane Hill in 1827, had three daughters and a son, and retired to Hertfordshire in 1830, presumably because of health problems; however, contemporary accounts also point to an indolence that seemed a significant part of his character. In the country, he hunted, fished, wrote poetry, and kept bees. He moved his family to Brittany in 1841.

While he was in France, Wells began to enjoy a heightened status among a small group of poets and artists in England. DANTE GABRIEL ROSSETTI read a copy of *Joseph and His Brethren* and, greatly impressed, began to champion Wells. Over the next two decades, a number of prominent critics and poets, including ALGERNON CHARLES SWINBURNE, GEORGE MEREDITH, and THEODORE WATTS-DUNTON, attempted to have the poem reprinted, succeeding in 1876. An edited and expanded version of *Joseph and His Brethren* was widely admired, but following the 1874 death of his wife, Wells had burned a collection of unpublished manuscripts, and was unable to capitalize on his brief burst of fame in order to establish himself as a major poet.

Wells died after a long illness on February 17, 1879, in Marseilles. Today, his poem has once more fallen into obscurity, although during its period of fame it was effectively required reading for Pre-Raphaelite circles.

Works about Charles Jeremiah Wells

Fredeman, William E., and Ira Bruce Nadel. *Victorian Poets Before 1850*. Detroit: Gale, 1984.

Johnston, Priscilla. "Charles Jeremiah Wells: An Early Keatsian Poet." *Keats-Shelley Journal* 26 (1977): 72–87.

Webbe, Cornelius, and Charles Wells. *Sonnets; Summer; Joseph and His Brethren*. New York: Garland, 1978.

West, Jane (1758–1852) *poet, novelist*

Born in London, Jane West, née Iliffe, was the daughter of John Iliffe and his wife, Jane. She was educated at home and began writing poetry as a girl. She published at least six books of poems before 1800. In 1783 she married Thomas West, a farmer from Northamptonshire in the English Midlands. Although she helped her husband run the farm, West also found time to write poetry, educational tracts, novels, and popular "conduct books," such as *Letters to a Young Man* (1801) and *Letters to a Young Lady* (1806), which advised young men and women how to behave. In 1793 she published her first novel, *The Advantages of Education; or, The History of Maria Williams*. Her novel *A Gossip's Story* (1796) is thought to have been an inspiration for JANE AUSTEN's *Sense and Sensibility*. She wrote a series of popular novels that were didactic but humorous, narrated by Prudentia Homespun, an elderly spinster. After 1810 West wrote historical fiction, such as *The*

Loyalists (1812) and *Alicia de Lacey* (1814), a historical romance. She said that she wanted to make historical characters "talk in the language of common life." Following the death of her husband in 1823, West wrote little else. Her final novel was *Ringrove; or, Old-fashioned Notions* (1827).

Wheeler, Anna (Anna Doyle Wheeler)
(1785–1848) *nonfiction writer*

Born in Limerick, Ireland, Anna Wheeler was the youngest daughter of the Angelican archdeacon Nicholas Doyle and his wife, Anna Dunbar Doyle. After her father died, Wheeler was raised by her mother's family, and at age 15, against her mother's wishes, she married Francis Massy Wheeler, who had inherited his family's estate at Ballywire.

Wheeler, who had six children, only two of whom survived past infancy, found her marriage unbearable. For a while she escaped by reading radical social and political philosophy, in particular the work of MARY WOLLSTONECRAFT. In 1812 Wheeler took her two daughters and fled to Guernsey, in the Channel Islands, where her uncle, Sir John Doyle, was governor.

From Guernsey she moved to Paris and then to London, where she moved in radical social circles, advocated equal education and employment opportunities for men and women, and fought for marriage and divorce laws that were fairer to women.

In 1825 Wheeler and her friend WILLIAM THOMPSON coauthored *The Appeal of One Half the Human Race, Women, Against the Pretensions of the Other Half, Men, to Restrain Them in Political and Thence in Civil and Domestic Slavery*. *The Appeal*, as it was more commonly called, was written in response to JAMES MILL's essay on government in the 1824 edition of the *Encyclopaedia Britannica*, in which he claimed that women should not be allowed to vote, "since their interests were covered by their husbands or fathers." It explains instead the historical causes for the oppression of women and argues for the equality of the sexes while directly attacking Mill: "But is it not strange that a philosopher, a lover of wisdom, avowedly founding his arguments on Utility, that is to say, on the tendency of actions or institutions to promote the greatest possible quantity of human happiness,—should deliberately in the very threshold of his argument put aside *one half* of the human race, of all ages and all characters and conditions as unentitled to consideration. . . ."

After *The Appeal*, Wheeler became a well-known advocate for women's rights and an eloquent lecturer. Her most famous speech, *Rights of Women*, delivered in 1829 at the Finsbury Square lecture chapel, attempted to disprove the argument of male superiority.

The scholar Dolores Dooley has called for a modern reappraisal of Wheeler's role in the history of feminism: "She stands as perhaps one of the earliest of women in social science and in her 'science for happiness', she offers a human project that in turn offers a major challenge and counterposition to any society governed by a philosophy of competitive individualism."

A Work about Anna Wheeler
Dooley, Dolores. *Equality in Community: Sexual Equality in the Writings of William Thompson and Anna Doyle Wheeler*. Cork, Ireland: Cork University Press, 1996.

White, Joseph Blanco (José Maria Blanco y Crespo) (1775–1841) *poet, journalist*

White was born in Seville, Spain. His father was Guilermo Blanco, originally William White. William White was an Irish Catholic who fled to Spain to escape religious persecution; he married Maria Gertrudis Crespo, a member of the Spanish aristocracy, though the family was impoverished by the time of her marriage to Blanco. While Joseph White's father was not a particularly astute businessman, he was known for his charitable works, volunteering at a local hospital and performing menial tasks out of a spirit of helping the sick and dying. White's mother was extremely religious and was happy when, at the age of twelve, her son decided to study for the priesthood.

White attended the Dominican College of Santo Tomás and the University of Seville. He was ordained a Roman Catholic priest in 1799, despite the fact that he had many doubts about his faith. White had to conceal his doubts carefully, however, because while not as powerful as it once was, the Inquisition was still a force in Spain and still concerned itself with deviations from doctrine on the part of the clergy. At the time, in fact, he wrote, "[B]elieving religion a fable, I still found myself compelled daily to act as a minister and promoter of imposture."

At first deterred by his love for his parents, Blanco finally left Spain in 1810 and emigrated to England. There he studied at Oxford University and became friends with the writer MATTHEW ARNOLD and JOHN CARDINAL NEWMAN. He was eventually ordained an Anglican minister in 1814. He continued to be plagued with doubts, however, disliking dogmatism in all its shapes, and eventually converted to Unitarianism. Suffering ill health from 1837 on, White died in 1841.

While in England, White founded and wrote for the Spanish-language magazine *El Español* (*The Spaniard*). Among the causes he championed was the independence of Spanish colonies in Latin America. He also wrote extensively on theology, including *Practical and Internal Evidence against Catholicism* (1825) and *Observations on Heresy and Orthodoxy* (1835). He is best remembered today for his sonnet "Night," which like much of his work, questions assumptions about the meaning of life and death. He imagines the first man who faced the night and wonders, "Did he not tremble for this lovely frame, / This glorious canopy of light and blue?" As frightened as he is, however, this first man to observe night realizes that "creation widened on his view. / Who could have thought what darkness lay concealed / within thy beams, O Sun!" The poem ends on a very dark note, as the poet exclaims, "Weak man! Why, to shun death, this anxious strife? / If Light can thus deceive, wherefore not Life?"

White, William Hale (Mark Rutherford)
(1831–1913) *novelist*

William Hale White was born in Bedford, England, to William White, a printer, and Mary Ann Chignall White. His father was a deacon and lay preacher in the Bunyan Meeting, a fundamentalist congregation begun by John Bunyan (1628–88), the 17th-century author of *Pilgrim's Progress,* who had lived in Bedford. (White's biography of Bunyan was published in 1905.) White came to distrust the moderate Calvinism that the Meeting now practiced, believing it failed to match the rigorous devotion of Bunyan's Puritanism. In 1851 he entered New College in London. The following year, White was expelled for questioning scriptural authority.

White worked chiefly as a clerk and a journalist, although he also preached. Arguing that lower-class men should be allowed to vote, he wrote *An Argument for the Extension of the Franchise* (1866).

White was 49 when his first novel, *The Autobiography of Mark Rutherford, Dissenting Minister* (1881), appeared. It was signed Mark Rutherford—a pseudonym announcing this new phase of White's career. The name itself, according to White's biographer Irvin Stock, was "invented and without special significance." (White's true name would remain hidden until 1896.) The novel is a lightly fictionalized account of White's own life, with Rutherford, like White, even suffering from hypochondria. However, differences between Rutherford's fictional life and White's real one did exist; for instance, Rutherford completes his college education. White's "sense of responsibility to personal truth" and to the expression of "deep personal feeling," as the critic John Middleton Murry noted in the *Daily News and Leader* in 1915, is apparent in the sincerity and urgency of Rutherford's account of religious crisis: "What reason for continuance as a preacher could I claim? . . . I trembled to anticipate the complete emptiness to which before long I should be reduced." Indeed, increasingly isolated from his congregation as his religious inspiration and conviction crumble, Rutherford rejects formal religion and pursues an independent course. He is loath, however, to divorce himself from human ties: "The desire for something like sympathy and love absolutely devoured me.... [I] clung to the hope that I might employ myself in some way which, however feebly, would help mankind a little to the realisation of an ideal." Eventually, Rutherford finds employment with a publisher of agnostic books—a character based on John Chapman, for whom White had worked. Having confessed his inadequacy at the job (and at life) to the publisher's niece (a character based on the novelist GEORGE ELIOT), Rutherford is redeemed by her kindness and finds his agnostic credo: "Blessed are they who heal us of self-despisings."

Mark Rutherford's Deliverance (1885) continues White's fictional autobiography. Rutherford the idealist is educated by life's harsh realities. Stock has remarked that the novel's "vivid and terrible picture of Victorian England . . . [is what] gives the work much of its value as history and accounts for much of its modest fame." In London, Rutherford discovers, "Hope, faith, and God seemed impossible amidst the smoke of the streets"; he refers to the city's "pollution" of "air, earth, and water." Rutherford is not the only one who endures an alienated existence. The "whole occupation all day long" of one friend, Clark, "was to write addresses [for newspapers to be delivered], . . . his hours being from nine o'clock to seven."

Another novel, *The Revolution in Tanner's Lane* (1887), is a historical account of Puritanism. It is divided into two halves, the first centering on Zachariah Coleman, an ardent Calvinist whose faith is undermined by a miserable marriage and the "weary pilgrimage" this and other events have made of his life. Coleman, therefore, hopes to shore up his faith by converting friends to it. In the novel's second half, set later during the time of White's childhood, George Allan (who, like Coleman, resembles White) confronts the brand of faith practiced in Bunyan Meeting. The two narratives are only lightly linked, in that Coleman is a friend of Allan's parents, and critics have carped at its split nature. E. A. Baker indeed has found structure a recurrent problem in White's novels, which "[dispense] with anything of the nature of a plot" and whose stories, even, "are broken and discrepant." But the novel's two parts are unified by the similar testing of faith that the two main characters undergo, and the critic John Lucas has even argued that, instead of "faulty construction," this organization succeeds in dramatizing White's "own sense of a crumbling [Puritan] tradition."

White's characters often seek ways out of their sense of incompleteness and alienation. In this they reflect their author. His fiction, the critic Catherine R. Harland has written, is "a reworking of the struggle of his own spiritual and emotional life," an attempt "to give meaning to human suffering and to create in imagination the solutions that eluded him in actual life."

Other Work by William Hale White

Clara Hopgood. Rutland, Vt.: Charles E. Tuttle, 1996.

A Work about William Hale White

Harland, Catherine R. *Mark Rutherford: The Mind and Art of William Hale White*. Columbus: Ohio State University Press, 1988.

Whyte-Melville, George John (1821–1878) novelist

George Whyte-Melville was born in Fife, Scotland, to John Whyte-Melville and Catherine Anne Osborne Whyte-Melville. He attended Eton and in 1839 became an officer in the British army. In 1847 he married Charlotte Hanbury; they later had one daughter. In 1855 Whyte-Melville fought in the Crimean War, in which Great Britain, France, and Turkey joined together to prevent Russia from taking control of Constantinople (Istanbul), the capital of the Turkish empire. In his book *The Interpreter* (1858), Whyte-Melville wrote a vivid account of the "butchery of the trenches" during the Siege of Sebastopol. Following the war, he settled in England to write and hunt. Many of his novels draw on his military experience and love of fox hunting. The hero of his first novel, *Digby Grand: An Autobiography* (1853), joins the army after attending Eton, as Whyte-Melville did. Of the many novels he wrote in the 1860s and 1870s, his most popular was *The Gladiators: A Tale of Rome and Judaea* (1863), about a young Briton who is enslaved by the Romans. Whyte-Melville was killed during a hunt when his horse stumbled and fell. Theodore Ralph, in his *American Song Treasury*, reports that the popular hunting song "D'Ye Ken John Peel" was written after the funeral in tribute to Whyte-Melville.

Wilde, Jane Francesca (Speranza) (1821–1896) *poet, essayist*

Jane Francesca Wilde, née Elgee, was born in Wexford, in southeast Ireland, to Charles Elgee, an attorney, and Sarah Kingsbury Elgee. As a young woman, she wrote articles under the pen name Speranza in support of the cause of Irish independence from England. One of her articles, "The Die Is Cast," published in 1848, stated that the Irish should use violence if necessary to drive out the English. In 1851 she married Robert Willis Wilde, a famous Irish eye surgeon. Their home in Dublin became a center for Irish and visiting English writers; among the guests who might be found at her weekly salons were BRAM STOKER, JOHN RUSKIN, and William Butler Yeats. The Wildes had a daughter and two sons, one of whom was the writer OSCAR WILDE.

In 1864 Francesca Wilde published a book titled *Poems* that dealt with Irish independence. Another book of poems followed in 1867. She might have been better known for her eccentric and witty personality than for her writings, but the writings were many. Personally superstitious, she collected folk charms and legends and published two books on them, in 1887 and 1890. She also published essays, including *Notes on Men, Women and Books* (1891) and *Social Studies* (1893). Wilde believed strongly that women had been enslaved by men for centuries and in her essays she urged them to break free.

Wilde, Oscar (1854–1900) *poet, novelist, playwright*

Oscar Wilde was born in Dublin to Sir William Wilde, a physician and an amateur antiquarian, and LADY JANE WILDE, a gifted poet and journalist who wrote under the pen name Speranza. Wilde was initially educated by his parents, particularly by his mother. His formal education began at Portora Royal School for Boys in Enniskillen, Ireland. At 17 Wilde enrolled in Trinity College, Dublin, where he was deeply influenced by the professor of classics, socialite, and famous public speaker Reverend John Pentland Mahaffy. Under Mahaffy's guidance, Wilde became a brilliant scholar and won a scholarship to Magdalen College, Oxford.

Wilde seriously began writing poetry at Oxford and was awarded the prestigious Newdigate Prize for poetry. Among his teachers were WALTER PATER and JOHN RUSKIN, two of the leading literary and artistic critics of the day. Under their influence Wilde became an advocate of AESTHETICISM, a movement that promoted the idea that art exists for its own beauty alone, not to fulfill some practical function. According to Ruskin and Pater, art is of central importance to life. Wilde was also attracted to Pater's demand that life be led with aesthetic intensity.

After Wilde received his degree in 1878, he moved to London and became the leading spokesman for aestheticism. He worked as an art reviewer, gave public lectures in the United States and Canada, and lived among the artists of Paris before finally deciding on a literary career. In 1883, while lecturing in Dublin, Wilde met and soon married Constance Mary Lloyd. To support his wife, Wilde edited *Woman's World* magazine—a position that offered not only a steady income, but also entrance into the literary world. Wilde's relationship with Constance steadily deteriorated, however, as he began leading a double life as a married man and a practicing homosexual. Wilde had a particularly troubled, long-lasting relationship with LORD ALFRED "Bosie" DOUGLAS, a young aristocrat.

Although Wilde was a regular contributor to the *Pall Mall Gazette* and *Dramatic View*, his first major publication was a collection of fairy tales written for his sons and influenced by the Danish writer Hans Christian Andersen, *The Happy Prince and Other Tales* (1888). Most critics received the work favorably. In 1889 Wilde retired from his position at *Woman's World* and published his first truly controversial work, "The Decay of Lying" (1889). Many of Wilde's ideas promoted Decadence, a radical offshoot of aestheticism, which demanded that art, particularly poetry, be free of the real world. The work, clearly a provocation of the Victorian establishment, disturbed many readers.

As his fame increased, Wilde's work became more provocative, especially with publication of *The Picture of Dorian Gray* (1891). His play *Salomé* (1893) was refused a license for production in London, although a French version was mounted in Paris in 1896. It was as a dramatist that Wilde found his greatest critical and popular success, with the sophisticated comedies *Lady Windermere's Fan* (1892), *A Woman of No Importance* (1893), *The Importance of Being Earnest* (1895), and *An Ideal Husband* (1895).

Wilde's personal life became more and more turbulent. Lord Douglas introduced Wilde to the underworld of male prostitutes, and his sexual debaucheries became the talk of London. When Bosie's father, the marquess of Queensberry, publicly insulted Wilde by calling him a sodomite, Wilde responded by initiating what proved to be a disastrous libel suit. After an enormous amount of evidence marshaled by the defense from testimonies of male prostitutes, Wilde's case backfired. He was arrested on charges of sodomy (then illegal in England) and prosecuted alongside the madam of the male brothel that Wilde used to frequent. Convicted, he was sentenced to two years of hard labor, the most severe punishment allowed for the crime.

After he was released, bankrupt, at age 42, Wilde left England, never to return. During the trial, Wilde's wife left him and changed her family name to protect the integrity of their children. While in prison, Wilde composed an autobiographical work, *De Profundis* (1905), in which he defended his art and sexual identity. His prison experience provided him the material for his best poem, "The Ballad of Reading Gaol" [jail] (1898), which describes the hanging of a murderer. Wilde died in poverty in Paris, virtually abandoned by all of his former friends, including Lord Douglas.

Critical Analysis

The Picture of Dorian Gray appeared first in *Lippincott's Magazine*. Its decadent themes, alien to the supposed wholesomeness of the Victorian society, created a controversy among readers and critics alike. Dorian Gray is a young hedonist, or pleasure-seeker, whose portrait is painted by Basil Hallward. Although Hallward is a mediocre painter, he is inspired by Dorian's angelic beauty and paints a masterpiece. Amazed by the perfection of the painting, Dorian utters a wish to be able to retain his physical appearance and have the picture age instead of himself. When he realizes that his wish has come true, he loses all restraint and begins experimenting with every sort of perverse pleasure imaginable. Eventually, he commits murder.

While the portrait takes on nightmarish features, Dorian remains untouched. When Hallward again sees the painting, he cannot believe it is his:

> An exclamation of horror broke from the painter's lips as he saw in the dim light the hideous face on the canvas grinning at him. There was something in its expression that filled him with disgust and loathing.... It was Dorian Gray's own face that he was look-

ing at! The horror, whatever it was, had not yet entirely spoiled that marvellous beauty.

In certain ways, the novel exposed the dark, ugly side of the Victorian society and humanity at large. The work was praised by some critics for its innovative form and exploration of new themes, while others viewed the work as "degenerate" and perverse. Whatever the case, Wilde's name became famous and notorious at the same time.

Wilde's comedies still give delight today. His first major play, *Lady Windermere's Fan,* satirizes high society. The happy marital lives of Lord and Lady Windermere are interrupted when a blackmailing divorcee is driven to self-sacrifice by maternal love. The play is also notable for its wit and delicate use of humor: "One should always be in love," insists one character, "That's the reason one should never marry."

The Importance of Being Earnest, Wilde's most farcical and popular work, pushes all social conventions aside. The feckless heroes of the play, Jack and Algernon, fall desperately in love with Gwendolyn and Cecily. The play focuses on their machinations as they seek the hands of their beloved. With all its absurdities—double lives, mislaid babies, and Gwendolyn's addiction to the name Earnest—the play criticizes the degenerate aristocracy, exposes the rigidity of the middle class, and satirizes social institutions like marriage and love. Although the play was tremendously popular and had a long run, it was not without its critics. "To become a spectator at one's life," Wilde replied to his critics, "is to escape the suffering of life."

Of all Wilde's works, "The Ballad of Reading Gaol" is his most realistic. As the critic H. E. Woodbridge notes, this "must be pronounced his best poem. . . . It contains few or no rhetorical flourishes, its diction is simple and poignant; . . . it is passionately sincere." In describing the execution central to the poem, the poet writes coldly and starkly:

> *They hanged him as a beast is hanged;*
> *They did not even toll*
> *A requiem that might have brought*
> *Rest to his startled soul.*
> * * * * * * * *
> *They stripped him of his canvas clothes,*
> *And gave him to the flies;*
> *They mocked the swollen purple throat,*
> *And the stark and staring eyes;*
> *And with laughter loud they heaped the shroud*
> *In which their convict lies.*

"Reading Gaol" contains one of the most famous line that Wilde wrote: "Yet each man kills the thing he loves."

Wilde's works are still widely read, studied, and appreciated; his aphorisms are much-quoted; and his plays are performed all over the world and have been adapted as films. "I was a man who stood in symbolic relation to the art and culture of my age," he wrote. "I had realized this for myself at the very dawn of my manhood and had forced my age to realize it afterwards." During his short literary career, Wilde did his best to shake the moral foundations of Victorian society. As the critic John Lahr notes, "To stand out in Victorian culture, Wilde had to stand against it."

Other Work by Oscar Wilde

Complete Works of Oscar Wilde: Stories, Poems, Plays, and Essays. New York: HarperCollins, 1989.

Works about Oscar Wilde

Ellmann, Richard. *Oscar Wilde.* New York: Penguin, 1987.
Goodman, Jonathan. *Oscar Wilde File.* London: Allison & Busby, 1988.
Holland, Merlin. *The Real Trial of Oscar Wilde.* New York: Harper Perennial, 2004.
———. *The Wilde Album.* London: Fourth Estate, 1997.
Knox, Melissa. *Oscar Wilde: A Long and Lovely Suicide.* New Haven, Conn.: Yale University Press, 1994.
Pearce, Joseph. *The Unmasking of Oscar Wilde.* Fort Collins, Colo.: Ignatius Press, 2005.

Williams, Helen Maria (1761–1827) poet, nonfiction writer

Helen Williams was born in London. Her father was Charles Williams, a soldier in the British army, and her mother was Helen Hay Williams. She was educated at home by her mother and in 1782 published her first poem, *Edwin and Eltruda*. Deeply committed to liberal ideals, she wrote poems about moral and political issues such as *Peru* (1784), which condemned Europe's exploitation of South American countries, and *Poem on the Bill Lately Passed for Regulating the Slave Trade* (1788). These early poems were widely read and provided her with a substantial income.

In 1788 Williams went to France to live with her sister, Cecilia, and remained there during the French Revolution. Although she supported the revolutionary leaders who overthrew and beheaded King Louis XVI, she was imprisoned by the Jacobins, the most extreme revolutionaries, when they violently pushed aside the more moderate Girondists in 1793 and began the Reign of Terror. Williams was eventually released, but some of her friends were sent to the guillotine for being insufficiently radical. Yet even after the violence and anarchy of the Reign of Terror, and despite the disillusionment of most intellectuals who had at first supported the Revolution, then seen its ideals betrayed, Williams remained committed to it.

During her years in France, Williams wrote several vivid, novelistic accounts of life in France after the Revolution. These included *Letters from France Containing Many New Anecdotes Relative to the French Revolution and the Present State of French Manners* (1792–96), *Sketches of the State of Manners and Opinions in the French Republic* (1801), and *A Narrative of the Events Which Have Taken Place in France* (1815). Although Williams's *Letters* are fascinating documents, and her descriptions of life in revolutionary France are riveting, she is considered a biased and unreliable historian. Toward the end of her life Williams moved to Amsterdam, but she returned to Paris, where she died in 1827.

A Work about Helen Williams

Shuter, Jane, ed. *Helen Williams and the French Revolution.* Austin, Tex.: Raintree Steck-Vaughn, 1996.

Wilson, John

See NORTH, CHRISTOPHER.

Wollstonecraft, Mary (1759–1797) nonfiction writer, novelist

Mary Wollstonecraft, often regarded as the founder of feminism, was born in London to the alcoholic and violent farmer Edward John Wollstonecraft and his wife, Elizabeth Dixon Wollstonecraft. Wollstonecraft experienced financial hardship while trying to run a school with her sisters, and worked as a governess after the school closed.

Faced with the limited career opportunities available to women, she became part of a circle of radicals that included the revolutionary Thomas Paine and the political writer WILLIAM GODWIN, with whom she had a long affair. During this period, she had a child by the writer and ex-soldier Gilbert Imlay, although the two did not marry. She went on to raise the child with Godwin, whom she eventually married while she was pregnant with their child Mary (later MARY SHELLEY). Wollstonecraft died giving birth to Mary.

Wollstonecraft depicts the oppression of women in her novel *Maria* (1788), composed while she was a governess. Renowned more for its feminism than for its artistic merits, the semiautobiographical novel is the story of Maria, a woman with a brutal father, who grows up to marry an aristocrat husband. However, Maria benefits more from her relationship with an intellectual named Henry, an invalid. After Henry's death, she is reconciled to life with her husband and becomes a tolerant, progressive landlord.

Wollstonecraft is best known for the philosophical tract *A Vindication of the Rights of Woman* (1792), in which she calls for both sexes to have the same legal rights: "For men and women, truth, if I understand the meaning of the word, must be the same." She argues that women have sacrificed physical and intellectual strength for beauty and refinement, and she seeks to change that with a "revolution in female manners." Women, she contends, should be allowed to be philosophers, physicians, businesspeople, and politicians. She also calls for a national education system to prepare women for a fuller role in society by teaching them to function as self-directed beings.

Wollstonecraft campaigned for more than women's rights. Like Godwin, she was interested in overall social reform. Thus in 1790 she wrote *Vindication of the Rights of Man* to answer to the conservative philosopher EDMUND BURKE's attack on the French Revolution in *Reflections on the Revolution in France*. Wollstonecraft's work was heavily influenced by Thomas Paine's call for individualism and resistance to oppressive customs.

Wollstonecraft herself was in France, near Paris, during the 1789 Reign of Terror, in which hundreds of people lost their lives at the order of the revolutionary government. In *An Historical and Moral View of the Origins and Progress of the French Revolution* (1794) she blames the Terror on the harshness of life under the old regime. Although she did not approve of the bloodshed, she remained committed to the Revolution's ideals.

Wollstonecraft's writings proved popular in the last half of the 19th century, as they appealed to the leaders and members of the women's suffrage movement. The biographer Eleanor Flexner calls Wollstonecraft "The woman who first effectively challenged the age-old image of her sex as lesser and subservient human beings" and notes that "It is not given to many books to exert as powerful an influence as the *Vindication* has."

Works about Mary Wollstonecraft

Flexner, Eleanor. *Mary Wollstonecraft*. New York: Coward, McCann & Geohegan, 1972.

Gordon, Lyndall. *Vindication: A Life of Mary Wollstonecraft*. New York: Harper Perennial, 2006.

Jacobs, Diane. *Her Own Woman: The Life of Mary Wollstonecraft*. Yucca Valley, Calif.: Citadel, 2003.

Taucherт, Ashley. *Mary Wollstonecraft and the Accent of the Feminine*. New York: Palgrave Macmillan, 2002.

Todd, Janet M. *Mary Wollstonecraft: A Revolutionary Life*. New York: Columbia University Press, 2002.

Wood, Ellen (1814–1887) *novelist*

Ellen Price was born on January 17 in Worcester, England, to Thomas Price, a glove manufacturer, and Elizabeth Evans Price. Ellen suffered from a spinal illness that partially paralyzed her as a child and left her a semi-invalid. In 1836 she married Henry Wood, a successful banker. The Woods, who had several children, spent the next 20 years in France. There Wood began writing short stories and literary sketches and contributing to magazines such as *Bentley's Miscellany* and the *New Monthly Magazine*. Because of her spinal condition, she had to lie on a couch while writing. In 1861 she published her first novel, *East Lynne*, a melodrama about an aristocratic heroine who suffers terrible consequences for adultery. The book went through four editions in six months and made Wood famous. It was also adapted as a play and performed for many years. In 1862 Wood published two more best-selling novels, both of which have melodramatic plots and clear moral messages. *Mrs. Halliburton's Troubles* is about a young widow who brings up her children in poverty after being cheated of her inheritance. *The Channings* is the story of two families. All of her novels were published under the name Mrs. Henry Wood. After her husband died in 1867, she became editor of the *Argosy* magazine, which serialized her novels. Wood's Johnny Ludlow stories, based on her rural childhood, also appeared in the magazine and were later published in three volumes. The narrator of the stories is the hero, Johnny, who tells the story of his life in episodes, with none of the melodrama typical of her novels.

A Work about Ellen Wood

Wynne, Deborah. *The Sensation Novel and the Victorian Family Magazine.* New York: St. Martin's Press, 2001.

Wordsworth, Dorothy (1771–1855)
diarist, poet

Dorothy Wordsworth was born in Cockermouth, Westmoreland, in northwest England. She was one of five children born to John Wordsworth, an attorney, and his wife, Anne Cookson Wordsworth. Dorothy was the younger sister, by less than a year, of the poet WILLIAM WORDSWORTH and as an adult became his devoted companion.

Wordsworth's mother died in 1778, and her father was unable to care for the children; he died in 1783. The boys were sent away to school and Dorothy was sent to live with relatives. From 1778 to 1788 Wordsworth lived with a variety of relatives, some of whom treated her like a servant rather than as family. During this time, she gained a scattered education. Wordsworth finally found a home with her uncle, William Cookson, with whom she lived until 1794. After she arrived at her uncle's home, Wordsworth was further tutored until, with the help of Cookson's wife, she was able to set up a small school. She saw little of her brothers during these years and especially missed her favorite, William.

In 1795, thanks to an inheritance, William was able to buy a home in Dorset, in southwest England. Despite the disapproval of their immediate family, who doubted William's ability to maintain his inheritance, Dorothy moved in with him, causing some social embarrassment at their unique living situation. Not long after, she moved with William to the county of Somerset (also in the southwest) to be near their friend SAMUEL TAYLOR COLERIDGE. The three friends were so spiritually and intellectually close that Coleridge later referred to them as "three persons with one soul." Dorothy Wordsworth wrote about their time in Somerset in her diary, known as the *Alfoxden Journal,* after the village where she and William lived.

In 1799 Wordsworth and her brother settled at Dove Cottage in Grasmere, in the Lake District of northwest England, where they lived for the rest of their lives, with occasional travels to Scotland and the Continent. Even after William's marriage to Wordsworth's friend Mary Hutchinson, the sister continued to live with the family and became like a second mother to her nieces and nephews.

Dorothy Wordsworth is known today primarily for her journals, although she did write poetry, some of which her brother published along with his own. Her journals were not published until 1894. The *Alfoxden Journal* was written in 1798 and was followed by the *Grasmere Journals* (1800–03), *Recollections of a Tour Made in Scotland,* (1804) and *Journal of a Tour on the Continent* (1820). Wordsworth's brother and Coleridge relied on her journals for inspiration and ideas. William's famous poem "I Wandered Lonely as a Cloud," composed in 1804, with its memorable images of daffodils, might have been inspired by this passage from his sister's journal, April 15, 1802:

> ". . . some [daffodils] rested their heads upon these stones as on a pillow for weariness, and the rest tossed and reeled and danced, and seemed as if they verily laughed with the wind that blew upon them over the lake. They looked so gay—ever-glancing, ever changing."

Wordsworth's journals are full of minutely observed moments of daily life, beautifully rendered. Her attachment to the natural world reveals her romantic sensibility: "The sea perfectly calm blue, streaked with deeper colour by the clouds, and tongues or points of sand; on our return of a gloomy red." Wordsworth, like her brother, was able to capture a sense of the sublime in nature: ". . . the sun was shining and the prospect looked so divinely beautiful. . . . It seemed more sacred than I had ever seen it, and yet more allied to human life." Her detailed descriptions of domestic life provide scholars with a great deal of information about daily existence in this period: We learn when she washed her hair, what the Wordsworths had for supper, and how they amused themselves.

She also writes about the living conditions of the lower class: "We met near Skelleth a pretty little Boy with a wallet over his shoulder.... He spoke gently and without complaint. When I asked him if he got enough to eat, he looked surprized, and said 'Nay.' He was 7 years old but seemed not more than 5." Although this scene is portrayed without comment, the reader can infer Wordsworth's dismay.

Coleridge said about her powers of observation: "Her eye [is] watchful in minutest observation of nature; and her taste [is] a perfect electrometer. It bends, protrudes, and draws in, at subtlest beauties." In fact, her most prominent feature were her eyes. THOMAS DE QUINCEY describes them vividly: "Her eyes were not soft, as Mrs. Wordsworth's nor were they fierce or bold; but they were wild and startling, and hurried in their motion."

Wordsworth actually never wrote anything for publication, but all her journals have been published. Her journals have most often been read in order to discover more about her brother—about his concerns and inspirations—but her writing is worthy of study in its own right. Dorothy's publisher, E. de Sélincourt, said that she was "probably ... the most distinguished of English writers who never wrote a line for the general public."

In 1829 Wordsworth was stricken with a severe illness, perhaps dysentery. She never truly recovered her health, so she could not take the long walks she loved so much, write, or travel. Beginning about 1835, her mind began to deteriorate. The last 20 years of her life were spent in a mental fog with brief periods of lucidity. She died at the age of 83, five years after her beloved brother's death.

William Wordsworth's "Lines Composed a Few Miles above Tintern Abbey" contains a lasting tribute to his relationship with his sister, whose perception, sensitivity, and appreciation of nature deeply influenced him:

> *My dear, dear Friend; and in thy voice I catch*
> *The language of my former heart, and read*
> *My former pleasures in the shooting lights*
> *Of thy wild eyes. Oh! Yet a little while*
> *May I behold in thee what I was once,*
> *My dear, dear Sister!*

Critical Analysis

Much critical debate in recent years has centered around the relationship between Dorothy and William Wordsworth, as revealed particularly in her unpublished writing. Some feminists believe that Wordsworth felt exploited by her brother and revealed her disappointment and anger in some of her poetry. Marjorie Levinson in *Wordsworth's Great Period Poems* (1986), for example, regards Wordsworth's "Thoughts on My Sickbed" as an outcry against her ideas having been "pilfered" by others. Earlier critics have read the poem quite differently, as it seems on the surface a coming to fruition of William Wordsworth's hope, articulated in his "Tintern Abbey" (1798), that his sister should, in times of sorrow, be comforted by the memory of their shared love of nature and by his capturing of those times in his poetry. The poem seems easily to support this interpretation, while much stretching and special pleading is needed to regard the poem as a protest.

"Thoughts on My Sickbed" was written in 1831, three years after Wordsworth fell ill and was confined to bed. She begins with a question, asking if her life has been "Pilfered of this sunny spring?" The question is simple enough: Will she miss the delights of this spring because she can no longer walk outside to enjoy it? She seems to refer to her brother's great autobiographical poem, "The Prelude," when she asks if spring's "prelusive sounds" will fail to touch her heart this year because of her circumstances.

After this stanza of questioning, Wordsworth protests, "Ah, say not so," and recalls how her now "feeble frame" has been "enriched" by her youthful communion with nature. As she invokes the beauty of these past encounters, she recalls, among other things, "The daffodil dancing in the breeze," a line that pays tribute to William's "I Wandered Lonely as a Cloud." She also seems to allude to William's "splendor in the grass," with "A promise of fruits and the splendid flower."

She goes further to say that even as a youth, free to roam, she did not experience the joy that she feels now from the "vernal air" and from the "first flowers of the year" that old friends have brought to her "unprompted and unbidden." She suddenly experiences "a power unfelt before" that bears her back in memory:

> No prisoner in this lonely room,
> I saw the green banks of the Wye
> Recalling thy prophetic words—
> Bard, brother, friend from infancy!

William's "prophetic words" were these:

> If solitude, or fear, or pain, or grief,
> Should be thy portion, with what healing
>   thoughts
> Of tender joy will thou remember me,
> And these my exhortations!

What she will remember, he says, is that "these steep woods and lofty cliffs,/And this green pastoral landscape, were to me/More dear, both for themselves and for thy sake."

Her poem concludes with a reference to one of William's "Lucy" poems, in which he describes his dead beloved: "No motion has she now, no force." Wordsworth says she has "No need of motion or of strength / Or even breathing air" to return in memory to their youth, to nature, and to the beautiful landscape both loved so much.

This is a lovely poem that has been misinterpreted by critics.

Works about Dorothy Wordsworth

Armstrong, Nancy, *Women in Romanticism: Mary Wollstonecraft, Dorothy Wordsworth, and Mary Shelley.* Totowa, N.J.: Barnes & Noble, 1989.

Cervelli, Kenneth R. *Dorothy Wordsworth's Ecology.* New York: Routledge, 2007.

Lee, Edmund. *Dorothy Wordsworth: The Story of a Sister's Love.* 1894. Reprint, Whitefish, Mont.: Kessinger, 2007.

Levin, Susan M. *Dorothy Wordsworth and Romanticism.* New Brunswick, N.J.: Rutgers University Press, 1987.

Wordsworth, William (1770–1850) *poet*

William Wordsworth was born at Cockermouth, Cumberland, in England's Lake District. He was one of five children of John Wordsworth, a lawyer, and his wife, Anne Cookson Wordsworth. When Wordsworth's mother died in 1778, the young boy was sent to grammar school in the village of Hawkshead. He often wandered the nearby countryside, which he alludes to in his long autobiographical poem *The Prelude* (1805).

In 1787 Wordsworth began his studies at Cambridge University, but he was not a particularly good student and preferred walks in the country to his studies. Trips to France, Switzerland, and Germany in 1790 had much more influence on his development than work done in the classroom.

In November 1791, after graduating, Wordsworth traveled again to France, hoping to improve his command of the language with the vague idea of becoming a language tutor. France was in upheaval following its Revolution; what kind of government would take the place of the old system had not been determined. In France, Wordsworth met Captain Michael Beaupuy, a Republican officer who influenced Wordsworth's thinking. In *The Prelude* Wordsworth says that he and Beaupuy talked of

> . . . the end
> Of civil government, and its wisest forms;
> Of ancient loyalty, and chartered rights,
> Custom and habit, novelty and change;
> Of self-respect, and virtue in the few
> For patrimonial honour set apart,
> And ignorance in the labouring multitude.

Wordsworth began his career as a writer in 1793 with the publication of *An Evening Walk,* "the history of a poet's evening," addressed to his sister DOROTHY WORDSWORTH. In the same year he published *Descriptive Sketches,* about the walking tour of the Alps he took in 1790. These works foreshadow Wordsworth's mature ability to evoke a landscape and highlight the link between humanity and the natural world.

In 1795 an inheritance from a friend allowed Wordsworth and his sister Dorothy to settle down at Racedown, Dorset. In the same year, Wordsworth met SAMUEL TAYLOR COLERIDGE, with whom he developed a deep friendship. Wordsworth and his sister subsequently moved to the county of Somerset to be near Coleridge, who lived in the village of Nether Stowey, Somerset. There, as a result of many hours of walking and talking together, the two poets collaborated to produce *Lyrical Ballads,* which marked the beginning of ROMANTICISM in England. The first edition, published anonymously in 1798, contained poems by both Wordsworth and Coleridge. Wordworth's were intended to show the poetry inherent in everyday objects and conversations, while Coleridge's dealt with supernatural subjects. "We Are Seven," for example, tells of a conversation between the speaker and a little girl in which neither can hear the other's view of reality. The girl is imperturbably sure that there are seven children in her family, even though two of them "in the churchyard lie," and she sits on their grave mounds to eat her supper. By the last stanza the speaker has abandoned euphemism:

> "But they are dead; those two are dead!
> "Their spirits are in heaven!"
> 'Twas throwing words away; for still
> The little Maid would have her will,
> And said, "Nay, we are seven!"

In 1800 a revised edition appeared. It included Wordsworth's famous Preface, which Coleridge had urged Wordsworth to write in order to clarify their intentions to choose incidents and situations from common life and to relate or describe them, throughout, as far as was possible in a selection of language really used by men, and, at the same time, to throw over them a certain coloring of imagination, whereby ordinary things should be presented to the mind in an unusual aspect.

The ideas about politics, humanity, and poetic diction expressed in the Preface and practiced in the poems were too radical for most reviewers, and the volume was roundly criticized.

Following the second edition of *Lyrical Ballads,* Wordsworth began to write *The Prelude,* a poem in which he attempted to describe the "growth of a poet's mind." This autobiographical work was not competed until 1805 and not published until after Wordsworth's death in 1850. The quality of the work as poetry is uneven. Some passages are dull and uninspired, while others are both beautifully written and sharply insightful, such as this famous description of how it felt to witness the optimistic beginnings of the French Revolution:

> *Bliss was it in that dawn to be alive,*
> *But to be young was very heaven; O times,*
> *In which the meagre, stale, forbidding ways*
> *Of custom, law, and statute took at once*
> *The attraction of a Country in Romance;*
> *When Reason seem'd the most to assert her rights. . . .*

In 1799 Wordsworth and Dorothy settled at Dove Cottage in Grasmere in the Lake district. There, Wordsworth began to plan a great philosophic poem on "Man, Nature, and Society," *The Recluse.* Although parts of the poem were written, the whole as Wordsworth had envisioned it was never completed. In 1802 Wordsworth inherited money owed to his father, who had died in 1783, and was thus able to marry. He wed Mary Hutchinson, a friend of Dorothy's.

In 1807 Wordsworth published *Poems in Two Volumes,* which contained much of the verse for which he is particularly remembered today, including "The Solitary Reaper," "I Wandered Lonely as a Cloud," "Sonnet Composed upon Westminster Bridge," and "Ode: Intimations of Immortality." As with *Lyrical Ballads,* this volume initially received many negative reviews.

From 1807 on, Wordsworth's poetic powers declined. Backing away from his youthful support of the French Revolution, Wordsworth became increasingly conservative: Later editions of *Lyrical Ballads,* for instance, contain poems celebrating capital punishment. Abandoning his pantheistic (finding the divine in all creation) views of a God within man and nature, Wordsworth became increasingly conventional in his religious beliefs. Even Wordsworth's language changed, becoming increasingly stilted. The philosopher Bertrand Russell described the feelings of many scholars when he wrote:

> In his youth Wordsworth sympathized with the French Revolution, went to France, wrote good poetry.... At this period he was called a "bad" man. Then he became "good," ... adopted correct principles, and wrote bad poetry.

In 1814 Wordsworth published "The Excursion," intended to be a part of the longer, philosophical poem, *The Recluse.* Its publication was greeted by Francis Jeffrey in the *Edinburgh Review* by the famous line, "This will never do!" While some passages rise to former heights of greatness, the poem is primarily of interest today as autobiography.

In 1843, after the death of Robert Southey, Wordsworth was named poet laureate of England. He was venerated by many younger writers, such as Matthew Arnold, but was criticized for his lapse into conservatism by some of the new generation of poets such as Robert Browning.

Critical Analysis

Most of the poetry for which Wordsworth is known today was written between 1793 and 1807. These are the poems in which Wordsworth seeks the truth about human nature and often finds it among the poor and suffering. These are the poems in which he tries to express his vision in the simple language of the everyday, and in which he seeks out the sublime in nature as a moral compass for humankind.

Among the greatest of Wordsworth's poems is "Ode: Intimations of Immortality." As the poem begins, the poet recalls the innocence of his youth and his capacity for seeing nature "Apparell'd in celestial light" but laments that he no longer sees as he once did: "There hath pass'd away a glory from the earth." He tries to rouse himself to enjoy the pastoral scene and chides himself for his sullenness "While Earth itself is adorning, / This sweet May-Morning." Still, he finds that he cannot recapture "the glory and the dream" of his youth.

From this feeling brought on by his observation of physical nature, the poet begins to articulate his philosophy of human nature. Birth, he says, is "but a sleep and a forgetting." The soul of a newborn child comes from heaven "trailing clouds of glory." Thus a young child is still suffused with divinity, still "Nature's priest" and the "best philosopher." As he ages, however, the child begins to lose his grasp on "the glories he has known," distracted by what Wordsworth in another poem, "The World Is Too Much With Us," called "getting and spending," the comings and goings of daily life. In fact, the poet says, children hold the "truths . . . which we are toiling all our lives to find."

Yet Wordsworth does not give up hope for humanity because "in our embers / Is something that doth live, / That nature yet remembers." We have, as the title suggests, "intimations of immortality":

> . . . in a season of calm weather
> Though inland far we be,
> Our souls have sight of that immortal sea
> Which brought us hither.

According to Wordsworth, all of our best choices, our finest stirrings, our ability to feel joy and to appreciate the truly sublime beauties of nature stem from this memory of our union with the divine, from which we came and toward which we are journeying. So, as the poet says in one of the most frequently quoted lines in the poem, "Though nothing can bring back the hour / Of splendor in the grass, of glory in the flower"—the intense perceptions of youth—there are strengths and joys in maturity also:

> We will grieve not, rather find
> Strength in what remains behind;
> In the primal sympathy
> Which having been must ever be;
> In the soothing thoughts that spring
> Out of human suffering;
> In the faith that looks through death,
> In years that bring the philosophic mind.

Although the beauties of nature no longer reveal themselves to the poet, in their celestial colors even the "meanest flower" provokes "Thoughts that do often lie too deep for tears." Thus the human capacity to suffer and survive, to wonder and wish, to love and cherish, all stem from the faded memory of the union with the divine force.

Other Work by William Wordsworth
William Wordsworth: The Major Works. New York: Oxford University Press, 2000.

Works about William Wordsworth
Bloom, Harold. *William Wordsworth.* New York: Chelsea House, 2004.
Davies, Hunter. *William Wordsworth.* London: Weidenfeld & Nicolson, 1997.
Mahoney, John. *William Wordsworth: A Poetic Life.* New York: Fordham University Press, 1997.
Roe, Nicholas. *The Politics of Nature: William Wordsworth and Some Contemporaries.* New York: Palgrave Macmillan, 2002.

Y-Z

Yates, Edmund Hodgson (1831–1894)
journalist, novelist

Edmund Yates was born in Edinburgh, Scotland, where his parents, Frederick Yates and Elizabeth Brunton, were on tour with a theater company. Yates was educated in England and Germany. From 1847 to 1872 he worked in the British Post Office while writing theater reviews, plays, and articles for literary journals on the side. In 1853 he married Louisa Wilkinson, with whom he had four children. Several comedies that Yates wrote were produced in 1857. He also became widely known as one of the first gossip columnists in England while editing the newspaper *Town Talk*.

During the 1860s, Yates began publishing novels, such as *Black Sheep!* (1867), a crime novel, and *The Rock Ahead* (1868). His books were fast-moving, cosmopolitan, and stylish, with crime and sex often central to the plot. Like his mentor CHARLES DICKENS, Yates went on a successful lecture and reading tour in the United States, where his novels were popular. In 1873 he became a correspondent for the *New York Herald*, and in 1874, he founded a new society magazine, *The World: A Journal for Men and Women*.

Meanwhile, he continued producing novels at a remarkable rate, including *The Impending Sword* (1874) and *The Silent Witness* (1875). He had also become editor of a monthly magazine, *Time*, where he worked from 1879 to 1884. Yates published an entertaining memoir, *Recollections and Experiences*, in 1884.

A Work about Edmund Yates

Edwards, P. O. *Dickens's "Young Men": George Augustus Sala, Edmund Yates and the World of Victorian Journalism.* New York: Cambridge University Press, 1997.

Yonge, Charlotte Mary (1823–1901)
novelist, children's writer, nonfiction writer

Charlotte Yonge was born in Otterbourne, near Winchester, England, to William Yonge, an officer in the British army who had fought at Waterloo, and Frances Mary Bargus Yonge. Both of Yonge's grandfathers were clergymen, and the Yonge household was a deeply religious one. She was educated at home and knew few people outside her family.

Yonge's life was quiet and uneventful. She was a teacher in the village school, as well as of Sunday school. She took only one trip away from Otterbourne, visiting Paris in 1869, and moved out of the house in which she was born only when she was nearly 40. Her hobby was botany, about which she was extremely knowledgeable.

In 1835, when Yonge was 12, the well-known theologian JOHN KEBLE was appointed to serve in the nearby parish of Hursley. Keble, along with JOHN NEWMAN, was an important leader of the OXFORD MOVEMENT, whose aim was to promote the Church of England as a divinely sponsored institution and to preserve it from increasing secularization and domination by the British government. The Oxford Movement, which also sought to reintroduce ritual and ceremonies that had been abandoned in the 17th century, influenced many writers, among them ALFRED, LORD TENNYSON, WILLIAM MORRIS, CHRISTINA ROSSETTI, as well as Charlotte Yonge. One result of the movement was to split the Anglican Church into the "Broad" (which was typically Protestant in its leanings), "Low" (which was evangelical and less concerned with ritual), and "High" (which tended to be more Catholic in nature). Inspired by Keble, who was almost a second father to her, Yonge was a follower of the High Church.

Yonge's first book, *Le Château de Melville*, written in French and published when she was 15, was intended as a fund-raiser for a local girls' school. Her first serious attempt at fiction was *Abbeychurch; or, Self-Control and Self-Conceit* (1844), in which the novel's main character, Lizzie Woodbourne, must learn to control her impulses with the help of a neighbor and her father, a vicar.

Yonge's first great success was *The Heir of Redclyffe* (1853), which details the spiritual struggle of Guy Morville. Yonge followed with *Heartsease; or, The Brother's Wife* (1854), in which the 16-year-old middle-class Violet struggles to win the approval and affection of her husband's aristocratic family. After several disasters and a fire that destroys the family home (along with a domineering, rich aunt), Violet succeeds in earning a place among the Martindales.

Equal in popularity to *The Heir of Redclyffe*, *The Daisy Chain; or, Aspirations* (1856) is the story of the motherless May family and how Ethel May and her siblings bring education and High Church Christianity to a group of quarry workers. As Yonge writes in the novel's preface, this book is "a Family Chronicle—a domestic record of home events, large and small, during those years of early life when the character is chiefly formed, and as an endeavour to trace the effects of those aspirations which are a part of every youthful nature. That the young should take one hint, to think whether their hopes and upward-breathings are truly upwards, and founded in lowliness, may be called the moral of the tale."

Although nearly all of Yonge's fictional works are about family and home life, most often enjoyed by women in the 19th century, her books had broader appeal. It is said that her works were the favorites of soldiers during the Crimean War (1853–56). Virtually everyone read her work, including such well-known figures as the American novelist Louisa May Alcott, Christina Rossetti, and William Morris. Yonge's influence can clearly be seen in the focus on brothers and sisters in Alcott's *Little Women* (1868–69) and *Little Men* (1871). In the former, Meg finds her sister Jo crying over a copy of *The Heir of Redclyffe*.

Yonge was an extraordinarily prolific writer. In addition to novels for adults, she turned out children's books, particularly historical novels; textbooks; history; and biography—more than 200 works in all. Between 1851 and 1890 she also edited a children's magazine, the *Monthly Packet*, and two Sunday-school publications.

Critical Analysis

Yonge wrote in the genre of domestic realism, and nearly all of her fiction deals with life in large families of the same class as her own, and especially with relations among brothers and sisters. Though usually didactic and deeply influenced by High Church principles, her fiction includes compelling characters and convincing dialogue. Many modern readers find Yonge's work a treasure trove of information about daily life in Victorian England.

To place the popularity of her work in context, it is important to note that the Victorian period was one of huge social, economic, and scientific change, which many people found disturbing. Yonge was popular largely because her works were conservative—even reactionary—and portrayed the old virtues as crucial to spiritual survival in the modern world. In the Victorian era, nostalgia for better days led writers like Yonge to idealize the age of chivalry as embodying virtues that were lost to the nineteenth century.

The Heir of Redclyffe tells the story of Sir Guy Morville, who fears his own downfall as a result of the family curse, a violent temper. He spends his life attempting to keep himself under control and to remain securely on the path of righteousness. Although he slips and struggles, Guy is a paradigm of virtue. He is generous, truthful, religious, and extraordinarily devoted to his wife:

> Guy was a very chivalrous lover; the polish and courtesy that sat so well on his frank, truthful manners, were even more remarkable in his courtship. . . . [He] treated her with a sort of reverential love and gentleness, while she looked up to him with ever-increasing honour.

In portraying Guy as she does, Yonge emphasizes the importance of morality over all other character traits. She contrasts Guy with his more brilliant and polished cousin Phillip, who is shown to be deficient. Guy's redemption is completed in his alliance with Amy Edmonstone, who is Yonge's ideal woman—subservient to husband and father, a moral compass for her husband and family. Guy regards Amy as "a guide and guard whose love might arm him, soothe him, and encourage him."

Guy Morville became a model of the masculine ideal for many in the Victorian era. According to the scholar Kate Saunders, "A whole generation of young people was inspired by the hero, Sir Guy Morville, a blueprint for the new 'macho' ideal of the age. Guy is moral, courageous, self-sacrificing, and places duty before his own self-interest. The Pre-Raphaelite artists William Morris and Edward Burne-Jones categorized Morville's goodness as "a pattern for actual life."

Nineteenth-century women also found models in Yonge's books. As the scholar Julia Courtney writes, "The ideas that she promulgated through her books, through her personal influence and through her letters were actually major ideas for a key generation of Victorian women—the women born in the second half of the 1840s who went on to become the first generation of women head teachers, who founded the Girls' High Schools, and who became the Principals of the new women's colleges at various universities."

Other Work by Charlotte Yonge
The Caged Lion. 1870. Reprint, Maclean, Va.: Indypublish, 2002.

Works about Charlotte Yonge
Dennis, Barbara. *Charlotte Yonge: Novelist of the Oxford Movement.* Lewiston, N.Y.: Edwin Mellin Press, 1992.
Hayter, Althea. *Charlotte Yonge.* Jackson, Miss.: Northcote House, 1996.

Zangwill, Israel (1864–1926) *novelist, short story writer, playwright*

Israel Zangwill was one of England's most popular writers in the last decade of the 19th century. He was born in London to Jewish immigrant parents from eastern Europe; his father, Moses Zangwill, a clothing peddler, came from Latvia and his mother, Ellen Hannah Marks Zangwill, from Poland. He began his schooling in Bristol, where his parents had moved shortly after his birth, but continued his studies at the Jew's Free School in London's East End when they moved back. His academic brilliance was such that he became a pupil-teacher before graduating. He proceeded to London University, where he graduated with honors in French, English, and "Mental and Moral Science."

An essay, "English Judaism," which he wrote for the *Jewish Quarterly Review,* convinced the Jewish Publication Society of Philadelphia to commission him to write a novel expanding on his description of contemporary Jewish ghetto life. This became *Children of the Ghetto* (1892), a novel of generational and cultural conflict among immigrant Jews in England; and it was immediately and immensely popular. The novel's first part, "Children of the Ghetto," primarily depicts the older generation of immigrant Jews as they try to manage their lives amid great poverty, while the second, "Grandchildren of the Ghetto," concerns the English-born second generation of Jews who have become assimilated and have prospered. Zangwill's skill in depicting the very real characters and their struggles, along with the humor that sustained them in their difficulties, appealed to a wide audience of non-Jews, for whom Zangwill included explanations of Jewish culture: "The Chasidim are the Corybantes or Salvationists of Judaism. In England their idiosyncrasies are limited to noisy jubilant services in their *Chevrah,* the worshippers dancing or leaning or standing or writhing or beating their heads against the wall as they will, and frisking like happy children in the presence of their Father."

Zangwill's best novel, *The King of Schnorrers* (1894), tells the story of a "schnorrer," a wheedler or beggar who can skillfully manipulate his victims into giving him what he wants, whether or not he is deserving of their largesse. In this case, Manasseh Bueno Barzillai Azevedo da Costa, an aristocratic Sephardic (Mediterranean) Jew, outwits the far richer Ashkenazi (Eastern European) Jew Joseph Brobstock, but meets his match with the Tedesco (German) Jew Yankelé, who wants to become his son-in-law. Because Yankelé exhibits schnorrering abilities equal to his own, Manesseh has to give in.

Mining again this rich vein of ghetto Jewish life and humor, Zangwill produced in 1898 a masterful collection of stories, *Dreamers of the Ghetto.* His play *The Melting Pot* (1908) made the title phrase popular as a description of the United States. Zangwill was to continue writing in many genres almost until the day of his death, but what he is mainly remembered for are the works produced in the especially prolific period of the 1890s. The critic Meri-Jane Rochelson has analyzed Zangwill's diminishing popularity: "There are a number of reasons for the eclipse of Zangwill's reputation after his death in 1926. These include the rise of modernism, which placed his fiction outside the literary canon, and the drily didactic quality of many of his later plays, which made them unsuccessful in their day and unlikely candidates for revival." Zangwill's writings, however, continue to interest those concerned with the history of the Jewish experience in England.

A Work about Israel Zangwill

Udelson, Joseph H. *Dreamer of the Ghetto: The Life and Works of Israel Zangwill.* Tuscaloosa: University of Alabama Press, 1990.

Selected Bibliography

Abrams, M. H., ed. *The Norton Anthology of English Literature.* 6th ed., Vol. 2. New York: W. W. Norton, 1993.

Adburgham, Alison. *Silver Fork Society: Fashionable Life and Literature from 1814.* London: Constable, 1983.

Altick, Richard D. *The English Common Reader: A Social History of the Mass Reading Public, 1800–1900.* 2d ed. Columbus: Ohio State University Press, 1998.

Ardis, Ann L. *New Women, New Novels: Feminism and Early Modernism.* New Brunswick, N.J.: Rutgers University Press, 1990.

Armstrong, Nancy. *Desire and Domestic Fiction: A Political History of the Novel.* New York: Oxford University Press, 1995.

Ashton, Rosemary. *Thomas and Jane Carlyle: Portrait of a Marriage.* London: Random House, 2003.

Ayres, Brenda. *Frances Trollope and the Novel of Social Change.* Westport, Conn.: Greenwood Press, 2001.

Baring-Gould, Sabine. *Curious Myths of the Middle Ages.* New York: Crescent Books, 1987.

Barros, Carolyn, and Johanna Smith, eds. *Life-Writings by British Women, 1660–1815: An Anthology.* Boston: Northeastern University Press, 2000.

Beer, John. *William Blake: A Literary Life.* New York: Palgrave Macmillan, 2007.

Belford, Barbara. *Bram Stoker and the Man Who Was Dracula.* New York: Da Capo, 2002.

Bellamy, Joan, et al., eds. *Women, Scholarship and Criticism, 1790–1900.* Manchester, England: Manchester University Press, 2001.

Berlin, Isaiah. *The Roots of Romanticism.* Princeton, N.J.: Princeton University Press, 2001.

Bieri, James. *Percy Bysshe Shelley: A Biography.* Baltimore: Johns Hopkins University Press, 2008.

Black, Eugene C., ed. *British Politics in the Nineteenth Century.* New York: Harper & Row, 1969.

Blades, John. *John Keats.* New York: Palgrave Macmillan, 2002.

Blain, Virginia, et al. *Feminist Companion to Literature in English: Women Writers from the Middle Ages to the Present.* New Haven, Conn.: Yale University Press, 1990.

Bloom, Harold. *The Visionary Company: A Reading of English Romantic Poetry.* Ithaca, N.Y.: Cornell University Press, 1971.

———, ed. *Classic Horror Writers.* Philadelphia: Chelsea House, 1993.

———. *Pre-Raphaelite Poets.* New York: Chelsea House, 1986.

———. *William Wordsworth.* New York: Chelsea House, 2004.

Blumenberg, Werner. *Karl Marx: An illustrated History.* New York: Verso Press, 2000.

Boas, Elizabeth Schutz. *Elizabeth Barrett Browning.* Whitefish, Mont.: Kessinger, 2005.

Bratton, J. S. *The Impact of Victorian Children's Fiction.* Totowa, N.J.: Barnes & Noble, 1981.

Brooks, Peter. *Henry James Goes to Paris.* Princeton, N.J.: Princeton University Press, 2007.

Browne, E. Janet. *Charles Darwin: The Power of Place.* Princeton, N.J.: Princeton University Press, 2003.

Buckley, Jerome H. *The Victorian Temper.* New York: Vintage, 1951.

Buckley, Jerome H., ed. *The Pre-Raphaelites: An Anthology.* Chicago: Academy Chicago, 1986.

Buckton, Oliver S. *Cruising with Robert Louis Stevenson: Travel, Narrative, and the Colonial Body.* Columbus: Ohio University Press, 2007.

Burroughs, Catherine, ed. *Women in British Romantic Theatre: Drama, Performance, and Society, 1790–1840.* Cambridge: Cambridge University Press, 2000.

Caine, Barbara. *Victorian Feminists.* New York: Oxford University Press, 1992.

Capaldi, Nicholas. *John Stuart Mill: A Biography.* Cambridge: Cambridge University Press, 2004.

Carpenter, Humphrey, and Mari Prichard. *The Oxford Companion to Children's Literature.* New York: Oxford University Press, 1984.

Carpenter, Angelica Shirley. *In the Garden: Essays in Honor of Frances Hodgson Burnett.* Lanham, Md.: Scarecrow Press, 2006.

Carretta, Vincent. *Equiano, the African: Biography of a Self-Made Man.* New York: Penguin, 2007.

Cervelli, Kenneth R. *Dorothy Wordsworth's Ecology.* New York: Routledge, 2007.

Chesterton, G. K. *The Victorian Age in Literature.* Notre Dame, Ind.: University of Notre Dame Press, 1962.

Child, Lincoln, ed. *Dark Banquet: A Feast of Twelve Great Ghost Stories.* New York: St. Martin's Press, 1985.

Chitham, Edward. *The Birth of Wuthering Heights: Emily Brontë at Work.* New York: Palgrave Macmillan, 2001.

Christie, William. *Samuel Taylor Coleridge: A Literary Life.* New York: Palgrave Macmillan, 2006.

Clery, E. J. *Women's Gothic: From Clara Reeve to Mary Shelley.* Horndon, England: Northcote House Publishers, 2000.

Cohen, Paula Marantz. *The Daughter's Dilemma: Family Process and the Nineteenth-Century Domestic Novel.* Ann Arbor: University of Michigan Press, 1991.

Colby, Vineta. *The Singular Anomaly: Women Novelists of the Nineteenth Century.* New York: New York University Press, 1970.

———. *Vernon Lee: A Literary Biography.* Charlottesville: University of Virginia Press, 2003.

Collingwood, Stuart Dodgson. *The Life and Letters of Lewis Carroll.* Whitefish, Mont.: Kessinger, 2004.

Cook, Jon. *Hazlitt in Love: A Fatal Attachment.* London: Short Books, 2007.

Cox, Jeffrey. *Poetry and Politics in the Cockney School: Keats, Shelley, Hunt, and Their Circle.* Cambridge, England: Cambridge University Press, 1998.

Cox, Michael, ed. *Victorian Tales of Mystery and Detection: An Oxford Anthology.* New York: Oxford University Press, 1992.

Crisp, Shelley Jean. *The Woman Poet Emerges: The Literary Tradition of Mary Coleridge, Alice Meynell, and Charlotte Mew.* Ann Arbor: University of Michigan Press, 1987.

Crumb, Lawrence N. *The Oxford Movement and Its Leaders.* Lanham, Md.: Scarecrow Press, 1990.

Cuddon, J. A. *The Penguin Dictionary of Literary Terms and Literary Theory.* 4th ed. New York: Penguin Books, 1999.

Cunningham, Valentine, ed. *The Victorians: An Anthology of Poetry and Poetics.* Malden, Mass.: Blackwell, 2000.

Daiches, David, ed. *The Penguin Companion to English Literature.* New York: Penguin, 1971.

Damon, S. Foster. *William Blake: His Philosophy and Symbols.* Whitefish, Mont.: Kessinger, 2006.

David, Deirdre. *Intellectual Women and Victorian Patriarchy: Harriet Martineau, Elizabeth Bar-

rett Browning, George Eliot. Ithaca, N.Y.: Cornell University Press, 1987.
Dossey, Barbara. *Florence Nightingale: Mystic, Visionary, Healer.* New York: Lippincott Williams & Wilkins, 2000.
Drabble, Margaret, ed. *The Oxford Companion to English Literature.* 6th ed. New York: Oxford University Press, 2000.
Edwards, Paul, ed. The Encyclopedia of Philosophy. New York: Macmillan, 1967.
Edwards, Peter David. *Idyllic Realism from Mary Russell Mitford to Hardy.* New York: St. Martin's Press, 1988.
Eisler, Benita. *Naked in the Marketplace: The Lives of George Sand.* Berkeley, Calif.: Counterpoint, 2006.
Ella, George Melvin. *William Cowper: The Man of God's Stamp.* Guelph, Canada: Joshua Press, 2001.
Ellis, Stickney S. *From Marlowe to Shaw.* London: Williams & Norgate, 1950.
———. *From Rousseau to Proust.* Freeport, N.Y.: Books for Librarians, 1968.
Fairweather, E. R. *The Oxford Movement.* New York: Oxford University Press, 1964.
Fairweather, Maria. *Madame de Staël.* New York: Carroll & Graf, 2006.
Fallis, Richard. *The Irish Renaissance.* Syracuse, N.Y.: Syracuse University Press, 1977.
Feldman, Paula R., ed. *British Women Poets of the Romantic Era: An Anthology.* Baltimore: Johns Hopkins University Press, 1997.
Feldman, Paula, and Theresa Kelley, eds. *Romantic Women Writers: Voices and Countervoices.* Hanover, N.H.: University Press of New England, 1995.
Fellows, Lawrence, and Janet Beller. *A Gentle War: The Story of the Salvation Army.* New York: Athenaeum, 1980.
Fraser, Rebecca. *Charlotte Brontë.* New York: Vintage, 2003.
Gagnier, Regenia. *Subjectivities: A History of Self-Representation in Britain, 1832–1920.* New York: Oxford University Press, 1991.
Galchinsky, Michael. *The Origin of the Modern Jewish Woman Writer: Romance and Reform in Victorian England.* Detroit: Wayne State University Press, 1996.
Gallagher, Catherine. *The Industrial Reformation of English Fiction: Social Discourse and Narrative Form 1832–1867.* Chicago: University of Chicago Press, 1985.
Gardner, Burdett. *Lesbian Imagination Victorian Style: A Psychological and Critical Study of Vernon Lee.* New York: Garland, 1981.
Garrett, Martin. *Elizabeth Barrett Browning and Robert Browning.* British Library Writers' Library Lives Series. Oxford: Oxford University Press, 2002.
Gaull, Marilyn. *English Romanticism: The Human Context.* New York: W. W. Norton, 1988.
Gilmour, David. *The Long Recessional: The Imperial Life of Rudyard Kipling.* New York: Farrar, Straus & Giroux, 2003.
Gordon, Lyndall. *Vindication: A Life of Mary Wollstonecraft.* New York: Harper Perennial, 2006.
Greenfield, John R., ed. *British Romantic Prose Writers, 1789–1832.* Detroit: Gale, 1991.
Guy, Josephine. *The Victorian Social Problem Novel: The Market, the Individual, and Communal Life.* New York: St. Martin's Press, 1996.
Halladay, Jean R. *Eight Late Victorian Poets Shaping the Artistic Sensibility of an Age.* Lewiston, N.Y.: Edwin Mellen Press, 1993.
Hardin, Terri. *The Pre-Raphaelites: Inspiration from the Past.* New York: Todtri Productions Limited, 1996.
Hardy, Barbara. *George Eliot: A Critic's Biography.* London: Continuum, 2006.
Hare, Augustus J. C., ed. *The Life and Letters of Maria Edgeworth.* Gloucester, England: Dodo Press, 2007.
Harlan, Elizabeth. *George Sand.* New Haven: Yale University Press, 2004.
Harris, Lanzen, ed. *Nineteenth Century Literature Criticism.* Vol. 6. Detroit: Gale, 1981.
Harvey, Sir Paul. *The Oxford Companion to English Literature.* 4th ed. New York: Oxford University Press, 1967.
Hawlin, Stefan. *Robert Browning: A Sourcebook.* London: Routledge, 2001.

Heilmann, Ann. *New Woman Fiction: Women Writing First-Wave Feminism.* New York: St. Martin's Press, 2000.

Henderson, John P., and John B. Davis. *The Life and Economics of David Ricardo.* New York: Springer, 1997.

Hendrickson, Robert. *British Literary Anecdotes.* New York: Facts On File, 1990.

Herold, J. Christopher. *Mistress to an Age: A Life of Madame de Staël.* New York: Grove, 2002.

Hewison, Robert, Ian Warrell, and Stephen Wildman. *Ruskin, Turner, and the Pre-Raphaelites.* London: Tate Gallery Publishing, 2000.

Hilton, Tim. *John Ruskin.* New Haven, Conn.: Yale University Press, 2002.

Holland, Merlin. *The Real Trial of Oscar Wilde.* New York: Harper Perennial, 2004.

Honderich, Ted. *The Oxford Companion to Philosophy.* New York: Oxford University Press, 1995.

Hoobler, Dorothy, and Thomas Hoobler. *The Monsters: Mary Shelley and the Curse of Frankenstein.* Boston: Back Bay Books, 2007.

Houghton, Walter E. *The Victorian Frame of Mind.* New Haven, Conn.: Yale University Press, 1957.

Howard, David, Jon Lucas, and John Goode, eds. *Traditions and Tolerance in Nineteenth-Century Fiction.* New York: Barnes & Noble, 1967.

Hughes, Kathryn. *George Eliot: The Last Victorian.* New York: Cooper Square Press, 2001.

Jacobs, Diane. *Her Own Woman: The Life of Mary Wollstonecraft.* Yucca Valley, Calif.: Citadel, 2003.

Jeal, Tim. *Stanley: The Impossible Life of Africa's Greatest Explorer.* New Haven: Yale University Press, 2007.

Jeffrey, Francis. *On the Lake Poets.* Washington, D.C.: Woodstock Books, 1998.

Johnson, George. *British Novelists Between the Wars.* Detroit: Gale Research, 1998.

Jones, Ann H. *Ideas and Innovations: Best Sellers of Jane Austen's Age.* New York: AMS Press, 1986.

Kemp, Peter, ed. *The Oxford Dictionary of Literary Quotations.* New York: Oxford University Press, 1998.

Kennedy, Richard S. and Donald S. Hair. *The Dramatic Imagination of Robert Browning: A Literary Life.* Columbia: University of Missouri Press, 2007.

Knoepflmacher, U. C. *Religious Humanism and the Victorian Novel: George Eliot, Walter Pater, and Samuel Butler.* Princeton, N.J.: Princeton University Press, 1965.

Kroeber, Karl. *Romantic Narrative Art.* Madison: University of Wisconsin Press, 1966.

Kunitz, Stanley J., ed. *British Authors of the Nineteenth Century.* New York: H. W. Wilson, 1936.

Lang, Andrew. *Custom and Myth.* London: Routledge, 1997.

Lang, Cecil B., ed. *The Pre-Raphaelites and Their Circle.* 2d ed. Chicago: University of Chicago Press, 1975.

Langley, Helen. *Benjamin Disraeli: Scenes from an Extraordinary Life.* Oxford: Bodelean Library, 2005.

Lapp, Robert Keith. *Contest for Cultural Authority: Hazlitt, Coleridge, and the Distresses of the Regency.* Detroit: Wayne State University, 1999.

Ledger, Sally, and Allison Ledger. *The New Woman: Fiction and Feminism at the Fin de Siècle.* Manchester, England: Manchester University Press, 1997.

Lee, Edmund. *Dorothy Wordsworth: The Story of a Sister's Love.* 1894. Reprint, Whitefish, Mont.: Kessinger, 2007.

Lellenberg, Jon, Daniel Stashower, and Charles Foley. *Arthur Conan Doyle: A Life in Letters.* New York: Penguin, 2007.

Logan, Deborah Anna. *The Hour and the Woman: Harriet Martineau's "Somewhat Remarkable" Life.* DeKalb: Northern Illinois University Press, 2002.

Lycett, Andrew. *The Man Who Created Sherlock Holmes: The Life and Times of Sir Arthur Conan Doyle.* New York: Free Press, 2007.

MacCarthy, Fiona. *Byron: Life and Legend.* New York: Farrar, Straus & Giroux, 2004.

Markos, Louis A. *Pressing Forward: Alfred, Lord Tennyson and the Victorian Age.* Ave Maria, Fla.: Sapienta Press of Ave Maria University, 2007.

Marcus, Sharon. *Between Women: Friendship, Desire, and Marriage in Victorian England.* Princeton, N.J.: Princeton University Press, 2007.

Marsh, Jan. *The Pre-Raphaelite Sisterhood.* New York: St. Martin's Press, 1985.

Matus, Jill L., ed. *The Cambridge Companion to Elizabeth Gaskell.* Cambridge: Cambridge University Press, 2007.

McCarthy, Fiona. *William Morris.* New York: Faber & Faber, 2003.

McGann, Jerome. *Dante Gabriel Rossetti and the Game that Must Be Lost.* New Haven, Conn.: Yale University Press, 2000.

McGavran, James Hold, ed. *Romanticism and Children's Literature in Nineteenth-Century England.* Athens: University of Georgia Press, 1991.

McIntyre, Ian. *Dirt and Diety: A Life of Robert Burns.* New York: HarperCollins, 1996.

Mighall, Robert. *A Geography of Victorian Gothic Fiction: Mapping History's Nightmares.* New York: Oxford University Press, 2000.

Moore, Thomas. *The Life and Death of Lord Edward Fitzgerald.* Whitefish, Mont.: Kessinger, 2007.

Morrow, John. *Thomas Carlyle.* London: Hambledon & London, 2007.

Muller, Jill. *Gerard Manley Hopkins and Victorian Catholicism: A Heart in Hiding.* London: Taylor & Francis, 2007.

Murphy, Patricia. *Time Is of the Essence: Temporality, Gender, and the New Woman.* Albany: State University of New York Press, 2001.

Myers, Sylvia Harcstark. *The Bluestocking Circle: Women, Friendship, and the Life of the Mind in Eighteenth-Century England.* New York: Oxford University Press, 1990.

Newman, James L. *Imperial Footprints: Henry Morton Stanley's African Journeys.* Dulles, Va.: Potomac Books, 2006.

Noakes, Vivian. *Edward Lear: The Life of a Wanderer.* London: Sutton, 2006.

Norton, Ricter. *Mistress of Udolpho: The Life of Ann Radcliffe.* Leicester, England: Leicester University Press, 1999.

Novick, Sheldon M. *Henry James: The Mature Master.* New York: Random House, 2007.

———. *Henry James: The Young Master.* New York: Random House, 2007.

O'Connell, Marvin. *The Oxford Conspirators: A History of the Oxford Movement, 1833–1845.* Lanham, Md.: University Press of America, 2000.

Orel, Harold. *Victorian Literary Critics: George Henry Lewes, Walter Bagehot, Richard Holt Hutton, Leslie Stephen, Andrew Lang, George Saintsbury, and Edmund Gosse.* New York: St. Martin's Press, 1984.

Ousby, Ian. *The Cambridge Guide to Literature in English.* New York: Cambridge University Press, 1999.

Palazzo, Lynda. *Christina Rossetti's Feminist Theology.* New York: Palgrave Macmillan, 2002.

Parker, Peter, ed. *A Reader's Guide to Twentieth Century Writers.* New York: Oxford University Press, 1996.

Pascal, Janet B., ed. *Beyond Baker Street.* New York: Oxford University Press, 2000.

Pearce, Joseph. *The Unmasking of Oscar Wilde.* Fort Collins, Colo.: Ignatius Press, 2005.

Perkins, David, ed. *English Romantic Writers.* New York: Harcourt, Brace & World, 1967.

Peterson, William. *Malthus: The Founder of Modern Demography.* Edison, N.J.: Transaction Publishers, 1998.

Photiadis, Constantin. *George Meredith: His Life, Genius, and Teaching.* Honolulu: University Press of the Pacific, 2004.

Pite, Ralph. *Thomas Hardy: The Guarded Life.* New York: Picador, 2007.

Pollard, Arthur, ed. *The Victorians.* Vol. 6 of *The Penguin History of Literature.* New York: Penguin Books, 1993.

Powell, Neil. *George Crabbe: An English Life, 1754–1832.* London: Random House, 2004.

Pratt, Linda Ray. *Matthew Arnold Revisited.* New York: Twayne, 2000.

Purinton, Marjean D. *Romantic Ideology Unmasked: The Mentally Constructed Tyrannies in Dramas of William Wordsworth, Lord Byron, Percy Shelley, and Joanna Baillie.* Newark: University of Delaware Press, 1994.

Quammen, David. *The Reluctant Mr. Darwin: An Intimate Portrait of Charles Darwin and the Making of His Theory of Evolution.* New York: Norton, 2007.

Reeves, Richard. *John Stuart Mill.* Conshohocken, Penn.: Atlantic Books, 2007.

Richards, Janet Radcliffe. *Human Nature after Darwin: A Philosophical Introduction.* London: Routledge, 2001.

Richardson, Angelique, and Chris Willis, eds. *The New Woman in Fiction and in Fact: Fin de Siècle Feminisms.* Foreword by Lyn Pykett. New York: Palgrave Macmillan, 2001.

Roe, Nicholas. *The Politics of Nature: William Wordsworth and Some Contemporaries.* New York: Palgrave Macmillan, 2002.

Rogers, Pat, ed. *The Oxford Illustrated History of English Literature.* New York: Oxford University Press, 1987.

Rosa, M. A. *The Silver-Fork School.* New York: Columbia University Press, 1936.

Rose, Phyllis. *Parallel Lives: Four Victorian Marriages.* New York: Random House, 1983.

Sanders, Andrew. *The Short Oxford History of English Literature.* Oxford, England: Oxford University Press, Clarendon Press, 1994.

Schaffer, Talia. *The Forgotten Female Aesthetes.* Charlottesville: University Press of Virginia, 2000.

Schaffer, Talia, and Kathy Psomiades, eds. *Women and British Aestheticism.* Charlottesville: University Press of Virginia, 1999.

Scheinberg, Cynthia. *Women's Poetry and Religion in Victorian England: Jewish Identity and Christian Culture.* Cambridge, England: Cambridge University Press, 2002.

Scheller, William. *Amazing Archaeologists and Their Finds.* Minneapolis: Oliver Press, 1994.

Schlueter, Paul, and June Schlueter, eds. *An Encyclopedia of British Women Writers.* Rev. eds. New Brunswick, N.J.: Rutgers University Press, 1998.

Schmidt, Michael. *Lives of the Poets.* New York: Alfred A. Knopf, 1999.

Schofield, Philip. *Utility and Democracy: The Political Thought of Jeremy Bentham.* Oxford: Oxford University Press, 2006.

Scott, Walter Sidney. *The Bluestocking Ladies.* London: J. Green, 1947.

Scullion, Adrienne, ed. *Female Playwrights of the Nineteenth Century.* London: J. M. Dent, 1996.

Shattock, Joanne. *Oxford Guide to British Women Writers.* New York: Oxford University Press, 1993.

Showalter, Elaine. *A Literature of Their Own: British Women Novelists from Brontë to Lessing.* Princeton, N.J.: Princeton University Press, 1976.

Siepmann, Katherine Baker, ed. *Benét's Reader's Encyclopedia.* 3d ed. New York: HarperCollins, 1987.

Simonton, Dean Keith. *Origins of Genius: Darwinian Perspectives on Creativity.* Oxford, England: Oxford University Press, 1999.

Skousen, Mark. *The Big Three in Economics: Adam Smith, Karl Marx, and John Maynard Keynes.* New York: M.E. Sharpe, 2007.

Slater, Michael. *Charles Dickens.* Very Interesting People Series. Oxford: Oxford University Press, 2007.

Smiley, Jane. *Charles Dickens.* London: Phoenix, 2003.

Smith, Margaret, ed. *Selected Letters of Charlotte Brontë.* New York: Oxford University Press, 2007.

Somervell, D. C. *English Thought in the Nineteenth Century.* New York: David McKay, 1965.

Speck, W. A. *Robert Southey: Entire Man of Letters.* New Haven, Conn.: Yale University Press, 2006.

Spender, Dale. *Mothers of the Novel: 100 Good Women Writers before Jane Austen.* London: Pandora, 1986.

Spense, John. *Becoming Jane Austen.* London: Continuum, 2007.

Stephen, Leslie, Sir. *The English Utilitarians.* Vol. 1. New York: A. M. Kelley, 1968.

Stephen, Leslie, and Sidney Lee, eds. *The Dictionary of National Biography.* Vol. 19. London: Oxford University Press, 1959.

Stevenson, Lionel. *The Pre-Raphaelite Poets.* Chapel Hill: University of North Carolina Press, 1972.

Stitt, Megan. *Metaphors of Change in the Language of Nineteenth-Century Fiction: Scott, Gaskell, and Kingsley.* New York: Oxford University Press, 1998.

Stott, Rebecca, and Simon Avery. *Elizabeth Barrett Browning: Studies in 18th and 19th Century Literature Series.* New York: Longman, 2003.

Strachey, Lytton. *Eminent Victorians.* New York: Random House, 1999.

Stringer, Jenny, ed. *The Oxford Companion to Twentieth-Century Literature in English.* New York: Oxford University Press, 1996.

Sullivan, Margaret C. *The Jane Austen Handbook: A Sensible Yet Elegant Guide to Her World.* Philadelphia: Quirk Books, 2007.

Sutherland, James. *The Oxford Book of Literary Anecdotes.* New York: Oxford University Press, 1975.

Sutherland, John, ed. *The Stanford Companion to Victorian Fiction.* Stanford, Calif.: Stanford University Press, 1990.

Taylor, D. J. *Thackeray: The Life of a Literary Man.* New York: Carroll & Graf, 2001.

Taylor, Jenny Bourne. *The Cambridge Companion to Wilkie Collins.* Cambridge: Cambridge University Press, 2006.

Thomas, Donald, and Henry Mayhew. *The Victorian Underworld.* New York: New York University Press, 1998.

Tomalin, Claire. *Thomas Hardy.* New York: Penguin, 2007.

Tucker, Herbert, ed. *A Companion to Victorian Literature.* Malden, Mass.: Blackwell, 1999.

Ty, Eleanor. *Empowering the Feminine: The Narratives of Mary Robinson, Jane West, and Amelia Opie, 1796–1812.* Toronto, Ontario: University of Toronto Press, 1998.

Untermeyer, Louis. *Lives of the Poets.* New York: Simon & Schuster, 1959.

Vaiss, Paul, ed. *From Oxford to the People: Reconsidering Newman and the Oxford Movement.* Harrisburg, Penn.: Morehouse, 1997.

Vendler, Helen. *The Odes of John Keats.* New York: Belknap Press, 2004.

Walters, J. Cuming. *Tennyson: Poet, Philosopher, Idealist: Studies of the Life, Work, and Teaching of the Poet Laureate.* Columbia, Mo.: Athena University Press, 2004.

Watson, George J. L. *Irish Identity and the Literary Revival.* 2d ed. Washington, D.C.: Catholic University of America Press, 1994.

Welch, Robert. *The Abbey Theatre, 1899–1999: Form and Pressure.* New York: Oxford University Press, 1999.

White, Stephen K. *Edmund Burke.* Lanham, Md.: Rowman & Littlefield Publishers, 2002.

Williams, Susan, ed. *The Lifted Veil: The Book of Fantastic Literature by Women, 1800–World War II.* New York: Caroll & Graf, 1992.

Wood, Christopher. *The Pre-Raphaelites.* New York: Seven Dials, 2001.

Woodring, Carl, ed. *The Columbia History of British Poetry.* New York: Columbia University Press, 1994.

Woodring, Carl, and James Shapiro, eds. *The Columbia Anthology of British Poetry.* New York: Columbia University Press, 1995.

Wright, Thomas. *The Life of William Cowper.* Honolulu: University Press of the Pacific, 2005.

Wu, Duncan. *Romanticism: An Anthology.* Cambridge, Mass.: Blackwell, 2000.

Wynne, Deborah. *The Sensation Novel and the Victorian Family Magazine.* New York: Palgrave Macmillan, 2001.

Zorn, Christa. *Vernon Lee: Aesthetics, History, and the Victorian Female Intellectual.* Columbus: Ohio University Press, 2003.

Index

Note: **Boldface** page numbers indicate main entries.

A

Abbeychurch; or, Self-Control and Self-Conceit (Yonge) 418
Abbey Theatre 193
"Abbot of Muchelnaye, The" (Alford) 7
Abdy, Maria 177
à Beckett, Gilbert **1,** 231
Abrams, M. H. 374
Absentee, The (Edgeworth) 129
Academy (magazine) 120, 269, 385
"Accursed Race, An" (Gaskell) 149
Ackroyd, Peter 246
Across the Plains (Stevenson) 367
Acton, Eliza **1–2**
Adam Bede (Eliot) 131, 132
Adams, Bertha Jane Leith **2**
Adams, Francis William Lauderdale **2–3**
Adams, George 160
Ada Reis (Lamb) 220
Addison, Joseph 43, 219, 385
Address of the United Irishmen to the Volunteers of Ireland (manifesto) 125
Adele (Kavanagh) 207
Adeline Mowbray; or, The Mother and Daughter (Opie) 293, 294
Adelphi Theatre 56
Admirals All and Other Verse (Newbolt) 282
"Adonais" (Shelley) 208, 352
"Advance of Women, The" (Corelli) 99
Advantages of Education, The (West) 402

Adventures of a Younger Son (Trelawney) 389
Adventures of Caleb Williams, The; or, Things as They Are (Godwin) 156
Adventures of Hajji Baba of Isphahan (Morier) 273
Adventures of Hugh Trevor, The (Holcroft) 181
Adventures of Philip, The (Thackeray) 384
Aeschylus 50
Aesop's Fables in Words of One Syllable (Aikin) 4
aestheticism **3–4**
    Gilbert (W. S.) on 152
    Hallam (Arthur) and 166
    Leverson (Ada) on 232
    O'Shaughnessy (Arthur) in 295
    Pater (Walter) and 3, 199, 302
    transition from, to Decadence 22, 407
    Wilde (Oscar) in 3, 406
aesthetics 228, 229, 301
African Millionaire, An (Allen) 7
"After a Parting" (Meynell) 261
Against the Stream (Charles) 82
Aggressive Christianity (Booth) 36
Agincourt (James) 196
Agnes (Oliphant) 293
Agnes Grey (Brontë) 42, 43
"Agnostic's Apology, An" (Stephen) 365
"Agnostic's Psalm, The" (Naden) 280
Aguilar, Grace **4**
"Ah, Bring It Not" (Radford) 317
Aikin, Anna Laetitia. *See* Barbauld, Anna Laetitia
Aikin, John 19, 20

Aikin, Lucy **4–5**
Ainsworth, William Harrison **5–6,** 56, 57, 143, 283, 296, 320
Ainsworth's Magazine 6
A Lady of England. *See* Tucker, Charlotte Maria
"Alaric at Rome" (Arnold) 8
Alastor (Shelley) 351
Alaya, Flavia 346
Albert (prince consort of Great Britain) 252, 381, 396–397
Alcestis (Todhunter) 388
Alcott, Louisa May 418
Alderson, Amelia. *See* Opie, Amelia Alderson
Aldrich, Ruth 147–148
Alexander, William **6**
Alford, Henry **6–7**
Alfoxden Journal (Wordsworth) 411
Alfred Hagart's Household (Smith) 357
Alice's Adventures in Wonderland (Carroll) 80–81, 193
Alicia de Lacey (West) 403
Allan Quartermain (Haggard) 164
Allen, Grant 400
Allen, Vivian 73
Allen, Walter 62
All for Jesus (Faber) 138
All in a Battle (Lathom) 224
All In All (Marston) 251
Allingham, Philip 5, 144
Allingham, William **7–8**
All Ireland Review (magazine) 291
Allison, Robert J. 136
All Sorts and Conditions of Men (Besant) 28

428

All the Year Round (magazine) 2, 28, 95, 114, 139
A.L.O.E. *See* Tucker, Charlotte Maria
Alone in London (Buchanan) 55
Altered States (Chayefsky) 368
Altiora Peto (Oliphant) 292
Alton Locke (Kingsley) 97, 212
Alwyn; or, The Gentleman Comedian (Holcroft) 180
Amateur Emigrant, The (Stevenson) 367
Ambassador, The (Craigie) 103
Ambassadors, The (James) 197, 198
America: A Prophesy (Blake) 31
American, The (James) 197
American Notes (Dickens) 113
American Scene, The (James) 197
American Song Treasury (Ralph) 406
Amis, Kingsley 385
Amours of Voyage (Clough) 87
Amy Herbert (Sewell) 345
Amymone: A Romance of the Days of Pericles (Linton) 236
Anastasius; or, Memoirs of a Greek, written at the Close of the Eighteenth Century (Hope) 182
"And Art Thou Come with Us to Dwell" (Greenwell) 163
Andersen, Hans Christian 187, 407
Anderson, Nancy Fix 237
"Andrea del Sarto" (Browning) 53
Androcles and the Lion (Shaw) 347
Angel in the House, The (Patmore) 303, 304
Anglican Church 284, 298–299, 380, 418
Anima Figura (Symonds) 375
Animal Magnetism (Inchbald) 192
Annals of a Quiet Neighborhood (Macdonald) 243
Annals of the Parish (Galt) 147
Annan, Noel 366
Anna St. Ives (Holcroft) 181
Annotated Alice (Gardner) 81
Anodos. *See* Coleridge, Mary Elizabeth
Anstruther, Ian 364
Anstruther-Thompson, Kit 228
Anthony, David 185
"Anticipation" (Hamilton) 166
antifeminism 74, 134, 237, 285
Anti-Jacobin Review, The (magazine) 75, 144, 263
Antiquary, The (Scott) 341
Anti-Suffrage League 99, 399
Antonina (Collins) 95
Apologia Pro Vita Sua (Newman) 284
Apostles 141, 166
Apostolicae Curae 380
Appeal, The (Wheeler and Thompson) 403

Appeal from the New to the Old Whigs (Burke) 60
Appreciations (Pater) 302
Archer, William 185–186
Ardath: The Story of a Dead Self (Corelli) 99
À Rebours (Huysman) 3
Argosy (magazine) 410
Argument for the Extension of the Franchise, An (White) 404
Argus (magazine) 399
Ariadne in Mantua (Lee) 229
Aristocracy and Evolution (Mallock) 245
Aristophanes 144
Arms and the Man (Shaw) 347
Armstrong, Isobel 234
Armstrong, Tim 169
Arnold, Mary. *See* Ward, Mary
Arnold, Matthew xiii, **8–10**
  Adams (Francis) and 3
  Broughton (Rhoda) and 50
  Clough (Arthur) and 9, 87
  father of 8, 11
  godfather of 210
  Hemans (Felicia Dorothea) and 176
  Henley (W. E.) and 178
  Hopkins (Gerard Manley) and 184
  Mallock (William Hurrell) on 245
  niece of 399
  Palgrave (Francis) and 301
  Saintsbury (George) and 335
  Swinburne (Algernon Charles) and 373
  Watson (William) and 399
  White (Joseph Blanco) and 404
  Wordsworth (William) and 8, 9, 415
Arnold, Thomas 8, **10–11**, 87, 189, 210, 399
Arrahna-Pogue (Boucicault) 39
Artists' and Amateurs' Magazine 332
art nouveau style 22
Art of Eloquence, The (Polwhele) 308
Ascent of Man, The (Blind) 33
Ashton, Rosemary 132
Ashton Morton (Meade) 256
As I Knew Them (Dixon) 118
Asolondo (Browning) 53
Aspen Court (Brooks) 49
Assommoir, L' (Zola) 270
Aston, John Partington 5
Astonishment!!! (Lathom) 224
Atalanta in Calydon (Swinburne) 373
Athelings, The (Oliphant) 292–293
Athenaeum (journal) 81, 117, 148, 160, 199, 202, 203, 207, 292, 385

Atonement of Leam Dundas, The (Linton) 237
At the Back of the North Wind (Macdonald) 242
Attila (James) 196
Auden, W. H. 184
"Auld Lang Syne" (Burns) 65
Aunt Hepsy's Foundling (Adams) 2
Aunt Judy's Magazine 137
Aurora Leigh (Browning) 51–52, 53, 141, 363
Austen, Jane xiii, **11–13**
  on Brunton (Mary) 55
  Burney (Frances) and 63
  Cholmondeley (Mary) and 83
  domestic novels by 120
  Eden (Emily) and 127
  Jewsbury (Maria Jane) and 203
  More (Hannah) and 272
  Opie (Amelia) and 294
  on Radcliffe (Ann) 315
  Roche (Regina) and 325
  on Scott (Sir Walter) 341
  Walford (Lucy) and 398
  West (Jane) and 402
Austen, Lady Anna 100
Austin, Alfred **13**, 41, 262
Austin, Lucy. *See* Gordon, Lucie Duff
Australian Essays (Adams) 3
Australian Heroine, An (Praed) 310
Australians, The (Adams) 3
Autobiography (Haydon) 172
Autobiography (Hunt) 190
Autobiography (Mill) 265
Autobiography (Taylor) 378
Autobiography (Trollope) 343
Autobiography, Poems and Songs (Johnston) 204
Autobiography 1800–75 (Taylor) 379
Autobiography of Christopher Kirkland, The (Linton) 237
Autobiography of Douglas, The (Douglas) 120
Autobiography of Mark Rutherford, Dissenting Minister, The (White) 404–405
"Autumnal Ode" (De Vere) 112
Autumn Swallows: A Book of Lyrics (Hopkins) 182
"Ave Atque Vale" (Swinburne) 373–374
Aveling, Edward 253
Awkward Age, The (James) 197
Ayesha (Morier) 273
Aylwin (Watts-Dunton) 400
Ayrshire Legatees, The (Galt) 147
Aytoun, William Edmondstoune **14**, 119
"Azalea, The" (Patmore) 304
Azeth the Egyptian (Linton) 236

B

Babbage, Charles **15–16**
Babbage, Henry 16
Bab Ballads, The (Gilbert) 151
Babe in Bohemia, A (Danby) 107
Babil and Bijou (Boucicault) 39
Back to Methuselah (Shaw) 347
Bacon, Francis 15
Bagehot, Walter **16–17**, 87
Bailey, Edward Battersby 239
Baillie, Joanna **17–18**, 19, 176
Baily, Leslie 151
Bain, Alexander 263
Baker, E. A. 405
Baker, H. Barton 323
Balder (Dobell) 119
Balfour, Mary. *See* Brunton, Mary
Ballade of Lovers, A (Probyn) 311
"Ballad of Athlone, A" (De Vere) 112
"Ballad of Burdens, A" (Swinburne) 373
"Ballad of Hell, A" (Davidson) 110
"Ballad of Past Meridian, A" (Meredith) 258
"Ballad of Reading Gaol, The" (Wilde) 407, 408
"Ballad of Trelawny" (Hawker) 171–172
Ballads and Songs (Davidson) 109
Ballads and Sonnets (Rossetti) 330
Ballads of Scotland (Aytoun) 14
Ballantyne, Robert Michael **18–19**
Balzac, Honoré de 121, 196, 297
Banker's Wife, The (Gore) 158
Banshee and Other Poems, The (Todhunter) 388
Barabbas: A Dream of the World's Tragedy (Corelli) 99
Barbara's History (Edwards) 129
Barbauld, Anna Laetitia 4, **19–21**, 326
Barchester novels (Trollope) 390, 391
Barchester Towers (Trollope) 390
Baring-Gould, Sabine 21
Barker, Juliet 45
Barnabys in America, The (Trollope) 393
Barnes, William **21–22**
Barony, The (Porter) 309
Barrack-Room Ballads (Kipling) 214–215
Barrett, Elizabeth. *See* Browning, Elizabeth Barrett
Barrie, J. M. 18, 147, 293
Barzun, Jacques 17
"Bas Bleu" (More) 34
Basil (Baillie) 17
Basil (Collins) 95
Battle Day and Other Poems, The (Jones) 205
"Battle of Blenheim, The" (Southey) 359
Battle of Marathon, The (Browning) 50

Baudelaire, Charles 3, 111, 178, 248, 269, 334, 374, 376–377
Beach of Falesá, The (Stevenson) 367
Beardsley, Aubrey Vincent **22–23**, 121, 231, 376
Beatty, Charles 157
Beaumarchais, Pierre 181
Beaumont, Thomas Barber 28
Beaupuy, Michael 413
"Because the Few with signal virtue crowned" (Milnes) 266
Beckman, Linda Hunt 234
Beddington, Ada. *See* Leverson, Ada
Beddoes, Thomas 23
Beddoes, Thomas Lovell 23
Beerbohm, Henry Maximilian 22, **23–25**, 118, 170, 179, 232
Beerbohm-Tree, Herbert 388
Beeton, Isabella 2, **25**
Behind the Scenes (Bulwer-Lytton) 58
Belcaro (Lee) 229
Beleaguered City, The (Oliphant) 293
Belfast Magazine 125
Belford, Barbara 369
Belgium and Western Germany in 1833 (Trollope) 392
Belinda (Broughton) 49
Belinda (Edgeworth) 128
Bell, Acton. *See* Brontë, Anne
Bell, Currer. *See* Brontë, Charlotte
Bell, E. M. 365
Bell, Ellis. *See* Brontë, Emily
Bell, Joseph 122
Bell, Vanessa 365
Bella Donna (Fitzgerald) 143
Bella Donna (Hichens) 179
Belloc, Bessie Rayner Parkes **25–26**, 35
Belloc, Hilaire 26
Belloc-Lowndes, Marie 26
Bells and Pomegranates (Browning) 53
Benefit of the Doubt, The (Pinero) 308
Bennett, James Gordon 363
Benson, A. C. 46
Bentham, Jeremy **26–27**, 157, 173, 252, 263, 264, 305
Benthamites 27
Bentley, Eric 78
Bentley's Miscellany (periodical) 6, 296, 410
Beowulf 335
Beppo the Conscript (Trollope) 394
Berkman, Joyce Avrech 338
Berwick, Mary. *See* Procter, Adelaide Anne
Besant, Annie Wood 27
Besant, Sir Walter **28–29**, 276
Beth Book, The (Grand) 161
Bethlehem (Faber) 138
"Betrothal, The" (Patmore) 303

"Better Land, The" (Hemans) 177
Bevington, Louisa Sarah **29**
Bevis: The Story of a Boy (Jefferies) 200
Bianca Cappello (Bulwer-Lytton) 58
Bible in Spain, The (Borrow) 38
"Bill's Paper Chase" (Jacobs) 195
Biographia Borealis; or, Lives of the Northern Worthies (Coleridge) 90
Biographia Literaria (Coleridge) 92–93
Biographical Sketches (Martineau) 253
Biographical Sketches of Cornwall (Polwhele) 309
Biographical Studies (Bagehot) 16
Birds of Jamaica (Gosse) 160
Birds of Passage (Blind) 33
"Birthday, A" (Rossetti) 328
Blachford, Mary. *See* Tighe, Mary
Black, Helen 250
Black, William **29–30**
Black Beauty (Sewell) 344
Black Cat, The (Todhunter) 388
Black-Eyed Susan (Jerrold) 202
Blackmore, Richard Doddridge **30**
Black Sheep! (Yates) 417
Black Sheep, The (Coyne) 102
Blackstone, Sir William 26
Black Tor, The (Fenn) 139
Blackwood, William 287
Blackwood's Magazine xiv, 14, 23, 90, 147, 149, 179, 202, 208, 238, 243, 287–288, 293, 296, 303, 332, 398
Blain, Virginia 134
Blake, William xii, 19, **30–33**, 64, 242, 325, 343, 374
Blanche Lisle and Other Poems (Webster) 401
Blanco y Crespo, José Maria. *See* White, Joseph Blanco
Bland, Fabian 281
Bland, Hubert 281
Blandford, Ann. *See* Edwards, Amelia
Blank Verse (Lamb) 218
Blaug, Mark 321
Bleak House (Dickens) 112, 114, 144, 190, 276
"Blessed Damozel, The" (Rossetti) 310, 329
Blessington, Lady Marguerite. *See* Gardiner, Marguerite
Blighted Life, A (Bulwer-Lytton) 58
Blind, Mathilde 33
"Blood is the Price of Heaven" (Faber) 138
Blood of the Vampire (Marryat) 249
Bloom, Harold 9
Bloomfield, Robert **33–34**
"Bluestocking Revels, The" (Hunt) 297
bluestocking writers **34–35**
Blunt, Wilfrid Scawen 296–297
Blythe, Ronald 173

Boarding Out and Pauper Schools (Smedley) 355
"Bob Burke's Duel with Ensign Brady" (Maginn) 244
"Bob the Fiddler" (Barnes) 22
Bodichon, Barbara 25, **35**, 132, 199
"Body's Beauty" (Rossetti) 329
Boehme, Jacob 242
Bog of Stars, The (O'Grady) 291
Boldrewood, Rolf **35-36**, 219
Bondman, The (Caine) 73
Bonfire of the Vanities (Wolfe) 392
Bonnie Kate (Adams) 2
Book of Ahania, The (Blake) 31
Book of a Thousand Nights and One Night, The (Burton) 67
Book of Highland Minstrelsy, A (Ogilvy) 291
Book of Nonsense Verse, A (Lear) 226
Book of Snobs, The (Thackeray) 383
Book of Thel, The (Blake) 31
Book of the Seasons, The (Howitt and Howitt) 187-188
Booth, Catherine **36**, 37
Booth, Charles **36-37**
Booth, Florence 68
Booth, William 36, **37**
Bootles' Baby: A Story of the Scarlet Lancers (Stannard) 364
Bootles' Children (Stannard) 364
Border and Bastille (Lawrence) 225
Borges, Jorge Luis 24-25
Borough, The (Crabbe) 102
Borrow, George Henry **37-38**, 400
Boscawen, Edward 34
Boscawen, Frances 34
Bostonians, The (James) 197
Botham, Mary. *See* Howitt, Mary
Bothie of Tober-na-Vuolich, The (Clough) 87
Bothwell (Swinburne) 373
Boucicault, Dion **38-39**
Bowdler, Thomas **39-40**
Bowles, William Lisle **40**
Box and Cox (Morton) 276
Boxiana (Egan) 130
Boyd, Elizabeth French 71
Braddon, Mary Elizabeth 30, **40-41**, 249, 343
Bradlaugh, Charles 27
Bradley, Katherine Harris. *See* Field, Michael
Brakespeare (Lawrence) 225
Brandes, G. M. C. 75
Bratton, J. S. 257
Breaking a Butterfly (Jones) 206
"Bredon Hill" (Housman) 185
Bride of Lammermoor, The (Scott) 5, 341

"Bride of the Greek Isle, The" (Hemans) 176-177
Brides' Tragedy, The (Beddoes) 23
Bridges, Robert **41-42**, 91, 183
Brief Reflections Relative to the Emigrant French Clergy (Burney) 62
Brief Summary, in Plain Language, of the Most Important Laws Concerning Women, A (Bodichon) 35
Briggs, Asa 356
Briggs, Julia 282
Brinton, Crane 366
British Anti-Slavery Society 311
British Novelists, The (Barbauld) 20
Brittain, Frederick 314
Brome, Vincent 276
Brontë, Anne **42-43**, 44, 46
Brontë, Charlotte 42, **43-46**
  biography of 150
  Byronic hero used by 326
  Condition of England novel by 97
  Craik (Mrs.) and 104
  Jewsbury (Geraldine) and 203
  Lewes (George Henry) and 234
  Sand (George) and 336
  Staël (Madame de) and 363
  Thackeray (William Makepeace) and 384
Brontë, Emily xi, 21, 42, 44, **46-48**, 315, 326, 336, 338
Bronze Soldier, The (Reynolds) 320
Brooke, Emma Frances 48
Brooks, Shirley **48-49**
Broomfield, Andrea 236
Brother of the Shadow, The (Praed) 310
Brothers Karamazov, The (Dostoyevsky) 88
Broughton, Rhoda **49-50**
Brown, Ford Madox 310, 329
Brown, John Mason 218
Brown, Thomas Edward **50**
Browne, Charlotte Elizabeth. *See* Tonna, Charlotte Elizabeth
Browne, Felicia Dorothea. *See* Hemans, Felicia Dorothea
Browne, Thomas Alexander. *See* Boldrewood, Rolf
"Brownies, The" (Ewing) 137
Browning, Elizabeth Barrett xiii, **50-52**
  Blind (Mathilde) and 33
  Bradley (Katherine Harris) and 141
  Hemans (Felicia Dorothea) and 176, 177
  husband of 51, 52, 53
  Meynell (Alice) and 261, 262
  Mitford (Mary Russell) and 267
  Ogilvy (Eliza) and 291
  Pfeiffer (Emily) and 306, 307

  Ritchie (Anne Thackeray) and 322
  Sand (George) and 51, 336
  Staël (Madame de) and 363
  Thackeray (William Makepeace) and 384
  Trollope (Thomas) and 394
Browning, Robert **52-54**
  Coleridge (Mary Elizabeth) and 91
  on Field (Michael) 140
  Forster (John) and 53, 143
  Henley (W. E.) and 178
  James (Henry) and 196
  Jameson (Anna Brownell) and 199
  Mew (Charlotte) and 260
  Meynell (Alice Christina) on 262
  Ritchie (Anne Thackeray) and 322
  Rossetti (Dante Gabriel) and 330
  Sharp (William) and 346
  Swinburne (Algernon Charles) and 373
  Webster (Augusta) and 401
  wife of 51, 52, 53
  Wordsworth (William) and 53, 415
Brunton, Mary **54-55**
Buchanan, Robert Williams **55-56**, 329, 373
Buckle, Henry Thomas 378
Buckley, Jerome Hamilton 245, 295, 310-311
Buckstone, John Baldwin **56**
Bulgarian Horrors and Questions of the East (Gladstone) 155
Bulwer-Lytton, Sir Edward George Earle **56-57**
  Collins (Wilkie) and 57, 95
  Fenn (George Manville) and 139
  Newgate crime novel by 57, 283
  on Patmore (Coventry) 303
  Reynolds (G. W. M.) and 320
  silver-fork novels by 57, 354, 355
  wife of 56, 58
Bulwer-Lytton, Rosina Wheeler 56, **58**
Bunyan, John 404
Burgin, G. B. 201
Burke, Edmund **58-60**, 62, 102, 110, 350, 366, 410
Burne-Jones, Edward 22, 118, 310, 373, 419
Burnett, Frances Eliza Hodgson **60-61**
Burney, Frances 11, 19, **61-63**, 119, 120
Burns, James **63-64**
Burns, Robert **64-66**
  Barnes (William) and 21
  biography of 238
  Cook (Eliza) and 98
  Cowper (William) and 100
  Crabbe (George) and 102
  Henley (W. E.) and 178
  Jeffrey (Francis) on 200

Burns and Oates (publishing firm) 63–64
Burns's Fireside Library 63
Burns stanza 65
Burroughs, Edgar Rice 166
Burstein, Miriam 372
Burton, Sir Richard Francis 66–67, 361
Butler, Josephine 67–68
Butler, Marilyn 167
Butler, Samuel 68–69, 347
Butt, Mary Martha. *See* Sherwood, Mary
Buxton, Harry 15
B.V. *See* Thomson, James
Byrne, Charlotte. *See* Dacre, Charlotte Byrne
Byron, George Gordon, Lord 69–72
   Arnold (Matthew) on 9
   on Baillie (Joanna) 18
   on Bowles (William Lisle) 40
   Craik (Mrs.) and 103
   De Vere (Aubrey Thomas) and 112
   on Frere (John) 144
   Galt (John) and 147
   Gardiner (Marguerite) and 148
   Hallam (Arthur) and 166
   on Hogg (James) 179
   on Hope (Thomas) 182
   Howitt (William) and 187
   Hunt (Leigh) and 189
   Jeffrey (Francis) on 201
   Lamb (Lady Caroline) and 70, 219–220
   Lee (Harriet) and 228
   Moore (Thomas) and 271
   North (Christopher) on 287
   Opie (Amelia) and 293
   Owenson (Sydney) and 297
   as romantic poet 70, 326
   Scott (Sir Walter) and 70, 340
   Shelley (Mary Wollstonecraft) and 70, 349
   Shelley (Percy Bysshe) and 70, 351, 352
   Southey (Robert) and 71, 359
   Trelawney (Edward) and 389
   Watson (William) and 399
Byronic hero 17, 70, 117, 220, 326
Byrrne, E. Fairfax. *See* Brooke, Emma Frances
By the Looking Glass (Webster) 401

C

Caesar and Cleopatra (Shaw) 347
Caine, T. H. Hall 73–74
Caird, Alice Mona 74
Caleb Williams (Holcroft) 181
Calendars of State Papers (Green) 162
Cambridge, Ada 74

Cambridge Apostles 141, 166
Camilla; or, A Picture of Youth (Burney) 62
Campbell, James 322
Campbell, Thomas 40, **75**
Campbellite sect 277
Canadian Naturalist, The (Gosse) 160
Candida (Shaw) 347
"Candidate, The: To the Authors of The Monthly Review" (Crabbe) 102
Canning, George 75–76, 144
Canterbury Tales, The (Chaucer) 87, 228
Canterbury Tales, The (Lee) 228
Canto the Third (Byron) 201
"Can Writing Be Taught?" (Lee) 229
Can You Forgive Her? (Trollope) 390, 391
Capital (Marx and Engels). *See Kapital, Das* (Marx and Engels)
Carlyle, Jane Welsh 76, 77, 145, 202, 336
Carlyle, Thomas xiii, 76–79
   Black (William) on 29
   Clough (Arthur) and 87
   Dickens (Charles) and 97
   Fitzgerald (Edward) and 141
   Forster (John) and 143
   Froude (James Anthony) and 78–79, 145
   on Gaskell (Elizabeth) 149
   Gordon (Lucie Duff) and 157
   on Jeffrey (Francis) 201
   Jewsbury (Geraldine) and 202
   Maginn (William) on 244
   Mill (John Stuart) and 78, 265
   Reade (Charles) and 318
   Stephen (Leslie) on 78, 366
   Trollope (Frances) and 393
Carlyle's Life in London (Froude) 78–79
"Carmilla" (Le Fanu) 230
Carmina Crucis (Greenwell) 163
Carpenter, Edward **79**, 133
Carr, Ezra Slocum 277
"Carrion Comfort" (Hopkins) 183
Carroll, Lewis xi, **79–82**, 193, 226, 282, 322
Carrots: Just a Little Boy (Molesworth) 267–268
Carte, Richard D'Oyly 151
"Casabianca" (Hemans) 177
Case of Rebellious Susan, The (Jones) 206
Cassandra (Nightingale) 287
Cassell's Magazine 139
Castaway, A (Webster) 401
"Castaway, The" (Cowper) 101
Caste (Robertson) 323
Castle of Otranto (Walpole) 315
Castle Rackrent (Edgeworth) 128
Castles of Athlin and Dunbayne, The (Radcliffe) 315
Castle Spectre, The (Lewis) 236

Catherine (Thackeray) 383
Cavalry Life (Stannard) 364
Cayley, Charles Bagot 327
Cecil, David 32, 48
Cecil; or, Adventures of a Coxcomb (Gore) 158
Cecilia; or, Memoirs of an Heiress (Burney) 62, 63
Celebrated Female Sovereigns (Jameson) 199
Censor (magazine) 89
Ceres' Runaway (Meynell) 262
"Chaldee Manuscript" (North and Lockhart) 287
Chambers, Robert **82**
Chambers, Sir Edmund 92
Channings, The (Wood) 410
Chaplet of Verses, A (Procter) 312
Chapman, George 208
Chapman, John 405
Chapters on Socialism (Taylor) 378
Character (Smiles) 356
Characteristics of Women, Moral, Poetical, and Historical (Jameson) 199
Characters of Shakespeare's Plays (Hazlitt) 173
"Charge of the Light Brigade, The" (Tennyson) 382
Charles, Elizabeth **82–83**
Charles Dickens: A Critical Study (Gissing) 153
Charles O'Malley (Lever) 232
Charlton, H. B. 13
Charnock, Richard Stephen 257
Chartism (Carlyle) 97
Chartist movement 97, 98, 205, 320–321
Chartist Songs (Jones) 205
Chastelard (Swinburne) 373
Château de Melville, Le (Yonge) 418
Chaucer, Geoffrey 87, 228
Chayefsky, Paddy 368
Chesterton, G. K. 195, 226, 348
Cheveley, or, the Man of Honour (Bulwer-Lytton) 58
Childe Harold's Pilgrimage (Byron) 70, 201, 326
Child of the Age, A (Adams) 2
Child of the Jago, A (Morrison) 276
Children of the Abbey, The (Roche) 325
Children of the Ghetto (Zangwill) 420
Children of the Mist (Phillpotts) 307
Children of the New Forest, The (Marryat) 250
Children of To-Morrow (Sharp) 346
Children's Kingdom, The (Meade) 257
Children's Treasury of English Song, The (Palgrave) 301
Child's Garden of Verses, A (Stevenson) 367

Chimes, The (Dickens) 246
Chimes at Midnight, The (à Beckett) 1
Chitty, Gill 332–333
Cholmondeley, Mary 50, **83**
"Christabel" (Coleridge) 92
Christian, The (Caine) 73
Christian Lady's Magazine 389
Christian Socialism 189, 212
Christian Year, The (Keble) 210
Christie Johnstone (Reade) 318
Christmas Carol, A (Dickens) 113
Christmas-Eve and Easter-Day (Browning) 53
Christmas Garland, A (Beerbohm) 24
Christ's Company (Dixon) 118
Christ's Entry into Jerusalem (Haydon) 172
Chronicles of Carlingford, The (Oliphant) 293
Chronicles of the Schonberg-Cotta Family, The (Charles) 82
Citizen of the World (Goldsmith) 167
City of Dreadful Night, The (Thomson) 387
City of Saints and Across the Rocky Mountains to California, The (Burton) 67
City of the Sorel, The (Douglas) 120
City Poems (Smith) 357
"Claim of Englishwomen to the Suffrage Constitutionally Considered, The" (Taylor) 378
Clara Lennox (Lee) 228
Clara Vaughan (Blackmore) 30
Clare, John **83–85**
Clarke, Charles Cowden 85
Clarke, Frances Elizabeth Bellenden. *See* Grand, Sarah
Clarke, Mary Victoria Cowden Novello **85**
Clarke, Norma 76
Clarkson, Thomas **85–86**
classicism 75
Classification of the Sciences, The (Spencer) 362
Clausen, Christopher 123
Cleopatra (Haggard) 165
Clerical Error, A (Jones) 206
Clive, Caroline **86**
Cloister and the Hearth, The (Reade) 318–319
"Cloud, The" (Shelley) 303
Clough, Arthur Hugh 9, 50, **87–88**, 145, 301, 357
Cobbe, Frances Power **88–89**
Cobbett, William **89**
"Cockney school" of poetry 189, 208, 287
Coelebs in Search of a Wife (More) 272
Coelina, ou l'enfant de mystère (Pixérécourt) 181

Cohen, Mathilde. *See* Blind, Mathilde
Cohen, Morton N. 80, 81
Colby, Vineta 229
Colenso, John William **89–90**
Coleridge, David Hartley **90**
Coleridge, Mary Elizabeth **91–92**
Coleridge, Samuel Taylor xiii–xiv, **92–94**
  aestheticism influenced by 3
  bipolar disorder in 23
  Bowles (William Lisle) and 40
  Burns (Robert) and 64
  Byron (Lord) and 71
  Clare (John) and 84
  on Clarkson (Thomas) 86
  on Cowper (William) 101
  De Quincey (Thomas) and 110
  De Vere (Aubrey Thomas) and 112
  Hazlitt (William) and 173, 174
  Keats (John) and 208
  as Lake Poet 217
  Lamb (Charles) and 94, 217, 218
  Landor (Walter Savage) and 222
  Mill (John Stuart) and 264
  as romantic poet 40, 92, 325, 414
  Shelley (Mary Wollstonecraft) and 349
  Shelley (Percy Bysshe) and 351
  son of 90
  Southey (Robert) and 92, 358, 359, 360
  Stoker (Bram) and 370
  Taylor (Henry) and 379
  Wordsworth (Dorothy) and 92, 411, 412
  Wordsworth (William) and 92, 93, 94, 414
Collected Poems (Brown) 50
Collected Poems (Browning) 53
Collected Poems (Bulwer-Lytton) 57
Collected Poems (Canning) 76
Colleen Bawn, The (Boucicault) 39
Collingwood, W. G. 332
Collins, John Churton 400
Collins, Mortimer **94**
Collins, William Wilkie xiii, **94–96**
  Bulwer-Lytton (Edward) and 57, 95
  Dickens (Charles) and 95, 114, 144
  Jerrold (Douglas) and 202
  Radcliffe (Ann) and 315
  sensation fiction by 30, 95, 343
Collinson, James 327
Colloms, Brenda 213
Colonial Magazine and East India Review 214
Colonial Reformer, A (Boldrewood) 36
Colour of Life, The (Meynell) 262
Colour Sergeant No. 1 Company (Adams) 2

"Come, ye thankful people, come" (Alford) 7
comedy of manners 63
Comet Club 246
Cometh Up As a Flower (Broughton) 49
Comic Annual, The (magazine) 181
Comic History of England, The (à Beckett) 1
Comic History of Rome, The (à Beckett) 1
Coming of Love, The (Watts-Dunton) 400
Coming Race, The (Bulwer-Lytton) 57
Commentary on Romans (Colenso) 90
"Commerce Defended" (Mill) 263
Commins, Saxe 368
Commonweal (magazine) 274
communism 134–135. *See also* Marxism
Communist League 254
Communist Manifesto, The (Engels and Marx) 134, 254
Complete Concordance to Shakespeare, The (Clarke) 85
Complete Indian Cook and Housekeeper, The (Steel) 365
Complete Poetical Works (Dobson) 119
Comte, Auguste 171
Condition of England novels **96–98**, 149, 371
Condition of the Working Class in England, The (Engels) 134
Condorcet, Jean-Marie 351
Confession of Stephen Whapshare, The (Brooke) 48
Confessions (Symons) 376
Confessions of an English Opium Eater (De Quincey) 110, 111
Confessions of a Thug (Taylor) 379
Confessions of a Young Man (Moore) 269
Confessions of Harry Lorrequer, The (Lever) 232
Confessions of the Nun of St. Omer, The (Dacre) 106
Coningsby (Disraeli) 116, 117
Conrad, Joseph 178, 198
Constant, Benjamin 362
Constantia de Valmont (Lee) 228
Contagious Diseases Act 67–68
Contarini Fleming (Disraeli) 116
Contemporary Review (journal) 171
"Continued" (Turner) 395
Contribution to the Critique of Political Economy (Marx) 255
"Conversation" (Cowper) 101
conversation novels 245
Conversations Introducing Poetry (Smith) 357
Conversations with Lord Byron (Gardiner) 148
Cook, Eliza xiv, **98**, 105
Cooper, Edith Emma. *See* Field, Michael

Cooper, Thomas **98**
Coote, Stephen 10
Coral Island, The: A Tale of the Pacific Ocean (Ballantyne) 18
Corelli, Marie **99–100**
Corinne (Staël) 221, 363
Cornhill Magazine 121, 178, 293, 322, 365, 384, 390
Cornish Ballads and Other Poems (Hawker) 172
Cornish national anthem 171–172
Corn Laws 321, 356
Cornwall, Barry. *See* Procter, Bryan Waller
"Correspondances" (Baudelaire) 377
Corruption and Intolerance (Moore) 271
Corvo, Baron. *See* Rolfe, Frederick William
Cottagers of Glenburnie (Hamilton) 167
"Cotter's Saturday Night, The" (Burns) 65
Courtney, C. P. 59–60
Courtney, Julia 419
Cousin, Victor 3
"Cousin Phillis" (Gaskell) 149
Cowper, William **100–101**, 359
Coyne, Joseph Stirling **101–102**, 202, 231
Crabbe, George **102–103**
Craigie, Pearl Mary 103
Craik, Mrs. **103–105**
Crane, David 389
Cranford (Gaskell) 149
"Creation" (O'Shaughnessy) 295
Creole, or Love's Fetters, The (Brooks) 49
Crescent and the Cross, The (Warburton) 398
Crichton, Michael 349
Crime of the Congo, The (Doyle) 122–123
Criminal, The (Ellis) 133
Crisis (Holcroft) 180
Crisis in Ireland, The (O'Grady) 291
Critical Review (periodical) 294, 360
Critiques and Addresses (Huxley) 191
Croker, John Wilson 20, 252
"Cromwell" (Arnold) 8
Cronin, Richard 84
Crook of the Bough, The (Dowie) 121
Cross, Ada. *See* Cambridge, Ada
"Crossing the Bar" (Tennyson) 382
Crotchet Castle (Peacock) 305–306
Crowe, Catherine **105**
Cruikshank, George 113
Cruikshank's Magazine 355
"Cry of the Children, The" (Browning) 51
Crystal Age, A (Hudson) 188
"Crystal Cup, The" (Stoker) 369
"Crystal Palace, The" (Davidson) 110
Cuchullin and His Contemporaries (O'Grady) 193
Cuckoo Clock, The (Molesworth) 268

Culture and Anarchy (Arnold) 9
Curiosa Mathematica (Carroll) 80
Currie, James 65
Curry, Kenneth 360
Curse of Eve, The (Steel) 365
Curse of Kahama, The (Southey) 359
"Cynara" (Dowson) 121

D

Dacre, Charlotte Byrne 17, **106–107**
Daily News (newspaper) 7, 107, 202, 224
Daily Telegraph (newspaper) 100, 118
Daisy Chain, The; or, Aspirations (Yonge) 418
Daisy Miller (James) 196–197
Dallas, Eneas Sweetland **107**
Dalton, Maria. *See* Roche, Maria Regina
Danby, Frank **107**
Dandy Dick (Pinero) 307
Dandy Family, The (Moncrieff) 268
"Dandy School, The" (Hazlitt) 354–355
Dangers of Coquetry, The (Opie) 294
Daniel Deronda (Eliot) 131, 132
Danvers Jewels (Cholmondeley) 83
Darby, Mary. *See* Robinson, Mary
"Dark Angel" (Johnson) 204
"Darkling Thrush, A" (Hardy) 168, 169
"Dark Rosaleen" (Mangan) 247
Darwin, Charles xiv, **107–109**
   Bagehot (Walter) and 16
   Butler (Samuel) and 68
   on Chambers (Robert) 82
   Huxley (T. H.) and 108, 190, 191
   James (Henry) and 196
   Kingsley (Charles) on 212
   on Lyell (Sir Charles) 239
   Malthus (Thomas) and 246
   Spencer (Herbert) and 29, 362
   Strauss (David Friedrich) and 371
Darwin, Erasmus 343
"Darwin among the Machines" (Butler) 68
"Dashwood's Drag" (Ouida) 296
Daughter of Heth, A (Black) 30
Daughter of the Stars (Brooks) 49
Daughters of Danaus, The (Caird) 74
Daughters of England, The (Ellis) 134
David, Elizabeth 2
David Balfour (Stevenson) 367
David Copperfield (Dickens) 97, 113, 383, 384
Davidson, John **109–110**
Davie, Donald 169
Davies, Augusta. *See* Webster, Augusta
Davies, Stevie 47
Davis, Emily Jane. *See* Pfeiffer, Emily Jane
Davis, Julia. *See* Danby, Frank

Dawick, John 308
Day and Night Songs (Allingham) 8
Day-Lewis, C. 185
Days and Nights (Symons) 376
Days of My Life, The (Haggard) 165
"Dead Love" (Siddal Rossetti) 354
Dead Man's Rock (Quiller-Couch) 314
"Dead Poet, The" (Douglas) 120
Dear Girl, The (Fitzgerald) 143
Death's Jest-Book, or, the Fool's Tragedy (Beddoes) 23
Debenham's Vow (Edwards) 129
Decadence 22, 407
Decade of Italian Women, A (Trollope) 394
Decay of Lying, The (Wilde) 3, 30, 407
Decorations (Dowson) 121
Deemster, The (Caine) 73
Deep Down (Ballantyne) 19
Deerbrook (Martineau) 252–253
"Defence of Guenevere, The" (Morris) 275
Defence of Guenevere and Other Poems, The (Morris) 273
Defence of Poetry (Shelley) 295–296, 305, 351
Defence of Usury (Bentham) 26
Defoe, Daniel 143, 308, 340
Deity (Montgomery) 269
de la Mare, Walter 261
Delphine (Staël) 363
Demers, Patricia 272
Democratic Federation 274
De Monfort (Baillie) 17–18
Denis Duval (Thackeray) 384
Departmental Ditties (Kipling) 214
"Departure of the Swallow, The" (Howitt) 187
De Profundis (Wilde) 407
De Quincey, Thomas 84, **110–111**, 181, 217, 412
Descent of Man and Selection in Relation to Sex, The (Darwin) 109
Descriptive Sketches (Wordsworth) 414
Deserted Daughter, The (Holcroft) 181
Desmond, Adrian 191
"Despair" (Cambridge) 74
Destiny (Ferrier) 140
De Vere, Aubrey Thomas Hunt **112**
Deverell, William Howell 354
Devil's Die, The (Allen) 7
Devil's Disciple, The (Shaw) 347
dialectical materialism 254
Diana of the Crossways (Meredith) 258, 289
Diana Tempest (Cholmondeley) 83
Diary (Haydon) 172
Diary (James) 196
Diary in America (Marryat) 250
Diary of an Ennuyee, The (Jameson) 199

Diary of Mrs. Kitty Trevylyan, The (Charles) 82
Dick, Eliza. *See* Ogilvy, Eliza
Dickens, Charles xii, xiii, **112–115**
   à Beckett (Gilbert) and 1
   Ainsworth (William Harrison) and 6
   on Bentham (Jeremy) 26
   biography of 143, 144
   Browning (Robert) and 53
   Bulwer-Lytton (Edward) and 56, 57
   Clarke (Mary) and 85
   Collins (Wilkie) and 95, 114, 144
   Condition of England novels by 97
   Egan (Pierce) and 130
   Forster (John) and 143–144
   Gaskell (Elizabeth) and 114, 149
   Gissing (George) on 153
   Gordon (Lucie Duff) and 157
   Gore (Catherine) and 158
   on Hawker (Robert Stephen) 172
   on Hunt (Leigh) 189–190
   James (Henry) and 198
   Jerrold (Douglas) and 202
   Lemon (Mark) and 231
   Linton (Eliza Lynn) and 236, 237
   on Malthus (Thomas) 246
   Meredith (George) and 257
   Meynell (Alice Christina) on 262
   Morrison (Arthur) and 276
   Newgate crime novel by 113, 283
   as parliamentary reporter 48, 113
   Procter (Adelaide Anne) and 311, 312
   Reade (Charles) and 319
   Reynolds (G. W. M.) and 320
   Scott (Sir Walter) and 342
   silver-fork school and 354
   Thackeray (William Makepeace) and 383, 384
   Trollope (Anthony) and 390
   Trollope (Frances) and 393
   Trollope (Thomas) and 394
   Yates (Edmund) and 417
Dickinson, Emily 328
Dictionary of National Biography (Stephen) 366
Did You Ever Send Your Wife to Camberwell? (Coyne) 102
Digby Grand: An Autobiography (Whyte-Melville) 406
Dilke, Lady Emilia Frances **115**
Dionysius. *See* Boucicault, Dion
"Dipsychus" (Clough) 87
Discarded Son, The (Roche) 325
Discipline (Brunton) 55
Discords (Egerton) 130
discussion novels 305
Disguises (Webster) 401

Disraeli, Benjamin 28, 39, 97, **115–117,** 155, 158, 354, 397
Dissertations and Discussions (Taylor) 378
"Dissertation upon Roast Pig, A" (Lamb) 218, 219
"Diverting History of John Gilpin, The" (Cowper) 100
"Divine Image, The" (Blake) 31
Dixon, Ella Hepworth **117–118**
Dixon, Richard Watson **118–119**
Dobell, Sydney Thompson **119**
Dobson, Henry Austin **119**
Doctor's Dilemma, The (Shaw) 347
Dodd Family Abroad, The (Lever) 232
Dodgson, Charles Lutwidge. *See* Carroll, Lewis
Dog of Flanders, A (Ouida) 296
Doll's House, A (Ibsen) 206
Dombey and Son (Dickens) 113
Domestic Manners of the Americans (Trollope) 392
domestic novels 4, **120,** 148–149, 150, 398, 418
Donaldson, William 6
Done on Both Sides (Morton) 276
Don Juan (Byron) 70, 71
Don Juan in Hell (Shaw) 347
Donne, John 100, 159, 327
Don Sebastian; or, The House of Braganza (Porter) 309
Dooley, Dolores 403
Dostoyevsky, Fyodor 88
Douglas, Lord Alfred Bruce **120,** 407
Douglass, Frederick 135
"Dover Beach" (Arnold) 9–10
Dowie, Menie Muriel **120–121**
Dowling, Richard 121
Dowson, Ernest Christopher **121–122,** 204, 317, 376
Doyle, Anna. *See* Wheeler, Anna
Doyle, Richard 231
Doyle, Sir Arthur Conan 57, **122–124,** 165, 224, 340
Doyle, Sir Francis Hastings 124
Dr. Phillips: A Maida Vale Idyll (Danby) 107
Dracula (film) 370
Dracula (Stoker) 230, 249, 369–370
"Drake's Drum" (Newbolt) 282
Drama in Muslin, A (Moore) 269
"Drama of Exile, A" (Browning) 51
Dramatic Review (journal) 251
Dramatic Studies (Webster) 401
Dramatis Personae (Browning) 53
Draper, Jonathan 90
Dream at Sea, The (Buckstone) 56
"Dream Children: A Reverie" (Lamb) 218
Dreamers of the Ghetto (Zangwill) 420

"Dream Land" (Rossetti) 326
Dream of Gerontius (Newman) 284
Dreamthorp (Smith) 357
Drennan, William **124–125**
Drury Lane Theatre xiv, 236
Dryden (Saintsbury) 335
Dryden, John 240, 340
Dublin University Magazine 49, 143, 230, 232, 398
Duke's Children, The (Trollope) 390
du Maurier, Daphne 126
du Maurier, George **125–126**
Dunne, Mary Chavelita. *See* Egerton, George
"Duns Scotus's Oxford" (Hopkins) 183, 184
Dupin, Amandine-Aurore-Lucille. *See* Sand, George
Duplicity (Holcroft) 181
Durant, Will 60
Duties of Clerks in Petty Sessions in Ireland, The (Stoker) 369
Duty (Smiles) 356
Dynasts, The (Hardy) 168, 169

E

Eagleton, Terry 255
Early Adventures in Persia, Susiana, and Babylonia (Layard) 225
Early Italian Poets (Rossetti) 329
Earthly Paradise (Morris) 274
Eastern Life, Past and Present (Martineau) 253
East Lynne (Wood) 343, 410
Easy Introduction to the Knowledge of Nature and Reading Holy Scriptures, An (Trimmer) 389
Ebb-Tide, The (Stevenson) 367
Echoes from Old Cornwall (Hawker) 172
Eclectic Review (periodical) 268, 357
Economist, The (journal) 16, 44, 256, 362
Eden, Emily **127–128**
Edgeworth, Maria **128–129**
   Austen (Jane) and 11
   Beddoes (Thomas Lovell) and 23
   domestic novels by 120
   on Hamilton (Elizabeth) 167
   on Inchbald (Elizabeth) 192
   Opie (Amelia) and 293
   Scott (Sir Walter) and 128, 342
Edgeworth, Richard Lovell 343
Edinburgh Magazine 5, 179
Edinburgh Review (journal) 44, 70, 103, 200, 201, 217, 240, 263, 271, 287, 357–358, 415
Edleston, John 70
Education and Employment of Women, The (Butler) 67

"Education of the World, The" (Temple) 380
"Edward Gibbon" (Bagehot) 16
Edwards, Amelia **129**
Edward VII (king of Great Britain) 259, 308, 314
Edwin and Eltruda (Williams) 409
Effie Ogilvie (Oliphant) 293
Egan, Pierce **130**, 268
Egan, Pierce (the Younger) 130
Egerton, George **130**
Egg, Augustus 95
Egoist, The (Meredith) 258, 259
Egypt Exploration Fund 129
Eichthal, Gustave d' 264
"1887" (Housman) 185
Eighteen Hundred and Eleven (Barbauld) 20
Eirenicon (Pusey) 313
Eleanor's Victory (Braddon) 41
Elegiac Sonnets and Other Poems (Smith) 357
"Elegy" (Seward) 344
Elgar, Sir Edward 284, 295
Elgee, Jane Francesca. *See* Wilde, Jane Francesca
Elgin, Lord 292
Elia. *See* Lamb, Charles
Eliot, George xiii, **130–133**
　biography of 33
　Bulwer-Lytton (Edward) and 56
　Craik (Mrs.) on 104
　Dilke (Lady Emilia) and 115
　domestic novels by 120
　James (Henry) and 196
　Jameson (Anna Brownell) and 199
　Jewsbury (Geraldine) and 203
　Lewes (George Henry) and 132, 234, 235
　Linton (Eliza Lynn) and 236
　Sand (George) and 336
　Scott (Sir Walter) and 342
　silver-fork school and 354
　Spencer (Herbert) and 131, 362
　Staël (Madame de) and 363
　Strauss (David Friedrich) and 131, 371
　Thackeray (William Makepeace) and 385
　Trollope (Anthony) and 390
　Trollope (Thomas) and 394
　White (William Hale) and 405
Eliot, T. S.
　Arnold (Matthew) and 9
　Barbauld (Anna Laetitia) and 20
　Clough (Arthur) and 87
　on Collins (Wilkie) 96
　on Davidson (John) 109
　on Kipling (Rudyard) 215
　on Swinburne (Algernon Charles) 373, 374
　on Symons (Arthur) 376
　on Tennyson (Alfred, Lord) 382
Elizabeth I (queen of England) 396
Eliza Cook's Journal (magazine) xiv, 98
Ellen Middleton (Fullerton) 146
Elliot, Hugh 362
Ellis, Henry Havelock **133**, 337, 376
Ellis, Sarah Stickney **133–134**
El Ombu (Hudson) 188
Elton, Oliver 182
Emancipation Act of 1833 86
Emerson, Ralph Waldo 87, 277, 278
Eminent Victorians (Strachey) 287
Emma (Austen) 11, 12, 55, 325
Emmeline; or, The Orphan of the Castle (Smith) 357
"Emmy" (Symons) 376
Empedocles on Etna, and Other Poems (Arnold) 8
Enchanted Castle, The (Nesbit) 282
Encyclopaedia Britannica 124, 263, 334, 400, 403
Endymion (Disraeli) 116
Endymion (Keats) 201, 208
Eneas Eunuchus (Maginn) 243
Enfranchisement of Women, The (Mill) 262, 264
Engels, Friedrich 78, **134–135**, 253, 254
"England, My Mother" (Watson) 400
England and the English (Bulwer-Lytton) 57
England in Time of War (Dobell) 119
English Bards and Scotch Reviewers (Byron) 70
English Constitution, The (Bagehot) 16
English Criticism of the Novel (Graham) 229
"English Judaism" (Zangwill) 420
English Laws for Women in the Nineteenth Century (Norton) 289
English Novel, The (Saintsbury) 335, 336
English Poems (Le Gallienne) 231
English Poetry of the Later Nineteenth Century (Evans) 376
English Utilitarians, The (Stephen) 366
Englishwoman (journal) 118
Englishwoman's Domestic Magazine 25
English Woman's Journal 25, 312
English Women of Letters (Kavanagh) 207
Engrafted Rose, The (Brooke) 48
Ennui (Edgeworth) 129
Enquiry Concerning Political Justice, An (Godwin) 156
Entangled (Brooke) 48
Eothen; or, Traces of Travel Brought Home from the East (Kinglake) 211, 398
Epic of Women and Other Poems (O'Shaughnessy) 295
Epicureanism 302–303
Episodes in a Life of Adventure (Oliphant) 292
Epistles, Odes and Other Poems (Moore) 271
Epistles on Women (Aikin) 4
Epistle to William Wilberforce Esq. On the Rejection of the Bill for Abolishing the Slave Trade 19–20
Equiano, Olaudah **135–136**
Erechtheus (Swinburne) 373
Erewhon (Butler) 68–69
Eric Brighteyes (Haggard) 165
Ernest Maltravers (Bulwer-Lytton) 57
Eros and Psyche (Bridges) 41
Errors of Innocence, The (Lee) 228
"Espousals, The" (Patmore) 303
Essay on Intuitive Morals (Cobbe) 88
Essay on Mind, An (Browning) 50
"Essay on Shelley" (Browning) 53
Essay on the Impolicy of the Slave Trade, An (Clarkson) 86
Essay on the Principle of Population as it affects the Future Improvement of Society, An (Malthus) 245–246
Essay on the Principles of Human Action, An (Hazlitt) 173–174
Essay on the Slavery and Commerce of the Human Species, An (Clarkson) 85–86
Essays and Lectures on Political Subjects (Fawcett) 139
Essays and Reviews (Temple) 380
Essays in Criticism (Arnold) 9
Essays in English Literature, 1780–1860 (Saintsbury) 334
Essays in London (James) 211
Essays of Elia, The (Lamb) 218, 219
Essays on Some Unsettled Questions of Political Economy (Mill) 264
Essays on the Microscope (Adams) 160
Essays on Woman's Work (Belloc) 26
Essence of Christianity (Feuerbach) 131
"Essence of Parliament, The" (Brooks) 49
Esther Waters (Moore) 269, 270
Estimate of the Religion of the Fashionable World, An (More) 272
Eternal City, The (Caine) 73
Ettrick Shepherd. *See* Hogg, James
Eugene Aram (Bulwer-Lytton) 57
Euphorion (Lee) 229
Euphranor (Fitzgerald) 141
Eustace Diamonds, The (Trollope) 390
Evan Harrington (Meredith) 258
Evans, B. Ifor 185, 376, 386
Evans, Mary Ann. *See* Eliot, George
Evans, Matilda Jane **136**

Evelina; or, The History of a Young Lady's Entrance into the World (Burney) 62, 63
Evenings at Home; or, The Juvenile Budget Opened (Barbauld and Aikin) 19–20
Evening Walk, An (Wordsworth) 414
"Eve of St. Agnes, The" (Keats) 208
Everett, Charles 27
Evidences of Christianity (Paley) 300
evolution 29, 33, 82, 108–109, 133, 159, 160–161, 191, 338, 362
Ewing, Juliana Horatia **136–137**
Examiner (newspaper) 38, 173, 189, 208, 400
"Excursion, The" (Wordsworth) 200–201, 415
Experience of Life, The (Sewell) 345
"Extempore Effusion, Upon the Death of James Hogg" (Wordsworth) 180

F

Faber, William **138**
Fabian Society 281, 347
Fabulous Histories (Trimmer) 389–390
Factors of Organic Evolution (Spencer) 362
"Factory Girl." *See* Johnston, Ellen
Faerie Queen, The (Spenser) 208, 212, 242, 388
Fair Country Maid, A (Brooke) 48
"Fairies, The" (Allingham) 7–8
Fairy Alice (Fitzgerald) 143
Fairy and Folk Tales of the Irish Peasantry (Yeats) 193
Fairy Book series (Lang) 224
"Faithful for Ever" (Patmore) 303
"Faithless Nelly Gray" (Hood) 181
Fall, Marcus. *See* Dowling, Richard
False Friend, The (Robinson) 324
Family Magazine 390
Family Shakespeare (Bowdler) 40
Fancy's Following (Coleridge) 91
Fancy's Guerdon (Coleridge) 91
Far Away and Long Ago (Hudson) 188
Far from the Madding Crowd (Hardy) 168
Farjeon, Benjamin Leopold **138–139**
Farjeon, Eleanor 139
Farjeon, Joseph 139
"Farmer's Boy, The" (Bloomfield) 33, 34
Farmer's Wife, The (Phillpotts) 307
Farrow, Anthony 270
Fashionable Life; or, Paris and London (Trollope) 393
Fatal Revenge; or, The Family of Montorio (Maturin) 255
Fate of Adelaide, The (Landon) 220–221
Father and Daughter, The (Opie) 294

Father and Son: A Study of Two Temperaments (Gosse) 159–160
Fawcett, Millicent Garrett **139**
Fawkes, Richard 38
Feldman, Paula R. 20
"Felicia Hemans" (Browning) 177
Felix Holt, The Radical (Eliot) 131
Female Advocate, The; or, An Attempt to Recover the Rights of Women from Male Usurpation (Radcliffe) 316
"Female Fashions of 1799" (Robinson) 324
Female Speaker, The (Barbauld) 20
feminism 285
of Aguilar (Grace) 4
of Belloc (Bessie) 25
of Blind (Mathilde) 33
of Bodichon (Barbara) 25, 35, 132, 199
of Brontë (Anne) 43
of Brooke (Emma) 48
of Browning (Elizabeth Barrett) 51
of Butler (Josephine) 67–68
of Caird (Mona) 74, 285
of Cholmondeley (Mary) 83
of Dixon (Ella Hepworth) 118, 285
of Dowie (Menie Muriel) 121
of Gaskell (Elizabeth) 149, 150, 199
of Linton (Eliza Lynn) 236, 285
of Mill (Harriet Taylor) 262–263
of Mill (John Stuart) 264, 265
of Procter (Adelaide Anne) 312
of Radcliffe (Mary Ann) 316
of Sand (George) 336, 337
of Schreiner (Olive) 285, 338, 339
of Staël (Madame de) 363
of Webster (Augusta) 401
of Wheeler (Anna) 403
of Wollstonecraft (Mary) 131–132, 409–410
feminist critics
on Austen (Jane) 13
on Burney (Frances) 62
on Dacre (Charlotte) 106
on Levy (Amy) 234
on Rossetti (Dante Gabriel) 330
on Wordsworth (Dorothy) 412
Fenn, George Manville **139–140**
Fergusson, Sir William 95
Fern's Hollow (Stretton) 371
Ferrier, Susan **140,** 354
Feuerbach, Ludwig 131, 254
Field, Michael **140–141**
Fielding, Henry 11, 56, 63
Fiery Dawn, The (Coleridge) 91
Fifty Years Ago (Besant) 29
Figaro in London (magazine) 1
"Fight, The" (Hazlitt) 174
Fighting the Fire (Ballantyne) 19

Final Cause of Women, The (Cobbe) 89
"Final Problem, The" (Doyle) 122
Finley, C. Stephen 332
Finn and His Companions (O'Grady) 291
Fires Which Have Occurred in Edinburgh (Chambers) 82
Firmilian: A Spasmodic Tragedy (Aytoun) 119
First, Ruth 338
First Book of Urizen, The (Blake) 31
First Year in Canterbury Settlement, A (Butler) 68
"Fish Answers, A" (Hunt) 190
Fitzgerald, Edward **141–143,** 383
Fitzgerald, Percy Hetherington **143**
Five Children and It (Nesbit) 281–282
Flaubert, Gustave 121
Fleet Street Eclogues (Davidson) 109
Fleishman, Avrom 318–319
Fleshly School of Poetry and Other Phenomena of the Day, The (Buchanan) 55, 329, 373
Flexner, Eleanor 410
Flight of the Eagle, The (O'Grady) 291
Flint, Kate 118
Florence, Ronald 254
Florence McCarthy: An Irish Tale (Owenson) 297, 298
Flowers of Evil (Baudelaire) 178, 269
Flowers of Passion (Moore) 269
Flowers of the Night (Pfeiffer) 307
Flying Leaves from East and West (Pfeiffer) 307
Fo'c's'le Yarns; The Doctor and Other Poems (Brown) 50
Foliage (Hunt) 189
Folle journée: ou, Le mariage de Figaro (Beaumarchais) 181
Follies of the Day, The (Holcroft) 181
Food of the Gods, The (Wells) 349
Footnote to History, A (Stevenson) 367
For a Song's Sake and Other Stories (Marston) 251
Ford, George 266
Foresters, The (North) 287
Forest Minstral, The; A Selection of Songs, Adopted to the Most Favourite Scottish Airs (Hogg) 179
Forest Minstrel, The (Howitt and Howitt) 187
Forest of Flowers, The (Buckstone) 56
Forest Sanctuary, The (Hemans) 177
Forest Songs and Other Poems (Todhunter) 388
"Forsaken Merman, The" (Arnold) 8
Forster, E. M. 79, 165
Forster, John 53, **143–144,** 221, 236
For the Defence (Farjeon) 139
Fortitude and Frailty (Holcroft) 180

Fortnightly Review (journal) 3, 170, 171, 334, 366
Fortunes of Nigel, The (Scott) 56, 341
Foul Play (Reade) 318
"Fountain" (Craigie) 103
"Fountain of Tears, The" (O'Shaughnessy) 295
Four Stages of Poetry, The (Peacock) 305
Fourteen Sonnets (Bowles) 40
Four Zoas, The (Blake) 32
Fragment on Government, A (Bentham) 26
"Fra Lippo Lippi" (Browning) 53
Framley Parsonage (Trollope) 390
Franc, Maud Jeanne. *See* Evans, Matilda Jane
Frances I (Kemble) 210
Frank, Katherine 214
Frankau, Julia Davis. *See* Danby, Frank
Frankenstein; or, The Modern Prometheus (Shelley) 326, 349–350
Fraser, Hugh 244
Fraser's Magazine 8, 56, 145, 244, 383
Freedman, Jonathan 198
Free Labour (Reade) 318
French Architects and Sculptors of the Eighteenth Century (Dilke) 115
French Painters of the Eighteenth Century (Dilke) 115
French Revolution, The (Carlyle) 77–78
French Revolution, The: A Prophesy (Blake) 31
Frere, John Hookham **144**
Freud, Sigmund 230
Friend of Humanity and the Knife-Grinder, The (Canning) 75–76
Frogs, The (Aristophanes) 144
From a Paris Scrapbook (Le Gallienne) 231
From Man to Man (Schreiner) 338
From One Generation to Another (Scott) 340
From the Hills of Dreams (Sharp) 346
From Village to Court (Morton) 276
Frost, Lucy 3
Froude, James Anthony 78–79, **144–145**, 245
Froude, Richard H. 298
Frozen Deep, The (Collins) 95
Fruits of Philosophy, The (Knowlton) 27
Fugitive Pieces in Verse and Prose (Doyle) 125
Fuller, Margaret 131, 132
Fullerton, Lady Georgiana **145–146**
Fun (magazine) 151
Further Records (Kemble) 211
Fuseli, Henry 293
Future of Missions and the Mission of the Future, The (Booth) 37

G

Gaelic League 193
Galbraith, J. K. 246
Gallery of Literary Characters (Maginn) 244
Gallia (Dowie) 121
Gallienne, Richard. *See* Le Gallienne, Richard
Galsworthy, John 188
Galt, John **147–148**
Ganz, Margaret 69
Garden of Allah, The (Hichens) 179
Garden of Fidelity, The (Steel) 365
Garden That I Love, The (Austin) 13
Gardiner, Marguerite **148**
Gardner, Helen 159
Gardner, Martin 81
Garibaldi, Giuseppe 292
Garnett, Edward 188
Garnett, Richard 90, 105, 233
Garrett, Millicent. *See* Fawcett, Millicent Garrett
Garrick, David 272, 324
Garrick Club 390
Garrison Romance, A (Adams) 2
Gaskell, Elizabeth xi, 97, 114, 120, 125, **148–151**, 199, 267
Gates, Barbara 320
Gatty, Juliana Horatia. *See* Ewing, Juliana Horatia
Gay Lord Quex, The (Pinero) 308
Gay Science, The (Dallas) 107
Gebir (Landor) 222
Genius Loci: Notes on Places (Lee) 229
Gentleman's Magazine 102, 309
Geoffrey Stirling (Adams) 2
Geological Evidences of the Antiquity of Man (Lyell) 239
George Alfred Henty: The Story of an Active Life (Fenn) 139
George Geith of Fen Court (Riddell) 322
George IV (king of Great Britain) 158, 271, 324
George Washington (Harrison) 171
Gerard's Monument (Pfeiffer) 306
Germ (magazine) 326, 329
German Ideology (Engels and Marx) 134
"German's Tale, The: Kruitzer" (Lee) 228
Gerould, G. H. 387
Gertrude of Wyoming (Campbell) 75
"Ghost and the Bone-Setter, The" (Le Fanu) 230
Giant Killer, The (Tucker) 394
Gibbon, Edward 240
Gide, André 180
Gilbert, William Schwenk **151–153**
Gilbert and Sullivan: Their Lives and Times (Baily) 151
Gilcrest, Alexander 32

Gillman, James 93
Girlhood of Shakespeare's Heroines, The (Clarke) 85
Girl in the Karpathians, A (Dowie) 121
"Girl of the Period" (Linton) 237
Gissing, George xii, **153–155**, 255, 285
Gladiators, The: A Tale of Rome and Judaea (Whyte-Melville) 406
Gladstone, William Ewart 16, 124, **155**, 399
Glan Alarch (Pfeiffer) 307
Gleanings from the Menagerie at Knowlsey, Illustrated Excursions in Italy (Lear) 225–226
Glenarvon (Lamb) 219–220
Globe (magazine) 94, 332
Goa and the Blue Mountains (Burton) 66
Goblin Market and Other Poems, The (Rossetti) 327
Godey's Lady's Book (magazine) 60
Godolphin, Mary. *See* Aikin, Lucy
"God's Grandeur" (Hopkins) 183, 184
Godwin, Mary Wollstonecraft. *See* Shelley, Mary Wollstonecraft
Godwin, William **155–156**
  Coleridge (Samuel Taylor) and 92
  daughter of 155, 349, 351, 409
  Hamilton (Elizabeth) and 167
  Holcroft (Thomas) and 180, 181
  Lee (Harriet) and 228
  Peacock (Thomas Love) on 305
  Shelley (Percy Bysshe) and 155, 351
  wife of 155, 409, 410
Goethe, Johann Wolfgang von 3, 38, 70, 234, 235, 251, 349, 358, 383
Gold! (Reade) 318
Golden Bowl, The (James) 197, 198
Golden Butterfly, The (Besant and Rice) 28
Golden Treasury, The (Palgrave) 301
"Goldfish, The" (Cholmondeley) 83
Golding, William 18
Goldsmith, Oliver 143, 167
"Golgotha" (Todhunter) 388
Gomery, Robert. *See* Montgomery, Robert
Gondoliers, The (Gilbert) 151
Goode, John 28, 29
Gordian Knot (Brooks) 49
Gordon, Charles George **156–157**
Gordon, Lucie Duff **157–158**
Gordon, Lyndall 45
Gore, Catherine **158–159**, 354
Gosse, Edmund William **159–160**, 165, 294, 295, 304, 374
Gosse, Philip Henry 108, 159, **160–161**
Gossip's Story, A (West) 402
gothic novels 44, 230, 235, 236, 315–316, 326

Gould, John 225
"Government" (Mill) 263, 403
Gower, Georgiana. *See* Fullerton, Lady Georgiana
Graham, Ennis. *See* Molesworth, Mary Louisa
Graham, Kenneth 229
Grahame, Kenneth 178, 282
Graham Hamilton (Lamb) 220
Grammar of Assent (Newman) 284
Grand, Sarah **161**, 285
"Grandchildren of the Ghetto" (Zangwill) 420
Grant, Anne **161–162**
Grantley Manor (Fullerton) 146
Grant's Almanac (publication) 246
Granville de Vigne: A Tale of the Day (Ouida) 296
Grasmere Journals (Wordsworth) 411
"Graves of a Household, The" (Hemans) 177
Gray, Donald 302
Great Expectations (Dickens) 112, 114
Great St. Benedict's (Meade) 257
Green, Mary Anne Everett **162**
Green, R. L. 268
Green, Roger 36
Green Carnation, The (Hichens) 179
Greene, Hugh 195
Green Mansions: A Romance of the Tropical Forest (Hudson) 188
"Green Tea" (Le Fanu) 230
Greenwell, Dora **162–163**
Gregory, Lady 193
Greig, Noel 79
Grein, J. T. 107
Gretna Green (Jones) 205
Greville, Charles Cavendish Fulke **163**
Greville Memoirs, The (Greville) 163
Grey, Josephine. *See* Butler, Josephine
Grey Lady, The (Scott) 340
Grif: A Story of Australian Life (Farjeon) 138
Griffith Gaunt; or, Jealousy (Reade) 318
Grossmith, George 151–152
Growth in Holiness (Faber) 138
Grundy, Bertha Jane. *See* Adams, Bertha Jane Leith
Gryll Grange (Peacock) 305
Guardian of Education (Trimmer) 390
Gulliver's Travels (Swift) 201
"Gunga Din" (Kipling) 215
"Gup": Sketches of Anglo-Indian Life and Character (Marryat) 249
Guy Domville (James) 197
Guy Fawkes (Ainsworth) 5
Guy Livingstone (Lawrence) 224
Guy Mannering (Scott) 140, 341
Gypsy Christ, The (Sharp) 346

Gypsy Girl, The (Jones) 205
Gypsy Mother, The (Jones) 205

H

Hadrian VII (Luke) 325
Hadrian VII (Rolfe) 325
Hagarene (Lawrence) 225
Haggard, Henry Rider **164–166**, 215
Half Sisters, The (Jewsbury) 202, 203
Hallam, Arthur Henry **166**, 381
Hamilton, Alexander 89
Hamilton, Elizabeth **166–167**
Hamilton, William Gerard 59
Hamiltons, The; or, The New Era (Gore) 158
Hampshire Days (Hudson) 188
Handley Cross (Surtees) 372
Handling of Words, and Other Studies in Literary Psychology, The (Lee) 229
Happy Prince and Other Tales, The (Wilde) 407
Hard Cash (Reade) 318
Harding's Luck (Nesbit) 282
Hard Times (Dickens) 26, 97, 112, 114
Hardy, Harriet. *See* Mill, Harriet Taylor
Hardy, Thomas **167–170**
 Barnes (William) and 21
 du Maurier (George) and 125
 Lang (Andrew) on 224
 Meredith (George) and 258
 on Mew (Charlotte) 260, 261
 Stephen (Leslie) and 365
Harland, Catherine R. 405
Harper's Weekly 168
Harrington (Edgeworth) 129
Harris, Frank 170
Harrison, Frederic **171**
Harrison, Mary St. Leger Kingsley. *See* Malet, Lucas
Harrold, Charles Frederick 77
Hartley, David 92
Harward, Nancy 310
Haunted and the Haunters, The (Bulwer-Lytton) 57
Havoc of a Smile, The (Walford) 398
Hawker, Robert Stephen **171–172**
Hawthorne, Nathaniel 5, 196
Haydon, Benjamin Robert 172
Hayek, Friedrich 263
Hayley, William 343
Haymarket Theatre xiv, 56
Hays, Mary 167
Hayter, Althea 96
Hazlitt, William **172–175**
 Godwin (William) and 156
 Haydon (Benjamin Robert) and 172
 Holcroft (Thomas) and 181
 Hood (Thomas) and 181

on Lake Poets 217
 Lamb (Charles) and 218
 North (Christopher) on 287
 Procter (Adelaide Anne) and 311
 Shelley (Mary Wollstonecraft) and 349
 on silver-fork school 354–355
Headlong Hall (Peacock) 294, 305
Head of the House of Coombe, The (Burnett) 61
Hearn, Lafcadio **175–176**
Heart of Mid-Lothian, The (Scott) 341, 342
"Hearts and Diamonds" (Burnett) 60
Heartsease; or, The Brother's Wife (Yonge) 418
Hearts of Controversy (Meynell) 262
Hearts of Oak (Jones) 206
Heather on Fire, The : A Tale of the Highland Clearances (Blind) 33
Heavenly Twin, The (Grand) 161
Hedda Gabler (Ibsen) 159
Hegel, Georg Wilhelm Friedrich 254, 371
Heilman, Robert B. 44
Heine, Heinrich 251
Heiress of Desmond, The (Owenson) 297
Heir of Redclyffe, The (Yonge) 418, 419
Heir Without a Heritage, An (Brooke) 48
Helbeck of Bannisdale (Ward) 399
Held in Bondage (Ouida) 296
Helena in Troas (Todhunter) 388
Helen Fleetwood: Tale of Factories (Tonna) 388–389
Hemans, Felicia Dorothea **176–177**, 326, 363
Henderson, Philip 292
Henderson, T. F. 178
Henley, William Ernest **177–179**, 215, 224, 276
Henry Esmond (Thackeray). *See History of Henry Esmond, The* (Thackeray)
Henslow, John Stevens 108
Henty, G. A. 139
Herbert, George 100
Herbert, Sidney 286
Hereward the Wake (Kingsley) 212
Hero and Leander, and Bacchus and Ariadne (Hunt) 189
Heroic Period, The (O'Grady) 193
Hext, Harrington. *See* Phillpotts, Eden
Hibbert, Christopher 117
Hichens, Robert Smythe **179**
Hidden Depths (Skene) 355
High Anglicanism 284, 418
"Higher Education of Women, The" (Linton) 237
Highlands and Other Poems, The (Grant) 162

High Tide on the Coast of Lincolnshire, The (Ingelow) 193
Hill, Geoffrey 185
Hillingdon Hall (Surtees) 372
Hillyer, Robert 41
Hilton, Tim 332
Hints Addressed to the Patrons and Directors of Public Schools (Hamilton) 167
Hireling Shepherd, The (Hunt) 310
Historical and Moral View of the Origins and Progress of the French Revolution, An (Wollstonecraft) 410
Historical Essay on Architecture, An (Hope) 182
Historical Odes (Dixon) 118
Historical Tales of Illustrious British Children (Strickland and Strickland) 372
History of a Week, The (Walford) 398
History of Brazil (Southey) 361
History of Chivalry, A (James) 196
History of Criticism, A (Saintsbury) 336
History of Criticism and Literary Taste in Europe from the Earliest Texts to the Present Day, A (Saintsbury) 334–335
History of Devonshire (Polwhele) 309
History of Elizabethan Literature (Saintsbury) 334
History of England (Macaulay) 145
History of England, The (Austen) 11
History of England from the Accession of James II (Macaulay) 241–242
History of England from the Death of Cardinal Wolsey to the Defeat of the Spanish Armada (Froude) 145
History of English Language and Literature (Chambers) 82
History of English Prosody from the Twelfth Century to the Present Day, A (Saintsbury) 334
History of English Thought in the Eighteenth Century (Stephen) 365–366
History of Henry Esmond, The (Thackeray) 383, 384, 385
History of India (Mill) 263
History of Ireland (O'Grady) 291
History of Ireland, The (Moore) 271
History of Ireland and the Irish People Under the Government of England (Smiles) 356
History of Mary Prince, The (Prince) 311
History of Sir Richard Calmady, The: A Romance (Malet) 244
History of the British Empire (Chambers) 82
History of the Church of England from the Abolition of the Roman Jurisdiction (Dixon) 118–119

History of the Fairchild Family, The (Sherwood) 353
History of the French Novel (Saintsbury) 335
History of the Rise, Progress, and Accomplishment of the Abolition of the Slave Trade, The (Clarkson) 86
History of the Robins, The (Trimmer) 389–390
Hitler, Adolf 78
Hit or Miss (Pocock) 308
H.M.S. Pinafore (Gilbert and Sullivan) 152
Hobbes, John Oliver. *See* Craigie, Pearl Mary
Hodge and His Masters (Jefferies) 200
Hodgson, Frances. *See* Burnett, Frances Eliza Hodgson
Hoeckley, Cheri Lin Larsen 312
Hogarth, George 113
Hogarth, William 119
Hogg, James xiv, **179–180**, 287
Hogg, Thomas Jefferson 351
Hohenlinden (Campbell) 75
Holcroft, Frances **180**
Holcroft, Thomas **180–181**, 293
Hole in the Wall, A (Morrison) 276
Holiday Time, or the School Boy's Frolic (Lathom) 224
Holmes series (Doyle) 122, 123–124
Holt, Lee E. 69
"Holy Eucharist, The: A Comfort to the Penitent" (Pusey) 312–313
Holy Living; or, What the Salvation Army Teaches about Sanctification (Booth) 37
Home, Cecil. *See* Webster, Augusta
Home; or, The Iron Rule (Ellis) 134
Home Influence: A Tale for Mothers and Daughters (Aguilar) 4
Homer 208, 220
Hood, Thomas 84, **181–182**, 231
Hook, Theodore 354
Hooligans (Gilbert) 152
Hope, Thomas **182**
Hope of the Family, The (Coyne) 102
Hopkins, Ellice **182–183**
Hopkins, Gerard Manley 22, 41, **183–185**, 302, 386, 387
Hoppenstand, Gary 195
Horace 348
Horseman's Manual, The (Surtees) 372
Hosts of the Lord (Steel) 365
"Hound of Heaven, The" (Thompson) 385–386
Hound of the Baskervilles, The (Doyle) 122, 123
Hour and the Man, The (Martineau) 253
Hour Before Dawn, The: An Appeal to Men (Butler) 68
Hours in a Library (Stephen) 365

Hours of Idleness (Byron) 70
Hours with Orientals (Tucker) 394
Household Furniture and Interior Decoration (Hope) 182
Household Management (Beeton) 2, 25
Household Words (journal) 95, 114, 129, 144, 231, 236, 237, 257, 312, 394
House of Arden, The: A Story for Children (Nesbit) 282
House of Life, The (Rossetti) 329
House of the Seven Gables (Hawthorne) 5
House of Usna, The (Sharp) 346
Housman, Alfred Edward **185–186**
Housman, Laurence 186
Howard, H. L. *See* Wells, Charles Jeremiah
"How do I love thee? Let me count the ways." (Browning) 52
Howells, William Dean 126
"How I Built Myself a House" (Hardy) 167
How I Found Livingstone (Stanley) 363–364
Howitt, Mary 149, **186–187**
Howitt, William **187–188**
Hudson, William Henry **188**
Hughes, Thomas 10, **188–189**
Hughes, Winifred 343
Hugh Roe O'Donnell (O'Grady) 291
Hume, David 365
Hungarian Brothers, The (Porter) 309
Hunley, J. D. 135
Hunt, James Henry Leigh **189–190**, 208, 287, 297, 305, 357
Hunt, William Holman 310, 329
Hunting of the Snark, The (Carroll) 80, 81
"Hurrahing in Harvest" (Hopkins) 183
Huxley, Aldous 57, 229
Huxley, Julian 109
Huxley, Thomas Henry 108, **190–191**, 202, 245, 365
Huysmans, J. K. 3
Hymns in Prose for Children (Barbauld) 19
"Hymn to Intellectual Beauty" (Shelley) 351
Hypatia (Kingsley) 212
Hypocrites, The (Jones) 206

I

"I Am" (Clare) 84, 85
Ibsen, Henrik 107, 159, 206, 307, 347
Ideala (Grand) 161
Ideal Husband, An (Wilde) 407
Idea of a University Defined (Newman) 284
"Idea of Comedy and the Uses of Comic Spirit, The" (Meredith) 258
Idler in France, The (Gardiner) 148
Idler in Italy, The (Gardiner) 148

Idle Thoughts of an Idle Fellow, The (Jerome) 201
Idylls of the King (Tennyson) 381
Idyls and Rhymes (Collins) 94
"I Know Your Lips Are Bought" (Symons) 377
Iliffe, Jane. *See* West, Jane
Illuminated Magazine 95, 231
Illustrated London News (newspaper) 1, 49, 81, 99, 231
Illustrations of Birds of Jamaica (Gosse) 160
Illustrations of Political Economy (Martineau) 82, 252
Illustrations of the Family of Psittacidae, or Parrots (Lear) 225
Images of Good and Evil (Symons) 376
Imaginary Conversations (Landor) 222–223
Imaginary Portraits (Pater) 302
Imagination and Fancy (Hunt) 190
Impending Sword, The (Yates) 417
Importance of Being Earnest, The (Wilde) 197, 407, 408
Impressions of a Wanderer in Italy, Switzerland, France, and Spain (Trollope) 394
Impressions of Greece (Milnes) 266
Improvisatore, The (Beddoes) 23
Improvisatrice and Other Poems, The (Landon) 220–221
"In a Minor Key" (Levy) 234
Inchbald, Elizabeth **192–193**, 293
In Darkest Africa (Stanley) 37
In Darkest England and the Way Out (Booth) 37
Independent Theater Society 107
Independent Theatre 141
Indiana (Sand) 336–337
Indian Pilgrim, The (Sherwood) 353
Indiscretion in the Life of a Lady, An (Hardy) 168
industrialism xi, 77, 120, 255, 286
Industrial Unrest and Trade Union Policy (Booth) 37
In Excelsis (Douglas) 120
Infant Custody Bill of 1839 289–290
Ingelow, Jean Orris **193**
In Haste and at Leisure (Linton) 237
Inheritance, The (Ferrier) 140
In His Own Image (Rolfe) 325
In Hospital (Henley) 178
Inland Voyage, An (Stevenson) 367
In Memoriam (Tennyson) 166, 381, 382
"In No Strange Land" (Thompson) 386
"In Nunhead Cemetery" (Mew) 260–261
In Prison and Out (Stretton) 371
Inquiry into the Time and Place of Homer in History, An (Gladstone) 155

Insane Root, The (Praed) 310
Intelligent Woman's Guide to Socialism, Capitalism, Sovietism, and Fascism (Shaw) 347
Interesting Narrative of the Life of Olaudah Equiano, Or Gustavus Vassa, The (Equiano) 135–136
Interpreter, The (Whyte-Melville) 406
In the Cage (James) 197
In the South Seas (Stevenson) 367
"Intimations of Immortality" (Wordsworth) 219, 415–416
"In token that thou shalt not fear" (Alford) 7
Introduction to the Principles of Morals and Legislation, An (Bentham) 26
Introduction to the Study of Robert Browning, An (Symons) 376
Introduction to Zoology (Gosse) 160
"Introductory Discourse" (Baillie) 17
Invasion of the Crimea, The (Kinglake) 211
Invention of Love, The (Stoppard) 186
"Invictus" (Lister) 178
Ireland, with Other Poems (Johnson) 204
Irish Home Reading Magazine 204
Irish Literary Renaissance **193–194**, 204, 270, 292
Irish Literary Society 204, 388
Irish Penny Journal 247
Irish potato famine of 1846 112, 247, 248
Irish Theatre, The (Kavanagh) 102
Iron, Ralph. *See* Schreiner, Olive Emilie Albertina
Iron Master, The (Pinero) 307
Irving, Henry 307, 369
Irving, Washington 196
Irwin, Joseph 236
Island Race, The (Newbolt) 282–283
Isles of Greece and Other Poems (Skene) 355
Ismael: An Oriental Tale, with Other Poems (Bulwer-Lytton) 56
Italian, The (Radcliffe) 315
Italian Mysteries, or More Secrets than One (Lathom) 224
It Is Never Too Late to Mend (Reade) 318, 319–320
It's Only Round the Corner (Jones) 206
Ivanhoe (Scott) 341, 342, 383
Ivory Gate, The (Collins) 94
"I Wandered Lonely as a Cloud" (Wordsworth) 411, 413, 415

J

"Jabberwocky" (Carroll) 81
Jack Hinton (Lever) 232
Jack Sheppard (Ainsworth) 5, 57, 283

Jacob Faithful (Marryat) 250
Jacobs, William Wymark **195–196**
James, Alice 196
James, George Payne **196**
James, Henry **196–198**
  Beerbohm (Max) on 24
  Broughton (Rhoda) and 50
  on Collins (Wilkie) 96
  du Maurier (George) and 125
  Gosse (Edmund) and 159
  Haggard (H. Rider) and 165
  Henley (W. E.) and 178
  on Kemble (Fanny) 211
  Kipling (Rudyard) and 215
  Lang (Andrew) on 224
  on Lee (Vernon) 228, 229
  on Ritchie (Anne Thackeray) 322
  Stephen (Leslie) and 365
  Stevenson (Robert Louis) and 196, 367, 368
  Ward (Mary) and 399
James, William 196
James Merle (Black) 29
Jameson, Anna Brownell **199**
Jane Eyre (Brontë) 42, 43, 44–45, 104, 234, 326, 336, 384
Japp, A. H. 395
Jefferies, Richard **199–200**
Jeffrey, Francis, Lord 103, **200–201**, 217, 415
"Jenny" (Rossetti) 329, 330–331
Jerden, William 220, 221
Jerome, Jerome Klapka **201–202**
Jerrold, Douglas William **202**, 231, 232
Jerusalem (Blake) 32
Jessica's First Prayer (Stretton) 371
Jessie Phillips: A Tale of the Present Day (Trollope) 393
Jewett, Sarah Orne 267
"Jewish Women and Women's Rights" (Levy) 233
Jewsbury, Geraldine Endsor 76, **202–203**, 336
Jewsbury, Maria Jane 202, **203–204**
Jilt, The (Boucicault) 39
Joan of Arc: An Epic Poem (Southey) 358
Joan the Maid (Charles) 82
John Bull's Other Island (Shaw) 347
John Halifax, Gentleman (Craik) 104
John Inglesant (Shorthouse) 354
John Keats (Bridges) 41
Johnny Gibb of Gushetneuk (Alexander) 6
John Ruskin (Harrison) 171
Johnson, Edgar 114
Johnson, Joseph 243
Johnson, Lionel Pigot 110, 121, **204**, 317, 376
Johnson, R. Brimley 253

Johnson, Samuel 19, 34, 62, 143, 272
Johnston, Ellen xii, **204–205**
John Stuart Mill and the Harriet Taylor Myth (Pappe) 263
John Woodvil (Lamb) 218
"Jolly Beggars, The" (Burns) 66
Jones, Ann 106
Jones, Ernest Charles **205**
Jones, Hannah **205–206**
Jones, Henry Arthur **206**
Jorrocks's Jaunts and Jollities (Surtees) 372
Joseph and His Brethren: A Scriptural Drama (Wells) 402
Josephine Butler Society 68
Joshua Marvel (Farjeon) 138
Journal of a Residence in America (Kemble) 211
Journal of a Residence on a Georgia Plantation in 1838–39 (Kemble) 211
Journal of a Tour on the Continent (Wordsworth) 411
Journal of a West India Proprietor (Lewis) 236
Journal of the Discovery of the Source of the Nile (Speke) 361
Journals and Correspondence (Eden) 127
Journey Made in the Summer of 1794, A (Radcliffe) 315
Journey Through Persia, Armenia, and Asia Minor to Constantinople in the Years 1808 and 1809, A (Morier) 273
Journey to Khatmandu, A (Oliphant) 292
Joyce, James 198, 247, 269
Jude the Obscure (Hardy) 168, 169
Judgment of Solomon, The (Haydon) 172
Julian and Maddalo (Shelley) 352
"Jumblies, The" (Lear) 226
Jump, Harriet 121
Jungle Book, The (Kipling) 215
Jurassic Park (Crichton) 349
Just So Stories (Kipling) 215
Juvenilia (Hunt) 189
Juvenilia (Lee) 229

K

Kant, Immanuel 3, 300
Kapital, Das (Marx and Engels) 134–135, 254, 255, 321
Kaplan, Cora 52
Kasîdah of Hâjî Abdû el-Yezdî, The (Burton) 67
"Kathaleen Ny-Houlahan" (Mangan) 248
Katherine Beresford (Jones) 205
Kavanagh, Julia 192, **207**
Kavanagh, Peter 102
Kean, Edmund 255
Keating, P. J. 276

Keats, John xiv, **207–210**
aestheticism influenced by 3
Arnold (Matthew) on 9
biography of 266
Bridges (Robert) on 41
Clarke (Mary) and 85
Hallam (Arthur) and 166
Haydon (Benjamin Robert) and 172
Hood (Thomas) and 181
Hopkins (Gerard Manley) and 184
Hunt (Leigh) and 189, 208
Jeffrey (Francis) on 201
North (Christopher) on 287
as romantic poet 207, 208, 209, 326
Shelley (Percy Bysshe) and 208, 352
Swinburne (Algernon Charles) and 374
Thompson (Francis) and 387
on Tighe (Mary) 388
Watson (William) and 399
Wells (Charles Jeremiah) and 402
Keble, John **210**, 298, 312, 418
Kelly, Patrick 6
Kelly, Richard 81
Kellys and the O'Kellys, The (Trollope) 390
Kemble, Fanny **210–211**
Kenilworth (Scott) 341
Key-Notes (Bevington) 29
Kidnapped (Stevenson) 367
Kilmarnock volume (Burns) 64
Kim (Kipling) 215
King, Charlotte. *See* Dacre, Charlotte Byrne
King, Sophia 106
"King George the Fourth" (Beerbohm) 23
Kinglake, Alexander William **211**, 398
King of Schnorrers, The (Zangwill) 420
Kingsley, Charles 97, 145, 161, 189, **211–213**, 244
Kingsley, Mary Henrietta **213–214**, 244
Kingsley, Mary St. Leger. *See* Malet, Lucas
King Solomon's Mines (Haggard) 164, 165
King's Own, The (Marryat) 250
"King's Tragedy, The" (Rossetti) 330
King with Two Faces, The (Coleridge) 91
Kipling, Joseph Rudyard **214–216**
Beerbohm (Max) on 24
Ewing (Juliana Horatia) and 137
Gosse (Edmund) and 159
Haggard (H. Rider) and 165, 215
Henley (W. E.) and 178, 215
Lang (Andrew) and 224
Newbolt (Henry) and 283
Steel (Flora Annie) and 364, 365
on Surtees (Robert Smith) 373
Kirby, Sarah. *See* Trimmer, Sarah Kirby

Kirchhoff, Frederick 274
Knight, Stephen 123
Knight of St. John, The (Porter) 309
Knowlton, Charles 27
Koizumi, Yakumo. *See* Hearn, Lafcadio
"Kubla Khan" (Coleridge) 92
Kunitz, Stanley 211, 379

L

Labour and Life of the People (Booth) 37
"Lachrymae Musarum" (Watson) 400
Ladies of Llangollen 344
Lady Audley's Secret (Braddon) 40, 41, 343
Lady Bird (Fullerton) 146
"Ladybird, The" (Smith) 357
Lady Falaise (Shorthouse) 354
"Lady Geraldine's Courtship" (Browning) 51
Lady Lindores (Oliphant) 293
"Lady Mary" (Alford) 7
Lady of Lyon, The (Bulwer-Lytton) 57
"Lady of Shalott, The" (Tennyson) 381, 382
Lady of the Lake, The (Scott) 340
Lady on the Drawing-Room Floor, The (Coleridge) 91
"Lady Poverty, The" (Meynell) 261–262
Lady's Magazine 267
Lady Windermere's Fan (Wilde) 407, 408
Lahr, John 408
Lair of the White Worm, The (Stoker) 369
Lake, Claude. *See* Blind, Mathilde
Lake, The (Moore) 269–270
Lake Poets **217**, 305, 360
Lake Regions of Central Africa, The (Burton) 66–67
Lalla Rookh (Moore) 271
Lamb, Charles **217–219**
Ainsworth (William Harrison) and 5
Carroll (Lewis) and 80
Clare (John) and 84
Coleridge (Samuel Taylor) and 94, 217, 218
Forster (John) and 143
Haydon (Benjamin Robert) and 172
Hood (Thomas) and 181
Mitford (Mary Russell) and 267
sister of 217, 218, 220
Lamb, Lady Caroline 58, 70, **219–220**, 293
Lamb, Mary Ann 217, 218, **220**
"Lamb, The" (Blake) 32
Lamb, William 219
Lambeth Opinions 380
Lamia, Isabella, The Eve of St. Agnes, and Other Poems (Keats) 201, 208

"Lamp of Life, The" (Ruskin) 332
"Lamp of Memory, The" (Ruskin) 333
Lancashire Witches, The (Ainsworth) 5
Land for the Laborers (Cooper) 98
"Landing of the Pilgrim Fathers, The" (Hemans) 177
Landon, Letitia Elizabeth 58, 177, **220–221**, 243
Landor, Walter Savage 148, 205, **221–223**, 236
Landscapes in Poetry (Palgrave) 301
Land Tenure Reform Association 265
Lane, John 231
Lang, Andrew 164, 165, **223–224**
Lang, Cecil B. 310
Laodicean, A (Hardy) 125
Lass and the Lady, The (Jones) 205
Last Chronicle of Barset, The (Trollope) 390, 391
Last Days of Pompeii, The (Bulwer-Lytton) 57
Last Essays of Elia (Lamb) 218
Last Man, The (Shelley) 349, 350
Last of the Barons, The (Bulwer-Lytton) 57
Last Poems (Browning) 51
Last Poems (Housman) 186
"Last Rose of Summer, The" (Moore) 271
"Last Sark, The" (Johnston) 204
"Last Stage Coachman, The" (Collins) 95
Last Tenant, The (Farjeon) 139
Last Words on Translating Homer (Arnold) 9
Later Poems (Meynell) 261
"Latest Decalogue, The" (Clough) 88
Lathom, Francis **224**
Latter-Day Pamphlets (Carlyle) 78
Laurella and Other Poems (Todhunter) 388
"Laus Veneris" (Swinburne) 373
Lavengro (Borrow) 38
Lawrence, George Alfred **224–225**
Lawrie Todd (Galt) 147
Lawson, Charlotte. *See* Riddell, Charlotte
Layard, Austen Henry **225**
Lay of the Last Minstrel, The (Scott) 340
Lay Sermons (Huxley) 191
Lays for the Dead (Opie) 294
Lays of Ancient Rome (Macaulay) 241
Lays of a Wild Harp (Cook) 98
Lays of Leisure Hours (Jewsbury) 203
Lays of the Cavaliers (Aytoun) 14
"Lead, Kindly Light" (Newman) 283
Leap Year (Buckstone) 56
Lear, Edward **225–227**, 248
Lectures Chiefly on the Dramatic Literature of the Age of Elizabeth (Hazlitt) 173

Lectures on the English Poets (Hazlitt) 173
Lee, Amice 187, 188
Lee, Harriet **227–228**
Lee, Sophia 228
Lee, Vernon **228–229**
Leech, John 202, 231
Lees, Edith 133
Le Fanu, Alicia 230
Le Fanu, Joseph Sheridan 49, **229–230**
"Legalization of Female Slavery in England, The" (Besant) 27
Le Gallienne, Richard **230–231**
Legends and Lyrics (Procter) 312
Legends of the Madonna (Jameson) 199
Leicester: An Autobiography (Adams) 2
Leigh, Arran 141
L.E.L. *See* Landon, Letitia Elizabeth
Lélia (Sand) 336
Lemon, Mark 48, 49, 101, 202, **231–232**, 256
Leopardi, Giacomo 387
Leo XIII (pope) 284, 380
Lessons for Children (Barbauld) 19
Letters (Dowson) 122
Letters and Journals of Lord Byron, with Notices of his Life (Moore) 271
Letters and Memorials (Carlyle) 145
Letters for Literary Ladies (Edgeworth) 128
Letters from Egypt, 1863–1869 (Gordon) 157
Letters from England (Southey) 360
Letters from France Containing Many New Anecdotes Relative to the French Revolution and the Present State of French Manners (Williams) 409
Letters from Spain and Portugal (Southey) 359, 360
Letters from the Cape (Gordon) 157
Letters from the Mountains (Grant) 162
Letters of Mary, Queen of Scots (Strickland) 372
Letters of Royal Ladies of Great Britain (Green) 162
Letters on the Elementary Principles of Education (Hamilton) 167
Letters to a Young Lady (West) 402
Letters to a Young Man (West) 402
"Letters to the Chartists" (Kingsley) 212
Letters to the Young (Jewsbury) 203
Letter to the Queen on Lord Chancellor Cranworth's Marriage and Divorce Bill, A (Norton) 289
Letter to the Women of England, on the Injustice of Mental Subordination, A (Robinson) 324
Lever, Charles James **232**
Leverson, Ada **232–233**

Levinson, Marjorie 412
Levy, Amy **233–234**
Lewes, George Henry 44, 132, **234–235**, 236, 357, 394
Lewis, C. S. 242, 282
Lewis, Matthew Gregory 106, **235–236**, 326
Liars, The (Jones) 206
Liberal (journal) 189
Liber Amoris, or, the New Pygmalion (Hazlitt) 173
Libertine, The (Dacre) 106
Library of Fathers of the Holy Catholic Church, Anterior to the Division of East and West (Pusey) 312
Liddell, Alice Pleasance 80
Liddell, Henry George 80
Lie, The (Jones) 206
Liebling, A. J. 130
Life Among My Ain Folk (Alexander) 6
Life and Adventures of Jonathan Whitlaw, The (Trollope) 393
Life and Death of Jason, The (Morris) 274
Life and Labour (Smiles) 356
Life and Labour of the People of London (Booth) 37
Life and Letters of Captain Marryat (Marryat) 249
Life and Letters of John Donne, The (Gosse) 159
Life and Letters of John Keats, The (Milnes) 266
Life and Times of Louis the Fourteenth, The (James) 196
Lifeboat, The (Ballantyne) 19
Life Drama, A (Smith) 357
Life in London; or, The Day and Night Scenes of Jerry Hawthorn, Esq. And Corinthian Tom (Egan) 130
Life in the Sickroom (Martineau) 253
Life of Algernon Charles Swinburne, The (Gosse) 159
Life of Cellini, The (Symonds) 376
Life of Charles Dickens (Forster) 144
Life of Charlotte Brontë, The (Gaskell) 149, 150
Life of His Royal Highness the Prince Consort, The (Martin) 252
Life of Jesus, The (Strauss) 131, 371
Life of Lord Edward Fitzgerald, The (Moore) 271
Life of Luther, A (Tucker) 394
Life of Michelangelo Buonarroti, The (Symonds) 376
Life of Napoleon Buonaparte (Hazlitt) 173
Life of Nelson, The (Southey) 359, 360–361
Life of Rossetti (Sharp) 345

Life of Sir Walter Scott, The (Luckhart) 238
Life of Thomas Hardy, The (Hardy) 168
Life of Thomas Holcroft, The (Hazlitt) 181
Life the Accuser (Brooke) 48
Light Freights (Jacobs) 195
Light Load, A (Radford) 317
Lights and Shadows of Scottish Life (North) 287
Lilith (Macdonald) 243
Lilly Dawson (Crowe) 105
limericks 225–226
"Lines Composed a Few Miles above Tintern Abbey" (Wordsworth) 412
"Lines in Imitation of Spenser" (Keats) 208
"Lines Written on the Death of Mrs. Hemans" (Abdy) 177
Linton, Eliza Lynn **236–237**
Lippincott's Magazine 407
Lister, Joseph 178
Lister, Thomas Henry 354
Literary Gazette (newspaper) 220, 243
Literary Geography (Sharp) 346
Literary Magnet (magazine) 221
Literary Studies (Bagehot) 16
Literature of Their Own, A (Sewell) 345
Little, Janet **237–238**
Little Dorrit (Dickens) 114
Little Henry and His Bearer (Sherwood) 353
Little Lord Fauntleroy (Burnett) 61
Little Ottleys, The (Leverson) 233
Little Princess, A (Burnett) 61
Little Schoolmaster Mark, The (Shorthouse) 354
Little Women (Alcott) 418
Litz, A. Walton 13
Liverpool Mercury (magazine) 73
Lives of Boulton and Watt (Smiles) 356
Lives of the Engineers (Smiles) 356
Lives of the Modern Saints (Faber) 138
Lives of the Princesses of England (Green) 162
Lives of the Queens of England (Strickland and Strickland) 372
Lives of the Queens of Scotland and English Princesses (Strickland) 372
Lives of the Saints (Baring-Gould) 21
Livingstone, David 363–364
Llangollen Vale (Seward) 344
Lloyd, Charles 312
Lob Low-by-the-Fire (Ewing) 137
local-color novels 267
Lockhart, John Gibson **238**, 287
Lodore (Shelley) 350
"Lois the Witch" (Gaskell) 149
Lombard Street: A Description of the Money Market (Bagehot) 16

London Assurance (Boucicault) 38
"London Churches" (Milnes) 266
London Labour and the London Poor (Mayhew) 256
London Magazine 5, 34, 90, 173, 181, 218, 379
London Nights (Symons) 376
"London Snow" (Bridges) 41–42
London Society (magazine) 249, 369
London Voluntaries (Henley) 178
Long Ago (Field) 141
Longman, Thomas 1
Longman's Magazine 224
Lord Byron and Some of His Contemporaries (Hunt) 189
Lord Derby (Saintsbury) 335
Lord of the Flies (Golding) 18
"Lords and Liveries" (Thackeray) 355
Lorna Doone (Blackmore) 30
Loss and Gain (Newman) 64
Loss of the Birkenhead, The (Doyle) 124
Lost and Saved (Norton) 289
"Lost Chord, A" (Procter) 312
Lost World, The (Doyle) 122
Lot, Parson. *See* Kingsley, Charles
"Lot of Women Under the Rule of Man, The" (Caird) 74
"Lotos-Eaters, The" (Tennyson) 381
Lottery of Marriage, The: A Novel (Trollope) 393
Louisa (Seward) 343
Lounger, The (magazine) 166
Louverture, Toussaint 253
"Love and Friendship" (Austen) 11
Love and His Masks (Dowie) 121
Love and Money (Howitt) 187
"Love In Mayfair" (Probyn) 311
Lover and Husband (Molesworth) 267
"Lover's Journey, The" (Crabbe) 103
Lovers' Vows (Inchbald) 192
"Love's Coming of Age" (Carpenter) 79
Love's Conflict (Marryat) 249
Love's Cross-Currents: A Year's Letters (Swinburne) 374
Love's Frailties (Holcroft) 181
Loves of the Poets, The (Jameson) 199
Love's Victory (Farjeon) 138
Lovett, William 320
Low Anglicanism 284, 418
Lowe, John Livingston 92
Loyalists, The (West) 402–403
Lucas, F. L. 304
Lucas, John 405
Luce, Morton 171
Lucretia (Bulwer-Lytton) 283
"Lucubratio Ebria" (Butler) 68
"Lucy" (Wordsworth) 90
Ludlow, John Malcolm 212
Luke, Peter 325

Luke the Labourer (Buckstone) 56
Luther: A Poem (Montgomery) 269
"Lycidas" (Milton) 352
Lyell, Sir Charles xiv, **238–239**
Lying Prophets (Phillpotts) 307
Lynn, Eliza. *See* Linton, Eliza Lynn
Lyrical Ballads (Wordsworth and Coleridge) 17, 64, 92, 325, 360, 414
Lyrical Tales (Robinson) 324
Lyrics (Douglas) 120

M

Macaulay, Thomas Babington 145, **240–242**
Macdermots of Ballycloran, The (Trollope) 390
MacDiarmid, Hugh 64
Macdonald, George 91, **242–243**, 282
Machiavelli, Niccolò 241
Mackay, Mary. *See* Corelli, Marie
Macleod, Fiona. *See* Sharp, William
MacMillan's Magazine 311
Macready, William 53, 57
MacVicar, Anne. *See* Grant, Anne
Madam How and Lady Why (Kingsley) 213
Madelaine (Opie) 294
Madeleine (Kavanagh) 207
Madoc (Southey) 359
Magazine of Art 178
Magic City, The (Nesbit) 282
Maginn, William **243–244**, 287, 309
Magistrate, The (Pinero) 307
Mahaffy, John Pentland 406
Mahratta Tale, A (Taylor) 379
Maiden Aunt, The (Smedley) 355
Maiden's Revenge, The (Ainsworth) 5
Maid Marian (Peacock) 305
Maid of Hamlet, The (Roche) 325
Maid of Sker, The (Blackmore) 30
Mair, John 305
Maitland, Caroline. *See* Radford, Dollie
Major Barbara (Shaw) 347
"Making of Viola" (Thompson) 385
Malcolm X 135
Malet, Lucas **244–245**
Mallarmé, Stéphane 178
Mallock, William Hurrell **245**
Malory, Thomas 212
Malthus, Thomas 156, **245–246**, 252, 264, 305
Mamet, David 392
Man and Superman (Shaw) 347
Man and Woman (Ellis) 133
Manchester (Saintsbury) 335
Manfred (Byron) 70, 326
Mangan, James Clarence **246–249**
Manilius 186

Manliness of Christ, The (Hughes) 189
Mano (Dixon) 118
Mansfield Park (Austen) 12
Man's Place in Nature (Huxley) 191
Man versus the State, The (Spencer) 362
"Man Who Would Be King, The" (Kipling) 215–216
Manx dialect 50
Manxman, The (Caine) 73
Many Cargoes (Jacobs) 195
"Margaret Fuller and Mary Wollstonecraft" (Eliot) 131
Margaret Percival (Sewell) 345
Margolis, John D. 245
Maria (Wollstonecraft) 409
Marian; or, The Light of Someone's Home (Evans) 136
Marian Withers (Jewsbury) 202
Mari Magno (Clough) 87
Marius the Epicurean (Pater) 302–303
Mark Rutherford's Deliverance (White) 405
Marlborough (Saintsbury) 335
Marmion (Scott) 340
Marriage (Ferrier) 140
"Marriage, As It Was, As It Is, and As It Should Be" (Besant) 27
Marriage of Heaven and Hell, The (Blake) 31
Married Life (Buckstone) 56
Married Woman's Property and Divorce Act of 1857 289
Married Women's Property Act of 1882 35, 98, 139
Marryat, Florence **249–250**, 251
Marryat, Frederick 249, **250–251**
Marsh, Jan 327
Marston, Eleanor 294
Marston, John 40
Marston, Philip Bourke **251**, 294
Martian, The (du Maurier) 125–126
Martin, Sir Theodore **251–252**
Martin Chuzzlewit (Dickens) 113
Martineau, Harriet xiv, 82, **252–253**, 267, 293
Marx, Eleanor **253–254**
Marx, Karl 134, 156, 253, **254–255**, 321, 362
Marxism 134–135, 254–255
Marxist critics 13, 150, 255
Mary Barton (Gaskell) 97, 149, 150
Mary Stuart (Swinburne) 373
Masks and Faces (Reade) 318
"Masque of Anarchy, The" (Shelley) 352
Masque of Finn, The (O'Grady) 291
"Masquerading, I. Before" (Probyn) 311
"Masquerading, II. After" (Probyn) 311
Master Builder, The (Ibsen) 159
Master Christian, The (Corelli) 99

Masterman Ready (Marryat) 250
Master of Ballantrae, The (Stevenson) 367
Master Timothy's Book-Case (Reynolds) 320
Mathias, Thomas James 308
Matilda, Rosa. *See* Dacre, Charlotte Byrne
Matthews, John T. 47
Matthiesen, Paul F. 160
Maturin, Charles Robert **255**
Maud (Tennyson) 387
Maugham, Somerset 174–175
"Maureen" (Todhunter) 388
Maurice, Fredrick Denison 212
Maxiner, Paul 368
Maxwell, John 41
May Carols (De Vere) 112
Mayfair (Pinero) 307
Mayhew, Henry Philip 101, 202, 231, 232, **255–256**
Mayor of Casterbridge, The (Hardy) 168
Mayson, Isabella. *See* Beeton, Isabella
Mazzini, Giuseppe 373
McCann, Jerome J. 374
McCarthy, Justin 310
McGann, Jerome 221
Meade, Lillie Thomasina **256–257**
Meaning of History, The (Harrison) 171
Medea of Euripides, The (Webster) 401
Medwin, Tom 350
Mehalah (Baring-Gould) 21
Melada, Ivan 230
Melbourne, William Lamb, Viscount 219, 241, 288–289
Melincourt (Peacock) 305
Mellor, Ann 176
Melmoth: The Wanderer (Maturin) 255
Melting Pot, The (Zangwill) 420
Melville, Herman 198
Memoir of Barry Lyndon, The (Thackeray) 384
Memoirs and Essays in Art, Literature, and Social Morals (Jameson) 199
Memoirs of an American Lady (Grant) 162
Memoirs of Great Commanders (James) 196
Memoirs of Horace Walpole and His Contemporaries (Warburton) 398
Memoirs of Modern Philosophers (Hamilton) 167
Memoirs of Mrs. Elizabeth Hamilton with Selections from her Correspondence and Unpublished Writings (Hamilton) 167
Memoirs of Prince Rupert and The Cavaliers, with Their Private Correspondence, The (Warburton) 398

Memoirs of Shelley (Peacock) 305
Memoirs of the Analytical Society (Babbage) 15
Memoirs of the Court of Charles I (Aikin) 4
Memoirs of the Court of James I (Aikin) 4
Memoirs of the Court of Queen Elizabeth (Aikin) 4
Memoirs of the Early Italian Painters and the Progress of Painting in Italy (Jameson) 199
Memoirs of the Life of William Collins, Esq., R.A., The (Collins) 95
Memorials of a Residence on the Continent, and Historical Poems (Milnes) 266
Men, Women, and Books (Hunt) 190
Men and Manners (Lathom) 224
Men and Women (Browning) 53
Mere Chance, A (Cambridge) 74
Meredith, George **257–259**, 289, 373, 401, 402
Merope (Arnold) 8
Merriman, Henry Seton. *See* Scott, Hugh Stowell
Merry England (magazine) 261, 385, 386
Messiah, The (Montgomery) 269
Mew, Charlotte **259–261**
Meynell, Alice Christina Thompson **261–262**, 332, 385
Meynell, Wilfred 261
Meysey-Wigley, Caroline. *See* Clive, Caroline
Michael and His Lost Angel (Jones) 206
Michael Armstrong, the Factory Boy (Trollope) 393
Microcosm (magazine) 75
Middle-Aged Lover, The (Fitzgerald) 143
Middlemarch (Eliot) xiii, 115, 131, 132
Midnight Bell, The (Lathom) 224
Midnight Hour, The (Inchbald) 192
Midsummer Cushion, The (Clare) 84
Mighall, Robert 321
Mighty Atom, The (Corelli) 99
Mikado, The (Gilbert and Sullivan) 152–153
Mill, Harriet Taylor 157, **262–263**, 264
Mill, James 26, **263**, 403
Mill, John Stuart **263–265**
  Bentham (Jeremy) and 27, 264
  on Browning (Robert) 52
  Carlyle (Thomas) and 78, 265
  Fawcett (Millicent) and 139
  Gordon (Lucie Duff) and 157
  Peacock (Thomas Love) and 305
  Stephen (Leslie) on 366
  Taylor (Helen) and 378
  wife of 262–263, 264
Millais, John Everett 8, 310, 329

Miller, Ann 177
Miller, Henry 164
Millgate, Michael 160
Mill on the Floss, The (Eliot) 104, 131, 336
Mills, Howard 103
Milnes, Richard Monckton **265–266**
"Milton" (Macaulay) 240
Milton, Frances. *See* Trollope, Frances Milton
Milton, John
    Bridges (Robert) on 41
    Browning (Elizabeth Barrett) and 51
    Cowper (William) and 100
    elegy by 352
    Henley (W. E.) and 178
    Hopkins (Gerard Manley) and 184
    Martineau (Harriet) and 252
    More (Hannah) and 271
    Newman (John Henry) and 283
    Shelley (Mary Wollstonecraft) and 349, 350
Milton Prosody (Bridges) 41
Mind (journal) 29
"Ministering Angels" (Procter) 311
Minnie's Mission: An Australian Temperance Tale (Evans) 136
Minor Poet and Other Verse, A (Levy) 233–234
Minstrelsy of the Scottish Border (Scott) 179, 340
Miscellaneous Essays (Saintsbury) 334
Miscellaneous Pieces in Prose (Barbauld and Aikin) 19
Miscellaneous Poems (Opie) 294
Miscellaneous Verses (Doyle) 124
Mischief of Monica, The (Walford) 398
Miser's Daughter, The (Ainsworth) 5
Misfortunes of Elphin, The (Peacock) 305
Miss Betty (Stoker) 369
Miss Brown (Lee) 229
Miss Cayley's Adventures (Allen) 7
Miss Oona McQuarrie (Smith) 357
Miss Stuart's Legacy (Steel) 365
Mistletoe, The (Robinson) 324
Mitchel, John 247
Mitchell, Charlotte 86
Mitchell, Sally 104
Mitford, Mary Russell **266–267**
Miyoshi, Masao 159, 346
Modern Apostle and Other Poems, A (Naden) 280
Modern Cookery (Acton) 1–2
Modern Greece (Hemans) 176
"Modern Griselda, The" (Edgeworth) 128
Modern Love (Meredith) 258
Modern Lover, A (Moore) 269
"Modern Major General" (Gilbert) 152

Modern Painters (Ruskin) 331, 332, 333
Moglen, Helene 45
Mogul Tale, The; or, The Descent of the Balloon (Inchbald) 192
Moir, Erskine. *See* Skene, Felicia Mary
Molesworth, Mary Louisa 137, **267–268**
Moncrieff, William Thomas 130, **268**
Money (Bulwer-Lytton) 57
Monk. *See* Lewis, Matthew Gregory
Monk, The (Lewis) 106, 235, 236
"Monkey's Paw, The" (Jacobs) 195
Monks and the Giants, The (Frere) 144
Monna Innominata (Rossetti) 52, 328
"Monody on Mrs. Hemans" (Sigourney) 177
"Monopoly" (Charles) 82
Montagu, Elizabeth 34
Montaigne, Michel de 219
"Mont Blanc" (Shelley) 351
Montesquieu, Charles-Louis de Secondat, baron de la Brède et de 167
Montgomery, James **268**
Montgomery, Robert **268–269**
Monthly Magazine 20, 113
Monthly Packet (magazine) 418
Monthly Repository (periodical) 252
Moody, Catherine. *See* Gore, Catherine
Moonstone, The (Collins) 95, 96
Moore, George Augustus 107, 232, **269–270**
Moore, John S. 57
Moore, Thomas 148, 201, **270–271**, 297
Moors and the Fens, The (Riddell) 322
"Mopsa the Fairy" (Ingelow) 193
Morality of Marriage and Other Essays, The (Caird) 74
Mordred (Newbolt) 282
More, Hannah 19, 34, 240, **271–273**, 309
More Poems (Housman) 186
Moreton, Lee. *See* Boucicault, Dion
Morgan, Lady. *See* Owenson, Sydney
Morgan, Peter F. 200
Morier, James Justinian **273**
Morning Chronicle (newspaper) 48, 113, 173, 236, 256, 383
Morning Post (newspaper) 116, 129, 258
Morris, Jane 329–330
Morris, William **273–275**
    Marx (Eleanor) and 253
    Marx (Karl) and 255
    in Pre-Raphaelite movement 118, 273, 310, 330, 373
    Ruskin (John) and 333
    Yonge (Charlotte Mary) and 418, 419
Morrison, Arthur **275–276**
Morrison, Roger 288
Morte d'Arthur (Malory) 212
Morton, John Maddison **276**

Moscow, or the Cossack's Daughter (Moncrieff) 268
"Motherhood Under Conditions of Dependence" (Caird) 74
Mothers of England, The (Ellis) 134
Mott, Lucretia 35
Mountain Bard, The (Hogg) 179
Mountains of California, The (Muir) 278
"Mouse's Petition, The" (Barbauld) 19
Mozley, Anne 45
Mr. Nightingale's Diary (Dickens and Lemon) 231
Mr. Smith, a Part of His Life (Walford) 398
Mr. Sponge's Sporting Tour (Surtees) 373
Mrs. Armytage; or, Female Domination (Gore) 158
Mrs. Dane's Defense (Jones) 206
Mrs. Halliburton's Troubles (Wood) 410
Mrs. Leicester's School (Lamb and Lamb) 220
Mrs. Lorimer, a Sketch in Black and White (Malet) 244
Mrs. Warren's Profession (Shaw) 347
Mudie, Charles Edward 276–277
Mudie's Circulating Library xi, **276–277**
Muir, John **277–279**
Mulock, Dinah Maria. *See* Craik, Mrs.
Mumford, Catherine. *See* Booth, Catherine
Mummer's Wife, A (Moore) 269
Munera Pulveris (Ruskin) 331
Munich, Adrienne 397
Munster Cottage Boy, The (Roche) 325
Murder of St. Thomas à Becket (Pocock) 308
Murger, Henri 125
Murphy, Anna Brownell. *See* Jameson, Anna Brownell
Murray-Prior, Rosa. *See* Praed, Rosa
Murry, John Middleton 404
Music and Moonlight (O'Shaughnessy) 295
Music Makers, The (Elgar) 295
My Adventure in the Flying Scotsman (Phillpotts) 307
My Brother, A. E. Housman (Housman) 186
My Brother's Wife (Edwards) 129
My Fair Lady (musical) 348
My First Fit of the Gout (Morton) 276
My Flirtations (Dixon) 118
"My Heart Shall Be Thy Garden" (Meynell) 261
My Ladies' Sonnets (Le Gallienne) 231
My Lady Ludlow (Gaskell) 150
"My Last Duchess" (Browning) 53, 401
My Life (Ellis) 133
My Life and Loves (Harris) 170

Index 447

My Life and Times (Jerome) 201–202
"My Sister's Sleep" (Rossetti) 329
Mystères du Paris, Les (Sue) 320
Mysteries of London (Reynolds) 320
Mysteries of the Court of London, The (Reynolds) 320
Mysteries of Udolpho, The (Radcliffe) 315–316
Mysterious Freebooter, The (Lathom) 224
Mysterious Marriage, or, The Heirship of Roselva, The (Lee) 228
Mystery of Edwin Drood, The (Dickens) 114
Mystery of Killard, The (Dowling) 121
"Mystic and Cavalier" (Johnson) 204
My World as in My Time (Newbolt) 283

N

Naden, Constance Caroline **280**
Nadine, The Study of a Woman (Praed) 310
"Nameless One, The" (Mangan) 248
Narrative of the Earl of Elgin's Mission to China and Japan in the Years 1857, '58, '59 (Oliphant) 292
Narrative of the Events Which Have Taken Place in France, A (Williams) 409
Nation (journal) 121, 247
"National Apostasy" (Keble) 210
"National Gallery, The" (Kingsley) 212
National Observer (magazine) 178, 276
National Reformer (newspaper) 27, 387
National Review (journal) 13, 16
National Society for Women's Suffrage 26
National Union of Women's Suffrage Societies 139
naturalistic novels 269
Naturalist's Sojourn in Jamaica, A (Gosse) 160
natural selection 108–109
"Nature of Gothic, The" (Ruskin) 333
Naval Officer, The; or, Scenes and Adventures in the Life of Frank Mildmay (Marryat) 250
Necessity of Atheism, The (Shelley and Hogg) 351
Necker, Louise Germaine. *See* Staël, Madame de
negative capability 209
Nelson, William 18
Nemesis of Fate, The (Froude) 145
Neo-Christianity 171
Nesbit, Edith **280–282**
Neville-Sington, Pamela 393
New and Old (Symonds) 375
"New Aspects of the Woman Question, The" (Grand) 285

Newbolt, Henry **282–283**
Newcomes, The (Thackeray) 384, 385
New Echoes, and Other Poems (Cook) 98
Newgate Calendar, The (periodical) 283
Newgate crime novels 5, 57, 113, **283**, 383
New Grub Street (Gissing) 153
New Ladies' Almanac (publication) 246
"Newly Dead and Newly Born" (Ogilvy) 291
Newman, Beth 48
Newman, John Henry Cardinal 64, 112, 183, **283–285**, 298, 312, 404, 418
New Minnesinger and Other Poems, The (Bradley) 141
New Monthly Magazine 5, 6, 57, 173, 268, 296, 410
New Paul and Virginia, The (Mallock) 245
New Peerage, or, Our Eyes May Deceive Us, The (Lee) 228
New Poems (Arnold) 8–9
New Poems (Thompson) 385
New Quarterly Magazine 168
New Republic, The (Mallock) 245
New Review (magazine) 178
News from Nowhere (Morris) 274
New Sporting Magazine 372
Newton, John 100
Newton Forster (Marryat) 250
New Woman novels 48, 74, 118, 130, 161, 237, **285**. *See also* feminism
"New Year's Eve" (Lamb) 219
New York Critic (magazine) 398
New York Herald (newspaper) 363, 417
"Night" (White) 404
Nightingale, Florence 87, **285–287**, 355
"Nightingale's Nest, The" (Clare) 84, 85
Nightmare Abbey (Peacock) 305
Night's Adventure, A (Robertson) 323
Night Side of Nature, The; or, Ghosts and Ghost Seers (Crowe) 105
IX Poems by V. (Clive) 86
Noakes, Vivien 226
Nobel Prize in literature 215, 348
Nobler Sex, The (Marryat) 249
Noctes Ambrosianae series (North) 287
Nocturnal Visit, The (Roche) 325
"Nonsense Cookery" (Lear) 227
nonsense poetry 225–227
Non Sequitur (Coleridge) 91
"Non Sum Qualis Eram Bonae Sub Regno Cynarae" (Dowson) 121
Nordan, Pierre 124
Norman Sinclair (Aytoun) 14
North, Christopher **287–288**
North and South (Gaskell) 97, 125, 149, 151
Northanger Abbey (Austen) xiii, 11, 63, 315

Northern Star (Chartist publication) 205
North of Scotland Gazette 6
Norton, Caroline Sheridan 258, **288–290**
Norton, George 288–289
Nosferatu (film) 370
Notes on a Cellar-Book (Saintsbury) 335
Notes on Matters Affecting the Health, Efficiency, and Hospital Administration of the British Army (Nightingale) 286
Notes on Men, Women and Books (Wilde) 406
Notes on Nursing (Nightingale) 286
Not So Bad as We Seem (Bulwer-Lytton) 95
Nottingham, Chris 133
Not Wisely But Too Well (Broughton) 49
Not Without Thorns (Molesworth) 267
Novalis 387
Novello, Alfred 85
Novello, Mary. *See* Clarke, Mary Victoria Cowden Novello
Novice of St. Dominick, The (Owenson) 297
"No Worst, There is None" (Hopkins) 183
Noyes, Russell 94, 208, 209
Nuovo, Victor 300–301

O

O'Briens and the O'Flahertys, The: A National Tale (Owenson) 297
Obscene Publications Act 67
Observations on Heresy and Orthodoxy (White) 404
Observations on Man, his Frame, his Duty and his Expectations (Hartley) 92
Observations on the Natural Claim of a Mother to the Custody of Her Children as Affected by the Common Law Rights of the Father (Norton) 289
O'Casey, Sean 39
Ocean, The (Gosse) 160
Ocean, The (Montgomery) 268
Oceanic Hydrozoa (Huxley) 190
Ockerbloom, Mary Mark 289
"October" (Radford) 317
Octoroon, The (Boucicault) 39
Odd Craft (Jacobs) 195
Odd Women, The (Gissing) 153, 154, 285
"Ode" (O'Shaughnessy) 295
"Ode: Intimations of Immortality" (Wordsworth) 219, 415–416
"Ode on a Grecian Urn" (Keats) 208
"Ode on the Day of the Coronation of King Edward VII" (Watson) 400
"Ode on the Death of the Duke of Wellington" (Tennyson) 381

Odes and Addresses to Great People (Hood and Reynolds) 181
Odes of Anacreon Translated into English Verse, with Notes (Moore) 270
"Ode to a Nightingale" (Keats) 208, 209
"Ode to Melancholy" (Keats) 208
"Ode to Psyche" (Keats) 208
"Ode to the West Wind" (Shelley) 352–353
"Ode Written in Dejection, near Naples" (Shelley) 352
O'Doherty, Ensign Morgan. *See* Maginn, William
O'Donnel: A National Tale (Owenson) 297
"Oenone" (Tennyson) 381
Of Population (Godwin) 156
"Oft, in the Stilly Night" (Moore) 271
"Often Rebuked, Yet Always Back Returning" (Brontë) 46
Ogilvy, Eliza **291**
O'Grady, Standish James 193, **291–292**
Old Age Pensions Act of 1908 37
Old Age Pensions and the Aged Poor (Booth) 37
"Old Arm-Chair, The" (Cook) 98
Old Corcoran's Money (Dowling) 121
Old Curiosity Shop, The (Dickens) 113
Old English Gentleman, The (Polwhele) 308
Old Familiar Faces (Watts-Dunton) 400
"Old Familiar Faces, The" (Lamb) 218
Old Friends with New Faces (Tucker) 394
Old John (Brown) 50
Old Kensington (Ritchie) 322
Old Manor House, The (Smith) 357
Old Mortality (Scott) 341
Old Saint Paul's (Ainsworth) 5
Old Sir Douglas (Norton) 289
Oliphant, Laurence **292**, 293
Oliphant, Margaret 120, **292–293**
Olive (Craik) 104
Oliver Cromwell (Harrison) 171
Oliver Twist (Dickens) 6, 57, 97, 113, 283, 393
Olney Hymns (Cowper) 100
Omnipresence of the Deity, The (Montgomery) 269
Omphalos: An Attempt to Untie the Geological Knot (Gosse) 160–161
"On Being Hard Up" (Jerome) 201
"On Being Idle" (Jerome) 201
"On Being in Love" (Jerome) 201
Once a Week (magazine) 139, 231, 258
Once! Twice! Thrice! and Away! (Probyn) 311
One I Know Best, The (Burnett) 61
"One of Two Millions in East London" (Besant) 29

One Too Many, The (Linton) 237
"On First Looking into Chapman's Homer" (Keats) 208
"On Happiness" (Little) 238
On Heroes, Hero-Worship and the Heroic in History (Carlyle) 78
On Liberty (Mill) 265
"On Literary Construction" (Lee) 229
"On moonlit heath and lonesome bank" (Housman) 185
"On Murder Considered as One of the Fine Arts" (De Quincey) 110
"On Prayer" (Coleridge) 90
"On Some Characteristics of Modern Poetry and on the Lyrical Poems of Alfred Tennyson" (Hallam) 166
"On Some Fossil Remains of Man" (Huxley) 191
"On Style" (Lee) 229
On the Art of Reading (Quiller-Couch) 314
On the Art of Writing (Quiller-Couch) 314
"On the Disadvantages of Intellectual Superiority" (Hazlitt) 173
"On the Eclipse of the Moon of October 1865" (Turner) 394–395
On the Economy of Machine and Manufacturing (Babbage) 15
On the Face of the Waters (Steel) 365
"On the Feeling of Immortality in Youth" (Hazlitt) 174
"On the Knocking at the Gate in *Macbeth*" (De Quincey) 110
"On the Natural History of the Man-Like Apes" (Huxley) 191
On the Origin of Species (Darwin) 68, 108–109, 191, 371
"On the Relations of Man to the Lower Animals" (Huxley) 191
"On This Day I Complete My Thirty-Sixth Year" (Byron) 71–72
On Translating Homer (Arnold) 9
"Onward, Christian Soldier" (Baring-Gould) 21
"Oona of the Dark Eyes and the Crying of Wind" (Sharp) 346
Open Air, The (Jefferies) 200
Ophelia (Millais) 310, 329
Opie, Amelia Alderson 267, **293–294**
Opie, John 293, 294
Ordeal of Richard Feverel, The (Meredith) 258, 259
Orel, Harold 160
Oriental tinting 225
Original Poetry by Victor and Cazire (Shelley and Shelley) 351
Origin of Species (Darwin). *See On the Origin of Species* (Darwin)

Orlando (Woolf) xiv
Orley Farm (Trollope) 390, 391
Ormond (Edgeworth) 129
Orphans (Oliphant) 293
Orwell, George 153, 154, 318
O'Shaughnessy, Arthur William Edgar **294–296**
Other Poems (Meynell) 261
"Other Side of a Mirror, The" (Coleridge) 91
Ouida **296–297**, 354
Our Mutual Friend (Dickens) 114, 144
Our National Parks (Muir) 278
Our Seven Homes: Autobiographical Reminiscences (Charles) 83
Our Soldier Boy (Fenn) 139
Our Village (Mitford) 267
Owenson, Sydney 220, **297–298**, 342
"Owl and the Pussy Cat, The" (Lear) 226, 227
Oxford and Cambridge Magazine 273
Oxford Book of Christian Verse, The (Cecil) 32
Oxford Book of English Ballads, The (Quiller-Couch) 314
Oxford Book of English Verse, The (Quiller-Couch) 314
Oxford Magazine 314
Oxford Movement 112, 138, 145, 210, 284, **298–299**, 312, 345, 418

P

Pagan Poems (Moore) 269
Pagan Review (journal) 346
Pageant and Other Poems, A (Rossetti) 327
Paget, Violet. *See* Lee, Vernon
Paine, Thomas 60, 92, 180, 272, 293, 351, 409, 410
Pair of Blue Eyes, A (Hardy) 168
Paley, William **300–301**, 366
Palgrave, Francis Turner **301**
Palliser novels (Trollope) 390
Pall Mall Gazette (newspaper) 7, 179, 334, 377, 407
Palm Leaves (Milnes) 266
Pansies (Probyn) 311
Pantisocracy 92, 358
Pappe, H. O. 263
Paracelsus (Browning) 53
Paradise Lost (Milton) 51, 349, 350
Parent's Assistant, The (Edgeworth) 128
Paris and the Parisians (Trollope) 392
Parker, Theodore 88
Parkes, Bessie. *See* Belloc, Bessie Rayner Parkes
Partial Portraits (James) 125
"Parting, A" (Procter) 312

Passages from the Life of a Philosopher (Babbage and Buxton) 15
Passages in the Life of Mrs. Margaret Maitland (Oliphant) 292
Passing of the Third Floor Back, The (Jerome) 201
Passions, The (Dacre) 106
Past and Present (Carlyle) 78, 393
Pastor's Fireside, The (Porter) 309
Pater, Walter Horatio **301–303**
    aestheticism influenced by 3, 199, 302
    caricature of 23
    Hopkins (Gerard Manley) and 183, 302
    on Lamb (Charles) 218
    Lee (Vernon) and 228
    Mallock (William Hurrell) on 245
    Wilde (Oscar) and 302, 303, 406
"Pathetic Hypothetics" (Mangan) 248
Patience (Gilbert and Sullivan) 152
Patience of Hope, The (Greenwell) 163
Patmore, Coventry 134, 294, **303–305**
Patmore, Derek 304
Patronage (Edgeworth) 128–129
Patten, Janice 17
Pattison, Emilia. *See* Dilke, Lady Emilia Frances
Pattison, Mark 366
Paul Clifford (Bulwer-Lytton) 56, 57, 283
Paul Ferroll (Clive) 86
Pauline (Browning) 52
Paul Kelver (Jerome) 201
Peacock, Thomas Love 245, 294, **305–306**
Pearsall, Ronald 123
Peck, G. W. 47
Peckham, Morse 76
Peg Woffington (Reade) 318
Pelham (Bulwer-Lytton) 57, 355
Pendennis (Thackeray) 244, 383
Penguin Short History of English Literature, The (Coote) 10
penny dreadfuls 283, 320
Pentateuch and the Book of Joshua Critically Examined, The (Colenso) 90
People's Charter 320
People's Palace 28, 276
People's Paper (Chartist publication) 205
Perambulating Philosopher. *See* à Beckett, Gilbert
Peregrine Pickle (Smollett) 318
Perils of Certain English Prisoners, The (Collins and Dickens) 95
Perils of the Nation (Tonna) 389
Perlycross (Blackmore) 30
Perrin, Noel 40
Persian Letters (Montesquieu) 167

Personal Narrative of a Pilgrimage to Mecca and Medina, A (Burton) 66
Personal Reminiscences in Book-Making (Ballantyne) 19
Personal Reminiscences of a Great Crusade (Butler) 67–68
Personal Reminiscences of Henry Irving (Stoker) 369
Persuasion (Austen) 12
Peru (Williams) 409
"Pervasion of Rouge, The" (Beerbohm) 23
Peter Ibbetson (du Maurier) 125
Peter Pan (Barrie) 18, 147, 293
Peter Plymley's Letters (Smith) 358
Peter Simple (Marryat) 250
Petronel (Marryat) 249
Pettit, Amanda Jo 2
Pfeiffer, Emily Jane **306–307**
Phantasmagoria; or, Sketches of Life and Character (Jewsbury) 203
Phantastes (Macdonald) 91, 243
Phantom Future, The (Scott) 340
Pharais (Sharp) 346
"Phaudrig Coohoore" (Le Fanu) 230
Phelan, James 384
Philip Van Artevelde (Taylor) 379
Phillpotts, Eden **307**
Philosophical Enquiry into our Ideas of the Sublime and Beautiful, A (Burke) 58–59
Philosophical Radicals 263
Phineas Finn (Trollope) 390, 391
Phineas Redux (Trollope) 390, 391
Phoenix and the Carpet, The (Nesbit) 282
Physics and Politics (Bagehot) 16
Physiology of Common Life, The (Lewes) 235
Piccadilly (Oliphant) 292
Pickwick Abroad (Reynolds) 320
Pickwick Married (Reynolds) 320
Pickwick Papers (Dickens) 113, 130, 144
Picture of Dorian Gray, The (Wilde) 3, 407–408
Pictures of Private Life (Ellis) 134
"Pied Beauty" (Hopkins) 183, 184
Pierrot of the Minute, The (Dowson) 121
Pigs in Clover (Danby) 107
Pilgrim's Progress (Bunyan) 404
Pinero, Arthur Wing xiv, **307–308**
"Pippa Passes" (Browning) 53
Pique (Ellis) 134
Pirate City (Ballantyne) 19
Pirates of Penzance (Gilbert and Sullivan) 152
Pixérécourt, Guilbert de 181
Plain Letter to the Lord Chancellor on the Infant Custody Bill, A (Norton) 289–290
Plain Speaker, The (Hazlitt) 173

Plain Tales from the Hills (Kipling) 214
Plato and Platonism (Pater) 302
Plays (Kemble) 211
Plays on the Passions (Baillie) 17–18
Plays Pleasant and Unpleasant (Shaw) 347
Plea of the Midsummer Fairies, The (Hood) 181
Pleasures of Hope, The (Campbell) 75
Plotz, Judith 137
Plymouth Brethren 159
Pocock, Isaac **308**
Poe, Edgar Allan 17, 111, 248, 368
Poem on the Bill Lately Passed for Regulating the Slave Trade (Williams) 409
Poems (Acton) 1
Poems (Allingham) 7–8
Poems (Arnold) 8
Poems (Barbauld) 19
Poems (Hemans) 176
Poems (Ingelow) 193
Poems (Kemble) 211
Poems (Meredith) 257
Poems (Meynell) 261
Poems (Robinson) 324
Poems (Rossetti) 329
Poems (Southey) 359
Poems (Tennyson) 381
Poems (Thompson) 385, 386
Poems (Wilde) 406
Poems, by Elizabeth Barrett (Browning) 51
Poems, Second Series (Arnold) 8
Poems, Wherein It Is Attempted to Describe Certain Views of Nature and of Rustic Manners (Baillie) 17
Poems and Ballads (Swinburne) 373
Poems and Ballads: Second Series (Swinburne) 373
Poems and Lyrics of the Joy of Earth (Meredith) 258
Poems by Currer, Ellis, and Acton Bell (Brontë sisters) 42, 44, 46
Poems by Melanter (Blackmore) 30
Poems by Two Brothers (Tennyson and Turner) 381, 394
Poems Chiefly in the Scottish Tradition (Burns) 64
Poems Chiefly Lyrical (Tennyson) 381
Poems Descriptive of Rural Life and Scenery (Clare) 84
Poems in Two Volumes (Wordsworth) 200, 414–415
Poems New and Old (Newbolt) 283
Poems of 1844 (Patmore) 303
Poems of Many Years (Milnes) 266
Poems of Rural Life in the Dorset Dialect (Barnes) 22

Poems of Ten Years, 1846–1855 (Ogilvy) 291
Poems of Walter Savage Landor, The (Landor) 221
poètes maudite (accursed poets) 248
Poetica Erotica (Symons) 377
Poetical Sketches (Blake) 31
Poetical Works (Adams) 3
Poetical Works (Bridges) 41
Poetical Works (Dowson) 121–122
Poetical Works (Little) 237
Poetical Works of Henry Alford (Alford) 7
Poetical Works of the Late Mrs. Mary Robinson (Robinson) 324
Poetical Works of the Late Thomas Little, Esq., The (Moore) 271
Poetics: An Essay on Poetry (Dallas) 107
Poetic Trifles (Polwhele) 308
Poetry for Children (Aikin) 4
Poison Belt, The (Doyle) 122
Poland, Homer, and Other Poems (Aytoun) 14
Political Economy for Beginners (Fawcett) 139
Politics for the People (journal) 212
Polonius (Fitzgerald) 141
Polwhele, Richard **308–309**
Pomegranates from the Punjab (Tucker) 394
Ponsonby, Caroline. *See* Lamb, Lady Caroline
Poor Law Board 286
Poor Law of 1842 150–151
Poor Man and the Lady, The (Hardy) 167–168
Pope, Alexander 40, 50, 71, 102
Pope-Bowles controversy 40
Popular Account of Discoveries at Nineveh and Its Remains, A (Layard) 225
Popular Rhymes of Scotland (Chambers) 82
Porcupine, Peter. *See* Cobbett, William
"Porphyria's Lover" (Browning) 53
Porter, Anna Maria **309**
Porter, Jane **309**
Portrait of a Lady, The (James) 197
Portraits and Sketches (Gosse) 159
positivism 171, 245
Post Haste (Ballantyne) 19
Potter's Thumb, The (Steel) 365
Pound, Ezra 87, 222
Power, Margaret. *See* Gardiner, Marguerite
Practical and Internal Evidence against Catholicism (White) 404
Practical Education (Edgeworth) 128
Praed, Rosa **309–310**

Prelude, The (Wordsworth) 413
Preludes (Meynell) 261
Pre-Raphaelite movement **310–311**
  aestheticism influenced by 3
  Beardsley (Aubrey) influenced by 22
  Buchanan (Robert) on 55
  Dixon (Richard Watson) in 118
  Lee (Vernon) on 229
  magazine of 326, 329
  Morris (William) in 118, 273, 310, 330, 373
  Oxford Movement and 298
  Pater (Walter) and 301
  Rossetti (Christina) in 310, 326
  Rossetti (Dante Gabriel) in 310, 329
  Ruskin (John) in 310
  Siddal (Elizabeth) in 329, 354
  Swinburne (Algernon Charles) in 310, 373, 374
  Wells (Charles Jeremiah) and 402
Price, Ellen. *See* Wood, Ellen
Pride and Prejudice (Austen) 11, 12, 13, 63
Priestley, J. B. 173, 305
Prime Minister, The (Trollope) 390
Prince, Mary **311**
Prince's Progress and Other Poems, The (Rossetti) 327
Prince's Quest, The (Watson) 399
Princess and the Curdie, The (Macdonald) 243
Princess and the Goblin, The (Macdonald) 242–243
Princess Casamassima, The (James) 197
Princess of Thule, A (Black) 30
Principles in Art (Patmore) 304
Principles of Biology, The (Spencer) 362
Principles of Geology (Lyell) 238–239
Principles of Moral and Political Philosophy, The (Paley) 300
Principles of Political Economy (Mill) 264
Principles of Political Economy and Taxation, The (Ricardo) 321
Principles of Psychology (Spencer) 362
Principles of Sociology, The (Spencer) 362
Prison Amusements (Montgomery) 268
Prisoner of Chillon and Other Poems, The (Byron) 201
Pritchett, V. S. 164–165
Private Memoirs and Confessions of a Justified Sinner, The (Hogg) 179–180
Private of the Buffs, The (Doyle) 124
Problem in Greek Ethics, A (Symonds) 376
Problem in Modern Ethics, A (Symonds) 376
Problems of Life and Mind (Lewes) 235

Probyn, May **311**
"Procrastination" (Crabbe) 102–103
Procter, Adelaide Anne **311–312**
Procter, Bryan Waller 311
"Proem" (Adams) 3
Professor, The (Brontë) 44
Progress (magazine) 253
Prometheus (Goethe) 251
Prometheus Bound (Aeschylus) 50
Prometheus Bound of Aeschylus, The (Webster) 401
Prometheus Unbound (Shelley) 352
Prophecy of St. Oran and Other Poems, The (Blind) 33
Prophet's Mantle, The (Bland) 281
Protestant Magazine 389
Proust, Marcel 198
Psyche; or, The Legend of Love (Tighe) 388
Puck of Pook's Hill (Kipling) 215
Punch (magazine) 1, 48, 49, 80, 94, 101, 125, 202, 231–232, 256, 383
Purgatory of Suicides, The (Cooper) 98
Puritan Commonwealth (Forster) 143
Puritanism 404, 405
Purple Land that England Lost, The (Hudson) 188
Pusey, Edward Bouverie 298, **312–313**
Puseyism 312
Pushkin, Aleksandr 70
Pygmalion (Shaw) 347, 348
Pykett, Lyn 47–48

Q

Q. *See* Jerrold, Douglas William; Quiller-Couch, Sir Arthur Thomas
Quadroon (Reid) 39
Quakers 293
Quarterly Review (magazine) 20, 47, 76, 86, 189, 252, 298, 343, 359, 379
Quayle, Eric 19
Queen Mab (Kavanagh) 207
Queen Mab (Shelley) 351
Queen Mother, The (Swinburne) 373
Queen's Wake, The: A Legendary Poem (Hogg) 179
Queen Victoria as I Knew Her (Martin) 252
Quentin Durward (Scott) 341
Question of Memory, A (Field) 141
Quest of the Golden Girl, The (Le Gallienne) 231
Quest of the Sangraal, The: Chant the First (Hawker) 172
Quiller-Couch, Sir Arthur Thomas **314**
Quincey, Thomas. *See* De Quincey, Thomas
Quintessence of Ibsenism, The (Shaw) 347
Quirk, Denise 98

R

Rabelais, François 251
Radcliffe, Ann 230, 235, **315–316**, 326
Radcliffe, Mary Ann **316**
Radford, Dollie **317**
Radford, Ernest 317
Raglan, Lord James 211
Railway Bill of 1844 155
Railway Children, The (Nesbit) 282
railway literature 63
Rainwater, Catherine 83
Ralph, Theodore 406
Rambles in Germany and Italy, in 1840, 1842, and 1843 (Shelley) 349
Rambles of a Rat, The (Tucker) 394
Ramée, Marie Louise de la. *See* Ouida
Ranthorpe (Lewes) 234
Rapparee, The (Boucicault) 39
Read, Herbert 46
Reade, Charles xiii, **317–320**
Ready-Money Mortiboy: A Matter-of-Fact Story (Besant and Rice) 28
Realities (Linton) 236
Real Sheridan, The (Fitzgerald) 143
Reasons for and against the Enfranchisement of Women (Bodichon) 35
Rebecca and Rowena (Thackeray) 383
Recluse, The (Wordsworth) 414, 415
Recluse of Norway, The (Porter) 309
Recollections and Experiences (Yates) 417
Recollections of a Scottish Novelist, The (Walford) 398
Recollections of a Tour Made in Scotland (Wordsworth) 411
Recollections of the Last Days of Shelley and Byron (Trelawney) 389
Record of a Girlhood (Kemble) 211
Records of Byron, Shelley and the Author (Trelawney) 389
Records of Later Life (Kemble) 211
Records of Women (Hemans) 176
Red as a Rose Is She (Broughton) 49
Red Fairy Book (Lang) 224
Redgauntlet (Scott) 341
Red Hugh's Captivity (O'Grady) 291
Red Pottage (Cholmondeley) 83
Red Redmaynes, The (Phillpotts) 307
Red Rowans (Steel) 365
Reeds Shaken with the Wind (Hawker) 172
Reflections on the Revolution in France (Burke) 59–60, 410
Reform Act of 1832 131, 132, 240, 263
Reform Act of 1867 78, 321
Reform Act of 1884 321
Reformer (periodical) 58
Reformers (sect) 37

Regency period 130, 158
Regency romance 320
Regency Theater 268
Reginald Hastings: A Tale of the Troubles (Warburton) 398
Reid, Mayne 39
Reliques of Robert Burns (Jeffrey) 200
Remains in Verse and Prose of Arthur Henry Hallam (Hallam) 166
"Remarks on the Education of Girls" (Belloc) 25
Reminiscences (Carlyle) 145
Renaissance Fancies and Studies (Lee) 229
Renaissance in Italy, The (Symonds) 375
Renaissance of Art in France, The (Dilke) 115
"Renascence of Wonder in English Poetry, The" (Watts-Dunton) 400
Rendall, Jane 25
"Renouncement" (Meynell) 261
Repentance, A (Craigie) 103
Representative, The (newspaper) 115, 117
"Requiem" (Stevenson) 367
Restoration of the Works of Art to Italy (Hemans) 176
Retrospect of Western Travel (Martineau) 252
"Return!" (Dobell) 119
Return of the Guards (Doyle) 124
Return of the Native, The (Hardy) 168–169
Review of the Divorce Bill of 1856, A (Norton) 289
Revolt of Hindostan, The (Jones) 205
Revolution in Tanner's Lane, The (White) 405
Rewards and Fairies (Kipling) 215
Reynolds, George William MacArthur **320–321**
Reynolds, J. H. 181
Reynolds, Sir Joshua 34, 62, 272, 293
Reynolds' Miscellany (magazine) 320
Reynolds News and Sunday Citizen 321
Reynolds's Weekly Newspaper 321
Rhodes, Cecil 337–338
Rhyme of the Lady of the Rock and How It Grew, The (Pfeiffer) 307
Rhymers' Club 121, 204, 231, 317, 376
Rhys, Jean 45
Rhythm of Life, The (Meynell) 262
Ricardo, David 255, 263, 264, **321**
Rice, James 27
Richards, Pearl. *See* Craigie, Pearl Mary
Richardson, LeeAnne 317
Richardson, Samuel 11, 20, 63
Richelieu (Bulwer-Lytton) 57
Richelieu (James) 196
Riddell, Charlotte **322**

Ridenour, George M. 71
Rienzi (Bulwer-Lytton) 57
Rienzi (Mitford) 267
Riess, Daniel 221
Rigby, Elizabeth 47
"Rights and Wrongs of Women" (Linton) 237
Rights of Women (Wheeler) 403
"Right to Ignore the State, The" (Spencer) 362
Rimbaud, Arthur 3, 248
"Rime of the Ancient Mariner, The" (Coleridge) 92, 93–94, 325, 370
Ring and the Book, The (Browning) 52, 53, 54
Ringrove; or, Old-fashioned Notions (West) 403
Ritchie, Anne Thackeray **322–323**, 384
Rivals, The (Sheridan) 369
"River, The" (Patmore) 303
Road to Ruin, The (Holcroft) 181
Road to Xanadu, The (Lowe) 92
Robber's Wife, The (Pocock) 308
Robbery Under Arms (Boldrewood) 35–36
Robert Elsmere (Ward) 399
Robertson, Agnes 38–39
Robertson, Thomas William **323**
Robin Hood and Little John (Egan) 130
Robinson, Mary 228, **323–324**
Robinson Crusoe; or, The Bold Buccaneers (Pocock) 308
Robinson Crusoe in Words of One Syllable (Aikin) 4
Rob Roy (Scott) 341, 342
Rob Roy Macgregor (Pocock) 308
Roche, Maria Regina **324–325**
Rochelson, Meri-Jane 420
Rock Ahead, The (Yates) 417
Rockite, The (Tonna) 389
Roderick, the Last of the Goths (Southey) 359
Roderick Hudson (James) 196
Rodin, Auguste 178
Rolfe, Frederick William **325**
"Roman, The: A Dramatic Poem" (Dobell) 119
Roman Catholic Relief Act of 1829 358
Romance of a Station, The (Praed) 310
Romance of Canvas Town, A (Boldrewood) 36
Romance of His Life, and Other Romances (Cholmondeley) 83
Romance of Natural History, The (Gosse) 160
Romance of the Forest, The (Radcliffe) 315
Romance of Two Worlds, A (Corelli) 99
Romantic Ballads and Poems of Phantasy (Sharp) 346

romanticism xii–xiii, **325–326**
    Blake (William) in 32, 325
    Bowles (William Lisle) and 40
    Burns (Robert) in 65
    Byron (Lord) in 70, 326
    Coleridge (Samuel Taylor) in 40, 92, 325, 414
    De Quincey (Thomas) in 110
    Hazlitt (William) in 173
    Hunt (Leigh) in 190
    Keats (John) in 207, 208, 209, 326
    Patmore (Coventry) in 303
    Ruskin (John) in 332
    Scott (Hugh) in 340
    Shelley (Mary Wollstonecraft) in 326, 349
    Shelley (Percy Bysshe) in 23, 326, 352
    Southey (Robert) in 40
    transition between classicism and 75
    transition from, to Victorianism 187
    Wordsworth (William) in 40, 92, 325–326, 414
Romantic '90s, The (Le Gallienne) 231
Romany Rye, The (Borrow) 38
Romola (Eliot) 131
Rookwood (Ainsworth) 5
Roosevelt, Theodore 215, 259, 278
Rosamund (Swinburne) 373
Rose, Blanche, and Violet (Lewes) 234
"Rose Aylmer" (Landor) 222
Rosemary Lane (Farjeon) 138
Rosenberg, John D. 77, 78, 333
Rose Turquand (Hopkins) 182
Rossetti, Christina **326–328**
    brother of 326, 328
    Browning (Elizabeth Barrett) and 52
    Greenwell (Dora) and 163
    Hopkins (Gerard Manley) and 184
    Ingelow (Jean) and 193
    Jewsbury (Geraldine) and 202
    Meynell (Alice) and 261
    Oxford Movement and 418
    in Pre-Raphaelite movement 310, 326
    Swinburne (Algernon Charles) and 373
    Webster (Augusta) and 401
Rossetti, Dante Gabriel **328–331**
    Allingham (William) and 8
    Caine (T. H. Hall) and 73
    caricature of 23
    Carroll (Lewis) and 80
    Fitzgerald (Edward) and 141
    Ingelow (Jean) and 193
    James (Henry) and 196
    Jewsbury (Geraldine) and 202

    Meynell (Alice Christina) and 261
    Morris (William) and 273, 330
    on O'Shaughnessy (Arthur) 295
    Pater (Walter) and 303
    in Pre-Raphaelite movement 310, 329
    Sharp (William) and 345
    sister of 326, 328
    Swinburne (Algernon Charles) and 373
    Watson (William) and 399
    Watts-Dunton (Theodore) and 400
    Wells (Charles Jeremiah) and 402
    wife of 329, 354
Rousseau, Jean-Jacques 34, 293, 350
Rowe, John Carlos 198
Rowlands, John. *See* Stanley, Henry Morton
Royal Court Theatre 307
Royal Society of Authors xii
Ruba'iya't of Omar Khayyám, The (Fitzgerald) 141–143
Rugby, Tennessee (Hughes) 189
"Rugby Chapel" (Arnold) 11
Rugby School 8, 10–11, 79, 87, 188–189, 210, 221, 224, 380
Ruined Cottage, The (Jones) 205
Rundle, Elizabeth. *See* Charles, Elizabeth
Rupert de Linsay (Bulwer-Lytton) 56
Rural Felicity (Buckstone) 56
Rural Life of England, The (Howitt) 188
Rural Muse, The (Clare) 84
Rural Tales, Ballads and Songs (Bloomfield) 34
Ruskin, John xiv, **331–333**
    aestheticism influenced by 3
    Black (William) and 29
    Coleridge (Mary Elizabeth) and 91
    on Haydon (Benjamin Robert) 172
    James (Henry) and 196
    Jewsbury (Geraldine) and 202
    on Lear (Edward) 226
    in Pre-Raphaelite movement 310
    on Rossetti (Dante Gabriel) 330
    on Stannard (Henrietta) 364
    on Swinburne (Algernon Charles) 373
    Wilde (Jane Francesca) and 406
    Wilde (Oscar) and 406
Russell, Bertrand 70, 415
Russell, George 159
Russell, Henry 98
Russian Shores of the Black Sea, The (Oliphant) 292
Russians of the South (Brooks) 48
Ruth (Gaskell) 149, 150–151
Rutherford, Mark. *See* White, William Hale
Ryan, W. P. 121

S

Sacred and Legendary Art (Jameson) 199
"Sad Fortunes of Reverend Amos Barton, The" (Eliot) 131
Sadleir, Michael 251
Sailing of Long-Ships and Other Poems, The (Newbolt) 283
Saint Joan (Shaw) 347
Saints and Sinners (Jones) 206
Saintsbury, George xiv, 309, **334–336**
Saint-Simon, Henri, comte de 264
Saint Simonian movement 202
Saints' Tragedy, The (Kingsley) 212
Salaman and Absal (Fitzgerald) 141
Salomé (Wilde) 22, 120, 407
Salvation Army 36, 37, 68
Sand, George 9, 51, 196, **336–337**
Sanger, Margaret 133
Sappho and Phaon (Robinson) 324
Sargent, John Singer 196
Sartor Resartus (Carlyle) 77
Satan; or, Intellect Without God (Montgomery) 269
Saturday Review (newspaper) 2, 23, 107, 129, 170, 237, 285, 334
Saunders, Kate 419
Savin, Maynard 323
Savoy (magazine) 22, 121, 376
Savoy Theatre 151
Scapegoat, The (Caine) 73
Scènes de la Vie de Bohème (Murger) 125
Scenes from a Silent World (Skene) 355
Scenes from Clerical Life (Eliot) 131
Schaffer, Talia 244
schauerroman 235
Scheinberg, Cynthia 234
Schiller, Friedrich 251
Schleiermacher, Friedrich Daniel Ernst 371
Schmidt, Michael 84, 101
"Scholar-Gypsy, The" (Arnold) 9
School for Husbands, or Molière's Life and Times, The (Bulwer-Lytton) 58
Schoolmistress, The (Pinero) 307
School of Arrogance, The (Holcroft) 181
"School of the Heart, The" (Alford) 7
Schreiner, Olive Emilie Albertina 133, **337–339**
scientific materialism 109
Scientific Spirit of the Age, The (Cobbe) 89
Scinde, or the Unhappy Valley (Burton) 66
"Scotch Milkmaid, the." *See* Little, Janet
Scots dialect 65, 238
Scots Magazine 147
Scots Musical Museum, The (Burns) 64
Scots Observer (magazine) 178
Scott, Ann 338

Index

Scott, Dixon 262
Scott, Hugh Stowell **339–340**
Scott, R. T. *See* Maginn, William
Scott, Sir Walter xiii, **340–343**
    Ainsworth (William Harrison) and 5
    on Baillie (Joanna) 18
    Blackmore (Richard) and 30
    Burns (Robert) and 64
    Byron (Lord) and 70, 340
    daughter of 238
    Edgeworth (Maria) and 128, 342
    Fenn (George Manville) and 139
    Ferrier (Susan) and 140
    Galt (John) and 147
    Gore (Catherine) and 158
    on Hawker (Robert Stephen) 172
    Hazlitt (William) and 173
    Hemans (Felicia Dorothea) and 176
    Hogg (James) and 179
    James (George Payne) and 196
    Lewis (Matthew Gregory) and 236
    Macaulay (Thomas) and 240
    Maginn (William) on 244
    Newman (John Henry) and 283
    North (Christopher) on 287
    Opie (Amelia) and 293
    Owenson (Sydney) and 297, 342
    Pocock (Isaac) and 308
    printing business of 18, 341
    on Radcliffe (Ann) 315
    Saintsbury (George) and 335
    Seward (Anna) and 344
    on Smith (Charlotte) 357
    son-in-law of 238
    Strickland (Agnes) and 372
    Thackeray (William Makepeace) and 342, 383
Scott, Sophia 238
Scottish Chiefs, The (Porter) 309
Scottish Pastorals, Poems, Songs, etc., Mostly Written in the Dialect of the South (Hogg) 179
Scouring of the White Horse, The; or, The Long Vacation Ramble of a London Clerk (Hughes) 189
Scribner's (magazine) 60
"Sculpture" (Bulwer-Lytton) 56
Seaboard Parish, The (Macdonald) 243
Search after Happiness, The (More) 271–272
Search after Proserpine, The (De Vere) 112
Seasons, The (Thomson) 83
Sea Urchins (Jacobs) 195
Second Journey Through Persia (Morier) 273
Second Jungle Book, The (Kipling) 215
Second Mrs. Tanqueray, The (Pinero) 307–308
Second Thoughts (Buckstone) 56

Second Thoughts of an Idle Fellow, The (Jerome) 201
Secret Agent, The (Coyne) 102
Secret Garden, The (Burnett) 61
Secular Society 27
Sedgwick, Adam 108
Select Collection of Original Scottish Airs (Burns) 65
Selected Poems (Browning) 53
Selection of Irish Melodies, A (Moore) 271
Self Control (Brunton) 55
Self-Help, with Illustrations of Character and Conduct (Smiles) 356
Sélincourt, E. de 412
Sellers, Peter 133
Semi-attached Couple, The (Eden) 127
Semi-detached House, The (Eden) 127
Semple, Robert 65
sensation drama 39
sensation fiction xiii, 120, 283, **343**
    by Blackmore (Richard) 30
    by Braddon (Mary Elizabeth) 40–41, 249, 343
    Clive (Caroline) and 86
    by Collins (Wilkie) 30, 95, 343
    by Marryat (Florence) 249
    by Ouida 296
    by Wood (Ellen) 249, 343
Sense and Sensibility (Austen) 11–12, 402
Sentence, The (Webster) 401
Sentimental Traveller, The: Notes on Places (Lee) 229
Separation of Mother and Child by the Law of Custody of Infants, Considered, The (Norton) 289
Seraphim and Other Poems, The (Browning) 50
Sergeant, Adeline 105
Series of Plays, In Which It Is Attempted to Delineate the Stronger Passions of the Mind, A (Baillie) 17–18
Servant's Friend, The (Trimmer) 390
Settlers in Canada, The (Marryat) 250
Seven Ages of Women, and Other Poems, The (Strickland) 372
Seven Lamps of Architecture, The (Ruskin) 331, 332–333
Seven Men (Beerbohm) 24
Seven Sleepers of Ephesus, The (Coleridge) 91
Severn, Joseph 208
Seward, Anna 309, **343–344**
Sewell, Anna 344
Sewell, Elizabeth Missing **344–345**
Sexual Inversion (Ellis) 133, 376
"Shade-Catchers, The" (Mew) 260
Shadow of a Crime, The (Caine) 73
Shadow of the Sword, The (Buchanan) 55
Shadwell, Thomas 335

Shaffer, Julie 63
Shairp, J. C. 210
Shakespeare, William xiii–xiv, 40, 85, 199, 209, 220, 252, 271, 283, 358, 387
Shakespeare Key, The: Unlocking the Treasures of His Style (Clarke) 85
Shakespeare's Heroines (Jameson) 199
Shalkhuaser, Marian 327
Shamrock, The (Stoker) 369
"Shamus O'Brien" (Le Fanu) 230
Sharp, Elizabeth 345–346
Sharp, William **345–346**
Shaving of Shagpat, The: An Arabian Entertainment (Meredith) 257–258
Shaw, George Bernard xiv, **347–349**
    Boucicault (Dion) and 39
    Danby (Frank) and 107
    Gosse (Edmund) and 159
    on Grand (Sarah) 161
    Harris (Frank) and 170
    Henley (W. E.) and 178
    Lee (Vernon) and 228
    on Le Gallienne (Richard) 231
    Marx (Karl) and 255
    Morris (William) and 274
    Pinero (Arthur Wing) and 308
She (Haggard) 164, 165
Sheick, William 83
Shelley, Elizabeth 351
Shelley, Mary Wollstonecraft **349–350**
    Baillie (Joanna) and 17
    Byron (Lord) and 70, 349
    Crowe (Catherine) and 105
    husband of 155, 349, 351
    Opie (Amelia) and 293
    parents of 155, 349, 351, 409
    Radcliffe (Ann) and 315
    in romanticism 326, 349
Shelley, Percy Bysshe xi, **350–353**
    Arnold (Matthew) on 9
    Beddoes (Thomas Lovell) and 23
    biography of 375
    Byron (Lord) and 70, 351, 352
    De Vere (Aubrey Thomas) and 112
    Godwin (William) and 155, 351
    Hallam (Arthur) and 166
    Hemans (Felicia Dorothea) and 176
    Hunt (Leigh) and 189
    Keats (John) and 208, 352
    on O'Shaughnessy (Arthur) 295–296
    Owenson (Sydney) and 297
    Patmore (Coventry) and 303
    Peacock (Thomas Love) and 305
    as romantic poet 23, 326, 352
    Thomson (James) and 387
    Trelawney (Edward) and 389
    Watson (William) and 399
    wife of 155, 349, 351

Shepherd's Calendar, The (Clare) 84
Shepherd's Life, A (Hudson) 188
Sheridan, Caroline. *See* Norton, Caroline Sheridan
Sheridan, Richard Brinsley 230, 288, 369
Sheridan, William 143
Sherlock Holmes series (Doyle) 122, 123–124
Sherwood, Mary **353**
"She Walks in Beauty" (Byron) 70
She Was Young and He Was Old (Molesworth) 267
Shipwrecked Stranger, The (Jones) 205
Shirley (Brontë) 44, 45, 97
"Shooting Niagara: and After?" (Carlyle) 78
Shorter Poems (Bridges) 41
Short History of English Literature, A (Saintsbury) 334
Short History of French Literature (Saintsbury) 334
Shorthouse, Joseph Henry **354**
Short Studies in Great Subjects (Froude) 145
Showalter, Elaine 345
Shrine of Death and Other Stories (Dilke) 115
Shrine of Love and Other Stories (Dilke) 115
Shropshire Lad, A (Housman) 185–186
"shudder novel" 235
Shuttle, The (Burnett) 61
"Siberia" (Mangan) 248
Sicilian Idyll, A (Todhunter) 388
Sicilian Romance, A (Radcliffe) 315
"Sick Rose, The" (Blake) 31
Siddal Rossetti, Elizabeth Eleanor 329, **354**
Sierra Club 277, 278
Sight and Sound (Field) 141
Sigourney, Lydia 177
Silas Marner (Eliot) 131
Silent Witness, The (Yates) 417
Silhouettes (Symons) 376
"Silly Novels by Lady Novelists" (Eliot) 131
Silverado Squatters, The (Stevenson) 367
silver-fork school 57, 117, 120, 148, 158, **354–355**
Silver King, The (Jones) 206
Silverland (Lawrence) 225
Silvertongue, Gabriel. *See* Montgomery, James
Simonidea (Landor) 222
Simple Story, A (Inchbald) 192
Simpson, Elizabeth. *See* Inchbald, Elizabeth
Simson, Habbie 65
Sinclair, May 118, 260

Sindh and the Races that Inhabit the Valley of the Indus (Burton) 66
Sing-Song (Rossetti) 327
Singular Anomaly, The (Colby) 229
Sinner's Comedy, The (Craigie) 103
"Sins of the Fathers, The" (Gissing) 153
Sir John Chiverton (Ainsworth and Aston) 5
Sir Nigel (Doyle) 123
Sir Percival (Shorthouse) 354
Sisters, Inisfail, and Other Poems, The (De Vere) 112
Sisters of Charity, Catholic and Protestant, At Home and Abroad (Jameson) 199
Sister Songs (Thompson) 385
Six Charles Danvers (Cholmondeley) 83
Six Dramas of Calderón (Fitzgerald) 141
"Sixth Sunday after Epiphany, The" (Keble) 210
Skene, Felicia Mary **355**
Sketches Among the Poor (Gaskell and Gaskell) 149
Sketches by Boz (Dickens) 113
Sketches of Natural History (Howitt) 187
Sketches of Rural Life in Aberdeenshire (Alexander) 6
Sketches of the State of Manners and Opinions in the French Republic (Williams) 409
"Skylark" (Clare) 84–85
Sloan, John 109
Smedley, Francis Edward **355**
Smedley, Menella Bute **355**
Smiles, Samuel **355–356**
Smith, Adam 255, 321
Smith, Alexander **356–357**
Smith, Barbara. *See* Bodichon, Barbara
Smith, Charlotte **357**
Smith, Sarah. *See* Stretton, Hesba
Smith, Sydney **357–358**
Smollett, Tobias 63, 318
"Snail, The" (Smith) 357
Snake's Pass, The (Stoker) 369
Snider, Clifton 226
"Snow" (Davidson) 110
Snow Waste, The (Webster) 401
Soames, Enoch 24–25
Social Darwinism 29, 362
socialism 134–135. *See also* Marxism
Socialist League 253, 274
social problem novels 148, 149, 393
social problem plays 308
Social Statics (Spencer) 362
Social Studies (Wilde) 406
Society (Robertson) 323
Society for Promoting Christian Knowledge 160
Society for Promoting the Employment of Women 312

Society for the Abolition of the Slave Trade 86
Society for the Diffusion of Useful Knowledge xiv
Society for the Suppression of Vice 67
Society in America (Martineau) 252
Society of Friends (Quakers) 293
Soldier's Wife, The (Reynolds) 320
"Soliloquy of the Spanish Cloister" (Browning) 53
"Solitary Reaper, The" (Wordsworth) 415
Some Emotions and a Moral (Craigie) 103
Something of Myself (Kipling) 215
Song and Book of Los, The (Blake) 31
"Song of Derivations, A" (Meynell) 261
"Song of the Factory-Slave" (Jones) 205
"Song of the Poorer Classes" (Jones) 205
"Song of the Shirt" (Hood) 181–182
Songs and Other Verses (Radford) 317
Songs and Sonnets (Blind) 33
Songs and Sonnets of Springtime (Naden) 280
Songs before Sunrise (Swinburne) 373
Songs of Experience (Blake) 19, 31, 32, 64
Songs of Innocence (Blake) 19, 31, 32, 64
Songs of Memory and Hope (Newbolt) 283
Songs of Salvation (Greenwell) 163
"Songs of Seven" (Ingelow) 193
Songs of the Army of the Night (Adams) 3
Songs of Two Nations (Swinburne) 373
Song-Tide and Other Poems (Marston) 251
"Sonnet Composed upon Westminster Bridge" (Wordsworth) 415
Sonnets (Douglas) 120
Sonnets and Songs (Pfeiffer) 307
Sonnets From the Portuguese (Browning) 52, 53
Sonnets on the War (Dobell) 119
"Sonnet V. To the River Tweed" (Bowles) 40
Son of Hagar, The (Caine) 73
Sophia (Buchanan) 55–56
Sordello (Browning) 53
Sorrows of Rosalie, The: A Tale with Other Poems (Norton) 288
Sorrows of Satan, The (Corelli) 99
Sorrows of Young Werther, The (Goethe) 349
"Soul's Beauty" (Rossetti) 329
Soul's Legend, The (Greenwell) 163
Southey, Robert **358–361**
    Bowles (William Lisle) and 40
    Byron (Lord) and 71, 359
    Coleridge (Samuel Taylor) and 92, 358, 359, 360
    De Quincey (Thomas) and 110

Hazlitt (William) and 174
  as Lake Poet 217, 360
  Lamb (Charles) and 218
  Opie (Amelia) and 293
  as poet laureate 359, 360, 361
  Scott (Sir Walter) and 340
  Wordsworth (William) and 359, 360, 415
"Southey's Colloquies on Society" (Macaulay) 240
Southworth, Emma 120
Sowers, The (Scott) 340
Spasmodic School 119
Spear, Jeffrey L. 333
Specimens of the British Poets (Campbell) 75
Spectator (periodical) 365, 385
Speedie, Julie 233
Speke, John Hanning 66, **361**
Spencer, Herbert 16, 29, 131, **361–362**
Spender, Dale 55
Spender, Stephen 185
Spenser, Edmund 208, 211–212, 242, 388
Speranza. *See* Wilde, Jane Francesca
Sphinx's Lawyer, The (Danby) 107
"Spider and the Fly, The" (Howitt) 187
Spielmann, M. H. 49
"Spirit, The" (Hunt) 190
Spirit of Judaism, The (Aguilar) 4
Spirit of Place, The (Meynell) 262
Spirit of the Age, The (Hazlitt) 173, 174
Spoils of Poynton, The (James) 197
Sporting Magazine 372
"Spring" (Hopkins) 183
"Spring and Fall" (Hopkins) 184
sprung rhythm 184
Squire, The (Pinero) 307
St. Clair, William 389
St. Irvyne (Shelley) 351
Staël, Madame de 221, **362–363**
Stafford, William 264, 265
Stalky & Co. (Kipling) 215
Stamp Act 59
Standard Habbie 65
Stanley, Henry Morton 37, **363–364**
Stannard, Henrietta Vaughan **364**
Stanton, Elizabeth Cady 35
"Stanzas from the Grande Chartreuse" (Arnold) 9
"Stanzas on the Death of Mrs. Hemans" (Landon) 177
Stark, Myra 287
"Stately Homes of England, The" (Hemans) 177
Statesman, The (Taylor) 379
Statesmen of the Commonwealth of England, The (Forster) 143
"Stealthy School of Criticism, The" (Rossetti) 329

"Steam Threshing Machine, The" (Turner) 395
Stedman, Edmund Clarence 119, 331
Steel, Flora Annie **364–365**
Steele, Richard 219, 385
Stephen, Leslie 78, 103, **365–366**
Stephenson, George 356
Stephenson, Glennis 220, 221
Sterne, Lawrence 384
Stevens, Catherine. *See* Crowe, Catherine
Stevenson, Elizabeth. *See* Gaskell, Elizabeth
Stevenson, John 271
Stevenson, Lionel 258–259
Stevenson, Pearce. *See* Norton, Caroline Sheridan
Stevenson, Robert Louis Balfour **366–368**
  Ballantyne (R. M.) and 18
  on Coleridge (Mary Elizabeth) 91
  Fenn (George Manville) and 139
  Haggard (H. Rider) and 164
  Henley (W. E.) and 178
  James (Henry) and 196, 367, 368
  Lang (Andrew) and 224
  Scott (Hugh) and 340
  Stephen (Leslie) and 365
Stewart, Mary Louisa. *See* Molesworth, Mary Louisa
Stickney, Sarah. *See* Ellis, Sarah Stickney
Stillingfleet, Benjamin 34
Stock, Irving 404
Stoddard, Richard 52
Stoker, Abraham 230, 249, **368–370**, 406
Stone, Elizabeth **370–371**
Stones of Venice, The (Ruskin) 331, 333
Stoppard, Tom 186
Stories from the History of the Jews (Tucker) 394
Stories of the Seen and Unseen (Oliphant) 293
Stories of Waterloo (Maginn) 244
Stories Toto Told Me (Rolfe) 325
Story of a Modern Woman, The (Dixon) 118
Story of an African Farm, The (Schreiner) 338–339
Story of a Needle, The (Tucker) 394
Story of Doom and Other Poems, A (Ingelow) 193
Story of Elizabeth, The (Ritchie) 322, 384
Story of My Boyhood and Youth, The (Muir) 278
Story of Rimini, The (Hunt) 189
Story of Sigurd the Volsung, The (Morris) 274, 275
Story of the Amulet, The (Nesbit) 282

"Story of the Four Little Children Who Went Round the World, The" (Lear) 226–227
Story of the Treasure Seekers, The (Nesbit) 281
Story of West Africa, The (Kingsley) 214
Stowe, Harriet Beecher 267, 389, 393
Strachey, Lytton 284, 287, 397
Strand (magazine) 122, 140
Strange Adventures of a Phaeton, The (Black) 30
Strange Case of Dr. Jekyll and Mr. Hyde, The (Stevenson) 367, 368
Strange Stories (Allen) 7
Strange Story, A (Bulwer-Lytton) 57
Strathern (Gardiner) 148
Strauss, David Friedrich 131, **371**
Strayed Reveller, and Other Poems, The (Arnold) 8
stream-of-consciousness style 198, 260, 269
Stretton, Hesba **371**
Strickland, Agnes **371–372**
Strickland, Elizabeth 372
Strictures of Modern Female Education (More) 272
Strictures on the Life and Writings of Pope (Bowles) 40
Strong, Emilia Frances. *See* Dilke, Lady Emilia Frances
Stuart of Dunleath (Norton) 289
Student's Manual of the History of India, A (Taylor) 379
Studies in Animal Life (Lewes) 235
Studies in Elizabethan Drama (Symons) 376
Studies in the History of the Renaissance (Pater) 301–302
Studies in the Psychology of Sex (Ellis) 133
Studies of the Eighteenth Century in Italy (Lee) 229
Study in Scarlet, A (Doyle) 122, 123
"Style" (Pater) 302
Subjection of Women, The (Mill and Mill) 262, 265
Sue, Eugene 320
Suggestions for the Improvement of the Nursing Service in Hospitals and on the Methods of Training Nurses for the Sick Poor (Nightingale) 286
Sullivan, Sir Arthur 151–153, 276, 312
Summer in Skye, A (Smith) 357
Summer Songs (Collins) 94
Sunday Magazine 281
Sunday Times 101, 268
Sunstein, Emily 350
Superfluous Woman, A (Brooke) 48
Supernatural Fiction Writers: Fantasy and Horror (Bleiler) 322

"Suppression of Variant Types" (Caird) 74
Surtees, Robert Smith 372–373
Susan Hopley; or Circumstantial Evidence (Crowe) 105
Sutherland, John 48, 96, 121, 296, 399
Swedenborg, Emanuel 31
Sweet Anne Page (Collins) 94
Sweet Lavender (Pinero) 307
Sweet Mace (Fenn) 139
Swift, Jonathan 143, 201, 240, 340, 384
Swinburne, Algernon Charles 373–375
    on aestheticism 3
    on Baring-Gould (Sabine) 21
    on Dixon (Richard Watson) 118
    on Fitzgerald (Edward) 141
    Gilbert (W. S.) on 152
    Gosse (Edmund) on 159, 374
    Morris (William) and 273, 373
    O'Shaughnessy (Arthur) and 294, 295
    in Pre-Raphaelite movement 310, 373, 374
    Watson (William) and 400
    Watts-Dunton (Theodore) and 374, 400, 401
    Wells (Charles Jeremiah) and 402
Swiss Family Robinson, The (Marryat) 250
Switzerland (Porter) 309
Sword and Gown (Lawrence) 225
Sybil; or, The Two Nations (Disraeli) 97, 116, 117
Sylvia's Lovers (Gaskell) 150
Sylvie and Bruno (Carroll) 80
Sylvie and Bruno Concluded (Carroll) 80
Symbolic Logic (Carroll) 80
Symbolist Movement in Literature, The (Symons) 376
Symonds, John Addington 375–376
Symons, Arthur William 84, 122, 204, 317, 328, 376–377, 385
Sympneumata: Evolutionary Forces Now Active in Man (Oliphant) 292
synesthesia 377
Synge, John Millington 39, 193
Synthetic Philosophy, The (Spencer) 362
System, The (Tonna) 388
System of Logic (Mill) 264
Szmurlo, Karyna 363

T

"Tableaux Parisiens" (Baudelaire) 178
"Table Talk" (Cowper) 101
Table Talk; or, Original Essays on Men and Manners (Hazlitt) 173
Taft, William Howard 278
"Tailor Re-tailored, The" (Carlyle) 77
Tait's Edinburgh Magazine 251

Taken from the Enemy (Newbolt) 282
Tale Bearers, The (Pritchett) 164–165
Tale of Mystery, A (Holcroft) 181
Tale of Rosamund Gray and Old Blind Margaret, A (Lamb) 218
Tale of Two Cities, A (Dickens) 57, 114
Tales (Crabbe) 102–103
Tales from Shakespeare (Lamb and Lamb) 220
Tales of Fashionable Life (Edgeworth) 128
Tales of Mean Streets (Morrison) 276
Tales of Orris (Ingelow) 193
Tales of the Punjab (Steel) 365
Tales of Wonder (Lewis and Scott) 236
Tam O'Shanter (Burns) 65–66
Tancred (Disraeli) 116, 117
Tarcissus: The Boy Martyr of Rome (Rolfe) 325
Task, The (Cowper) 100–101
Task of Social Hygiene, The (Ellis) 133
Taylor, Brian 200
Taylor, Harriet. *See* Mill, Harriet Taylor
Taylor, Helen 378
Taylor, Philip Meadows 378–379
Taylor, Sir Henry 379–380
Taylor, William 38
Teacher of the Violin, The (Shorthouse) 354
Tell Me a Story (Molesworth) 267
Temper (Marryat) 249
Temple, Frederick 380
Temple Bar (magazine) 83
Temporal Power (Corelli) 99
Tenant of Wildfell Hall, The (Brontë) 42
Tenniel, John 80, 231
Tennyson, Alfred, Lord xiii, 380–383
    Alford (Henry) and 7
    brother of 381, 394
    on Bulwer-Lytton (Edward) 56
    Carroll (Lewis) and 80
    Charles (Elizabeth) and 82
    Coleridge (Mary Elizabeth) and 91
    Fitzgerald (Edward) and 141
    Forster (John) and 143
    Hallam (Arthur) and 166, 381
    Henley (W. E.) and 178
    Ingelow (Jean) and 193
    James (Henry) and 196
    Lear (Edward) and 226
    Meynell (Alice Christina) on 262
    Milnes (Richard Monckton) and 265
    Oxford Movement and 299, 418
    Palgrave (Francis) and 301
    as poet laureate 13, 51, 262, 381
    Ritchie (Anne Thackeray) and 322
    on Swinburne (Algernon Charles) 374

Thackeray (William Makepeace) and 383
Thompson (Francis) and 387
Thomson (James) and 387
Watson (William) and 399, 400
Tennyson, Charles. *See* Turner, Charles Tennyson
Tennyson, G. B. 79, 302
Tennyson's Selected Lyrics (Palgrave) 301
"Terribly Strange Bed, A" (Collins) 95
Tess of the D'Urbervilles (Hardy) 168, 169
Testament of Beauty, The (Bridges) 41
Thackeray, Anne. *See* Ritchie, Anne Thackeray
Thackeray, Harriet 365
Thackeray, William Makepeace 383–385
    on Bulwer-Lytton (Edward) 56
    daughters of. *See* Ritchie, Anne Thackeray; Thackeray, Harriet
    Fitzgerald (Edward) and 141, 383
    Gordon (Lucie Duff) and 157
    Gore (Catherine) and 158
    Jerrold (Douglas) and 202
    Maginn (William) and 243–244
    on Mayhew (Henry) 256
    Scott (Sir Walter) and 342, 383
    silver-fork school and 354, 355
    Trollope (Anthony) and 390
    writing for *Punch* 232, 383
Thaddeus of Warsaw (Porter) 309
Thalaba the Destroyer (Southey) 359
"Thames Embankment, The" (Davidson) 110
That Lass o' Lowrie's (Burnett) 60
Theatre Royal 39
Thelma: A Society Novel (Corelli) 99
"Theory of the Beautiful, A" (Todhunter) 388
Theosophical Society 27
There Is No Death (Marryat) 249
"There Is No God, the Wicked Sayeth" (Clough) 88
Theresa Marchmont; or, The Maid of Honour (Gore) 158
Thespis (Gilbert and Sullivan) 151
"Thirty Bob a Week" (Davidson) 109
Thomas, Dylan 185
Thompson, Alice Christina. *See* Meynell, Alice Christina Thompson
Thompson, E. P. 255
Thompson, Francis 112, 262, 385–387
Thompson, Julian 96
Thompson, William 403
Thomson, James 83, 387
Thomson, Patricia 336
Thoreau, Henry David 277
"Thorn, The" (Wordsworth) 326
Thornycroft, Hamo 159
Thorpe, Clarence DeWitt 209

"Thou Art Indeed Just, Lord" (Hopkins) 183
Thoughts at Fourscore (Cooper) 98
Thoughts on Art, Philosophy and Religion (Dobell) 119
Thoughts on Man (Godwin) 156
"Thoughts on My Sickbed" (Wordsworth) 412–413
Thoughts on the Causes of the Present Discontents (Burke) 59
Thoughts on the Importance of Manners of the Great to General Society (More) 272
Thoughts on the Necessity of Improving the Conditions of the Slave (Clarkson) 86
Thousand Miles up the Nile, A (Edwards) 129
Three Commanders, The (Kingston) 214
Three Cousins, The (Trollope) 393
Three Essays on Religion (Taylor) 378
Three Histories, The (Jewsbury) 203
Three Lieutenants, The (Kingston) 214
Three Men in a Boat (to Say Nothing of the Dog) (Jerome) 201
Three Men on the Bummel (Jerome) 201
Three Midshipmen, The (Kingston) 214
Three Northern Love Stories (Morris) 274
Three Paths, The (Kavanagh) 207
Three Plays for Puritans (Shaw) 347
Three Strangers, The (Lee) 228
Three Times Dead (Braddon) 40
Thrift (Smiles) 356
Through a Needle's Eye (Stretton) 371
Through Fire and Flame (Baring-Gould) 21
Through the Dark Continent (Stanley) 364
Through the Looking-Glass and What Alice Found There (Carroll) 80
"Through the Magic Door" (Doyle) 340
Through the Shadows: A Test of Truth (Skene) 355
Thuggis (secret society of criminals) 379
"Thyrsis" (Arnold) 8–9, 87
"Thyrza" poems (Byron) 70
Ticheburn, Cheviot. *See* Ainsworth, William Harrison
Ticonderoga (James) 196
Tighe, James 246
Tighe, Mary **387–388**
Time (magazine) 417
Time and Tide (Ruskin) 331–332
Times (newspaper) 1, 13, 107, 116, 158, 182, 183, 200, 292, 331, 379, 393
"Times of Erasmus and Luther, The" (Froude) 145
Timko, Michael 87
Tippos Sultaun (Taylor) 379

Tiw: A View of the Roots and Stems of the English as a Teutonic Tongue (Barnes) 21
"To a Fish" (Hunt) 190
"To a Louse" (Burns) 65
"To a Mouse" (Burns) 65
"To an Athlete Dying Young" (Housman) 186
Today (journal) 281
Todhunter, John **388**
"To George Sand. A Desire" (Browning) 336
"To Homer" (Coleridge) 90
Tolkien, J. R. R. 224, 242
Tom and Jerry; Or, Life in London (Egan) 130, 268
Tom and Jerry; or, Life in London (Moncrieff) 268
"To Marguerite—Continued" (Arnold) 8
Tom Brown at Oxford (Hughes) 189
Tom Brown's School Days (Hughes) 10, 189
Tom Burke of Ours (Lever) 232
Tom Jones (Fielding) 56
"To My Native Land" (Mangan) 246
Tonna, Charlotte Elizabeth **388–389**
Too Good for Him (Marryat) 249
Tooke, John 180
Too Strange Not to Be True (Fullerton) 146
Torch (journal) 29
Toryism and the Tory Democracy (O'Grady) 291
"To Shakespeare" (Coleridge) 90
Toward Democracy (Carpenter) 79
Tower of London, The (Ainsworth) 5
Townsend, J. Benjamin 110
Toyland (O'Shaughnessy and Marston) 294
"Toys, The" (Patmore) 304–305
Tract 90 (Newman) 284
Tractarian Movement. *See* Oxford Movement
Tract for the Times (Newman) 284
Traditions of Edinburgh (Chambers) 82
Traditions of Tuscany in Verse (Ogilvy) 291
Trafford, F. G. *See* Riddell, Charlotte
Tragic Muse, The (James) 197
Train (monthly) 80
Training of Children (Booth) 37
Transition (Brooke) 48
Translation of the Letters of a Hindoo Rajah (Hamilton) 167
Translations from Camoens, and Other Poets, with Original Poetry (Hemans) 176
Travels in West Africa (Kingsley) 213–214

Travels with a Donkey (Stevenson) 367
Treasure Island (Stevenson) 18, 164, 178, 367
"Treasure of the Deep, The" (Hemans) 177
Treasury of Sacred Song (Palgrave) 301
Trelawney, Edward John **389**
Trelawny of the "Wells" (Pinero) 307, 308
Tressady (Ward) 399
Trial by Jury (Gilbert and Sullivan) 151, 152
Trials of Margaret Lyndsay, The (North) 287
Trifles of Helicon (King and King) 106
Trilby (du Maurier) 125
Trilling, Lionel 9
Trimmer, Sarah Kirby **389–390**
"Triumph of Time, The" (Swinburne) 374–375
Trollope, Anthony 56, 57, 343, **390–392**, 393
Trollope, Frances Milton 390, **392–393**
Trollope, Thomas Adolphus 392, **393–394**
True Manliness (Hopkins) 183
True Story of Joshua Davidson, Christian and Communist, The (Linton) 237
True Sun (magazine) 143
Tryal, The (Baillie) 17
Tucker, Charlotte Maria **394**
Turner, Charles Tennyson 381, **394–395**
Turner, J. W. M. 293, 331, 332
Turn of the Screw, The (James) 197
Twain, Mark 392
"Twenty Golden Years Ago" (Mangan) 248
Twitchell, James 370
Two Destinies (Doyle) 124
Two Farmers, The (Trimmer) 390
Two Friends, The (Gardiner) 148
£200 a Year (Pinero) 307
Twopenny Post Bag, The (Moore) 271
"Two Races of Men, The" (Lamb) 218
"Tyger, The" (Blake) 32
Tynan, Katharine 178
Tysdahl, B. J. 156

U

Ulrick the Ready (O'Grady) 291
"Ulysses" (Tennyson) 382
Uncle Silas (Le Fanu) 230
Underneath the Bough (Field) 141
Under the Aspens (Pfeiffer) 307
Under the Greenwood Tree (Hardy) 168
"Under the Hill" (Beardsley) 22
Under the Microscope (Swinburne) 373
Under the Red Flag (Braddon) 41
Under the Sunset (Stoker) 369

Undertones (Buchanan) 55
Under Two Flags (Ouida) 296
Undying One, and Other Poems, The (Norton) 288
"Uniformity of Change" (Lyell) 239
Unitarianism 88, 149, 293, 404
United Irishmen 124–125
universalism 242
Unknown Eros, The (Patmore) 304–305
Unsex'd Females, The: A Poem (Polwhele) 308–309
Untermeyer, Louis 260
Unto This Last (Ruskin) 331
Unwin, Mary 100, 101
Ups and Downs (Boldrewood) 35
Up the Murray (Cambridge) 74
Use of Sunshine, The (Smedley) 355
Ussher, James 239
utilitarianism 3, 26, 77, 116, 262, 263, 264, 285, 300
utopian novels 68, 188, 274

V

"V." *See* Clive, Caroline
Vagabundulis Libellus (Symonds) 375
Valentine (Sand) 336
Valentine's Eve (Opie) 294
Valisneria (Pfeiffer) 306
Valperga (Shelley) 349
Vanity Fair (Thackeray) 354, 383, 384–385
Vanolis, Bysshe. *See* Thomson, James
Vassa, Gustavus. *See* Equiano, Olaudah
Vaughan, Henrietta. *See* Stannard, Henrietta Vaughan
Vendetta (Corelli) 99
"Venus Verticordia" (Rossetti) 329
Verlaine, Paul 121, 178, 377
Vermont Vale; or, Home Pictures in Australia (Evans) 136
Verses (Dowson) 121
Verses (Symonds) 375
Very Strange but Very True (Lathom) 224
Very Stressful! (Bulwer-Lytton) 58
Vesey, Elizabeth 34
Vespers of Palermo, The (Hemans) 176
Vestiges of the Natural History of Creation (Chambers) 82
Vicar of Lansdowne, The (Roche) 325
Vicar of Wrexhill, The (Trollope) 392, 393
Victims of Society, The (Gardiner) 148
Victoria, queen of Great Britain, empress of India **396–397**
    chaplain to 212
    confidant to 219
    consort of 252, 381, 396–397
    on Corelli (Marie) 99
    Disraeli (Benjamin) and 117, 397
    on Eliot (George) 132
    lake named in honor of 361
    Martin (Theodore) and 252
    Newbolt (Henry) on 282
    Nightingale (Florence) and 286
    on Smith (Sydney) 357
    Strickland (Agnes) and 372
    Tennyson (Alfred, Lord) and 381
    Walford (Lucy) and 398
Victorianism 187, 356, 396
Victorian Women Poets: An Anthology (Leighton and Reynolds) 29
Victoria Press 312
Victoria Regia (Procter) 312
Victories of Love, The (Patmore) 303
Victorine (Buckstone) 56
Vienna and the Austrians (Trollope) 392
Viereck, G. S. 120
Views in Rome and Its Environs (Lear) 225
Vignettes in Rhyme (Dobson) 119
Village, The (Crabbe) 102
Village Minstrel and Other Poems, The (Clare) 84
village novels 267
Village of Mariendorpt, The (Porter) 309
Villette (Brontë) 44, 46
Villon, François 178
Vindication of Natural Society, A (Burke) 58, 59
Vindication of the English Constitution in a Letter to a Noble and Learned Lord by Disraeli, the Younger, A (Disraeli) 116
Vindication of the Rights of Man (Wollstonecraft) 410
Vindication of the Rights of Woman, A (Wollstonecraft) 409–410
Virginians, The (Thackeray) 384
Virginibus Puerisque (Stevenson) 367
"Vision of Connaught in the Thirteenth Century, A" (Mangan) 247
Vision of Judgement, The (Byron) 71
Vision of the Daughters of Albion (Blake) 31
Visit to Italy, A (Trollope) 392
"Visit to the Cholera Districts of Bermondsey, A" (Mayhew) 256
Vivian Grey (Disraeli) 115, 117
"Vocabulary of the Gruesome" (Hearn) 175
"Voice of Encouragement, A—A New Year's Lay" (Mangan) 248–249
Voltaire 92, 358
Volumes in Folio (Le Gallienne) 231
Voyage of Captain Popanilla, The (Disraeli) 116

W

W. & R. Chambers (publishing house) 82
Wages of Sin, The: A Novel (Malet) 244
"Wake of William Orr, The" (Drennan) 124–125
Walford, Lucy **398**
Walks in Edinburgh (Chambers) 82
Wallace, William 309
Walpole, Horace 34, 235, 240, 315
Wanderer, The; or, Female Difficulties (Burney) 62
Wanderer of Switzerland, The (Montgomery) 268
Warburton, Eliot **398**
War Cry (periodical) 36
Ward, Ann. *See* Radcliffe, Ann
Ward, Mary 354, **399**
Ward, Plumer 354
Warden, The (Trollope) 390, 391
Warner, Val 260
"Warning, A" (Procter) 312
"Warning Voice, A" (Mangan) 247
Warnock, Robert 348–349
Warrior's Return, The (Opie) 294
"Washing-Day" (Barbauld) 20
Washington Square (James) 125, 197
"Wasp, The" (Davidson) 110
Waste Land, The (Eliot) 20
Water-Babies, The (Kingsley) 212, 213
Watson, John William **399–400**
Watson, Melvin 47
Watts, Alaric 203
Watts-Dunton, Theodore 374, **400–401**, 402
Wat Tyler (Southey) 358
Waugh, Evelyn 133
Waverley novels (Scott) 30, 147, 308, 341, 342
Waverly (Scott) 128, 341
Way of All Flesh, The (Butler) 69
Way We Live Now, The (Trollope) 390, 391–392
"Weal and Woe in Garvelach" (Martineau) 252
"We Are Seven" (Wordsworth) 326, 414
Webb, Beatrice Potter 36, 37
Webster, Augusta **401**
Webster, Flora Annie. *See* Steel, Flora Annie
Weeds and Wildflowers (Bulwer-Lytton) 56
Weir, Peter 102
Weird Stories (Riddell) 322
Weir of Hermiston (Stevenson) 367
Weldon, Fay 385
Well at the World's End, The (Morris) 275
Wells, Charles Jeremiah **402**
Wells, H. G. 24, 57, 118, 165, 170, 178, 228, 349

Welsh, Jane. *See* Carlyle, Jane Welsh
Welsh Melodies (Hemans) 176
Werner, or, The Inheritance (Byron) 228
West, Jane **402–403**
West African Studies (Kingsley) 214
Westminster Review (periodical) 27, 131, 264, 378
Westward Ho! (Kingsley) 212–213
Wet Magic, The (Nesbit) 282
Wharton, Edith 228
What I Remember (Fawcett) 139
What Led to the Discovery of the Source of the Nile (Speke) 361
What Maisie Knew (James) 197
Wheeler, Anna 58, **403**
Wheeler, Michael 332
Wheeler, Rosina. *See* Bulwer-Lytton, Rosina Wheeler
"When I Am Dead, My Dearest" (Rossetti) 328
"Where, oh! where, on his restless wing" (Acton) 1
Whibley, Charles 111
Whims and Oddities (Hood) 181
Whinfield, E. H. 142
Whisperer, The (Montgomery) 268
Whistler, James McNeill 152, 178, 196
White, Joseph Blanco **403–404**
White, William Hale **404–405**
White Company, The (Doyle) 122, 123
White Cross Army 182–183
"White Heliotrope" (Symons) 377
"White Peacock, The" (Sharp) 346
"White Ship, The" (Rossetti) 330
Whitman, Walt 79, 159, 178, 376
Whittier, John Greenleaf 163
Why Paul Ferroll Killed His Wife (Clive) 86
Why Should We Fear the Romish Priests? (Kingsley) 212
Whyte, Violet. *See* Stannard, Henrietta Vaughan
Whyte, W. 81
Whyte-Melville, George John **405–406**
Why Women Desire the Franchise (Cobbe) 89
Wide Sargasso Sea (Rhys) 45
Widow Barnaby, The (Trollope) 393
Widowers' Houses (Shaw) 347
Widow Married, The (Trollope) 393
"Wife a-Lost, The" (Barnes) 22
Wife and the Lover, The (Holcroft) 180
Wife of a Million, The (Lathom) 224
Wilde, Jane Francesca **406**
Wilde, Oscar xiv, **406–408**
　　in aestheticism 3, 406
　　Beardsley (Aubrey) and 22
　　biography of 170
　　on Black (William) 30

Boucicault (Dion) and 38
caricature of 23
on Corelli (Marie) 99
Douglas (Lord Alfred) and 120, 407
Dowson (Ernest) and 121
Gilbert (W. S.) on 152
Godwin (William) and 156
Harris (Frank) and 170
Hichens (Robert) on 179
James (Henry) and 197
on Kipling (Rudyard) 215
Lee (Vernon) and 228
Le Gallienne (Richard) and 231
Leverson (Ada) and 232, 233
mother of 406
Pater (Walter) and 302, 303, 406
Praed (Rosa) and 310
Symons (Arthur) and 376
Wild Irish Boy, The (Maturin) 255
Wild Irish Girl, The (Owenson) 297, 298
Wild Thyme (Egerton) 130
William Blake (Symons) 376
William Langshawe, The Cotton Lord (Stone) 370
Williams, Helen Maria **409**
Williams, Judith 45
Williams, Orlo 69
Williams, Raymond xiv, 255, 323
William Sharp: A Memoir (Sharp) 345–346
William the Silent (Harrison) 171
Wilson, Angus 215
Wilson, Jean Moorcroft 400
Wilson, John. *See* North, Christopher
Wilson, Margaret. *See* Oliphant, Margaret
"Windhover, The" (Hopkins) 183–184
Windsor Castle (Ainsworth) 5
Wind Voices (Marston) 251
Winged Destiny (Sharp) 346
Winged Victory, The (Grand) 161
Wings and Stings (Tucker) 394
Wings of Azreal, The (Caird) 74
Wings of the Dove, The (James) 197
Winter, John Strange. *See* Stannard, Henrietta Vaughan
"Winter in Brighton" (Collins) 94
Winter Studies and Summer Rambles in Canada (Jameson) 199
Wisdom of the Wise, The (Craigie) 103
"Witch, The" (Coleridge) 91
"Witch of Fife, The" (Hogg) 179
With Edged Tools (Scott) 340
"With the Straw Carrier" (Turner) 395
Wives and Daughters (Gaskell) 150
Wives of England, The (Ellis) 134
Wolfe, Tom 392
Wolff, Robert Lee 245
Wollstonecraft, Mary **409–410**

Burke (Edmund) and 60
daughter of 155, 349, 351, 409
Eliot (George) on 131–132
Holcroft (Thomas) and 180
husband of 155, 409, 410
Mathias (Thomas James) on 308
More (Hannah) on 272
Opie (Amelia) and 293
Polwhele (Richard) on 308–309
Radcliffe (Mary Ann) and 316
Wheeler (Anna) and 403
Woman in White, The (Collins) 57, 95–96, 343
Woman of No Importance, A (Wilde) 407
Woman's Friendship, A (Cambridge) 74
"Woman's Question, A" (Procter) 312
Woman's Thoughts about Women, A (Craik) 104
Woman's Work and Woman's Culture (Butler) 67
Woman's World (magazine) 118, 406–407
Woman Who Did, The (Allen) 7
Women (Maturin) 255
Women Adventures (Dowie) 121
Women and Labour (Schreiner) 338
Women and Work (Bodichon) 35
Women as They Are; or, Manners of the Day (Gore) 158
Women in France during the Eighteenth Century (Kavanagh) 207
Women of Christianity Exemplary for Acts of Piety and Charity (Kavanagh) 207
Women of England, The (Ellis) 134
Women of Israel, The (Aguilar) 4
Women's Enfranchisement League 338
women's suffrage movement 26, 35, 115, 118, 132, 139, 162, 262, 365, 378, 399, 401, 410
Women's Trade Union League 115, 253
Women's Victory, The (Fawcett) 139
Women's Writing of the Victorian Period: 1837–1901 (Jump) 121
Wood, Annie. *See* Besant, Annie Wood
Wood, Ellen 249, 343, **410–411**
Wood, Mary Anne. *See* Green, Mary Anne Everett
Wood beyond the World, The (Morris) 275
Woodbridge, H. E. 408
Woodbury, G. E. 112
Wood Magic (Jefferies) 200
Wood Spirit, The (Jones) 205
Woolf, Virginia xiv, 23–24, 198, 259, 260, 269, 306, 323, 327, 365
Wordsworth, Dorothy 92, 173, 217, **411–413**, 414
"Wordsworth, Tennyson, and Browning, or Pure, Ornate, and Grotesque Art in English Poetry" (Bagehot) 16–17

Wordsworth, William xi, xii, **413–416**
   Alford (Henry) and 7
   Arnold (Matthew) and 8, 9, 415
   Bagehot (Walter) on 16–17
   Baillie (Joanna) and 17
   Barbauld (Anna Laetitia) and 19
   Bowles (William Lisle) and 40
   Browning (Robert) and 53, 415
   Burns (Robert) and 64
   Byron (Lord) and 71
   Coleridge (Hartley) and 90
   Coleridge (Samuel Taylor) and 92, 93, 94, 414
   Crabbe (George) and 102
   De Quincey (Thomas) and 110
   De Vere (Aubrey Thomas) and 112
   Faber (William) and 138
   Hallam (Arthur) and 166
   Haydon (Benjamin Robert) and 172
   Hazlitt (William) and 173, 174
   Hemans (Felicia Dorothea) and 176
   on Hogg (James) 179, 180
   Jeffrey (Francis) on 200–201, 217, 415
   Keats (John) and 208
   as Lake Poet 217
   Lamb (Charles) and 218, 219
   Landor (Walter Savage) and 222
   Muir (John) and 277, 278
   North (Christopher) on 287
   Opie (Amelia) and 293
   Peacock (Thomas Love) on 305
   as poet laureate 51, 381, 415
   Procter (Adelaide Anne) and 311
   as romantic poet 40, 92, 325–326, 414
   Shelley (Mary Wollstonecraft) and 349
   Shelley (Percy Bysshe) and 351
   sister of 411, 412, 413, 414
   Southey (Robert) and 359, 360, 415
   Stephen (Leslie) on 366
   Taylor (Henry) and 379
   Watson (William) on 400

Wordsworth's Grave (Watson) 400
Wordsworth's Great Period Poems (Levinson) 412
Workers in the Dawn (Gissing) 153
Working-Class Movement in America, The (Marx and Aveling) 253–254
Working Men's Institutes xiv, 332, 344
"Workmen of England" (Kingsley) 212
Works (Swift) 201
Works of Anna Laetitia Barbauld, with a Memoir by Lucy Aikin (Aikin) 4–5
Works of Max Beerbohm, The (Beerbohm) 23
World, The (Montgomery) 268
World, The (magazine) 417
"World Is Too Much With Us, The" (Wordsworth) 415
World of Dreams, The (Ellis) 133
World of Girls, A (Meade) 257
"World-Strangeness" (Watson) 399–400
Wouldbegoods, The (Nesbit) 281
Wreath of Indian Stories, A (Tucker) 394
Wreck, The (Buckstone) 56
"Wreck of the Deutschland, The" (Hopkins) 183
Wrongs of Woman, The (Tonna) 389
Wuthering Heights (Brontë) 21, 43, 46–48, 326, 336, 338
Wyndham, Violet 232
Wynman, Margaret. *See* Dixon, Ella Hepworth
Wynn, Charles 359
Wyss, Jonathan 250

X

"Xantippe" (Levy) 233, 234
Xantippe and Other Verse (Levy) 233

Y

Yates, Edmund Hodgson 80, **417**
Yeast (Kingsley) 212
Yeats, William Butler
   on Allingham (William) 8
   Dixon (Ella Hepworth) on 118
   Dowson (Ernest) and 121, 122
   Gosse (Edmund) and 159
   Henley (W. E.) and 178
   in Irish Literary Renaissance 193
   Johnson (Lionel) and 204
   Le Gallienne (Richard) and 231
   Radford (Dollie) and 317
   Sharp (William) and 346
   Symons (Arthur) and 376
   Todhunter (John) and 388
   Wilde (Jane Francesca) and 406
Yellow Book (magazine) 22, 23, 121, 130, 231, 232, 325, 376
"Yellowhammer, The" (Clare) 84
Ye Mariners of England (Campbell) 75
Yendys, Sydney. *See* Dobell, Sydney Thompson
Yes or No (Pocock) 308
"Yes Thou Art Gone" (Brontë) 42
Yonge, Charlotte Mary **417–419**
Yosemite, The (Muir) 278
Young Castellan, The (Fenn) 139
Young Duke (Disraeli) 117
Young England 116
Young Fur Traders, The (Ballantyne) 18
Young Heiress, The: A Novel (Trollope) 393
"Young Lady's Lamentation on the Loss of Her Sister by Marriage, A" (Little) 237–238
Young Lives (Le Gallienne) 231
Young Men and Old Women (Inchbald) 192
Young Milliner, The (Stone) 370–371
Young Mistley (Scott) 340
Youth's Magazine 193

Z

Zangwill, Israel xii, **419–420**
Zanoni (Bulwer-Lytton) 57
Zastrozzi (Shelley) 351
Zoe: The History of Two Lives (Jewsbury) 202
Zofloya; or, The Moor (Dacre) 106
Zohrab the Hostage (Morier) 273
Zola, Émile 269, 270
Zuleika Dobson (Beerbohm) 24, 118